Routing and Switching Essentials
Companion Guide

Cisco Networking Academy

KT-498-516

Cisco Press

800 East 96th Street

Indianapolis, Indiana 46240 USA

Routing and Switching Essentials Companion Guide

Cisco Networking Academy

Copyright© 2014 Cisco Systems, Inc.

Published by:
Cisco Press
800 East 96th Street
Indianapolis, IN 46240 USA

Printed in the United States of America

Third Printing: September 2015

Library of Congress Control Number: 2013956689

ISBN-13: 978-1-58713-318-3
ISBN-10: 1-58713-318-0

Publisher	Paul Boger
Associate Publisher	Dave Dusthimer
Business Operation Manager, Cisco Press	Jan Cornelssen
Executive Editor	Mary Beth Ray
Managing Editor	Sandra Schroeder
Development Editor	Ellie C. Bru
Project Editor	Mandie Frank
Copy Editor	Apostrophe Editing Services
Technical Editor	Kathleen Page
Editorial Assistant	Vanessa Evans
Designer	Mark Shirar
Composition	Bumpy Design
Indexer	Ken Johnson
Proofreader	Dan Knott

Warning and Disclaimer

This book is designed to provide information about the Cisco Networking Academy Routing and Switching Essentials course. Every effort has been made to make this book as complete and as accurate as possible, but no warranty or fitness is implied.

The information is provided on an "as is" basis. The authors, Cisco Press, and Cisco Systems, Inc. shall have neither liability nor responsibility to any person or entity with respect to any loss or damages arising from the information contained in this book or from the use of the discs or programs that may accompany it.

The opinions expressed in this book belong to the author and are not necessarily those of Cisco Systems, Inc.

Trademark Acknowledgements

All terms mentioned in this book that are known to be trademarks or service marks have been appropriately capitalized. Cisco Press or Cisco Systems, Inc., cannot attest to the accuracy of this information. Use of a term in this book should not be regarded as affecting the validity of any trademark or service mark.

Special Sales

For information about buying this title in bulk quantities, or for special sales opportunities (which may include electronic versions; custom cover designs; and content particular to your business, training goals, marketing focus, or branding interests), please contact our corporate sales department at corpsales@pearsoned.com or (800) 382-3419.

For government sales inquiries, please contact governmentsales@pearsoned.com.

For questions about sales outside the U.S., please contact international@pearsoned.com.

Feedback Information

At Cisco Press, our goal is to create in-depth technical books of the highest quality and value. Each book is crafted with care and precision, undergoing rigorous development that involves the unique expertise of members from the professional technical community.

Readers' feedback is a natural continuation of this process. If you have any comments regarding how we could improve the quality of this book, or otherwise alter it to better suit your needs, you can contact us through email at feedback@ciscopress.com. Please make sure to include the book title and ISBN in your message.

We greatly appreciate your assistance.

CISCO

Americas Headquarters
Cisco Systems, Inc.
170 West Tasman Drive
San Jose, CA 95134-1706
USA
www.cisco.com
Tel: 408 526-4000
800 553-NETS (6387)
Fax: 408 527-0883

Asia Pacific Headquarters
Cisco Systems, Inc.
168 Robinson Road
#28-01 Capital Tower
Singapore 068912
www.cisco.com
Tel: +65 6317 7777
Fax: +65 6317 7799

Europe Headquarters
Cisco Systems International BV
Haarlerbergpark
Haarlerbergweg 13-19
1101 CH Amsterdam
The Netherlands
www-europe.cisco.com
Tel: +31 0 800 020 0791
Fax: +31 0 20 357 1100

Cisco has more than 200 offices worldwide. Addresses, phone numbers, and fax numbers are listed on the Cisco Website at **www.cisco.com/go/offices**.

©2007 Cisco Systems, Inc. All rights reserved. CCVP, the Cisco logo, and the Cisco Square Bridge logo are trademarks of Cisco Systems, Inc.; Changing the Way We Work, Live, Play, and Learn is a service mark of Cisco Systems, Inc.; and Access Registrar, Aironet, BPX, Catalyst, CCDA, CCDP, CCIE, CCIP, CCNA, CCNP, CCSP, Cisco, the Cisco Certified Internetwork Expert logo, Cisco IOS, Cisco Press, Cisco Systems, Cisco Systems Capital, the Cisco Systems logo, Cisco Unity, Enterprise/Solver, EtherChannel, EtherFast, EtherSwitch, Fast Step, Follow Me Browsing, FormShare, GigaDrive, GigaStack, HomeLink, Internet Quotient, IOS, IP/TV, iQ Expertise, the iQ logo, iQ Net Readiness Scorecard, iQuick Study, LightStream, Linksys, MeetingPlace, MGX, Networking Academy, Network Registrar, Packet, PIX, ProConnect, RateMUX, ScriptShare, SlideCast, SMARTnet, StackWise, The Fastest Way to Increase Your Internet Quotient, and TransPath are registered trademarks of Cisco Systems, Inc. and/or its affiliates in the United States and certain other countries.

All other trademarks mentioned in this document or Website are the property of their respective owners. The use of the word partner does not imply a partnership relationship between Cisco and any other company. (0609R)

About the Contributing Authors

Scott Empson is the chair of the Bachelor of Applied Information Systems Technology degree program at the Northern Alberta Institute of Technology in Edmonton, Alberta, Canada, where he teaches Cisco routing, switching, network design, and leadership courses in a variety of different programs (certificate, diploma, and applied degree) at the postsecondary level.

Scott is also the program coordinator of the Cisco Networking Academy Program at NAIT, an Area Support Centre for the province of Alberta. He has been with the Cisco Academy since 2000.

He has a Masters of Education degree along with three undergraduate degrees: a Bachelor of Arts, with a major in English; a Bachelor of Education, again with a major in English/Language Arts; and a Bachelor of Applied Information Systems Technology, with a major in Network Management. He currently holds several industry certifications, including CCNP, CCDP, CCAI, C|EH and Network+. Before instructing at NAIT, he was a junior/senior high school English/Language Arts/ Computer Science teacher at different schools throughout Northern Alberta.

Scott lives in Edmonton, Alberta, with his wife Trina and two children, Zachariah and Shaelyn.

Cheryl Schmidt is a professor at Florida State College at Jacksonville in Jacksonville, Florida, where she teaches courses in networking and PC repair. She has been teaching the academy curriculum since one of the earliest versions.

Cheryl has authored multiple books in such areas as PC repair, networking, and voice over IP. Cheryl also participates on a Cisco Academy team as a subject matter expert on a team that develops state-of-the-art assessments and courseware.

Outside of her academic responsibilities, Cheryl is currently pursuing a Ph.D. in information technology. She enjoys spending time with her family, grandkids, and granddog. She enjoys reading, biking, hiking, and puzzles.

Contents at a Glance

Contents

Icons Used in This Book

IP Phone	Phone	Cisco CallManager	100BaseT Hub	Wireless Router
Route/Switch Processor	Cisco ASA 5500	Printer	Cisco 5500 Family	Access Point
Router	Workgroup Switch	PC	Laptop	Modem
Headquarters	Branch Office	File/Application Server	Hub	Network Cloud / Line: Ethernet

Syntax Conventions

The conventions used to present command syntax in this book are the same conventions used in the IOS Command Reference. The Command Reference describes these conventions as follows:

- **Boldface** indicates commands and keywords that are entered literally as shown. In actual configuration examples and output (not general command syntax), boldface indicates commands that are manually input by the user (such as a **show** command).

- *Italics* indicate arguments for which you supply actual values.

- Vertical bars (|) separate alternative, mutually exclusive elements.

- Square brackets ([ ]) indicate an optional element.

- Braces ({ }) indicate a required choice.

- Braces within brackets ([{ }]) indicate a required choice within an optional element.

Introduction

Routing and Switching Essentials Companion Guide is the official supplemental textbook for the Cisco Network Academy CCNA Routing and Switching Essentials course. Cisco Networking Academy is a comprehensive program that delivers information technology skills to students around the world. The curriculum emphasizes real-world practical application, while providing opportunities for you to gain the skills and hands-on experience needed to design, install, operate, and maintain networks in small- to medium-sized businesses, as well as enterprise and service provider environments.

As a textbook, this book provides a ready reference to explain the same networking concepts, technologies, protocols, and devices as the online curriculum. This book emphasizes key topics, terms, and activities and provides some alternative explanations and examples as compared with the course. You can use the online curriculum as directed by your instructor and then use this Companion Guide's study tools to help solidify your understanding of all the topics.

Who Should Read This Book

This book is intended for students enrolled in the Cisco Networking Academy Routing and Switching Essentials course. The book, as well as the course, is designed as an introduction to data network technology for those pursuing careers as network professionals as well as those who need only an introduction to network technology for professional growth. Topics are presented concisely, starting with the most fundamental concepts and progressing to a comprehensive understanding of network communication. The content of this text provides the foundation for additional Cisco Academy courses, and preparation for the CCENT and CCNA Routing and Switching certifications.

Book Features

The educational features of this book focus on supporting topic coverage, readability, and practice of the course material to facilitate your full understanding of the course material.

Topic Coverage

The following features give you a thorough overview of the topics covered in each chapter so that you can make constructive use of your study time:

- **Objectives:** Listed at the beginning of each chapter, the objectives reference the core concepts covered in the chapter. The objectives match the objectives stated in the corresponding chapters of the online curriculum; however, the question format in the Companion Guide encourages you to think about finding the answers as you read the chapter.

- **"How-to" feature:** When this book covers a set of steps that you need to perform for certain tasks, the text lists the steps as a how-to list. When you are studying, the icon helps you easily refer to this feature as you skim through the book.

- **Notes:** These are short sidebars that point out interesting facts, timesaving methods, and important safety issues.

- **Chapter summaries:** At the end of each chapter is a summary of the chapter's key concepts. It provides a synopsis of the chapter and serves as a study aid.

- **Practice:** At the end of chapter there is a full list of all the Labs, Class Activities, and Packet Tracer Activities to refer back to for study time.

Readability

The following features have been updated to assist your understanding of the networking vocabulary:

- **Key terms:** Each chapter begins with a list of key terms, along with a page-number reference from inside the chapter. The terms are listed in the order in which they are explained in the chapter. This handy reference allows you to find a term, flip to the page where the term appears, and see the term used in context. The Glossary defines all the key terms.

- **Glossary:** This book contains an all-new Glossary with almost 200 terms.

Practice

Practice makes perfect. This new Companion Guide offers you ample opportunities to put what you learn into practice. You will find the following features valuable and effective in reinforcing the instruction that you receive:

- **Check Your Understanding questions and answer key:** Updated review questions are presented at the end of each chapter as a self-assessment tool. These questions match the style of questions that you see in the online course. Appendix A, "Answers to the 'Check Your Understanding' Questions," provides an answer key to all the questions and includes an explanation of each answer.

- **Labs and activities:** Throughout each chapter, you will be directed back to the online course to take advantage of the activities created to reinforce concepts. In addition, at the end of each chapter, there is a "Practice" section that collects a list of all the labs and activities to provide practice with the topics introduced in this chapter. The labs and class activities are available in the companion *Routing and Switching Essentials Lab Manual* (ISBN 978-1-58713-320-6). The Packet Tracer Activities PKA files are found in the online course.

- **Page references to online course:** After headings, you will see, for example, (1.1.2.3). This number refers to the page number in the online course so that you can easily jump to that spot online to view a video, practice an activity, perform a lab, or review a topic.

Lab Manual

The supplementary book *Routing and Switching Essentials Lab Manual*, by Cisco Press (ISBN 978-1-58713-320-6), contains all the labs and class activities from the course.

Practice and Study Guide

Additional Study Guide exercises, activities, and scenarios are available in the new *CCENT Practice and Study Guide* (978-158713-345-9) and *CCNA Routing and Switching Practice and Study Guide* (978-158713-344-2) books by Allan Johnson. Each Practice and Study Guide coordinates with the recommended curriculum sequence—the CCENT edition follows the course outlines for *Introduction to Networks* and *Routing and Switching Essentials*. The CCNA edition follows the course outlines for *Scaling Networks* and *Connecting Networks*.

About Packet Tracer Software and Activities

Interspersed throughout the chapters you'll find many activities to work with the Cisco Packet Tracer tool. Packet Tracer allows you to create networks, visualize how packets flow in the network, and use basic testing tools to determine whether the network would work. When you see this icon, you can use Packet Tracer with the listed file to perform a task suggested in this book. The activity files are available in the course. Packet Tracer software is available only through the Cisco Networking Academy website. Ask your instructor for access to Packet Tracer.

How This Book Is Organized

This book corresponds closely to the Cisco Academy Routing and Switching Essentials course and is divided into 11 chapters, one appendix, and a glossary of key terms:

- **Chapter 1, "Introduction to Switched Networks":** Introduces the concept of a switched network, reviews how a switch operates, and provides an overview of how the convergence of data, voice, and video traffic affects a switched network. Chapter 1 examines switch network design models and explains the benefits of implementing a switch network based on a hierarchical design. Switch features are also discussed.

- **Chapter 2, "Basic Switching Concepts and Configuration":** Basic switch concepts covered include the following: what happens when power is applied to a switch, switch troubleshooting tips, best practices for switch security, and the purpose of assigning an IP address, mask, and default gateway to a switch. The chapter also presents IOS commands used to configure a switch with an IP address, mask, default, and gateway for remote access including SSH access.

- **Chapter 3, "VLANs":** Examines the features and benefits provided by switch VLANs and trunks. Specific concepts include native VLAN, DTP, security issues, and best practices for implementation. Hands-on activities include configuration and troubleshooting of VLANs and trunks.

- **Chapter 4, "Routing Concepts":** Introduces the lowest layer of the TCP/IP model: the transport layer. This layer is essentially the equivalent of the OSI data link layer and the physical layer. The chapter discusses how this layer prepares network layer packets for transmission, controls access to the physical media, and transports the data across various media. This chapter includes a description of the encapsulation protocols and processes that occur as data travels across the LAN and the WAN as well as the media used.

- **Chapter 5, "Inter-VLAN Routing":** Examines the methods used to route between VLANs including using a Layer 3 switch. Explores the concept of a Layer 3 routed port. Includes configuration of inter-VLAN routing using multiple interfaces, router-on-a-stick, and a Layer 3 switch. Issues related to routing between VLANs are also discussed.

- **Chapter 6, "Static Routing":** Introduces the function of the network layer— routing—and the basic device that performs this function—the router. The important routing concepts related to addressing, path determination, and data packets for both IPv4 and IPv6 will be presented. The chapter also introduces the construction of a router and the basic router configuration.

- **Chapter 7, "Routing Dynamically":** Introduces Transmission Control Protocol (TCP) and User Datagram Protocol (UDP) and examines how each transports information across the network. It explores how TCP uses segmentation, the three-way handshake, and expectational acknowledgments to ensure reliable delivery of data. It also examines the best-effort delivery mechanism provided by UDP and describes when this would be preferred over TCP.

- **Chapter 8, "Single-Area OSPF":** Focuses on IPv4 and IPv6 network addressing, including the types of addresses and address assignment. It describes how to use the address mask or prefix length to determine the number of subnetworks and hosts in a network. This chapter also introduces Internet Control Message Protocol (ICMP) tools, such as ping and trace.

- **Chapter 9, "Access Control Lists":** Examines how to improve network performance by optimally dividing the IP address space based on network requirements. It explores the calculation of valid host addresses and the determination of both subnet and subnet broadcast addresses. This chapter examines subnetting for both IPv4 and IPv6.

- **Chapter 10, "DHCP":** Introduces DHCPv4 and DHCPv6 including explanation, configuration, and troubleshooting. The chapter examines the different methods an IPv6 client might obtain an IPv6 address with or without a DHCPv6 server.

- **Chapter 11, "Network Address Translation for IPv4":** Explains the concept of private and public IP addressing and when Network Address Translation (NAT) would be used. Advantages, disadvantages, and types of NAT are also covered. Configuration and troubleshooting of the various NAT types is an integral part of the chapter.

- **Appendix A, "Answers to the 'Check Your Understanding' Questions":** This appendix lists the answers to the "Check Your Understanding" review questions that are included at the end of each chapter.

- **Glossary:** The glossary provides you with definitions for all the key terms identified in each chapter.

CHAPTER 1

Introduction to Switched Networks

Objectives

Upon completion of this chapter, you will be able to answer the following questions:

- How do switched networks support small to medium-sized businesses?

- How has the convergence of data, voice, and video affected switched networks?

- What benefits are provided by creating networks based on a structured hierarchical design model?

- What are the two most commonly used Cisco hierarchical design models?

- What are the layers found in the Cisco hierarchical design model?

- What switch form factors are available?

- How do Layer 2 switches build and use a MAC address table to forward data?

- What is the difference between a collision domain and a broadcast domain?

Key Terms

This chapter uses the following key terms. You can find the definitions in the Glossary.

converged network   page 3

hierarchical   page 6

modularity   page 6

resiliency   page 7

flexibility   page 7

access layer   page 8

distribution layer   page 8

core layer   page 8

three-tier campus network design   page 8

two-tier campus network design   page 9

collapsed core network design   page 9

fixed configuration switch   page 13

modular configuration switch   page 13

stackable configuration switch   page 13

ingress   page 15

egress   page 15

MAC address table   page 16

application-specific-integrated circuit (ASIC)   page 19

store-and-forward switching   page 19

cut-through switching   page 19

frame-check-sequence (FCS)   page 20

collision domain   page 22

microsegmentation   page 23

broadcast domain   page 23

Introduction (1.0.1.1)

Modern networks continue to evolve to keep pace with the changing way organizations carry out their daily business. Users now expect instant access to company resources from anywhere and at any time. These resources not only include traditional data but also video and voice. There is also an increasing need for collaboration technologies that allow real-time sharing of resources between multiple remote individuals as though they were at the same physical location.

Different devices must seamlessly work together to provide a fast, secure, and reliable connection between hosts. LAN switches provide the connection point for end users into the enterprise network and are also primarily responsible for the control of information within the LAN environment. Routers facilitate the movement of information between LANs and are generally unaware of individual hosts. All advanced services depend on the availability of a robust routing and switching infrastructure on which they can build. This infrastructure must be carefully designed, deployed, and managed to provide a necessary stable platform.

This chapter begins an examination of the flow of traffic in a modern network. It examines some of the current network design models and the way LAN switches build forwarding tables and use the MAC address information to efficiently switch data between hosts.

Class Activity 1.0.1.2: Sent or Received Instructions

Individually, or in groups (per the instructor's decision), discuss various ways hosts send and receive data, voice, and streaming video.

Develop a matrix (table) listing network data types that can be sent and received. Provide five examples.

> **Note**
>
> For an example of the matrix, see the document prepared for this modeling activity.

Save your work in either hard- or soft-copy format. Be prepared to discuss your matrix and statements in a class discussion.

LAN Design (1.1)

Hiring managers want networking professionals, even entry level ones, to be able to design a LAN. Why is this so important? If someone knows how to design something, it means that person knows and understands the components that comprise the object. By knowing how to design a LAN, a network professional knows the network components and how those components interact with one another. The professional would also know what products to buy to expand the network.

Converged Networks (1.1.1)

The words *converged network* can mean several things to a network engineer: (1) a single network designed to handle voice, video, and data; (2) an internal network where the Layer 3 devices, such as routers, have a complete routing table to be able to accurately and efficiently send data to a remote destination; and (3) a switch network that has completed calculations that result in a single path through the switch network. In this chapter, we explore the first description.

Growing Complexity of Networks (1.1.1.1)

Our digital world is changing. The ability to access the Internet and the corporate network is no longer confined to physical offices, geographic locations, or time zones. In today's globalized workplace, employees can access resources from anywhere in the world and information must be available at any time, and on any device. These requirements drive the need to build next-generation networks that are secure, reliable, and highly available.

These next generation networks must not only support current expectations and equipment, but must also be able to integrate legacy platforms. Figure 1-1 shows some common legacy devices that must often be incorporated into network design. Figure 1-2 illustrates some of the newer platforms (converged networks) that help to provide access to the network anytime, anywhere, and on any device.

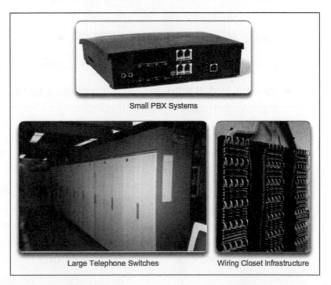

Small PBX Systems

Large Telephone Switches

Wiring Closet Infrastructure

Figure 1-1   Legacy Components

Unified Communication - Media
Convergence Server

Cisco Catalyst 2960 LAN Base
Switches

Cisco Unified IP Phones

Figure 1-2   Converged Network Components

Elements of a Converged Network (1.1.1.2)

To support collaboration, business networks employ converged solutions using
voice systems, IP phones, voice gateways, video support, and video conferencing
(Figure 1-3). Including data services, a converged network with collaboration support
may include features such as the following:

- **Call control:** Telephone call processing, caller ID, call transfer, hold, and
  conference

- **Voice messaging:** Voicemail

- **Mobility:** Receive important calls wherever you are

- **Automated attendant:** Serve customers faster by routing calls directly to the
  right department or individual

One of the primary benefits of transitioning to the converged network is that there
is just one physical network to install and manage. This results in substantial savings
over the installation and management of separate voice, video, and data networks.
Such a converged network solution integrates IT management so that any moves,
additions, and changes are completed with an intuitive management interface. A converged network solution also provides PC softphone application support, as well as
point-to-point video so that users can enjoy personal communications with the same
ease of administration and use as a voice call.

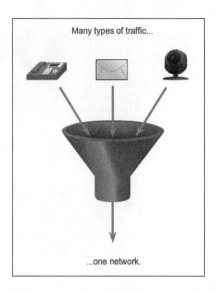

Figure 1-3   Network Traffic Convergence

The convergence of services onto the network has resulted in an evolution in networks from a traditional data transport role, to a super-highway for data, voice, and video communication. This one physical network must be properly designed and implemented to allow the reliable handling of the various types of information that it must carry. A structured design is required to allow management of this complex environment.

Play the online video to view a few of the collaboration services in action.

Video

Video 1.1.1.2: A Typical Work Day Transformed with People-Centric Collaboration

Go to course section 1.1.1.2. Click on the second graphic, and play the video to see how people can work more efficiently with collaboration tools.

Borderless Switched Networks (1.1.1.3)

With the increasing demands of the converged network, the network must be developed with an architectural approach that embeds intelligence, simplifies operations, and is scalable to meet future demands. One of the more recent developments in network design is illustrated by the Cisco Borderless Network architecture illustrated in Figure 1-4.

The Cisco Borderless Network is a network architecture that combines several innovations and design considerations to allow organizations to connect anyone, anywhere, anytime, and on any device securely, reliably, and seamlessly. This architecture is designed to address IT and business challenges, such as supporting the converged network and changing work patterns.

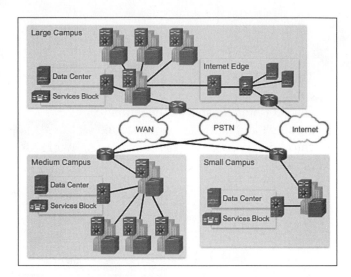

Figure 1-4 Borderless Switched Networks

The Cisco Borderless Network is built on an infrastructure of scalable and resilient hardware and software. It enables different elements, from access switches to wireless access points, to work together and allow users to access resources from any place at any time, providing optimization, scalability, and security to collaboration and virtualization.

Play the online video to learn more about the evolution of the Cisco Borderless Network.

Video

Video 1.1.1.3: Evolution of Borderless Networks

Go to course section 1.1.1.3. Click on the second graphic and play the video to see how a borderless network affects businesses.

Hierarchy in the Borderless Switched Network (1.1.1.4)

Creating a borderless switched network requires that sound network design principles are used to ensure maximum availability, flexibility, security, and manageability. The borderless switched network must deliver on current requirements and future required services and technologies. Borderless switched network design guidelines are built upon the following principles:

- *Hierarchical:* Facilitates understanding the role of each device at every tier, simplifies deployment, operation, and management, and reduces fault domains at every tier

- *Modularity:* Allows seamless network expansion and integrated service enablement on an on-demand basis

- *Resiliency:* Satisfies user expectations for keeping the network always on

- *Flexibility:* Allows intelligent traffic load sharing by using all network resources

These are not independent principles. Understanding how each principle fits in the context of the others is critical. Designing a borderless switched network in a hierarchical fashion creates a foundation that allows network designers to overlay security, mobility, and unified communication features. Two time-tested and proven hierarchical design frameworks for campus networks are the three-tier layer and the two-tier layer models, as illustrated in Figure 1-5.

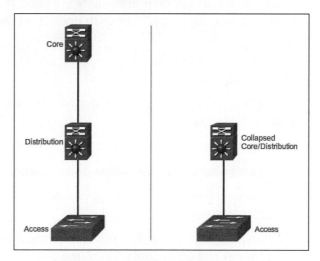

Figure 1-5 Switch Network Design Models

The three critical layers within these tiered designs are the access, distribution, and core layers. Each layer can be seen as a well-defined, structured module with specific roles and functions in the campus network. Introducing modularity into the campus hierarchical design further ensures that the campus network remains resilient and flexible enough to provide critical network services. Modularity also helps to allow for growth and changes that occur over time.

Core Distribution Access (1.1.1.5)

There are three layers of distribution access:

- Access layer

- Distribution layer

- Core layer

These will be discussed in greater detail in this section.

Access Layer

The *access layer* represents the network edge, where traffic enters or exits the campus network. Traditionally, the primary function of an access layer switch is to provide network access to the user. Access layer switches connect to distribution layer switches, which implement network foundation technologies such as routing, quality of service, and security.

To meet network application and end-user demand, the next-generation switching platforms now provide more converged, integrated, and intelligent services to various types of endpoints at the network edge. Building intelligence into access layer switches allows applications to operate on the network more efficiently and securely.

Distribution Layer

The *distribution layer* interfaces between the access layer and the core layer to provide many important functions, including:

- Aggregating large-scale wiring closet networks
- Aggregating Layer 2 broadcast domains and Layer 3 routing boundaries
- Providing intelligent switching, routing, and network access policy functions to access the rest of the network
- Providing high availability through redundant distribution layer switches to the end-user and equal cost paths to the core
- Providing differentiated services to various classes of service applications at the edge of the network

Core Layer

The *core layer* is the network backbone. It connects several layers of the campus network. The core layer serves as the aggregator for all of the other campus blocks and ties the campus together with the rest of the network. The primary purpose of the core layer is to provide fault isolation and high-speed backbone connectivity.

Figure 1-6 shows a *three-tier campus network design* for organizations where the access, distribution, and core are each separate layers. To build a simplified, scalable, cost-effective, and efficient physical cable layout design, the recommendation is to build an extended-star physical network topology from a centralized building location to all other buildings on the same campus.

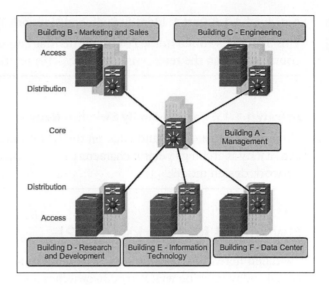

Figure 1-6   Three-Tier Campus Network Design

In some cases, because of a lack of physical or network scalability restrictions, maintaining a separate distribution and core layer is not required. In smaller campus locations where there are fewer users accessing the network or in campus sites consisting of a single building, separate core and distribution layers may not be needed. In this scenario, the recommendation is the alternate *two-tier campus network design*, also known as the *collapsed core network design.*

Figure 1-7 shows a two-tier campus network design example for an enterprise campus where the distribution and core layers are collapsed into a single layer.

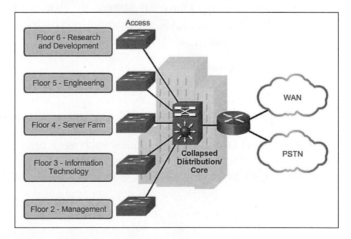

Figure 1-7   Two-Tier Campus Network Design

Interactive Graphic

Activity 1.1.1.6 Part 1: Identify Switched Network Terminology

This activity is found in the course in the first graphic in 1.1.1.6. Go to the online course to match the term with the switch characteristic.

Interactive Graphic

Activity 1.1.1.6 Part 2: Identify Switched Network Layer Functions

Go to the course online and click on the second graphic. Perform the practice activity by matching specific characteristics to one of the three layers of the switch network design model.

Switched Networks (1.1.2)

Switched networks are important when deploying wired LANs. A network professional today must be well-versed in switches and LAN technology in order to add commonly deployed devices such as PCs, printers, video cameras, phones, copiers, and scanners. Sharing and accessing network devices is common in both the home and business network.

Role of Switched Networks (1.1.2.1)

The role of switched networks has evolved dramatically in the last two decades. It was not long ago that flat Layer 2 switched networks were the norm. Flat Layer 2 data networks relied on the basic properties of Ethernet and the widespread use of hub repeaters to propagate LAN traffic throughout an organization. As shown in Figure 1-8, networks have fundamentally changed to switched LANs in a hierarchical network. A switched LAN allows more flexibility, traffic management, and additional features, such as:

- Quality of service
- Additional security
- Support for wireless networking and connectivity
- Support for new technologies, such as IP telephony and mobility services

Figure 1-9 shows the hierarchical design used in the borderless switched network.

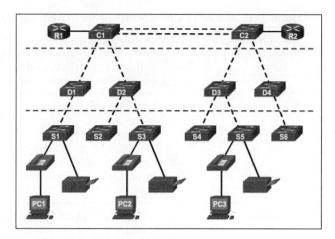

Figure 1-8   Hierarchical Networks

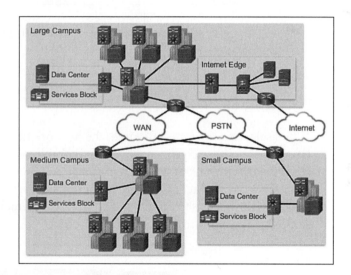

Figure 1-9   Three-Tier Design in Borderless Switched Networks

Form Factors (1.1.2.2)

There are various types of switches used in business networks. It is important to deploy the appropriate types of switches based on network requirements. Table 1-1 highlights some common business considerations when selecting switch equipment.

Table 1-1   Business Considerations for Switch Selection

Switch Feature	Business Consideration
Cost	The cost of a switch will depend on the number and speed of the interfaces, supported features, and expansion capability.
Port density	Network switches must support the appropriate number of devices on the network.
Power	It is now common to power access points, IP phones, and even compact switches using Power over Ethernet (PoE). In addition to PoE considerations, some chassis-based switches support redundant power supplies.
Reliability	The switch should provide continuous access to the network.
Port speed	The speed of the network connection is of primary concern to the end users.
Frame buffers	The capability of the switch to store frames is important in a network where there may be congested ports to servers or other areas of the network.
Scalability	The number of users on a network typically grows over time; therefore, the switch should provide the opportunity for growth.

When selecting the type of switch, the network designer must choose between a fixed or a modular configuration, and stackable or non-stackable. Another consideration is the thickness of the switch, which is expressed in number of rack units. This is important for switches that are mounted in a rack. For example, the fixed configuration switches shown in Figure 1-10 are all 1 rack unit (1U). These options are sometimes referred to as switch form factors.

Features and options are limited to those that originally come with the switch.

Figure 1-10   Fixed Configuration Switches

Fixed Configuration Switches

Fixed configuration switches do not support features or options beyond those that originally came with the switch (refer to Figure 1-10). The particular model determines the features and options available. For example, a 24-port gigabit fixed switch cannot support additional ports. There are typically different configuration choices that vary in how many and what types of ports are included with a fixed configuration switch.

Modular Configuration Switches

Modular configuration switches offer more flexibility in their configuration. Modular configuration switches typically come with different sized chassis that allow for the installation of different numbers of modular line cards (Figure 1-11). The line cards actually contain the ports. The line card fits into the switch chassis the way that expansion cards fit into a PC. The larger the chassis, the more modules it can support. There can be many different chassis sizes to choose from. A modular switch with a 24-port line card supports an additional 24-port line card, to bring the total number of ports up to 48.

The chassis accepts line cards that contain the ports.

Figure 1-11   Modular Configuration Switches

Stackable Configuration Switches

Stackable configuration switches can be interconnected using a special cable that provides high-bandwidth throughput between the switches (Figure 1-12). Cisco StackWise technology allows the interconnection of up to nine switches. Switches can be stacked one on top of the other with cables connecting the switches in a daisy chain fashion. The stacked switches effectively operate as a single larger switch. Stackable switches are desirable where fault tolerance and bandwidth availability are critical and a modular switch is too costly to implement. Using cross-connected connections, the network can recover quickly if a single switch fails. Stackable switches use a special port for interconnections. Many Cisco stackable switches also support StackPower technology, which enables power sharing among stack members.

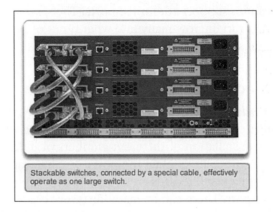

Stackable switches, connected by a special cable, effectively operate as one large switch.

Figure 1-12   Stackable Configuration Switches

Activity 1.1.2.3: Identify Switch Hardware

Go to the online course to match the term to the switch selection criteria.

The Switched Environment (1.2)

One of the most exciting functions of networking is the switched environment because businesses are always adding devices to the wired network, and they will do so through a switch. Learning how switches operate is important to someone entering the networking profession.

Frame Forwarding (1.2.1)

On Ethernet networks, frames contain a source MAC address and a destination MAC address. Switches receive a frame from the source device and quickly forward it toward the destination device.

Switching as a General Concept in Networking and Telecommunications (1.2.1.1)

The concept of switching and forwarding frames is universal in networking and telecommunications. Various types of switches are used in LANs, WANs, and the public switched telephone network (PSTN). The fundamental concept of switching refers to a device making a decision based on two criteria:

- Ingress port
- Destination address

The decision on how a switch forwards traffic is made in relation to the flow of that traffic. The term *ingress* is used to describe a frame entering a device on a specific port. The term *egress* is used to describe frames leaving the device through a particular port.

When a switch makes a decision, it is based on the ingress port and the destination address of the message.

A LAN switch maintains a table that it uses to determine how to forward traffic through the switch.

Interactive Graphic

Activity 1.2.1.1: LAN Switch Forwarding Operation

Go to the course online to see an animation of how a switch forwards a frame based on the destination MAC address. Click the Play button to begin.

In the animated example:

- If a message enters switch port 1 and has a destination address of EA, then the switch forwards the traffic out port 4.

- If a message enters switch port 5 and has a destination address of EE, then the switch forwards the traffic out port 1.

- If a message enters switch port 3 and has a destination address of AB, then the switch forwards the traffic out port 6.

The only intelligence of the LAN switch is its capability to use its table to forward traffic based on the ingress port and the destination address of a message. With a LAN switch, there is only one master switching table that describes a strict association between addresses and ports; therefore, a message with a given destination address always exits the same egress port, regardless of the ingress port it enters.

Cisco LAN switches forward Ethernet frames based on the destination MAC address of the frames.

Dynamically Populating a Switch MAC Address Table (1.2.1.2)

Switches use MAC addresses to direct network communications through the switch to the appropriate outbound port toward the destination. A switch is made up of integrated circuits and accompanying software that controls the data paths through the switch. For a switch to know which port to use to transmit a frame, it must first learn which devices exist on each port. As the switch learns the relationship of ports to devices, it builds a table called a *MAC address table,* or content addressable memory (CAM) table. CAM is a special type of memory used in high-speed searching applications.

LAN switches determine how to handle incoming data frames by maintaining the MAC address table. A switch builds its MAC address table by recording the MAC address of each device connected to each of its ports. The switch uses the information in the MAC address table to send frames destined for a specific device out the port, which has been assigned to that device.

An easy way to remember how a switch operates is the following saying: A switch learns on "source" and forwards based on "destination." This means that a switch populates the MAC address table based on source MAC addresses. As frames enter the switch, the switch "learns" the source MAC address of the received frame and adds the MAC address to the MAC address table or refreshes the age timer of an existing MAC address table entry.

To forward the frame, the switch examines the destination MAC address and compares it to addresses found in the MAC address table. If the address is in the table, the frame is forwarded out the port associated with the MAC address in the table. When the destination MAC address is not found in the MAC address table, the switch forwards the frame out of all ports (flooding) except for the ingress port of the frame. In networks with multiple interconnected switches, the MAC address table contains multiple MAC addresses for a single port connected to the other switches.

The following steps describe the process of building the MAC address table:

Step 1.   The switch receives a frame from PC 1 on Port 1 (Figure 1-13).

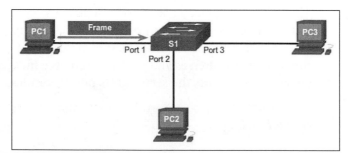

Figure 1-13   Building a MAC Address Table: PC1 Sends Frame to Port 1

Step 2.   The switch examines the source MAC address and compares it to the MAC address table.

■ If the address is not in the MAC address table, it associates the source MAC address of PC 1 with the ingress port (Port 1) in the MAC address table (Figure 1-14).

■ If the MAC address table already has an entry for that source address, it resets the aging timer. An entry for a MAC address is typically kept for five minutes.

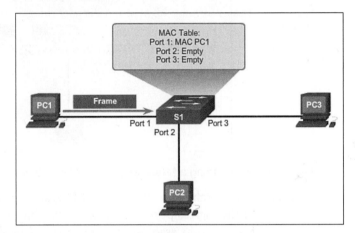

Figure 1-14 Building a MAC Address Table: S1 Adds MAC Address Heard Through Port 1

Step 3. After the switch has recorded the source address information, the switch examines the destination MAC address.

■ If the destination address is not in the MAC table or if it's a broadcast MAC address, as indicated by all Fs, the switch floods the frame to all ports, except the ingress port (Figure 1-15).

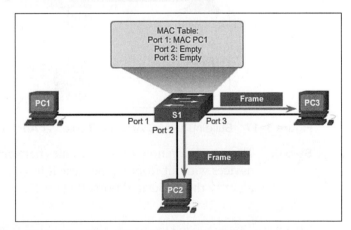

Figure 1-15 Building a MAC Address Table: S1 Broadcasts the Frame

Step 4.   The destination device (PC 3) replies to the frame with a unicast frame addressed to PC 1 (Figure 1-16).

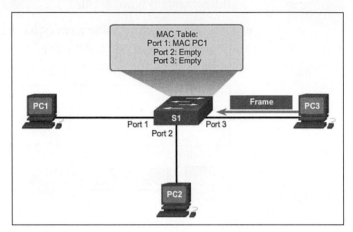

Figure 1-16   Building a MAC Address Table: PC3 Sends a Reply Frame

Step 5.   The switch enters the source MAC address of PC 3 and the port number of the ingress port into the address table. The destination address of the frame and its associated egress port is found in the MAC address table (Figure 1-17).

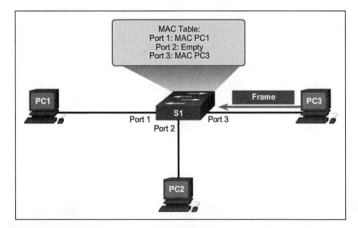

Figure 1-17   Building a MAC Address Table: S1 Adds the MAC Address for PC3

Step 6.   The switch can now forward frames between these source and destination devices without flooding because it has entries in the address table that identify the associated ports (Figure 1-18).

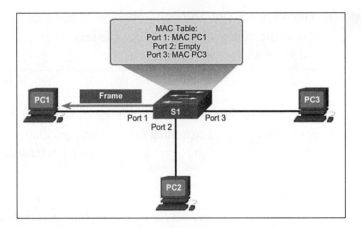

Figure 1-18   Building a MAC Address Table: S1 Sends the Frame to Port 1

Switch Forwarding Methods (1.2.1.3)

Commonly, in earlier networks, as they grew, enterprises began to experience slower network performance. Ethernet bridges (an early version of a switch) were added to networks to limit the size of the collision domains. In the 1990s, advancements in integrated circuit technologies allowed for LAN switches to replace Ethernet bridges. These LAN switches were able to move the Layer 2 forwarding decisions from software to *application-specific-integrated circuits (ASICs)*. ASICs reduce the packet-handling time within the device, and allow the device to handle an increased number of ports without degrading performance. This method of forwarding data frames at Layer 2 was referred to as *store-and-forward switching*. This term distinguished it from cut-through switching.

As shown in the online video, the store-and-forward method makes a forwarding decision on a frame after it has received the entire frame and then checked the frame for errors.

Video 1.2.1.3: Store-and-Forward Switching

Video

Go to the course online to see an animation of how a store-and-forward switch works.

By contrast, the *cut-through switching method*, as shown in the online video, begins the forwarding process after the destination MAC address of an incoming frame and the egress port has been determined.

Video

Video 1.2.1.3: Cut-Through Switching

Go to the course online. Click on the second graphic to see an animation of how a cut-through switch works.

Store-and-Forward Switching (1.2.1.4)

Store-and-forward switching has two primary characteristics that distinguish it from cut-through: error checking and automatic buffering.

Error Checking

A switch using store-and-forward switching performs an error check on an incoming frame. After receiving the entire frame on the ingress port, as shown in Figure 1-19, the switch compares the *frame-check-sequence (FCS)* value in the last field of the datagram against its own FCS calculations. The FCS is an error checking process that helps to ensure that the frame is free of physical and data-link errors. If the frame is error-free, the switch forwards the frame. Otherwise, the frame is dropped.

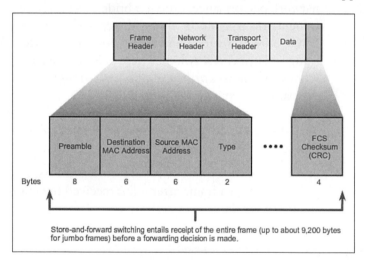

Figure 1-19   Store-and-Forward Switching

Automatic Buffering

The ingress port buffering process used by store-and-forward switches provides the flexibility to support any mix of Ethernet speeds. For example, handling an incoming frame traveling into a 100 Mb/s Ethernet port that must be sent out a 1 Gb/s interface would require using the store-and-forward method. With any mismatch in speeds between the ingress and egress ports, the switch stores the entire frame in a buffer, computes the FCS check, forwards the frame to the egress port buffer and then sends the frame.

Store-and-forward switching is Cisco's primary LAN switching method.

A store-and-forward switch drops frames that do not pass the FCS check, therefore it does not forward invalid frames. By contrast, a cut-through switch may forward invalid frames because no FCS check is performed.

Cut-Through Switching (1.2.1.5)

An advantage to cut-through switching is the capability of the switch to start forwarding a frame earlier than store-and-forward switching. There are two primary characteristics of cut-through switching: rapid frame forwarding and invalid frame processing.

Rapid Frame Forwarding

As indicated in Figure 1-20, a switch using the cut-through method can make a forwarding decision as soon as it has looked up the destination MAC address of the frame in its MAC address table. The switch does not have to wait for the rest of the frame to enter the ingress port before making its forwarding decision.

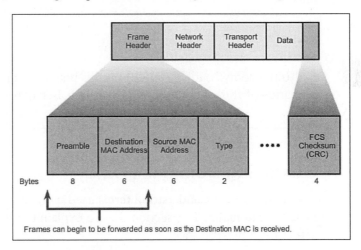

Figure 1-20   Cut-Through Switching

With today's MAC controllers and ASICs, a switch using the cut-through method can quickly decide whether it needs to examine a larger portion of a frame's headers for additional filtering purposes. For example, the switch can analyze past the first 14 bytes (the source MAC address, destination MAC, and the EtherType fields), and examine an additional 40 bytes in order to perform more sophisticated functions relative to IPv4 Layers 3 and 4.

The cut-through switching method does not drop most invalid frames. Frames with errors are forwarded to other segments of the network. If there is a high error rate (invalid frames) in the network, cut-through switching can have a negative impact on bandwidth; thus, clogging up bandwidth with damaged and invalid frames.

Fragment Free

Fragment free switching is a modified form of cut-through switching in which the switch waits for the collision window (64 bytes) to pass before forwarding the frame. This means each frame will be checked into the data field to make sure no fragmentation has occurred. Fragment free mode provides better error checking than cut-through, with practically no increase in latency.

With a lower latency speed advantage of cut-through switching, it is more appropriate for extremely demanding, high-performance computing (HPC) applications that require process-to-process latencies of 10 microseconds or less.

Interactive Graphic

Activity 1.2.1.6: Frame Forwarding Methods

Go to the online course to indicate whether each given action is performed by store-and-forward or cut-through switching. Use the online curriculum to check your answer.

Interactive Graphic

Activity 1.2.1.7: Switch It!

Go to the course outline to perform this practice activity where you have multiple scenarios of frames going through a switch. Select how the switch will handle the frame.

Switching Domains (1.2.2)

Two commonly misunderstood terms used with switching are collision domains and broadcast domains. This section tries to explain these two important concepts that affect LAN performance.

Collision Domains (1.2.2.1)

In hub-based Ethernet segments, network devices compete for the medium, because devices must take turns when transmitting. The network segments that share the same bandwidth between devices are known as *collision domains*, because when two or more devices within that segment try to communicate at the same time, collisions may occur.

It is possible, however, to use networking devices such as switches, which operate at the data link layer of the OSI model to divide a network into segments and reduce the number of devices that compete for bandwidth. Each port on a switch is a new segment because the devices plugged into the ports do not compete with each other for bandwidth. The result is that each port represents a new collision domain. More bandwidth is available to the devices on a segment, and collisions in one collision domain do not interfere with the other segments. This is also known as *microsegmentation*.

As shown in the Figure 1-21, each switch port connects to a single PC or server, and each switch port represents a separate collision domain.

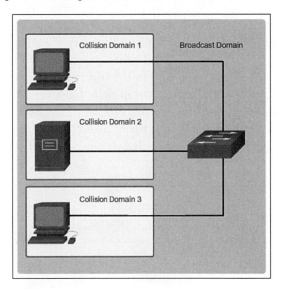

Figure 1-21   Collision Domains

Broadcast Domains (1.2.2.2)

Although switches filter most frames based on MAC addresses, they do not filter broadcast frames. For other switches on the LAN to receive broadcast frames, switches must flood these frames out all ports. A collection of interconnected switches forms a single *broadcast domain*. A network layer device, such as a router, can divide a Layer 2 broadcast domain. Routers are used to segment both collision and broadcast domains.

When a device sends a Layer 2 broadcast, the destination MAC address in the frame is set to all binary ones. A frame with a destination MAC address of all binary ones is received by all devices in the broadcast domain.

The Layer 2 broadcast domain is referred to as the MAC broadcast domain. The MAC broadcast domain consists of all devices on the LAN that receive broadcast frames from a host.

Interactive
Graphic

Activity 1.2.2.2: Broadcast Domains

Go to the online curriculum, and click Play to see this in the first half of the animation.

Watch how a switch broadcasts a frame out all ports except the port that received the frame.

When a switch receives a broadcast frame, the switch forwards the frame out each of the switch ports, except the ingress port where the broadcast frame was received. Each device connected to the switch receives a copy of the broadcast frame and processes it, as shown in the top broadcast domain in Figure 1-22. Broadcasts are sometimes necessary for initially locating other devices and network services, but they also reduce network efficiency. Network bandwidth is used to propagate the broadcast traffic. Too many broadcasts and a heavy traffic load on a network can result in congestion: a slowdown in the network performance.

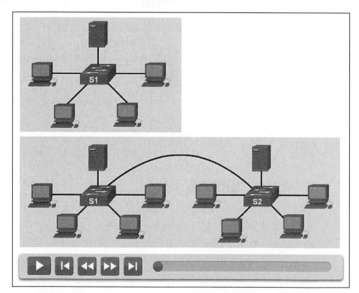

Figure 1-22   Broadcast Domains

When two switches are connected together, the broadcast domain is increased, as seen in the second (bottom) broadcast domain shown in Figure 1-22. In this case, a broadcast frame is forwarded to all connected ports on switch S1. Switch S1 is connected to switch S2. The frame is then also propagated to all devices connected to switch S2.

Alleviating Network Congestion (1.2.2.3)

LAN switches have special characteristics that make them effective at alleviating network congestion. First, they allow the segmentation of a LAN into separate collision domains. Each port of the switch represents a separate collision domain and provides the full bandwidth to the device or devices that are connected to that port. Second, they provide full-duplex communication between devices. A full-duplex connection can carry transmitted and received signals at the same time. Full-duplex connections have dramatically increased LAN network performance and are required for 1 Gb/s Ethernet speeds and higher.

Switches interconnect LAN segments (collision domains), use a table of MAC addresses to determine the segment to which the frame is to be sent, and can lessen or eliminate collisions entirely. Table 1-2 shows some important characteristics of switches that contribute to alleviating network congestion.

Table 1-2   Switch Characteristics That Help with Congestion

Characteristic	Explanation
High port density	Switches have high-port densities: 24- and 48-port switches are often just 1 rack unit (1.75 inches) in height and operate at speeds of 100 Mb/s, 1 Gb/s, and 10 Gb/s. Large enterprise switches may support hundreds of ports.
Large frame buffers	The ability to store more received frames before having to start dropping them is useful, particularly when there may be congested ports to servers or other parts of the network.
Port speed	Depending on the cost of a switch, it may be possible to support a mixture of speeds. Ports of 100 Mb/s and 1 or 10 Gb/s are common. (100 Gb/s is also possible.)
Fast internal switching	Having fast internal forwarding capabilities allows high performance. The method that is used may be a fast internal bus or shared memory, which affects the overall performance of the switch.
Low per-port cost	Switches provide high-port density at a lower cost. For this reason, LAN switches can accommodate network designs featuring fewer users per segment, therefore, increasing the average available bandwidth per user.

Activity 1.2.2.4: Circle the Domain

Go to the online course to view nine network topologies. On each graphic, draw a circle around the devices that make up each broadcast or collision domain as directed.

Summary (1.3)

Class Activity 1.3.1.1: It's Network Access Time

Use Packet Tracer for this activity. Internet connectivity is not required in this design. Work with a classmate to create two network designs to accommodate the following scenarios:

Scenario 1 – Classroom Design (LAN)

- 15 student end devices represented by 1 or 2 PCs

- 1 instructor end device preferably represented by a server

- Stream video presentations over a LAN connection

Scenario 2 – Administrative Design (WAN)

- All requirements as listed in Scenario 1

- Access to and from a remote administrative server for video presentations and pushed updates for network application software

Both the LAN and WAN designs should fit on to one Packet Tracer file screen. All intermediary devices should be labeled with the switch model (or name) and the router model (or name).

Save your work and be ready to justify your device decisions and layout to your instructor and the class.

Interactive Graphic

Activity 1.3.1.2: Basic Switch Configurations

Configuring switches is a common practice for LAN technicians, and practice is the key to becoming proficient. This Syntax Checker activity reviews basic switch configurations from the first course.

Go to the course outline to perform this practice activity.

Packet Tracer ☐ Activity

Packet Tracer Activity 1.3.1.3: Skills Integration Challenge

As a recently hired LAN technician, your network manager has asked you to demonstrate your ability to configure a small LAN. Your tasks include configuring initial settings on two switches using the Cisco IOS and configuring IP address parameters on host devices to provide end-to-end connectivity. You are to use two switches and two hosts/PCs on a cabled and powered network.

We have seen that the trend in networks is toward convergence using a single set of wires and devices to handle voice, video, and data transmission. In addition, there has been a dramatic shift in the way businesses operate. No longer are employees constrained to physical offices or by geographic boundaries. Resources must now be seamlessly available anytime and anywhere. The Cisco Borderless Network architecture enables different elements, from access switches to wireless access points, to work together and allow users to access resources from any place at any time.

The traditional three-layer hierarchical design model divides the network into core, distribution, and access layers, and allows each portion of the network to be optimized for specific functionality. It provides modularity, resiliency, and flexibility, which provides a foundation that allows network designers to overlay security, mobility, and unified communication features. In some networks, having a separate core and distribution layer is not required. In these networks, the functionality of the core layer and the distribution layer are often collapsed together.

Cisco LAN switches use ASICs to forward frames based on the destination MAC address. Before this can be accomplished, the switch must first use the source MAC address of incoming frames to build a MAC address table in content-addressable memory (CAM). If the destination MAC address is contained in this table, the frame is forwarded only to the specific destination port. In cases where the destination MAC address is not found in the MAC address table, the frames are flooded out all ports except the one on which the frame was received.

Switches use either store-and-forward or cut-through switching. Store-and-forward reads the entire frame into a buffer and checks the CRC before forwarding the frame. Cut-through switching only reads the first portion of the frame and starts forwarding it as soon as the destination address is read. Although this is extremely fast, no error checking is done on the frame before forwarding.

Every port on a switch forms a separate collision domain allowing for extremely high-speed full-duplex communication. Switch ports do not block broadcasts, and connecting switches together can extend the size of the broadcast domain often resulting in degraded network performance.

Practice

The following activities provide practice with the topics introduced in this chapter. The Class Activities are available in the companion *Routing and Switching Essential Lab Manual* (978-1-58713-320-6). The Packet Tracer Activities PKA files are found in the online course.

Class Activities

Class Activity 1.0.1.2: Sent or Received Instructions

Class Activity 1.3.1.1: It's Network Access Time

Packet Tracer Activities

Packet Tracer Activity1.3.1.3: Skills Integration Challenge

Check Your Understanding Questions

Complete all the review questions listed here to test your understanding of the topics and concepts in this chapter. The appendix, "Answers to the 'Check Your Understanding' Questions," lists the answers.

1. Which three options correctly associate a layer of the hierarchical design model with the function of that layer? (Choose three.)

   A. Core - end device connectivity

   B. Distribution - aggregation and traffic control

   C. Access - end device connectivity

   D. Distribution - high speed backbone

   E. Access - aggregation of traffic

   F. Core - high speed backbone

2. Which hierarchical network design goal is to provide a way for the network to always be accessible?

   A. hierarchical

   B. modularity

   C. resiliency

   D. flexibility

3. Which two layers of the hierarchical network design model are commonly combined into a single layer in a small-to-medium sized network architecture? (Choose two.)

    A. access

    B. data link

    C. network

    D. distribution

    E. application

    F. core

4. What is convergence as it relates to network design?

    A. Implementation of an access-distribution-core layer design model for all sites in a corporation

    B. A centralized point in the network design where all traffic aggregates before transmission to the destination

    C. The combining of voice and video with traditional network traffic

    D. Designing a network in such a way that each tier has a specific function and upgrade path

5. What are three benefits of a converged network? (Choose three.)

    A. Voice and data support staff are combined.

    B. Network design is simplified.

    C. Network configuration is simplified.

    D. Voice, video, and data traffic use one physical network.

    E. Maintenance is simpler than hierarchical networks.

    F. Network moves, adds, and changes are simplified.

6. Which two terms are correctly defined? (Choose two.)

    A. Internal switching rate - processing capability of a switch that quantifies how much data it can process per second

    B. Port density - capability to use multiple switch ports concurrently for higher throughput data communication

    C. Rack unit - number of ports that can fit in a specific switch

    D. Cut-through switching - the transmission of a frame after the destination MAC address has been examined and processed

    E. Modular configuration switch - only support features or options that ship with the device

7. A switch that uses MAC addresses to forward frames operates at which layer of the OSI model?

   A. Layer 1

   B. Layer 2

   C. Layer 3

   D. Layer 4

8. A switch has just been powered on. PC1 connects to port 1; PC2 connects to port 2. If PC1 sends data to PC2, how will the switch process the frame?

   A. The switch forwards the frame based on the MAC address of PC2.

   B. The switch adds the MAC address of PC1 (that is received on the ingress port) to the switch MAC address table.

   C. The switch forwards the frame to all switch ports including ports 1 and 2.

   D. The switch adds the IP address of PC2 (that is sent through the egress port) to the switch MAC address table.

9. What function is most likely to be provided by a Cisco access layer switch?

   A. PoE

   B. Routing

   C. Link aggregation

   D. Fault isolation

10. Use the abbreviated MAC addresses in the MAC address table to determine the correct answer. A PC connected to port Gi0/3 sends data to a PC connected to port Gi0/5. When the switch receives the data, what will the switch do to process the frame?

Port	MAC address
Gi0/3	AA
Gi0/7	AB

    A. Add the destination MAC address to the switch MAC address table.

    B. Forward the data out all ports except for port Gi0/3.

    C. Forward the data to port Gi0/3.

    D. Forward the data out all ports.

    E. Add both the source and destination MAC addresses to the switch MAC address table.

11. Use the abbreviated MAC addresses in the MAC address table to determine the correct answer. A PC connected to port Gi0/4 sends data to a PC connected to port Gi0/3. When the switch receives the data, what will the switch do first to process the frame?

Port	MAC address
Gi0/3	AA
Gi0/7	AB

A. Add the source MAC address to the switch MAC address table.

B. Forward the data out all ports except for port 4.

C. Forward the data to port 5.

D. Forward the data out all ports.

E. Add both the source and destination MAC addresses to the switch MAC address table.

F. Add the destination MAC address to the switch MAC address table.

CHAPTER 2

Basic Switching Concepts and Configuration

Objectives

Upon completion of this chapter, you will be able to answer the following questions:

- What are the steps a switch takes after power is applied?

- What is the function of the boot loader if the operating system is corrupt or missing?

- How might the switch LEDs help with troubleshooting?

- What are the steps taken to configure a Cisco switch with an IP address, subnet mask, and default gateway?

- What interface is used to apply an IP address to a Cisco switch?

- What functionality is available once a switch has an IP address and default gateway?

- What type of customization can be applied to a switch port?

- What tools can be used to troubleshoot a Layer 1 or 2 problem?

- What steps are required to configure a switch for SSH access?

- What are some common security attacks that affect switches?

- What mitigation tools could be used on a Cisco switch to prevent or react to a security attack?

- What are best practices for switch security?

- What steps are required to configure switch security?

- What is the purpose of NTP?

Key Terms

This chapter uses the following key terms. You can find the definitions in the Glossary.

Introduction (2.0.1.1)

Switches are used to connect multiple devices on the same network. In a properly designed network, LAN switches are responsible for directing and controlling the data flow at the access layer to networked resources.

Cisco switches are self-configuring and no additional configurations are necessary for them to function out of the box. However, Cisco switches run Cisco IOS, and can be manually configured to better meet the needs of the network. This includes adjusting port speed and bandwidth, as well as implementing security requirements.

Additionally, Cisco switches can be managed both locally and remotely. To remotely manage a switch, it needs to have an IP address and default gateway configured. These are just two of the configurations discussed in this chapter.

Switches operate at the access layer where client network devices connect directly to the network and IT departments want uncomplicated network access for the users. The access layer is one of the most vulnerable areas of the network because it is so exposed to the user. Switches need to be configured to be resilient to attacks of all types while they are protecting user data and allowing for high speed connections. Port security is one of the security features Cisco managed switches provide.

This chapter examines some of the basic switch configuration settings required to maintain a secure, available, switched LAN environment.

Class Activity 2.0.1.2: Stand by Me

Scenario

When you arrived to class today, you were given a number by your instructor to use for this introductory class activity.

When class begins, your instructor will ask certain students with specific numbers to stand. Your job is to record the standing students' numbers for each scenario.

Scenario 1: Students with numbers starting with the number 5 should stand. Record the numbers of the standing students.

Scenario 2: Students with numbers ending in B should stand. Record the numbers of the standing students.

Scenario 3: Students with the number 504C should stand. Record the number of the standing student.

At the end of this activity, divide into small groups and record answers to the Reflection questions on the PDF contained in the online course.

Save your work and be prepared to share it with another student or the entire class.

Basic Switch Configuration (2.1)

Switches are one of the most numerous devices installed onto the corporate network infrastructure. Configuring them can be fun and challenging. Knowing how switches normally boot and load an operating system is also important.

Switch Boot Sequence (2.1.1.1)

After a Cisco switch is powered on, it goes through the following boot sequence:

Step 1. First, the switch loads a power-on self-test (POST) program stored in ROM. POST checks the CPU subsystem. It tests the CPU, DRAM, and the portion of the flash device that makes up the flash file system.

Step 2. Next, the switch loads the boot loader software. The *boot loader* is a small program stored in ROM and is run immediately after POST successfully completes.

Step 3. The boot loader performs low-level CPU initialization. It initializes the CPU registers that control where physical memory is mapped, the quantity of memory, and memory speed.

Step 4. The boot loader initializes the flash file system on the system board.

Step 5. Finally, the boot loader locates and loads a default IOS operating system software image into memory and hands control of the switch over to the IOS.

The boot loader finds the Cisco IOS image on the switch using the following process: The switch attempts to automatically boot by using information in the BOOT environment variable. If this variable is not set, the switch attempts to load and execute the first executable file it can by performing a recursive, depth-first search throughout the flash file system. In a depth-first search of a directory, each encountered subdirectory is completely searched before continuing the search in the original directory. On Catalyst 2960 Series switches, the image file is normally contained in a directory that has the same name as the image file (excluding the .bin file extension).

The IOS operating system then initializes the interfaces using the Cisco IOS commands found in the configuration file, startup configuration, which is stored in NVRAM.

In Figure 2-1, the BOOT environment variable is set using the **boot system** global configuration mode command. Use the **show bootvar** command (**show boot** in older IOS versions) to see the current IOS boot file version.

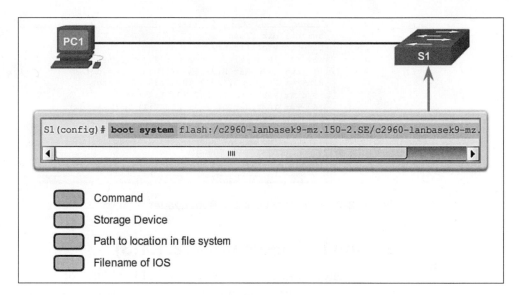

Figure 2-1   Configure BOOT Environment Variable

Recovering from a System Crash (2.1.1.2)

The boot loader provides access into the switch if the operating system cannot be used because of missing or damaged system files. The boot loader has a command line that provides access to files stored in flash memory.

The boot loader can be accessed through a console connection using these steps:

Step 1.   Connect a console cable from the PC to the switch console port. Configure terminal emulation software to connect to the switch.

Step 2.   Unplug the switch power cord.

Step 3.   Reconnect the power cord to the switch and within 15 seconds press and hold down the Mode button while the System LED is still flashing green.

Step 4.   Continue pressing the Mode button until the System LED turns briefly amber and then solid green; then release the Mode button.

Step 5.   The boot loader `switch:` prompt appears in the terminal emulation software on the PC.

The **boot loader** command line supports commands to format the flash file system, reinstall the operating system software, and recover from a lost or forgotten password. For example, the **dir** command can be used to view a list of files within a specified directory as shown in Figure 2-2.

```
switch: dir flash:
Directory of flash:/
 3 -rwx 1839 Mar 01 2002 00:48:15 config.text
11 -rwx 1140 Mar 01 2002 04:18:48 vlan.dat
21 -rwx 26 Mar 01 2002 00:01:39 env_vars
 9 drwx 768 Mar 01 2002 23:11:42 html
16 -rwx 1037 Mar 01 2002 00:01:11 config.text
14 -rwx 1099 Mar 01 2002 01:14:05 homepage.htm
22 -rwx 96 Mar 01 2002 00:01:39 system_env_vars
17 drwx 192 Mar 06 2002 23:22:03 c2960-lanbase-mz.122-25.FX

15998976 bytes total (6397440 bytes free)
```

Figure 2-2   Directory Listing in Boot Loader

Switch LED Indicators (2.1.1.3)

Cisco Catalyst switches have several status LED indicator lights. You can use the switch LEDs to quickly monitor switch activity and its performance. Switches of different models and feature sets will have different LEDs, and their placement on the front panel of the switch may also vary.

Figure 2-3 shows the switch LEDs and the Mode button for a Cisco Catalyst 2960 switch. The Mode button is used to toggle through port status, port duplex, port speed, and PoE (if supported) status of the port LEDs.

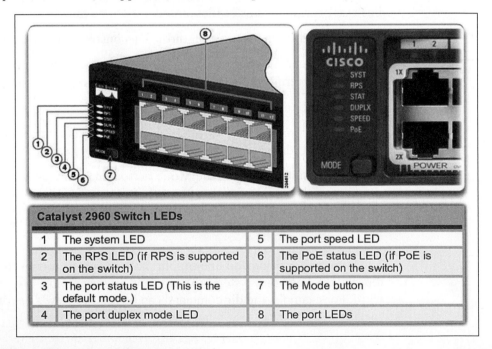

	Catalyst 2960 Switch LEDs		
1	The system LED	5	The port speed LED
2	The RPS LED (if RPS is supported on the switch)	6	The PoE status LED (if PoE is supported on the switch)
3	The port status LED (This is the default mode.)	7	The Mode button
4	The port duplex mode LED	8	The port LEDs

Figure 2-3   Cisco 2960 Switch LEDs

Table 2-1 contains the purpose of the Cisco 2960 switch LED indicators, and the meaning of their colors.

Table 2-1   Purpose of Cisco Switch LEDs

System LED	Shows whether the system is receiving power and is functioning properly. If the LED is off, it means the system is not powered. If the LED is green, the system is operating normally. If the LED is amber, the system is receiving power but is not functioning properly.
Redundant Power System (RPS) LED	Shows the RPS status. If the LED is off, the RPS is off or not properly connected. If the LED is green, the RPS is connected and ready to provide backup power. If the LED is blinking green, the RPS is connected but is unavailable because it is providing power to another device. If the LED is amber, the RPS is in standby mode or in a fault condition. If the LED is blinking amber, the internal power supply in the switch has failed, and the RPS is providing power.
Port Status LED	Indicates that the port status mode is selected when the LED is green. This is the default mode. When selected, the port LEDs will display colors with different meanings. If the LED is off, there is no link, or the port was administratively shut down. If the LED is green, a link is present. If the LED is blinking green, there is activity and the port is sending or receiving data. If the LED is alternating green-amber, there is a link fault. If the LED is amber, the port is blocked to ensure a loop does not exist in the forwarding domain and is not forwarding data (typically, ports will remain in this state for the first 30 seconds after being activated). If the LED is blinking amber, the port is blocked to prevent a possible loop in the forwarding domain.
Port Duplex LED	Indicates the port duplex mode is selected when the LED is green. When selected, port LEDs that are off are in half-duplex mode. If the port LED is green, the port is in full-duplex mode.
Port Speed LED	Indicates the port speed mode is selected. When selected, the port LEDs will display colors with different meanings. If the LED is off, the port is operating at 10 Mb/s. If the LED is green, the port is operating at 100 Mb/s. If the LED is blinking green, the port is operating at 1000 Mb/s.
Power over Ethernet (PoE) Mode LED	If PoE is supported, a PoE mode LED will be present. If the LED is off, it indicates the PoE mode is not selected and none of the ports have been denied power or placed in a fault condition. If the LED is blinking amber, the PoE mode is not selected but at least one of the ports has been denied power, or has a PoE fault. If the LED is green, it indicates the PoE mode is selected and the port LEDs will display colors with different meanings. If the port LED is off, PoE is off. If the port LED is green, PoE is being provided to a device. If the port LED is alternating green-amber, PoE is denied because providing power to the powered device will exceed the switch power capacity. If the LED is blinking amber, PoE is off due to a fault. If the LED is amber, PoE for the port has been disabled.

Preparing for Basic Switch Management (2.1.1.4)

To prepare a switch for remote management access, the switch must be configured with an IP address and a subnet mask. Keep in mind that to manage the switch from a remote network, the switch must be configured with a default gateway. This is very similar to configuring the IP address information on host devices. In Figure 2-4, the *switch virtual interface (SVI)* on S1 should be assigned an IP address. The SVI is a virtual interface, not a physical port on the switch.

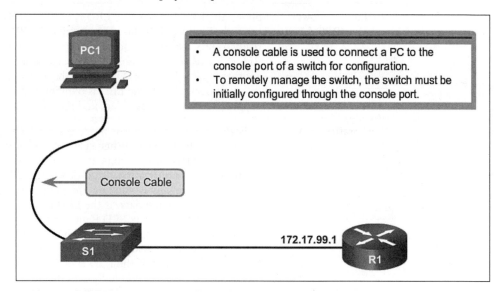

Figure 2-4   Preparing for Remote Switch Management

SVI is a concept related to VLANs. VLANs are numbered logical groups to which physical ports can be assigned. Configurations and settings applied to a VLAN are also applied to all the ports assigned to that VLAN.

By default, the switch is configured to have the management of the switch controlled through VLAN 1. All ports are assigned to VLAN 1 by default. For security purposes, it is considered a best practice to use a VLAN other than VLAN 1 for the management VLAN. Furthermore, it is also a best practice to use a VLAN that is not used by end devices such as users and printers.

Note

These IP settings are only for remote management access to the switch; assigning an IP address to the switch does not allow the switch to route Layer 3 packets.

Configuring Basic Switch Management Access with IPv4 (2.1.1.5)

Step 1. Configure the Management Interface.

■ An IP address and subnet mask is configured on the management SVI of the switch from VLAN interface configuration mode. As shown in Table 2-2, the **interface vlan 99** command is used to enter interface configuration mode. The **ip address** command is used to configure the IP address. The **no shutdown** command enables the interface.

Table 2-2   Configure the Switch Management Interface

Enter global configuration mode.	`S1# configure terminal`
Enter interface configuration mode for the SVI.	`S1(config)# interface vlan 99`
Configure the management interface IP address.	`S1(config-if)# ip address 172.17.99.11 255.255.0.0`
Enable the management interface.	`S1(config-if)# no shutdown`
Return to privileged EXEC mode.	`S1(config-if)# end`
Save the running config to the startup config.	`S1# copy running-config startup-config`

■ In this example, VLAN 99 is configured with the IP address and mask of 172.17.99.11. To create a VLAN with the *vlan_id* of 99 and associate it to an interface, use the following commands:

```
S1(config)# vlan vlan_id
S1(config-vlan)# name vlan_name
S1(config)# end
S1(config)# config terminal
S1(config)# interface interface_id
S1(config-if)# switchport mode access
S1(config-if)# switchport access vlan vlan_id
```

Note

The SVI for VLAN 99 will not appear as "up/up" until VLAN 99 is created, the IP address assigned to the SVI, the **no shutdown** command entered, and either (1) a device is connected to an access port associated with VLAN 99 (not a best practice) or (2) a trunk link (covered in the VLAN chapter) connects to another network device such as a switch.

Step 2.   Configure the Default Gateway.

■ The switch should be configured with a default gateway if the switch will be managed remotely from networks not directly connected. The default gateway is the first Layer 3 device (such as a router) on the same management VLAN network to which the switch connects. The switch will forward IP packets with destination IP addresses outside the local network to the default gateway. As shown in Table 2-3 and Figure 2-5, R1 is the default gateway for S1. The interface on R1 connected to the switch has IP address 172.17.99.1. This address is the default gateway address for S1.

Table 2-3   Commands to Configure a Switch Default Gateway

Enter global configuration mode.	`S1# configure terminal`
Configure the switch default gateway.	`S1(config)# ip default-gateway 172.17.99.1`
Return to privileged EXEC mode.	`S1(config)# end`
Save the running config to the startup config.	`S1# copy running-config startup-config`

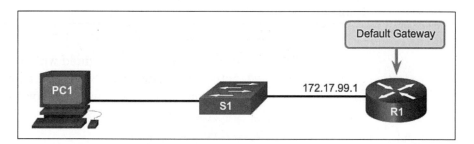

Figure 2-5   Configuring the Switch Default Gateway

■ To configure the default gateway for the switch, use the **ip default-gateway** command. Enter the IP address of the default gateway. The default gateway is the IP address of the router interface to which the switch connects. Use the following command to backup the configuration: **copy running-config startup-config**.

Step 3.   Verify the Configuration.

■ As shown in Figure 2-6, the **show ip interface brief** command is useful when determining the status of both physical and virtual interfaces. The output shown in Figure 2-6 confirms that interface VLAN 99 has been configured with an IP address and a subnet mask, and that FastEthernet port Fa0/18 has been assigned to the VLAN 99 management interface. Both interfaces are now "up/up" and operational.

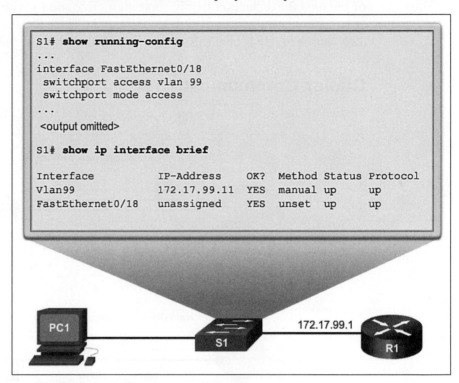

```
S1# show running-config
...
interface FastEthernet0/18
 switchport access vlan 99
 switchport mode access
...
 <output omitted>

S1# show ip interface brief

Interface          IP-Address      OK?  Method Status Protocol
Vlan99             172.17.99.11    YES  manual up     up
FastEthernet0/18   unassigned      YES  unset  up     up
```

172.17.99.1

Figure 2-6   Verifying the Switch Management Interface Configuration

Lab 2.1.1.6: Basic Switch Configuration

In this lab, you will complete the following objectives:

- Part 1: Cable the Network and Verify the Default Switch Configuration
- Part 2: Configure Basic Network Device Settings
- Part 3: Verify and Test Network Connectivity
- Part 4: Manage the MAC Address Table

Configure Switch Ports (2.1.2)

Port configuration starts with the basics of duplex and speed. Sometimes switch ports must manually have their duplex mode and speed manually configured. Most of the time the technician simply connects a cable and lets the network device and switch automatically negotiate these parameters. There are also times when things go awry and there are issues. This section helps you with these basic concepts.

Duplex Communication (2.1.2.1)

Figure 2-7 illustrates full-duplex and half-duplex communication.

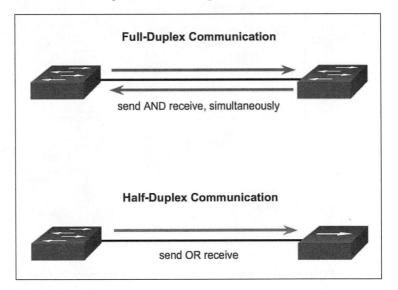

Figure 2-7   Duplex Modes

Full-duplex communication improves the performance of a switched LAN. Full-duplex communication increases effective bandwidth by allowing both ends of a connection to transmit and receive data simultaneously. This is also known as bidirectional communication. This method of optimizing network performance requires micro-segmentation. A micro-segmented LAN is created when a switch port has only one device connected and is operating at full-duplex. This results in a micro size collision domain of a single device. Because there is only one device connected, a micro-segmented LAN is collision free.

Unlike full-duplex communication, half-duplex communication is unidirectional. Sending and receiving data does not occur at the same time. Half-duplex communication creates performance issues because data can flow in only one direction at a time, often resulting in collisions. Half-duplex connections are typically seen in older hardware, such as hubs. Full-duplex communication has replaced half-duplex in most hardware.

Most Ethernet and Fast Ethernet NICs sold today offer full-duplex capability. Gigabit Ethernet and 10Gb NICs require full-duplex connections to operate. In full-duplex mode, the collision detection circuit on the NIC is disabled. Frames that are sent by the two connected devices cannot collide because the devices use two separate circuits in the network cable. Full-duplex connections require a switch that supports full-duplex configuration, or a direct connection using an Ethernet cable between two devices.

Standard, shared hub-based Ethernet configuration efficiency is typically rated at 50 to 60 percent of the stated bandwidth. Full-duplex offers 100 percent efficiency in both directions (transmitting and receiving). This results in a 200 percent potential use of the stated bandwidth.

Configure Switch Ports at the Physical Layer (2.1.2.2)

Just as a network card in a PC can have specific conditions such as duplex and speed set, so too can a switch port. This section examines how to configure specific parameters on a Cisco switch port and introduces auto-MDIX.

Duplex and Speed

Switch ports can be manually configured with specific duplex and speed settings. Use the **duplex** interface configuration mode command to manually specify the duplex mode for a switch port. Use the **speed** interface configuration mode command to manually specify the speed for a switch port. In Figure 2-8 and Table 2-4, port F0/1 on switch S1 and S2 are manually configured with the **full** keyword for the **duplex** command and the **100** keyword for the **speed** command.

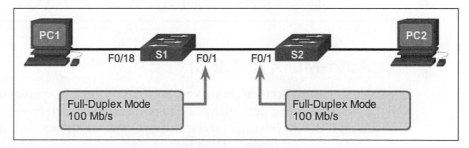

Figure 2-8   Manually Configure Duplex and Speed

Table 2-4   Cisco Switch Port Configuration

Enter global configuration mode.	S1# **configure terminal**
Enter interface configuration mode.	S1(config)# **interface fastethernet 0/1**
Configure the interface duplex mode.	S1(config-if)# **duplex full**
Configure the interface speed.	S1(config-if)# **speed 100**
Return to privileged EXEC mode.	S1(config-if)# **end**
Save the running config to the startup config.	S1# **copy running-config startup-config**

The default setting for both duplex and speed for switch ports on Cisco Catalyst 2960 and 3560 switches is auto. The 10/100/1000 ports operate in either half- or full-duplex mode when they are set to 10 or 100 Mb/s, but when they are set to 1000 Mb/s (1 Gb/s), they operate only in full-duplex mode. When troubleshooting switch port issues, the duplex and speed settings should be checked.

Note

Mismatched settings for the duplex mode and speed of switch ports can cause connectivity issues. Auto negotiation failure creates mismatched settings. Cisco recommends using the **auto** command for duplex and manually configuring interface speed using the **speed** command in order to avoid connectivity issues between devices.

All fiber optic ports, such as 100BASE-FX ports, operate only at one preset speed and are always full-duplex.

Interactive Graphic

Activity 2.1.2.2: Configure Switch Port Duplex and Speed

Access the second figure in the online course to use the Syntax Checker to practice configuring port Fa0/1 of switch S1.

Auto-MDIX (2.1.2.3)

Until recently, certain cable types (straight-through or crossover) were required when connecting devices. Switch-to-switch or switch-to-router connections required using different Ethernet cables. Using the *automatic medium-dependent interface crossover (auto-MDIX)* feature on an interface eliminates this problem. When auto-MDIX is enabled, the interface automatically detects the required cable connection type (straight-through or crossover) and configures the connection appropriately. When connecting to switches without the auto-MDIX feature, straight-through cables must be used to connect to devices such as servers, workstations, or routers. Crossover cables must be used to connect a switch to another switch or repeater.

With auto-MDIX enabled, either type of cable can be used to connect to other devices, and the interface automatically corrects for any incorrect cabling. On newer Cisco routers and switches, the **mdix auto** interface configuration mode command enables the feature. When using auto-MDIX on an interface, the interface speed and duplex must be set to **auto** so that the feature operates correctly.

Figure 2-9 shows the topology, and Table 2-5 shows the commands to enable auto-MDIX.

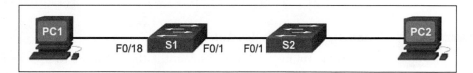

Figure 2-9   Configure Auto-MDIX

Table 2-5   Cisco Switch Auto-MDIX Commands

Enter global configuration mode.	`S1# configure terminal`
Enter interface configuration mode.	`S1(config)# interface fastethernet 0/1`
Configure the interface to automatically negotiate the duplex mode with the connected device.	`S1(config-if)# duplex auto`
Configure the interface to automatically negotiate speed with the connected device.	`S1(config-if)# speed auto`
Enable auto-MDIX on the interface.	`S1(config-if)# mdix auto`
Return to privileged EXEC mode.	`S1(config-if)# end`
Save the running config to the startup config.	`S1# copy running-config startup-config`

Note

The auto-MDIX feature is enabled by default on Catalyst 2960 and Catalyst 3560 switches but is not available on the older Catalyst 2950 and Catalyst 3550 switches.

To examine the auto-MDIX setting for a specific interface, use the **show controllers ethernet-controller** command with the argument `interface-id` and the **phy** keyword. To limit the output to lines referencing auto-MDIX, use the **include Auto-MDIX** filter. As shown in Figure 2-10, the output indicates On or Off for the feature.

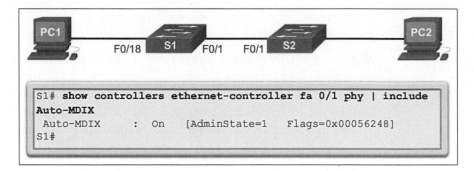

Figure 2-10   Verify Auto-MDIX

Activity 2.1.2.3: Enable Auto-MDIX

Go to the online course and select the third graphic to use the Syntax Checker to practice configuring the FastEthernet 0/1 interface on S2 for auto-MDIX.

Verifying Switch Port Configuration (2.1.2.4)

Table 2-6 describes some of the options for the **show** command that are helpful in verifying common configurable switch features.

Table 2-6   Switch Verification Commands

Display interface status and configuration.	S1# `show interfaces [interface-id]`
Display current startup configuration.	S1# `show startup-config`
Display current operating configuration.	S1# `show running-config`
Display information about the flash file system.	S1# `show flash:`
Display status of system hardware and software.	S1# `show version`
Display a history of commands entered.	S1# `show history`
Display IP information about an interface.	S1# `show ip [interface-id]`
Display the MAC address table.	S1# `show mac-address-table` OR S1# `show mac address-table`

Look at the sample abbreviated output from the **show running-config** command. Use this command to verify that the switch has been correctly configured. As seen in the output for S1, some key information is shown:

- Fast Ethernet 0/18 interface configured with the management VLAN 99

- VLAN 99 configured with an IP address of 172.17.99.11 255.255.0.0

- Default gateway set to 172.17.99.1

```
S1# show running-config
Building configuration…

Current configuration : 1664 bytes
!
<output omitted>
!
interface FastEthernet0/18
 switchport access vlan 99
 switchport mode access
!
<output omitted>
!
interface Vlan99
 ip address 172.17.99.11 255.255.0.0
!
<output omitted>
!
ip default-gateway 172.17.99.1
!
<output omitted>
```

The **show interfaces** command is another commonly used command, which displays status and statistics information on the network interfaces of the switch. The **show interfaces** command is frequently used when configuring and monitoring network devices.

Look at the output from the **show interfaces fastethernet 0/18** command. The first line in the output indicates that the FastEthernet 0/18 interface is up/up meaning that it is operational. Further down the output shows that the duplex is full and the speed is 100 Mb/s.

```
S1# show interfaces fastethernet 0/18
FastEthernet0/18 is up, line protocol is up (connected)
  Hardware is Fast Ethernet, address is 0cd9.96e8.8a01 (bia 0cd9.96e8.8a01)
  MTU 1500 bytes, BW 100000 Kbit/sec, DLY 100 usec,
      reliability 255/255, txload 1/255, rxload 1/255
  Encapsulation ARPA, loopback not set
  Keepalive set (10 sec)
  Full-duplex, 100Mb/s, media type is 10/100BaseTX
  input flow-control is off, output flow-control is unsupported
  ARP type: ARPA, ARP Timeout 04:00:00
```

```
Last input 00:00:01, output 00:00:06, output hang never
Last clearing of "show interface" counters never
Input queue: 0/75/0/0 (size/max/drops/flushes);
Total output drops: 0
Queueing strategy: fifo
Output queue: 0/40 (size/max)
5 minute input rate 0 bits/sec, 0 packets/sec
5 minute output rate 0 bits/sec, 0 packets/sec
   25994 packets input, 2013962 bytes, 0 no buffer
   Received 22213 broadcasts (21934 multicasts)
   0 runts, 0 giants, 0 throttles
   0 input errors, 0 CRC, 0 frame, 0 overrun, 0 ignored
   0 watchdog, 21934 multicast, 0 pause input
   0 input packets with dribble condition detected
   7203 packets output, 771291 bytes, 0 underruns
<output omitted>
```

Network Access Layer Issues (2.1.2.5)

The output from the **show interfaces** command can be used to detect common media issues. One of the most important parts of this output is the display of the line and data link protocol status. The following output and Table 2-7 indicate the summary line to check the status of an interface.

```
S1# show interfaces fastethernet 0/18
FastEthernet0/18 is up, line protocol is up (connected)
 Hardware is Fast Ethernet, address is 0022.91c4.0301 (bia 0022.91c4.0e01)
 MTU 1500 bytes, BW 100000 Kbit/sec, DLY 100 usec,
<output omitted>
```

Table 2-7   Verify the Status of a Switch Interface

Interface Status	Line Protocol Status	Link State
Up	Up	Operational
Down	Down	Interface problem

The first parameter (FastEthernet0/1 is up) refers to the hardware layer and, essentially, reflects whether the interface is receiving the carrier detect signal from the other end. The second parameter (line protocol is up) refers to the data link layer and reflects whether the data link layer protocol keepalives are being received.

Based on the output of the **show interfaces** command, possible problems can be fixed as follows:

- If the interface is up and the line protocol is down, a problem exists. There could be an encapsulation type mismatch, the interface on the other end could be error-disabled, or there could be a hardware problem.

- If the line protocol and the interface are both down, a cable is not attached or some other interface problem exists. For example, in a back-to-back connection (a connection where the transmitter of one device connects directly to the receiver of another device without a transmission media between the two devices), one end of the connection may be administratively down.

- If the interface is administratively down, it has been manually disabled (the **shutdown** command has been issued) in the active configuration.

The following output shows an example of **show interfaces** command. The example shows counters and statistics for the FastEthernet0/1 interface.

```
S1# show interfaces fastethernet0/1
FastEthernet0/1 is up, line protocol is up
 Hardware is Fast Ethernet, address is 0022.91c4.0e01 (bia
    0022.91c4.0e01)MTU 1500 bytes, BW 100000 Kbit, DLY 100 usec,
<output omitted>
   2295197 packets input, 305539992 bytes, 0 no buffer
   Received 1925500 broadcasts, 0 runts, 0 giants, 0 throttles
   3 input errors, 3 CRC, 0 frame, 0 overrun, 0 ignored
   0 watchdog, 68 multicast, 0 pause input
   0 input packets with dribble condition detected
   3594664 packets output, 436549843 bytes, 0 underruns
   8 output errors, 1790 collisions, 10 interface resets
   0 unknown protocol drops
   0 babbles, 235 late collision, 0 deferred
<output omitted>
```

Some media errors are not severe enough to cause the circuit to fail but do cause network performance issues. Table 2-8 explains some of these common errors that can be detected using the **show interfaces** command.

Table 2-8   Network Access Layer Issues

Input Errors	Total number of errors. It includes runts, giants, no buffer, CRC, frame, overrun, and ignored counts.
Runts	Packets that are discarded because they are smaller than the minimum packet size for the medium. For instance, any Ethernet packet that is less than 64 bytes is considered a runt.
Giants	Packets that are discarded because they exceed the maximum packet size for the medium. For example, any Ethernet packet that is greater than 1,518 bytes is considered a giant.

continues

Table 2-8   (continued)

CRC errors	CRC errors are generated when the calculated checksum is not the same as the checksum received.
Output Errors	The sum of all errors that prevented the final transmission of datagrams out of the interface that is being examined.
Collisions	The number of messages retransmitted because of an Ethernet collision.
Late Collisions	A collision that occurs after 512 bits of the frame have been transmitted.

"Input errors" is the sum of all errors in datagrams that were received on the interface being examined. This includes runts, giants, CRC, no buffer, frame, overrun, and ignored counts. The reported input errors from the **show interfaces** command include the following:

- **Runt Frames:** Ethernet frames that are shorter than the 64-byte minimum allowed length are called runts. Malfunctioning NICs are the usual cause of excessive runt frames, but they can be caused by improperly or unterminated cables which can also cause excessive collisions.

- **Giants:** Ethernet frames that are longer than the maximum allowed length are called giants. Giants are caused by the same issues as those that cause runts.

- **CRC errors:** On Ethernet and serial interfaces, CRC errors usually indicate a media or cable error. Common causes include electrical interference, loose or damaged connections, or using the incorrect cabling type. If you see many CRC errors, there is too much noise on the link and you should inspect the cable for damage and length. You should also search for and eliminate noise sources, if possible.

"Output errors" is the sum of all errors that prevented the final transmission of datagrams out of an interface that is being examined. The reported output errors from the **show interfaces** command include the following:

- **Collisions:** Collisions in half-duplex operations are completely normal, and you should not worry about them, as long as you can tolerate the performance when half-duplex mode is used. However, you should never see collisions in a properly designed and configured network that uses full-duplex communication. It is highly recommended that you use full-duplex unless you have older or legacy equipment that requires half-duplex.

- **Late collisions:** A late collision refers to a collision that occurs after 512 bits of the frame (the preamble) have been transmitted. Excessive cable lengths are the most common cause of late collisions. Another common cause is duplex misconfiguration. For example, you could have one end of a connection configured for full-duplex and the other for half-duplex. You would see late collisions on the interface that is configured for half-duplex. In that case, you must configure the same duplex setting on both ends. A properly designed and configured network should never have late collisions.

Troubleshooting Network Access Layer Issues (2.1.2.6)

Most issues that affect a switched network are encountered during the original implementation. Theoretically, after it is installed, a network continues to operate without problems. However, cabling gets damaged, configurations change, and new devices are connected to the switch that require switch configuration changes. Ongoing maintenance and troubleshooting of the network infrastructure is required.

To troubleshoot these issues when you have no connection or a bad connection between a switch and another device, follow this general process, as shown in Figure 2-11, and explained thereafter.

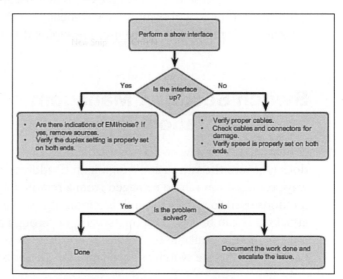

Figure 2-11   Troubleshooting Switch Media Issues

Use the **show interfaces** command to check the interface status.

If the interface is down:

- Check to make sure that the proper cables are being used. Additionally, check the cable and connectors for damage. If a bad or incorrect cable is suspected, replace the cable.

- If the interface is still down, the problem may be due to a mismatch in speed setting. The speed of an interface is typically auto-negotiated; therefore, even if speed is manually configured on one interface, the connecting interface should auto-negotiate accordingly. If a speed mismatch does occur through misconfiguration or a hardware or software issue, then that may result in the interface going down. Manually set the same speed on both connection ends if an auto negotiation problem is suspected.

If the interface is up, but issues with connectivity are still present:

- Using the **show interfaces** command, check for indications of excessive noise. Indications may include an increase in the counters for runts, giants, and CRC errors. If there is excessive noise, first find and remove the source of the noise, if possible. Also, verify that the cable does not exceed the maximum cable length and check the type of cable that is used. For copper cable, it is recommended that you use at least Category 5.

- If noise is not an issue, check for excessive collisions. If there are collisions or late collisions, verify the duplex settings on both ends of the connection. Much like the speed setting, the duplex setting is usually auto-negotiated. If there does appear to be a duplex mismatch, manually set the duplex on both connection ends. It is recommended to use full-duplex if both sides support it.

Switch Security: Management and Implementation (2.2)

When you take a new switch out of the box, the first thing the network engineer does is secure the switch and assign it an IP address, subnet mask, and default gateway so the switch can be managed from a remote location. Learning the different methods used to secure a switch is important. Also important is learning the types of attacks that can be launched on, toward, or through a switch. By understanding the attacks and the available tools and countermeasures, a technician can be better prepared to secure the switch and make use of the tools and security commands.

Secure Remote Access (2.2.1)

There are different methods that can be used to secure a switch including Telnet and SSH. Telnet has already been covered, but SSH is a much better method used to securely manage the switch from a remote location.

SSH Operation (2.2.1.1)

Secure Shell (SSH) is a protocol that provides a secure (encrypted) management connection to a remote device. SSH should replace Telnet for management connections. Telnet is an older protocol that uses insecure plaintext transmission of both the login authentication (username and password) and the data transmitted between the communicating devices. SSH provides security for remote connections by providing strong encryption when a device is authenticated (username and password) and also for the transmitted data between the communicating devices. SSH is assigned to TCP port 22. Telnet is assigned to TCP port 23.

Look at the online course, and select the first graphic to see how an attacker can monitor packets using a product such as Wireshark. A Telnet stream can be targeted to capture the username and password.

In the following output, you can see how the attacker can capture the username and password of the administrator from the plaintext Telnet session.

```
...........
User Access verification
username: .................P.........vt100..BBoobb

.

Password: cisco

.

R1> eenn

.

Password: class

.

R1#
```

Click on the third graphic in the online course to see a Wireshark view of an SSH session. The attacker can track the session using the IP address of the administrator device.

However, if a Wireshark capture is made on the SSH session, the fourth graphic in the online course shows how the username and password are encrypted.

To enable SSH on a Catalyst 2960 switch, the switch must be using a version of the IOS software including cryptographic (encrypted) features and capabilities. In the following output, use the **show version** command on the switch to see which IOS the switch is currently running, and IOS filename that includes the combination "k9" supports cryptographic (encrypted) features and capabilities.

```
S1> show version
Cisco IOS Software, C2960 Software (C2960-LANBASEK9-M),
Version 15.0(@)SE, RELEASE SOFTWARE (fc1)

<output omitted>
```

Configuring SSH (2.2.1.2)

Before configuring SSH, the switch must be minimally configured with a unique hostname and the correct network connectivity settings.

- **Verify SSH support:** Use the **show ip ssh** command to verify that the switch supports SSH. If the switch is not running an IOS that supports cryptographic features, this command is unrecognized.

- **Configure the IP domain:** Configure the IP domain name of the network using the **ip domain-name** *domain-name* global configuration mode command. In Figure 2-12, the *domain-name* value is **cisco.com**.

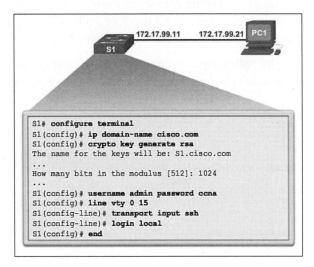

Figure 2-12   Configure SSH for Remote Management

- **Generate RSA key pairs:** Generating an RSA key pair automatically enables SSH. Use the **crypto key generate rsa** global configuration mode command to enable the SSH server on the switch and generate an RSA key pair. When generating RSA keys, the administrator is prompted to enter a modulus length. Cisco recommends a minimum modulus size of 1024 bits (refer to the sample configuration in Figure 2-12). A longer modulus length is more secure, but it takes longer to generate and use.

Note

To delete the RSA key pair, use the **crypto key zeroize rsa** global configuration mode command. After the RSA key pair is deleted, the SSH server is automatically disabled.

- **Configure user authentication:** The SSH server can authenticate users locally or using an authentication server. To use the local authentication method, create a username and password pair using the **username** *username* **password** *password* global configuration mode command. In the example, the user **admin** is assigned the password **ccna**.

- **Configure the vty lines:** Enable the SSH protocol on the vty lines using the **transport input ssh** line configuration mode command. The Catalyst 2960 has vty lines ranging from 0 to 15. This configuration prevents non-SSH (such as Telnet) connections and limits the switch to accept only SSH connections. Use the **line vty** global configuration mode command and then the **login local** line configuration mode command to require local authentication for SSH connections from the local username database.

Interactive Graphic

Activity 2.2.1.2: Configure SSH

Go to the online course and select the second graphic to use the Syntax Checker to configure SSH on switch S1.

Verifying SSH (2.2.1.3)

On a PC, an SSH client, such as PuTTY, is used to connect to an SSH server. For the examples in Figures 2-16 to 2-18, the following have been configured:

- SSH enabled on switch S1

- Interface VLAN 99 (SVI) with IP address 172.17.99.11 on switch S1

- PC1 with IP address 172.17.99.21

In Figure 2-13, the PC initiates an SSH connection to the SVI VLAN IP address of S1.

In Figure 2-14, the user has been prompted for a username and password. Using the configuration from the previous example, the username **admin** and password **ccna** are entered. After entering the correct combination, the user is connected via SSH to the CLI on the Catalyst 2960 switch.

Figure 2-13   Configure PuTTY with SSH Client Connection Parameters

Figure 2-14   Remote Management SSH Connection

To display the version and configuration data for SSH on the device that you configured as an SSH server, use the **show ip ssh** command. In the example, SSH version 2 is enabled. To check the SSH connections to the device, use the **show ssh** command (see Figure 2-15).

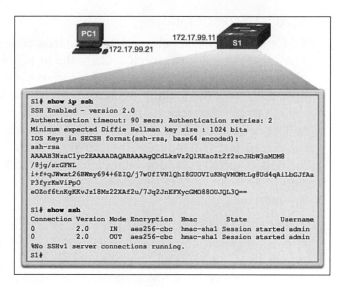

```
S1# show ip ssh
SSH Enabled - version 2.0
Authentication timeout: 90 secs; Authentication retries: 2
Minimum expected Diffie Hellman key size : 1024 bits
IOS Keys in SECSH format(ash-rsa, base64 encoded):
ssh-rsa
AAAAB3NzaC1yc2EAAAADAQABAAAAgQCdLksVz2QlREsoZt2f2scJHbW3aMDM8
/8jg/srGFNL
i+f+qJWwxt26BWmy694+6ZIQ/j7wUfIVN1QhI8GUOVIuKNqVMOMtLg8Ud4qAiLbGJfAa
P3fyrKmViPpO
eOZof6tnKgKKvJz18Mz22XAf2u/7Jq2JnEFXycGMO88OUJQL3Q==

S1# show ssh
Connection Version Mode Encryption  Hmac       State           Username
0             2.0   IN  aes256-cbc  hmac-sha1  Session started  admin
0             2.0   OUT aes256-cbc  hmac-sha1  Session started  admin
%No SSHv1 server connections running.
S1#
```

Figure 2-15   Verify SSH Status and Settings

Packet Tracer Activity 2.2.1.4: Configuring SSH

SSH should replace Telnet for management connections. Telnet uses insecure plaintext communications. SSH provides security for remote connections by providing strong encryption of all transmitted data between devices. In this activity, you will secure a remote switch with password encryption and SSH.

Security Concerns in LANs (2.2.2)

Wired LANs are a common source of attack because so much information can be gained about the wired network using free downloadable tools. By examining downloaded frames, attackers can determine IP addresses of network devices, protocols being used, valid server names and IP addresses, etc. With this information an attacker can launch further attacks or even insert a rogue device. This section introduces the types of attacks and countermeasures to be performed on a wired LAN.

Common Security Attacks: MAC Address Flooding (2.2.2.1)

Basic switch security does not stop malicious attacks. Security is a layered process that is essentially never complete. The more aware networking professionals within an organization are regarding security attacks and the dangers they pose, the better. Some types of security attacks are described here, but the details of how some of these attacks work are beyond the scope of this course. More detailed information is found in the CCNA WAN Protocols course and the CCNA Security course.

MAC Address Flooding

All Catalyst switch models use a MAC address table for Layer 2 switching. The MAC address table in a switch contains the MAC addresses associated with each physical port and the associated VLAN for each port. As a frame arrives on a switch port, the source MAC address is recorded in the MAC address table. The switch then examines the received destination MAC address and looks in the MAC address table to see if it contains the destination MAC address. If an entry already exists for the destination MAC address, the switch forwards the frame to the correct port. If the destination MAC address does not exist in the MAC address table, the switch floods the frame out of every port on the switch, except the port where the frame was received.

The MAC address flooding behavior of a switch for unknown addresses can be used to attack a switch. This type of attack is called a *MAC address table overflow attack*. MAC address table overflow attacks are sometimes referred to as *MAC flooding attacks* and CAM table overflow attacks. The following figures show how this type of attack works.

In Figure 2-16, host A sends traffic to host B. The switch receives the frames and looks up the destination MAC address in its MAC address table. If the switch cannot find the destination MAC in the MAC address table, the switch then copies the frame and floods (broadcasts) it out of every switch port, except the port where it was received.

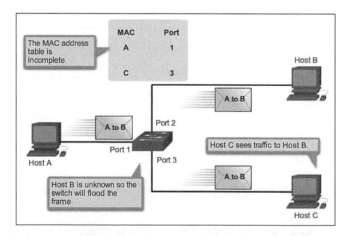

Figure 2-16   MAC Address Flooding - Switch Floods Frame for Unknown MAC

In Figure 2-17, host B receives the frame and sends a reply to host A. The switch then learns that the MAC address for host B is located on port 2 and records that information into the MAC address table.

Host C also receives the frame from host A to host B, but because the destination MAC address of that frame is host B, host C drops that frame.

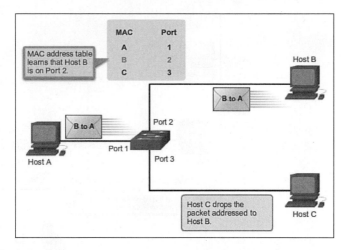

Figure 2-17   MAC Address Flooding - Switch Records MAC Address

As shown in Figure 2-18, any frame sent by host A (or any other host) to host B is forwarded to port 2 of the switch and not broadcasted out every port.

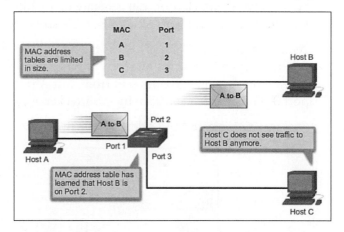

Figure 2-18   MAC Address Flooding - Switch Uses MAC Address Table to Forward Traffic

MAC address tables are limited in size. MAC flooding attacks make use of this limitation to overwhelm the switch with fake source MAC addresses until the switch MAC address table is full.

As shown in Figure 2-19, an attacker at host C can send frames with fake, randomly-generated source and destination MAC addresses to the switch. The switch updates the MAC address table with the information in the fake frames. When the MAC address table is full of fake MAC addresses, the switch enters into what is known as fail-open mode. In this mode, the switch broadcasts all frames to all machines on the network. As a result, the attacker can see all of the frames.

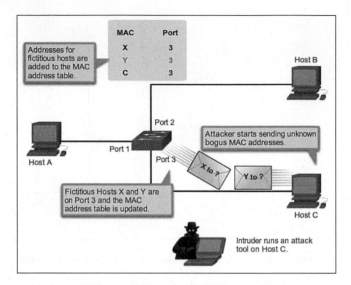

Figure 2-19   MAC Address Flooding Attack - Attacker Launches Attack

Some network attack tools can generate up to 155,000 MAC entries on a switch per minute. The maximum MAC address table size is switch model-dependent.

As shown in Figure 2-20, as long as the MAC address table on the switch remains full, the switch broadcasts all received frames out of every port except the ingress port. In this example, frames sent from host A to host B are also broadcast out of port 3 on the switch and seen by the attacker at host C.

One way to mitigate MAC address table overflow attacks is to configure port security.

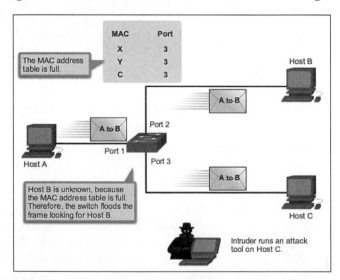

Figure 2-20   MAC Address Flooding Attack - Attacker Sees Broadcasts

Common Security Attacks: DHCP Spoofing (2.2.2.2)

DHCP is the protocol that automatically assigns a host a valid IP address out of a DHCP pool. DHCP has always been the main protocol used within industry for allocating clients IP addresses. Two types of DHCP attacks can be performed against a switched network: DHCP starvation attacks and DHCP spoofing, as shown in Figure 2-21.

In *DHCP starvation attacks*, an attacker floods the DHCP server with DHCP requests to use all the available IP addresses that the DHCP server can issue. After these IP addresses are issued, the server cannot issue any more addresses, and this situation produces a *denial-of-service (DoS) attack* as new clients cannot obtain network access. A DoS attack is any attack that is used to overload specific devices and network services with illegitimate traffic, thereby preventing legitimate traffic from reaching those resources.

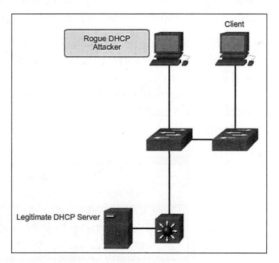

Figure 2-21 DHCP Spoofing and Starvation Attack

In *DHCP spoofing attacks*, an attacker configures a fake DHCP server on the network to issue IP addresses to clients. The normal reason for this attack is to force the clients to use false Domain Name System (DNS) or Windows Internet Naming Service (WINS) servers and to make the clients use the attacker, or a machine under the control of the attacker, as their default gateway.

DHCP starvation is often used before a DHCP spoofing attack to deny service to the legitimate DHCP server, making it easier to introduce a fake DHCP server into the network.

To mitigate DHCP attacks, use the DHCP snooping and port security features on the Cisco Catalyst switches. These features are covered in a later topic.

Common Security Attacks: Leveraging CDP (2.2.2.3)

The *Cisco Discovery Protocol (CDP)* is a proprietary protocol that all Cisco devices can be configured to use. CDP discovers other Cisco devices that are directly connected, which allows the devices to auto-configure their connection. In some cases, this simplifies configuration and connectivity.

By default, most Cisco routers and switches have CDP enabled on all ports. CDP information is sent in periodic, unencrypted broadcasts. This information is updated locally in the CDP database of each device. Even though CDP is a Layer 2 protocol, all Cisco devices can use CDP to communicate and share device information with an adjacent Cisco device; however, this information cannot be shared beyond a single, adjacent Cisco device.

CDP contains information about the device, such as the IP address, software version, platform, capabilities, and the native VLAN. This information can be used by an attacker to find ways to attack the network, typically in the form of a DoS attack.

Figure 2-22 shows a portion of a Wireshark capture showing the contents of a CDP packet. The Cisco IOS software version discovered via CDP, in particular, would allow the attacker to determine whether there were any security vulnerabilities specific to that particular version of IOS. Also, because CDP is not authenticated, an attacker could craft bogus CDP packets and send them to a directly-connected Cisco device.

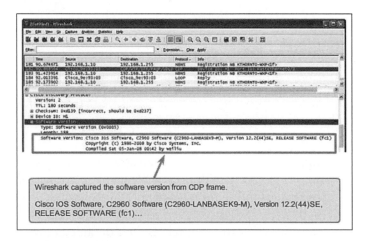

Figure 2-22   Wireshark CDP Packet Capture

Note

It is recommended that you disable the use of CDP on devices or ports that do not need to use it by using the **no cdp run** global configuration mode command. CDP can be disabled on a per port basis.

Telnet Attacks

The Telnet protocol is insecure and can be used by an attacker to gain remote access to a Cisco network device. There are tools available that allow an attacker to launch a brute force password-cracking attack against the vty lines on the switch.

Brute Force Password Attack

A *brute force password attack* tries to crack a password on another device. The first phase of a brute force password attack starts with the attacker using a list of common passwords and a program designed to try to establish a Telnet session using each word on the dictionary list. If the password is not discovered by the first phase, a second phase begins. In the second phase of a brute force attack, the attacker uses a program that creates sequential character combinations in an attempt to guess the password. Given enough time, a brute force password attack can crack almost all passwords used.

To mitigate against brute force password attacks, use strong passwords that are changed frequently. A strong password should have a mix of uppercase and lowercase letters and should include numerals and symbols (special characters). Access to the vty lines can also be limited using an access control list (ACL) that designates what IP address(es) are allowed access to the vty lines.

Telnet DoS Attack

Telnet can also be used to launch a DoS attack. In a *Telnet DoS attack*, the attacker exploits a flaw in the Telnet server software running on the switch that renders the Telnet service unavailable. This sort of attack prevents an administrator from remotely accessing switch management functions. This can be combined with other direct attacks on the network as part of a coordinated attempt to prevent the network administrator from accessing core devices during the breach.

Vulnerabilities in the Telnet service that permit DoS attacks to occur are usually addressed in security patches that are included in newer Cisco IOS revisions.

Note

It is a best practice to use SSH, rather than Telnet for remote management connections.

Activity 2.2.2.4: Common Security Attacks

Go to the online course to perform the practice activity where you match the type of attack to the description.

Security Best Practices (2.2.3)

With so many devices being attached to the wired network, network security is even more important today. Security starts the moment you take a network device, such as a switch, out of the box for the first time. Now that some of the common attacks have been covered, next is what a network administrator can do to protect and counteract those attacks.

Best Practices (2.2.3.1)

Defending your network against attack requires vigilance and education. The following are best practices for securing a network:

- Develop a written security policy for the organization.

- Shut down unused services and ports.

- Use strong passwords and change them often.

- Control physical access to devices.

- Avoid using standard insecure HTTP websites, especially for login screens; instead use the more secure HTTPS.

- Perform backups and test the backed up files on a regular basis.

- Educate employees about social engineering attacks, and develop policies to validate identities over the phone, via email, and in person.

- Encrypt and password-protect sensitive data.

- Implement security hardware and software, such as firewalls.

- Keep software up-to-date by installing security patches weekly or daily, if possible.

These methods are only a starting point for security management. Organizations must remain vigilant at all times to defend against continually evolving threats. Use network security tools to measure the vulnerability of the current network.

Network Security Tools and Testing (2.2.3.2)

Network security tools help a network administrator test a network for weaknesses. Some tools allow an administrator to assume the role of an attacker. Using one of these tools, an administrator can launch an attack against the network and audit the results to determine how to adjust security policies to mitigate those types of attacks. Security auditing and penetration testing are two basic functions that network security tools perform.

Network security testing techniques may be manually initiated by the administrator. Other tests are highly automated. Regardless of the type of testing, the staff that sets up and conducts the security testing should have extensive security and networking knowledge. This includes expertise in the following areas:

- Network security

- Firewalls

- Intrusion prevention systems

- Operating systems

- Programming

- Networking protocols (such as TCP/IP)

Network Security Audits (2.2.3.3)

Network security tools allow a network administrator to perform a security audit of a network. A *security audit* reveals the type of information an attacker can gather simply by monitoring network traffic.

For example, network security auditing tools allow an administrator to flood the MAC address table with fictitious MAC addresses. This is followed by an audit of the switch ports as the switch starts flooding traffic out of all ports. During the audit, the legitimate MAC address mappings are aged out and replaced with fictitious MAC address mappings. This determines which ports are compromised and not correctly configured to prevent this type of attack.

Timing is an important factor in performing the audit successfully. Different switches support varying numbers of MAC addresses in their MAC table. It can be difficult to determine the ideal amount of spoofed MAC addresses to send to the switch. A network administrator also has to contend with the age-out period of the MAC address table. If the spoofed MAC addresses start to age out while performing a network audit, valid MAC addresses start to populate the MAC address table, and limiting the data that can be monitored with a network auditing tool.

Network security tools can also be used for penetration testing against a network. *Penetration testing* is a simulated attack against the network to determine how vulnerable it would be in a real attack. This allows a network administrator to identify weaknesses within the configuration of networking devices and make changes to make the devices more resilient to attacks. There are numerous attacks that an administrator can perform, and most tool suites come with extensive documentation detailing the syntax needed to execute the desired attack.

Because penetration tests can have adverse effects on the network, they are carried out under very controlled conditions, following documented procedures detailed in a comprehensive network security policy. An off-line test bed network that mimics the actual production network is the ideal. The test bed network can be used by networking staff to perform network penetration tests.

Switch Port Security (2.2.4)

Port security is the process of enabling specific commands on switch ports to protect against unauthorized wired devices being attached to the network. An easy way for an intruder to gain access to a corporate network is to plug into an unused Ethernet jack or to unplug an authorized device and use that connector. Cisco provides ways to protect against such behavior.

Secure Unused Ports (2.2.4.1)

The first step in port security is to be aware of ports that are not currently being used on the switch.

Disable Unused Ports

A simple method that many administrators use to help secure the network from unauthorized access is to disable all unused ports on a switch. For example, if a Catalyst 2960 switch has 24 ports and there are three Fast Ethernet connections in use, it is good practice to disable the 21 unused ports. Navigate to each unused port and issue the Cisco IOS **shutdown** command. If a port later on needs to be reactivated, it can be enabled with the **no shutdown** command. Figure 2-23 shows partial output for this configuration.

It is simple to make configuration changes to multiple ports on a switch. If a range of ports must be configured, use the **interface range** command.

```
Switch(config)# interface range type module/first-number - last-number
```

The process of enabling and disabling ports can be time-consuming, but it enhances security on the network and is well worth the effort.

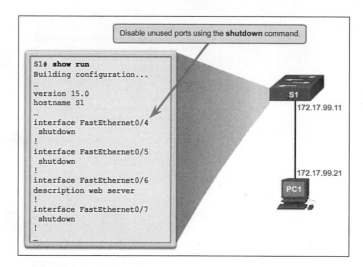

Figure 2-23   Disable Unused Switch Ports

DHCP Snooping (2.2.4.2)

DHCP snooping is a Cisco Catalyst feature that determines which devices attached to switch ports can respond to DHCP requests. DHCP snooping can be used to prevent unauthorized DHCP messages that contain information such as IP address-related data being provided to legitimate network devices.

As part of the DHCP configuration process, switch ports can be identified as trusted and untrusted. *Trusted ports* can source any type of DHCP message; *untrusted ports* can source DHCP requests only. This configuration protects the network from someone attacking a device by acting as a rogue DHCP server. Trusted ports host a DHCP server or can be an uplink toward the DHCP server. If a rogue device on an untrusted port attempts to send a DHCP response packet into the network, the port is shut down. This feature can be coupled with DHCP options in which switch information, such as the port ID of the DHCP request, can be inserted into the DHCP request packet.

As shown in Figures 2-24 and 2-25, untrusted ports are those not explicitly configured as trusted. A DHCP binding table is built for untrusted ports. Each entry contains a client MAC address, IP address, lease time, binding type, VLAN number, and port ID recorded as clients make DHCP requests. The table is then used to filter subsequent DHCP traffic. From a DHCP snooping perspective, untrusted access ports should not send any DHCP server responses.

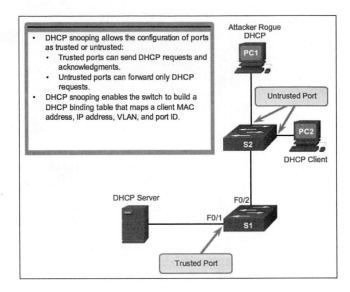

Figure 2-24   DHCP Snooping Operation

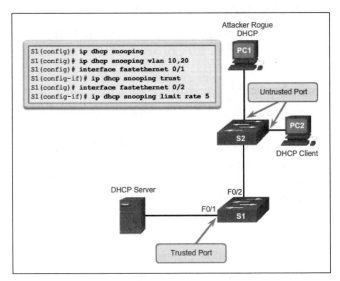

Figure 2-25   DHCP Snooping Configuration

These steps illustrate how to configure DHCP snooping on a Catalyst 2960 switch:

Step 1.   Enable DHCP snooping using the **ip dhcp snooping** global configuration mode command.

Step 2.   Enable DHCP snooping for specific VLANs using the **ip dhcp snooping vlan** *number* command.

Step 3. Define ports as trusted at the interface level by defining the trusted ports using the **ip dhcp snooping trust** command.

Optional Step 4. Limit the rate at which an attacker can continually send bogus DHCP requests through untrusted ports to the DHCP server using the **ip dhcp snooping limit rate** *rate* command.

Port Security: Operation (2.2.4.3)

All switch ports (interfaces) should be secured before the switch is deployed for production use. One way to secure ports is by implementing a feature called port security. Cisco *port security* limits the number of valid MAC addresses allowed on a port. The MAC addresses of legitimate devices are allowed access, while other MAC addresses are denied.

Port Security

Port security can be configured to allow one or more MAC addresses. If the number of MAC addresses allowed on the port is limited to one, then only the device with that specific MAC address can successfully connect to the port.

If a port is configured as a secure port and the maximum number of MAC addresses is reached, any additional attempts to connect by unknown MAC addresses will generate a security violation.

Note

Remember that when implementing port security on a switch port to:

■ Turn port security on before doing any other commands.

■ Specify a single MAC address or a group of valid MAC addresses allowed on the port.

■ Specify that a port automatically shuts down if unauthorized MAC addresses are detected.

Secure MAC Address Types

There are a number of ways to configure port security. The type of secure address is based on the configuration and includes:

■ *Static secure MAC addresses:* MAC addresses that are manually configured on a port by using the **switchport port-security mac-address** *mac-address* interface configuration mode command. MAC addresses configured in this way are stored in the address table and are added to the running configuration on the switch.

- *Dynamic secure MAC addresses:* MAC addresses that are dynamically learned and stored only in the address table. MAC addresses configured in this way are removed when the switch restarts.

- *Sticky secure MAC addresses:* MAC addresses that can be dynamically learned or manually configured stored in the address table, and added to the running configuration.

Sticky Secure MAC addresses

To configure an interface to convert dynamically learned MAC addresses to sticky secure MAC addresses and add them to the running configuration, you must enable sticky learning. Sticky learning is enabled on an interface by using the **switchport port-security mac-address sticky** interface configuration mode command.

When this command is entered, the switch converts all dynamically learned MAC addresses, including those that were dynamically learned before sticky learning was enabled, to sticky secure MAC addresses. All sticky secure MAC addresses are added to the address table and to the running configuration.

Sticky secure MAC addresses can also be manually defined. When sticky secure MAC addresses are configured by using the **switchport port-security mac-address sticky** `mac-address` interface configuration mode command, all specified addresses are added to the address table and the running configuration.

If the sticky secure MAC addresses are saved to the startup configuration file, then when the switch restarts or the interface shuts down, the interface does not need to relearn the addresses. If the sticky secure addresses are not saved, they will be lost.

If sticky learning is disabled by using the **no switchport port-security mac-address sticky** interface configuration mode command, the sticky secure MAC addresses remain part of the address table but are removed from the running configuration.

The following list shows the characteristics of sticky secure MAC addresses.

Note

On a switch port, **switchport port-security** commands will not function until port security is enabled.

- Learned dynamically, converted to sticky secure MAC addresses stored in the running-config.

- Removed from the running-config if port security is disabled.

- Lost when the switch reboots (power cycled).

- Saving sticky secure MAC addresses in the startup-config makes them permanent, and the switch retains them after a reboot.

- Disabling sticky learning converts sticky MAC addresses to dynamic secure addresses and removes them from the running-config.

Port Security: Violation Modes (2.2.4.4)

It is a security violation when either of these situations occurs:

- The maximum number of secure MAC addresses have been added to the address table for that interface, and a station whose MAC address is not in the address table attempts to access the interface.

- An address learned or configured on one secure interface is seen on another secure interface in the same VLAN.

An interface can be configured for one of three violation modes, specifying the action to be taken if a violation occurs. Table 2-9 presents which kinds of data traffic are forwarded when one of the following security violation modes are configured on a port:

- **Protect:** When the number of secure MAC addresses reaches the limit allowed on the port, packets with unknown source addresses are dropped until a sufficient number of secure MAC addresses are removed or the number of maximum allowable addresses is increased. There is no notification that a security violation has occurred.

- **Restrict:** When the number of secure MAC addresses reaches the limit allowed on the port, packets with unknown source addresses are dropped until a sufficient number of secure MAC addresses are removed or the number of maximum allowable addresses is increased. In this mode, there is a notification that a security violation has occurred.

- **Shutdown:** In this (default) violation mode, a port security violation causes the interface to immediately become error-disabled and turns off the port LED. It increments the violation counter. When a secure port is in the error-disabled state, it can be brought out of this state by entering the **shutdown** and **no shutdown** interface configuration mode commands.

Security violations occur in these situations:

- A station with MAC address that is not in the address table attempts to access the interface when the table is full.

- An address is being used on two secure interfaces in the same VLAN.

Table 2-9 Security Violations Modes

Violation Mode	Forwards Traffic	Sends Syslog Message	Displays Error Message	Increases Violation Counter	Shuts Down Port
Protect	No	No	No	No	No
Restrict	No	Yes	No	Yes	No
Shutdown	No	No	No	Yes	Yes

To change the violation mode on a switch port, use the **switchport port-security violation** {*protect* | *restrict* |*shutdown*} interface configuration mode command.

Port Security: Configuring (2.2.4.5)

Table 2-10 summarizes the default port security configuration on a Cisco Catalyst switch.

Table 2-10 Port Security Default Settings

Feature	Default Setting
Port security	Disabled on a port
Maximum number of secure MAC addresses	1
Violation mode	Shutdown. The port shuts down when the maximum number of secure MAC addresses is exceeded.
Sticky address learning	Disabled

Figure 2-26 shows the topology used when configuring F0/18 on the S1 switch. Table 2-11 shows the Cisco IOS CLI commands needed to configure port security on the Fast Ethernet F0/18 port on the S1 switch. Notice that the example does not specify a violation mode. In this example, the violation mode is the default mode of shutdown.

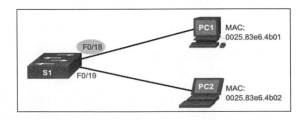

Figure 2-26 Port Security Configuration Topology

Table 2-11   Cisco Switch IOS CLI Commands for Dynamic Port Security

Specify the interface to be configured for port security.	`S1(config)# interface fastethernet 0/18`
Set the interface mode to access.	`S1(config-if)# switchport mode access`
Enable port security on the interface.	`S1(config-if)# switchport port-security`

Table 2-12 shows the commands needed to enable sticky secure MAC addresses for port security on Fast Ethernet port 0/19 of switch S1. As stated earlier, a specific maximum number of secure MAC addresses can be manually configured. In this example, the Cisco IOS command syntax is used to set the maximum number of MAC addresses to 50 for port 0/19. The violation mode is set to the default mode of shutdown.

Table 2-12   Cisco Switch IOS CLI Commands for Sticky Port Security

Specify the interface to be configured for port security.	`S1(config)# interface fastethernet 0/19`
Set the interface mode to access.	`S1(config-if)# switchport mode access`
Enable port security on the interface.	`S1(config-if)# switchport port-security`
Set the maximum number of secure addresses allowed on the port.	`S1(config-if)# switchport port-security maximum 50`
Enable sticky learning.	`S1(config-if)# switchport port-security mac-address sticky`

Port Security: Verifying (2.2.4.6)

Many students make the mistake of forgetting to enable port security before doing the specific port security options. For any configuration step, verification is important. It is especially important when configuring port security.

Verify Port Security

After configuring port security on a switch, check each interface to verify that the port security is set correctly, and check to ensure that the static MAC addresses have been configured correctly.

Verify Port Security Settings

To display port security settings for the switch or for the specified interface, use the **show port-security [interface** *interface-id*] command. The output for the dynamic port security configuration is shown as follows. By default, there is one MAC address allowed on this port.

```
S1# show port-security interface fastethernet 0/18
Port Security                  : Enabled
Port Status                    : Secure-up
Violation Mode                 : Shutdown
Aging Time                     : 0 mins
Aging Type                     : Absolute
SecureStatic Address Aging     : Disabled
Maximum MAC Addresses          : 1
Total MAC Addresses            : 1
Configured MAC Addresses       : 0
Sticky MAC Addresses           : 0
Last Source Address:Vlan       : 0025.83e6.4b01:1
Security Violation Count       : 0
```

Taking a look at the port after the configuration has been applied shows the values for the sticky port security settings. The maximum number of addresses is set to 50 as configured.

```
S1# show port-security interface fastethernet 0/19
Port Security                  : Enabled
Port Status                    : Secure-up
Violation Mode                 : Shutdown
Aging Time                     : 0 mins
Aging Type                     : Absolute
SecureStatic Address Aging     : Disabled
Maximum MAC Addresses          : 50
Total MAC Addresses            : 1
Configured MAC Addresses       : 0
Sticky MAC Addresses           : 1
Last Source Address:Vlan       : 0025.83e6.4b02:1
Security Violation Count       : 0
```

Note

The MAC address in the previous output as 0025.83e6.4b02:1 is identified as a sticky MAC address.

Sticky MAC addresses are added to the MAC address table and to the running configuration. As shown in the output, the sticky MAC address for PC2 has been automatically added to the running configuration for S1.

```
S1# show run | begin FastEthernet 0/19
interface FastEthernet0/19
 switchport mode access
 switchport port-security
```

```
switchport port-security maximum 50
switchport port-security mac-address sticky
switchport port-security sticky 0025.83e6.4b02
```

Verify Secure MAC Addresses

To display all secure MAC addresses configured on all switch interfaces, or on a specified interface with aging information for each, use the **show port-security address** command. As shown in the output, the secure MAC addresses are listed along with the types.

```
S1# show port-security address
Secure Mac Address Table
------------------------------------------------------------
Vlan   Mac Address      Type            Ports   Remaining Age
                                                (mins)
----   -----------      ----            -----   ---------------
1      0025.83e6.4b01   SecureDynamic   Fa0/18   -
1      0025.83e6.4b02   SecureSticky    Fa0/19   -
------------------------------------------------------------
```

Ports in Error Disabled State (2.2.4.7)

When a port is configured with port security, a violation can cause the port to become error disabled. When a port is error disabled, it is effectively shut down and no traffic is sent or received on that port. A series of port security related messages display on the console as shown.

```
Sep 20 06:44:54.966: %PM-4-ERR_DISABLE: psecure-violation
error detected on Fa0/18, putting Fa0/18 in err-disable state
Sep 20 06:44:54.966: %PORT_SECURITY-2-PSECURE_VIOLATION:
Security violation occurred, caused by MAC address
000c.292b.4c75 on port FastEthernet0/18.
Sep 20 06:44:53.973: %LINEPROTO-5-PPDOWN: Line protocol on
Interface FastEthernet0/18, changed state to down
Sep 20 06:44:56.971: %LINK-3-UPDOWN: Interface
FastEthernet0/18, changed state to down
```

Note

Notice in the output how the port protocol and link status changed to down.

Another indication that a port security violation has occurred is that the switch port LED will change to orange. The **show interfaces** command identifies the port status as err-disabled as shown in the following output. The output of the **show port-security interface** command now shows the port status as secure-shutdown.

Because the port security violation mode is set to `shutdown`, the port with the security violation goes to the error disabled state.

```
S1# show interfaces fastethernet 0/18 status
Port Name    Status          Vlan  Duplex   Speed     Type
Fa0/18       err-disabled    1     auto     auto      10/100BaseTX


S1# show port-security interface fastethernet 0/18
    Port Security              : Enabled
    Port Status                : Secure-shutdown
    Violation Mode             : Shutdown
    Aging Time                 : 0 mins
    Aging Type                 : Absolute
    SecureStatic Address Aging : Disabled
    Maximum MAC Addresses      : 1
    Total MAC Addresses        : 0
    Configured MAC Addresses   : 0
    Sticky MAC Addresses       : 0
    Last Source Address:Vlan   : 000c.292b.4c75:1
    Security Violation Count   : 1
```

The administrator should determine what caused the security violation before re-enabling the port. If an unauthorized device is connected to a secure port, the port should not be re-enabled until the security threat is eliminated. To re-enable the port, use the **shutdown** interface configuration mode command. Then, use the **no shutdown** interface configuration command to make the port operational, as shown in the following output.

```
S1(config)# interface FastEthernet 0/18
S1(config-if)# shutdown
Sep 20 06:57:28.532: %LINK-5-CHANGED: Interface
FastEthernet0/18, changed state to administratively down
S1(config-if)# no shutdown
Sep 20 06:57:48.186: %LINK-3-UPDOWN: Interface
FastEthernet0/18, changed state to up
Sep 20 06:57:49.193: %LINEPROTO-5-UPDOWN: Line protocol on
Interface FastEthernet0/18, changed state to up
```

Network Time Protocol (NTP) (2.2.4.8)

Having the correct time within networks is important. Correct time stamps are required to accurately track network events such as security violations. Additionally, clock synchronization is critical for the correct interpretation of events within syslog data files as well as for digital certificates.

Network Time Protocol (NTP) is a protocol that is used to synchronize the clocks of computer systems over packet-switched, variable-latency data networks. NTP allows network devices to synchronize their time settings with an NTP server. A group of NTP clients that obtain time and date information from a single source will have more consistent time settings.

A secure method of providing clocking for the network is for network administrators to implement their own private network master clocks, synchronized to UTC, using satellite or radio. However, if network administrators do not want to implement their own master clocks because of cost or other reasons, other clock sources are available on the Internet. NTP can get the correct time from an internal or external time source including the following:

- Local master clock

- Master clock on the Internet

- GPS or atomic clock

A network device can be configured as either an NTP server or an NTP client. To allow the software clock to be synchronized by an NTP time server, use the **ntp server** *ip-address* command in global configuration mode. A sample configuration is shown in Figure 2-27. Router R2 is configured as an NTP client, while router R1 serves as an authoritative NTP server.

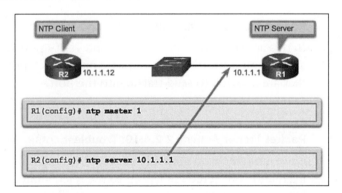

Figure 2-27   Configuring NTP

To configure a device as having an NTP master clock to which peers can synchronize themselves, use the **ntp master** [*stratum*] command in global configuration mode. The stratum value is a number from 1 to 15 and indicates the NTP stratum number that the system will claim. If the system is configured as an NTP master and no stratum number is specified, it will default to stratum 8. If the NTP master cannot reach any clock with a lower stratum number, the system will claim to be synchronized at the configured stratum number, and other systems will be willing to synchronize to it using NTP.

Figure 2-28 displays the verification of NTP. To display the status of NTP associations, use the **show ntp associations** command in privileged EXEC mode. This command will indicate the IP address of any peer devices that are synchronized to this peer, statically configured peers, and stratum number. The **show ntp status** user EXEC command can be used to display such information as the NTP synchronization status, the peer that the device is synchronized to, and in which NTP strata the device is functioning.

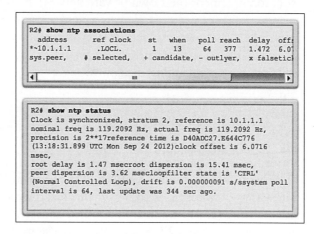

Figure 2-28   Verifying NTP

Packet Tracer Activity 2.2.4.9: Configuring Switch Port Security

In this activity, you will configure and verify port security on a switch. Port security allows you to restrict ingress traffic on a switch port by limiting the MAC addresses that are allowed to send traffic into the port.

Packet Tracer Activity 2.2.4.10: Troubleshooting Switch Port Security

The employee who normally uses PC1 brought his laptop from home, disconnected PC1, and connected the laptop to the telecommunication outlet. After reminding him of the security policy that does not allow personal devices on the network, you now must reconnect PC1 and re-enable the port.

Lab 2.2.4.11: Configuring Switch Security Features

In this lab, you will complete the following objectives:

- Part 1: Set Up the Topology and Initialize Devices
- Part 2: Configure Basic Device Settings and Verify Connectivity
- Part 3: Configure and Verify SSH Access on S1
- Part 4: Configure and Verify Security Features on S1

Summary (2.3)

Now that you are getting the sense of what network administrators do to configure basic features and security features on a switch, you are ready to look back and review all you have learned. Then perform the activity and skills integration challenge to prove to yourself you are ready to move to the next chapter.

Class Activity 2.3.1.1: Switch Trio

Scenario

You are the network administrator for a small- to medium-sized business. Corporate headquarters for your business has mandated that on all switches in all offices, security must be implemented. The memorandum delivered to you this morning states:

"By Monday, April 18, 20xx, the first three ports of all configurable switches located in all offices must be secured with MAC addresses—one address will be reserved for the PC, one address will be reserved for the laptop in the office, and one address will be reserved for the office server.

If security is breached, we ask you to shut the affected port down until the reason for the breach can be certified.

Please implement this policy no later than the date stated in this memorandum. For questions, call 1.800.555.1212. Thank you. The Network Management Team."

Work with a partner in the class and create a Packet Tracer example to test this new security policy. After you have created your file, test it with at least one device to ensure it is operational or validated.

Save your work and be prepared to share it with the entire class.

Packet Tracer Activity 2.3.1.2: Skills Integration Challenge

The network administrator asked you to configure a new switch. In this activity, you will use a list of requirements to configure the new switch with initial settings, SSH, and port security.

When a Cisco LAN switch is first powered on, it goes through the following boot sequence:

Step 1.   First, the switch loads a power-on self-test (POST) program stored in ROM. POST checks the CPU subsystem. It tests the CPU, DRAM, and the portion of the flash device that makes up the flash file system.

Step 2. Next, the switch loads the boot loader software. The boot loader is a small program stored in ROM and is run immediately after POST successfully completes.

Step 3. The boot loader performs low-level CPU initialization. It initializes the CPU registers, which control where physical memory is mapped, the quantity of memory, and its speed.

Step 4. The boot loader initializes the flash file system on the system board.

Step 5. Finally, the boot loader locates and loads a default IOS operating system software image into memory and hands control of the switch over to the IOS.

The specific Cisco IOS file that is loaded is specified by the BOOT environmental variable. After the Cisco IOS is loaded it uses the commands found in the startup-config file to initialize and configure the interfaces. If the Cisco IOS files are missing or damaged, the boot loader program can be used to reload or recover from the problem.

The operational status of the switch is displayed by a series of LEDs on the front panel. These LEDs display such things as port status, duplex, and speed.

An IP address is configured on the SVI of the management VLAN to allow for remote configuration of the device. A default gateway belonging to the management VLAN must be configured on the switch using the **ip default-gateway** command. If the default gateway is not properly configured, remote management is not possible. It is recommended that Secure Shell (SSH) be used to provide a secure (encrypted) management connection to a remote device to prevent the sniffing of unencrypted user names and passwords which is possible when using protocols such as Telnet.

One of the advantages of a switch is that it allows full-duplex communication between devices effectively doubling the communication rate. Although it is possible to specify the speed and duplex settings of a switch interface, it is recommended that the switch be allowed to set these parameters automatically to avoid errors.

Switch port security is a requirement to prevent such attacks as MAC Address Flooding and DHCP Spoofing. Switch ports should be configured to allow only frames with specific source MAC addresses to enter. Frames from unknown source MAC addresses should be denied and cause the port to shut down to prevent further attacks.

Port security is only one defense against network compromise. There are 10 best practices that represent the best insurance for a network:

- Develop a written security policy for the organization.
- Shut down unused services and ports.

- Use strong passwords and change them often.

- Control physical access to devices.

- Avoid using standard insecure HTTP websites, especially for login screens. Instead use the more secure HTTPS.

- Perform backups and test the backed up files on a regular basis.

- Educate employees about social engineering attacks, and develop policies to validate identities over the phone, via email, and in person.

- Encrypt sensitive data and protect it with a strong password.

- Implement security hardware and software, such as firewalls.

- Keep IOS software up-to-date by installing security patches weekly or daily, if possible.

These methods are only a starting point for security management. Organizations must remain vigilant at all times to defend against continually evolving threats.

NTP is used to synchronize the date and time among network devices. NTP clients can synchronize their time settings with an NTP server. Clock synchronization is important when using system log messages for verification and troubleshooting.

Practice

The following activities provide practice with the topics introduced in this chapter. The Labs and Class Activities are available in the companion *Routing and Switching Essentials Lab Manual* (9781587133206). You can find the Packet Tracer Activities PKA files in the online course.

Class Activities

Class Activity 2.0.1.2: Stand by Me

Class Activity 2.3.1.1: Switch Trio

Labs

Lab 2.1.1.6: Basic Switch Configuration

Lab 2.2.4.11: Configuring Switch Security Features

Packet Tracer Activities

Packet Tracer Activity 2.2.1.4: Configuring SSH

Packet Tracer Activity 2.2.4.9: Configuring Switch Port Security

Packet Tracer Activity 2.2.4.10: Troubleshooting Switch Port Security

Packet Tracer Activity 2.3.1.2: Skills Integration Challenge

Check Your Understanding Questions

Complete all the review questions listed here to test your understanding of the topics and concepts in this chapter. The appendix, "Answers to the 'Check Your Understanding' Questions," lists the answers.

1. Which three options correctly associate the command with the paired behavior? (Choose three.)

   A. **switchport port-security violation protect**: Frames with unknown source addresses are dropped and a notification is sent.

   B. **switchport port-security violation restrict**: Frames with unknown source addresses are dropped and no notification is sent.

   C. **switchport port-security violation shutdown**: Frames with unknown source addresses result in the port becoming error-disabled, and a notification is sent.

   D. **switchport port-security mac-address sticky**: Allows dynamically learned MAC addresses to be stored in the running-configuration.

   E. **switchport port-security maximum**: Defines the number of MAC addresses associated with a port.

2. What is the effect of entering the following command on a Fast Ethernet switch port?

   ```
   SW1(config-if)# duplex full
   ```

   A. The connected device communicates in two directions, but only one direction at a time.

   B. The switch port returns to its default configuration.

   C. If the device connected to this port is also set for full duplex, the device participates in collision-free communication.

   D. The efficiency of this configuration is typically rated at 50 to 60 percent.

   E. The connected device should be configured as half duplex.

3. Which two tasks does autonegotiation in an Ethernet network accomplish? (Choose two.)

   A. Sets the link speed

   B. Sets the IP address

   C. Sets the link duplex mode

   D. Sets MAC address assignments on switch port

   E. Sets the ring speed

4. Why should a default gateway be assigned to a switch?

   A. So that there can be remote connectivity to the switch via such programs as Telnet and ping

   B. So that frames can be sent through the switch to the router

   C. So that frames generated from workstations and destined for remote networks can pass to a higher level

   D. So that other networks can be accessed from the command prompt of the switch

5. The network administrator wants to configure an IP address on a Cisco switch. How does the network administrator assign the IP address?

   A. In privileged EXEC mode

   B. On the switch interface FastEthernet0/0

   C. On the management VLAN

   D. On the physical interface connected to the router or next-hop device

6. Which option correctly associates the Layer 2 security attack with the description?

   A. MAC address flooding: Broadcast requests for IP addresses with spoofed MAC addresses.

   B. DHCP starvation: Using proprietary Cisco protocols to gain information about a switch.

   C. CDP attack: The attacker fills the switch MAC address table with invalid MAC addresses.

   D. Telnet attack: Using brute force password attacks to gain access to a switch.

7. What is an advantage of using SSH over Telnet when remotely connecting to a switch?

    A. Encryption

    B. More connection lines

    C. Connection-oriented services

    D. Username and password authentication

8. Consider the configuration. Which two commands are not needed on the switch in order for a remote network administrator to access the switch using SSH?

    A. `Switch(config)# ip domain-name mydomain.com`

    B. `Switch(config)# crypto key generate rsa`

    C. `Switch(config)# ip ssh version 2`

    D. `Switch(config)# line vty 0 15`

    E. `Switch(config-if)# transport input ssh`

9. What is an advantage of having the correct date and time on a network device?

    A. Network administrators are provided with correct timestamps on log messages.

    B. When working at the console prompt, the network administrator has a good idea how long the configuration or troubleshooting process is taking.

    C. Other devices can use CDP to discover neighbor device information if the time and date are synchronized between the two devices.

    D. Secure remote connectivity can be accomplished if the date and time are accurate.

10. What is the purpose of DHCP snooping?

    A. Ensures devices are configured for automatic IP address assignment

    B. Prevents unauthorized DHCP servers

    C. Prevents DHCP messages from going across a trunk

    D. Prevents DHCP messages from being sent to another network

11. What is a Cisco best practice for deploying switches?

    A. When a server connects to a switch, the switch port should have the port speed manually configured, but the autonegotiation feature used for duplex.

    B. A compound word should be used as a password on an infrastructure network device such as a switch.

    C. Telnet should be used whenever possible on the switch vty lines.

    D. The enable secret password should be used when configuring a switch to use SSH on the vty lines.

12. When would auto-MDIX be best to use?

    A. When a switch connects to a router

    B. When a switch connects to another switch

    C. When any device connects to an access layer switch

    D. When the cable type is unknown

CHAPTER 3

VLANs

Objectives

Upon completion of this chapter, you will be able to answer the following questions:

- What is a VLAN and what benefits are provided by implementing VLANs?

- What are the different types of VLANs?

- When would you use a trunk?

- How does a trunk work?

- What is the purpose of the native VLAN?

- How do you configure VLANs and trunks?

- What is DTP and when should you use it?

- What commands would be used to troubleshoot VLANs and trunks?

- What types of security issues are related to VLANs and trunks and how would you mitigate these issues?

- What are the best practices to use when implementing VLANs and trunks?

Key Terms

This chapter uses the following key terms. You can find the definitions in the Glossary.

Introduction (3.0.1.1)

Network performance is a key factor in the productivity of an organization. One of the technologies used to improve network performance is the separation of large broadcast domains into smaller ones. By design, Layer 3 devices such as routers will block broadcast traffic at an interface. However, routers normally have a limited number of LAN interfaces. A router's primary role is to move information between networks, not provide network access to end devices.

The role of providing access into a LAN is normally reserved for an access layer switch. A *virtual local area network (VLAN)* can be created on a Layer 2 switch to reduce the size of broadcast domains, similar to a Layer 3 device. VLANs are commonly incorporated into network design making it easier for a network to support the goals of an organization. While VLANs are primarily used within switched local area networks, modern implementations of VLANs allow them to span WLANs, MANs, and WANs.

This chapter will cover how to configure, manage, and troubleshoot VLANs and VLAN trunks. It will also examine security considerations and strategies relating to VLANs and trunks, and best practices for VLAN design.

Class Activity 3.0.1.2: Vacation Station

Scenario

You have purchased a vacation home at the beach for rental purposes. There are three identical floors on each level of the home. Each floor offers one digital television for renters to use.

According to the local Internet service provider, only three stations may be offered within a television package. It is your job to decide which television packages you offer your guests.

- Divide the class into groups of three students per group.

- Choose three different stations to make one subscription package for each floor of your rental home.

- Complete the PDF for this activity.

- Share your completed group-reflection answers with the class.

VLAN Segmentation (3.1)

One way of breaking a larger network into smaller sections is by implementing VLANs. VLANs allow segmentation, or breaking a large network into smaller ones.

VLAN Definitions (3.1.1.1)

Within a switched internetwork, VLANs provide segmentation and organizational flexibility. VLANs provide a way to group devices within a LAN. A group of devices within a VLAN communicate as if they were attached to the same wire. VLANs are based on logical connections, instead of physical connections.

VLANs allow an administrator to segment networks based on factors such as function, project team, or application, without regard for the physical location of the user or device as shown in Figure 3-1. Devices within a VLAN act as if they are in their own independent network, even if they share a common infrastructure with other VLANs. Any switch port can belong to a VLAN, and unicast, broadcast, and multicast packets are forwarded and flooded only to end stations within the VLAN where the packets are sourced. Each VLAN is considered a separate logical network, and packets destined for stations that do not belong to the VLAN must be forwarded through a device that supports routing.

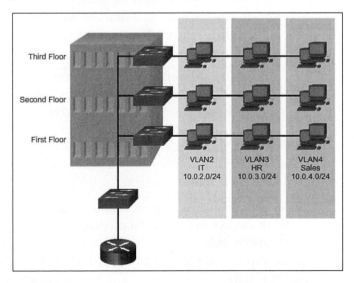

Figure 3-1   VLAN Groups

A VLAN creates a logical broadcast domain that can span multiple physical LAN segments. VLANs improve network performance by separating large broadcast domains into smaller ones. If a device in one VLAN sends a broadcast Ethernet frame, all devices in the VLAN receive the frame, but devices in other VLANs do not.

VLANs enable the implementation of access and security policies according to specific groupings of users. Each switch port can be assigned to only one VLAN (with the exception of a port connected to an IP phone or to another switch).

Benefits of VLANs (3.1.1.2)

User productivity and network adaptability are important for business growth and success. VLANs make it easier to design a network to support the goals of an organization. The primary benefits of using VLANs are as follows:

- **Security:** Groups that have sensitive data are separated from the rest of the network, decreasing the chances of confidential information breaches. As shown in Figure 3-2, faculty computers are on VLAN 10 and completely separated from student and guest data traffic.

- **Cost reduction:** Cost savings result from reduced need for expensive network upgrades and more efficient use of existing bandwidth and uplinks.

- **Better performance:** Dividing flat Layer 2 networks into multiple logical workgroups (broadcast domains) reduces unnecessary traffic on the network and boosts performance.

- **Shrink broadcast domains:** Dividing a network into VLANs reduces the number of devices in the broadcast domain. As shown in Figure 3-2, there are six computers on this network, but there are three broadcast domains: Faculty, Student, and Guest.

- **Improved IT staff efficiency:** VLANs make it easier to manage the network because users with similar network requirements share the same VLAN. When a new switch is provisioned, all the policies and procedures already configured for the particular VLAN are implemented when the ports are assigned. It is also easy for the IT staff to identify the function of a VLAN by giving it an appropriate name. In Figure 3-2, for easy identification VLAN 10 has been named "Faculty," VLAN 20 is named "Student," and VLAN 30 "Guest."

- **Simpler project and application management:** VLANs aggregate users and network devices to support business or geographic requirements. Having separate functions makes managing a project or working with a specialized application easier; an example of such an application is an e-learning development platform for faculty.

Each VLAN in a switched network corresponds to an IP network; therefore, VLAN design must take into consideration the implementation of a hierarchical network addressing scheme. A hierarchical network addressing scheme means that IP network numbers are applied to network segments or VLANs in an orderly fashion that takes the network as a whole into consideration. Blocks of contiguous network addresses are reserved for and configured on devices in a specific area of the network, as shown in Figure 3-2.

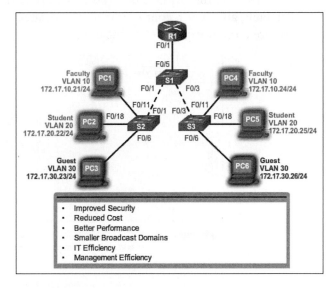

Figure 3-2   Benefits of VLANs

Types of VLANs (3.1.1.3)

There are a number of distinct types of VLANs used in modern networks. Some VLAN types are defined by traffic classes. Other types of VLANs are defined by the specific function that they serve.

Data VLAN

A *data VLAN* is a VLAN that is configured to carry user-generated traffic. A VLAN carrying voice or management traffic would not be part of a data VLAN. It is common practice to separate voice and management traffic from data traffic. A data VLAN, is sometimes referred to as a user VLAN. Data VLANs are used to separate the network into groups of users or devices.

Default VLAN

All switch ports become a part of the *default VLAN* after the initial boot up of a switch loading the default configuration. Switch ports that participate in the default VLAN are part of the same broadcast domain. This allows any device connected to any switch port to communicate with other devices on other switch ports. The default VLAN for Cisco switches is VLAN 1. In Figure 3-3, the **show vlan brief** command was issued on a switch running the default configuration. Notice that all ports are assigned to VLAN 1 by default.

VLAN 1 has all the features of any VLAN, except it cannot be renamed or deleted. By default, all Layer 2 control traffic is associated with VLAN 1. In Figure 3-3, all ports are currently assigned to the default VLAN 1.

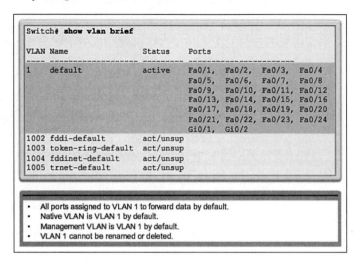

Figure 3-3 Default VLAN 1

Native VLAN

A *native VLAN* is assigned to an 802.1Q *trunk* port. Trunk ports are the links between switches that support the transmission of traffic associated with more than one VLAN. An 802.1Q trunk port supports traffic coming from many VLANs (tagged traffic), as well as traffic that does not come from a VLAN (untagged traffic). The 802.1Q trunk port places untagged traffic on the native VLAN, which by default is VLAN 1.

Native VLANs are defined in the IEEE 802.1Q specification to maintain backward compatibility with untagged traffic common to legacy LAN scenarios. A native VLAN serves as a common identifier on opposite ends of a trunk link.

It is a best practice to configure the native VLAN as an unused VLAN, distinct from VLAN 1 and other VLANs. In fact, it is not unusual to dedicate a fixed VLAN to serve the role of the native VLAN for all trunk ports in the switched domain. Look at Figure 3-4.

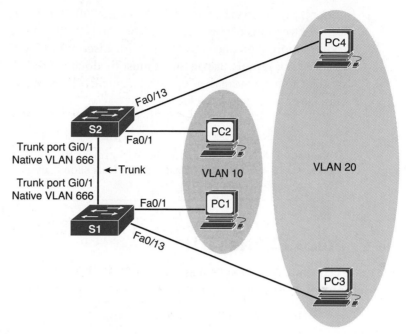

Traffic from VLANs 10 and 20 cross the trunk. A tag is added with the VLAN number before the data leaves the switch port. An unused VLAN number is configured as the native VLAN.

Figure 3-4   Native VLAN

PC1 and PC2 are in VLAN 10. PC3 and PC4 are in VLAN 20. Traffic from both VLANs crosses the trunk link that is configured between the two switches. If PC1 was sending traffic to PC2, as the data leaves the S1 Gi0/1 port, the S1 switch would "tag" the traffic with VLAN 10. When S2 receives the tag, the switch removes it and sends the data on to PC2. The native VLAN should be an unused VLAN, as shown in Figure 3-4. If any devices were configured in the native VLAN, the switches would not tag the traffic before it is placed on the trunk link.

Management VLAN

A *management VLAN* is any VLAN configured to access the management capabilities of a switch. VLAN 1 is the management VLAN by default. To create the management VLAN, the switch virtual interface (SVI) of that VLAN is assigned an IP address and subnet mask, allowing the switch to be managed via HTTP, Telnet, SSH, or SNMP.

Note

Because the out-of-the-box configuration of a Cisco switch has VLAN 1 as the default VLAN, VLAN 1 would be a bad choice for the management VLAN.

In the past, the management VLAN for a 2960 switch was the only active SVI. On 15.x versions of the Cisco IOS for Catalyst 2960 Series switches, it is possible to have more than one active SVI. With Cisco IOS 15.x, the particular active SVI assigned for remote management must be documented. Although theoretically a switch can have more than one management VLAN, having more than one increases exposure to network attacks.

Note

If the native VLAN is the same as the management VLAN, a security risk exists. The native VLAN, when used, and the management VLAN should always be a VLAN number distinct from any other VLANs.

Voice VLANs (3.1.1.4)

A separate VLAN known as a *voice VLAN* is needed to support Voice over IP (VoIP). VoIP traffic requires:

- Assured bandwidth to ensure voice quality
- Transmission priority over other types of network traffic
- Capability to be routed around congested areas on the network
- Delay of less than 150 ms across the network

To meet these requirements, the entire network has to be designed to support VoIP. The details of how to configure a network to support VoIP are beyond the scope of this course, but it is useful to summarize how a voice VLAN works between a switch, a Cisco IP phone, and a computer.

In Figure 3-5, VLAN 150 is designed to carry voice traffic. The student computer PC5 is attached to the Cisco IP phone, and the phone is attached to switch S3. PC5 is in VLAN 20, which is used for student data.

Packet Tracer Activity 3.1.1.5: Who Hears the Broadcast?

In this activity, a 24-port Catalyst 2960 switch is fully populated. All ports are in use. You will observe broadcast traffic in a VLAN implementation and answer some reflection questions.

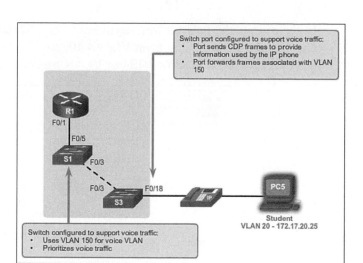

Figure 3-5   Voice VLAN

VLANs in a Multiswitched Environment (3.1.2)

Even a small business might have more than one switch. Multiple switch configuration and design influences network performance. Trunks are commonly used to connect a switch to a switch or to another network device such as a router.

VLAN Trunks (3.1.2.1)

A VLAN trunk, or trunk, is a point-to-point link between two network devices that carries more than one VLAN. A VLAN trunk extends VLANs across two or more network devices. Cisco supports IEEE 802.1Q for coordinating trunks on Fast Ethernet, Gigabit Ethernet, and 10-Gigabit Ethernet interfaces.

VLANs would not be very useful without VLAN trunks. VLAN trunks allow all VLAN traffic to propagate between switches, so that devices which are in the same VLAN, but connected to different switches, can communicate without the intervention of a router.

A VLAN trunk does not belong to a specific VLAN; rather, it is a conduit for multiple VLANs between switches and routers. A trunk could also be used between a network device and server or other device that is equipped with an appropriate 802.1Q-capable NIC. By default, on a Cisco Catalyst switch, all VLANs are supported on a trunk port.

In Figure 3-6, the links between switches S1 and S2, and S1 and S3 are configured to transmit traffic coming from VLANs 10, 20, 30, and 99 across the network. This network could not function without VLAN trunks.

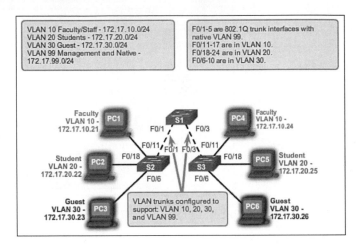

Figure 3-6 Trunks

Controlling Broadcast Domains with VLANs (3.1.2.2)

Recall that a broadcast domain includes all of the devices that receive a broadcast. When a switch is bought, removed from the packaging, and powered on, all devices attached to the switch are part of the same network or broadcast domain. When VLANs are implemented, each VLAN is its own broadcast domain. Let's examine that concept because VLANs are commonly implemented in business.

Network Without VLANs

In normal operation, when a switch receives a broadcast frame on one of its ports, it forwards the frame out all other ports except the port where the broadcast was received.

Activity 3.1.2.2: Traffic Without VLAN Segmentation

Go to the online curriculum and access the first graphic. Press the Play button in order to see what happens when PC1 sends a Layer 2 broadcast.

In the animation, the entire network is configured in the same subnet (172.17.40.0/24) and no VLANs are configured. As a result, when the faculty computer (PC1) sends out a broadcast frame, switch S2 sends that broadcast frame out all of its ports. Eventually the entire network receives the broadcast because the network is one broadcast domain.

Network with VLANs

Interactive Graphic

Activity 3.1.2.2: Traffic with VLAN Segmentation

Go to the course outline and access the second graphic to see how the traffic changes when segmentation has been implemented.

As shown in the animation, the network has been segmented using two VLANs: Faculty devices are assigned to VLAN 10 and Student devices are assigned to VLAN 20. When a broadcast frame is sent from the faculty computer, PC1, to switch S2, the switch forwards that broadcast frame only to those switch ports configured to support VLAN 10.

The ports that comprise the connection between switches S2 and S1 (ports F0/1), and between S1 and S3 (ports F0/3) are trunks and have been configured to support all the VLANs in the network.

When S1 receives the broadcast frame on port F0/1, S1 forwards that broadcast frame out of the only other port configured to support VLAN 10, which is port F0/3. When S3 receives the broadcast frame on port F0/3, it forwards that broadcast frame out of the only other port configured to support VLAN 10, which is port F0/11. The broadcast frame arrives at the only other computer in the network configured in VLAN 10, which is faculty computer PC4.

Figure 3-7 shows a network design without using segmentation compared to how it looks with VLAN segmentation, as shown in Figure 3-8. Notice how the network with the VLAN segmentation design has different network numbers for the two VLANs. Also notice how a trunk must be used to carry multiple VLANs across a single link. By implementing a trunk, any future VLAN or any PC related to assembly line production can be carried between the two switches.

When VLANs are implemented on a switch, the transmission of unicast, multicast, and broadcast traffic from a host in a particular VLAN are restricted to the devices that are in that VLAN.

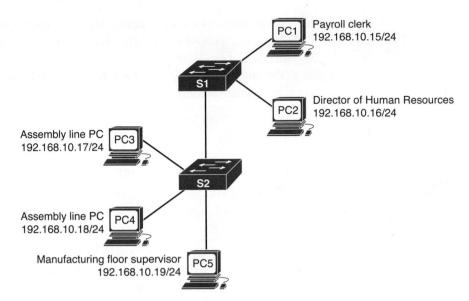

Figure 3-7   Network without Segmentation

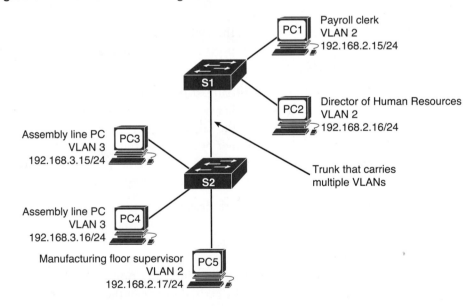

Figure 3-8   Networks with Segmentation

Tagging Ethernet Frames for VLAN Identification (3.1.2.3)

Layer 2 devices use the Ethernet frame header information to forward packets. The standard Ethernet frame header does not contain information about the VLAN to which the frame belongs; thus, when Ethernet frames are placed on a trunk, information about the VLANs to which they belong must be added. This process, called *tagging*, is accomplished by using the IEEE 802.1Q header specified in the IEEE 802.1Q standard. The 802.1Q header includes a 4-byte tag inserted within the original Ethernet frame header, specifying the VLAN to which the frame belongs, as shown in Figure 3-9.

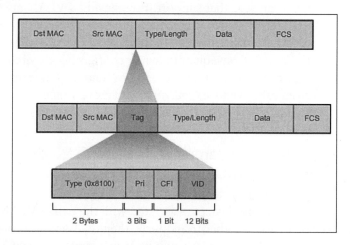

Figure 3-9   Fields in an Ethernet 802.1Q Frame

When the switch receives a frame on a port configured in access mode and assigned a VLAN, the switch inserts a VLAN tag in the frame header, recalculates the FCS, and sends the tagged frame out of a trunk port.

VLAN Tag Field Details

The VLAN tag field consists of a Type field, a tag control information field, and the FCS field:

- **Type:** A 2-byte value called the tag protocol ID (TPID) value. For Ethernet, it is set to hexadecimal 0x8100.

- **User priority:** A 3-bit value that supports level or service implementation.

- **Canonical Format Identifier (CFI):** A 1-bit identifier that enables Token Ring frames to be carried across Ethernet links.

- **VLAN ID (VID):** A 12-bit VLAN identification number that supports up to 4096 VLAN IDs.

After the switch inserts the Type and tag control information fields, it recalculates the FCS values and inserts the new FCS into the frame.

Native VLANs and 802.1Q Tagging (3.1.2.4)

Native VLANs frequently baffle students. Keep in mind that all trunks have a native VLAN whether you configure it or not. It is best if you control the VLAN ID used as the native VLAN on a trunk. You will learn why in this section.

Tagged Frames on the Native VLAN

Some devices that support trunking add a VLAN tag to native VLAN traffic. Control traffic sent on the native VLAN should not be tagged. If an 802.1Q trunk port receives a tagged frame with the VLAN ID the same as the native VLAN, it drops the frame. Consequently, when configuring a switch port on a Cisco switch, configure devices so that they do not send tagged frames on the native VLAN. Devices from other vendors that support tagged frames on the native VLAN include IP phones, servers, routers, and non-Cisco switches.

Untagged Frames on the Native VLAN

When a Cisco switch trunk port receives untagged frames (which are unusual in a well-designed network), the switch forwards those frames to the native VLAN. If there are no devices associated with the native VLAN (which is not unusual) and there are no other trunk ports, then the frame is dropped. The default native VLAN is VLAN 1 on a Cisco switch. When configuring an 802.1Q trunk port, a default Port VLAN ID (PVID) is assigned the value of the native VLAN ID. All untagged traffic coming in or out of the 802.1Q port is forwarded based on the PVID value. For example, if VLAN 99 is configured as the native VLAN, the PVID is 99 and all untagged traffic is forwarded to VLAN 99. If the native VLAN has not been reconfigured, the PVID value is set to VLAN 1.

In Figure 3-10, PC1 is connected by a hub to an 802.1Q trunk link. PC1 sends untagged traffic which the switches associate with the native VLAN configured on the trunk ports, and forward accordingly. Tagged traffic on the trunk received by PC1 is dropped. This scenario reflects poor network design for several reasons: it uses a hub, it has a host connected to a trunk link, and it implies that the switches have access ports assigned to the native VLAN. But it illustrates the motivation for the IEEE 802.1Q specification for native VLANs as a means of handling legacy scenarios. A better designed network without a hub is shown in Figure 3-11.

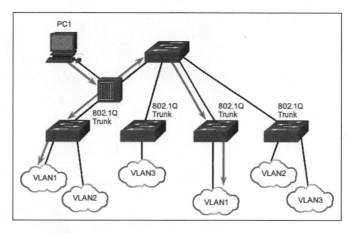

Figure 3-10   Native VLAN on 802.1Q Trunk

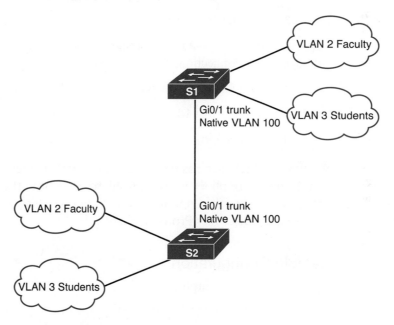

Figure 3-11   Better Native VLAN Design

Voice VLAN Tagging (3.1.2.5)

As shown in Figure 3-12, the F0/18 port on S3 is configured to be in voice mode so that voice frames will be tagged with VLAN 150. Data frames coming through the Cisco IP phone from PC5 are left untagged. Data frames destined for PC5 coming from port F0/18 are tagged with VLAN 20 on the way to the phone. The phone strips the VLAN tag before the data is forwarded to PC5.

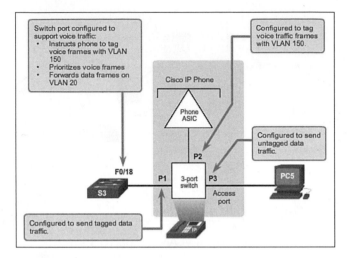

Figure 3-12   Voice VLAN Tagging

The Cisco IP phone contains an integrated three-port 10/100 switch. The ports provide dedicated connections to these devices:

- Port 1 connects to the switch or other VoIP device.

- Port 2 is an internal 10/100 interface that carries the IP phone traffic.

- Port 3 (access port) connects to a PC or other device.

When the switch port has been configured with a voice VLAN, the link between the switch and the IP phone acts as a trunk to carry both the tagged voice traffic and untagged data traffic. Communication between the switch and IP phone is facilitated by the Cisco Discovery Protocol (CDP).

Sample Configuration

Look at the sample output.

```
S1# show interfaces fa0/18 switchport
Name: Fa0/18
Switchport: Enabled
Administrative Mode: static access
Operational Mode: down
Administrative Trunking Encapsulation: dot1q
Negotiation of Trunking: Off
Access Mode VLAN: 20 (student)
Trunking Native Mode VLAN: 1 (default)
Administrative Native VLAN tagging: enabled
Voice VLAN: 150 (voice)
<output omitted>
```

A discussion of voice Cisco IOS commands are beyond the scope of this course, but the highlighted areas in the sample output show the F0/18 interface configured with a VLAN configured for data (VLAN 20) and a VLAN configured for voice (VLAN 150).

Activity 3.1.2.6: Predict Switch Behavior

Go to the online curriculum and select the three graphics to practice with VLANs and trunks.

Packet Tracer
☐ Activity

Packet Tracer Activity 3.1.2.7: Investigating a VLAN Implementation

In this activity, you will observe how broadcast traffic is forwarded by the switches when VLANs are configured and when VLANs are not configured.

VLAN Implementations (3.2)

VLANs allow multiple networks to exist on one or more switches. Companies commonly use VLANs to separate a user network from other networks such as a voice network, printer/copier network, and guest network.

VLAN Ranges on Catalyst Switches (3.2.1.1)

Different Cisco Catalyst switches support various numbers of VLANs. The number of supported VLANs is large enough to accommodate the needs of most organizations. For example, the Catalyst 2960 and 3560 Series switches support more than 4000 VLANs. Normal range VLANs on these switches are numbered 1 to 1005 and extended range VLANs are numbered 1006 to 4094. Figure 3-13 illustrates the available VLAN IDs on a Catalyst 2960 switch running Cisco IOS Release 15.x.

```
Switch# show vlan brief

VLAN Name                             Status    Ports
---- -------------------------------- --------- -------------------------------
1    default                          active    Fa0/1,  Fa0/2,  Fa0/3,  Fa0/4
                                                Fa0/5,  Fa0/6,  Fa0/7,  Fa0/8
                                                Fa0/9,  Fa0/10, Fa0/11, Fa0/12
                                                Fa0/13, Fa0/14, Fa0/15, Fa0/16
                                                Fa0/17, Fa0/18, Fa0/19, Fa0/20
                                                Fa0/21, Fa0/22, Fa0/23, Fa0/24
                                                Gi0/1, Gi0/2
1002 fddi-default                     act/unsup
1003 token-ring-default               act/unsup
1004 fddinet-default                  act/unsup
1005 trnet-default                    act/unsup
```

Figure 3-13   Normal VLAN ID Range

Normal Range VLANs

Used in small- and medium-sized business and enterprise networks.

- Identified by a VLAN ID between 1 and 1005.

- IDs 1002 through 1005 are reserved for Token Ring and FDDI VLANs.

- IDs 1 and 1002 to 1005 are automatically created and cannot be removed.

- Configurations are stored within a VLAN database file, called *vlan.dat*. The `vlan.dat` file is located in the flash memory of the switch.

- The *VLAN Trunking Protocol (VTP)* is a Cisco-proprietary Layer 2 protocol used to manage VLAN configurations between switches; VTP can learn and store only normal range VLANs.

Extended Range VLANs

- Enable service providers to extend their infrastructure to a greater number of customers. Some global enterprises could be large enough to need extended range VLAN IDs.

- Are identified by a VLAN ID between 1006 and 4094.

- Configurations are not written to the `vlan.dat` file.

- Support fewer VLAN features than normal range VLANs.

- Are, by default, saved in the running configuration file.

- VTP does not learn extended range VLANs.

Note

Because there are 12 bits in the VLAN ID field of the IEEE 802.1Q header, 4096 is the upper boundary for the number of VLANs available on Catalyst switches.

Creating a VLAN (3.2.1.2)

When configuring normal range VLANs, the configuration details are stored in flash memory on the switch in a file called vlan.dat. Flash memory is persistent and does not require the **copy running-config startup-config** command. However, because other details are often configured on a Cisco switch at the same time that VLANs are created, it is good practice to save running configuration changes to the startup configuration.

Table 3-1 displays the Cisco IOS command syntax used to add a VLAN to a switch and give it a name.

Note

Naming each VLAN is considered a best practice in switch configuration.

Table 3-1   Commands Used to Create a VLAN

Enter global configuration mode.	`S1# configure terminal`
Create a VLAN with a valid VLAN ID number.	`S1(config)# vlan vlan-id`
Specify a unique name to identify the VLAN.	`S1(config-vlan)# name vlan-name`
Return to the privileged EXEC mode.	`S1(config-vlan)# end`

Figure 3-14 shows how the student VLAN (VLAN 20) is configured on switch S1. In the topology example, the student computer (PC1) has not been associated with a VLAN yet, but it does have an IP address of 172.17.20.22.

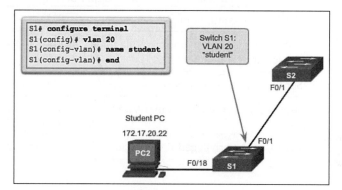

Figure 3-14   Sample VLAN Configuration

Interactive Graphic

Activity 3.2.1.2: VLAN Creation and Verification

Go to the online course and click on the third graphic to use the Syntax Checker to create a VLAN and use the **show vlan brief** command to display the contents of the `vlan.dat` file.

In addition to entering a single VLAN ID, a series of VLAN IDs can be entered separated by commas, or a range of VLAN IDs separated by hyphens using the **vlan** `vlan-id` command. For example, use the following command to create VLANs 100, 102, 105, 106, and 107:

```
S1(config)# vlan 100,102,105-107
```

Assigning Ports to VLANs (3.2.1.3)

After creating a VLAN, the next step is to assign ports to the VLAN. An access port can belong to only one VLAN at a time; one exception to this rule is that of a port connected to an IP phone, in which case, there are two VLANs associated with the port: one for voice and one for data.

Table 3-2 displays the syntax for defining a port to be an access port and assigning it to a VLAN. The **switchport mode access** command is optional, but strongly recommended as a security best practice. With this command, the interface changes to permanent access mode.

Note

Use the **interface range** command to simultaneously configure multiple interfaces.

Table 3-2   Commands Used to Assign Ports to VLANs

Enter global configuration mode.	S1# **configure terminal**
Enter interface configuration mode for a particular port number.	S1(config)# **interface** *interface_id*
Set the port to access mode.	S1(config-if)# **switchport mode access**
Assign the port to a particular VLAN.	S1(config-if)# **switchport access vlan** *vlan-id*
Return to the privileged EXEC mode.	S1(config-if)# **end**

In Figure 3-15, VLAN 20 is assigned to port F0/18 on switch S1; therefore, the student computer (PC2) is in VLAN 20. When VLAN 20 is configured on other switches, the network administrator knows to configure the other student computers to be in the same subnet as PC2 (172.17.20.0/24).

Interactive Graphic

Activity 3.2.1.3: Assign Ports to a VLAN and Verify

Go to the online curriculum to the third graphic and use the Syntax Checker to assign a VLAN to a particular interface and use the **show vlan brief** command to display the contents of the vlan.dat file.

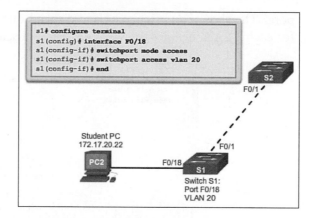

Figure 3-15   Sample VLAN Interface Configuration

The **switchport access vlan** command forces the creation of a VLAN if it does not already exist on the switch. For example, VLAN 30 is not present in the **show vlan brief** output of the switch. If the **switchport access vlan 30** command is entered on any interface with no previous configuration, then the switch displays the following:

```
% Access VLAN does not exist. Creating vlan 30
```

Changing VLAN Port Membership (3.2.1.4)

There are a number of ways to change VLAN port membership. Table 3-3 shows the syntax for changing a switch port to VLAN 1 membership with the **no switchport access vlan** interface configuration mode command.

Table 3-3   Remove **VLAN** Configuration Commands

Enter global configuration mode.	S1# **configure terminal**
Enter interface configuration mode for a particular port number.	S1(config)# **interface** *interface_id*
Assign the port to a particular VLAN.	S1(config-if)# **no switchport access vlan** *vlan-id*
Return to the privileged EXEC mode.	S1(config-if)# **end**

Interface F0/18 was previously assigned to VLAN 20. The **no switchport access vlan** command is entered for interface F0/18. Examine the output in the **show vlan brief** command that immediately follows as shown in Figure 3-16. The **show vlan brief** command displays the VLAN assignment and membership type for all switch ports. The **show vlan brief** command displays one line for each VLAN. The output for each VLAN includes the VLAN name, status, and switch ports.

```
S1(config)# int fa0/18
S1(config-if)# no switchport access vlan
S1(config-if)# end
S1# show vlan brief

VLAN Name               Status    Ports
---- ------------------ -------   -------------------------------
1    default            active    Fa0/1, Fa0/2, Fa0/3, Fa0/4
                                  Fa0/5, Fa0/6, Fa0/7, Fa0/8
                                  Fa0/9, Fa0/10, Fa0/11, Fa0/12
                                  Fa0/13, Fa0/14, Fa0/15, Fa0/16
                                  Fa0/17, Fa0/18, Fa0/19, Fa0/20
                                  Fa0/21, Fa0/22, Fa0/23, Fa0/24
                                  Gi0/1, Gi0/2
20   student            active
1002 fddi-default       act/unsup
1003 token-ring-default act/unsup
1004 fddinet-default    act/unsup
1005 trnet-default      act/unsup
S1#
```

Figure 3-16   Sample Interface Removal of a VLAN

VLAN 20 is still active, even though no ports are assigned to it. The **show interfaces fa0/18 switchport** output verifies that the access VLAN for interface F0/18 has been reset to VLAN 1.

```
S1# show interfaces fa0/18 switchport
Name: Fa0/18
Switchport: Enabled
Administrative Mode: static access
Operational Mode: down
Administrative Trunking Encapsulation: dot1q
Negotiation of Trunking: Off
Access Mode VLAN: 1 (default)
Trunking Native Mode VLAN: 1 (default)
<output omitted>
```

A port can easily have its VLAN membership changed. It is not necessary to first remove a port from a VLAN to change its VLAN membership. When an access port has its VLAN membership reassigned to another existing VLAN, the new VLAN membership simply replaces the previous VLAN membership. In the following output, port F0/11 is assigned to VLAN 20.

```
S1# config t
S1(config)# interface fastethernet0/11
S1(config-if)# switchport mode access
S1(config-if)# switchport access vlan 20
% Access VLAN does not exist. Creating vlan 20
S1(config-if)# end
S1# show vlan brief
```

```
VLAN Name                     Status    Ports
---- ----------------------   --------- -------------------------
1    default                  active    Fa0/1,  Fa0/2,  Fa0/3,  Fa0/4
                                        Fa0/5,  Fa0/6,  Fa0/7,  Fa0/8
                                        Fa0/9,  Fa0/10, Fa0/12, Fa0/13
                                        Fa0/14, Fa0/15, Fa0/16, Fa0/17
                                        Fa0/18, Fa0/19, Fa0/20, Fa0/21
                                        Fa0/22, Fa0/23, Fa0/24, Gig1/1
                                        Gig1/2
20   VLAN0020                 active    Fa0/11
1002 fddi-default             act/unsup
1003 token-ring-default       act/unsup
1004 fddinet-default          act/unsup
1005 trnet-default            act/unsup
```

Activity 3.2.1.4: Changing VLAN Port Membership

Go to the online curriculum and click on the fifth graphic to use the Syntax Checker to change VLAN port membership.

Deleting VLANs (3.2.1.5)

In Figure 3-17, the **no vlan** `vlan-id` global configuration mode command is used to remove VLAN 20 from the switch. Switch S1 had a minimal configuration with all ports in VLAN 1 and an unused VLAN 20 in the VLAN database. The **show vlan brief** command verifies that VLAN 20 is no longer present in the `vlan.dat` file after using the **no vlan 20** command.

```
S1# conf t
S1(config)# no vlan 20
S1(config)# end
S1#
S1# sh vlan brief

VLAN Name                  Status    Ports
---- ------------------    --------- -----------------------------------
1    default               active    Fa0/1, Fa0/2, Fa0/3, Fa0/4
                                     Fa0/5, Fa0/6, Fa0/7, Fa0/8
                                     Fa0/9, Fa0/10, Fa0/12, Fa0/13
                                     Fa0/14, Fa0/15, Fa0/16, Fa0/17
                                     Fa0/18, Fa0/19, Fa0/20, Fa0/21
                                     Fa0/22, Fa0/23, Fa0/24, Gi0/1
                                     Gi0/2
1002 fddi-default          act/unsup
1003 token-ring-default    act/unsup
1004 fddinet-default       act/unsup
1005 trnet-default         act/unsup
S1#
```

Figure 3-17   Deleting a VLAN

Caution

Before deleting a VLAN, be sure to first reassign all member ports to a different VLAN. Any ports that are not moved to an active VLAN are unable to communicate with other hosts after the VLAN is deleted and until they are assigned to an active VLAN.

Alternatively, the entire `vlan.dat` file can be deleted using the **delete flash:vlan.dat** privileged EXEC mode command. The abbreviated command version (**delete vlan.dat**) can be used if the `vlan.dat` file has not been moved from its default location. After issuing this command and reloading the switch, the previously configured VLANs are no longer present. This effectively places the switch into its factory default condition concerning VLAN configurations.

Note

For a Cisco Catalyst switch, the **erase startup-config** command must accompany the **delete vlan.dat** command prior to using the **reload** command to restore the switch to its factory default condition.

Verifying VLAN Information (3.2.1.6)

After a VLAN is configured, VLAN configurations can be validated using Cisco IOS **show** commands.

Table 3-4 shows common **show vlan** command options.

Table 3-4   The `show vlan` Command Options

`show vlan [brief	id vlan-id	name vlan-name	summary]`	
Display one line for each VLAN with the VLAN name, status, and associated ports.	`brief`
Display information about a single VLAN identified by the VLAN ID number, which can be a number between 1 and 4094.	`id vlan-id`
Display information about a single VLAN identified by a VLAN name. The VLAN name is an ASCII string from 1 to 32 characters.	`name vlan-name`
Display VLAN summary information.	`summary`

Table 3-5 shows common **show interfaces** command options.

Table 3-5   The `show interfaces` Command Options

`show interfaces [interface-id | vlan vlan-id] | switchport`	
Valid interfaces include physical ports (including type, module, and port number) and port channels. The port-channel range is 1 to 6.	`interface-id`
VLAN identification, which is a number from 1 to 4094.	`vlan vlan-id`
Display the administrative and operational status of a switch port, including port blocking and port protection settings.	`switchport`

In Figure 3-18, the **show vlan name student** command produces output that is not easily interpreted. The preferable option is to use the **show vlan brief** command. The **show vlan summary** command displays the count of all configured VLANs. The output in Figure 3-18 shows seven VLANs.

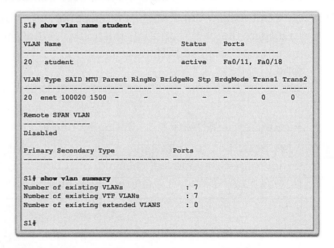

```
S1# show vlan name student

VLAN Name                             Status    Ports
---- -------------------------------- --------- --------------
20   student                          active    Fa0/11, Fa0/18

VLAN Type SAID MTU Parent RingNo BridgeNo Stp BrdgMode Trans1 Trans2
---- -------------------- ------ ------ ------ ---- -------- ------
20   enet 100020 1500 -       -      -        -   -        0      0

Remote SPAN VLAN
----------------
Disabled

Primary Secondary Type               Ports
------- --------- ------------------ ------------------------

S1# show vlan summary
Number of existing VLANs              : 7
Number of existing VTP VLANs          : 7
Number of existing extended VLANS     : 0

S1#
```

Figure 3-18   Using the **show vlan** Command

The **show interfaces vlan** `vlan-id` command displays details that are beyond the scope of this course. The important information appears on the second line in the output, indicating that VLAN 20 is up.

```
S1# show interfaces vlan 20
Vlan 20 is up, line protocol is down
  Hardware is EtherSVI, address is 001c.57ec.0641 (bia 001c.57ec.0641)
  MTU 1500 bytes, BW 1000000 Kbit, DLY 10 usec,
      reliability 255/255, txload 1/255, rxload 1/255
  Encapsulation ARPA, loopback not set
Last input never, output never, output hang never
  Last clearing of "show interface" counters never
  Input queue: 0/75/0/0 (size/max/drops/flushes);
```

```
        Total output drops: 0
        Queueing strategy: fifo
        Output queue: 0/40 (size/max)
        5 minute input rate 0 bits/sec, 0 packets/sec
        5 minute output rate 0 bits/sec, 0 packets/sec
          0 packets input, 0 bytes, 0 no buffer
          Received 0 broadcasts (0 IP multicast)
          0 runts, 0 giants, 0 throttles
          0 input errors, 0 CRC, 0 frame, 0 overrun, 0 ignored
          0 packets output, 0 bytes, 0 underruns
          0 output errors, 0 interface resets
          0 output buffer failures, 0 output buffers swapped out
      <output omitted>
```

Interactive Graphic

Activity 3.2.1.6: Using the show interfaces Command

Go to the online curriculum and select the fourth graphic to use the Syntax Checker to display the switch port information using the **show interfaces** *interface-id* **switchport** command. This command can be used to verify VLAN assignments and mode.

Packet Tracer Activity 3.2.1.6: Configuring VLANs

VLANs are helpful in the administration of logical groups, allowing members of a group to be easily moved, changed, or added. This activity focuses on creating and naming VLANs, and assigning access ports to specific VLANs.

VLAN Trunks (3.2.2)

Trunks are commonly used between switches and other network devices such as a router, another switch, or a server. A network technician must be very familiar with configuring a trunk and ensuring it works properly.

Configuring IEEE 802.1Q Trunk Links (3.2.2.1)

A VLAN trunk is an OSI Layer 2 link between two switches that carries traffic for all VLANs (unless the allowed VLAN list is restricted manually or dynamically). To enable trunk links, configure the ports on either end of the physical link with parallel sets of commands.

To configure a switch port on one end of a trunk link, use the **switchport mode trunk** command. With this command, the interface changes to permanent trunking mode. The port enters into a Dynamic Trunking Protocol (DTP) negotiation to convert the link into a trunk link even if the interface connecting to it does not agree to the change. DTP is described in the next topic. In this course, the **switchport mode trunk** command is the only method implemented for trunk configuration.

The Cisco IOS command syntax to specify a native VLAN (other than VLAN 1) is shown in Table 3-6. In the example, VLAN 99 is configured as the native VLAN using the **switchport trunk native vlan 99** command.

Use the Cisco IOS **switchport trunk allowed vlan** *vlan-list* command to specify the list of VLANs to be allowed on the trunk link.

Table 3-6   Switch Port Trunk Commands

Enter global configuration mode.	S1# `configure terminal`
Enter interface configuration mode for a particular port number.	S1(config)# `interface` *interface_id*
Optionally, put the trunk in the appropriate trunking mode if the switch supports more than one mode.	S1(config-if)# `switchport trunk encapsulation [dot1q	isl]`
Force the link to be a trunk link.	S1(config-if)# `switchport mode trunk`
Specify a native VLAN for untagged 802.1Q frames.	S1(config-if)# `switchport trunk native vlan` *vlan_id*
Specify the list of VLANs to be allowed on the trunk link.	S1(config-if)# `switchport trunk allowed vlan` *vlan-list*
Return to the privileged EXEC mode.	S1(config-if)# `end`

In Figure 3-19, VLANs 10, 20, and 30 support the Faculty, Student, and Guest computers (PC1, PC2, and PC3). The F0/1 port on switch S1 is configured as a trunk port and forwards traffic for VLANs 10, 20, and 30. VLAN 99 is configured as the native VLAN.

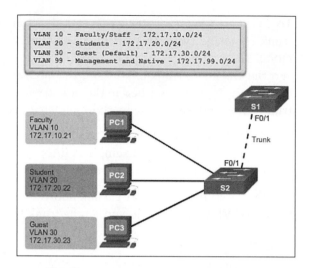

```
VLAN 10 - Faculty/Staff - 172.17.10.0/24
VLAN 20 - Students - 172.17.20.0/24
VLAN 30 - Guest (Default) - 172.17.30.0/24
VLAN 99 - Management and Native - 172.17.99.0/24
```

Figure 3-19   Sample VLAN Design

Look at the configuration of port F0/1 on switch S1 as a trunk port. The native VLAN is changed to VLAN 99 and the allowed VLAN list is restricted to 10, 20, and 30. If the native VLAN is not allowed on the trunk link, the trunk will not allow any data traffic for the native VLAN.

```
S1(config)# interface fastethernet0/1
S1(config-if)# switchport mode trunk
S1(config-if)# switchport trunk native vlan 99
S1(config-if)# switchport trunk allowed vlan 10,20,30
S1(config-if)# end
```

Note

This configuration assumes the use of Cisco Catalyst 2960 switches, which automatically use 802.1Q encapsulation on trunk links. Other switches may require manual configuration of the encapsulation. Always configure both ends of a trunk link with the same native VLAN. If 802.1Q trunk configuration is not the same on both ends, Cisco IOS Software reports errors.

Resetting the Trunk to Default State (3.2.2.2)

Table 3-7 shows the commands to remove the allowed VLANs and reset the native VLAN of the trunk. When reset to the default state, the trunk allows all VLANs and uses VLAN 1 as the native VLAN.

Table 3-7   Resetting Configures Values on Trunk Lines

Enter global configuration mode.	`S1# configure terminal`
Enter interface configuration mode for a particular port number.	`S1(config)# interface interface_id`
Set trunk to allow all VLANs.	`S1(config-if)# no switchport trunk allowed vlan`
Reset the native VLAN to the default.	`S1(config-if)# no switchport trunk native vlan`
Configure the port in access mode.	`S1(config-if)# switchport mode access`
Optionally, remove the trunk mode if it was entered.	`S1(config-if)# no switchport trunk encapsulation [dot1q	isl]`
Return to the privileged EXEC mode.	`S1(config-if)# end`

The command to reset the switch port to an access port and, in effect, delete the trunk configuration is also shown.

The following output shows the commands used to reset all trunking characteristics of a trunking interface to the default settings. The **show interfaces f0/1 switchport** command reveals that the trunk has been reconfigured to a default state.

```
S1(config)# interface f0/1
S1(config-if)# no switchport trunk allowed vlan
S1(config-if)# no switchport trunk native vlan
S1(config-if)# end
S1# show interfaces f0/1 switchport
Name: Fa0/1
Switchport: Enabled
Administrative Mode: trunk
Operational Mode: trunk
Administrative Trunking Encapsulation: dot1q
Operational Trunking Encapsulation: dot1q
Negotiation of Trunking: On
Access Mode VLAN: 1 (default)
Trunking Native Mode VLAN: 1 (default)
Administrative Native VLAN tagging: enabled
<output omitted>
Administrative private-vlan trunk mappings: none
Operational private-vlan: none
Trunking VLANs Enabled: All
Pruning VLANs Enabled: 2-1001
<output omitted>
```

The following sample output shows the commands used to remove the trunk feature from the F0/1 switch port on switch S1. The **show interfaces f0/1 switchport** command reveals that the F0/1 interface is now in static access mode.

```
S1(config)# interface f0/1
S1(config-if)# switchport mode access
S1(config-if)# end
S1# show interfaces f0/1 switchport
Name: Fa0/1
Switchport: Enabled
Administrative Mode: static access
Operational Mode: static access
Administrative Trunking Encapsulation: dot1q
Operational Trunking Encapsulation: native
Negotiation of Trunking: Off
Access Mode VLAN: 1 (default)
Trunking Native Mode VLAN: 1 (default)
Administrative Native VLAN tagging: enabled
<output omitted>
```

Verifying Trunk Configuration (3.2.2.3)

The following output displays the configuration of switch port F0/1 on switch S1. The configuration is verified with the **show interfaces** *interface-ID* **switchport** command.

```
S1(config)# interface f0/1
S1(config-if)# switchport mode trunk
S1(config-if)# switchport trunk native vlan 99
S1(config-if)# end
S1# show interfaces f0/1 switchport
Name: Fa0/1
Switchport: Enabled
Administrative Mode: trunk
Operational Mode: trunk
Administrative Trunking Encapsulation: dot1q
Operational Trunking Encapsulation: dot1q
Negotiation of Trunking: On
Access Mode VLAN: 1 (default)
Trunking Native Mode VLAN: 99 (VLAN0099)
Administrative Native VLAN tagging: enabled
Voice VLAN: none
Administrative private-vlan host-association: none
Administrative private-vlan mapping: none
Administrative private-vlan trunk native VLAN: none
```

```
Administrative private-vlan trunk Native VLAN tagging: enabled
Administrative private-vlan trunk normal VLANs: none
Administrative private-vlan trunk associations: none
Administrative private-vlan trunk mappings: none
Operational private-vlan: none
Trunking VLANs Enabled: All
Pruning VLANs Enabled: 2-1001
<output omitted>
```

The top highlighted area shows that port F0/1 has its administrative mode set to **trunk**. The port is in trunking mode. The next highlighted area verifies that the native VLAN is VLAN 99. Further down in the output, the bottom highlighted area shows that all VLANs are enabled on the trunk.

Activity 3.2.2.3: Configuring and Verifying a Trunk

Go to the online curriculum and select the second graphic to use the Syntax Checker to configure a trunk supporting all VLANs on interface F0/1, with native VLAN 99. Verify the trunk configuration with the **show interfaces f0/1 switchport** command.

Packet Tracer Activity 3.2.2.4: Configuring Trunks

VLAN trunks are required to pass VLAN information between switches. A port on a switch is either an access port or a trunk port. Access ports carry traffic from a specific VLAN assigned to the port. A trunk port by default is a member of all VLANs; therefore, it carries traffic for all VLANs. This activity focuses on creating trunk ports and assigning them to a native VLAN other than the default.

Lab 3.2.2.5: Configuring VLANs and Trunking

In this lab, you will complete the following objectives:

- Part 1: Build the Network and Configure Basic Device Settings
- Part 2: Create VLANs and Assign Switch Ports
- Part 3: Maintain VLAN Port Assignments and the VLAN Database
- Part 4: Configure an 802.1Q Trunk Between the Switches
- Part 5: Delete the VLAN Database

Dynamic Trunking Protocol (3.2.3)

The *Dynamic Trunking Protocol (DTP)* is used to negotiate forming a trunk between two Cisco devices. DTP causes increased traffic, and is enabled by default, but may be disabled.

Introduction to DTP (3.2.3.1)

Ethernet trunk interfaces support different trunking modes. An interface can be set to trunking or nontrunking, or to negotiate trunking with the neighbor interface. Trunk negotiation is managed by the Dynamic Trunking Protocol (DTP), which operates on a point-to-point basis only, between network devices.

DTP is a Cisco proprietary protocol that is automatically enabled on Catalyst 2960 and Catalyst 3560 Series switches. Switches from other vendors do not support DTP. DTP manages trunk negotiation only if the port on the neighbor switch is configured in a trunk mode that supports DTP.

Caution

Some internetworking devices might forward DTP frames improperly, which can cause misconfigurations. To avoid this, turn off DTP on interfaces on a Cisco switch connected to devices that do not support DTP.

The default DTP configuration for Cisco Catalyst 2960 and 3560 switches is dynamic auto as shown in Figure 3-20 on interface F0/3 of switches S1 and S3.

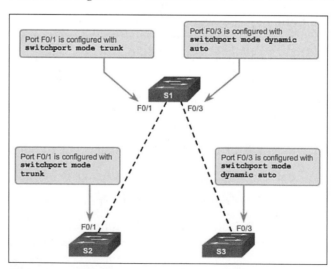

Figure 3-20   Initial DTP Configuration

To enable trunking from a Cisco switch to a device that does not support DTP, use the **switchport mode trunk** and **switchport nonegotiate** interface configuration mode commands. This causes the interface to become a trunk but not generate DTP frames.

In Figure 3-21, the link between switches S1 and S2 becomes a trunk because the F0/1 ports on switches S1 and S2 are configured to ignore all DTP advertisements, and to come up in and stay in trunk port mode. The F0/3 ports on switches S1 and S3 are set to dynamic auto, so the negotiation results in the access mode state. This creates an inactive trunk link. When configuring a port to be in trunk mode, there is no ambiguity about which state the trunk is in; it is always on. With this configuration, it is easy to remember which state the trunk ports are in; if the port is supposed to be a trunk, the mode is set to trunk.

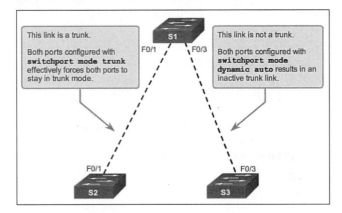

Figure 3-21   DTP Interaction Results

Negotiated Interface Modes (3.2.3.2)

Ethernet interfaces on Catalyst 2960 and Catalyst 3560 Series switches support different trunking modes with the help of DTP:

- **switchport mode access:** Puts the interface (access port) into permanent nontrunking mode and negotiates to convert the link into a nontrunk link. The interface becomes a nontrunk interface, regardless of whether the neighboring interface is a trunk interface.

- **switchport mode dynamic auto:** Makes the interface able to convert the link to a trunk link. The interface becomes a trunk interface if the neighboring interface is set to trunk or desirable mode. The default switchport mode for newer Cisco switch Ethernet interfaces is **dynamic auto**. Note that if two Cisco switches are left to the common default setting of **auto**, a trunk will never form.

- **switchport mode dynamic desirable:** Makes the interface actively attempt to convert the link to a trunk link. The interface becomes a trunk interface if the neighboring interface is set to trunk, desirable, or auto mode. This is the default switchport mode on older switches, such as the Catalyst 2950 and 3550 Series switches.

- **switchport mode trunk:** Puts the interface into permanent trunking mode and negotiates to convert the neighboring link into a trunk link. The interface becomes a trunk interface even if the neighboring interface is not a trunk interface.

- **switchport nonegotiate:** Prevents the interface from generating DTP frames. You can use this command only when the interface switchport mode is **access** or **trunk**. You must manually configure the neighboring interface as a trunk interface to establish a trunk link.

Table 3-8 illustrates the results of the DTP configuration options on opposite ends of a trunk link connected to Catalyst 2960 switch ports.

Table 3-8   DTP Negotiated Interface Modes

	Dynamic Auto	Dynamic Desirable	Trunk	Access
Dynamic Auto	Access	Trunk	Trunk	Access
Dynamic Desirable	Trunk	Trunk	Trunk	Access
Trunk	Trunk	Trunk	Trunk	Limited connectivity
Access	Access	Access	Limited connectivity	Access

Note

Configure trunk links statically whenever possible.

The default DTP mode is dependent on the Cisco IOS Software version and on the platform. To determine the current DTP mode, issue the **show dtp interface** command, as shown in the following output.

```
S1# show dtp interface f0/1
DTP information for FastEthernet0/1:
  TOS/TAS/TNS:                          TRUNK/ON/TRUNK
  TOT/TAT/TNT:                          802.1Q/802.1Q/802.1Q
```

```
    Neighbor address 1:                            0CD996D23F81
    Neighbor address 2:                            000000000000
    Hello timer expiration (sec/state):            12/RUNNING
    Access timer expiration (sec/state):           never/STOPPED
    Negotiation timer expiration (sec/state):      never/STOPPED
    Multidrop timer expiration (sec/state):        never/STOPPED
    FSM state:                                     S6:TRUNK
    # times multi & trunk                          0
    Enabled:                                       yes
    In STP:                                        no
<output omitted>
```

Interactive Graphic

Activity 3.2.3.2: Configuring and Verifying DTP

Go to the curriculum and click on the third graphic in order to use the Syntax Checker to determine the DTP mode on interface F0/1.

Note

A general best practice is to set the interface to **trunk** and **nonegotiate** when a trunk link is required. On links where trunking is not intended, DTP should be turned off.

Interactive Graphic

Activity 3.2.3.3: Predict DTP Behavior

Go to the course outline to perform this practice activity where you will select whether a link will become a trunk link or an access link.

Troubleshoot VLANs and Trunks (3.2.4)

When first learning about switches, students have trouble knowing where to start troubleshooting. Pay particular attention to the **show** commands in this section to verify your configurations using the described techniques instead of simply using the **show running-configuration** command.

IP Addressing Issues with VLAN (3.2.4.1)

Each VLAN must correspond to a unique IP subnet. If two devices in the same VLAN have different subnet addresses, they cannot communicate. This is a common problem, and it is easy to solve by identifying the incorrect configuration and changing the subnet address to the correct one.

In Figure 3-22, PC1 cannot connect to the web/TFTP server shown.

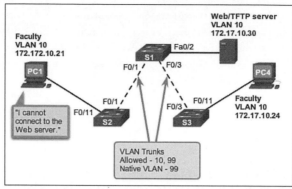

Figure 3-22   IP Issue Within a VLAN

A check of the IP configuration settings of PC1 shown in Figure 3-23 reveals the most common error in configuring VLANs: an incorrectly configured IP address. PC1 is configured with an IP address of 172.172.10.21, but it should have been configured with 172.17.10.21.

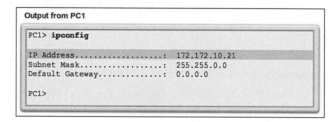

Figure 3-23   Incorrect IP Address Problem

The PC1 Fast Ethernet configuration dialog box shows the updated IP address of 172.17.10.21. In Figure 3-24, the output on the bottom reveals that PC1 has regained connectivity to the web/TFTP server found at IP address 172.17.10.30.

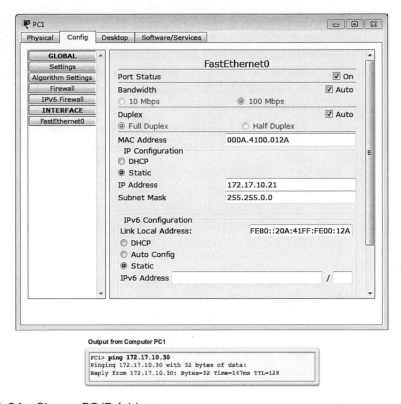

Output from Computer PC1

```
PC1> ping 172.17.10.30
Pinging 172.17.10.30 with 32 bytes of data:
Reply from 172.17.10.30: Bytes-32 Time-147ms TTL-128
```

Figure 3-24   Change PC IP Address

Missing VLANs (3.2.4.2)

If there is still no connection between devices in a VLAN, but IP addressing issues have been ruled out, see the flowchart in Figure 3-25 to troubleshoot.

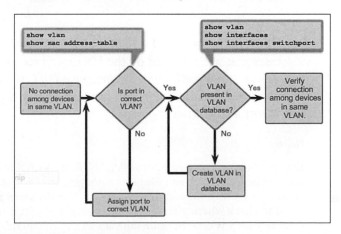

Figure 3-25   Missing VLAN Flowchart

- As shown in Figure 3-25, use the **show vlan** command to check whether the port belongs to the expected VLAN. If the port is assigned to the wrong VLAN, use the **switchport access vlan** command to correct the VLAN membership on a particular port. Use the **show mac address-table** command to check which addresses were learned on a particular port of the switch and to which VLAN that port is assigned, as shown in the following output.

```
S1# show mac address-table interface fastethernet 0/1
          Mac Address Table
-------------------------------------

Vlan    Mac Address      Type       Ports
----    -------------    -------    -----
10      000c.296a.a21c   DYNAMIC    Fa0/1
10      000f.34f9.9181   DYNAMIC    Fa0/1
      Total MAC addresses for this criterion: 2
```

- **Total Mac Addresses for this criterion:** If the VLAN to which the port is assigned is deleted, the port becomes inactive. Use the **show vlan** or **show interfaces switchport** command to verify whether a VLAN is active.

```
S1# show interfaces fastethernet0/1 switchport
Name: Fa0/1
Switchport: Enabled
Administrative Mode: static access
Operational Mode: static access
Administrative Trunking Encapsulation: dot1q
Operational Trunking Encapsulation: native
Negotiation of Trunking: Off
Access Mode VLAN: 10 (Inactive)
Trunking Native Mode VLAN: 1 (default)
Administrative Native VLAN tagging: enabled
<output omitted>
```

In the previous example of a MAC address table, the output shows the MAC addresses that were learned on the F0/1 interface. It can be seen that MAC address 000c.296a.a21c was learned on interface F0/1 in VLAN 10. If this number is not the expected VLAN number, change the port VLAN membership using the **switchport access vlan** command.

Note

Each port in a switch belongs to a VLAN. If the VLAN to which the port belongs is deleted, the port becomes inactive. All ports belonging to the VLAN that was deleted are unable to communicate with the rest of the network. Use the **show interface f0/1 switchport** command to check whether the port is inactive. If the port is inactive, it is not functional until the missing VLAN is created using the **vlan** *vlan_id* command.

Introduction to Troubleshooting Trunks (3.2.4.3)

A common task of a network administrator is to troubleshoot trunk link formation or links incorrectly behaving as trunk links. Sometimes a switch port may behave like a trunk port even if it is not configured as a trunk port. For example, an access port might accept frames from VLANs different from the VLAN to which it is assigned. This is called *VLAN leaking*, which is caused by a mismatched native VLAN or misconfigured trunk.

Figure 3-26 displays a flowchart of general trunk troubleshooting guidelines.

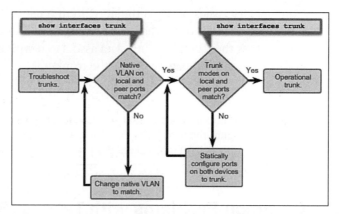

Figure 3-26   Trunk Troubleshooting Flowchart

To troubleshoot issues when a trunk is not forming or when VLAN leaking is occurring, proceed as follows:

■ Use the **show interfaces trunk** command to check whether the local and peer native VLANs match. If the native VLAN does not match on both sides, VLAN leaking occurs.

■ Use the **show interfaces trunk** command to check whether a trunk has been established between switches. Statically configure trunk links whenever possible. Cisco Catalyst switch ports use DTP by default and attempt to negotiate a trunk link.

To display the status of the trunk, determine the native VLAN used on that trunk link and verify trunk establishment using the **show interfaces trunk** command. The following output shows that the native VLAN on one side of the trunk link was changed to VLAN 2. If one end of the trunk is configured as native VLAN 99 and the other end is configured as native VLAN 2, a frame sent from VLAN 99 on one side is received on VLAN 2 on the other side. VLAN 99 leaks into the VLAN 2 segment.

```
SW1# show interfaces f0/1 trunk

Port        Mode      Encapsulation    Status     Native vlan
Fa0/1       auto      802.1q           trunking  2
<output omitted>
```

CDP displays a notification of a native VLAN mismatch on a trunk link with this message:

```
*Mar 1 06:45:26.232: %CDP-4-NATIVE_VLAN_MISMATCH: Native VLAN mismatch discovered on
    FastEthernet0/1 (2), with S2 FastEthernet0/1 (99).
```

Connectivity issues occur in the network if a native VLAN mismatch exists. Data traffic for VLANs, other than the two native VLANs configured, successfully propagates across the trunk link, but data associated with either of the native VLANs does not successfully propagate across the trunk link.

Note

The previous output indicates that there is an active trunk despite the native VLAN mismatch. Configure the native VLAN to be the same VLAN on both sides of the link to correct this behavior so that VLAN leaking does not occur.

Common Problems with Trunks (3.2.4.4)

Trunking issues are usually associated with incorrect configurations, shown in Table 3-9.

Table 3-9   Common Problems with Trunks

Problem	Result	Example
Native VLAN mismatch	Poses a security risk and creates unintended results	One port is defined as native VLAN 99 and the opposite trunk end is defined as native VLAN 100.
Trunk mode mismatch	Causes loss of network connectivity	One end of the trunk is configured as trunk mode "off" and the other as trunk mode "on."
Allowed VLANs on trunks	Causes unexpected traffic or no traffic to be sent over the trunk	The list of allowed VLANs does not support current VLAN trunking requirements.

When configuring VLANs and trunks on a switched infrastructure, the following types of configuration errors are the most common:

- **Native VLAN mismatches:** Trunk ports are configured with different native VLANs. This configuration error generates console notifications, and causes control and management traffic to be misdirected. This poses a security risk.

- **Trunk mode mismatches:** One trunk port is configured with trunk mode off and the other with trunk mode on. This configuration error causes the trunk link to stop working.

- **Allowed VLANs on trunks:** The list of allowed VLANs on a trunk has not been updated with the current VLAN trunking requirements. In this situation, unexpected traffic or no traffic is sent over the trunk.

If an issue with a trunk is discovered and if the cause is unknown, start troubleshooting by examining the trunks for a native VLAN mismatch. If that is not the cause, check for trunk mode mismatches, and finally check for the allowed VLAN list on the trunk. The next two sections examine how to fix the common problems with trunks.

Trunk Mode Mismatches (3.2.4.5)

Trunk links are normally configured statically with the **switchport mode trunk** command. Cisco Catalyst switch trunk ports use DTP to negotiate the state of the link. When a port on a trunk link is configured with a trunk mode that is incompatible with the neighboring trunk port, a trunk link fails to form between the two switches.

In Figure 3-27, PC4 cannot connect to the internal web server. The topology indicates a valid configuration. Why is there a problem?

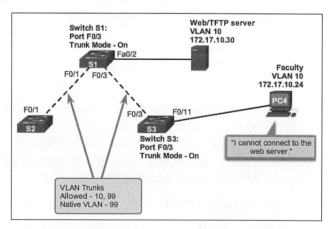

Figure 3-27 Trunk Scenario Topology

Check the status of the trunk ports on switch S1 using the **show interfaces trunk** command. The following output reveals that interface Fa0/3 on switch S1 is not currently a trunk link. Examining the F0/3 interface reveals that the switch port is actually in dynamic auto mode.

Output from Switch S1:

```
S1# show interfaces trunk
Port         Mode      Encapsulation    Status      Native vlan
Fa0/1        on        802.1q           trunking    99
Port         Vlans allowed on trunk
Fa0/1        10,99
Port         Vlans allowed and active in management domain
Fa0/1        10,99
Port         Vlans in spanning tree forwarding state and not pruned
Fa0/1        10,99


S1# show interfaces f0/3 switchport
Name: Fa0/3
Switchport: Enabled
Administrative Mode: dynamic auto
<output omitted>
```

An examination of the trunks on switch S3 reveals that there are no active trunk ports. Further checking reveals that the Fa0/3 interface is also in dynamic auto mode. This explains why the trunk is down as shown in the output.

Output from Switch S3:

```
S3# show interfaces trunk


S3#
S3# show interfaces f0/3 switchport
Name: Fa0/3
Switchport: Enabled
Administrative Mode: dynamic auto
<output omitted>
```

To resolve the issue, reconfigure the trunk mode of the F0/3 ports on switches S1 and S3, as shown in the following output. After the configuration change, the output of the **show interfaces** command indicates that the port on switch S1 is now in trunking mode. The output from PC4 indicates that it has regained connectivity to the Web/TFTP server found at IP address 172.17.10.30.

Output from Switch S1:

```
S1# config terminal
S1(config)# interface fastethernet0/3
```

```
S1(config-if)# switchport mode trunk
S1(config-if)# end
S1# show interfaces fa0/3 switchport
Name: Fa0/3
Switchport: Enabled
Administrative Mode: trunk
<output omitted>
```

Output from Switch S3:

```
S3# config terminal
S3(config)# interface fastethernet0/3
S3(config-if)# switchport mode trunk
S3(config-if)# end
S3# show interfaces fa0/3 switchport
Name: Fa0/3
Switchport: Enabled
Administrative Mode: trunk
<output omitted>
S3# show interfaces trunk
Port        Mode    Encapsulation  Status        Native vlan
Fa0/3       on      802.1q         trunking      99
Port        Vlans allowed on trunk
Fa0/3       10,99
Port        Vlans allowed and active in management domain
Fa0/3       10,99
Port        Vlans in spanning tree forwarding state and not pruned
Fa0/3       10,99
```

Output from Computer PC4:

```
Pc4> ping 172.17.10.30
Pinging 172.17.10.30 with 32 bytes of data:
Reply from 172.17.10.30: bytes=32 time=147ms TTL=128
<output omitted>
```

Incorrect VLAN List (3.2.4.6)

For traffic from a VLAN to be transmitted across a trunk, it must be allowed on the trunk. To do so, use the **switchport trunk allowed vlan** *vlan-id* command.

In Figure 3-28, VLAN 20 (Student) and PC5 have been added to the network. The documentation has been updated to show that the VLANs allowed on the trunk are 10, 20, and 99. In this scenario, PC5 cannot connect to the student email server.

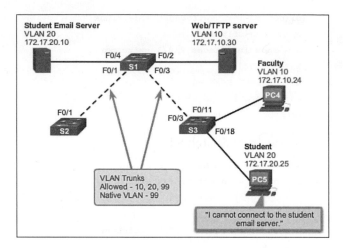

Figure 3-28   Incorrect VLAN List Scenario Topology

Check the trunk ports on switch S3 using the **show interfaces trunk** command as shown in the output that follows.

Output from Switch S3:

```
S3# show interfaces trunk
Port        Mode        Encapsulation    Status      Native vlan
Fa0/3       on          802.1q            trunking  99
Port        Vlans allowed on trunk
Fa0/3       10,20,99
Port        Vlans allowed and active in management domain
Fa0/3       10,20,99
Port        Vlans in spanning tree forwarding state and not pruned
Fa0/3       10,20,99
```

The command reveals that the interface F0/3 on switch S3 is correctly configured to allow VLANs 10, 20, and 99 as shown in the output.

An examination of the F0/3 interface on switch S1 reveals that interfaces F0/1 and F0/3 allow only VLANs 10 and 99. Someone updated the documentation but forgot to reconfigure the ports on the S1 switch, as shown in the output.

Output from Switch S1:

```
S1# show interfaces trunk
Port        Mode        Encapsulation    Status      Native vlan
Fa0/1       on          802.1q
Fa0/3       on          802.1q            trunking  99
Port        Vlans allowed on trunk
Fa0/1       10,99
Fa0/3       10,99
<output omitted>
```

Reconfigure F0/1 and F0/3 on switch S1 using the **switchport trunk allowed vlan 10,20,99** command as shown in the following output. The output shows that VLANs 10, 20, and 99 are now added to the F0/1 and F0/3 ports on switch S1. The **show interfaces trunk** command is an excellent tool for revealing common trunking problems.

Output from Switch S1:

```
S1# config terminal
S1(config)# interface f0/1
S1(config-if)# switchport trunk allowed vlan 10,20,99
S1(config-if)# interface f0/3
S1(config-if)# switchport trunk allowed vlan 10,20,99
S1# show interface trunk

Port        Mode      Encapsulation    Status     Native vlan
Fa0/1       on        802.1q
Fa0/3       on        802.1q           trunking   99
Port        Vlans allowed on trunk
Fa0/1       10,20,99
Fa0/3       10,20,99
<output omitted>
```

PC5 has regained connectivity to the student email server found at IP address 172.17.20.10.

Output from Computer PC5:

```
PC5> ping 172.17.20.10
Pinging 172.17.20.10 with 32 bytes of data:
Reply from 172.17.20.10: bytes=32 time=147ms TTL=128
<output omitted>
```

Packet Tracer Activity 3.2.4.7: Troubleshooting a VLAN Implementation: Scenario 1

In this activity, you will troubleshoot connectivity problems between PCs on the same VLAN. The activity is complete when PCs on the same VLAN can ping each other. Any solution you implement must conform to the Addressing Table.

Packet Tracer Activity 3.2.4.8: Troubleshooting a VLAN Implementation: Scenario 2

In this activity, you will troubleshoot a misconfigured VLAN environment. The initial network has errors. Your objective is to locate and correct the errors in the configurations and establish end-to-end connectivity. Your final configuration should match the Topology diagram and Addressing Table. The native VLAN for this topology is VLAN 56.

Lab 3.2.4.9: Troubleshooting VLAN Configurations

In this lab, you will complete the following objectives:

Part 1: Build the Network and Configure Basic Device Settings

Part 2: Troubleshoot VLAN 10

Part 3: Troubleshoot VLAN 20

VLAN Security and Design (3.3)

Learning what attacks can occur and how to design the switch network to mitigate these attacks is important to a network technician. Because VLANs are commonly configured in a business environment, VLANs are a common security target.

Switch Spoofing Attack (3.3.1.1)

There are a number of different types of VLAN attacks in modern switched networks. The VLAN architecture simplifies network maintenance and improves performance, but it also opens the door to abuse. It is important to understand the general methodology behind these attacks and the primary approaches to mitigate them.

VLAN hopping enables traffic from one VLAN to be seen by another VLAN. *Switch spoofing* is a type of VLAN hopping attack that works by taking advantage of an incorrectly configured trunk port. By default, trunk ports have access to all VLANs and pass traffic for multiple VLANs across the same physical link, generally between switches.

Activity 3.3.1.1: Switch Spoofing Attack

Go to the online curriculum, and click the Play button in the graphic to see an animation of a switch spoofing attack.

In a basic switch spoofing attack, the attacker takes advantage of the fact that the default configuration of the switch port is dynamic auto. The network attacker configures a system to spoof itself as a switch. This spoofing requires that the network attacker be capable of emulating 802.1Q and DTP messages. By tricking a switch into thinking that another switch is attempting to form a trunk, an attacker can gain access to all the VLANs allowed on the trunk port.

The best way to prevent a basic switch spoofing attack is to turn off trunking on all ports, except the ones that specifically require trunking. On the required trunking ports, disable DTP, and manually enable trunking.

Double-Tagging Attack (3.3.1.2)

Another type of VLAN attack is a *double-tagging* (or double-encapsulated) VLAN hopping attack. This type of attack takes advantage of the way that hardware on most switches operates. Most switches perform only one level of 802.1Q de-encapsulation, which allows an attacker to embed a hidden 802.1Q tag inside the frame. This tag allows the frame to be forwarded to a VLAN that the original 802.1Q tag did not specify as shown in Figure 3-29. An important characteristic of the double-encapsulated VLAN hopping attack is that it works even if trunk ports are disabled, because a host typically sends a frame on a segment that is not a trunk link.

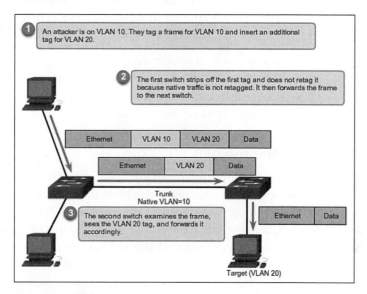

Figure 3-29   Double-Tagging Attack

A double-tagging VLAN hopping attack follows three steps:

Step 1.   The attacker sends a double-tagged 802.1Q frame to the switch. The outer header has the VLAN tag of the attacker, which is the same as the native VLAN of the trunk port. The assumption is that the switch processes the frame received from the attacker as if it were on a trunk port or a port with a voice VLAN. (A switch should not receive a tagged Ethernet frame on an access port.) For the purposes of this example, assume that the native VLAN is VLAN 10. The inner tag is the victim VLAN; in this case, it is VLAN 20.

Step 2.   The frame arrives on the switch, which looks at the first 4-byte 802.1Q tag. The switch sees that the frame is destined for VLAN 10, which is the native VLAN. The switch forwards the packet out on all VLAN 10 ports after stripping the VLAN 10 tag. On the trunk port, the VLAN 10 tag is stripped, and the packet is not retagged because it is part of the native VLAN. At this point, the VLAN 20 tag is still intact and has not been inspected by the first switch.

Step 3.   The second switch looks only at the inner 802.1Q tag that the attacker sent and sees that the frame is destined for VLAN 20, the target VLAN. The second switch sends the frame on to the victim port or floods it, depending on whether there is an existing MAC address table entry for the victim host.

This type of attack is unidirectional and works only when the attacker is connected to a port residing in the same VLAN as the native VLAN of the trunk port. Thwarting this type of attack is not as easy as stopping basic VLAN hopping attacks.

The best approach to mitigating double-tagging attacks is to ensure that the native VLAN of the trunk ports is different from the VLAN of any user ports. In fact, it is considered a security best practice to use a fixed VLAN that is distinct from all user VLANs in the switched network as the native VLAN for all 802.1Q trunks.

PVLAN Edge (3.3.1.3)

Some applications require that no traffic be forwarded at Layer 2 between ports on the same switch so that one neighbor does not see the traffic generated by another neighbor. In such an environment, the use of the *Private VLAN (PVLAN) Edge* feature, also known as protected ports, ensures that there is no exchange of unicast, broadcast, or multicast traffic between these ports on the switch, as shown in Figure 3-30.

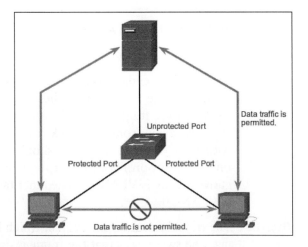

Figure 3-30   PVLAN Edge

The PVLAN Edge feature has the following characteristics:

- A protected port does not forward any traffic (unicast, multicast, or broadcast) to any other port that is also a protected port, except for control traffic. Data traffic cannot be forwarded between protected ports at Layer 2.

- Forwarding behavior between a protected port and a nonprotected port proceeds as usual.

- Protected ports must be manually configured.

To configure the PVLAN Edge feature, enter the **switchport protected** command in interface configuration mode as shown in the output that follows.

```
S1(config)# interface g0/1
S1(config-if)# switchport protected
S1(config-if)# end
S1# show interfaces g0/1 switchport
Name: G0/1
Switchport: Enabled
Administrative Mode: dynamic auto
Operational Mode: down
Administrative Trunking Encapsulation: dot1q
Negotiation of Trunking: On
Access Mode VLAN: 1 (default)
Trunking Native Mode VLAN: 1 (default)
Administrative Native VLAN tagging: enabled
Voice VLAN: none
<output omitted>

Protected: true
Unknown unicast blocked: disabled
Unknown multicast blocked: disabled
Appliance trust: none
```

To disable protected port, use the **no switchport protected** interface configuration mode command. To verify the configuration of the PVLAN Edge feature, use the **show interfaces** *interface-id* **switchport** global configuration mode command.

Activity 3.3.1.3: Configure and Verify the PVLAN Edge Feature

Interactive Graphic

Go to the online curriculum, and click on the third graphic to use the Syntax Checker to configure the PVLAN Edge feature on interface G0/1 and verify the configuration.

Interactive
Graphic

Activity 3.3.1.4: Identify the Type of VLAN Attack

Go to the course outline to perform this practice activity. Drag the type of attack to the description.

Design Best Practices for VLANs (3.3.2)

Because VLANs are a common security target, designing VLANs with security in mind is being proactive. Here are some best practices to use before you create the first VLAN on a switch.

VLAN Design Guidelines (3.3.2.1)

Cisco switches have a factory configuration in which default VLANs are preconfigured to support various media and protocol types. The default Ethernet VLAN is VLAN 1. It is a security best practice to configure all the ports on all switches to be associated with VLANs other than VLAN 1. This is usually done by configuring all unused ports to a *black hole VLAN* that is not used for anything on the network. All used ports are associated with VLANs distinct from VLAN 1 and distinct from the black hole VLAN. It is also a good practice to shut down unused switch ports to prevent unauthorized access.

A good security practice is to separate management and user data traffic. The management VLAN, which is VLAN 1 by default, should be changed to a separate, distinct VLAN. To communicate remotely with a Cisco switch for management purposes, the switch must have an IP address configured on the management VLAN. Users in other VLANs would not be able to establish remote access sessions to the switch unless they were routed into the management VLAN, providing an additional layer of security. Also, the switch should be configured to accept only encrypted SSH sessions for remote management.

All control traffic is sent on VLAN 1. Therefore, when the native VLAN is changed to something other than VLAN 1, all control traffic is tagged on IEEE 802.1Q VLAN trunks (tagged with VLAN ID 1). A recommended security practice is to change the native VLAN to a different VLAN than VLAN 1. The native VLAN should also be distinct from all user VLANs. Ensure that the native VLAN for an 802.1Q trunk is the same on both ends of the trunk link.

DTP offers four switch port modes: access, trunk, dynamic auto, and dynamic desirable. A general guideline is to disable autonegotiation. As a port security best practice, do not use the dynamic auto or dynamic desirable switch port modes.

Finally, voice traffic has stringent QoS requirements. If user PCs and IP phones are on the same VLAN, each tries to use the available bandwidth without considering the other device. To avoid this conflict, it is good practice to use separate VLANs for IP telephony and data traffic.

Lab 3.3.2.2: Implementing VLAN Security

In this lab, you will complete the following objectives:

Part 1: Build the Network and Configure Basic Device Settings

Part 2: Implement VLAN Security on the Switches

Summary (3.4)

This chapter thoroughly covered VLANs: how to design and create VLANs and how to transmit those VLANs to other network devices such as other switches using a trunk link. Security risks associated with VLANs and how to mitigate those risks with some proactive designs and configurations were also covered. This section helps you to determine if you learned the main points as well as the finer details of the chapter.

Class Activity 3.4.1.1: VLAN Plan

Scenario

You are designing a VLAN switched network for your small- to medium-sized business.

Your business owns space on two floors of a high-rise building. The following elements need VLAN consideration and access for planning purposes:

- Management
- Finance
- Sales
- Human Resources
- Network administrator
- General visitors to your business location

You have two Cisco 3560-24PS switches.

Use a word processing software program to design your VLAN-switched network scheme.

Section 1 of your design should include the regular names of your departments, suggested VLAN names and numbers, and which switch ports would be assigned to each VLAN.

Section 2 of your design should list how security would be planned for this switched network.

When your VLAN plan is finished, complete the reflection questions from this activity's PDF.

Save your work. Be able to explain and discuss your VLAN design with another group or with the class.

Packet Tracer
☐ Activity

Packet Tracer Activity 3.4.1.2: Skills Integration Challenge

In this activity, two switches are completely configured. On a third switch, you are responsible for assigning IP addressing to the SVI, configuring VLANs, assigning VLANs to interfaces, configuring trunking, and performing basic switch security.

This chapter introduced VLANs. VLANs are based on logical connections, instead of physical connections. VLANs are a mechanism to allow network administrators to create logical broadcast domains that can span across a single switch or multiple switches, regardless of physical proximity. This function is useful to reduce the size of broadcast domains or to allow groups or users to be logically grouped without the need to be physically located in the same place.

There are several types of VLANs:

- Default VLAN

- Management VLAN

- Native VLAN

- User/Data VLANs

- Black Hole VLAN

- Voice VLAN

On a Cisco switch, VLAN 1 is the default Ethernet VLAN, the default native VLAN, and the default management VLAN. Best practices suggest that the native and management VLANs be moved to another distinct VLAN and that unused switch ports be moved to a "black hole" VLAN for increased security.

The **switchport access vlan** command is used to create a VLAN on a switch. After creating a VLAN, the next step is to assign ports to the VLAN. The **show vlan brief** command displays the VLAN assignment and membership type for all switch ports. Each VLAN must correspond to a unique IP subnet.

Use the **show vlan** command to check whether the port belongs to the expected VLAN. If the port is assigned to the wrong VLAN, use the **switchport access vlan** command to correct the VLAN membership. Use the **show mac address-table** command to check which addresses were learned on a particular port of the switch and to which VLAN that port is assigned.

A port on a switch is either an access port or a trunk port. Access ports carry traffic from a specific VLAN assigned to the port. A trunk port by default is a member of all VLANs; therefore, it carries traffic for all VLANs.

VLAN trunks facilitate inter-switch communication by carrying traffic associated with multiple VLANs. IEEE 802.1Q frame tagging differentiates between Ethernet frames associated with distinct VLANs as they traverse common trunk links. To enable trunk links, use the **switchport mode trunk** command. Use the **show interfaces trunk** command to check whether a trunk has been established between switches.

Trunk negotiation is managed by the Dynamic Trunking Protocol (DTP), which operates on a point-to-point basis only, between network devices. DTP is a Cisco proprietary protocol that is automatically enabled on Catalyst 2960 and Catalyst 3560 Series switches.

To place a switch into its factory default condition with 1 default VLAN, use the command **delete flash:vlan.dat** and **erase startup-config**.

This chapter also examined the configuration, verification, and troubleshooting of VLANs and trunks using the Cisco IOS CLI and explored basic security and design considerations in the context of VLANs.

Practice

The following activities provide practice with the topics introduced in this chapter. The Labs and Class Activities are available in the companion *Introduction to Routing and Switching Essentials Lab Manual* (978-1-58713-320-6). You can find the Packet Tracer Activities PKA files in the online course.

Class Activities

Class Activity 3.0.1.2: Vacation Station

Class Activity 3.4.1.1: VLAN Plan

Labs

Lab 3.2.2.5: Configuring VLANs and Trunking

Lab 3.2.4.9: Troubleshooting VLAN Configurations

Lab 3.3.2.2: Implementing VLAN Security

Packet Tracer Activities

Packet Tracer Activity 3.1.1.5: Who Hears the Broadcast?

Packet Tracer Activity 3.1.2.7: Investigating a VLAN Implementation

Packet Tracer Activity 3.2.1.6: Configuring VLANs

Packet Tracer Activity 3.2.2.4: Configuring Trunks

Packet Tracer Activity 3.2.4.7: Troubleshooting a VLAN Implementation: Scenario 1

Packet Tracer Activity 3.2.4.8: Troubleshooting a VLAN Implementation: Scenario 2

Packet Tracer Activity 3.4.1.2: Skills Integration Challenge

Check Your Understanding Questions

Complete all the review questions listed here to test your understanding of the topics and concepts in this chapter. The appendix, "Answers to the 'Check Your Understanding' Questions," lists the answers.

1. What is the difference between an access port and a trunk port?

   A. A trunk port belongs to a single VLAN; an access port provides access for multiple VLANs between switches.

   B. An access port can have a native VLAN, but a trunk port cannot.

   C. An access port can have only one device attached.

   D. Multiple VLANs traverse a trunk port, but an access port can belong to a single VLAN.

2. Switch S1 and Switch S2 are both configured with ports in the Faculty, Students, Voice, Guest, Printing, and Admin VLANs. Each VLAN contains 12 users. How many subnets are needed to address the VLANs?

   A. 1

   B. 2

   C. 4

   D. 6

   E. 8

   F. 12

   G. 24

3. What mechanism is used to achieve the separation between different VLANs as they cross a trunk link?

   A. VLAN tagging using 802.1Q protocol

   B. VLAN tagging using 802.1p protocol

   C. VLAN multiplexing

   D. VLAN set as a native VLAN

4. What are two options to consider when configuring a trunk link between two switches? (Choose two.)

   A. The **switchport nonegotiate** command must be configured for trunks that use DTP.

   B. Port security cannot be configured on the trunk interfaces.

   C. The native VLAN must be the same on both ends of the trunk.

   D. Different encapsulation types can be configured on both ends of the trunk link.

   E. Trunk ports can be configured only on Gigabit Ethernet interfaces.

5. A 24-port switch has been configured to support three VLANs named Sales, Marketing, and Finance. Each VLAN spans four ports on the switch. The network administrator has deleted the Marketing VLAN from the switch. What two statements describe the status of the ports associated with this VLAN? (Choose two.)

   A. The ports are inactive.

   B. The ports are administratively disabled.

   C. The ports will become trunks to carry data from all remaining VLANs.

   D. The ports will remain part of the Marketing VLAN until reassigned to another VLAN.

   E. The ports were released from the Marketing VLAN and automatically reassigned to VLAN 1.

6. Which three statements are true about hosts that are configured in the same VLAN? (Choose three.)

   A. Hosts in the same VLAN must be on the same IP subnet.

   B. Hosts in different VLANs can communicate with the aid of only the Layer 2 switch.

   C. Hosts in the same VLAN share the same broadcast domain.

   D. Hosts in the same VLAN share the same collision domain.

   E. Hosts in the same VLAN comply with the same security policy.

   F. Hosts in the same VLAN must be on the same physical segment.

7. Refer to Figure 3-8. Host PC3 is unable to transfer data because it does not have the MAC address of the destination host. If PC3 sends out an ARP request broadcast, which of the other hosts will see the message?

   A. Only PC3

   B. Only PC4

   C. Only PC4 and PC5

   D. PC1, PC2, PC4, and PC5

   E. PC1, PC2, PC3, PC4, and PC5

8. With each listed characteristic on the right, indicate in the blank on the left whether it reflects a normal range VLAN, an extended range VLAN, or VLAN 1. Use N for normal range VLAN, E for extended range VLAN, and 1 for VLAN 1.

   _____ 1–1005

   _____ 1006–4094

   _____ Stored in vlan.dat

   _____ Default management VLAN

   _____ Default native VLAN

   _____ All ports are a member of by default

   _____ Stored in running configuration file

9. Refer to the following configuration. Host 1 is connected to interface Fa0/4 with IP address 192.168.1.22/28. Host 2 is connected to interface Fa0/5 with IP address 192.168.1.33/28. Host 3 is connected to interface F0/6 with IP address 192.168.1.30/28. Select the three statements that describe the success of pinging from one host to another. (Choose three.)

```
Switch(config)# vlan 10
Switch(config-vlan)# name Faculty
Switch(config-vlan)# vlan 20
Switch(config-vlan)# name Staff
Switch(config-vlan)# interface range fa0/4 , fa0/6
Switch(config-if-range)# switchport mode access
Switch(config-if-range)# switchport access vlan 10
Switch(config-if-range)# interface fa0/5
Switch(config-if)# switchport mode access
Switch(config-if)# switchport access vlan 20
```

A. Host 1 can ping Host 2.

B. Host 1 cannot ping Host 2.

C. Host 1 can ping Host 3.

D. Host 1 cannot ping Host 3.

E. Host 2 can ping Host 3.

F. Host 2 cannot ping Host 3.

10. Which three options accurately associate the Catalyst switch command with the result? (Choose three.)

A. **show vlan id** *vlan-id*: displays information about a specific VLAN.

B. **show vlan:** displays detailed information about all VLANs on the switch.

C. **show vlan brief:** displays detailed information about all VLANs on the switch.

D. **show interfaces fa0/1 switchport:** displays information about a specific port.

E. **show interfaces fa0/1:** displays VLAN information about a specific port.

11. Match the commands with the correct descriptions.

_____   **switchport mode trunk**

_____   **switchport mode dynamic desirable**

_____   **switchport nonegotiate**

_____   **switchport mode access**

A. Configures the port to negotiate a trunk

B. Configures the trunk to not send DTP packets

C. Configures the port as a permanent 802.1Q trunk

D. Disables trunk mode

12. Match the problem definition with the correct problem description.

_____   Native VLAN mismatch

_____   Trunk mode mismatch

_____   Incorrect VLAN list

_____   VLAN subnet conflict

A. Both switches are configured to dynamic auto and will not negotiate a link.

B. Not all the VLANs needed are allowed to traverse a trunk.

C. PCs on the same VLAN are not sharing the same address space.

D. The VLAN configured for untagged frames is not the same on two switches connected by a trunk.

13. The _____ protocol is an industry standard for trunking.

14. Which Layer 2 security issue sends a frame destined for one VLAN to a different VLAN by adding more than one VLAN ID to the header?

A. Double-tagging

B. Switch spoofing

C. PVLAN edge

D. Plaintext vty access

15. Which two design considerations are best practices for switch VLAN design? (Choose two.)

A. Unused ports should be left to the default configuration.

B. The native VLAN should be an unused VLAN.

C. All unused ports should be configured as a part of the black hole VLAN.

D. All unused ports should be configured as a part of the native VLAN.

E. A server should always be configured as a protected port.

F. The management VLAN should be a VLAN not used by any type of user traffic.

G. Disable DTP messages.

CHAPTER 4

Routing Concepts

Objectives

Upon completion of this chapter, you will be able to answer the following questions:

- What are the primary functions and features of a router?

- How do you connect devices together in a small routed network?

- How do you use the CLI to configure a router to route between two directly connected networks?

- How do you verify connectivity between two directly connected networks on a router?

- What is the encapsulation and de-encapsulation process used by routers when switching packets between interfaces?

- How does a router determine which path to follow?

- What do directly connected networks look like in a routing table?

- How is a routing table created:

  - Using directly connected routes?

  - Using static routes?

  - Using a dynamic routing protocol?

Key Terms

This chapter uses the following key terms. You can find the definitions in the Glossary.

Introduction (4.0.1.1)

Networks allow people to communicate, collaborate, and interact in many ways. Networks are used to access web pages, talk using IP telephones, participate in video conferences, compete in interactive gaming, shop using the Internet, complete online coursework, and more.

Ethernet switches function at the data link layer, Layer 2, and are used to forward Ethernet frames between devices within the same network. However, when the source IP and destination IP addresses are on different networks, the Ethernet frame must be sent to a router. A *router* connects one network to another network. The router is responsible for the delivery of packets across different networks. The destination of the IP packet might be a web server in another country or an email server on the local area network.

The router uses its routing table to determine the best path to use to forward a packet. It is the responsibility of the routers to deliver those packets in a timely manner. The effectiveness of internetwork communications depends, to a large degree, on the capability of routers to forward packets in the most efficient way possible.

When a host sends a packet to a device on a different IP network, the packet is forwarded to the default gateway because a host device cannot communicate directly with devices outside of the local network. The *default gateway* is the destination that routes traffic from the local network to devices on remote networks. It is often used to connect a local network to the Internet.

This chapter will also answer the question, "What does a router do with a packet received from one network and destined for another network?" Details of the routing table will be examined including connected, static, and dynamic routes.

Because the router can route packets between networks, devices on different networks can communicate. This chapter will introduce the router, its role in the networks, its main hardware and software components, and the routing process.

Class Activity 4.0.1.2: Do We Really Need a Map?

This modeling activity asks you to research travel directions from source to destination. Its purpose is to compare those types of directions to network routing directions.

Scenario

Using the Internet and Google Maps, located at `http://maps.google.com`, find a route between the capital city of your country and some other distant town or between two places within your own city. Pay close attention to the driving or walking directions Google Maps suggests.

Notice that in many cases, Google Maps suggests more than one route between the two locations you chose. It also allows you to put additional constraints on the route, such as avoiding highways or tolls.

Copy at least two route instructions supplied by Google Maps for this activity. Place your copies into a word processing document and save it for use with the next step.

Open the .pdf accompanying this modeling activity and complete it with a fellow student. Discuss the reflection questions listed on the .pdf and record your answers.

Be prepared to present your answers to the class.

Functions of a Router (4.1.1)

This section will discuss all of the various functions and uses of a router.

Characteristics of a Network (4.1.1.1)

Networks have had a significant impact on our lives. They have changed the way we live, work, and play. Networks allow us to communicate, collaborate, and interact in ways we never did before. We use the network in a variety of ways, including web applications, IP telephony, video conferencing, interactive gaming, electronic commerce, education, and more.

As shown in Figure 4-1, there are many key structures and performance-related characteristics referred to when discussing networks:

- **Topology:** There are physical and logical topologies. The *physical topology* is the arrangement of the cables, network devices, and end systems. It describes how the network devices are actually interconnected with wires and cables. The *logical topology* is the path over which the data is transferred in a network. It describes how the network devices appear connected to network users.

- **Speed:** Speed is a measure of the data rate in bits per second (b/s) of a given link in the network. Although the term "speed" is commonly used when referring to the network bandwidth, it is not technically accurate. The actual speed that the bits are transmitted does not vary over the same medium. The difference in bandwidth is due to the number of bits transmitted per second, not how fast they travel over a wire or wireless medium.

- **Cost:** Cost indicates the general expense for purchasing of network components, and installation and maintenance of the network.

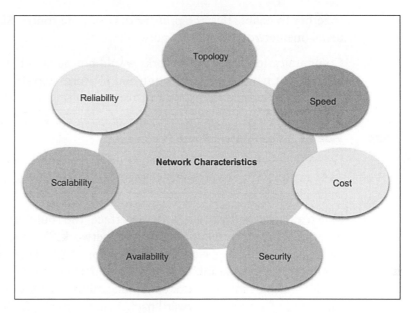

Figure 4-1   Network Characteristics

- **Security:** Security indicates how protected the network is, including the information that is transmitted over the network. The subject of security is important, and techniques and practices are constantly evolving. Consider security whenever actions are taken that affect the network.

- *Availability:* Availability is a measure of the probability that the network is available for use when it is required.

- *Scalability:* Scalability indicates how easily the network can accommodate more users and data transmission requirements. If a network design is optimized to only meet current requirements, it can be very difficult and expensive to meet new needs when the network grows.

- *Reliability:* Reliability indicates the dependability of the components that make up the network, such as the routers, switches, PCs, and servers. Reliability is often measured as a probability of failure or as the mean time between failures (MTBF).

These characteristics and attributes provide a means to compare different networking solutions.

Why Routing? (4.1.1.2)

How does clicking a link in a web browser return the desired information in mere seconds? Although there are many devices and technologies collaboratively working together to enable this, the primary device is the router. Stated simply, a router connects one network to another network.

Communication between networks would not be possible without a router determining the best path to the destination and forwarding traffic to the next router along that path. The router is responsible for the routing of traffic between networks.

Video

Video 4.1.1.2: Routers Route Packets

Go to the course and play the animation of a packet being sent through a Cisco 1841 router from sender to receiver.

When a packet arrives on a router interface, the router uses its routing table to determine how to reach the destination network. The destination of the IP packet might be a web server in another country or an email server on the local area network. It is the responsibility of routers to deliver those packets efficiently. The effectiveness of internetwork communications depends, to a large degree, on the capability of routers to forward packets in the most efficient way possible.

Routers Are Computers (4.1.1.3)

Most network-capable devices (i.e., computers, tablets, and smartphones) require the following components to operate, as shown in Figure 4-2:

- Central processing unit (CPU)

- Operating system (OS)

- Memory and storage (RAM, ROM, NVRAM, Flash, and hard drive)

A router is essentially a specialized computer. It requires a CPU and memory to temporarily and permanently store data to execute operating system instructions, such as system initialization, routing functions, and switching functions.

Note

Cisco devices use the Cisco Internetwork Operating System (IOS) as the system software.

Table 4-1 summarizes the types of router memory, the volatility, and examples of what is stored in each.

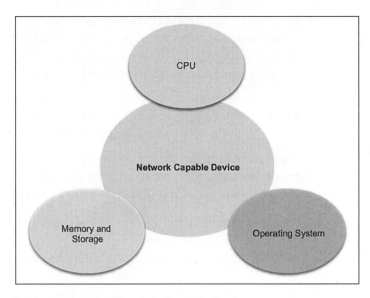

Figure 4-2   Components of a Network-Capable Device

Table 4-1   Router Memory

Memory	Volatile/Nonvolatile	Stores
RAM	Volatile	▪ Running IOS ▪ Running Configuration File ▪ IP Routing and ARP Tables ▪ Packet Buffer
ROM	Non-Volatile	▪ Bootup instructions ▪ Basic Diagnostic Software ▪ Limited IOS
NVRAM	Non-Volatile	▪ Startup configuration file
Flash	Non-Volatile	▪ IOS ▪ Other System Files

Routers store data using:

▪ *Random-access memory (RAM)*: Provides temporary storage for various applications and processes including the running IOS, the running configuration file, various tables (i.e., IP routing table, Ethernet ARP table) and buffers for packet processing. RAM is referred to as volatile because it loses its contents when power is turned off.

- *Read-only memory (ROM)*: Provides permanent storage for bootup instructions, basic diagnostic software, and a limited IOS in case the router cannot load the full-featured IOS. ROM is firmware and referred to as nonvolatile because it does not lose its contents when power is turned off.

- *Nonvolatile random-access memory (NVRAM)*: Provides permanent storage for the startup configuration file (startup-config). NVRAM is non-volatile and does not lose its contents when power is turned off.

- *Flash memory*: Provides permanent storage for the IOS and other system-related files. The IOS is copied from flash into RAM during the bootup process. Flash is non-volatile and does not lose its contents when power is turned off.

Unlike a computer, a router does not have video adapters or sound card adapters. Instead, routers have specialized ports and network interface cards to interconnect devices to other networks. Figure 4-3 identifies some of these ports and interfaces.

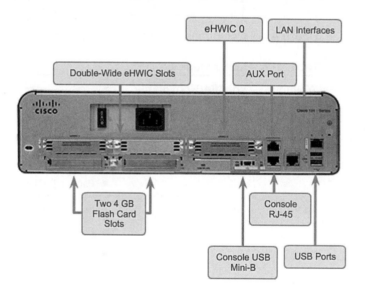

Figure 4-3   Back Panel of a Router

Routers Interconnect Networks (4.1.1.4)

Most users are unaware of the presence of numerous routers on their own network or on the Internet. Users expect to be able to access web pages, send emails, and download music, regardless of whether the server accessed is on their own network or on another network. Networking professionals know that it is the router that is responsible for forwarding packets from network to network, from the original source to the final destination.

A router connects multiple networks, which means that it has multiple interfaces that each belong to a different IP network. When a router receives an IP packet on one interface, it determines which interface to use to forward the packet to the destination. The interface that the router uses to forward the packet may be the final destination, or it may be a network connected to another router that is used to reach the destination network.

Video 4.1.1.4: Routers Connect

Go to the course and play the animation of a packet being sent through two Cisco routers. R1 and R2 are responsible for receiving the packet on one network and forwarding the packet out another network toward the destination network.

Each network that a router connects to typically requires a separate interface. These interfaces are used to connect a combination of both local-area networks (LANs) and wide-area networks (WANs). LANs are commonly Ethernet networks that contain devices, such as PCs, printers, and servers. WANs are used to connect networks over a large geographical area. For example, a WAN connection is commonly used to connect a LAN to the Internet service provider (ISP) network.

Notice that each site in Figure 4-4 requires the use of a router to interconnect to other sites. Even the Home Office requires a router. In this topology, the router located at the Home Office is a specialized device that performs multiple services for the home network.

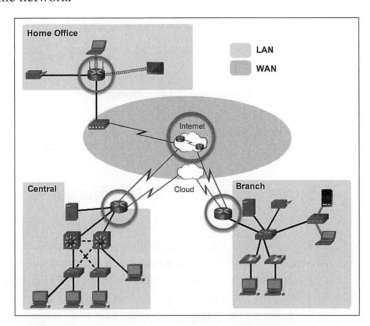

Figure 4-4   The Router Connection

Routers Choose Best Paths (4.1.1.5)

The primary functions of a router are to

- Determine the best path to send packets

- Forward packets toward their destination

The router uses its routing table to determine the best path to use to forward a packet. When the router receives a packet, it examines the destination address of the packet and uses the routing table to search for the best path to that network. The routing table also includes the interface to be used to forward packets for each known network. When a match is found, the router encapsulates the packet into the data link frame of the outgoing or exit interface, and the packet is forwarded toward its destination.

It is possible for a router to receive a packet that is encapsulated in one type of data link frame, and to forward the packet out of an interface that uses a different type of data link frame. For example, a router may receive a packet on an Ethernet interface, but must forward the packet out of an interface configured with the Point-to-Point Protocol (PPP). The data link encapsulation depends on the type of interface on the router and the type of medium to which it connects. The different data link technologies that a router can connect to include Ethernet, PPP, Frame Relay, DSL, cable, and wireless (802.11, Bluetooth).

Note

Routers use static routes and dynamic routing protocols to learn about remote networks and build their routing tables.

Video

Video 4.1.1.5: How the Router Works

Go to the course and play the animation of a packet being sent through two routers from sender to receiver.

Packet-Forwarding Mechanisms (4.1.1.6)

Routers support three packet-forwarding mechanisms:

- *Process switching* (see Figure 4-5): An older packet-forwarding mechanism still available for Cisco routers. When a packet arrives on an interface, it is forwarded to the control plane where the CPU matches the destination address with an entry in its routing table, and then determines the exit interface and forwards the packet. It is important to understand that the router does this for every packet, even if the destination is the same for a stream of packets. This process-switching mechanism is very slow and rarely implemented in modern networks.

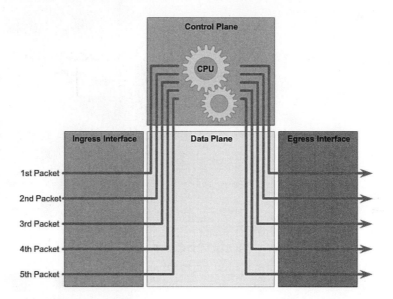

Figure 4-5 Process Switching

- *Fast switching* **(see Figure 4-6):** This is a common packet-forwarding mechanism, which uses a fast-switching cache to store next-hop information. When a packet arrives on an interface, it is forwarded to the control plane where the CPU searches for a match in the fast-switching cache. If it is not there, it is process-switched and forwarded to the exit interface. The flow information for the packet is also stored in the fast-switching cache. If another packet going to the same destination arrives on an interface, the next-hop information in the cache is reused without CPU intervention.

- *Cisco Express Forwarding (CEF)* **(see Figure 4-7):** CEF is the most recent and preferred Cisco IOS packet-forwarding mechanism. Like fast switching, CEF builds a Forwarding Information Base (FIB), and an adjacency table. However, the table entries are not packet-triggered like fast switching but change-triggered such as when something changes in the network topology. Therefore, when a network has converged, the FIB and adjacency tables contain all the information a router would have to consider when forwarding a packet. The FIB contains precomputed reverse lookups, next hop information for routes including the interface and Layer 2 information. Cisco Express Forwarding is the fastest forwarding mechanism and the preferred choice on Cisco routers.

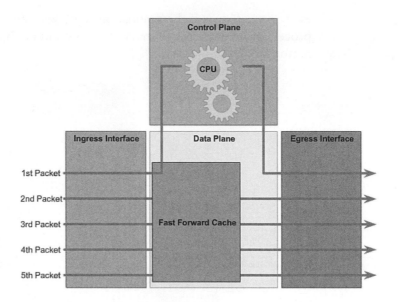

Figure 4-6 Fast Switching

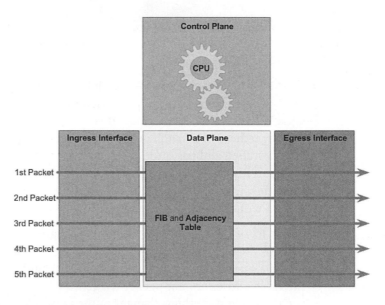

Figure 4-7 Cisco Express Forwarding

Figures 4-5 through 4-7 illustrate the differences between the three packet-forwarding mechanisms. Assume that a traffic flow consisting of five packets are all going to the same destination. As shown in Figure 4-5, with process switching, each packet must be processed by the CPU individually. Contrast this with fast switching, as shown in Figure 4-6. With fast switching, notice how only the first packet of a flow is process-switched and added to the fast-switching cache. The next four packets are quickly processed based on the information in the fast-switching cache. Finally, in Figure 4-7, CEF builds the FIB and adjacency tables after the network has converged. All five packets are quickly processed in the data plane.

A common analogy used to describe the three packet-forwarding mechanisms is as follows:

- Process switching solves a problem by doing math long hand, even if it is the identical problem.

- Fast switching solves a problem by doing math long hand one time and remembering the answer for subsequent identical problems.

- CEF solves every possible problem ahead of time in a spreadsheet.

Interactive Graphic

Activity 4.1.1.7 Part 1: Identify Router Components

This matching activity allows you to check your knowledge of router memory.

Go to the course and perform the activity (4.1.1.7 Part 1) where you will match the memory type with its appropriate memory functions.

Interactive Graphic

Activity 4.1.1.7 Part 2: Identify Router Components

This matching activity allows you to check your knowledge of router components.

Go to the course and perform the activity (4.1.1.7 Part 2) where you will match port/slot name to the letter that corresponds to the appropriate back panel location.

Packet Tracer □ Activity

Packet Tracer Activity 4.1.1.8: Using Traceroute to Discover the Network

The company you work for has acquired a new branch location. You asked for a topology map of the new location, but apparently one does not exist. However, you have username and password information for the new branch's networking devices and you know the web address for the new branch's server. Therefore, you will verify connectivity and use the **tracert** command to determine the path to the location. You will connect to the edge router of the new location to determine the devices and networks attached. As a part of this process, you will use various **show** commands to gather the necessary information to finish documenting the IP addressing scheme and create a diagram of the topology.

Lab 4.1.1.9: Mapping the Internet

In this lab, you will complete the following objectives:

- Part 1: Determine Network Connectivity to a Destination Host

- Part 2: Trace a Route to a Remote Server Using Tracert

Connect Devices (4.1.2)

This section will discuss connecting to various devices, including networks and gateways.

Connect to a Network (4.1.2.1)

Network devices and end users typically connect to a network using a wired Ethernet or wireless connection. Refer to Figure 4-8 as a sample reference topology.

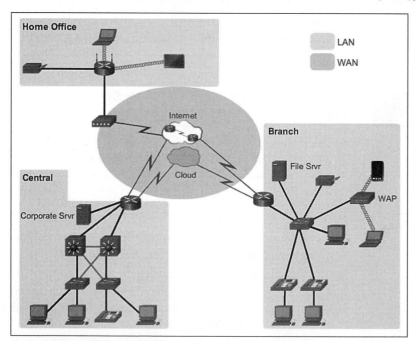

Figure 4-8   Sample LAN and WAN Connections

The LANs in the figure serve as an example of how users and network devices could connect to networks.

Home office devices can connect as follows:

- Laptops and tablets connect wirelessly to a home router.

- A network printer connects using an Ethernet cable to the switch port on the home router.

- The home router connects to the service provider cable modem using an Ethernet cable.

- The cable modem connects to the Internet service provider (ISP) network.

The Branch site devices connect as follows:

- Corporate resources (i.e., file servers and printers) connect to Layer 2 switches using Ethernet cables.

- Desktop PCs and voice over IP (VoIP) phones connect to Layer 2 switches using Ethernet cables.

- Laptops and smartphones connect wirelessly to wireless access points (WAPs).

- The WAPs connect to switches using Ethernet cables.

- Layer 2 switches connect to an Ethernet interface on the edge router using Ethernet cables. An edge router is a device that sits at the edge or boundary of a network and routes between that network and another, such as between a LAN and a WAN.

- The edge router connects to a WAN service provider (SP).

- The edge router also connects to an ISP for backup purposes.

The Central site devices connect as follows:

- Desktop PCs and VoIP phones connect to Layer 2 switches using Ethernet cables.

- Layer 2 switches connect redundantly to multilayer Layer 3 switches using Ethernet fiber-optic cables (orange connections).

- Layer 3 multilayer switches connect to an Ethernet interface on the edge router using Ethernet cables.

- The corporate website server is connected using an Ethernet cable to the edge router interface.

- The edge router connects to a WAN SP.

- The edge router also connects to an ISP for backup purposes.

In the Branch and Central LANs, hosts are connected either directly or indirectly (via WAPs) to the network infrastructure using a Layer 2 switch.

Default Gateways (4.1.2.2)

To enable network access, devices must be configured with IP address information to identify the appropriate

- *IP address*: Identifies a unique host on a local network

- *Subnet mask*: Identifies with which network subnet the host can communicate

- **Default gateway:** Identifies the router to send a packet to when the destination is not on the same local network subnet

When a host sends a packet to a device that is on the same IP network, the packet is simply forwarded out of the host interface to the destination device.

When a host sends a packet to a device on a different IP network, then the packet is forwarded to the default gateway, because a host device cannot communicate directly with devices outside of the local network. The default gateway is the destination that routes traffic from the local network to devices on remote networks. It is often used to connect a local network to the Internet.

The default gateway is usually the address of the interface on the router connected to the local network. The router maintains routing table entries of all connected networks as well as entries of remote networks, and determines the best path to reach those destinations.

Using Figure 4-9 as an example, if PC1 sends a packet to the Web Server located at 176.16.1.99, it would discover that the Web Server is not on the local network and it, therefore, must send the packet to the Media Access Control (MAC) address of its default gateway. The Packet protocol data unit (PDU) in Figure 4-9 identifies the source and destination IP and MAC addresses.

NOTE

A router is also usually configured with its own default gateway. This is sometimes known as the Gateway of Last Resort.

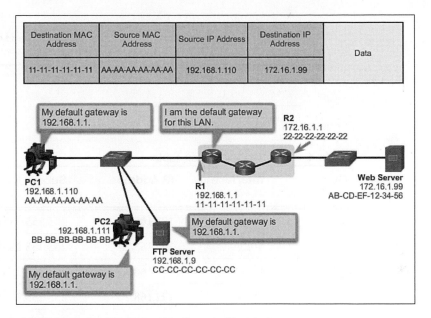

Figure 4-9   Getting the Pieces to the Correct Network

Document Network Addressing (4.1.2.3)

When designing a new network or mapping an existing network, document the network. At a minimum, the documentation should identify

- Device names
- Interfaces used in the design
- IP addresses and subnet masks
- Default gateway addresses

This information is captured by creating two useful network documents:

- *Topology diagram*: Provides a visual reference that indicates the physical connectivity and logical Layer 3 addressing. Often created using software, such as Microsoft Visio.

- An *addressing table*: A table that captures device names, interfaces, IPv4 addresses, subnet masks, and default gateway addresses.

Figure 4-10 is an example of a topology diagram. Table 4-2 is an example of an addressing table.

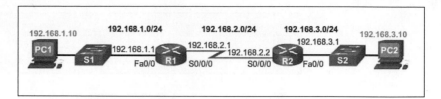

Figure 4-10   Documenting Network Addressing

Table 4-2   Network Address Table

Device	Interface	IP Address	Subnet Mask	Default Gateway
R1	Fa0/0	192.168.1.1	255.255.255.0	N/A
	S0/0/0	192.168.2.1	255.255.255.0	N/A
R2	Fa0/0	192.168.3.1	255.255.255.0	N/A
	S0/0/0	192.168.2.2	255.255.255.0	N/A
PC1	N/A	192.168.1.10	255.255.255.0	192.168.1.1
PC2	N/A	192.168.3.10	255.255.255.0	192.168.3.1

Enable IP on a Host (4.1.2.4)

A host can be assigned IP address information either

- *Statically*: The host is manually assigned the correct IP address, subnet mask, and default gateway. The DNS server IP address can also be configured.

- *Dynamically*: IP address information is provided by a server using the Dynamic Host Configuration Protocol (DHCP). The DHCP server provides a valid IP address, subnet mask, and default gateway for end devices. Other information may be provided by the server.

Figure 4-11 and Figure 4-12 provide static and dynamic IPv4 address configuration examples.

Statically assigned addresses are commonly used to identify specific network resources, such as network servers and printers. They can also be used in smaller networks with few hosts. However, most host devices acquire their IPv4 address information by accessing a DHCP server. In large enterprises, dedicated DHCP servers providing services to many LANs are implemented. In a smaller branch or small office setting, DHCP services can be provided by a Cisco Catalyst switch or a Cisco ISR.

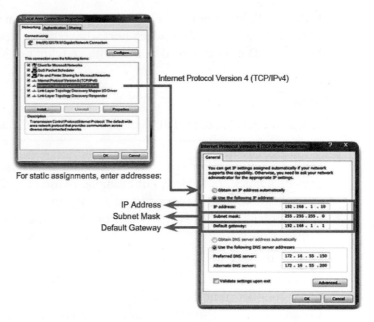

Figure 4-11   Statically Assigning an IP Address

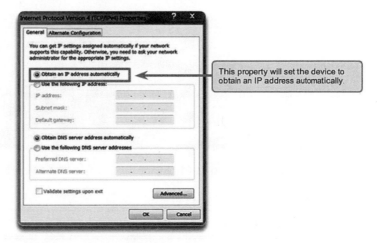

Figure 4-12   Dynamically Assigning an IP Address

Device LEDs (4.1.2.5)

Host computers connect to a wired network using a network interface and RJ-45 Ethernet cable. Most network interfaces have one or two LED link indicators next to the interface. Typically, a green LED means a good connection while a blinking green LED indicates network activity.

If the link light is not on, then there may be a problem with either the network cable or the network itself. The switch port where the connection terminates would also have an LED indicator lit. If one or both ends are not lit, try a different network cable.

Note

The actual function of the LEDs varies between computer manufacturers.

Similarly, network infrastructure devices commonly use multiple LED indicators to provide a quick status view. For example, a Cisco Catalyst 2960 switch has several status LEDs to help monitor system activity and performance. These LEDs are generally lit green when the switch is functioning normally and lit amber when there is a malfunction.

Cisco ISRs use various LED indicators to provide status information. A Cisco 1941 router is shown in Figure 4-13. The LEDs on the router help the network administrator conduct some basic troubleshooting. Each device has a unique set of LEDs. Consult the device-specific documentation for an accurate description of the LEDs. Table 4-3 following the figure shows the color and description of each LED.

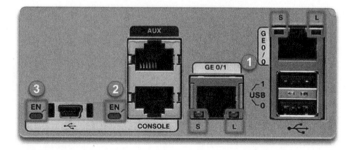

Figure 4-13 Cisco 1941 LEDs

Table 4-3 Cisco 1941 LEDs

Cisco 1941 LEDs

#	Port	LED	Color	Description
1	GE0/0 and GE0/1	S (Speed)	1 blink + pause	Port operating at 10 Mb/s
			2 blink + pause	Port operating at 100 Mb/s
			3 blink + pause	Port operating at 1000 Mb/s
		L (Link)	Green	Link is active
			Off	Link is inactive

Cisco 1941 LEDs

#	Port	LED	Color	Description
2	Console	EN	Green	Port is active
			Off	Port is inactive
3	USB	EN	Green	Port is active
			Off	Port is inactive

Console Access (4.1.2.6)

In a production environment, infrastructure devices are commonly accessed remotely using Secure Shell (SSH) or HyperText Transfer Protocol Secure (HTTPS). Console access is really only required when initially configuring a device, or if remote access fails.

Console access requires

- *Console cable*: RJ-45-to-DB-9 console cable

- *Terminal emulation software*: Tera Term, PuTTY, and HyperTerminal

The cable is connected between the serial port of the host and the console port on the device. Most computers and notebooks no longer include built-in serial ports. If the host does not have a serial port, the USB port can be used to establish a console connection. A special USB-to-RS-232 compatible serial port adapter is required when using the USB port.

The Cisco ISR G2 supports a USB serial console connection. To establish connectivity, a USB Type-A to USB Type-B (mini-B USB) is required, as well as an operating system device driver. This device driver is available from www.cisco.com. Although these routers have two console ports, only one console port can be active at a time. When a cable is plugged into the USB console port, the RJ-45 port becomes inactive. When the USB cable is removed from the USB port, the RJ-45 port becomes active.

Table 4-4 summarizes the console connection requirements. Figure 4-14 displays the various ports and cables required.

Table 4-4   Console Connection Requirements

Port on Computer	Cable Required	Port on ISR	Terminal Emulation
Serial Port	RJ-45 to DB-9 console cable		
USB Type-A Port	USB to RS-232 compatible serial port adapter	RJ-45 Console Port	
	Adapter may require a software driver		Tera Term
	RJ-45 to DB-9 console cable		PuTTY
	USB Type-A to USB Type-B (mini USB)	USB Type-B (Mini-B USB)	
	A device driver is required and available from cisco.com.		

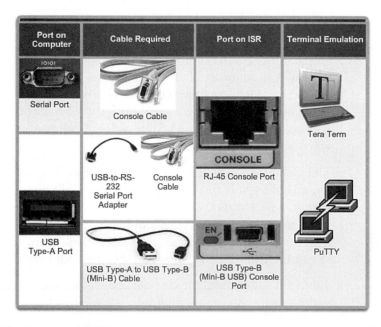

Figure 4-14   Ports and Cables

Enable IP on a Switch (4.1.2.7)

Network infrastructure devices require IP addresses to enable remote management. Using the device IP address, the network administrator can remotely connect to the device using Telnet, SSH, HTTP, or HTTPS.

A switch does not have a dedicated interface to which an IP address can be assigned. Instead, the IP address information is configured on a virtual interface called a *switched virtual interface (SVI)*.

For example, in Figure 4-15, the SVI on the Layer 2 switch S1 is assigned the IP address 192.168.10.2/24 and a default gateway of the router located at 192.168.10.1.

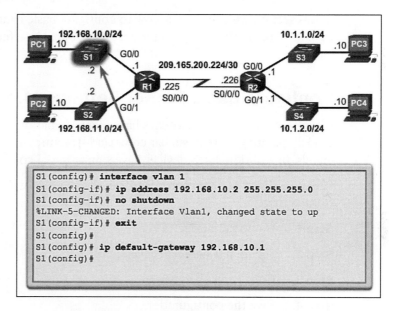

Figure 4-15   Configure the Management SVI of S2

Interactive Graphic

Activity 4.1.2.7: Configure the Switch Management Interface

Go to the course online to use the Syntax Checker in Figure 2 to configure the Layer 2 switch S2.

Interactive Graphic

Activity 4.1.2.8: Document Network Addressing

Go to the course online and complete the activity on documenting network addresses.

> **Packet Tracer**
> ☐ **Activity**

Packet Tracer Activity 4.1.2.9: Documenting the Network

Background/Scenario

Your job is to document the addressing scheme and connections used in the Central portion of the network. You will need to use a variety of commands to gather the required information.

Go to the course online to complete this Packet Tracer Activity.

Basic Settings on a Router (4.1.3)

In this section we will discuss how to configure basic router settings, as well as configuration on an IPv4 router interface, IPv6 router interface, and an IPv4 loopback interface.

Configure Basic Router Settings (4.1.3.1)

Cisco routers and Cisco switches have many similarities. They support a similar modal operating system, similar command structures, and many of the same commands. In addition, both devices have similar initial configuration steps.

When configuring a Cisco switch or router, the following basic tasks should be performed first:

Step 1. Name the device.

Step 2. Secure management access.

Step 3. Configure a banner.

Step 4. Save the configuration.

Looking at each step individually you have

- **Name the device:** Distinguishes it from other routers. (See Figure 4-16.)

- **Secure management access:** Secures privileged EXEC, user EXEC, and Telnet access, and encrypts passwords to their highest level. (See Figure 4-17.)

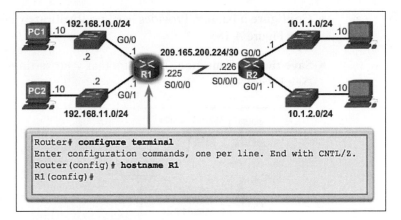

```
Router# configure terminal
Enter configuration commands, one per line. End with CNTL/Z.
Router(config)# hostname R1
R1(config)#
```

Figure 4-16   Name the Device

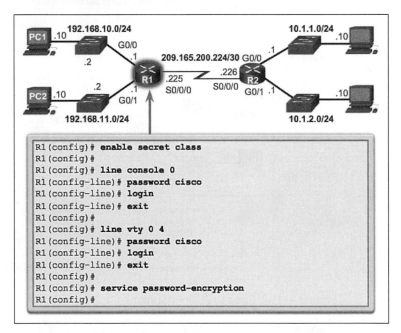

```
R1(config)# enable secret class
R1(config)#
R1(config)# line console 0
R1(config-line)# password cisco
R1(config-line)# login
R1(config-line)# exit
R1(config)#
R1(config)# line vty 0 4
R1(config-line)# password cisco
R1(config-line)# login
R1(config-line)# exit
R1(config)#
R1(config)# service password-encryption
R1(config)#
```

Figure 4-17   Secure Management Access

- **Configure a banner:** Provides legal notification of unauthorized access. (See Figure 4-18.)

- **Save the configuration:** To ensure that your settings are not lost. (See Figure 4-19.)

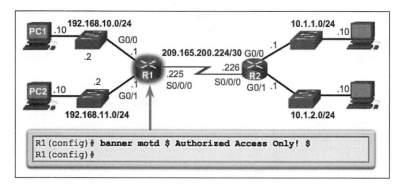

```
R1(config)# banner motd $ Authorized Access Only! $
R1(config)#
```

Figure 4-18   Configure a Banner

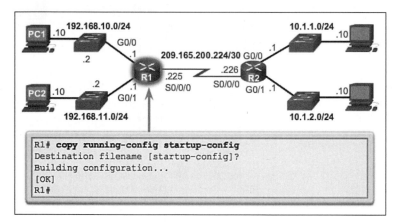

```
R1# copy running-config startup-config
Destination filename [startup-config]?
Building configuration...
[OK]
R1#
```

Figure 4-19   Save the Configuration

Note

Always save the changes on a router and verify the basic configuration and router operations.

Interactive Graphic

Activity 4.1.3.1: Configure Basic Settings on a Router

Go to the course online to use the Syntax Checker in the fifth figure to configure router R2.

Configure an IPv4 Router Interface (4.1.3.2)

One distinguishing feature between switches and routers is the type of interfaces supported by each. For example, Layer 2 switches support LANs and, therefore, have multiple FastEthernet or Gigabit Ethernet ports.

Routers support LANs and WANs and can interconnect different types of networks; therefore, they support many types of interfaces. For example, G2 ISRs have one or two integrated Gigabit Ethernet interfaces and *High-Speed WAN Interface Card (HWIC)* slots to accommodate other types of network interfaces, including serial, DSL, and cable interfaces.

To be available, an interface must be

- **If using IPv4, configured with an address and a subnet mask:** Use the **ip address** *ip-address subnet-mask* interface configuration command.

- **Activated:** By default, LAN and WAN interfaces are not activated (**shutdown**). To enable an interface, it must be activated using the **no shutdown** command. (This is similar to powering on the interface.) The interface must also be connected to another device (a hub, a switch, or another router) for the physical layer to be active.

Optionally, the interface could also be configured with a short description. It is good practice to configure a description on each interface. The description text is limited to 240 characters. On production networks, a description can be helpful in troubleshooting by providing information about the type of network to which the interface is connected. If the interface connects to an ISP or service carrier, it is helpful to enter the third-party connection and contact information.

Depending on the type of interface, additional parameters may be required. For example, in the lab environment, the serial interface connecting to the serial cable end labeled DCE must be configured with the **clock rate** command.

Note

Accidentally using the **clock rate** command on a DTE interface generates a `%Error: This command applies only to DCE interface` message.

 In summary, to configure an IPv4 router interface you should

Step 1.   Enter into the interface configuration mode.

Step 2.   Add a short description about the interface.

Step 3.   Add an IPv4 address and subnet mask.

Step 4.   Add a clock rate if it is a serial interface with a DCE cable plugged into it.

Step 5.   Activate the interface.

Figures 4-20 through 4-22 provide examples of configuring the router interfaces of R1.

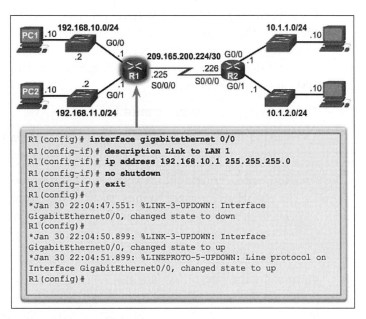

Figure 4-20   Configuring the G0/0 Interface

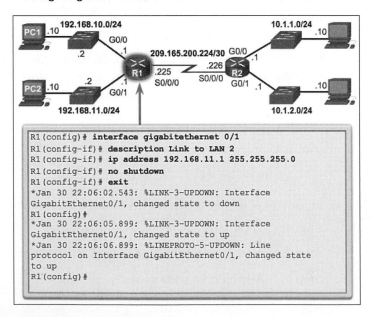

Figure 4-21   Configuring the G0/1 Interface

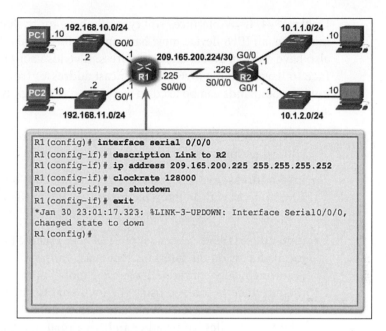

Figure 4-22 Configuring the S0/0/0 Interface

Activity 4.1.3.2: Configure Basic Settings on a Router

Go to the course online to use the Syntax Checker in the fourth figure to configure router R2.

Configure an IPv6 Router Interface (4.1.3.3)

Configuring an IPv6 interface is similar to configuring an interface for IPv4. Most IPv6 configuration and verification commands in the Cisco IOS are similar to their IPv4 counterparts. In many cases, the only difference uses **ipv6** in place of **ip** in commands.

An IPv6 interface must be

- **Configured with IPv6 address and subnet mask:** Use the **ipv6 address** *ipv6-address/prefix-length* [**link-local** | **eui-64**] interface configuration command.

- **Activated:** The interface must be activated using the **no shutdown** command.

Note

An interface can generate its own IPv6 link-local address without having a global unicast address by using the **ipv6 enable** interface configuration command.

Unlike IPv4, IPv6 interfaces will typically have more than one IPv6 address. At a minimum, an IPv6 device must have an IPv6 link-local address but will most likely also have an IPv6 global unicast address. IPv6 also supports the ability for an interface to have multiple IPv6 global unicast addresses from the same subnet. The following commands can be used to statically create a global unicast or link-local IPv6 address:

- **ipv6 address** *ipv6-address/prefix-length*: Creates a global unicast IPv6 address as specified.

- **ipv6 address** *ipv6-address/prefix-length* **eui-64**: Configures a global unicast IPv6 address with an interface identifier (ID) in the low-order 64 bits of the IPv6 address using the EUI-64 process.

- **ipv6 address** *ipv6-address/prefix-length* **link-local**: Configures a static link-local address on the interface that is used instead of the link-local address that is automatically configured when the global unicast IPv6 address is assigned to the interface or enabled using the **ipv6 enable** interface command. Recall, the **ipv6 enable** interface command is used to automatically create an IPv6 link-local address regardless of whether an IPv6 global unicast address has been assigned.

In the example topology shown in Figure 4-23, R1 must be configured to support the following IPv6 network addresses:

- 2001:0DB8:ACAD:0001:/64 or 2001:DB8:ACAD:1::/64

- 2001:0DB8:ACAD:0002:/64 or 2001:DB8:ACAD:2::/64

- 2001:0DB8:ACAD:0003:/64 or 2001:DB8:ACAD:3::/64

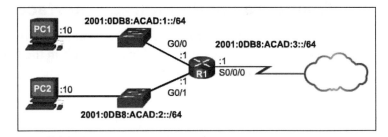

Figure 4-23 IPv6 Topology

When the router is configured using the **ipv6 unicast-routing** global configuration command, the router begins sending ICMPv6 Router Advertisement messages out the interface. This enables a PC connected to the interface to automatically configure an IPv6 address and to set a default gateway without needing the services of a DHCPv6 server. Alternatively, a PC connected to the IPv6 network can get its IPv6 address statically assigned, as shown in Figure 4-24. Notice that the default gateway address configured for PC1 is the IPv6 global unicast address of the R1 Gigabit-Ethernet 0/0 interface.

Figure 4-24   Statically Assign an IPv6 Address to PC1

In summary, to configure an IPv6 router interface you should

Step 1.   Be in the interface configuration mode.

Step 2.   Add a short description about the interface.

Step 3.   Add an IPv6 address and subnet mask.

Step 4.   Add a clock rate if it is a serial interface with a DCE cable plugged into it.

Step 5.   Activate the interface.

The router interfaces in the example topology must be configured and enabled as shown in Figures 4-25 through 4-27.

Activity 4.1.3.3: Configure Basic Settings on a Router

Go to the course online to use the Syntax Checker in the sixth figure to configure the IPv6 global unicast addresses on router R2.

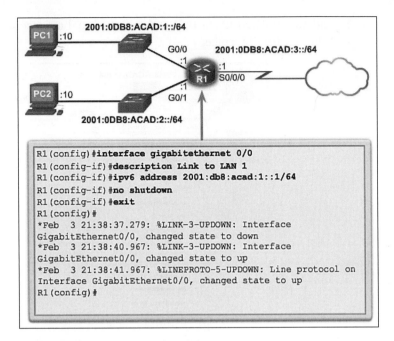

Figure 4-25   Configuring the R1 G0/0 Interface

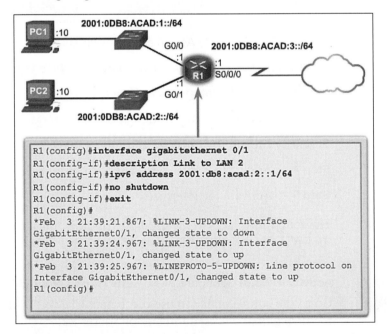

Figure 4-26   Configuring the R1 G0/1 Interface

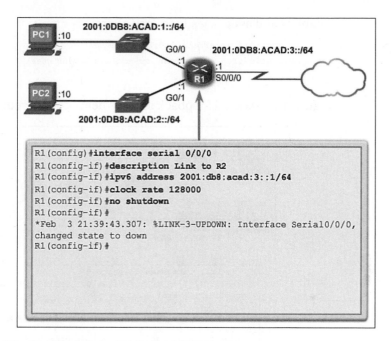

Figure 4-27   Configuring the R1 Serial 0/0/0 Interface

Configure an IPv4 Loopback Interface (4.1.3.4)

Another common configuration of Cisco IOS routers is enabling a loopback interface.

The *loopback interface* is a logical interface internal to the router. It is not assigned to a physical port and can therefore never be connected to any other device. It is considered a software interface that is automatically placed in an UP state, as long as the router is functioning.

The loopback interface is useful in testing and managing a Cisco IOS device because it ensures that at least one interface will always be available. For example, it can be used for testing purposes, such as testing internal routing processes, by emulating networks behind the router.

In addition, the IPv4 address assigned to the loopback interface can be significant to processes on the router that use an interface IPv4 address for identification purposes, such as the Open Shortest Path First (OSPF) routing process. By enabling a loopback interface, the router will use the always available loopback interface address for identification, rather than an IP address assigned to a physical port that may go down.

Enabling and assigning a loopback address is simple:

```
Router(config)# interface loopback number
Router(config-if)# ip address ip-address subnet-mask
Router(config-if)# exit
```

Figure 4-28 shows a loopback address being configured.

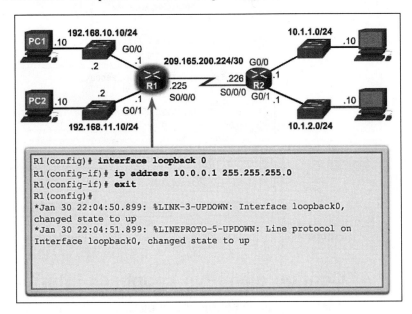

Figure 4-28 Configure the R1 Loopback0 Interface

Multiple loopback interfaces can be enabled on a router. The IPv4 address for each loopback interface must be unique and unused by any other interface.

Packet Tracer Activity 4.1.3.5: Configuring IPv4 and IPv6 Interfaces

Background/Scenario

Routers R1 and R2 each have two LANs. Your task is to configure the appropriate addressing on each device and verify connectivity between the LANs.

Go to the course online to complete this lab activity.

Verify Connectivity of Directly Connected Networks (4.1.4)

When trying to verify connectivity, the **show** commands should be used.

Verify Interface Settings (4.1.4.1)

There are several **show** commands that can be used to verify the operation and configuration of an interface.

The following three commands are especially useful to quickly identify an interface status:

- **show ip interface brief:** Displays a summary for all interfaces including the IPv4 address of the interface and current operational status.

- **show ip route:** Displays the contents of the IPv4 routing table stored in RAM. In Cisco IOS 15, active interfaces should appear in the routing table with two related entries identified by the code 'c' (Connected) or 'L' (Local). In previous IOS versions, only a single entry with the code 'c' will appear.

- **show running-config interface** *interface-id*: Displays the commands configured on the specified interface.

Figure 4-29 displays the output of the **show ip interface brief** command.

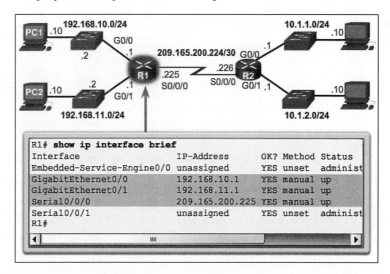

Figure 4-29   show ip interface brief Command Output

The output reveals that the LAN interfaces and the WAN link are all activated and operational as indicated by the Status of "up" and Protocol of "up". A different output would indicate a problem with either the configuration or the cabling. Note that in Figure 4-29, the Embedded-Service-Engine0/0 interface is displayed because Cisco ISRs G2 have dual core CPUs on the motherboard. The Embedded-Service-Engine0/0 interface is outside the scope of this course.

Interactive Graphic

Activity 4.1.4.1 Part 1: Verify Connectivity of Directly Connected Networks

Go to the course online to use the slider bar in the first graphic to see the entire output of the **show ip interface brief** command.

Figure 4-30 displays the output of the **show ip route** command.

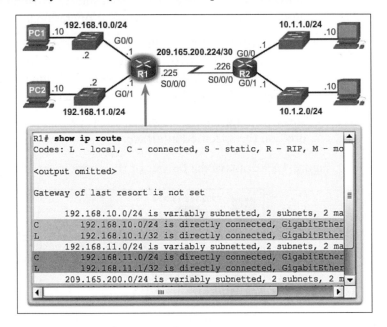

Figure 4-30   show ip route Command Output

Notice the three directly connected network entries and the three local host route interface entries. A local host route has an administrative distance of 0. It also has a /32 mask for IPv4, and a /128 mask for IPv6. The local host route is for routes on the router owning the IP address. It is used to allow the router to process packets destined to that IP.

Interactive Graphic

Activity 4.1.4.1 Part 2: Verify Connectivity of Directly Connected Networks

Go to the course online to use the slider bars in the second graphic to see the entire output of the **show ip route** command.

Figure 4-31 displays the output of the **show running-config interface** command.

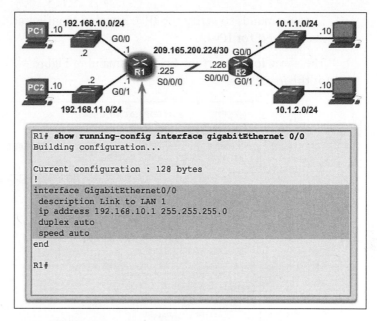

Figure 4-31   show running-config interface Command Output

The output displays the current commands configured on the specified interface.

The following two commands are used to gather more detailed interface information:

- **show interfaces:** Displays interface information and packet flow count for all interfaces on the device

- **show ip interface:** Displays the IPv4 related information for all interfaces on a router

Activity 4.1.4.1 Part 3: Verify Router Interfaces

Go to the course online to use the Syntax Checker in the fourth graphic to verify the interfaces on R1.

Activity 4.1.4.1 Part 4: Verify Router IP Interfaces

Go to the course online to use the Syntax Checker in the fifth graphic to verify the GigabitEthernet 0/0 IP interface settings.

Verify IPv6 Interface Settings (4.1.4.2)

The commands to verify the IPv6 interface configuration are similar to the commands used for IPv4.

The **show ipv6 interface brief** command in Figure 4-32 displays a summary for each of the interfaces.

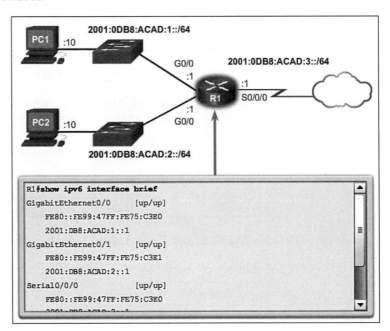

Figure 4-32   show ipv6 interface brief Command Output

The [up/up] output on the same line as the interface name indicates the Layer 1/ Layer 2 interface state. This is the same as the Status and Protocol columns in the equivalent IPv4 command.

The output displays two configured IPv6 addresses per interface. One address is the IPv6 global unicast address that was manually entered. The other address, which begins with FE80, is the link-local unicast address for the interface. A link-local address is automatically added to an interface whenever a global unicast address is assigned. An IPv6 network interface is required to have a link-local address, but not necessarily a global unicast address.

Activity 4.1.4.2 Part 1: Verify Connectivity of Directly Connected Networks

Go to the course online to use the slider bar in the first graphic to see the entire output of the **show ipv6 interface brief** command.

The **show ipv6 interface gigabitethernet 0/0** command output shown in Figure 4-33 displays the interface status and all of the IPv6 addresses belonging to the interface. Along with the link local address and global unicast address, the output includes the multicast addresses assigned to the interface, beginning with prefix FF02.

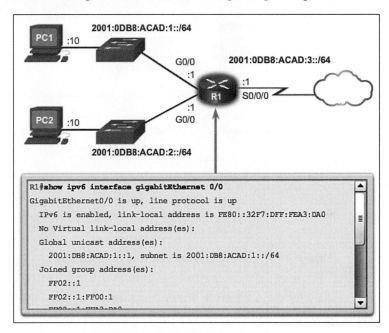

Figure 4-33   show ipv6 interface gigabitethernet Command Output

Activity 4.1.4.2 Part 2: Verify Connectivity of Directly Connected Networks

Go to the course online to use the slider bar in the second graphic to see the entire output of the **show ipv6 interface gigabitethernet** command.

The **show ipv6 route** command shown in Figure 4-34 can be used to verify that IPv6 networks, and specific IPv6 interface addresses have been installed in the IPv6 routing table. The **show ipv6 route** command will only display IPv6 networks, not IPv4 networks.

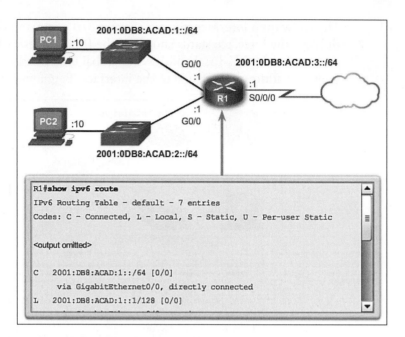

Figure 4-34   show ipv6 route Command Output

Activity 4.1.4.2 Part 3: Verify Connectivity of Directly Connected Networks

Go to the course online to use the slider bar in the third graphic to see the entire output of the **show ipv6 route** command.

Within the routing table, a 'c' next to a route indicates that this is a directly connected network. When the router interface is configured with a global unicast address and is in the "up/up" state, the IPv6 prefix and prefix length is added to the IPv6 routing table as a connected route.

The IPv6 global unicast address configured on the interface is also installed in the routing table as a local route. The local route has a /128 prefix. Local routes are used by the routing table to efficiently process packets with the interface address of the router as the destination.

The **ping** command for IPv6 is identical to the command used with IPv4 except that an IPv6 address is used. As shown in Figure 4-35, the **ping** command is used to verify Layer 3 connectivity between R1 and PC1.

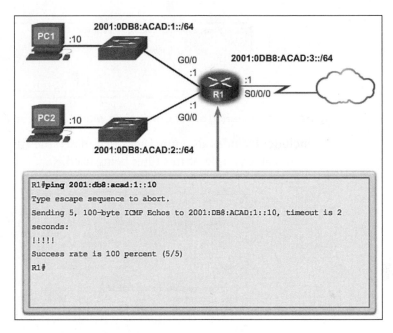

```
R1#ping 2001:db8:acad:1::10
Type escape sequence to abort.
Sending 5, 100-byte ICMP Echos to 2001:DB8:ACAD:1::10, timeout is 2
seconds:
!!!!!
Success rate is 100 percent (5/5)
R1#
```

Figure 4-35 **ping** Command Output

Other useful IPv6 verification commands include

- **show interface**
- **show ipv6 routers**

Filter Show **Command Output (4.1.4.3)**

Commands that generate multiple screens of output are, by default, paused after 24 lines. At the end of the paused output, the `--More--` text displays. Pressing **Enter** displays the next line, and pressing the spacebar displays the next set of lines. Use the **terminal length** `number` command to specify the number of lines to be displayed. A value of 0 (zero) prevents the router from pausing between screens of output.

Another useful feature that improves the user experience in the command-line interface (CLI) is the filtering of **show** output. Filtering commands can be used to display specific sections of output. To enable the filtering command, enter a pipe (|) character after the **show** command and then enter a filtering parameter and a filtering expression.

The filtering parameters that can be configured after the pipe include

- **section:** Shows entire section that starts with the filtering expression. Figure 4-36 shows us an example of this filter being used.

```
R1# show running-config | section line vty
line vty 0 4
 password 7 030752180500
 login
 transport input all
R1#
```

Figure 4-36 Filtering **show** Commands with | Section Parameter

- **include:** Includes all output lines that match the filtering expression. Figure 4-37 shows an example of this filter being used.

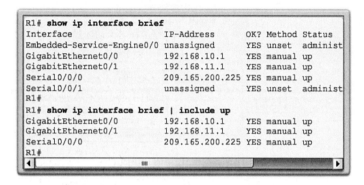

Figure 4-37 Filtering **show** Commands with | Include Parameter

Activity 4.1.4.3 Part 1: Filtering show **Commands Using the** | **Parameter**

Go to the course online to use the slider bar in the second graphic to see the entire output of the **show ip interface** command.

- **exclude:** Excludes all output lines that match the filtering expression. Figure 4-38 shows an example of this filter being used.

```
R1# show ip interface brief
Interface                    IP-Address       OK? Method Status
Embedded-Service-Engine0/0   unassigned       YES unset  administ
GigabitEthernet0/0           192.168.10.1     YES manual up
GigabitEthernet0/1           192.168.11.1     YES manual up
Serial0/0/0                  209.165.200.225  YES manual up
Serial0/0/1                  unassigned       YES unset  administ

R1# show ip interface brief | exclude unassigned
Interface                    IP-Address       OK? Method Status
GigabitEthernet0/0           192.168.10.1     YES manual up
GigabitEthernet0/1           192.168.11.1     YES manual up
Serial0/0/0                  209.165.200.225  YES manual up

R1#
```

Figure 4-38 Filtering **show** Commands with | Exclude Parameter

Activity 4.1.4.3 Part 2: Filtering show **Commands Using the** | **Parameter**

Go to the course online to use the slider bar in the third graphic to see the entire output of the **show ip interface brief** command.

- **begin:** Shows all the output lines from a certain point, starting with the line that matches the filtering expression. Figure 4-39 shows an example of this filter being used.

```
R1# show ip route | begin Gateway
Gateway of last resort is not set

      192.168.10.0/24 is variably subnetted, 2 subnets, 2 masks
C        192.168.10.0/24 is directly connected, GigabitEthernet0/0
L        192.168.10.1/32 is directly connected, GigabitEthernet0/0
      192.168.11.0/24 is variably subnetted, 2 subnets, 2 masks
C        192.168.11.0/24 is directly connected, GigabitEthernet0/1
L        192.168.11.1/32 is directly connected, GigabitEthernet0/1
      209.165.200.0/24 is variably subnetted, 2 subnets, 2 masks
C        209.165.200.224/30 is directly connected, Serial0/0/0
L        209.165.200.225/32 is directly connected, Serial0/0/0
R1#
```

Figure 4-39   Filtering **show** Commands with | Begin Parameter

Note

Output filters can be used in combination with any **show** command.

Activity 4.1.4.3 Part 3: Verify Router IP Interfaces

Go to the course online to use the Syntax Checker in the fifth graphic to verify Router interface settings using the pipe parameter.

Command History Feature (4.1.4.4)

The command history feature is useful because it temporarily stores the list of executed commands to be recalled.

To recall commands in the history buffer, press **Ctrl+P** or the **Up Arrow** key. The command output begins with the most recent command. Repeat the key sequence to recall successively older commands. To return to more recent commands in the history buffer, press **Ctrl+N** or the **Down Arrow** key. Repeat the key sequence to recall successively more recent commands.

By default, command history is enabled, and the system captures the last 10 command lines in its history buffer. Use the **show history** privileged EXEC command to display the contents of the buffer.

It is also practical to increase the number of command lines that the history buffer records during the current terminal session only. Use the **terminal history size** user EXEC command to increase or decrease the size of the buffer.

Figure 4-40 displays a sample of the **terminal history size** and **show history** commands.

```
R1# terminal history size 200
R1#
R1# show history
  show ip interface brief
  show interface g0/0
  show ip interface g0/1
  show ip route
  show ip route 209.165.200.224
  show running-config interface s0/0/0
  terminal history size 200
  show history
R1#
```

Figure 4-40   Command History Feature

Activity 4.1.4.4: The Command History Feature

Go to the course online to use the Syntax Checker in the second graphic to practice the two EXEC commands.

Packet Tracer Activity 4.1.4.5: Configuring and Verifying a Small Network

Background/Scenario

In this activity, you will configure a router with basic settings including IP addressing. You will also configure a switch for remote management and configure the PCs. After you have successfully verified connectivity, you will use **show** commands to gather information about the network.

Go to the course online to complete this lab activity.

Lab 4.1.4.6: Configuring Basic Router Settings with IOS CLI

In this lab, you will complete the following objectives:

- Part 1: Set Up the Topology and Initialize Devices
- Part 2: Configure Devices and Verify Connectivity
- Part 3: Display Router Information
- Part 4: Configure IPv6 and Verify Connectivity

Lab 4.1.4.7: Configuring Basic Router Settings with CCP

In this lab, you will complete the following objectives:

- Part 1: Set Up the Topology and Initialize Devices

- Part 2: Configure Devices and Verify Connectivity

- Part 3: Configure Router to Allow CCP Access

- Part 4: (Optional) Install and Setup CCP on PC-A

- Part 5: Configure R1 Settings Using CCP

- Part 6: Use CCP Utilities

Switching Packets Between Networks (4.2.1)

Many IT professionals, both novice and veteran, can become confused when discussing the concept of moving packets between interfaces of a router. Even though this movement takes place on a router, it is still called switching. It may also be called route switching so as not to be confused with packet switching that occurs at Layer 2 of the OSI.

Router Switching Function (4.2.1.1)

A primary function of a router is to forward packets toward their destination. This is accomplished by using a switching function, which is the process used by a router to accept a packet on one interface and forward it out of another interface. A key responsibility of the switching function is to encapsulate packets in the appropriate data link frame type for the outgoing data link.

> **Note**
>
> In this context, the term "switching" literally means moving packets from source to destination and should not be confused with the function of a Layer 2 switch.

After the router has determined the exit interface using the path determination function, the router must encapsulate the packet into the data link frame of the outgoing interface.

What does a router do with a packet received from one network and destined for another network? The router performs the following three major steps:

Step 1.   De-encapsulates the Layer 3 packet by removing the Layer 2 frame header and trailer.

Step 2.   Examines the destination IP address of the IP packet to find the best path in the routing table.

Step 3.   If the router finds a path to the destination, it encapsulates the Layer 3 packet into a new Layer 2 frame and forwards the frame out the exit interface.

As shown in Figure 4-41, devices have Layer 3 IPv4 addresses, and Ethernet interfaces have Layer 2 data link addresses. For example, PC1 is configured with IPv4 address 192.168.1.10 and an example MAC address of 0A-10. As a packet travels from the source device to the final destination device, the Layer 3 IP addresses do not change. However, the Layer 2 data link addresses change at every hop as the packet is de-encapsulated and re-encapsulated in a new frame by each router. It is likely that the packet is encapsulated in a different type of Layer 2 frame than the one in which it was received. For example, an Ethernet encapsulated frame might be received by the router on a FastEthernet interface and then processed to be forwarded out of a serial interface as a Point-to-Point Protocol (PPP) encapsulated frame.

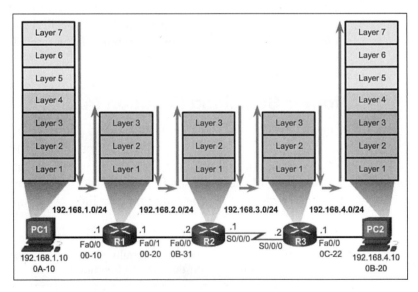

Figure 4-41   Encapsulating and De-Encapsulating Packets

Send a Packet (4.2.1.2)

Video 4.2.1.2: PC1 Sends a Packet to PC2

Go to the online course and play the animation of a packet being sent through three routers from sender to receiver.

In the animation in the online course, PC1 is sending a packet to PC2. PC1 must determine if the destination IPv4 address is on the same network. PC1 determines its own subnet by doing an AND operation on its own IPv4 address and subnet mask. This produces the network address that PC1 belongs to. Next, PC1 does this same AND operation using the packet destination IPv4 address and the PC1 subnet mask.

If the destination network address is the same network as PC1, then PC1 does not use the default gateway. Instead, PC1 refers to its ARP cache for the MAC address of the device with that destination IPv4 address. If the MAC address is not in the cache, then PC1 generates an ARP request to acquire the address to complete the packet and send it to the destination. If the destination network address is on a different network, then PC1 forwards the packet to its default gateway.

To determine the MAC address of the default gateway, PC1 checks its ARP table for the IPv4 address of the default gateway and its associated MAC address.

If an ARP entry does not exist in the ARP table for the default gateway, PC1 sends an ARP request. Router R1 sends back an ARP reply. PC1 can then forward the packet to the MAC address of the default gateway, the Fa0/0 interface of router R1.

A similar process is used for IPv6 packets. Instead of the ARP process, IPv6 address resolution uses ICMPv6 Neighbor Solicitation and Neighbor Advertisement messages. IPv6-to-MAC address mapping are kept in a table similar to the ARP cache, called the neighbor cache.

Forward to the Next Hop (4.2.1.3)

Video 4.2.1.3: R1 Forwards the Packet to R2

Video

Go to the online course and play the animation of a packet being sent through three routers from sender to receiver.

The following processes take place when R1 receives the Ethernet frame from PC1:

1. R1 examines the destination MAC address, which matches the MAC address of the receiving interface, FastEthernet 0/0. R1, therefore, copies the frame into its buffer.

2. R1 identifies the Ethernet Type field as 0x800, which means that the Ethernet frame contains an IPv4 packet in the data portion of the frame.

3. R1 de-encapsulates the Ethernet frame.

4. Because the destination IPv4 address of the packet does not match any of the directly connected networks of R1, R1 consults its routing table to route this packet. R1 searches the routing table for a network address that would include

the destination IPv4 address of the packet as a host address within that network. In this example, the routing table has a route for the 192.168.4.0/24 network. The destination IPv4 address of the packet is 192.168.4.10, which is a host IPv4 address on that network.

The route that R1 finds to the 192.168.4.0/24 network has a next-hop IPv4 address of 192.168.2.2 and an exit interface of FastEthernet 0/1. This means that the IPv4 packet is encapsulated in a new Ethernet frame with the destination MAC address of the IPv4 address of the next-hop router.

Because the exit interface is on an Ethernet network, R1 must resolve the next-hop IPv4 address with a destination MAC address using ARP:

1. R1 looks up the next-hop IPv4 address of 192.168.2.2 in its ARP cache. If the entry is not in the ARP cache, R1 would send an ARP request out of its FastEthernet 0/1 interface, and R2 would send back an ARP reply. R1 would then update its ARP cache with an entry for 192.168.2.2 and the associated MAC address.

2. The IPv4 packet is now encapsulated into a new Ethernet frame and forwarded out the FastEthernet 0/1 interface of R1.

Packet Routing (4.2.1.4)

Video

Video 4.2.1.4: R2 Forwards the Packet to R3

Go to the online course and play the animation of a packet being sent through three routers from sender to receiver.

The following processes take place when R2 receives the frame on its Fa0/0 interface:

1. R2 examines the destination MAC address, which matches the MAC address of the receiving interface, FastEthernet 0/0. R2, therefore, copies the frame into its buffer.

2. R2 identifies the Ethernet Type field as 0x800, which means that the Ethernet frame contains an IPv4 packet in the data portion of the frame.

3. R2 de-encapsulates the Ethernet frame.

4. Because the destination IPv4 address of the packet does not match any of the interface addresses of R2, R2 consults its routing table to route this packet. R2 searches the routing table for the destination IPv4 address of the packet using the same process R1 used.

5. The routing table of R2 has a route to the 192.168.4.0/24 network, with a next-hop IPv4 address of 192.168.3.2 and an exit interface of Serial 0/0/0. Because the exit interface is not an Ethernet network, R2 does not have to resolve the next-hop IPv4 address with a destination MAC address.

6. The IPv4 packet is now encapsulated into a new data link frame and sent out the Serial 0/0/0 exit interface.

When the interface is a point-to-point (P2P) serial connection, the router encapsulates the IPv4 packet into the proper data link frame format used by the exit interface (HDLC, PPP, etc.). Because there are no MAC addresses on serial interfaces, R2 sets the data link destination address to an equivalent of a broadcast.

Reach the Destination (4.2.1.5)

Video 4.2.1.5: R3 Forwards the Packet to PC2

Video

Go to the online course and play the animation of a packet being sent through three routers from sender to receiver.

The following processes take place when the frame arrives at R3:

1. R3 copies the data link PPP frame into its buffer.

2. R3 de-encapsulates the data link PPP frame.

3. R3 searches the routing table for the destination IPv4 address of the packet. The routing table has a route to a directly connected network on R3. This means that the packet can be sent directly to the destination device and does not need to be sent to another router.

Because the exit interface is a directly connected Ethernet network, R3 must resolve the destination IPv4 address of the packet with a destination MAC address:

1. R3 searches for the destination IPv4 address of the packet in its Address Resolution Protocol (ARP) cache. If the entry is not in the ARP cache, R3 sends an ARP request out of its FastEthernet 0/0 interface. PC2 sends back an ARP reply with its MAC address. R3 then updates its ARP cache with an entry for 192.168.4.10 and the MAC address that is returned in the ARP reply.

2. The IPv4 packet is encapsulated into a new Ethernet data link frame and sent out the FastEthernet 0/0 interface of R3.

3. When PC2 receives the frame, it examines the destination MAC address, which matches the MAC address of the receiving interface, its Ethernet network interface card (NIC). PC2, therefore, copies the rest of the frame into its buffer.

4. PC2 identifies the Ethernet Type field as 0x800, which means that the Ethernet frame contains an IPv4 packet in the data portion of the frame.

5. PC2 de-encapsulates the Ethernet frame and passes the IPv4 packet to the IPv4 process of its operating system.

Interactive Graphic

Activity 4.2.1.6 Part 1: Match Layer 2 and Layer 3 Addressing

Go to the online course and perform the activity (4.2.1.6 Part 1) where you will place the MAC and IP addresses in the appropriate field in the frame.

Interactive Graphic

Activity 4.2.1.6 Part 2: Match Layer 2 and Layer 3 Addressing

Go to the online course and perform the activity (4.2.1.6 Part 2) where you will place the MAC and IP addresses in the appropriate field in the frame.

Path Determination (4.2.2)

If switching packets between router interfaces is a primary function of a router, then the other primary function of a router is for the router to determine the best path to use when sending packets from source to destination.

Routing Decisions (4.2.2.1)

A primary function of a router is to determine the best path to use to send packets. To determine the best path, the router searches its routing table for a network address that matches the destination IP address of the packet.

The routing table search results in one of three path determinations:

- *Directly connected network*: If the destination IP address of the packet belongs to a device on a network that is directly connected to one of the interfaces of the router, that packet is forwarded directly to the destination device. This means that the destination IP address of the packet is a host address on the same network as the interface of the router.

- *Remote network*: If the destination IP address of the packet belongs to a remote network, then the packet is forwarded to another router. Remote networks can only be reached by forwarding packets to another router.

- **No route determined:** If the destination IP address of the packet does not belong to either a connected or remote network, the router determines if there is a Gateway of Last Resort available. A *Gateway of Last Resort* is set when a default route is configured on a router. If there is a default route, the packet is forwarded to the Gateway of Last Resort. If the router does not have a default route, then the packet is discarded. If the packet is discarded, the router sends an ICMP unreachable message to the source IP address of the packet.

The logic flowchart in Figure 4-42 illustrates the router packet-forwarding decision process.

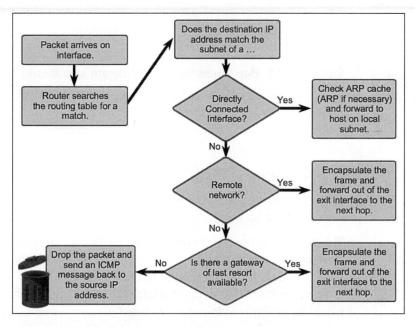

Figure 4-42   Packet Forward Decision Process

Best Path (4.2.2.2)

Determining the best path involves the evaluation of multiple paths to the same destination network and selecting the optimum or shortest path to reach that network. Whenever multiple paths to the same network exist, each path uses a different exit interface on the router to reach that network.

The best path is selected by a routing protocol based on the value or metric it uses to determine the distance to reach a network. A *metric* is the quantitative value used to measure the distance to a given network. The *best path* to a network is the path with the lowest metric.

Dynamic routing protocols typically use their own rules and metrics to build and update routing tables. The routing algorithm generates a value, or a metric, for each path through the network. Metrics can be based on either a single characteristic or several characteristics of a path. Some routing protocols can base route selection on multiple metrics, combining them into a single metric.

The following lists some dynamic protocols and the metrics they use:

- **Routing Information Protocol (RIP):** Hop count
- **Open Shortest Path First (OSPF):** The Cisco cost based on cumulative bandwidth from source to destination
- **Enhanced Interior Gateway Routing Protocol (EIGRP):** Bandwidth, delay, load, and reliability

Video

Video 4.2.2.2: Hop Count Versus Bandwidth as a Metric

Go to the online course and play the animation showing how a network path may be different depending on the metric being used.

Load Balancing (4.2.2.3)

What happens if a routing table has two or more paths with identical metrics to the same destination network?

When a router has two or more paths to a destination with equal cost metrics, then the router forwards the packets using both paths equally. This is called equal cost *load balancing*. The routing table contains the single destination network but has multiple exit interfaces, one for each equal cost path. The router forwards packets using the multiple exit interfaces listed in the routing table.

If configured correctly, load balancing can increase the effectiveness and performance of the network. Equal cost load balancing can be configured to use both dynamic routing protocols and static routes.

Only EIGRP supports *unequal cost load balancing*.

Video

Video 4.2.2.3: Load Balancing

Go to the online course and play the animation showing an example of equal cost load balancing.

Administrative Distance (4.2.2.4)

It is possible for a router to be configured with multiple routing protocols and static routes. If this occurs, the routing table may have more than one route source for the same destination network. For example, if both RIP and EIGRP are configured on a router, both routing protocols may learn of the same destination network. However, each routing protocol may decide on a different path to reach the destination based on that routing protocol's metrics. RIP chooses a path based on hop count, whereas EIGRP chooses a path based on its composite metric. How does the router know which route to use?

Cisco IOS uses what is known as the *administrative distance (AD)* to determine the route to install into the IP routing table. The AD represents the "trustworthiness" of the route; the lower the AD, the more trustworthy the route source. AD is a number between 0 and 255. For example, a static route has an AD of 1, whereas an EIGRP-discovered route has an AD of 90. Given two separate routes to the same destination, the router chooses the route with the lowest AD. When a router has the choice of a static route and an EIGRP route, the static route takes precedence. Similarly, a directly connected route with an AD of 0 takes precedence over a static route with an AD of 1. If the administrative distance is 255, the router does not believe the source of that route and does not install that route into the routing table. Table 4-5 lists various routing protocols and their associated ADs.

Table 4-5 Default Administrative Distances

Route Source	Administrative Distance
Connected	0
Static	1
EIGRP summary route	5
External BGP	20
Internal EIGRP	90
IGRP	100
OSPF	110
IS-IS	115
RIP	120
External EIGRP	170
Internal BGP	200
Unknown	255

Interactive Graphic

Activity 4.2.2.5: Order the Steps in the Packet-Forwarding Process

Go to the course online and complete the activity of ordering the steps in the packet-forwarding process.

Analyze the Routing Table (4.3.1)

The *routing table* is used to store information about known directly connected and remote networks. If a network is not listed in the routing table, the router will have no knowledge of that network. Reaching that network will then be impossible. All Cisco IT professionals must understand and analyze the routing table.

The Routing Table (4.3.1.1)

The routing table of a router stores information about

- **Directly connected routes:** These routes come from the active router interfaces. Routers add a directly connected route when an interface is configured with an IP address and is activated.

- **Remote routes:** These are remote networks connected to other routers. Routes to these networks can either be statically configured or dynamically configured using dynamic routing protocols.

Specifically, a routing table is a data file in RAM that is used to store route information about directly connected and remote networks. The routing table contains network or next hop associations. These associations tell a router that a particular destination can be optimally reached by sending the packet to a specific router that represents the next hop on the way to the final destination. The next hop association can also be the outgoing or exit interface to the next destination.

Figure 4-43 identifies the directly connected networks and remote networks of router R1.

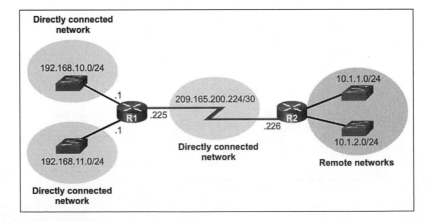

Figure 4-43   Directly Connected and Remote Network Routes

Routing Table Sources (4.3.1.2)

On a Cisco IOS router, the **show ip route** command can be used to display the IPv4 routing table of a router. A router provides additional route information, including how the route was learned, how long the route has been in the table, and which specific interface to use to get to a predefined destination.

Entries in the routing table can be added as

- **Local route interfaces:** Added when an interface is configured and active. This entry is only displayed in IOS 15 or newer for IPv4 routes and all IOS releases for IPv6 routes.

- **Directly connected interfaces:** Added to the routing table when an interface is configured and active.

- **Static routes:** Added when a route is manually configured and the exit interface is active.

- **Dynamic routing protocol:** Added when routing protocols that dynamically learn about the network, such as EIGRP or OSPF, are implemented and networks are identified.

The sources of the routing table entries are identified by a code. The code identifies how the route was learned. For instance, common codes include

- **L:** Identifies the address assigned to a router's interface. This allows the router to efficiently determine when it receives a packet for the interface instead of being forwarded.

- **C:** Identifies a directly connected network.

- **S:** Identifies a static route created to reach a specific network.

- **D:** Identifies a dynamically learned network from another router using EIGRP.

- **O:** Identifies a dynamically learned network from another router using the OSPF routing protocol.

> **NOTE**
>
> There are other codes as part of the routing table, which are beyond the scope of this chapter.

Figure 4-44 shows the routing table of R1 in a simple network.

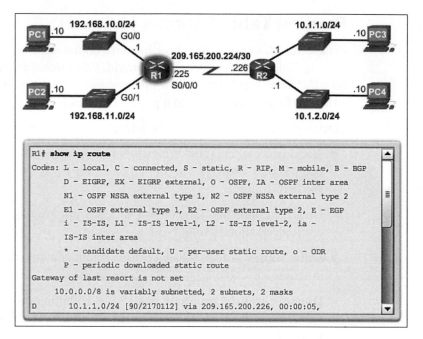

Figure 4-44   Routing Table of R1

Activity 4.3.1.2: Routing Table of R1

Go to the online course and use the slider bar to see the entire output of the **show ip route** command.

Remote Network Routing Entries (4.3.1.3)

As a network administrator, it is imperative to know how to interpret the content of an IPv4 and IPv6 routing table. Figure 4-45 displays an IPv4 routing table entry on R1 for the route to remote network 10.1.1.0.

The entry identifies the following information:

- **Route source:** Identifies how the route was learned.

- **Destination network:** Identifies the address of the remote network.

- **Administrative distance:** Identifies the trustworthiness of the route source. Lower values indicate preferred route source.

- **Metric:** Identifies the value assigned to reach the remote network. Lower values indicate preferred routes.

- **Next hop:** Identifies the IPv4 address of the next router to forward the packet to.

- **Route timestamp:** Identifies how much time has passed since the route was learned.

- **Outgoing interface:** Identifies the exit interface to use to forward a packet toward the final destination.

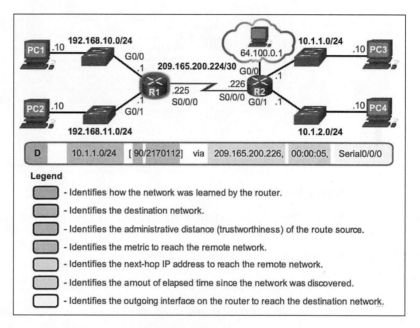

Figure 4-45 Remote Network Entry Identifiers

Interactive
Graphic

Activity 4.3.1.4: Interpret the Content of a Routing Table Entry

Go to the online course and complete the activity of creating a routing table entry.

Directly Connected Routes (4.3.2)

The most reliable network that a router will know about is one that it is directly connected to.

Directly Connected Interfaces (4.3.2.1)

A newly deployed router without any configured interfaces has an empty routing table, as shown in Figure 4-46.

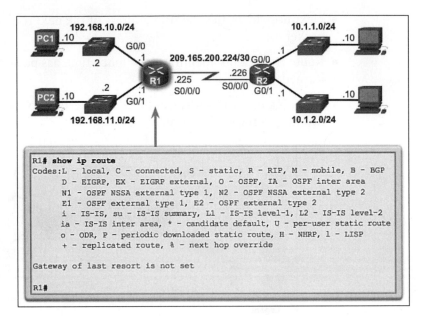

Figure 4-46   Empty Routing Table

Before the interface state is considered up/up and added to the IPv4 routing table, the interface must

- Be assigned a valid IPv4 or IPv6 address

- Be activated with the **no shutdown** command

- Receive a carrier signal from another device (router, switch, host, etc.)

When the interface is up, the network of that interface is added to the routing table as a directly connected network.

Directly Connected Routing Table Entries (4.3.2.2)

An active, properly configured, directly connected interface actually creates two routing table entries. Figure 4-47 displays the IPv4 routing table entries on R1 for the directly connected network 192.168.10.0.

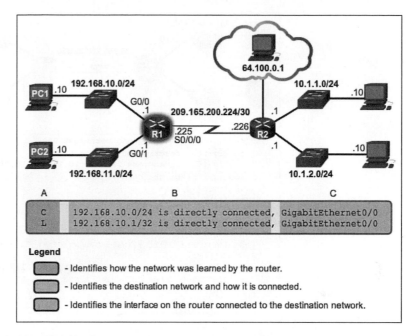

Figure 4-47   Directly Connected Network Entry Identifiers

The routing table entry for directly connected interfaces is simpler than the entries for remote networks. The entries contain the following information:

- **Route source:** Identifies how the route was learned. Directly connected interfaces have two route source codes. 'C' identifies a directly connected network. 'L' identifies the IPv4 address assigned to the router's interface.

- **Destination network:** The address of the remote network.

- **Outgoing interface:** Identifies the exit interface to use when forwarding packets to the destination network.

- Prior to IOS 15, local route routing table entries (L) were not displayed in the IPv4 routing table. Local route (L) entries have always been a part of the IPv6 routing table.

Directly Connected Examples (4.3.2.3)

The examples in Figures 4-48 through 4-50 show the steps to configure and activate the interfaces attached to R1. Notice the Layer 1 and 2 informational messages generated as each interface is activated.

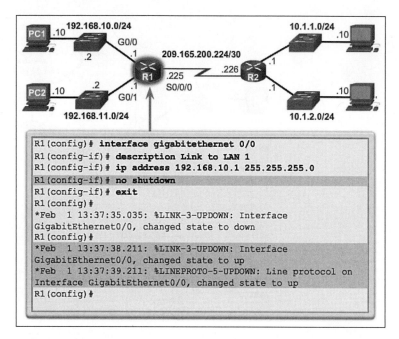

Figure 4-48   Configuring a Directly Connected Gigabit Ethernet Interface

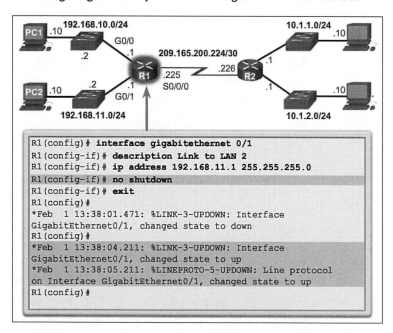

Figure 4-49   Configuring a Directly Connected Gigabit Ethernet Interface

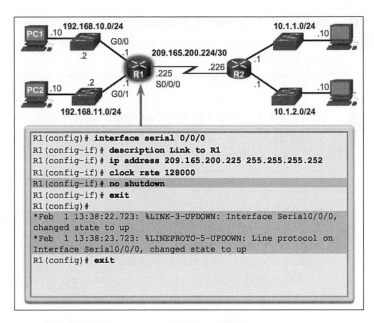

Figure 4-50   Configuring a Directly Connected Serial Interface. As Each Interface Is Added, the Routing Table Automatically Adds the Connected (C) and Local (L) Entries.

Figure 4-51 and Example 4-1 provide an example of the routing table with the directly connected interfaces of R1 configured and activated.

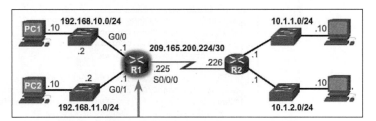

Figure 4-51   Verifying the Directly Connected Routing Table Entries

Example 4-1   Verifying Directly Connected Routing Table Entries

```
R1#  show ip route | begin Gateway
Gateway of last resort is not set


      192.168.10.0/24 is variably subnetted, 2 subnets, 2 masks
C     192.168.10.0/24 is directly connected, GigabitEthernet0/0
L     192.168.10.1/32 is directly connected, GigabitEthernet0/0
      192.168.11.0/24 is variably subnetted, 2 subnets, 2 masks
C     192.168.11.0/24 is directly connected, GigabitEthernet0/1
L     192.168.11.1/32 is directly connected, GigabitEthernet0/1
```

Activity 4.3.2.3 Part 1: Verifying the Directly Connected Routing Table Entries

Go to the online course and use the slider bar to see the entire output of the **show ip route** command.

Activity 4.3.2.3 Part 2: The Command History Feature

Go to the course online to use the Syntax Checker in the fifth graphic to configure and activate the directly connected interfaces on R2.

Directly Connected IPv6 Example (4.3.2.4)

The example in Figure 4-52 shows the configuration steps for the directly connected interfaces of R1 with the indicated IPv6 addresses. Notice the Layer 1 and Layer 2 informational messages generated as each interface is configured and activated.

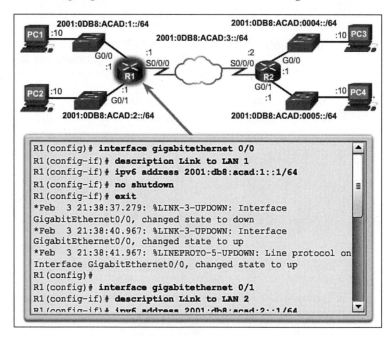

Figure 4-52   Configure the R1 Directly Connected IPv6 Interfaces

Activity 4.3.2.4 (Part 1): Configure the R1 Directly Connected IPv6 Interfaces

Go to the online course and use the slider bar in the first graphic to see the entire output of the configuration of directly connected IPv6 interfaces.

The **show ipv6 route** command shown in Figure 4-53 is used to verify that IPv6 networks and specific IPv6 interface addresses have been installed in the IPv6 routing table. Like IPv4, a 'c' next to a route indicates that this is a directly connected network. An 'L' indicates the local route. In an IPv6 network, the local route has a /128 prefix. Local routes are used by the routing table to efficiently process packets with a destination address of the interface of the router.

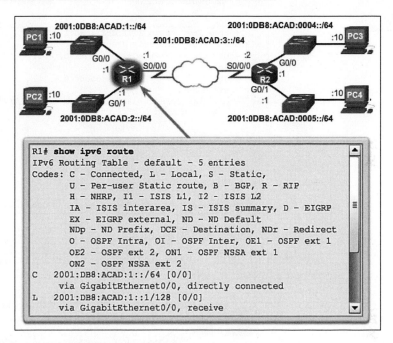

Figure 4-53 Show the IPv6 Route Table

Activity 4.3.2.4 Part 2: Show the IPv6 Route Table

Go to the online course and use the slider bar in the second graphic to see the entire output of the **show ipv6 route** command.

Notice that there is also a route installed to the FF00::/8 network. This route is required for multicast routing.

Figure 4-54 displays how the **show ipv6 route** command can be combined with a specific network destination to display the details of how that route was learned by the router.

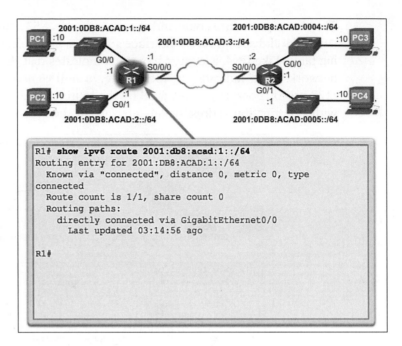

Figure 4-54 Show an IPv6 Route Entry

Figure 4-55 displays how connectivity to R2 can be verified using the **ping** command.

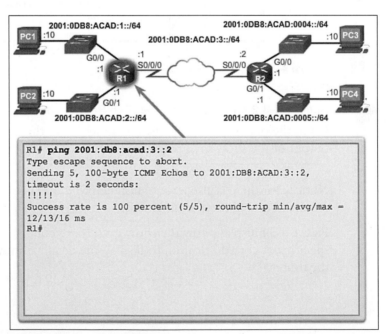

Figure 4-55 Test Connectivity to R2 S0/0/0

In Figure 4-56, notice what happens when the G0/0 LAN interface of R2 is the target of the **ping** command. The pings are unsuccessful. This is because R1 does not have an entry in the routing table to reach the 2001:DB8:ACAD:4::/64 network.

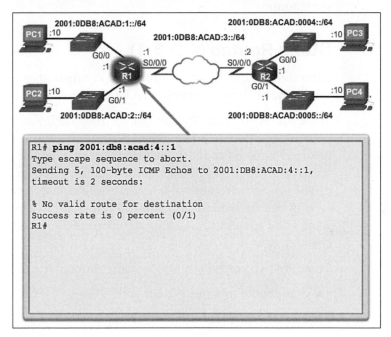

```
R1# ping 2001:db8:acad:4::1
Type escape sequence to abort.
Sending 5, 100-byte ICMP Echos to 2001:DB8:ACAD:4::1,
timeout is 2 seconds:

% No valid route for destination
Success rate is 0 percent (0/1)
R1#
```

Figure 4-56   Test Connectivity to R2 G0/0

R1 requires additional information to reach a remote network. Remote network route entries can be added to the routing table using either

- Static routing

- Dynamic routing protocols

Packet Tracer
☐ Activity

Packet Tracer Activity 4.3.2.5: Investigating Directly Connected Routes

Background

The network in the activity is already configured. You will log in to the routers and use **show** commands to discover and answer the questions about the directly connected routes.

Go to the online course to complete this lab activity.

Statically Learned Routes (4.3.3)

After directly connected routes, the most reliable route that a router can learn is a static route.

Static Routes (4.3.3.1)

After directly connected interfaces are configured and added to the routing table, then static or dynamic routing can be implemented.

Static routes are manually configured. They define an explicit path between two networking devices. Unlike a dynamic routing protocol, static routes are not automatically updated and must be manually reconfigured if the network topology changes. The benefits of using static routes include improved security and resource efficiency. Static routes use less bandwidth than dynamic routing protocols, and no CPU cycles are used to calculate and communicate routes. The main disadvantage to using static routes is the lack of automatic reconfiguration if the network topology changes.

There are two common types of static routes in the routing table:

- Static route to a specific network
- Default static route

A static route can be configured to reach a specific remote network. IPv4 static routes are configured using the **ip route** `network mask {next-hop-ip | exit-intf}` global configuration command. A static route is identified in the routing table with the code 's'.

A default static route is similar to a default gateway on a host. The default static route specifies the exit point to use when the routing table does not contain a path for the destination network.

A default static route is useful when a router has only one exit point to another router, such as when the router connects to a central router or service provider.

To configure an IPv4 default static route, use the **ip route 0.0.0.0 0.0.0.0** `{exit-intf | next-hop-ip}` global configuration command.

Static Route Examples (4.3.3.2)

Activity 4.3.3.2 Part 1: Entering and Verifying a Static Default Route

Go to the online course and use the slider bar in the first graphic to see the entire output of the **show ip route** command.

Figure 4-57 shows the configuration of an IPv4 default static route on R1 to the Serial 0/0/0 interface. Notice that the configuration of the route generated an 's⋆' entry in the routing table. The 's' signifies that the route source is a static route while the asterisk (*) identifies this route as a possible candidate to be the default route. In fact, it has been chosen as the default route as evidenced by the line that reads, "Gateway of Last Resort is 0.0.0.0 to network 0.0.0.0."

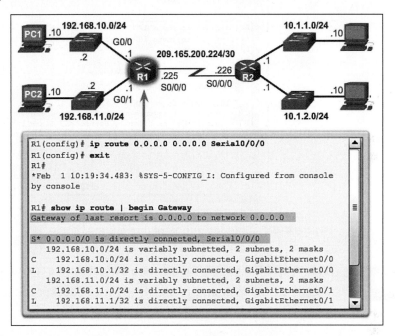

Figure 4-57   Entering and Verifying a Static Default Route

Activity 4.3.3.2 Part 2: Entering and Verifying a Static Route

Go to the online course and use the slider bar in the second graphic to see the entire output of the **show ip route** command.

Figure 4-58 shows the configuration of two static routes from R2 to reach the two LANs on R1. The route to 192.168.10.0/24 has been configured using the exit interface while the route to 192.168.11.0/24 has been configured using the next hop IPv4 address. Although both are acceptable, there are some differences in how they operate. For instance, notice how different they look in the routing table. Also notice that because these static routes were to specific networks, the output indicates that the Gateway of Last Resort is not set.

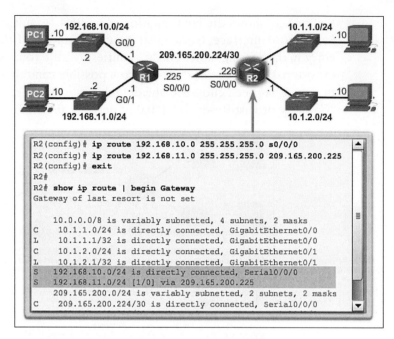

Figure 4-58   Entering and Verifying a Static Route

Activity 4.3.3.2 Part 3: Configure a Default Static Route on R1

Go to the online course to use the Syntax Checker in the third graphic to configure a default static route on router R1 going to R2.

Activity 4.3.3.2 Part 4: Configure Static Routes on R2

Go to the online course to use the Syntax Checker in the fourth graphic to configure static routes on router R2 to reach the R1 LANs.

Static IPv6 Route Examples (4.3.3.3)

Like IPv4, IPv6 supports static and default static routes. They are used and configured like IPv4 static routes.

To configure a default static IPv6 route, use the **ipv6 route ::/0** {*ipv6-address* | *interface-type interface-number*} global configuration command.

Figure 4-59 shows the configuration of a default static route on R1 to the Serial 0/0/0 interface.

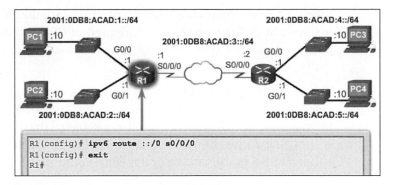

Figure 4-59 Entering and Verifying an IPv6 Static Default Route

Notice in the output shown in Figure 4-60 that the default static route configuration generated an 's' entry in the routing table. The 's' signifies that the route source is a static route. Unlike the IPv4 static route, there is no asterisk (*) or Gateway of Last Resort explicitly identified.

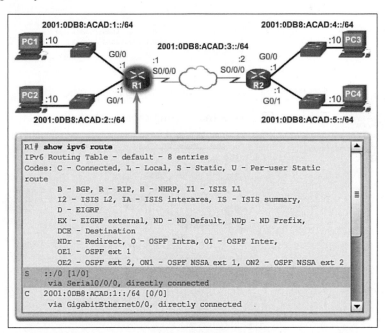

Figure 4-60 Entering and Verifying an IPv6 Static Default Route

Activity 4.3.3.3 Part 1: Entering and Verifying an IPv6 Static Default Route

Go to the online course and use the slider bar in the second graphic to see the entire output of the **show ip route** command.

Like IPv4, static routes are routes explicitly configured to reach a specific remote network. Static IPv6 routes are configured using the **ipv6 route** *ipv6-prefix/ prefix-length {ipv6-address|interface-type interface-number}* global configuration command.

The example in Figure 4-61 shows the configuration of two static routes from R2 to reach the two LANs on R1. The route to the 2001:0DB8:ACAD:2::/64 LAN is configured with an exit interface, while the route to the 2001:0DB8:ACAD:1::/64 LAN is configured with the next hop IPv6 address. The next hop IPv6 address can be either an IPv6 global unicast or link-local address.

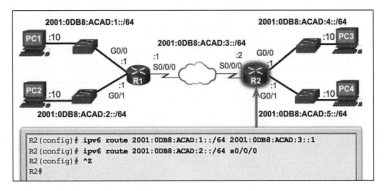

Figure 4-61   Entering and Verifying IPv6 Static Routes

Figure 4-62 shows the routing table with the new static routes installed.

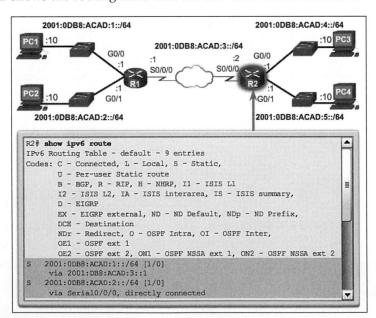

Figure 4-62   Entering and Verifying IPv6 Static Routes

Activity 4.3.3.3 Part 2: Entering and Verifying IPv6 Static Routes

Go to the online course and use the slider bar in the fourth graphic to see the entire output of the **show ipv6 route** command.

Figure 4-63 confirms remote network connectivity to the 2001:0DB8:ACAD:4::/64 LAN on R2 from R1.2.

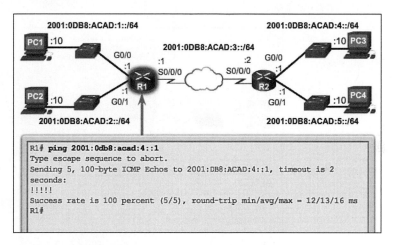

Figure 4-63   Verifying Remote Network Connectivity

Dynamic Routing Protocols (4.3.4)

For larger networks, the use of static routes alone may not be very efficient. Dynamic routing protocols can be used to allow routers to automatically exchange information in order to create entries for the routing table

Dynamic Routing (4.3.4.1)

Dynamic routing protocols are used by routers to share information about the reachability and status of remote networks. Dynamic routing protocols perform several activities, including network discovery and maintaining routing tables.

Network discovery is the capability of a routing protocol to share information about the networks that it knows about with other routers that are also using the same routing protocol. Instead of depending on manually configured static routes to remote networks on every router, a dynamic routing protocol allows the routers to automatically learn about these networks from other routers. These networks, and the best path to each, are added to the routing table of the router, and identified as a network learned by a specific dynamic routing protocol.

During network discovery, routers exchange routes and update their routing tables. Routers have converged after they have finished exchanging and updating their routing tables. Routers then maintain the networks in their routing tables.

Figure 4-64 provides a simple scenario of how two neighboring routers would initially exchange routing information. In this simplified message, exchange R1 introduces itself and the networks it can reach. R2 responds and provides R1 with its networks.

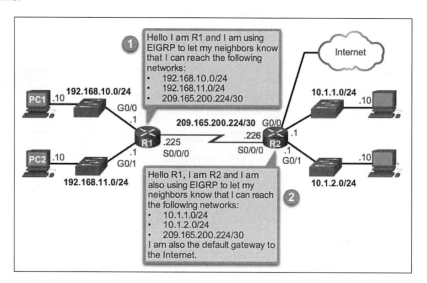

Figure 4-64   Dynamic Routing Scenario

IPv4 Routing Protocols (4.3.4.2)

A router running a dynamic routing protocol does not only make a best path determination to a network, but it also determines a new best path if the initial path becomes unusable (or if the topology changes). For these reasons, dynamic routing protocols have an advantage over static routes. Routers that use dynamic routing protocols automatically share routing information with other routers and compensate for any topology changes without involving the network administrator.

Cisco ISR routers can support a variety of dynamic IPv4 routing protocols including

- **EIGRP:** Enhanced Interior Gateway Routing Protocol
- **OSPF:** Open Shortest Path First
- **IS-IS:** Intermediate System-to-Intermediate System
- **RIP:** Routing Information Protocol

To determine which routing protocols are supported by the IOS, use the **router ?** command in global configuration mode, as shown in Figure 4-65.

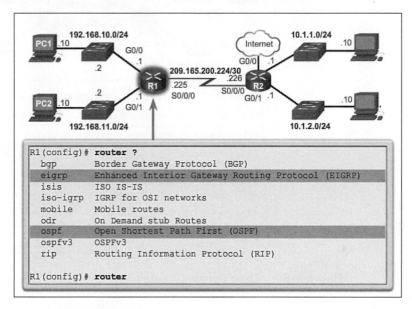

Figure 4-65   Supported IPv4 Routing Protocols

The focus of this course is on EIGRP and OSPF. RIP will be discussed only for legacy reasons; the other routing protocols supported by the IOS are beyond the scope of the CCNA certification.

IPv4 Dynamic Routing Examples (4.3.4.3)

In this dynamic routing example, assume that R1 and R2 have been configured to support the dynamic routing protocol EIGRP. The routers also advertise directly connected networks. R2 advertises that it is the default gateway to other networks.

Figure 4-66 shows the topography of a network that has been configured with a dynamic routing protocol.

The output in Figure 4-66 displays the routing table of R1 after the routers have exchanged updates and converged. Along with the connected and link local interfaces, there are three 'D' entries in the routing table.

- The entry beginning with 'D*EX' identifies that the source of this entry was EIGRP ('D'). The route is a candidate to be a default route ('*'), and the route is an external route ('*EX') forwarded by EIGRP.

- The other two 'D' entries are routes installed in the routing table based on the update from R2 advertising its LANs.

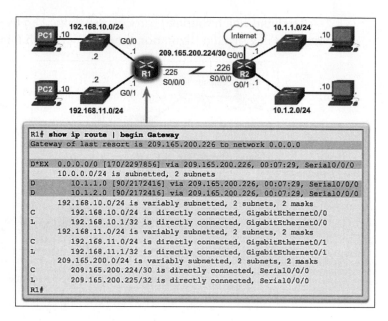

Figure 4-66 Verify Dynamic Routes

IPv6 Routing Protocols (4.3.4.4)

As shown in Figure 4-67, ISR routers can support dynamic IPv6 routing protocols including

- RIPng (RIP next generation)
- OSPFv3
- EIGRP for IPv6

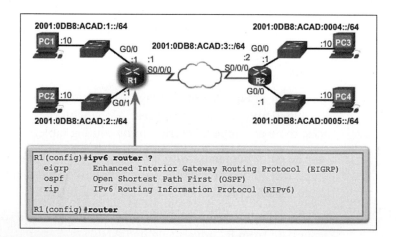

Figure 4-67 Supported IPv6 Routing Protocols

Support for dynamic IPv6 routing protocols is dependent on hardware and IOS version. Most of the modifications in the routing protocols are to support the longer IPv6 addresses and different header structures.

To enable IPv6 routers to forward traffic, you must configure the **ipv6 unicast-routing** global configuration command.

IPv6 Dynamic Routing Examples (4.3.4.5)

Routers R1 and R2 have been configured with the dynamic routing protocol EIGRP for IPv6. (This is the IPv6 equivalent of EIGRP for IPv4.)

To view the routing table on R1, enter the **show ipv6 route** command, as shown in Figure 4-68. The output in the figure displays the routing table of R1 after the routers have exchanged updates and converged. Along with the connected and local routes, there are two D entries (EIGRP routes) in the routing table.

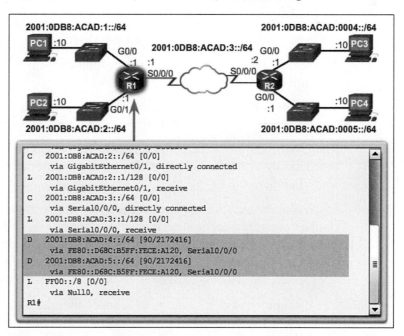

Figure 4-68   Verify Dynamic Routes

Activity 4.3.4.5: Verify Dynamic Routes

Go to the online course and use the slider bar to see the entire output of the **show ipv6 route** command.

Summary (4.4)

Class Activity 4.4.1.1: We Really Could Use a Map!

Scenario

Use the Ashland and Richmond routing tables shown in the file provided with this activity.

With the help of a classmate, draw a network topology using the information from the tables.

To assist you with this activity, follow these guidelines:

- **Start with the Ashland router:** Use its routing table to identify ports and IP addresses and networks.

- **Add the Richmond router:** Use its routing table to identify ports and IP addresses and networks.

- Add any other intermediary and end devices as specified by the tables.

In addition, record answers from your group to the reflection questions provided with this activity.

Be prepared to share your work with another group and the class.

There are many key structures and performance-related characteristics referred to when discussing networks: topology, speed, cost, security, availability, scalability, and reliability.

Cisco routers and Cisco switches have many similarities. They support a similar modal operating system, similar command structures, and many of the same commands. One distinguishing feature between switches and routers is the type of interfaces supported by each. When an interface is configured on both devices, the appropriate **show** commands need to be used to verify a working interface.

The main purpose of a router is to connect multiple networks and forward packets from one network to the next. This means that a router typically has multiple interfaces. Each interface is a member or host on a different IP network.

Cisco IOS uses what is known as the administrative distance (AD) to determine the route to install into the IP routing table. The routing table is a list of networks known by the router. The routing table includes network addresses for its own interfaces, which are the directly connected networks, as well as network addresses for remote networks. A remote network is a network that can only be reached by forwarding the packet to another router.

Remote networks are added to the routing table in two ways: either by the network administrator manually configuring static routes or by implementing a dynamic routing protocol. Static routes do not have as much overhead as dynamic routing protocols; however, static routes can require more maintenance if the topology is constantly changing or is unstable.

Dynamic routing protocols automatically adjust to changes without any intervention from the network administrator. Dynamic routing protocols require more CPU processing and also use a certain amount of link capacity for routing updates and messages. In many cases, a routing table will contain both static and dynamic routes.

Routers make their primary forwarding decision at Layer 3, the Network layer. However, router interfaces participate in Layers 1, 2, and 3. Layer 3 IP packets are encapsulated into a Layer 2 data link frame and encoded into bits at Layer 1. Router interfaces participate in Layer 2 processes associated with their encapsulation. For example, an Ethernet interface on a router participates in the ARP process like other hosts on that LAN.

The Cisco IP routing table is not a flat database. The routing table is actually a hierarchical structure that is used to speed up the lookup process when locating routes and forwarding packets.

Components of the IPv6 routing table are very similar to the IPv4 routing table. For instance, it is populated using directly connected interfaces, static routes, and dynamically learned routes.

Practice

The following activities provide practice with the topics introduced in this chapter. The Labs and Class Activities are available in the companion *Routing and Switching Essentials Lab Manual* (978-1-58713-320-6). You can find the Packet Tracer Activities PKA files in the online course.

Class Activities

Class Activity 4.0.1.2: Do We Really Need a Map?

Class Activity 4.4.1.1: We Really Could Use a Map!

Labs

Lab 4.1.1.9: Mapping the Internet

Lab 4.1.4.6: Configuring Basic Router Settings with IOS CLI

Lab 4.1.4.7: Configuring Basic Router Settings with CCP

Packet Tracer Activities

Packet Tracer Activity 4.1.1.8: Using Traceroute to Discover the Network

Packet Tracer Activity 4.1.2.9: Documenting the Network

Packet Tracer Activity 4.1.3.5: Configuring IPv4 and IPv6 Interfaces

Packet Tracer Activity 4.1.4.5: Configuring and Verifying a Small Network

Packet Tracer Activity 4.3.2.5: Investigating Directly Connected Routes

Check Your Understanding Questions

Complete all the review questions listed here to test your understanding of the topics and concepts in this chapter. The appendix, "Answers to the 'Check Your Understanding' Questions," lists the answers.

1. Which two statements correctly describe the components of a router? (Choose two.)

   A. RAM permanently stores the configuration file used during the boot sequence.

   B. ROM contains diagnostics executed on hardware modules.

   C. NVRAM stores a backup copy of the IOS used during the boot sequence.

   D. Flash memory does not lose its contents during a reboot.

   E. ROM contains the most current and most complete version of the IOS.

   F. Flash contains boot system commands to identify the location of the IOS.

2. Which three statements describe features of Cisco devices that perform routing? (Choose three.)

   A. The IP address of a LAN interface on a Layer 3 device provides the default gateway for hosts connected to that LAN.

   B. A routing protocol must be enabled in order for a Layer 3 device to build a routing table.

   C. Routing tables are volatile. When power is removed from a Layer 3 device, the routing table ceases to exist.

   D. A routing table is automatically created for directly connected, active LAN and WAN interfaces.

   E. A directly connected Layer 3 interface must be manually added to the routing table in order for routing to be enabled on that interface.

3. What address and prefix length is used when configuring an IPv6 default static route?

   A. ::/0

   B. ::1/128

   C. 0.0.0.0/0

   D. FF02::1/8

4. What is the purpose of a routing protocol?

   A. It is used to build and maintain ARP tables.

   B. It provides a method for segmenting and reassembling data packets.

   C. It allows an administrator to devise an addressing scheme for the network.

   D. It allows a router to share information about known networks with other routers.

   E. It provides a procedure for encoding and decoding data into bits for packet forwarding.

5. Which tasks can be accomplished by using the command history feature? (Choose two.)

   A. View a list of commands entered in a previous session.

   B. Recall up to 15 command lines by default.

   C. Set the command history buffer size.

   D. Recall previously entered commands.

   E. Save command lines in a log file for future reference.

6. During the process of encapsulation, how does the PC determine if the packet is destined for a host on a remote network?

   A. By checking the ARP cache for the destination host MAC address

   B. By querying the DNS server for the information of the destination host

   C. By sending a broadcast to the local LAN segment to see if there is any response

   D. By performing the AND operation on the destination IP address and its own subnet mask

7. When a router learns that multiple paths are available to a destination network from the same routing protocol, which factor is considered by a router to choose the best path to forward a packet?

   A. The lowest metric

   B. The order of paths on the routing table

   C. The fastest bandwidth of exiting interfaces

   D. The reliability value of the neighboring routers

8. Which two statements describe characteristics of load balancing? (Choose two.)

   A. Load balancing occurs when a router sends the same packet to different destination networks.

   B. Load balancing occurs when the same number of packets is sent over static and dynamic routes.

   C. Load balancing allows a router to forward packets over multiple paths to the same destination network.

   D. Unequal cost load balancing is supported by EIGRP.

   E. If multiple paths with different metrics to a destination exist, the router cannot support load balancing.

9. What is a Gateway of Last Resort?

   A. The IP address of another router

   B. The IP address of the Internet provider

   C. A term to describe a default gateway on a host device

   D. Where dropped packets are sent

10. Refer to the exhibit.

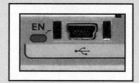

What is the purpose of the router port that is shown?

    A. To back up the IOS

    B. To configure the router

    C. To run an IOS from an alternative location

    D. To connect to a port on a switch

11. What code is used in the routing table to identify routes learned through EIGRP?

    A. C

    B. D

    C. L

    D. O

    E. S

12. Which two statements describe static routes? (Choose two.)

    A. They are created in interface configuration mode.

    B. They require manual reconfiguration to accommodate network changes.

    C. They automatically become the default gateway of the router.

    D. They are identified in the routing table with the prefix *S*.

    E. They are automatically updated whenever an interface is reconfigured or shut down.

13. The output of the **show ip route** command contains the following entry: S 10.2.0.0 [1/0] via 172.16.2.2. What value is indicated by the 1 in the [1/0] portion of the output?

    A. Metric

    B. Number of hops

    C. Administrative distance

    D. Interface ID through which the network can be reached

CHAPTER 5

Inter-VLAN Routing

Objectives

Upon completion of this chapter, you will be able to answer the following questions:

- What are the three methods used to route between VLANs?

- What is a disadvantage to the legacy method used to route between VLANs?

- What is a disadvantage to using router-on-a-stick to route between VLANs?

- What is different about routing between VLANs using a Layer 3 switch?

- How do you configure a router for routing between VLANs using either the legacy method or router-on-a-stick?

- How do you configure a switch when routing between VLANs using the legacy method, router-on-a-stick, or a multilayer switch?

- What kind of router, switch, and IP addressing issues arise when configuring routing between VLANs?

- What are the most important **show** commands used when routing between VLANs?

Key Terms

This chapter uses the following key terms. You can find the definitions in the Glossary.

Introduction (5.0.1.1)

We have seen that using VLANs to segment a switched network provides improved performance, manageability, and security. Trunks are used to carry information from multiple VLANs between network devices such as switch to switch, switch to router, or switch to server. However, because these VLANs have segmented the network, a Layer 3 process is required to allow traffic to move from one network segment to another.

This Layer 3 routing process can either be implemented using a router or a Layer 3 switch interface. The use of a Layer 3 device provides a method for controlling the flow of traffic between network segments, including network segments created by VLANs.

This chapter focuses on the methods used for the implementation of inter-VLAN routing. It includes configurations for both the use of a router and a Layer 3 switch. It also describes issues encountered when implementing inter-VLAN routing and standard troubleshooting techniques.

Class Activity 5.0.1.2: Switching to Local Network Channels

Scenario

You work for a small- to medium-size business. As the network administrator, you are responsible for ensuring that your network operates efficiently and securely.

Several years ago, you created VLANs on your only switch for two of your departments, Accounting and Sales. As the business has grown, it has become apparent that sometimes these two departments must share company files and network resources.

You discuss this scenario with network administrators in a few branches of your company. They tell you to consider using inter-VLAN routing.

- Research the concept of inter-VLAN routing.

- Design a simple presentation to show your manager how you would use inter-VLAN routing to allow the Accounting and Sales departments to remain separate, but share company files and network resources.

Inter-VLAN Routing Configuration (5.1)

Seldom would any company have VLANs that are not routed. Communication between VLANs is common, such as between PCs that are on a separate VLAN from printers and copiers, IP phones, or access points. A technician must be very familiar with the concept of and configuration of VLANs, trunking, and routing between VLANs.

What Is Inter-VLAN Routing? (5.1.1.1)

VLANs are used to segment switched networks. Layer 2 switches, such as the Catalyst 2960 Series, can be configured with over 4,000 VLANs. However, Layer 2 switches have very limited IPv4 and IPv6 functionality and cannot perform the routing function of routers. While Layer 2 switches are gaining more IP functionality, such as the ability to perform static routing, these Layer 2 switches do not support dynamic routing. With the large number of VLANs possible on these switches, static routing is insufficient.

A VLAN is a broadcast domain, so computers on separate VLANs are unable to communicate without the intervention of a routing device. Any device that supports Layer 3 routing, such as a router or a multilayer switch, can be used to perform the necessary routing functionality. Regardless of the device used, the process of forwarding network traffic from one VLAN to another VLAN using routing is known as *inter-VLAN routing*. Figure 5-1 shows a router performing inter-VLAN routing for VLANs 10 and 30.

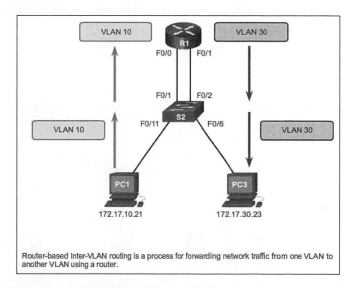

Figure 5-1   What Is Inter-VLAN Routing?

Legacy Inter-VLAN Routing (5.1.1.2)

Historically, the first solution for inter-VLAN routing relied on routers with multiple physical interfaces. Each interface had to be connected to a separate network (VLAN) and configured with a distinct subnet.

In this legacy approach, inter-VLAN routing is performed by connecting different physical router interfaces to different physical switch ports. The switch ports connected to the router are placed in access mode and each physical interface is assigned to a different VLAN. Each router interface can then accept traffic from the VLAN associated with the switch interface that it is connected to, and traffic can be routed to the other VLANs connected to the other interfaces.

Note

The topology uses parallel links to build the trunks between the switches to achieve link aggregation and redundancy. However, redundant links make the topology more complex and may introduce connectivity issues if not properly managed. Protocols and techniques, such as spanning tree and EtherChannel should be implemented to manage redundant links. These techniques are beyond the scope of this chapter.

Interactive Graphic

Activity 5.1.1.2: Legacy Inter-VLAN Routing Animation

Go to the online curriculum and access the graphic. Click the Play button to view an animation of legacy inter-VLAN routing.

As shown in the animation and Figure 5-2, the following steps are taken for PC1 to communicate with PC3.

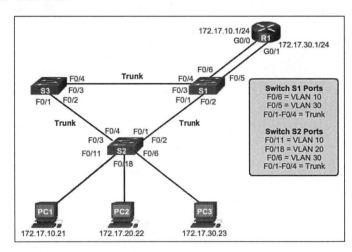

Figure 5-2   Legacy Inter-VLAN Routing

Step 1.   PC1 on VLAN 10 is communicating with PC3 on VLAN 30 through router R1.

Step 2.   PC1 and PC3 are on different VLANs and have IP addresses on different subnets.

Step 3.   Router R1 has a separate interface configured for each of the VLANs.

Step 4.   PC1 sends unicast traffic destined for PC3 to switch S2 on VLAN 10, where it is then forwarded out the trunk interface to switch S1.

Step 5.   Switch S1 then forwards the unicast traffic to router R1 on interface G0/0.

Step 6.   The router routes the unicast traffic through its interface G0/1, which is connected to VLAN 30.

Step 7.   The router forwards the unicast traffic to switch S1 on VLAN 30.

Step 8.   Switch S1 then forwards the unicast traffic to switch S2 through the active trunk link, after which switch S2 can then forward the unicast traffic to PC3 on VLAN 30.

In this example, the router was configured with two separate physical interfaces to interact with the different VLANs and perform the routing.

Note

This method of inter-VLAN routing is not efficient and is generally no longer implemented in switched networks. It is shown in this course for explanation purposes only.

Router-on-a-Stick Inter-VLAN Routing (5.1.1.3)

While legacy inter-VLAN routing requires multiple physical interfaces on both the router and the switch, a more common, present-day implementation of inter-VLAN routing does not. Instead, some router software permits configuring an interface as a trunk link, meaning only one physical interface is required on the router and the switch to route packets between multiple VLANs.

"Router-on-a-stick" is a type of router configuration in which a single physical router interface routes traffic between multiple VLANs on a network. As seen in Figure 5-3, the router is connected to switch S1 using a single, physical network connection (a trunk).

The router interface is configured to operate as a trunk link and is connected to a switch port that is configured in trunk mode. The router performs inter-VLAN routing by accepting VLAN-tagged traffic on the trunk interface coming from the adjacent switch, and then internally routing between the VLANs using subinterfaces. Note that each VLAN has a separate subinterface. The router then forwards the routed traffic, VLAN-tagged for the destination VLAN, out the same physical interface as it used to receive the traffic.

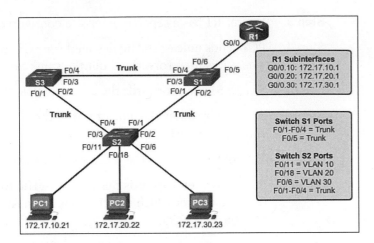

Figure 5-3   Router-on-a-Stick Inter-VLAN Routing

Subinterfaces are software-based virtual interfaces, associated with a single physical interface. Subinterfaces are configured in software on a router and each subinterface is independently configured with an IP address and VLAN assignment. Subinterfaces are configured for different subnets corresponding to their VLAN assignment to facilitate logical routing. After a routing decision is made based on the destination VLAN, the data frames are VLAN-tagged and sent back out the physical interface.

Interactive Graphic

Activity 5.1.1.3: Router-on-a-Stick Inter-VLAN Routing Animation

Go to the online curriculum and click the Play button to view an animation of how a router-on-a-stick performs its routing function.

As shown in the animation and Figure 5-3, the following steps are taken for PC1 on VLAN 10 to communicate with PC3 on VLAN 30.

Step 1.   PC1 on VLAN 10 is communicating with PC3 on VLAN 30 through router R1 using a single, physical router interface.

Step 2.   PC1 sends its unicast traffic to switch S2.

Step 3.   Switch S2 then tags the unicast traffic as originating on VLAN 10 and forwards the unicast traffic out its trunk link to switch S1.

Step 4.   Switch S1 forwards the tagged traffic out the other trunk interface on port F0/5 to the interface on router R1.

Step 5.   Router R1 accepts the tagged unicast traffic on VLAN 10 and routes it to VLAN 30 using its configured subinterfaces.

Step 6.   The unicast traffic is tagged with VLAN 30 as it is sent out the router interface to switch S1.

Step 7. Switch S1 forwards the tagged unicast traffic out the other trunk link to switch S2.

Step 8. Switch S2 removes the VLAN tag of the unicast frame and forwards the frame out to PC3 on port F0/6.

Note

The router-on-a-stick method of inter-VLAN routing does not scale beyond 50 VLANs.

Multilayer Switch Inter-VLAN Routing (5.1.1.4)

The router-on-a-stick implementation of inter-VLAN routing requires only one physical interface on a router and one interface on a switch, simplifying the cabling of the router. However, in other implementations of inter-VLAN routing, a dedicated router is not required.

Multilayer switches can perform Layer 2 and Layer 3 functions, replacing the need for dedicated routers to perform basic routing on a network. Multilayer switches support dynamic routing and inter-VLAN routing.

Interactive Graphic

Activity 5.1.1.4: Switch Inter-VLAN Routing

Go to the online curriculum and click the Play button in the graphic to see an animation of how switch-based inter-VLAN routing occurs.

As shown in the animation and Figure 5-4, communication between PC1 and PC3 stays within the multilayer switch when using it to perform inter-VLAN routing.

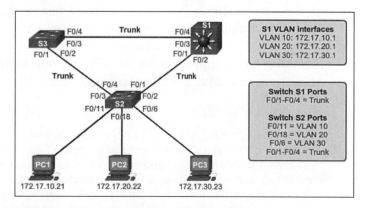

Figure 5-4 Multilayer Switch-Based Inter-VLAN Routing

Step 1. PC1 on VLAN 10 is communicating with PC3 on VLAN 30 through switch S1 using VLAN interfaces configured for each VLAN.

Step 2. PC1 sends its unicast traffic to switch S2.

Step 3. Switch S2 tags the unicast traffic as originating on VLAN 10 as it forwards the unicast traffic out its trunk link to switch S1.

Step 4. Switch S1 removes the VLAN tag and forwards the unicast traffic to the VLAN 10 interface.

Step 5. Switch S1 routes the unicast traffic to its VLAN 30 interface.

Step 6. Switch S1 then retags the unicast traffic with VLAN 30 and forwards it out the trunk link back to switch S2.

Step 7. Switch S2 removes the VLAN tag of the unicast frame and forwards the frame out to PC3 on port F0/6.

Note

To enable a multilayer switch to perform routing functions, the multilayer switch must have IP routing enabled.

Multilayer switching is more scalable than any other inter-VLAN routing implementation. This is because routers have a limited number of available ports to connect to networks. Additionally, for interfaces that are configured as a trunk line, limited amounts of traffic can be accommodated on that interface at one time.

With a multilayer switch, traffic is routed internal to the switch device, which means packets are not filtered down a single trunk line to obtain new VLAN-tagging information. A multilayer switch does not, however, completely replace the functionality of a router. Routers support a significant number of additional features, such as the capability to implement greater security controls. Rather, a multilayer switch can be thought of as a Layer 2 device that is upgraded to have some routing capabilities.

Note

In this course, configuring inter-VLAN routing on a switch is restricted to configuring static routes on a 2960 switch, which is the only routing functionality supported on the 2960 switches. The 2960 switch supports up to 16 static routes (including user-configured routes and the default route) and any directly connected routes and default routes for the management interface; the 2960 switch can have an IP address assigned to each switch virtual interface (SVI). For a full-featured, relatively inexpensive multilayer switch, the Cisco Catalyst 3560 Series switches support the EIGRP, OSPF, and BGP routing protocols.

Interactive Graphic

Activity 5.1.1.5: Identify the Types of Inter-VLAN routing

Go to the online curriculum and click on the first graphic. Select whether the network design uses legacy routing between VLANs, router-on-a-stick, or a multilayer switch to route between VLANs. Do the same for the second and third graphics.

Configure Legacy Inter-VLAN Routing (5.1.2)

Not all routers and router IOS versions support subinterfaces, so take a little time to learn the traditional method of routing each VLAN through a physical router interface.

Configure Legacy Inter-VLAN Routing: Preparation (5.1.2.1)

Legacy inter-VLAN routing requires routers to have multiple physical interfaces. The router accomplishes the routing by having each of its physical interfaces connected to a unique VLAN. Each interface is also configured with an IP address for the subnet associated with the particular VLAN to which it is connected. By configuring the IP addresses on the physical interfaces, network devices connected to each of the VLANs can communicate with the router using the physical interface connected to the same VLAN. In this configuration, network devices can use the router as a gateway to access the devices connected to the other VLANs.

The routing process requires the source device to determine if the destination device is local or remote to the local subnet. The source device accomplishes this by comparing the source and destination IP addresses against the subnet mask. When the destination IP address has been determined to be on a remote network, the source device must identify where it needs to forward the packet to reach the destination device. The source device examines the local routing table to determine where it needs to send the data. Devices use their default gateway as the Layer 2 destination for all traffic that must leave the local subnet. The default gateway is the route that the device uses when it has no other explicitly defined route to the destination network. The IP address of the router interface on the local subnet acts as the default gateway for the sending device.

When the source device has determined that the packet must travel through the local router interface on the connected VLAN, the source device sends out an ARP request to determine the MAC address of the local router interface. When the router sends its ARP reply back to the source device, the source device can use the MAC address to finish framing the packet before it sends it out on the network as unicast traffic.

Because the Ethernet frame has the destination MAC address of the router interface, the switch knows exactly which switch port to forward the unicast traffic out of to reach the router interface for that VLAN. When the frame arrives at the router, the router removes the source and destination MAC address information and examines the destination IP address of the packet. The router compares the destination address to entries in its routing table to determine where it needs to forward the data to reach its final destination. If the router determines that the destination network is another locally connected network, as is the case with inter-VLAN routing, the router sends an ARP request out the interface physically connected to the destination VLAN. The destination device responds back to the router with its MAC address, which the router then uses to frame the packet. (The router frames the packet by adding another header with the MAC address for the router as the Layer 2 source address and the newly discovered MAC address of the destination device.) The router then sends the unicast traffic to the switch, which forwards it out the port where the destination device is connected.

Interactive Graphic

Activity 5.1.2.1: Legacy Inter-VLAN Routing Step-by-Step

Go to the online curriculum and click the Play button in the graphic to view how legacy inter-VLAN routing is accomplished.

Even though there are many steps in the process of inter-VLAN routing, when two devices on different VLANs communicate through a router, the entire process happens in a fraction of a second.

Configure Legacy Inter-VLAN Routing: Switch Configuration (5.1.2.2)

To configure legacy inter-VLAN routing, start by configuring the switch.

As shown in Figure 5-5, router R1 is connected to switch ports F0/4 and F0/5, which have been configured for VLANs 10 and 30, respectively.

```
S1(config)# vlan 10
S1(config-vlan)# vlan 30
S1(config-vlan)# interface f0/11
S1(config-if)# switchport mode access
S1(config-if)# switchport access vlan 10
S1(config-vlan)# interface f0/4
S1(config-if)# switchport mode access
S1(config-if)# switchport access vlan 10
S1(config-vlan)# interface f0/6
S1(config-if)# switchport mode access
S1(config-if)# switchport access vlan 30
```

```
S1(config-vlan)# interface f0/5
S1(config-if)# switchport mode access
S1(config-if)# switchport access vlan 30
S1(config-if)# end
S1# copy running-config startup-config
```

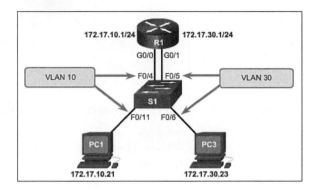

Figure 5-5   Configuring Legacy Inter-VLAN Routing on a Switch

Use the **vlan** *vlan_id* global configuration mode command to create VLANs. In this example, VLANs 10 and 30 were created on switch S1.

After the VLANs have been created, the switch ports are assigned to the appropriate VLANs. The **switchport mode access** and **switchport access vlan** *vlan_id* commands are executed from interface configuration mode on the switch for each interface to which the router connects.

In this example, interfaces F0/4 and F0/11 have been assigned to VLAN 10 using the **switchport access vlan 10** command. The same process is used to assign interface F0/5 and F0/6 on switch S1 to VLAN 30.

Finally, to protect the configuration so that it is not lost after a reload of the switch, the **copy running-config startup-config** command is executed to back up the running configuration to the startup configuration.

Configure Legacy Inter-VLAN Routing: Router Interface Configuration (5.1.2.3)

Next, the router can be configured to perform inter-VLAN routing.

Router interfaces are configured in a manner similar to configuring VLAN interfaces on switches. To configure a specific interface, change to interface configuration mode from global configuration mode.

As shown in Figure 5-6, each interface is configured with an IP address using the **ip address** *ip_address subnet_mask* command in interface configuration mode.

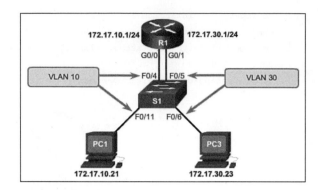

Figure 5-6 Configuring Legacy Inter-VLAN Routing on a Router

```
R1(config)# interface g0/0
R1(config-if)# ip address 172.17.10.1 255.255.255.0
R1(config-if)# no shutdown
*Mar 20 01:42:12.951: %LINK-3-UPDOWN: Interface GigabitEthernet0/0,
    changed state to up
*Mar 20 01:42:13.951: %LINEPROTO-5-UPDOWN: Line protocol on Interface
    GigabitEthernet0/0, changed state to up
R1(config-if)# interface g0/1
R1(config-if)# ip address 172.17.30.1 255.255.255.0
R1(config-if)# no shutdown
*Mar 20 01:25:54.951: %LINK-3-UPDOWN: Interface GigabitEthernet0/1,
    changed state to up
*Mar 20 01:42:55.951: %LINEPROTO-5-UPDOWN: Line protocol on Interface
    GigabitEthernet0/1, changed state to up
R1(config-if)# end
R1# copy running-config startup-config
```

In the example, interface G0/0 is configured with IP address 172.17.10.1 and subnet mask 255.255.255.0 using the **ip address 172.17.10.1 255.255.255.0** command.

Router interfaces are disabled by default and must be enabled using the **no shutdown** command before they are used. After the **no shutdown** interface configuration mode command has been issued, a notification displays, indicating that the interface state has changed to up. This indicates that the interface is now enabled.

The process is repeated for all router interfaces. Each router interface must be assigned to a unique subnet for routing to occur. In this example, the other router interface, G0/1, has been configured to use IP address 172.17.30.1, which is on a different subnet than interface G0/0.

After the IP addresses are assigned to the physical interfaces and the interfaces are enabled, the router is capable of performing inter-VLAN routing. Routes are automatically added to the routing table when a router Ethernet interface is "up and up" and an IP address has been assigned.

Examine the routing table using the **show ip route** command.

In Figure 5-7, there are two routes visible in the routing table. One route is to the 172.17.10.0 subnet, which is attached to the local interface G0/0. The other route is to the 172.17.30.0 subnet, which is attached to the local interface G0/1. The router uses this routing table to determine where to send the traffic it receives. For example, if the router receives a packet on interface G0/0 destined for the 172.17.30.0 subnet, the router would identify that it should send the packet out interface G0/1 to reach hosts on the 172.17.30.0 subnet.

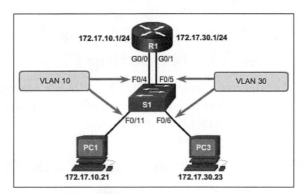

Figure 5-7 Configuring Legacy Inter-VLAN Routing - Routing Table

```
R1# show ip route
Codes:     L - local, C - connected, S - static, R - RIP, M - mobile,
           B - BGP, D - EIGRP, EX - EIGRP external, O - OSPF,
           IA - OSPF inter area, N1 - OSPF NSSA external type 1,
           N2 - OSPF NSSA external type 2, E1 - OSPF external type 1,
           E2 - OSPF external type 2, i - IS-IS, su - IS-IS summary,
           L1 - IS-IS level-1, L2 - IS-IS level-2,
           ia - IS-IS inter area, * - candidate default,
           U - per-user static route, o - ODR,
           P - periodic downloaded static route, H - NHRP, l - LISP,
           + - replicated route, % - next hop override

Gateway of last resort is not set

      172.17.0.0/16 is variably subnetted, 4 subnets, 2 masks
C        172.17.10.0/24 is directly connected, GigabitEthernet0/0
L        172.17.10.1/32 is directly connected, GigabitEthernet0/0
C        172.17.30.0/24 is directly connected, GigabitEthernet0/1
L        172.17.30.1/32 is directly connected, GigabitEthernet0/1
```

Notice the letter C to the left of each of the route entries for the VLANs. This letter indicates that the route is local for a connected interface. Using the output in this example, if traffic were destined for the 172.17.30.0 subnet, the router would forward the traffic out interface G0/1.

Lab 5.1.2.4: Configuring Per-Interface Inter-VLAN Routing

In this lab, you will complete the following objectives:

- Part 1: Build the Network and Configure Basic Device Settings
- Part 2: Configure Switches with VLANs and Trunking
- Part 3: Verify Trunking, VLANs, Routing, and Connectivity

Configure Router-on-a-Stick Inter-VLAN Routing (5.1.3)

Configuring router-on-a-stick inter-VLAN routing is more common then configuring the legacy method that uses one physical interface per VLAN. Routers have a specific number of Ethernet ports and are rarely upgraded to include more.

Configure Router-on-a-Stick: Preparation (5.1.3.1)

Legacy inter-VLAN routing using physical interfaces has a significant limitation. Routers have a limited number of physical interfaces to connect to different VLANs. As the number of VLANs increases on a network, having one physical router interface per VLAN quickly exhausts the physical interface capacity of a router. An alternative in larger networks is to use VLAN trunking and subinterfaces. Remember that a trunk carries multiple VLANs on the same link. VLAN trunking allows a single physical router interface to route traffic for multiple VLANs. This technique is termed router-on-a-stick and uses virtual subinterfaces on the router to overcome the hardware limitations based on physical router interfaces.

Subinterfaces are software-based virtual interfaces that are assigned to physical interfaces. Each subinterface is configured independently with its own IP address and subnet mask. This allows a single physical interface to simultaneously be part of multiple logical networks.

When configuring inter-VLAN routing using the router-on-a-stick model, the physical interface of the router must be connected to a trunk link on the adjacent switch. On the router, subinterfaces are created for each unique VLAN on the network. Each subinterface is assigned an IP address specific to its subnet/VLAN and is also configured to tag frames for that VLAN. This way, the router can keep the traffic from each subinterface separated as it traverses the trunk link back to the switch.

Functionally, the router-on-a-stick model is the same as using the legacy inter-VLAN routing model, but instead of using the physical interfaces to perform the routing, subinterfaces of a single physical interface are used.

In Figure 5-8, PC1 wants to communicate with PC3. PC1 is on VLAN 10 and PC3 is on VLAN 30. For PC1 to communicate with PC3, PC1 must have its data routed through router R1 via subinterfaces.

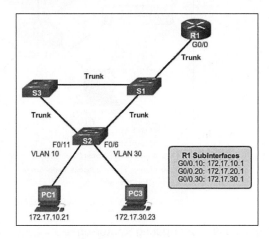

Figure 5-8   Router Subinterfaces and Inter-VLAN Routing

Interactive
Graphic

Activity 5.1.3.1: Router-on-a-Stick Inter-VLAN Routing Step-by-Step

Go to the curriculum and click the Play button in the graphic to see an animation of how subinterfaces are used to route between VLANs. When the animation pauses, read the text to the left of the topology. Click Play again to continue the animation.

Using trunk links and subinterfaces decreases the number of router and switch ports used. Not only can this save money, it can also reduce configuration complexity. Consequently, the router subinterface approach can scale to a much larger number of VLANs than a configuration with one physical interface per VLAN design.

Configure Router-on-a-Stick: Switch Configuration (5.1.3.2)

To enable inter-VLAN routing using router-on-a stick, start by enabling trunking on the switch port that is connected to the router.

In Figure 5-9, router R1 is connected to switch S1 on trunk port F0/5. VLANs 10 and 30 are added to switch S1.

Because switch port F0/5 is configured as a trunk port, the port does not need to be assigned to any VLAN. To configure switch port F0/5 as a trunk port, execute the **switchport mode trunk** command in interface configuration mode for port F0/5.

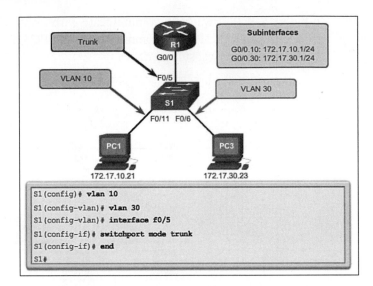

Figure 5-9 Configuring Router-on-a-Stick Inter-VLAN Routing - Switch

Note

The router does not support the Dynamic Trunking Protocol (DTP), which is used by switches, so the following commands cannot be used on a router: **switchport mode dynamic auto** or **switchport mode dynamic desirable**.

The router can now be configured to perform inter-VLAN routing.

Configure Router-on-a-Stick: Router Subinterface Configuration (5.1.3.3)

The configuration of the router is different when a router-on-a-stick configuration is used compared to legacy inter-VLAN routing. Figure 5-10 shows that multiple subinterfaces are configured.

```
R1(config)# interface g0/0.10
R1(config-subif)# encapsulation dot1q 10
R1(config-subif)# ip address 172.17.10.1 255.255.255.0
R1(config-subif)# interface g0/0.30
R1(config-subif)# encapsulation dot1q 30
R1(config-subif)# ip address 172.17.30.1 255.255.255.0
R1(config-subif)# interface g0/0
R1(config-if)# no shutdown
*Mar 20 00:20:59.299: %LINK-3UPDOWN: Interface GigabitEthernet0/0,
changed state to down
```

```
*Mar 20 00:21:02.919: %LINK-3UPDOWN: Interface GigabitEthernet0/0,
changed state to up
*Mar 20 00:21:03.919: %LINEPROTO-5-UPDOWN: Line protocol on Interface
GigabitEthernet0/0, changed state to up
```

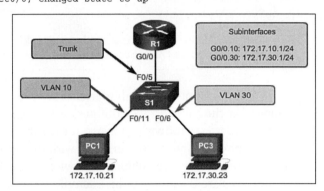

Figure 5-10   Configuring Router-on-a-Stick Inter-VLAN Routing - Router

Each subinterface is created using the **interface** *interface_id*
subinterface_id global configuration mode command. The syntax for the subinterface is the physical interface, in this case **g0/0**, followed by a period and a subinterface number. The subinterface number is configurable, but it typically reflects the VLAN number. In this example, the subinterfaces use **10** and **30** as subinterface numbers to make it easier to remember the VLANs with which they are associated. Subinterface GigabitEthernet0/0.10 is created using the **interface g0/0.10** global configuration mode command.

Before assigning an IP address to a subinterface, the subinterface must be configured to operate on a specific VLAN using the **encapsulation dot1q** *vlan_id* command. In this example, subinterface G0/0.10 is assigned to VLAN 10 so the *vlan_id* argument is **10** (**encapsulation dot1q 10**).

Note

There is a **native** keyword option that can be appended to this command to set the IEEE 802.1Q native VLAN. In this example the **native** keyword option was excluded to leave the native VLAN default to VLAN 1. The particular native VLAN number on the router must always match the native VLAN number assigned on the trunked switch port.

Next, assign the IP address for the subinterface using the **ip address** *ip_address*
subnet_mask subinterface configuration mode command. In this example, subinterface G0/0.10 is assigned the IP address 172.17.10.1 using the **ip address 172.17.10.1 255.255.255.0** command.

This process is repeated for all router subinterfaces required to route between the VLANs configured on the network. Each router subinterface must be assigned an IP address on a unique subnet for routing to occur. For example, the other router sub-interface, G0/0.30, is configured to use IP address 172.17.30.1, which is on a different subnet from subinterface G0/0.10.

Note

A router will not allow subinterfaces to be assigned IP addresses in the same subnetwork. Also, after subinterfaces have been configured, they must be enabled.

Unlike a physical interface, subinterfaces are not enabled with the **no shutdown** command at the subinterface configuration mode level of the Cisco IOS software. Entering the **no shutdown** command at the subinterface level has no effect. Instead, when the physical interface is enabled with the **no shutdown** command, all the configured subinterfaces are enabled. Likewise, if the physical interface is disabled, all subinterfaces are disabled. In this example, the command **no shutdown** is entered in interface configuration mode for interface G0/0, which in turn, enables all of the configured subinterfaces.

After the physical interface has been enabled, the individual subinterfaces can be administratively shut down with the **shutdown** command.

Configure Router-on-a-Stick: Verifying Subinterfaces (5.1.3.4)

By default, Cisco routers are configured to route traffic between local interfaces including local subinterfaces. As a result, routing does not specifically need to be enabled.

In Figure 5-11, the **show vlans** command displays information about the Cisco IOS VLAN subinterfaces. The output shows the two VLAN subinterfaces, Gigabit-Ethernet0/0.10 and GigabitEthernet0/0.30.

Next, examine the routing table using the **show ip route** command (see Figure 5-12).

In Figure 5-12, the routes defined in the routing table indicate that they are associated with specific subinterfaces, rather than separate physical interfaces. There are two routes in the routing table. One route is to the 172.17.10.0 subnet, which is attached to the local subinterface G0/0.10. The other route is to the 172.17.30.0 subnet, which is attached to the local subinterface G0/0.30. The router uses this routing table to determine where to send the traffic it receives. For example, if the router received a packet on subinterface G0/0.10 destined for the 172.17.30.0 subnet, the router would identify that it should send the packet out subinterface G0/0.30 to the 172.17.30.0 subnet.

```
R1# show vlans
<output omitted>
Virtual LAN ID:  10 (IEEE 802.1Q Encapsulation)

  vLAN Trunk Interface:   GigabitEthernet0/0.10

  Protocols Configured:   Address:      Received:   Transmitted:
         IP               172.17.10.1        11            18
<output omitted>
Virtual LAN ID:  30 (IEEE 802.1Q Encapsulation)

  vLAN Trunk Interface:   GigabitEthernet0/0.30

  Protocols Configured:   Address:      Received:   Transmitted:
         IP               172.17.30.1        11             8
<output omitted>
```

Figure 5-11   Verifying Router-on-a-Stick Inter-VLAN Routing - VLANs

```
R1# show ip route
Codes: L - local, C - connected, S - static, R - RIP,M - mobile,
       B - BGP
       D - EIGRP, EX - EIGRP external, O - OSPF,
       IA - OSPF inter area
       N1 - OSPF NSSA external type 1,
       N2 - OSPF NSSA external type 2
       E1 - OSPF external type 1, E2 - OSPF external type 2
       i - IS-IS, su - IS-IS summary, L1 - IS-IS level-1,
       L2 - IS-IS level-2
       ia - IS-IS inter area, * - candidate default,
       U - per-user static route
       o - ODR, P - periodic downloaded static route, H - NHRP,
       l - LISP
       + - replicated route, % - next hop override

Gateway of last resort is not set

    172.17.0.0/16 is variably subnetted, 4 subnets, 2 masks
C      172.17.10.0/24 is directly connected, GigabitEthernet0/0.10
L      172.17.10.1/32 is directly connected, GigabitEthernet0/0.10
C      172.17.30.0/24 is directly connected, GigabitEthernet0/0.30
L      172.17.30.1/32 is directly connected, GigabitEthernet0/0.30
```

Figure 5-12   Verifying Router-on-a-Stick Inter-VLAN Routing - Routing Table

Activity 5.1.3.4: Configuring Router-on-a-Stick Inter-VLAN Routing Step-by-Step

Go to the online curriculum and select the third graphic to use the Syntax Checker to configure and verify router-on-a-stick on R1.

Configure Router-on-a-Stick: Verifying Routing (5.1.3.5)

After the router and switch have been configured to perform inter-VLAN routing, the next step is to verify host-to-host connectivity. Access to devices on remote VLANs can be tested using the **ping** command.

For the example shown in Figure 5-13, a **ping** and a **tracert** are initiated from PC1 to the destination address of PC3.

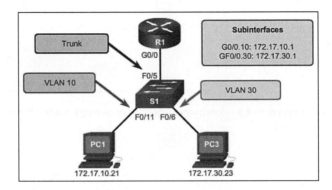

Figure 5-13   Verifying Router-on-a-Stick Inter-VLAN Routing

```
PC1> ping 172.17.30.23

Pinging 172.17.30.23 with 32 bytes of data:

Reply from 172.17.30.23: bytes=32 time=17ms TTL=127
Reply from 172.17.30.23: bytes=32 time=15ms TTL=127
Reply from 172.17.30.23: bytes=32 time=18ms TTL=127
Reply from 172.17.30.23: bytes=32 time=19ms TTL=127

Ping statistics for 172.17.30.23:
     Packets: Sent = 4, Received = 4, lost = 0 (0% loss),
Approximate round trip times in milli-seconds:
     Minimum = 15ms, Maximum = 19ms, Average = 17ms

PC1> tracert 172.17.30.23

Tracing route to 172.17.30.23 over a maximum of 30 hops:

   1    9 ms     7 ms     9 ms     172.17.10.1
   2   16 ms    15 ms    16 ms     172.17.30.23

Trace complete.
```

Ping Test

The **ping** command sends an ICMP echo request to the destination address. When a host receives an ICMP echo request, it responds with an ICMP echo reply to confirm that it received the ICMP echo request. The **ping** command calculates the elapsed time using the difference between the time the echo request was sent and the time the echo reply was received. This elapsed time is used to determine the latency of the connection. Successfully receiving a reply confirms that there is a path between the sending device and the receiving device.

Tracert Test

Tracert is a useful utility for confirming the routed path taken between two devices. On UNIX systems, the utility is specified by **traceroute**. Tracert also uses ICMP to determine the path taken, but it uses ICMP echo requests with specific time-to-live values defined on the frame. The time-to-live value determines exactly how many router hops away the ICMP echo is allowed to reach. The first ICMP echo request is sent with a time-to-live value set to expire at the first router on route to the destination device.

When the ICMP echo request times out on the first route, an ICMP message is sent back from the router to the originating device. The device records the response from the router and proceeds to send out another ICMP echo request, but this time with a greater time-to-live value. This allows the ICMP echo request to traverse the first router and reach the second device on route to the final destination. The process repeats recursively until finally the ICMP echo request is sent all the way to the final destination device. After the **tracert** utility finishes running, it displays a list of ingress router interfaces that the ICMP echo request reached on its way to the destination.

In the example, the **ping** utility was able to send an ICMP echo request to the IP address of PC3. Also, the **tracert** utility confirms that the path to PC3 is through the 172.17.10.1 subinterface IP address of router R1.

<table>
<tr><td>Packet Tracer
□ **Activity**</td><td>**Packet Tracer Activity 5.1.3.6: Configuring Router-on-a-Stick Inter-VLAN Routing**</td></tr>
</table>

In this activity, you will check for connectivity prior to implementing inter-VLAN routing. You will then configure VLANs and inter-VLAN routing. Finally, you will enable trunking and verify connectivity between VLANs.

Lab 5.1.3.7: Configuring 801.2Q Trunk-Based Inter-VLAN Routing

In this lab, you will complete the following objectives:

- Part 1: Build the Network and Configure Basic Device Settings
- Part 2: Configure Switches with VLANs and Trunking
- Part 3: Configure Trunk-Based Inter-VLAN Routing

Troubleshoot Inter-VLAN Routing (5.2)

No task is complete without knowing what common issues might occur and how to verify that a problem is actually fixed. The next few sections examine issues found in both the router and the switch when configuring inter-VLAN routing.

Inter-VLAN Configuration Issues (5.2.1)

Because inter-VLAN routing involves configuring either (1) multiple switch access ports and multiple router interfaces, (2) a switch trunk port and router subinterfaces, or (3) a multilayer switch with routing between VLANs, multiple issues can arise on either the switch or the router. IP addressing misconfigurations might also occur. Switch and router misconfigurations are covered first.

Switch Port Issues (5.2.1.1)

There are several common switch misconfigurations that can arise when configuring routing between multiple VLANs.

When using the legacy routing model for inter-VLAN routing, ensure that the switch ports that connect to the router interfaces are configured with the correct VLANs and are configured for access mode as a security best practice. If a switch port is not configured for the correct VLAN, devices configured on that VLAN cannot connect to the router interface; therefore, those devices are unable to send data to the other VLANs.

As shown in the Figure 5-14 topology, PC1 and router R1 interface G0/0 are configured to be on the same logical subnet, as indicated by their IP address assignment. However, the switch port F0/4 that connects to router R1 interface G0/0 has not been configured and remains in the default VLAN. Because router R1 is on a different VLAN than PC1, they are unable to communicate.

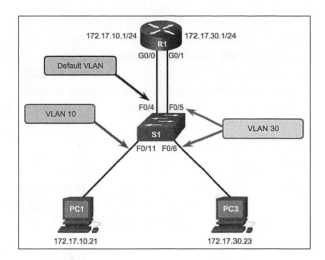

Figure 5-14   Switch Configuration Issues When Using Legacy Inter-VLAN Routing Between VLANs

To correct this problem, execute the **switchport access vlan 10** interface configuration mode command on switch port F0/4 on switch S1. When the switch port is configured for the correct VLAN, PC1 can communicate with router R1 interface G0/0, which allows it to access the other VLANs connected to router R1.

The Figure 5-15 topology shows the router-on-a-stick routing model. However, interface F0/5 on switch S1 is not configured as a trunk and is left in the default VLAN for the port. As a result, the router is unable to route between VLANs because each of its configured subinterfaces is unable to send or receive VLAN-tagged traffic.

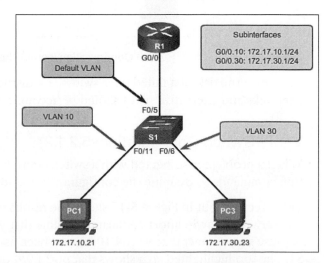

Figure 5-15   A Switch Configuration Issue When Using Router-on-a-Stick

To correct this problem, issue the **switchport mode trunk** interface configuration mode command on switch port F0/5 on S1. This converts the interface to a trunk port, allowing a trunk to be established between R1 and S1. When the trunk is successfully established, devices connected to each of the VLANs are able to communicate with the subinterface assigned to their VLAN, thus enabling inter-VLAN routing. If a problem still exists, check the native VLAN configuration on both the switch trunk port and the appropriate router subinterface. Ensure the native VLAN numbers are the same on both devices.

The Figure 5-16 topology shows the trunk link between S1 and S2 is down. Because there is no redundant connection or path between the devices, all devices connected to S2 are unable to reach router R1. As a result, all devices connected to S2 are unable to route to other VLANs through R1.

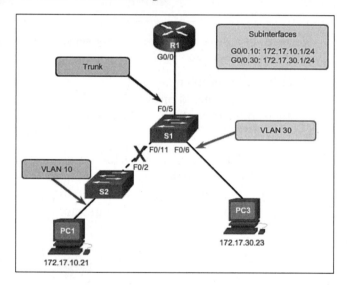

Figure 5-16   Another Switch Configuration Issue When Using Router-on-a-Stick

To reduce the risk of a failed inter-switch link disrupting inter-VLAN routing, redundant links and alternative paths should be accounted for within the network design.

Verify Switch Configuration (5.2.1.2)

When a problem is suspected with a switch configuration, use the various verification commands to examine the configuration and identify the problem.

The screen output in Figure 5-17 shows the results of the **show interfaces** *interface-id* **switchport** command. Assume that you have issued these commands because you suspect that VLAN 10 has not been assigned to port F0/4 on switch S1. The top highlighted area shows that port F0/4 on switch S1 is in access mode, but it does not show that it has been directly assigned to VLAN 10. The bottom highlighted area confirms that port F0/4 is still set to the default VLAN. The **show running-config** and the **show interfaces** *interface-id* **switchport** commands are useful for identifying VLAN assignment and port configuration issues.

```
S1# show interfaces FastEthernet 0/4 switchport
Name: Fa0/4
Switchport: Enabled
Administrative Mode: static access
Operational Mode: up
Administrative Trunking Encapsulation: dot1q
Operational Trunking Encapsulation: native
Negotiation of Trunking: On
Access Mode VLAN: 1 (default)
Trunking Native Mode VLAN: 1 (default)
<output omitted>
S1#
```

Figure 5-17   Incorrect Switch VLAN

The following output shows that after a device configuration has changed, communication between router R1 and switch S1 has stopped. The link between the router and the switch is supposed to be a trunk link. The screen output shows the results of the **show interfaces** *interface_id* **switchport** and the **show running-config** commands. The top highlighted area confirms that port F0/4 on switch S1 is in access mode, not trunk mode. The bottom highlighted area also confirms that port F0/4 has been configured for access mode.

```
S1# show interfaces f0/4 switchport
Name: Fa0/4
Switchport: Enabled
Administrative Mode: static access
Operational Mode: down
Administrative Trunking Encapsulation: dot1q
Operational Trunking Encapsulation: native
<output omitted>

S1# show running-config
Building configuration…
<output omitted>
interface FastEthernet0/4
 switchport mode access
<output omitted>
```

Interface Issues (5.2.1.3)

When enabling inter-VLAN routing on a router, one of the most common configuration errors is to connect the physical router interface to the wrong switch port. This places the router interface in the incorrect VLAN and prevents it from reaching the other devices within the same subnet.

As shown in Figure 5-18, router R1 interface G0/0 is connected to switch S1 port F0/9. Switch port F0/9 is configured for the default VLAN, not VLAN 10. This prevents PC1 from being able to communicate with the router interface. Therefore, it is unable to route to VLAN 30.

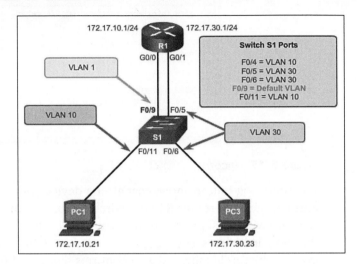

Figure 5-18   Legacy Routing Between VLANs Issues

To correct this problem, physically connect the router R1 interface G0/0 to switch S1 port F0/4. This puts the router interface in the correct VLAN and allows inter-VLAN routing. Alternately, change the VLAN assignment of switch port F0/9 to VLAN 10. This also allows PC1 to communicate with router R1 interface G0/0.

Verify Router Configuration (5.2.1.4)

With router-on-a-stick configurations, a common problem is assigning the wrong VLAN ID to the subinterface.

As shown in Figure 5-19, router R1 has been configured with the wrong VLAN on subinterface G0/0.10, preventing devices configured on VLAN 10 from communicating with subinterface G0/0.10. This subsequently prevents those devices from being able to send data to other VLANs on the network.

Using the **show interfaces** and the **show running-config** commands can be useful in troubleshooting this type of issue, as shown in Figure 5-19.

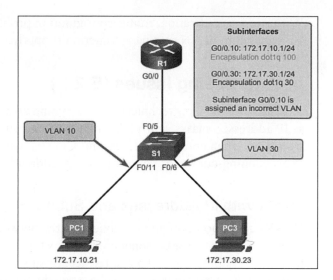

Figure 5-19   Incorrect VLAN on a Router Subinterface

The **show interfaces** command produces a lot of output, making it sometimes difficult to see the problem, as shown in the following output. However, the top highlighted section shows that the subinterface G0/0.10 on router R1 uses VLAN 100.

```
R1# show interfaces
<output omitted>
GigabitEthernet0/0.10 is up, line protocol is down (disabled)
 Encapsulation 802.1Q Virtual LAN, Vlan ID 100
 ARP type: ARPA, ARP Timeout 04:00:00,
 Last clearing of "show interface" counters never
<output omitted>


R1# show running-config
<output omitted>
interface GigabitEthernet0/0.10
 encapsulation dot1q 100
 ip address 172.17.10.1 255.255.255.0
!
interface GigabitEthernet0/0.30
<output omitted>
```

The **show running-config** command confirms that subinterface G0/0.10 on router R1 has been configured to allow access to VLAN 100 traffic and not VLAN 10.

To correct this problem, configure subinterface G0/0.10 to be on the correct VLAN using the **encapsulation dot1q 10** subinterface configuration mode command. When the subinterface has been assigned to the correct VLAN, it is accessible by devices on that VLAN, and the router can perform inter-VLAN routing.

With proper verification, router configuration problems are quickly addressed, allowing inter-VLAN routing to function properly.

IP Addressing Issues (5.2.2)

Students and industry technicians make typing errors when entering numbers such as IP addresses, masks, and VLAN numbers. A technician must be extremely conscientious when entering numbers and knowing what commands to use (besides **show running-config**, of course) to verify addressing-related configurations.

Errors with IP Addresses and Subnet Masks (5.2.2.1)

VLANs correspond to unique subnets on the network. For inter-VLAN routing to operate, a router must be connected to all VLANs, either by separate physical interfaces or by subinterfaces. Each interface, or subinterface, must be assigned an IP address that corresponds to the subnet to which it is connected. This permits devices on the VLAN to communicate with the router interface and enables the routing of traffic to other VLANs connected to the router.

The following are some common IP addressing errors:

- As shown in Figure 5-20, router R1 has been configured with an incorrect IP address on interface G0/0. This prevents PC1 from being able to communicate with router R1 on VLAN 10. To correct this problem, assign the correct IP address to router R1 interface G0/0 using the **ip address 172.17.10.1 255.255.255.0** command. After the router interface has been assigned the correct IP address, PC1 can use the router interface as a default gateway for accessing other VLANs.

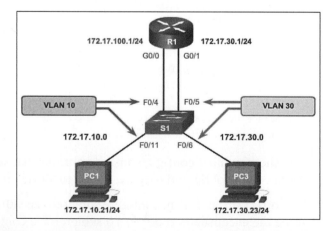

Figure 5-20   IP Addressing Issue with Legacy Routing Between VLANs

- In Figure 5-21, PC1 has been configured with an incorrect IP address for the subnet associated with VLAN 10. This prevents PC1 from being able to communicate with router R1 on VLAN 10. To correct this problem, assign the correct IP address to PC1. Depending on the type of PC being used, the configuration details may be different.

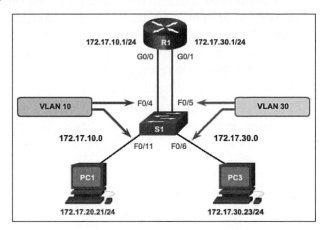

Figure 5-21   Host IP Addressing Issue with Legacy Routing Between VLANs

- In Figure 5-22, PC1 has been configured with the incorrect subnet mask. According to the subnet mask configured for PC1, PC1 is on the 172.17.0.0 network. The result is that PC1 calculates that PC3, with the IP address 172.17.30.23, is on the same subnet as PC1. PC1 does not forward traffic destined for PC3 to router R1 interface G0/0; therefore, the traffic never reaches PC3. To correct this problem, change the subnet mask on PC1 to 255.255.255.0. Depending on the type of PC being used, the configuration details can be different.

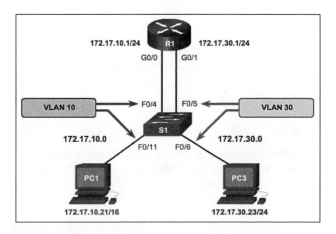

Figure 5-22   IP Addressing Corrected

Verifying IP Address and Subnet Mask Configuration Issues (5.2.2.2)

Each interface, or subinterface, must be assigned an IP address corresponding to the subnet to which it is connected. A common error is to incorrectly configure an IP address for a subinterface. The following output displays the output of the **show running-config** command. The highlighted area shows that subinterface G0/0.10 on router R1 has an IP address of 172.17.20.1. The VLAN for this subinterface should support VLAN 10 traffic. The IP address has been configured incorrectly. The **show ip interface** command is useful in this setting. The second highlight shows the incorrect IP address.

```
R1# show running-config
Building configuration...
<output omitted>
!
interface GigabitEthernet0/0.10
 encapsulation dot1q 10
 ip address 172.17.20.1 255.255.255.0
!
interface GigabitEthernet0/0.30
<output omitted>

R1# show ip interface

<output omitted>

GigabitEthernet0/0.10 is up, line protocol is up

  Internet address is 172.17.20.1/24

  Broadcast address is 255.255.255.255

<output omitted>
```

Sometimes it is the end-user device, such as a personal computer, that is improperly configured. Figure 5-23 shows the displayed IP configuration for PC1. The IP address is 172.17.20.21, with a subnet mask of 255.255.255.0. But in this scenario, PC1 should be in VLAN 10, with an address of 172.17.10.21 and a subnet mask of 255.255.255.0.

Note

Although configuring subinterface IDs to match the VLAN number makes it easier to manage inter-VLAN configuration, it is not a requirement. When troubleshooting addressing issues, ensure that the subinterface is configured with the correct address for that VLAN.

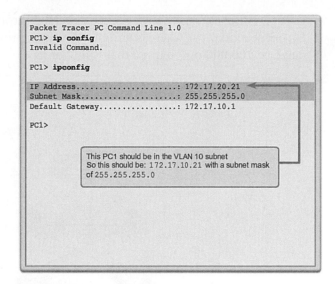

```
Packet Tracer PC Command Line 1.0
PC1> ip config
Invalid Command.

PC1> ipconfig

IP Address.....................: 172.17.20.21
Subnet Mask....................: 255.255.255.0
Default Gateway................: 172.17.10.1

PC1>


            This PC1 should be in the VLAN 10 subnet
            So this should be: 172.17.10.21 with a subnet mask
            of 255.255.255.0
```

Figure 5-23   PC IP Addressing Issue

Activity 5.2.2.3: Identify the Solution to the Inter-VLAN Routing Issue

Go to the online curriculum to select the command used to troubleshoot an inter-VLAN problem. Select each graphic, analyze the output, and select the command that produced the output.

Packet Tracer Activity 5.2.2.4: Troubleshooting Inter-VLAN Routing

In this activity, you will troubleshoot connectivity problems caused by improper configurations related to VLANs and inter-VLAN routing.

Layer 3 Switching (5.3)

Layer 3 switching is the ability for routing to be enabled on a switch. Layer 3 switching is so much easier to configure inter-VLAN routing than either of the other two methods. Layer 3 switching is very common in industry and, as such, those hiring entry-level network professionals expect a technician to have a working knowledge of Layer 3 switches and how to configure them for inter-VLAN routing.

Introduction to Layer 3 Switching (5.3.1.1)

Router-on-a-stick is simple to implement because routers are usually available in every network. As shown in Figure 5-24, most enterprise networks use multilayer switches to achieve high-packet processing rates using hardware-based switching.

Layer 3 switches usually have packet-switching throughputs in the millions of packets per second (pps), whereas traditional routers provide packet switching in the range of 100,000 pps to more than 1 million pps.

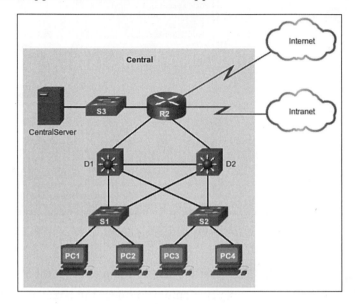

Figure 5-24   Layer 3 Switching in a Corporate Environment

All Catalyst multilayer switches support the following types of Layer 3 interfaces:

- **Routed port:** A pure Layer 3 interface similar to a physical interface on a Cisco IOS router.

- **Switch virtual interface (SVI):** A virtual VLAN interface for inter-VLAN routing. In other words, SVIs are the virtual-routed VLAN interfaces.

High-performance switches, such as the Catalyst 6500 and Catalyst 4500, perform almost every function involving OSI Layer 3 and higher using hardware-based switching that is based on Cisco Express Forwarding.

All Layer 3 Cisco Catalyst switches support routing protocols, but several models of Catalyst switches require enhanced software for specific routing protocol features. Catalyst 2960 Series switches running IOS Release 12.2(55) or later support static routing.

Catalyst switches use different default settings for interfaces. All members of the Catalyst 3560 and 4500 families of switches use Layer 2 interfaces by default. Members of the Catalyst 6500 family of switches running Cisco IOS use Layer 3 interfaces by default. Default interface configurations do not appear in the running or startup configuration. Depending on which Catalyst family of switches is used, the **switchport** or **no switchport** interface configuration mode commands might be present in the running config or startup configuration files.

Inter-VLAN Routing with Switch Virtual Interfaces (5.3.1.2, 5.3.1.3)

In the early days of switched networks, switching was fast (often at hardware speed, meaning the speed was equivalent to the time it took to physically receive and forward frames onto other ports) and routing was slow (routing had to be processed in software). This prompted network designers to extend the switched portion of the network as much as possible. Access, distribution, and core layers were often configured to communicate at Layer 2. This topology created loop issues. To solve these issues, spanning-tree technologies were used to prevent loops while still enabling flexibility and redundancy in inter-switch connections.

However, as network technologies have evolved, routing has become faster and cheaper. Today, routing can be performed at hardware speed. One consequence of this evolution is that routing can be transferred to the core and the distribution layers without impacting network performance.

Many users are in separate VLANs, and each VLAN is usually a separate subnet. Therefore, it is logical to configure the distribution switches as Layer 3 gateways for the users of each access switch VLAN as shown in Figure 5-25. This implies that each distribution switch must have IP addresses matching each access switch VLAN.

Layer 3 (routed) ports (or sometimes called simply *routed ports*) are normally implemented between the distribution and the core layer.

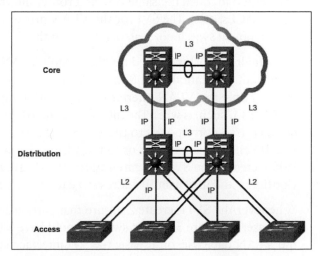

Figure 5-25   Switched Network Design

> **Note**
>
> A Layer 3 (routed) port on a switch does *not* belong to a VLAN; it is *not* configured for access or trunk mode; it *can* be any normal Layer 2 port, but converted to a Layer 3 port and have an IP address assigned.

The network architecture depicted is not dependent on spanning tree because there are no physical loops in the Layer 2 portion of the topology.

An SVI is a virtual interface that is configured within a multilayer switch, as shown in Figure 5-26.

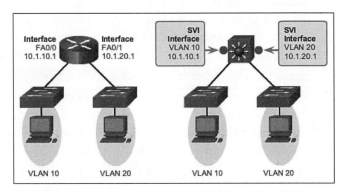

Figure 5-26   Switched Virtual Interfaces

An SVI can be created for any VLAN that exists on the switch. An SVI is considered to be virtual because there is no physical port dedicated to the interface. It can perform the same functions for the VLAN as a router interface would, and can be configured in much the same way as a router interface (i.e., IP address, inbound/outbound ACLs, etc.). The SVI for the VLAN provides Layer 3 processing for packets to or from all switch ports associated with that VLAN.

By default, an SVI is created for the default VLAN (VLAN 1) to permit remote switch administration. Additional SVIs must be explicitly created. SVIs are created the first time the VLAN interface configuration mode is entered for a particular VLAN SVI, such as when the **interface vlan 10** command is entered. The VLAN number used corresponds to the VLAN tag associated with data frames on an 802.1Q encapsulated trunk or to the VLAN ID (VID) configured for an access port. When creating an SVI as a gateway for VLAN 10, name the SVI interface VLAN 10. Configure and assign an IP address to each VLAN SVI.

Whenever the SVI is created, ensure that particular VLAN is present in the VLAN database. In Figure 5-26, the switch should have VLAN 10 and VLAN 20 present in the VLAN database; otherwise, the SVI interface stays down.

The following are some of the reasons to configure an SVI:

- To provide a gateway for a VLAN so that traffic can be routed into or out of that VLAN

- To provide Layer 3 IP connectivity to the switch

- To support routing protocol and bridging configurations

The following are some of the advantages of SVIs (the only disadvantage is that multilayer switches are more expensive):

- It is much faster than router-on-a-stick, because everything is hardware switched and routed.

- No need for external links from the switch to the router for routing.

- Not limited to one link. Layer 2 EtherChannels can be used between the switches to get more bandwidth.

- Latency is much lower, because it does not need to leave the switch.

Inter-VLAN Routing with Routed Ports (5.3.1.4)

Remember that routed ports are commonly used between the distribution and core layer switches in the hierarchical switch design mode. Routed ports are commonly implemented on multilayer switches.

Routed Ports and Access Ports on a Switch

A routed port is a physical port that acts similarly to an interface on a router. Unlike an access port, a routed port is not associated with a particular VLAN. A routed port behaves like a regular router interface. Also, because Layer 2 functionality has been removed, Layer 2 protocols, such as STP, do not function on a routed interface. However, some protocols, such as LACP and EtherChannel, do function at Layer 3.

Unlike Cisco IOS routers, routed ports on a Cisco IOS switch do not support subinterfaces.

Routed ports are used for point-to-point links. Connecting a WAN router or a security device to a switch routed port are examples of how a routed port might be used. In a switched network, routed ports are mostly configured between switches in the core and distribution layer. Figure 5-27 illustrates an example of routed ports in a campus switched network.

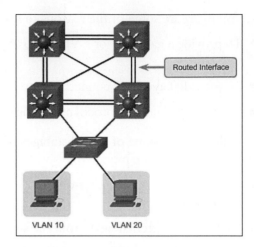

Figure 5-27   Switch Routed Ports

To configure routed ports, use the **no switchport** interface configuration mode command on the appropriate ports. For example, the default configuration of the interfaces on Catalyst 3560 switches are Layer 2 interfaces, so they must be manually configured as routed ports. In addition, assign an IP address and other Layer 3 parameters as necessary to the routed port. After assigning the IP address, verify that IP routing is globally enabled and that applicable routing protocols and/or static routes are configured.

Following are some of the advantages of routed ports:

- A multilayer switch can have SVIs and routed ports in a single switch.

- Multilayer switches forward either Layer 2 or Layer 3 traffic in hardware, helping to perform routing faster.

Note

Routed ports are not supported on Catalyst 2960 Series switches.

Configuring Static Routes on a Catalyst 2960 (5.3.1.5)

A Catalyst 2960 switch can function as a Layer 3 device and route between VLANs and a limited number of static routes.

The Cisco Switch Database Manager (SDM) provides multiple templates for the 2960 switch. The templates can be enabled to support specific roles depending on how the switch is used in the network. For example, the sdm lanbase-routing template can be enabled to allow the switch to route between VLANs and to support static routing.

In Figure 5-28, the **show sdm prefer** command is entered on switch S1, and the default template is applied. The default template is the factory default setting for a Catalyst 2960 switch. The default template does not support static routing. If IPv6 addressing has been enabled, the template will be dual-ipv4-and-ipv6 default.

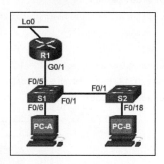

Figure 5-28   Switch Database Manager Template

```
S1# show sdm prefer
 The current template is "default" template.
 The selected template optimizes the resources in
 the switch to support this level of features for
 0 routed interfaces and 255 VLANs.

   number of unicast mac addresses:        8K
   number of IPv4 IGMP groups:             0.25K
   number of IPv4/MAC qos aces:            0.125K
   number of IPv4/MAC security aces:       0.375K
```

The SDM template can be changed in global configuration mode with the **sdm prefer** command.

Note

In Figures 5-29, 5-30, 5-32, and 5-33, the **do** command is used to execute user EXEC or privilege EXEC commands from other router configuration modes.

In Figure 5-29, the SDM template options are displayed with the **sdm prefer ?** command. The SDM template is changed to lanbase-routing. The switch must be reloaded for the new template to take effect.

```
S1# configure terminal
Enter configuration commands, one per line. End with CNTL/Z.
S1(config)# sdm prefer ?
  default               Default bias
  dual-ipv4-and-ipv6    Supports both IPv4 and IPv6
  lanbase-routing       Supports both IPv4 and IPv6 Static Routing
  qos                   QoS bias
```

```
S1(config)# sdm prefer lanbase-routing
Changes to the running SDM preferences have been stored, but cannot
take effect until the next reload.
Use 'show sdm prefer' to see what SDM preference is currently active.
S1(config)# do reload
System configuration has been modified. Save? [yes/no]: yes
Building configuration...
[OK]
Proceed with reload? [confirm]
*Mar 20 00:10:24.557: %SYS-5-RELOAD: Reload requested by console.
Reload Reason: Reload command.
```

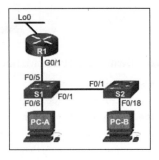

Figure 5-29   Switch SDM Template

In Figure 5-30, the lanbase-routing template is active on S1. With this template, static routing is supported for up to 750 static routes.

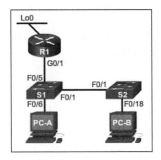

Figure 5-30   2960 Static Route Support

```
S1# show sdm prefer
  The current template is "lanbase-routing" template.
  The selected template optimizes the resources in
  the switch to support this level of features for
  0 routed interfaces and 255 VLANs.

  number of unicast mac addresses:                      4K
  number of IPv4 IGMP groups + multicast routes:        0.25K
  number of IPv4 unicast routes:                        0.75K
```

```
    number of directly-connected IPv4 hosts:          0.75K
    number of indirect IPv4 routes:                   16
  number of IPv6 multicast groups:                    0.375K
  number of directly-connected IPv6 addresses:        0.75K
  number of direct IPv6 unicast routes:               16
  number of IPv4 policy based routing aces:           0
  number of IPv4/MAC qos aces:                        0.125K
  number of IPv4/MAC security aces:                   0.375K
  number of IPv6 policy based routing aces:           0
  number of IPv6 qos aces:                            0.375K
  number of IPv6 security aces:                       127
```

In Figure 5-31, interface F0/6 on S1 is assigned to VLAN 2. The SVIs for VLANs 1 and 2 are also configured with IP addresses 192.168.1.1/24 and 192.168.2.1/24, respectively. IP routing is enabled with the **ip routing** global configuration mode command.

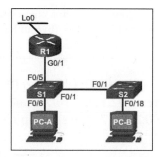

Figure 5-31   Enabling IPv4 Routing Functionality on a 2960 Switch

```
S1(config)# interface f0/6
S1(config-if)# switchport mode access
S1(config-if)# switchport access vlan 2
S1(config-if)# interface vlan 1
S1(config-if)# ip address 192.168.1.1 255.255.255.0
S1(config-if)# interface vlan 2
S1(config-if)# ip address 192.168.2.1 255.255.255.0
S1(config-if)# no shutdown
Mar 20 01:00:25.021: %LINEPROTO-5-UPDOWN: Line protocol on Interface
Vlan2, changed state to up
S1(config)# ip routing
S1(config)# do show ip route

Codes:    L - local, C - connected, S - static, R - RIP, M - mobile,
      B - BGP, D - EIGRP, EX - EIGRP external, O - OSPF,
      IA - OSPF inter area, N1 - OSPF NSSA external type 1,
      N2 - OSPF NSSA external type 2, E1 - OSPF external type 1,
      E2 - OSPF external type 2, i - IS-IS, su - IS-IS summary,
```

```
            L1 - IS-IS level-1,L2 - IS-IS level-2,
            ia - IS-IS inter area, * - candidate default,
            U - per-user static route, o - ODR,
            P - periodic downloaded static route, H - NHRP, 1 - LISP
            + - replicated route, % - next hop override

Gateway of last resort is not set

        192.168.1.0/24 is variably subnetted, 2 subnets, 2 masks
C           192.168.1.0/24 is directly connected, Vlan1
L           192.168.1.1/32 is directly connected, Vlan1
        192.168.2.0/24 is variably subnetted, 2 subnets, 2 masks
C           192.168.2.0/24 is directly connected, Vlan2
L           192.168.2.1/32 is directly connected, Vlan2
```

Note

The **ip routing** command is automatically enabled on Cisco routers; however, the corresponding command for IPv6, **ipv6 unicast-routing**, is disabled, by default, on Cisco routers and switches.

In Figure 5-32, router R1 has two IPv4 networks configured: interface G0/1 has IP address 192.168.1.10/24, and loopback interface Lo0 has IP address 209.165.200.225/27. The **show ip route** command output is displayed.

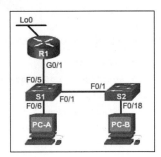

Figure 5-32 Router Participating in Routing with a Switch

```
R1# show ip route

Codes:   L - local, C - connected, S - static, R - RIP, M - mobile,
       B - BGP, D - EIGRP, EX - EIGRP external, O - OSPF,
       IA - OSPF inter area, N1 - OSPF NSSA external type 1,
       N2 - OSPF NSSA external type 2, E1 - OSPF external type 1,
       E2 - OSPF external type 2, i - IS-IS, su - IS-IS summary,
       L1 - IS-IS level-1,L2 - IS-IS level-2,
       ia - IS-IS inter area, * - candidate default,
       U - per-user static route, o - ODR,
```

```
          P - periodic downloaded static route, H - NHRP, 1 - LISP
          + - replicated route, % - next hop override

Gateway of last resort is not set

          192.168.1.0/24 is variably subnetted, 2 subnets, 2 masks
C              192.168.1.0/24 is directly connected, GigabitEthernet0/1
L              192.168.1.10/32 is directly connected, GigabitEthernet0/1
          209.165.200.0/24 is variably subnetted, 2 subnets, 2 masks
C              209.165.200.224/27 is directly connected, Loopback0
L              209.165.200.225/32 is directly connected, Loopback0
```

A default route is configured on S1 in Figure 5-33. The **show ip route** command output is displayed.

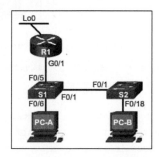

Figure 5-33   Configuring a Static Route on a 2960 Switch

```
S1(config)# ip route 0.0.0.0 0.0.0.0 192.168.1.10
S1(config)# do show ip route

Codes:    L - local, C - connected, S - static, R - RIP, M - mobile,
       B - BGP, D - EIGRP, EX - EIGRP external, O - OSPF,
       IA - OSPF inter area, N1 - OSPF NSSA external type 1,
       N2 - OSPF NSSA external type 2, E1 - OSPF external type 1,
       E2 - OSPF external type 2, i - IS-IS, su - IS-IS summary,
       L1 - IS-IS level-1,L2 - IS-IS level-2,
       ia - IS-IS inter area, * - candidate default,
       U - per-user static route, o - ODR,
       P - periodic downloaded static route, H - NHRP, 1 - LISP
       + - replicated route, % - next hop override

Gateway of last resort is 192.168.1.10 to network 0.0.0.0

S*    0.0.0.0/0 [1/0] via 192.168.1.10
          192.168.1.0/24 is variably subnetted, 2 subnets, 2 masks
C          192.168.1.0/24 is directly connected, Vlan1
L          192.168.1.1/32 is directly connected, Vlan1
```

```
       192.168.2.0/24 is variably subnetted, 2 subnets, 2 masks
C          192.168.2.0/24 is directly connected, Vlan2
L          192.168.2.1/32 is directly connected, Vlan2
```

A static route to the remote network 192.168.2.0/24 (VLAN 2) is configured on R1 in Figure 5-34. The **show ip route** command output is displayed.

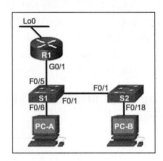

Figure 5-34   Final Routing Table on the Router

```
R1# ip route 192.168.2.0 255.255.255.0 g0/1
R1(config)# do show ip route

Codes:   L - local, C - connected, S - static, R - RIP, M - mobile,
     B - BGP, D - EIGRP, EX - EIGRP external, O - OSPF,
     IA - OSPF inter area, N1 - OSPF NSSA external type 1,
     N2 - OSPF NSSA external type 2, E1 - OSPF external type 1,
     E2 - OSPF external type 2, i - IS-IS, su - IS-IS summary,
     L1 - IS-IS level-1,L2 - IS-IS level-2,
     ia - IS-IS inter area, * - candidate default,
     U - per-user static route, o - ODR,
     P - periodic downloaded static route, H - NHRP, 1 - LISP
     + - replicated route, % - next hop override

Gateway of last resort is not set

     192.168.1.0/24 is variably subnetted, 2 subnets, 2 masks
C        192.168.1.0/24 is directly connected, GigabitEthernet0/1
L        192.168.1.10/32 is directly connected, GigabitEthernet0/1
S    192.168.2.0/24 is directly connected, GigabitEthernet0/1
     209.165.200.0/24 is variably subnetted, 2 subnets, 2 masks
C        209.165.200.224/27 is directly connected, Loopback0
L        209.165.200.225/32 is directly connected, Loopback0
```

In Figure 5-35, PC-A is configured with IP address 192.168.2.2/24 in VLAN 2 and PC-B is configured with IP address 192.168.1.2/24 in VLAN 1. PC-B is able to ping both PC-A and the loopback interface on R1.

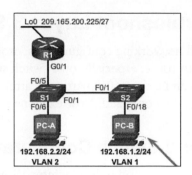

Figure 5-35   Host Connectivity

```
Microsoft Windows [version 6.1.7601]
Copyright <c> 2009 Microsoft Corporation. All rights reserved.
C:\Users\NetAcad> ping 192.168.2.2

Pinging 192.168.2.2 with 32 bytes of data:
Reply from 192.168.2.2: bytes=32 time=2ms TTL=127
Reply from 192.168.2.2: bytes=32 time=1ms TTL=127
Reply from 192.168.2.2: bytes=32 time=1ms TTL=127
Reply from 192.168.2.2: bytes=32 time=1ms TTL=127

Ping statistics for 192.168.2.2:
    Packets: Sent = 4, Received = 4, lost = 0 (0% loss),
Approximate round trip times in milli-seconds:
    Minimum = 1ms, Maximum = 2ms, Average = 1ms


C:\Users\NetAcad> ping 209.165.200.225
Pinging 209.165.200.225 with 32 bytes of data:
Reply from 209.165.200.225: bytes=32 time=2ms TTL=127
Reply from 209.165.200.225: bytes=32 time=1ms TTL=127
Reply from 209.165.200.225: bytes=32 time=1ms TTL=127
Reply from 209.165.200.225: bytes=32 time=1ms TTL=127

Ping statistics for 209.165.200.225:
    Packets: Sent = 4, Received = 4, lost = 0 (0% loss),
Approximate round trip times in milli-seconds:
    Minimum = 1ms, Maximum = 1ms, Average = 1ms
```

Interactive Graphic

Activity 5.3.1.5: Static Routing on a 2960

Go online and click on the ninth graphic in order to use the Syntax Checker to configure static routing on S1.

Troubleshoot Layer 3 Switching (5.3.2)

As in all networking configurations, problems can occur when using a multilayer switch to route, especially on a switch such as the 2960 model where only static routes can be done. Pay particular attention to your static route parameters when entering the command. Now examine some of the other issues that might occur.

Layer 3 Switch Configuration Issues (5.3.2.1)

The issues common to legacy inter-VLAN routing and router-on-a-stick inter-VLAN routing are also manifested in the context of Layer 3 switching. To troubleshoot Layer 3 switching issues, the following items should be checked for accuracy:

- **VLANs:** VLANs must be defined across all the switches. VLANs must be enabled on the trunk ports. Ports must be in the right VLANs.

- **SVIs:** SVI must have the correct IP address or subnet mask. SVI must be up. SVI must match with the VLAN number.

- **Routing:** Routing must be enabled. Each interface or network should be added to the routing protocol.

- **Hosts:** Hosts must have the correct IP address or subnet mask. Hosts must have a default gateway associated with an SVI or routed port.

To troubleshoot the Layer 3 switching problems, be familiar with the implementation and design layout of the topology such as shown in Figure 5-36.

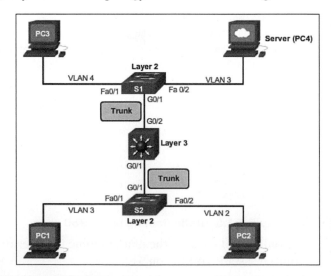

Figure 5-36   Layer 3 Switch Topology

Example: Troubleshooting Layer 3 Switching (5.3.2.2)

Company XYZ is adding a new floor, floor 5, to the network as shown in Figure 5-37. Based on this, the current requirements are to make sure the users on floor 5 can communicate with users on other floors. Currently, users on floor 5 cannot communicate with users on other floors. The following is an implementation plan to install a new VLAN for users on floor 5 and to ensure the VLAN is routing to other VLANs.

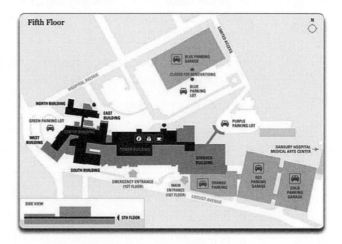

Figure 5-37   Layer 3 Switching Implementation and Troubleshooting Plan

There are four steps to implementing a new VLAN:

Step 1.   Create a new VLAN 500 on the fifth floor switch and on the distribution switches. Name this VLAN.

Step 2.   Identify the ports needed for the users and switches. Set the **switchport access vlan** command to **500** and ensure that the trunk between the distribution switches is properly configured and that VLAN 500 is allowed on the trunk.

Step 3.   Create an SVI interface on the distribution switches and ensure that IP addresses are assigned.

Step 4.   Verify connectivity.

The troubleshooting plan checks for the following:

Step 1.   Verify that all VLANs have been created:

- Was the VLAN created on all the switches?
- Verify with the **show vlan** command.

Step 2.   Ensure that ports are in the right VLAN and trunking is working as expected:

- Did all access ports have the **switchport access VLAN 500** command added?

- Were there any other ports that should have been added? If so, make those changes.

- Were these ports previously used? If so, ensure that there are no extra commands enabled on these ports that can cause conflicts. If not, is the port enabled?

- Are any user ports set to trunks? If so, issue the **switchport mode access** command.

- Are the trunk ports set to trunk mode?

- Is manual pruning of VLANs configured? If so, ensure that the trunks necessary to carry VLAN 500 traffic have the VLAN in the allowed statements.

Step 3.   Verify SVI configurations (if necessary):

- Is the SVI already created with the correct IP address and subnet mask?

- Is it enabled?

- Is routing enabled?

- Is this SVI added in the routing protocol?

Step 4.   Verify connectivity:

- Are all the links between switches in trunk mode?

- Is VLAN 500 allowed on all trunks?

- Is spanning-tree blocking any of the participating links?

- Are the ports enabled?

- Do the hosts have the right default gateways assigned?

- Ensure that the default route or some routing protocol is enabled, if necessary.

Interactive Graphic

Activity 5.3.2.3: Troubleshoot Layer 3 Switching Issues

Go to the online curriculum and look at the Layer 3 topology shown in the first graphic. Click on the second, third, and fourth graphic to see various command outputs and determine the issue.

Lab 5.3.2.4: Troubleshooting Inter-VLAN Routing

In this lab, you will complete the following objectives:

- Part 1: Build the Network and Load Device Configurations

- Part 2: Troubleshoot the Inter-VLAN Routing Configuration

- Part 3: Verify VLAN Configuration, Port Assignment, and Trunking

- Part 4: Test Layer 3 Connectivity

Summary (5.4)

Routing between VLANs is both challenging and fun on a router and/or a multilayer switch. Take a moment to review what you have learned with a class activity, reviewing the main points, and quizzing yourself on critical material.

Class Activity 5.4.1.1: The Inside Track

Your company has just purchased a three-level building. You are the network administrator and must design the company inter-VLAN routing network scheme to serve a few employees on each floor.

Floor 1 is occupied by the HR Department, Floor 2 is occupied by the IT Department, and Floor 3 is occupied by the Sales Department. All Departments must be able to communicate with each other, but at the same time have their own separate working networks.

You brought three Cisco 2960 switches and a Cisco 1941 series router from the old office location to serve network connectivity in the new building. New equipment is non-negotiable.

Refer to the PDF for this activity for further instructions.

Packet Tracer Activity 5.4.1.2: Skills Integration Challenge

In this activity, you will demonstrate and reinforce your ability to implement inter-VLAN routing, including configuring IP addresses, VLANs, trunking, and subinterfaces.

Inter-VLAN routing is the process of routing traffic between different VLANs, using either a dedicated router or a multilayer switch. Inter-VLAN routing facilitates communication between devices isolated by VLAN boundaries.

Legacy inter-VLAN routing depended on a physical router port being available for each configured VLAN. This has been replaced by the router-on-a-stick topology that relies on an external router with subinterfaces trunked to a Layer 2 switch. With the router-on-a-stick option, appropriate IP addressing and VLAN information must be configured on each logical subinterface, and a trunk encapsulation must be configured to match that of the trunking interface of the switch.

Another option is multilayer inter-vlan option using Layer 3 switching. Layer 3 switching involves SVIs and routed ports. Layer 3 switching is normally configured at the distribution and core layers of the hierarchical design model. Layer 3 switching with SVIs is a form of inter-VLAN routing. A routed port is a physical port that acts similarly to an interface on a router. Unlike an access port, a routed port is not associated with a particular VLAN.

Catalyst 2960 switches can be used in multilayer inter-vlan routing. These switches support static routing, but dynamic routing protocols are not supported. SDM templates are required for enabling IP routing on 2960 switches.

Troubleshooting inter-VLAN routing with a router or a Layer 3 switch are similar. Common errors involve VLAN, trunk, Layer 3 interface, and IP address configurations.

Practice

The following activities provide practice with the topics introduced in this chapter. The Labs and Class Activities are available in the companion *Routing and Switching Essentials Lab Manual* (978-1-58713-320-6). You can find the Packet Tracer Activities PKA files in the online course.

Class Activities

Class Activity 5.0.1.2: Switching to Local Network Channels

Class Activity 5.4.1.1: The Inside Track

Labs

Lab 5.1.2.4: Configuring Per-Interface Inter-VLAN Routing

Lab 5.1.3.7: Configuring 801.2Q Trunk-Based Inter-VLAN Routing

Lab 5.3.2.4: Troubleshooting Inter-VLAN Routing

Packet Tracer
☐ Activity

Packet Tracer Activities

Packet Tracer 5.1.3.6: Configuring Router-on-a-Stick Inter-VLAN Routing

Packet Tracer 5.2.2.4: Troubleshooting Inter-VLAN Routing

Packet Tracer 5.4.1.2: Skills Integration Challenge

Check Your Understanding Questions

Complete all the review questions listed here to test your understanding of the topics and concepts in this chapter. The appendix, "Answers to the 'Check Your Understanding' Questions," lists the answers.

1. Classify each item as either physical interface or subinterface.

    _____   one physical interface for many VLANs

    _____   bandwidth contention

    _____   access mode switch port connection

    _____   complex cable configuration

    _____   trunk mode switch port connection

    _____   one physical interface per VLAN

2. Classify each item as either router-on-a-stick, Layer 3 switch routing, or both.

    _____   subinterfaces

    _____   all VLANs share a single cable

    _____   multiple SVIs

    _____   faster

    _____   trunk mode switch port connection

    _____   an IP address per VLAN

    _____   routed port

3. What are three advantages of having a single trunk link on a switch and subinterfaces on the router instead of individual VLAN links between a switch that has three VLANs and a router to route between the VLANs? (Choose three.)

    A. It would free two switch and router ports.

    B. It would reduce the complexity of the cabling runs.

    C. It would increase the amount of bandwidth available for inter-VLAN routing.

    D. It would allow for less complex troubleshooting of inter-VLAN routing issues.

    E. It would allow adding more VLANs without requiring more cabling or switch ports.

    F. It would allow for less-complex configuration of inter-VLAN routing.

4. What condition is required to enable Layer 3 switching?

    A. The Layer 3 switch must have IP routing enabled.

    B. All participating switches must have unique VLAN numbers.

    C. All routed subnets must be on the same VLAN.

    D. Inter-VLAN portions of Layer 3 switching must use router-on-a-stick.

5. When implementing router-on-a-stick, what is necessary for establishing communication between VLANs?

    A. Multiple switch ports to connect to a single router interface

    B. Native VLAN IP address that is configured on the router physical interface

    C. All trunk ports configured in access mode

    D. Router subinterfaces

6. How does the router-on-a-stick model for inter-VLAN routing differ from traditional routing?

    A. The router-on-a-stick model uses multiple physical interfaces on the router, each configured with a different Layer 3 address.

    B. The router-on-a-stick model uses a single physical interface on the router with only the **no shutdown** command issued.

    C. The router-on-a-stick model uses subinterfaces on the router with only the **no shutdown** command issued on the physical interface.

    D. The router-on-a-stick model uses subinterfaces on the switch with only the **no shutdown** command issued on the physical interface.

7. Which command does the network administrator use to determine whether inter-VLAN communication is functioning?

    A. **show vlan**

    B. **ping**

    C. **ipconfig**

    D. **show interfaces**

8. Which three options are valid inter-VLAN routing methods? (Choose three.)

    A. Traditional routing

    B. Spanning-tree routing

    C. Router-on-a-stick

    D. 802.1Q routing

    E. Multilayer switch-based routing

9. A network technician is configuring a router to support inter-VLAN routing. After entering interface G0/0 configuration mode, the network administrator attempts to enter the command **encapsulation dot1q 10**. The router refuses to accept this command. What could account for this failure?

   A. Router port G0/0 is not physically connected to the switch.

   B. VLAN0001 has been renamed.

   C. R1 interface G0/0 was configured for subinterface operation.

   D. This command can be configured only on router subinterfaces.

   E. Interface G0/0 on the switch is shut down.

10. How many physical interfaces are required to perform inter-VLAN routing with each method indicated?

    Legacy inter-VLAN routing: _____

    Router-on-a-stick: _____

    Multilayer switching: _____

11. What command would be used to determine if all SVIs were "up and up" on a multilayer switch?

    A. **show vlans**

    B. **show ip interface brief**

    C. **show running-config**

    D. **show interface switchport**

12. A router-on-a-stick configuration will not allow PC1 on VLAN 10 to communicate with PC2 on VLAN 11. Which two of the following could be the problem? (Choose two.)

    A. The physical port on the router is shut down.

    B. The switch SVI is not "up and up."

    C. The port between the switch and the router is not a routed port.

    D. The port between the switch and the router has been placed in access mode.

    E. One or both of the router subinterfaces have been configured with an IP address in a different network.

CHAPTER 6

Static Routing

Objectives

Upon completion of this chapter, you will be able to answer the following questions:

- What are the advantages and disadvantages of static routing?

- Why are there different types of static routes?

- How do you configure IPv4 and IPv6 static routes by specifying a next-hop address?

- How do you configure an IPv4 and IPv6 Default Route?

- How do you use legacy classful addressing in a network implementation?

- What is the purpose of CIDR and how is it used to replace classful addressing?

- How do you design and implement a hierarchical addressing scheme?

- How do you configure an IPv4 and IPv6 summary network address to reduce the number of routing table updates?

- How do you configure a floating static route to provide a backup connection?

- How does a router process packets when a static route is configured?

- How do you troubleshoot common static and default route configuration issues?

Key Terms

This chapter uses the following key terms. You can find the definitions in the Glossary.

Introduction (6.0.1.1)

Routing is at the core of every data network, moving information across an internetwork from source to destination. *Routers* are the devices responsible for the transfer of packets from one network to the next. Routers learn about remote networks either dynamically using routing protocols, or manually using *static routes*. In many cases, routers use a combination of both dynamic routing protocols and static routes. This chapter focuses on static routing. Static routes are very common and do not require the same amount of processing and overhead as dynamic routing protocols.

In this chapter, sample topologies will be used to configure IPv4 and IPv6 static routes and to present troubleshooting techniques. In the process, several important IOS commands and the resulting output will be examined. An introduction to the routing table using both directly connected networks and static routes will be included.

This chapter will also contrast classful routing and the widely implemented classless routing methods. It will cover *Classless Inter-Domain Routing (CIDR)* and the *variable-length subnet mask (VLSM)* methods. CIDR and VLSM have helped conserve the IPv4 address space using subnetting and summarization techniques.

Class Activity 6.0.1.2: Which Way Should We Go

A huge sporting event is about to take place in your city. To attend the event, you make concise plans to arrive at the sports arena on time to see the entire game. There are two routes you can take to drive to the event:

- **Highway route:** It is easy to follow, and fast driving speeds are allowed.

- **Alternative, direct route:** You found this route using a city map. Depending on conditions, such as the amount of traffic or congestion, this just may be the way to get to the arena on time!

With a partner, discuss these options. Choose a preferred route to arrive at the arena in time to see every second of the huge sporting event.

Compare your optional preferences to network traffic, which route would you choose to deliver data communications for your small- to medium-sized business? Would it be the fastest, easiest route or the alternative, direct route? Justify your choice.

Complete the modeling activity .pdf found in the online course and be prepared to justify your answers to the class or with another group.

Static Routing (6.1.1)

Static routes are user-defined routes that cause packets moving between a source and a destination to take a specific path.

Reach Remote Networks (6.1.1.1)

A router can learn about remote networks in one of two ways:

- **Manually:** Remote networks are manually entered into the route table using static routes.

- **Dynamically:** Remote routes are automatically learned using a dynamic routing protocol.

Figure 6-1 provides a sample scenario of static routing.

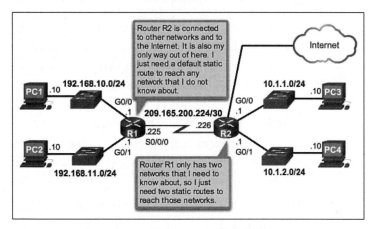

Figure 6-1   Static and Default Route Scenario

A network administrator can manually configure a static route to reach a specific network. Unlike a dynamic routing protocol, static routes are not automatically updated and must be manually reconfigured any time the network topology changes. A static route does not change until the administrator manually reconfigures it.

Why Use Static Routing? (6.1.1.2)

Static routing provides some advantages over dynamic routing, including:

- Static routes are not advertised over the network, resulting in better security.

- Static routes use less bandwidth than dynamic routing protocols; no CPU cycles are used to calculate and communicate routes.

- The path a static route uses to send data is known.

Static routing has the following disadvantages:

- Initial configuration and maintenance is time-consuming.

- Configuration is error-prone, especially in large networks.

Administrator intervention is required to maintain changing route information.

Does not scale well with growing networks; maintenance becomes cumbersome.

Requires complete knowledge of the whole network for proper implementation.

In Table 6-1, dynamic and static routing features are compared. Notice that the advantages of one method are the disadvantages of the other.

Table 6-1 Dynamic versus Static Routing

	Dynamic Routing	**Static Routing**
Configuration Complexity	Generally independent of the network size	Increases with network size
Topology Changes	Automatically adapts to topology changes	Administrator intervention required
Scaling	Suitable for simple and complex topologies	Suitable for simple topologies
Security	Less secure	More secure
Resource Usage	Uses CPU, memory, and link bandwidth	No extra resources needed
Predictability	Route depends on the current topology	Route to destination is always the same

Static routes are useful for smaller networks with only one path to an outside network. They also provide security in a larger network for certain types of traffic or links to other networks that need more control. It is important to understand that static and dynamic routing are not mutually exclusive. Rather, most networks use a combination of dynamic routing protocols and static routes. This may result in the router having multiple paths to a destination network via static routes and dynamically learned routes. However, the *administrative distance (AD)* of a static route is 1. Therefore, a static route will take precedence over all dynamically learned routes.

When to Use Static Routes (6.1.1.3)

Static routing has three primary uses:

- Providing ease of routing table maintenance in smaller networks that are not expected to grow significantly.

- Routing to and from stub networks. A *stub network* is a network accessed by a single route, and the router has only one neighbor.

- Using a single default route to represent a path to any network that does not have a more specific match with another route in the routing table. Default routes are used to send traffic to any destination beyond the next upstream router.

Figure 6-2 shows an example of a stub network connection and a default route connection. Notice in the figure that any network attached to R1 would have only one way to reach other destinations, whether to networks attached to R2 or to destinations beyond R2. This means that network 172.16.3.0 is a stub network and R1 is a *stub router*. Running a routing protocol between R2 and R1 is a waste of resources.

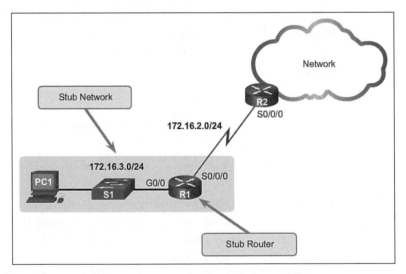

Figure 6-2   Stub Networks and Stub Routers

In this example, a static route can be configured on R2 to reach the R1 LAN. Additionally, because R1 has only one way to send out non-local traffic, a *default static route* can be configured on R1 to point to R2 as the *next hop* for all other networks.

Interactive Graphic

Activity 6.1.1.4: Identify the Advantages and Disadvantages of Static Routing

Go to the course online to perform this activity identifying advantages and disadvantages of static routing.

Types of Static Routes

There are several types of static routes which all have different uses. This section describes the different kinds of static routes and where they are to be used.

Static Route Applications (6.1.2.1)

Static routes are most often used to connect to a specific network or to provide a *Gateway of Last Resort* for a stub network. They can also be used to:

- Reduce the number of routes advertised by summarizing several contiguous networks as one static route

- Create a backup route in case a primary route link fails

The following types of IPv4 and IPv6 static routes will be discussed:

- Standard static route

- Default static route

- *Summary static route*

- *Floating static route*

Standard Static Route (6.1.2.2)

Both IPv4 and IPv6 support the configuration of static routes. Static routes are useful when connecting to a specific remote network.

- Figure 6-3 shows that R2 can be configured with a static route to reach the stub network 172.16.3.0/24.

Figure 6-3 is highlighting a stub network, but in fact, a static route can be used to connect to any network.

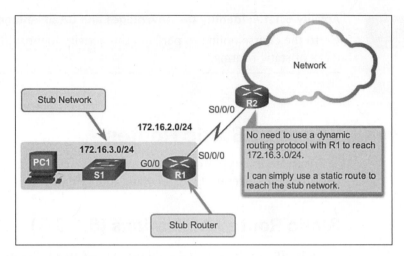

Figure 6-3   Connecting to a Stub Network

Default Static Route (6.1.2.3)

A default static route is a route that matches all packets. A default route identifies the gateway IP address to which the router sends all IP packets that it does not have a learned or static route. A default static route is simply a static route with 0.0.0.0/0 as the destination IPv4 address. Configuring a default static route creates a Gateway of Last Resort.

Note

All routes that identify a specific destination with a larger subnet mask take precedence over the default route.

Default static routes are used

- When no other routes in the routing table match the packet destination IP address. In other words, when a more specific match does not exist. A common use is when connecting a company's edge router to the ISP network.

- When a router has only one other router to which it is connected. This condition is known as a stub router.

Summary Static Route (6.1.2.4)

To reduce the number of routing table entries, multiple static routes can be summarized into a single static route if

- The destination networks are contiguous and can be summarized into a single network address.

- The multiple static routes all use the same *exit interface* or next-hop IP address.

In Figure 6-4, R1 would require four separate static routes to reach the 172.20.0.0/16 to 172.23.0.0/16 networks. Instead, one summary static route can be configured and still provide connectivity to those networks.

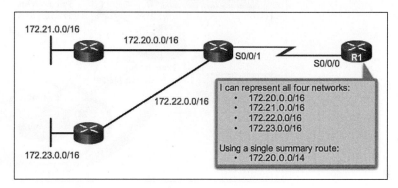

Figure 6-4   Using One Summary Static Route

Floating Static Route (6.1.2.5)

Another type of static route is a floating static route. Floating static routes are static routes that are used to provide a backup path to a primary static or *dynamic route*, in the event of a link failure. The floating static route is only used when the primary route is not available.

To accomplish this, the floating static route is configured with a higher administrative distance than the primary route. Recall that the administrative distance represents the trustworthiness of a route. If multiple paths to the destination exist, the router will choose the path with the lowest administrative distance.

For example, assume that an administrator wants to create a floating static route as a backup to an EIGRP-learned route. The floating static route must be configured with a higher administrative distance than EIGRP. EIGRP has an administrative distance of 90. If the floating static route is configured with an administrative distance of 95, the dynamic route learned through EIGRP is preferred to the floating static route. If the EIGRP-learned route is lost, the floating static route is used in its place.

In Figure 6-5, the *Branch router* typically forwards all traffic to the *HQ router* over the private WAN link.

In this example, the routers exchange route information using EIGRP. A floating static route, with an administrative distance of 91 or higher, could be configured to serve as a backup route. If the private WAN link fails and the EIGRP route disappears from the routing table, the router selects the floating static route as the best path to reach the HQ LAN.

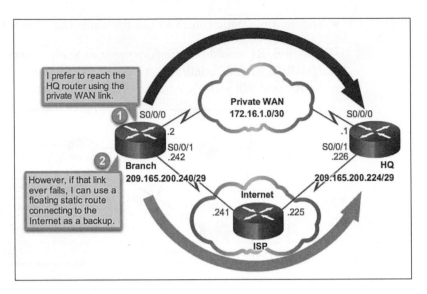

Figure 6-5   Configuring a Backup Route

Activity 6.1.2.6: Identify the Type of Static Route

Go to the course online to perform this activity identifying the type of static route being used.

Configure IPv4 Static Routes (6.2.1)

This section deals with the **ip route** command and how it is used to create static routes.

ip route **Command (6.2.1.1)**

Static routes are configured using the **ip route** global configuration command. The syntax of the command is:

```
Router(config)# ip route network-address subnet-mask {ip-address|interface-type
    interface-number[ip-address]} [distance] [name name] [permanent] [tagtag]
```

The following parameters are required to configure static routing:

- *network-address*: Destination network address of the remote network to be added to the routing table, often this is referred to as the prefix.

- *subnet-mask*: *Subnet mask*, or just mask, of the remote network to be added to the routing table. The subnet mask can be modified to summarize a group of networks.

One or both of the following parameters must also be used:

- *ip-address*: The IP address of the connecting router to use to forward the packet to the remote destination network. Commonly referred to as the next hop.

- *exit-intf*: The outgoing interface to use to forward the packet to the next hop.

Table 6-2 highlights the different parameters of the **ip route** command and gives a brief description of these parameters.

Table 6-2   ip route Command Syntax

Parameter	Description
network-address	Destination network address of the remote network to be added to the routing table
subnet-mask	<ul><li>Subnet mask of the remote network to be added to the routing table</li><li>The subnet mask can be modified to summarize a group of networks</li></ul>
ip-address	<ul><li>Commonly referred to as the next-hop router's IP address</li><li>Typically used when connecting to a broadcast media (i.e., Ethernet).</li><li>Commonly creates a *recursive lookup*</li></ul>
exit-intf	<ul><li>Use the outgoing interface to forward packets to the destination network</li><li>Also referred to as a directly attached static route</li><li>Typically used when connecting in a point-to-point configuration</li></ul>

The command syntax commonly used is

```
ip route network-address subnet-mask {ip-address | exit-intf}
```

The *distance* parameter is used to create a floating static route by setting an administrative distance that is higher than a dynamically learned route. The remaining parameters are not relevant for this chapter or for CCNA studies.

Next-Hop Options (6.2.1.2)

Figures 6-6, 6-7, and 6-8 show the routing tables of Routers R1, R2, and R3.

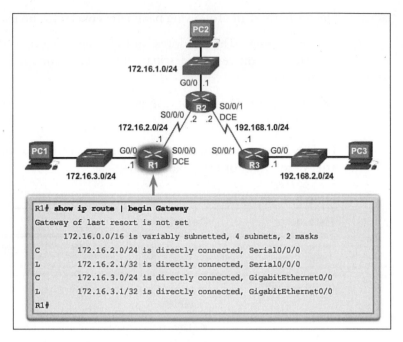

Figure 6-6 Routing Table of R1

First you have R1's routing table.

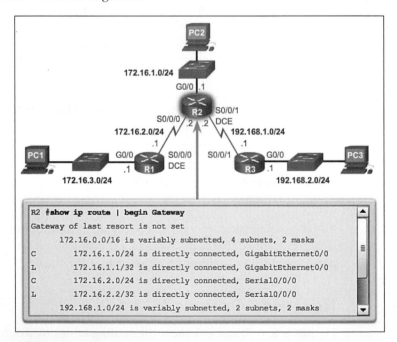

Figure 6-7 Routing Table of R2

Then you have R2's routing table.

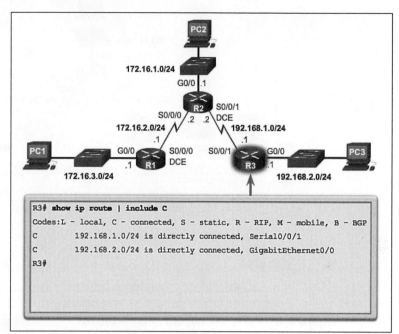

Figure 6-8   Routing Table of R3

Finally you have the routing table for R3.

In this example, Figures 6-6 through 6-8 display the routing tables of R1, R2, and R3. Notice that each router has entries only for directly connected networks and their associated local addresses. None of the routers have any knowledge of any networks beyond their directly connected interfaces.

For example, R1 has no knowledge of networks

- 172.16.1.0/24: LAN on R2

- 192.168.1.0/24: Serial network between R2 and R3

- 192.168.2.0/24: LAN on R3

Figure 6-9 displays a successful ping from R1 to R2

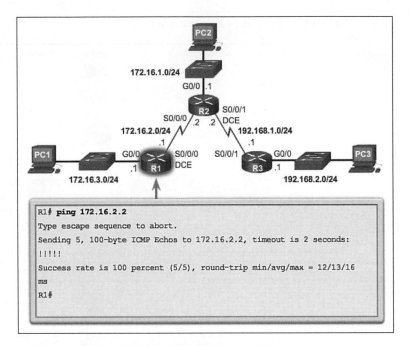

Figure 6-9 Verify Connectivity from R1 to R2

Figure 6-10 displays an unsuccessful ping to the R3 LAN. This is because R1 does not have an entry in its routing table for the R3 LAN network.

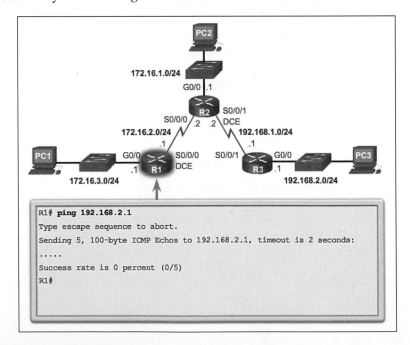

Figure 6-10 Verify Connectivity from R1 to the R3 LAN

The next hop can be identified by an IP address, exit interface, or both. How the destination is specified creates one of the three following route types:

- **Next-hop route:** Only the next-hop IP address is specified.

- *Directly connected static route*: Only the router exit interface is specified.

- *Fully specified static route*: The next-hop IP address and exit interface are specified.

Configure a Next-Hop Static Route (6.2.1.3)

In a next-hop static route, only the next-hop IP address is specified. The output interface is derived from the next hop.

In Figure 6-11, three next-hop static routes are configured on R1 using the IP address of the next hop, R2.

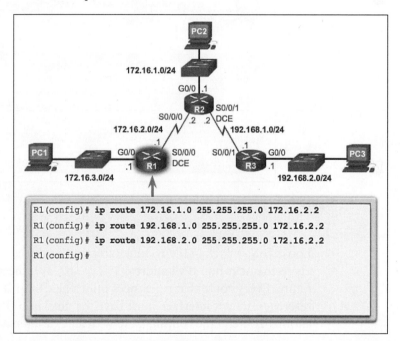

Figure 6-11   Configuring Next-Hop Static Routes on R1

Before any packet is forwarded by a router, the routing table process must determine the exit interface to use to forward the packet. This is known as route resolvability. The route resolvability process will vary depending upon the type of forwarding mechanism being used by the router. CEF (Cisco Express Forwarding) is the default behavior on most platforms running IOS 12.0 or later.

Interactive Graphic

Activity 6.2.1.3: Verify the Routing Table of R1

Go to the course online, and use the slider bar in the second graphic to see the entire output of the **show ip route** command.

Figure 6-12 details the basic packet-forwarding process in the routing table for R1 without the use of CEF.

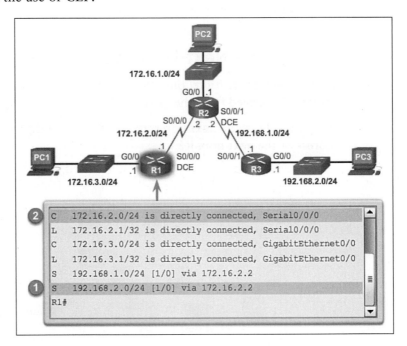

Figure 6-12   Verifying the Routing Table of R1

When a packet is destined for the 192.168.2.0/24 network, R1

1. Looks for a match in the routing table and finds that it has to forward the packets to the next-hop IPv4 address 172.16.2.2, as indicated by the label 1 in the figure. Every route that references only a next-hop IPv4 address and does not reference an exit interface must have the next-hop IPv4 address resolved using another route in the routing table with an exit interface.

2. R1 must now determine how to reach 172.16.2.2; therefore, it searches a second time for a 172.16.2.2 match. In this case, the IPv4 address matches the route for the directly connected network 172.16.2.0/24 with the exit interface Serial 0/0/0, as indicated by the label 2 in the figure. This lookup tells the routing table process that this packet is forwarded out of that interface.

It actually takes two routing table lookup processes to forward any packet to the 192.168.2.0/24 network. When the router performs multiple lookups in the routing table before forwarding a packet, it is performing a process known as a recursive lookup. Because recursive lookups consume router resources, they should be avoided when possible.

A recursive static route is valid (that is, it is a candidate for insertion in the routing table) only when the specified next hop resolves, either directly or indirectly, to a valid exit interface.

NOTE

CEF provides optimized lookup for efficient packet forwarding by using two main data structures stored in the data plane: a *Forwarding Information Base (FIB)*, which is a copy of the routing table and an adjacency table that includes Layer 2 addressing information. The information combined in both of these tables work together, so there is no recursive lookup needed for next-hop IP address lookups. In other words, a static route using a next-hop IP requires only a single lookup when CEF is enabled on the router.

Interactive
Graphic

Activity 6.2.1.3 Part 1: Configure Next-Hop Static Routes on R2

Go to the course online to use the Syntax Checker in the third graphic to configure next-hop static routes on router R2.

Interactive
Graphic

Activity 6.2.1.3 Part 2: Configure Next-Hop Static Routes on R3

Go to the course online to use the Syntax Checker in the fourth graphic to configure next-hop static routes on router R2.

Configure a Directly Connected Static Route (6.2.1.4)

When configuring a static route, another option is to use the exit interface to specify the next-hop address. In older IOS versions, prior to CEF, this method is used to avoid the recursive lookup problem.

Figure 6-13 shows three directly connected static routes are configured on R1 using the exit interface.

The routing table for R1 in Figure 6-14 shows that when a packet is destined for the 192.168.2.0/24 network, R1 looks for a match in the routing table, and finds that it can forward the packet out of its Serial 0/0/0 interface. No other lookups are required.

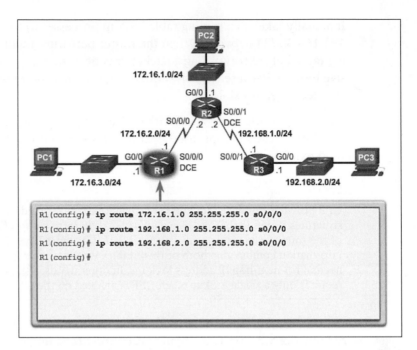

Figure 6-13   Configure Directly Connected Static Routes on R1

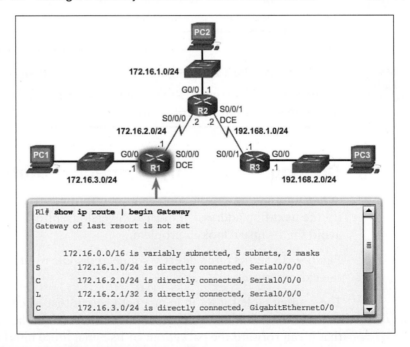

Figure 6-14   Verify the Routing Table of R1

Activity 6.2.1.4 Part 1: Verify the Routing Table of R1

Go to the course online to use the slider bar in the second graphic to see the entire output of the **show ip route | begin Gateway** command.

Notice how the routing table looks different for the route configured with an exit interface than the route configured with a recursive entry.

Configuring a directly connected static route with an exit interface allows the routing table to resolve the exit interface in a single search, instead of two searches. Although the routing table entry indicates "directly connected," the administrative distance of the static route is still 1. Only a directly connected interface can have an administrative distance of 0.

> **Note**
>
> For *point-to-point interfaces*, you can use static routes that point to the exit interface or to the next-hop address. For *multipoint/broadcast interfaces*, it is more suitable to use static routes that point to a next-hop address.

Activity 6.2.1.4 Part 2: Configure Directly Connected Static Routes on R2

Go to the course online to use the Syntax Checker in the third graphic to create a static route using an exit interface.

Activity 6.2.1.4 Part 3: Configure Directly Connected Static Routes on R3

Go to the course online to use the Syntax Checker in the fourth graphic to create a static route using an exit interface.

Although static routes that use only an exit interface on point-to-point networks are common, the use of the default CEF forwarding mechanism makes this practice unnecessary.

Configure a Fully Specified Static Route (6.2.1.5)

In a fully specified static route, both the output interface and the next-hop IP address are specified. This is another type of static route that is used in older IOSs, prior to CEF. This form of static route is used when the output interface is a multi-access interface and it is necessary to explicitly identify the next hop. The next hop must be directly connected to the specified exit interface.

As shown in Figure 6-15, suppose that the network link between R1 and R2 is an Ethernet link and that the GigabitEthernet 0/1 interface of R1 is connected to that network. CEF is not enabled.

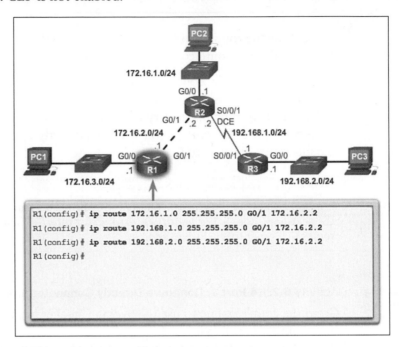

Figure 6-15 Configure Fully Specified Static Routes on R1

To eliminate the recursive lookup, a directly connected static route can be implemented using the following command:

```
R1(config)# ip route 192.168.2.0 255.255.255.0 GigabitEthernet 0/1
```

However, this may cause unexpected or inconsistent results. The difference between an Ethernet multi-access network and a point-to-point serial network is that a point-to-point network has only one other device on that network, the router at the other end of the link. With Ethernet networks, there may be many different devices sharing the same multi-access network, including hosts and even multiple routers. By only designating the Ethernet exit interface in the static route, the router will not have sufficient information to determine which device is the next-hop device.

R1 knows that the packet needs to be encapsulated in an Ethernet frame and sent out the GigabitEthernet 0/1 interface. However, R1 does not know the next-hop IPv4 address and therefore it cannot determine the destination MAC address for the Ethernet frame.

Depending upon the topology and the configurations on other routers, this static route may or may not work. It is recommended that when the exit interface is an

Ethernet network, that a fully specified static route is used including both the exit interface and the next-hop address.

As shown in Figure 6-16, when forwarding packets to R2, the exit interface is GigabitEthernet 0/1 and the next-hop IPv4 address is 172.16.2.2.

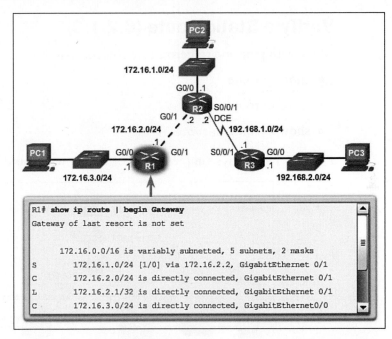

Figure 6-16   Verify the Routing Table of R1

Activity 6.2.1.5 Part 1: Configure a Fully Specified Static Route

Go to the course online to use the slider bar in the second graphic to see the entire output of the **show ip route | begin Gateway** command.

> **Note**
>
> With the use of CEF, a fully specified static route is no longer necessary. A static route using a next-hop address should be used.

Activity 6.2.1.5 Part 2: Configure Fully Specified Static Routes on R2

Go to the course online to use the Syntax Checker in the third graphic to create a fully specified static route.

Interactive Graphic

Activity 6.2.1.5 Part 3: Configure Fully Specified Static Routes on R3

Go to the course online to use the Syntax Checker in the fourth graphic to create a fully specified static route.

Verify a Static Route (6.2.1.6)

Along with **ping** and **traceroute**, useful commands to verify static routes include

- **show ip route**
- **show ip route static**
- **show ip route** *network*

Figure 6-17 displays sample output of the **show ip route static** command.

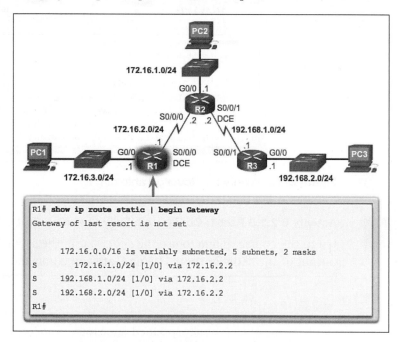

Figure 6-17 Verify the Routing Table of R1

In the example, the output is filtered using the pipe and **begin** parameter. The output reflects the use of static routes using the next-hop address. Figure 6-18 displays sample output of the **show ip route 192.168.2.1** command.

Figure 6-19 verifies the **ip route** configuration in the running configuration.

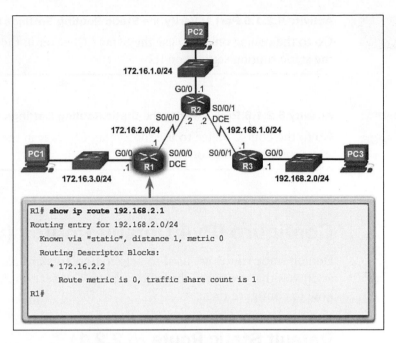

Figure 6-18   Verify a Specific Entry in the Routing Table of R1

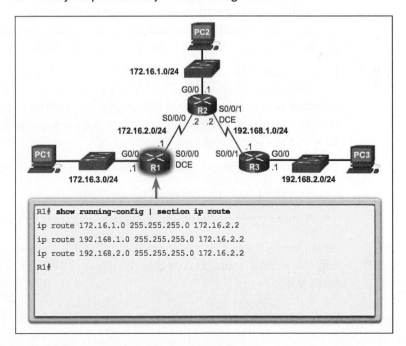

Figure 6-19   Verify the Static Route Configuration

Interactive Graphic

Activity 6.2.1.6 Part 1: Verify the Static Routing Settings on R2

Go to the course online to use the Syntax Checker in the fourth graphic to verify the static routing settings on R2

Interactive Graphic

Activity 6.2.1.6 Part 2: Verify the Static Routing Settings on R3

Go to the course online to use the Syntax Checker in the fifth graphic to verify the static routing settings on R3.

Configure IPv4 Default Routes (6.2.2)

Default static routes are used to help routers forward packets that have destination addresses that are not in the routing table. This section describes static routes and how to configure them.

Default Static Route (6.2.2.1)

A default route is a static route that matches all packets. Rather than storing all routes to all networks in the routing table, a router can store a single default route to represent any network that is not in the routing table.

Routers commonly use default routes that are either configured locally or learned from another router, using a dynamic routing protocol. A default route is used when no other routes in the routing table match the destination IP address of the packet. In other words, if a more specific match does not exist, then the default route is used as the Gateway of Last Resort.

Default static routes are commonly used when connecting

- An edge router to a service provider network

- A stub router (a router with only one upstream neighbor router)

As shown in Table 6-3, the command syntax for a default static route is similar to any other static route, except that the network address is `0.0.0.0` and the subnet mask is `0.0.0.0`.

Table 6-3 Default Static Route Syntax

Router(config)#**ip route 0.0.0.0 0.0.0.0** *{ip address | exit-intf }*

Parameter	Description
0.0.0.0	Matches any network address
0.0.0.0	Matches any subnet mask
ip-address	▪ Commonly referred to as the next-hop router's IP address ▪ Typically used when connecting to a broadcast media (i.e., Ethernet). ▪ Commonly creates a recursive lookup
exit-intf	▪ Use the outgoing interface to forward packets to the destination network ▪ Also referred to as a directly attached static route ▪ Typically used when connecting in a point-to-point configuration

The basic command syntax of a default static route is

ip route 0.0.0.0 0.0.0.0 *{ip-address| exit-intf}*

Note

An IPv4 default static route is commonly referred to as a *quad-zero route*.

Configure a Default Static Route (6.2.2.2)

In Figure 6-20, R1 can be configured with three static routes to reach all of the remote networks in the example topology. However, R1 is a stub router because it is connected only to R2. Therefore, it would be more efficient to configure a default static route.

The example in Figure 6-20 configures a default static route on R1. With the configuration shown in the example, any packets not matching more specific route entries are forwarded to 172.16.2.2.

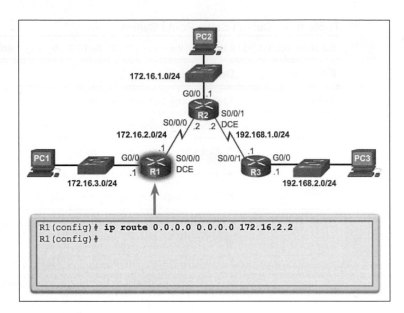

Figure 6-20   Configuring a Default Static Route

Verify a Default Static Route (6.2.2.3)

In Figure 6-21, the **show ip route static** command output displays the contents of the routing table. Note the asterisk (*) next to the route with code 's'. As displayed in the Codes table in the figure, the asterisk indicates that this static route is a candidate default route, which is why it is selected as the Gateway of Last Resort.

Activity 6.2.2.3: Verifying the Routing Table of R1

Go to the course online, and use the slider bar in the graphic to see the entire output of the **show ip route static** command.

The key to this configuration is the /0 mask. Recall that the subnet mask in a routing table determines how many bits must match between the destination IP address of the packet and the route in the routing table. A binary 1 indicates that the bits must match. A binary 0 indicates that the bits do not have to match. A /0 mask in this route entry indicates that none of the bits are required to match. The default static route matches all packets for which a more specific match does not exist.

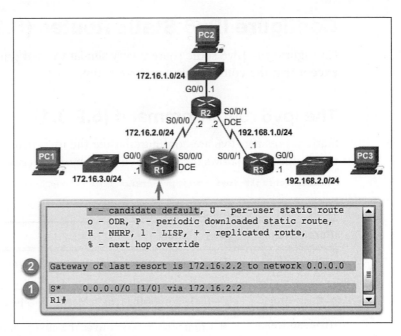

Figure 6-21   Verifying the Routing Table of R1

Packet Tracer Activity 6.2.2.4: Configuring IPv4 Static and Default Routes

Background/Scenario

In this activity, you will configure static and default routes. A static route is a route that is entered manually by the network administrator to create a route that is reliable and safe. There are four different static routes that are used in this activity: a recursive static route, a directly connected static route, a fully specified static route, and a default route.

Go to the course online to complete this Packet Tracer activity

Lab 6.2.2.5: Configuring IPv4 Static and Default Routes

In this lab, you will complete the following objectives:

- Part 1: Set Up the Topology and Initialize Devices
- Part 2: Configure Basic Device Settings and Verify Connectivity
- Part 3: Configure Static Routes
- Part 4: Configure and Verify a Default Route

Configure IPv6 Static Routes (6.2.3)

Configuring an IPv6 static route is very similar to configuring IPv4 static routes except that the command is now **ipv6 route**.

The ipv6 route **Command (6.2.3.1)**

Static routes for IPv6 are configured using the **ipv6 route** global configuration command. Table 6-4 shows the simplified version of the command syntax:

```
Router(config)# ipv6 routeipv6-prefix/prefix-length{ipv6-address| exit-intf}
```

Table 6-4   IPv6 Command Syntax

Parameter	Description
ipv6-prefix	Destination network address of the remote network to be added to the routing table.
prefix-length	Prefix length of the remote network to be added to the routing table.
ipv6-address	■ Commonly referred to as the next-hop router's IP address. ■ Typically used when connecting to a broadcast media (i.e., Ethernet). ■ Commonly creates a recursive lookup.
exit-intf	■ Use the outgoing interface to forward packets to the destination network. ■ Also referred to as a directly attached static route. ■ Typically used when connecting in a point-to-point configuration.

Most of parameters are identical to the IPv4 version of the command. IPv6 static routes can also be implemented as

- Standard IPv6 static route
- Default IPv6 static route
- Summary IPv6 static route
- Floating IPv6 static route

As with IPv4, these routes can be configured as recursive, directly connected, or fully specified.

The **ipv6 unicast-routing** global configuration command must be configured to enable the router to forward IPv6 packets. Figure 6-22 displays the enabling of IPv6 unicast routing.

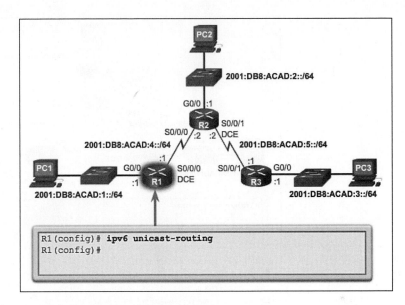

Figure 6-22   Enabling IPv6 Unicast Routing

Activity 6.2.3.1 Part 1: Enabling IPv6 Unicast Routing on R2

Go to the course online to use the Syntax Checker in the third graphic to enable IPv6 unicast routing on R2.

Activity 6.2.3.1 Part 2: Enabling IPv6 Unicast Routing on R3

Go to the course online to use the Syntax Checker in the fourth graphic to enable IPv6 unicast routing on R3.

Next-Hop Options (6.2.3.2)

In this example, Figures 6-23 through 6-25 display the routing tables of R1, R2, and R3.

Activity 6.2.3.2 Part1: Verifying the Routing Table of R1

Go to the course online, and use the slider bar in the first graphic to see the entire output of the **show ipv6 route** command.

Each router has entries only for directly connected networks and their associated local addresses.

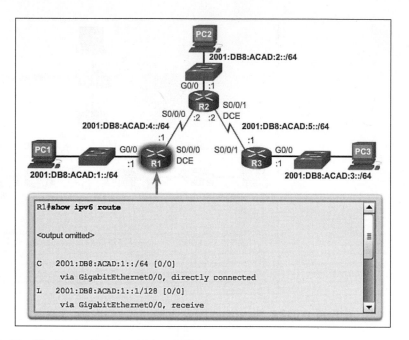

Figure 6-23 Verify the Routing Table of R1

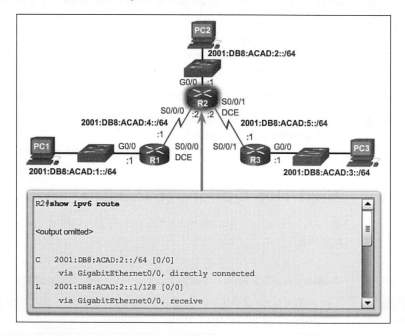

Figure 6-24 Verify the Routing Table of R2

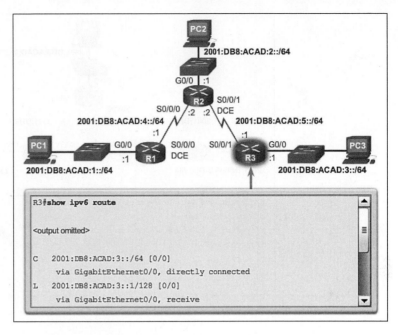

Figure 6-25   Verify the Routing Table of R3

Activity 6.2.3.2 Part 2: Verifying the Routing Table of R2

Go to the course online, and use the slider bar in the second graphic to see the entire output of the **show ipv6 route** command.

None of the routers have any knowledge of any networks beyond their directly connected interfaces.

Activity 6.2.3.2 Part 3: Verifying the Routing Table of R3

Go to the course online, and use the slider bar in the third graphic to see the entire output of the **show ipv6 route** command.

For example, R1 has no knowledge of networks:

- 2001:DB8:ACAD:2::/64: LAN on R2
- 2001:DB8:ACAD:5::/64: Serial network between R2 and R3
- 2001:DB8:ACAD:3::/64: LAN on R3

Figure 6-26 displays a successful ping from R1 to R2.

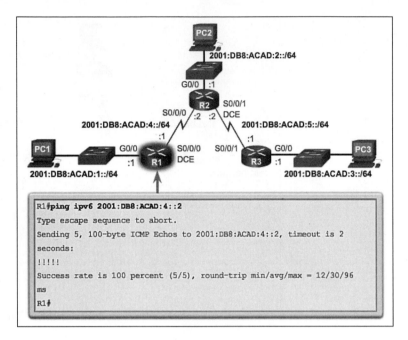

Figure 6-26   Verify Connectivity from R1 to R2

Figure 6-27 displays an unsuccessful ping to the R3 LAN. This is because R1 does not have an entry in its routing table for that network.

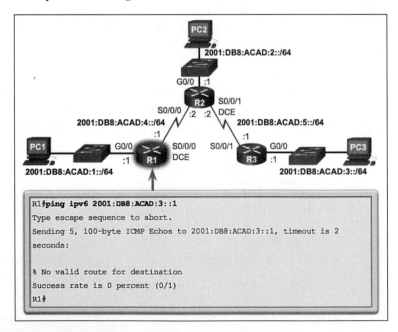

Figure 6-27   Verify Connectivity from R1 to the R3 LAN

The next hop can be identified by an IPv6 address, exit interface, or both. How the destination is specified creates one of three route types:

- **Next-hop static IPv6 route:** Only the next-hop IPv6 address is specified.

- **Directly connected static IPv6 route:** Only the router exit interface is specified.

- **Fully specified static IPv6 route:** The next-hop IPv6 address and exit interface are specified.

Configure a Next-Hop Static IPv6 Route (6.2.3.3)

In a next-hop static route, only the next-hop IPv6 address is specified. The output interface is derived from the next hop. For instance, in Figure 6-28, three next-hop static routes are configured on R1.

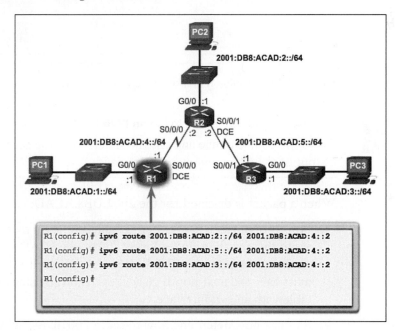

Figure 6-28   Configure Next-Hop Static IPv6 Routes

As with IPv4, before any packet is forwarded by the router, the routing table process must resolve the route to determine the exit interface to use to forward the packet. The route resolvability process will vary depending upon the type of forwarding mechanism being used by the router. Cisco Express Forwarding (CEF) is the default behavior on most platforms running IOS 12.0 or later.

Figure 6-29 details the basic packet-forwarding route resolvability process in the routing table for R1 without the use of CEF.

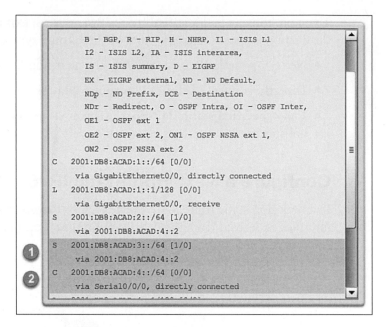

Figure 6-29   Verifying an IPv6 Next-Hop Lookup

Activity 6.2.3.3 Part 1: Verifying an IPv6 Next-Hop Lookup

Go to the course online and use the slider bar in the second graphic to see the entire output of the **show ipv6 route** command.

When a packet is destined for the 2001:DB8:ACAD:3::/64 network, R1:

1. Looks for a match in the routing table and finds that it has to forward the packets to the next-hop IPv6 address 2001:DB8:ACAD:4::2. Every route that references only a next-hop IPv6 address and does not reference an exit interface must have the next-hop IPv6 address resolved using another route in the routing table with an exit interface.

2. R1 must now determine how to reach 2001:DB8:ACAD:4::2; therefore, it searches a second time looking for a match. In this case, the IPv6 address matches the route for the directly connected network 2001:DB8:ACAD:4::/64 with the exit interface Serial 0/0/0. This lookup tells the routing table process that this packet is forwarded out of that interface.

Therefore, it actually takes two routing table lookup processes to forward any packet to the 2001:DB8:ACAD:3::/64 network. When the router has to perform multiple lookups in the routing table before forwarding a packet, it is performing a process known as a recursive lookup.

A recursive static IPv6 route is valid (that is, it is a candidate for insertion in the routing table) only when the specified next hop resolves, either directly or indirectly, to a valid exit interface.

Interactive Graphic

Activity 6.2.3.3 Part 2: Configuring Next-Hop Static IPv6 on R2

Go to the course online to use the Syntax Checker in the third graphic to configure Next-Hop Static IPv6 Routes on R2.

Interactive Graphic

Activity 6.2.3.3 Part 3: Configuring Next-Hop Static IPv6 on R3

Go to the course online to use the Syntax Checker in the fourth graphic to configure Next-Hop Static IPv6 Routes on R3.

Configure a Directly Connected Static IPv6 Route (6.2.3.4)

When configuring a static route on point-to-point networks, an alternative to using the next-hop IPv6 address is to specify the exit interface. This is an alternative used in older IOSs or whenever CEF is disabled, to avoid the recursive lookup problem.

For instance, in Figure 6-30, three directly connected static routes are configured on R1 using the exit interface.

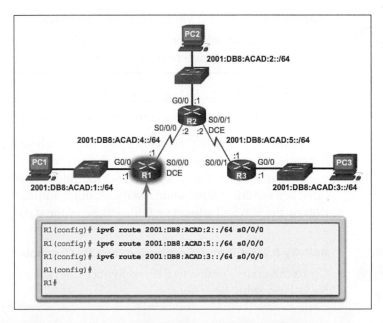

Figure 6-30 Configure Directly Connected Static IPv6 Routes on R1

The IPv6 routing table for R1 in Figure 6-31 shows that when a packet is destined for the 2001:DB8:ACAD:3::/64 network, R1 looks for a match in the routing table and finds that it can forward the packet out of its Serial 0/0/0 interface. No other lookups are required.

```
R1# show ipv6 route
IPv6 Routing Table - default - 8 entries
Codes: C - Connected, L - Local, S - Static, U - Per-
user Static route
       B - BGP, R - RIP, I1 - ISIS L1, I2 - ISIS L2
       IA - ISIS interarea, IS - ISIS summary, D -
EIGRP, EX - EIGRP external
       ND - ND Default, NDp - ND Prefix, DCE -
Destination, NDr - Redirect
       O - OSPF Intra, OI - OSPF Inter, OE1 - OSPF ext
1, OE2 - OSPF ext 2
       ON1 - OSPF NSSA ext 1, ON2 - OSPF NSSA ext 2
C   2001:DB8:ACAD:1::/64 [0/0]
     via GigabitEthernet0/0, directly connected
L   2001:DB8:ACAD:1::1/128 [0/0]
     via GigabitEthernet0/0, receive
S   2001:DB8:ACAD:2::/64 [1/0]
     via Serial0/0/0, directly connected
S   2001:DB8:ACAD:3::/64 [1/0]
     via Serial0/0/0, directly connected
```

Figure 6-31   Verifying the Routing Table of R1

Activity 6.2.3.4 Part 1: Verifying an IPv6 Next-Hop Lookup

Go to the course online, and use the slider bar in the second graphic to see the entire output of the **show ipv6 route** command.

Notice how the routing table looks different for the route configured with an exit interface than the route configured with a recursive entry.

Configuring a directly connected static route with an exit interface allows the routing table to resolve the exit interface in a single search instead of two searches. Recall that with the use of the CEF forwarding mechanism, static routes with an exit interface are considered unnecessary. A single lookup is performed using a combination of the FIB and adjacency table stored in the data plane.

Activity 6.2.3.4 Part 2: Configuring Directly Connected Static IPv6 Routes

Go to the course online to use the Syntax Checker in the third graphic to configure Next-Hop Static IPv6 Routes.

Activity 6.2.3.4 Part 3: Configuring Next-Hop Static IPv6 on R3

Go to the course online to use the Syntax Checker in the fourth graphic to configure Directly Connected Static IPv6 Routes.

Configure a Fully Specified Static IPv6 Route (6.2.3.5)

In a fully specified static route, both the output interface and the next-hop IPv6 address are specified. Similar to fully specified static routes used with IPv4, this would be used if CEF were not enabled on the router and the exit interface was on a multi-access network. With CEF, a static route using only a next-hop IPv6 address would be the preferred method even when the exit interface is a multi-access network.

Unlike IPv4, there is a situation in IPv6 when a fully specified static route must be used. If the IPv6 static route uses an IPv6 link-local address as the next-hop address, a fully specified static route including the exit interface must be used. Figure 6-32 shows an example of a fully qualified IPv6 static route using an IPv6 link-local address as the next-hop address.

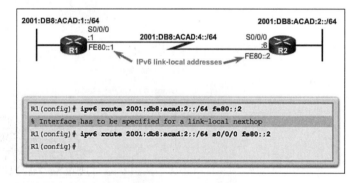

Figure 6-32   Configure Fully Specified Static IPv6 Routes on R1

The reason a fully specified static route must be used is because IPv6 link-local addresses are not contained in the IPv6 routing table. Link-local addresses are only unique on a given link or network. The next-hop link-local address may be a valid address on multiple networks connected to the router. Therefore, it is necessary that the exit interface be included.

In Figure 6-32, a fully specified static route is configured using R2's link-local address as the next-hop address. Notice that IOS requires that an exit interface be specified.

The following output shows the IPv6 routing table entry for this route. Notice that both the next-hop link-local address and the exit interface are included.

```
R1# show ipv6 route static | begin 2001:DB8:ACAD:2::/64
S    2001:DB8:ACAD:2::/64 [1/0]
     via FE80::2, Serial0/0/0
```

Activity 6.2.3.5: Configure a Fully Specified Static IPv6 Route on R2

Go to the course online to use the Syntax Checker in the third graphic to configure Next-Hop Static IPv6 Routes.

Verify IPv6 Static Routes (6.2.3.6)

Along with **ping** and **traceroute**, useful commands to verify static routes include

- **show ipv6 route**
- **show ipv6 route static**
- **show ipv6 route** *network*

Figure 6-33 displays sample output of the **show ipv6 route static** command. The output reflects the use of static routes using next-hop global unicast addresses.

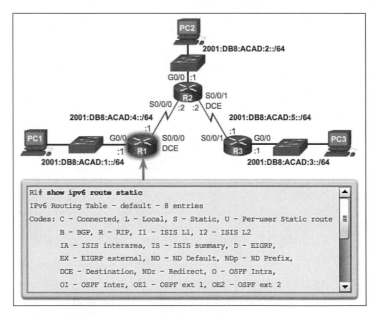

Figure 6-33 Verify the Routing Table of R1

Activity 6.2.3.6: Verifying the Routing Table of R1

Go to the course online, and use the slider bar in the first graphic to see the entire output of the **show ipv6 route static** command.

Figure 6-34 displays sample output from the **show ip route 2001:DB8:ACAD:3::** command.

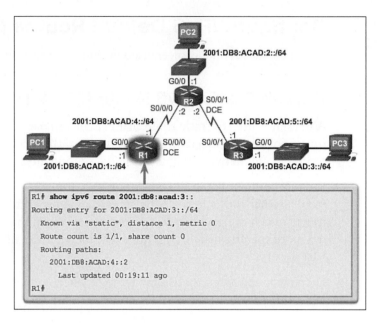

Figure 6-34   View a Specific Entry in the Routing Table

Figure 6-35 verifies the **ipv6 route** configuration in the running configuration.

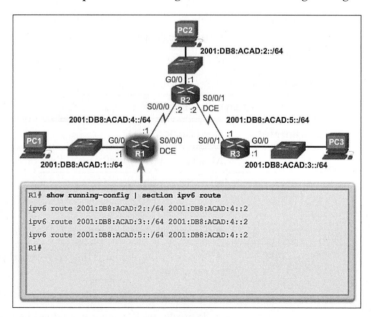

Figure 6-35   Verify the Static Route Configuration

Configure IPv6 Default Routes (6.2.4)

A default static route is often used in simple router topologies.

Default Static IPv6 Route (6.2.4.1)

A default route is a static route that matches all packets. Instead of routers storing routes for all of the networks in the Internet, they can store a single default route to represent any network that is not in the routing table.

Routers commonly use default routes that are either configured locally or learned from another router, using a dynamic routing protocol. They are used when no other routes match the packet's destination IP address in the routing table. In other words, if a more specific match does not exist, then use the default route as the Gateway of Last Resort.

Default static routes are commonly used when connecting

- A company's edge router to a service provider network.

- A router with only an upstream neighbor router. The router has no other neighbors and is, therefore, referred to as a stub router.

As shown in Table 6-5, the command syntax for a default static route is similar to any other static route, except that the ipv6-prefix/prefix-length is `::/0`, which matches all routes.

Table 6-5   Default Static IPv6 Route Syntax

```
Router(config)#ip route ::/0 {ip address | exit-intf }
```

Parameter	Description
`::/0`	Matches any IPv6 Prefix regardless of prefix length
ip-address	- Commonly referred to as the next-hop router's IPv6 address - Typically used when connecting to a broadcast media (i.e. Ethernet). - Commonly creates a recursive lookup
exit-intf	- Use the outgoing interface to forward packets to the destination network - Also referred to as a directly attached static route - Typically used when connecting in a point-to-point configuration

The basic command syntax of a default static route is

```
ipv6 route ::/0 {ipv6-address | exit-intf}
```

Configure a Default Static IPv6 Route (6.2.4.2)

The example in Figure 6-36 displays a configuration for a default static IPv6 route on R1.

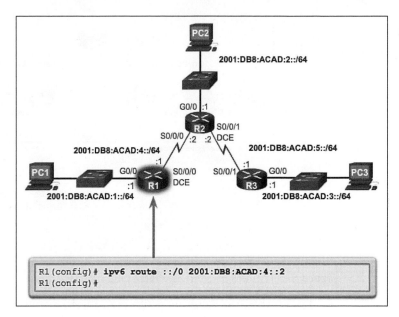

Figure 6-36   Configuring a Default Static IPv6 Route

R1 can be configured with three static routes to reach all of the remote networks in our topology. However, R1 is a stub router because it is connected to only R2. Therefore, it would be more efficient to configure a default static IPv6 route.

Verify a Default Static Route (6.2.4.3)

In Figure 6-37, the **show ipv6 route static** command output displays the contents of the routing table.

Unlike IPv4, IPv6 does not explicitly state that the default IPv6 is the Gateway of Last Resort.

Interactive Graphic

Activity 6.2.4.6: Verifying the Routing Table of R1

Go to the course online, and use the slider bar in the first graphic to see the entire output of the **show ipv6 route static** command.

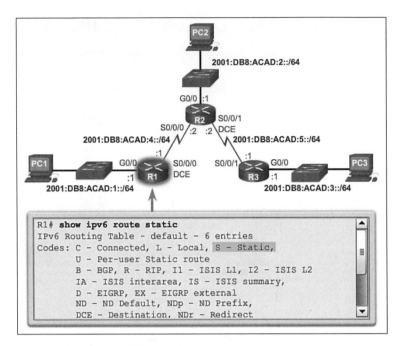

Figure 6-37 Verifying the Routing Table of R1

The key to this configuration is the `::/0` mask. Recall that the ipv6 prefix-length in a routing table determines how many bits must match between the destination IP address of the packet and the route in the routing table. The `::/0` mask indicates that none of the bits are required to match. As long as a more specific match does not exist, the default static IPv6 route matches all packets.

Figure 6-38 displays a successful ping to the R3 LAN interface.

Packet Tracer
☐ Activity

Packet Tracer Activity 6.2.4.4: Configuring IPv6 Static and Default Routes

In this activity, you will configure IPv6 static and default routes. A static route is a route that is entered manually by the network administrator to create a route that is reliable and safe. There are four different static routes used in this activity: a recursive static route; a directly connected static route; a fully specified static route; and a default route.

Go to the course online to complete this Packet Tracer activity.

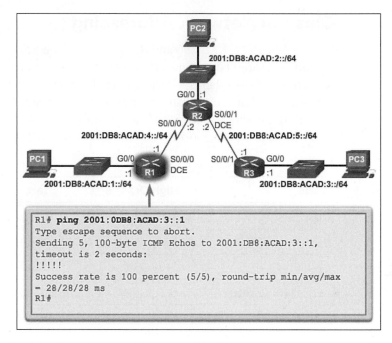

Figure 6-38   Verifying Connectivity to the R3 LAN

  Lab 6.2.4.5: Configuring IPv6 Static and Default Routes

In this lab, you will complete the following objectives:

- Part 1: Build the Network and Configure Basic Device Settings

- Part 2: Configure IPv6 Static and Default Routes

Review of CIDR and VLSM (6.3)

Classless Interdomain Routing (CIDR) was introduced to improve both address space utilization and routing scalability in the Internet. It was needed because of the rapid growth of the Internet and growth of the IP routing tables held in the Internet routers.

VLSM enables an organization to use more than one subnet mask within the same network address space. VLSM allows you to conserve IP addresses and efficiently use the available address space.

Classful Network Addressing (6.3.1.1)

Released in 1981, RFC 790 and RFC 791 describe how IPv4 network addresses were initially allocated based on a classification system. In the original specification of IPv4, the authors established the classes to provide three different sizes of networks for large, medium, and small organizations. As a result, class A, B, and C addresses were defined with a specific format for the *high order bits*. High order bits are the far-left bits in a 32-bit address, as shown in Table 6-6.

Table 6-6 High Order Bits

Class	High Order Bits	Start	End
Class A	0xxxxxxx	0.0.0.0	127.255.255.255
Class B	10xxxxxx	128.0.0.0	191.255.255.255
Class C	110xxxxx	192.0.0.0	223.255.255.255
Class D (Multicast)	1110xxxx	224.0.0.0	239.255.255.255
Class E (Reserved)	1111	240.0.0.0	255.255.255.255

- *Class A addresses* begin with 0: Intended for large organizations; includes all addresses from 0.0.0.0 (**00000000**) to 127.255.255.255 (**01111111**). The 0.0.0.0 address is reserved for default routing and the 127.0.0.0 address is reserved for loopback testing.

- *Class B addresses* begin with 10: Intended for medium-to-large organizations; includes all addresses from 128.0.0.0 (**10000000**) to 191.255.255.255 (**10111111**).

- *Class C addresses* begin with 110: Intended for small-to-medium organizations; includes all addresses from 192.0.0.0 (**11000000**) to 223.255.255.255 (**11011111**).

The remaining addresses were reserved for multicasting and future uses.

- *Class D Multicast addresses* begin with 1110: *Multicast addresses* are used to identify a group of hosts that are part of a multicast group. This helps reduce the amount of packet processing that is done by hosts, particularly on broadcast media (i.e., Ethernet LANs). Routing protocols, such as RIPv2, EIGRP, and OSPF, use designated multicast addresses (RIP = 224.0.0.9, EIGRP = 224.0.0.10, OSPF = 224.0.0.5, and 224.0.0.6).

- *Class E Reserved IP addresses* begin with 1111: These addresses were reserved for experimental and future use.

Classful Subnet Masks (6.3.1.2)

As specified in RFC 790, each network class has a default subnet mask associated with it.

As shown in Figure 6-39, class A networks used the first octet to identify the network portion of the address. This is translated to a 255.0.0.0 classful subnet mask. Because only 7 bits were left in the first octet (remember, the first bit is always 0), this made 2 to the 7th power, or 128 networks. The actual number is 126 networks, because there are two reserved class A addresses (i.e., 0.0.0.0/8 and 127.0.0.0/8). With 24 bits in the host portion, each class A address had the potential for over 16 million individual host addresses.

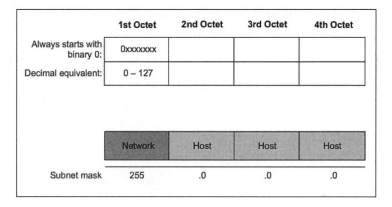

Figure 6-39   Class A Networks

As shown in Figure 6-40, class B networks used the first two octets to identify the network portion of the network address. With the first two bits already established as 1 and 0, 14 bits remained in the first two octets for assigning networks, which resulted in 16,384 class B network addresses. Because each class B network address contained 16 bits in the host portion, it controlled 65,534 addresses. (Recall that two addresses were reserved for the network and broadcast addresses.)

As shown in Figure 6-41, class C networks used the first three octets to identify the network portion of the network address. With the first three bits established as 1 and 1 and 0, 21 bits remained for assigning networks for over 2 million class C networks. But, each class C network only had 8 bits in the host portion, or 254 possible host addresses.

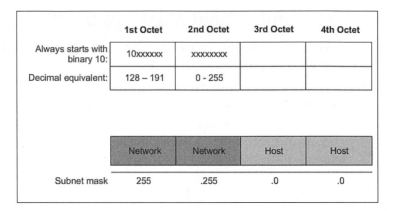

Figure 6-40   Class B Networks

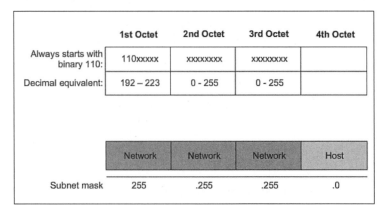

Figure 6-41   Class C Networks

An advantage of assigning specific default subnet masks to each class is that it made routing update messages smaller. *Classful routing protocols* do not include the subnet mask information in their updates. The receiving router applies the default mask based on the value of the first octet which identifies the class.

Classful Routing Protocol Example (6.3.1.3)

Using classful IP addresses meant that the subnet mask of a network address could be determined by the value of the first octet, or more accurately, the first three bits of the address. Routing protocols, such as RIPv1, only need to propagate the network address of known routes and do not need to include the subnet mask in the routing update. This is due to the router receiving the routing update determining the subnet mask simply by examining the value of the first octet in the network address, or by applying its ingress interface mask for subnetted routes. The subnet mask was directly related to the network address.

In Figure 6-42, R1 sends an update to R2. In the example, R1 knows that subnet 172.16.1.0 belongs to the same major classful network as the outgoing interface. Therefore, it sends a RIP update to R2 containing subnet 172.16.1.0. When R2 receives the update, it applies the receiving interface subnet mask (/24) to the update and adds 172.16.1.0 to the routing table.

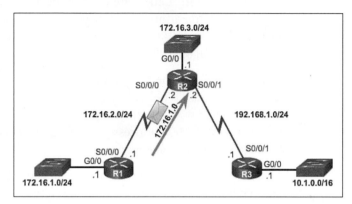

Figure 6-42 Classful Routing Updates

In Figure 6-43, R2 sends an update to R3. When sending updates to R3, R2 summarizes subnets 172.16.1.0/24, 172.16.2.0/24, and 172.16.3.0/24 into the major classful network 172.16.0.0. Because R3 does not have any subnets that belong to 172.16.0.0, it applies the classful mask for a class B network, which is /16.

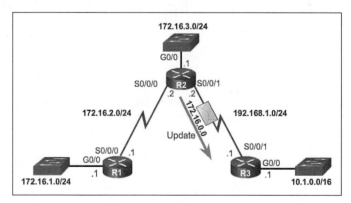

Figure 6-43 Classful Routing Updates

Classful Addressing Waste (6.3.1.4)

The classful addressing specified in RFCs 790 and 791 resulted in a tremendous waste of address space. In the early days of the Internet, organizations were assigned an entire classful network address from the A, B, or C class.

As illustrated in Figure 6-44

- Class A had 50% of the total address space. However, only 126 organizations could be assigned a class A network address. Ridiculously, each of these organizations could provide addresses for up to 16 million hosts. Very large organizations were allocated entire class A address blocks. Some companies and governmental organizations still have class A addresses. For example, General Electric owns 3.0.0.0/8, Apple Computer owns 17.0.0.0/8, and the U.S. Postal Service owns 56.0.0.0/8.

- Class B had 25% of the total address space. Up to 16,384 organizations could be assigned a class B network address and each of these networks could support up to 65,534 hosts. Only the largest organizations and governments could ever hope to use all 65,000 addresses. Like class A networks, many IP addresses in the class B address space were wasted.

- Class C had 12.5 % of the total address space. Many more organizations were able to get class C networks, but were limited in the total number of hosts that they could connect. In fact, in many cases, class C addresses were often too small for most midsize organizations.

- Classes D and E are used for multicasting and reserved addresses.

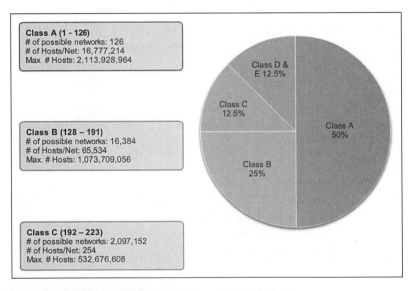

Figure 6-44   Classful IP Address Allocation = Inefficient

The overall result was that the classful addressing was a very wasteful addressing scheme. A better network addressing solution had to be developed. For this reason, Classless Inter-Domain Routing (CIDR) was introduced in 1993.

CIDR (6.3.2)

In 1993, as part of a process to slow down the growth of routing tables and to also slow down the use of IPv4 addresses, CIDR was introduced, and forever changed subnetting and IPv4 address management.

Classless Inter-Domain Routing (6.3.2.1)

Just as the Internet was growing at an exponential rate in the early 1990s, so were the size of the routing tables that were maintained by Internet routers under classful IP addressing. For this reason, the IETF introduced CIDR in RFC 1517 in 1993.

CIDR replaced the classful network assignments and address classes (A, B, and C) became obsolete. Using CIDR, the network address is no longer determined by the value of the first octet. Instead, the network portion of the address is determined by the subnet mask, also known as the *network prefix*, or *prefix length* (i.e., /8, /19, etc.).

ISPs are no longer limited to a /8, /16, or /24 subnet mask. They can now more efficiently allocate address space using any prefix length, starting with /8 and larger (i.e., /8, /9, /10, etc.). Figure 6-45 shows how blocks of IP addresses can be assigned to a network based on the requirements of the customer, ranging from a few hosts to hundreds or thousands of hosts.

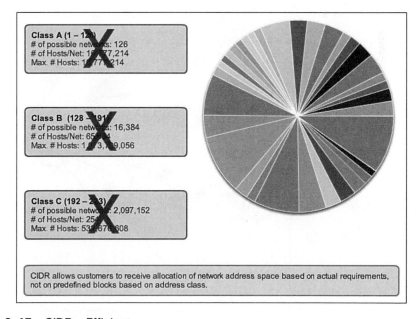

Figure 6-45   CIDR = Efficient

CIDR also reduces the size of routing tables and manages the IPv4 address space more efficiently using

- *Route summarization*: Also known as *prefix aggregation*, routes are summarized into a single route to help reduce the size of routing tables. For instance, one summary static route can replace several specific static route statements.

- *Supernetting*: Occurs when the route summarization mask is a smaller value than the default traditional classful mask.

Note

A supernet is always a route summary, but a route summary is not always a supernet.

CIDR and Route Summarization (6.3.2.2)

In Figure 6-46, notice that ISP1 has four customers, and that each customer has a variable amount of IP address space. The address space of the four customers can be summarized into one advertisement to ISP2. The 192.168.0.0/20 summarized or aggregated route includes all the networks belonging to Customers A, B, C, and D. This type of route is known as a supernet route. A supernet summarizes multiple network addresses with a mask that is smaller than the classful mask.

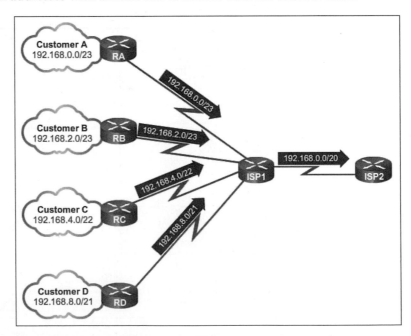

Figure 6-46   Summarizing Supernet Routes

Determining the summary route and subnet mask for a group of networks can be done in the following three steps:

Step 1.   List the networks in binary format.

Step 2.   Count the number of far-left matching bits. This identifies the prefix length or subnet mask for the summarized route.

Step 3.   Copy the matching bits and then add zero bits to the rest of the address to determine the summarized network address.

The summarized network address and subnet mask can now be used as the summary route for this group of networks.

Summary routes can be configured by both static routes and *classless routing protocols*.

Static Routing CIDR Example (6.3.2.3)

Creating smaller routing tables makes the routing table lookup process more efficient, because there are fewer routes to search. If one static route can be used instead of multiple static routes, the size of the routing table is reduced. In many cases, a single static route can be used to represent dozens, hundreds, or even thousands of routes.

Summary CIDR routes can be configured using static routes. This helps to reduce the size of routing tables.

In Figure 6-47, R1 has been configured to reach the identified networks in the topology. Although acceptable, it would be more efficient to configure a summary static route.

Figure 6-48 provides a solution using CIDR summarization. The six static route entries could be reduced to a 172.16.0.0/13 entry. The example removes the six static route entries and replaces them with a summary static route.

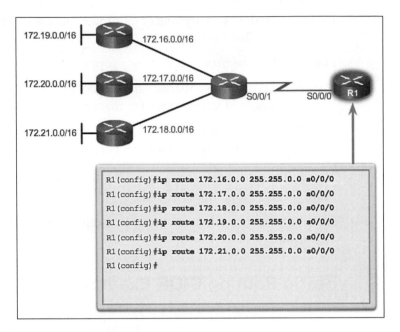

Figure 6-47 Six Static Routes

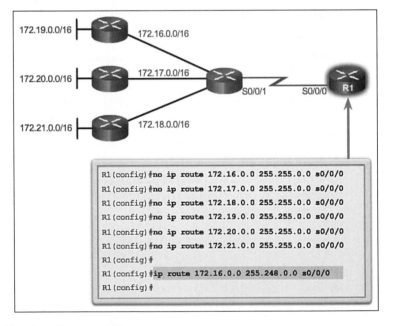

Figure 6-48 One Summary Route

Classless Routing Protocol Example (6.3.2.4)

Classful routing protocols cannot send supernet routes. This is because the receiving router automatically applies the default classful subnet mask to the network address in the routing update. If the topology in Figure 6-49 contained a classful routing protocol, then R3 would only install 172.16.0.0/16 in the routing table.

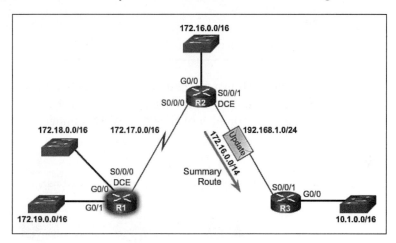

Figure 6-49   Classless Routing Update

Propagating VLSM and supernet routes requires a classless routing protocol such as RIPv2, OSPF, or EIGRP. Classless routing protocols advertise network addresses with their associated subnet masks. With a classless routing protocol, R2 can summarize networks 172.16.0.0/16, 172.17.0.0/16, 172.18.0.0/16, and 172.19.0.0/16 and advertise a supernet summary static route 172.16.0.0/14 to R3. R3 then installs the supernet route 172.16.0.0/14 in its routing table.

Note

When a supernet route is in a routing table, for example, as a static route, a classful routing protocol does not include that route in its updates.

VLSM (6.3.3)

All network administrators have to become very comfortable working with VLSM when creating and managing IP address plans. This skill set should be practiced on a regular basis so that it becomes second nature.

Fixed-Length Subnet Masking (6.3.3.1)

With *fixed-length subnet masking (FLSM)*, the same number of addresses is allocated for each subnet. If all the subnets have the same requirements for the number of hosts, these fixed size address blocks would be sufficient. However, most often that is not the case.

Note

FLSM is also referred to as traditional subnetting.

The topology shown in Figure 6-50 requires that network address 192.168.20.0/24 be subnetted into seven subnets: one subnet for each of the four LANs (Building A to D), and one for each of the three WAN connections between routers.

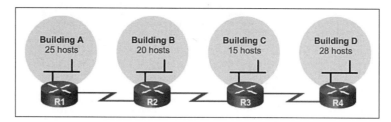

Figure 6-50   Network Topology: Basic Subnets

Figure 6-51 highlights how traditional subnetting can borrow 3 bits from the host portion in the last octet to meet the subnet requirement of seven subnets. For example, under the Host portion, the Subnet portion highlights how borrowing 3 bits creates 8 subnets, while the Host portion highlights 5 host bits providing 30 usable host IP addresses per subnet. This scheme creates the needed subnets and meets the host requirement of the largest LAN.

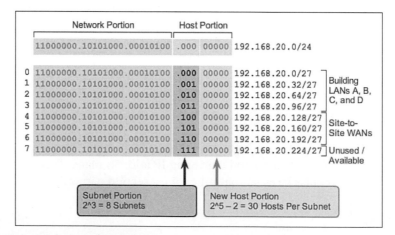

Figure 6-51   Basic Subnet Scheme

Although this traditional subnetting meets the needs of the largest LAN and divides the address space into an adequate number of subnets, it results in significant waste of unused addresses.

For example, only 2 addresses are needed in each subnet for the three WAN links. Because each subnet has 30 usable addresses, there are 28 unused addresses in each of these subnets. As shown in Figure 6-52, this results in 84 unused addresses (28 x 3). Further, this limits future growth by reducing the total number of subnets available. This inefficient use of addresses is characteristic of traditional subnetting of classful networks.

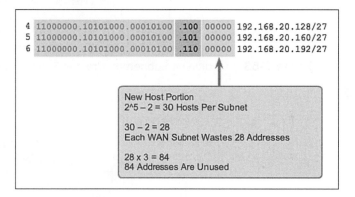

Figure 6-52 Unused Addresses on WAN Subnets

Applying a traditional subnetting scheme to this scenario is not very efficient and is wasteful. In fact, this example is a good model for showing how subnetting a subnet can be used to maximize address utilization. Subnetting a subnet, or using variable-length subnet mask (VLSM), was designed to avoid wasting addresses.

Variable-Length Subnet Masking (6.3.3.2)

In traditional subnetting, the same subnet mask is applied for all the subnets. This means that each subnet has the same number of available host addresses.

As illustrated in Figure 6-53, traditional subnetting creates subnets of equal size. Each subnet in a traditional scheme uses the same subnet mask.

With VLSM the subnet mask length varies depending on how many bits have been borrowed for a particular subnet, thus the "variable" part of variable-length subnet mask. As shown in Figure 6-54, VLSM allows a network space to be divided into unequal parts.

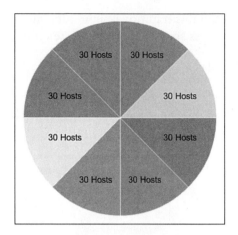

Figure 6-53   Traditional Subnetting Creates Equal-Sized Subnets

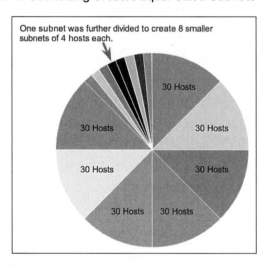

Figure 6-54   Subnets of Varying Sizes

VLSM subnetting is similar to traditional subnetting in that bits are borrowed to create subnets. The formulas to calculate the number of hosts per subnet and the number of subnets created still apply. The difference is that subnetting is not a single pass activity. With VLSM, the network is first subnetted, and then the subnets are subnetted again. This process can be repeated multiple times to create subnets of various sizes.

VLSM in Action (6.3.3.3)

VLSM allows the use of different masks for each subnet. After a network address is subnetted, those subnets can be further subnetted. VLSM is simply subnetting a subnet. VLSM can be thought of as sub-subnetting.

Video 6.3.3.3: VLSM Subnets

Video

Go to the course and play the animation of VLSM being performed on a network diagram.

The movie in the online curriculum shows the network 10.0.0.0/8 that has been subnetted using the subnet mask of /16, which makes 256 subnets. That is 10.0.0.0/16, 10.1.0.0/16, 10.2.0.0/16, ..., 10.255.0.0/16. Four of these /16 subnets are displayed in the movie's first graphic. Any of these /16 subnets can be subnetted further.

In the video

- The 10.1.0.0/16 subnet is subnetted again with the /24 mask.

- The 10.2.0.0/16 subnet is subnetted again with the /24 mask.

- The 10.3.0.0/16 subnet is subnetted again with the /28 mask.

- The 10.4.0.0/16 subnet is subnetted again with the /20 mask.

Individual host addresses are assigned from the addresses of "sub-subnets". For example, the video shows the 10.1.0.0/16 subnet divided into /24 subnets. The 10.1.4.10 address would now be a member of the more specific subnet 10.1.4.0/24.

Subnetting Subnets (6.3.3.4)

Another way to view the VLSM subnets is to list each subnet and its sub-subnets.

In Figure 6-55, the 10.0.0.0/8 network is the starting address space and is subnetted with a /16 mask. Borrowing 8 bits (going from /8 to /16) creates 256 subnets that range from 10.0.0.0/16 to 10.255.0.0/16.

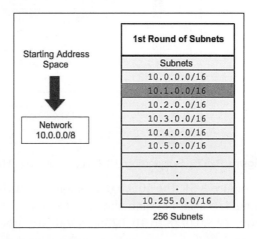

Figure 6-55 Subnetting 10.0.0.0/8 to 10.0.0.0/16

In Figure 6-56, the 10.1.0.0/16 subnet is further subnetted by borrowing 8 more bits. This creates 256 subnets with a /24 mask. This mask allows 254 host addresses per subnet. The subnets ranging from 10.1.0.0/24 to 10.1.255.0/24 are subnets of the subnet 10.1.0.0/16.

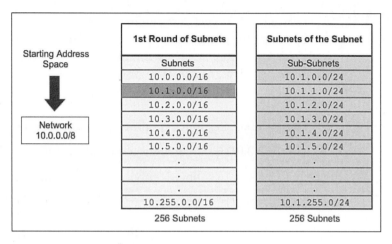

Figure 6-56   Subnetting 10.1.0.0/16 to 10.1.0.0/24

In Figure 6-57, the 10.2.0.0/16 subnet is also further subnetted with a /24 mask allowing 254 host addresses per subnet. The subnets ranging from 10.2.0.0/24 to 10.2.255.0/24 are subnets of the subnet 10.2.0.0/16.

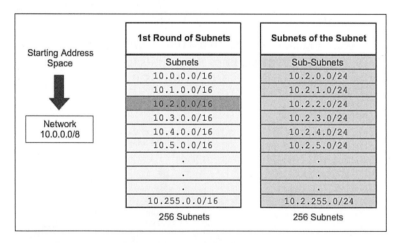

Figure 6-57   Subnetting 10.2.0.0/16 to 10.2.0.0/24

In Figure 6-58, the 10.3.0.0/16 subnet is further subnetted with a /28 mask, thus creating 4,096 subnets and allowing 14 host addresses per subnet. The subnets ranging from 10.3.0.0/28 to 10.3.255.240/28 are subnets of the subnet 10.3.0.0/16.

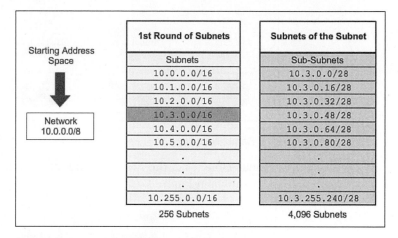

Figure 6-58   Subnetting 10.3.0.0/16 to 10.3.0.0/28

In Figure 6-59, the 10.4.0.0/16 subnet is further subnetted with a /20 mask, thus creating 16 subnets and allowing 4,094 host addresses per subnet. The subnets ranging from 10.4.0.0/20 to 10.4.240.0/20 are subnets of the subnet 10.4.0.0/16. These /20 subnets are big enough to subnet even further, allowing more networks.

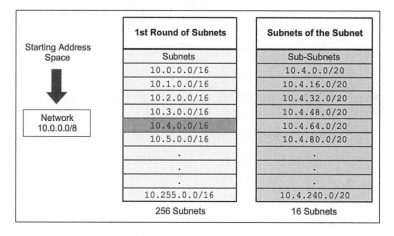

Figure 6-59   Subnetting 10.4.0.0/16 to 10.4.0.0/20

VLSM Example (6.3.3.5)

Careful consideration must be given to the design of a network addressing scheme. For example, the sample topology in Figure 6-60 requires seven subnets.

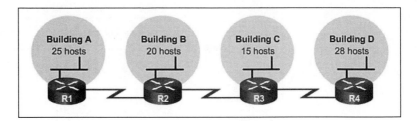

Figure 6-60 Basic Topology

Using traditional subnetting, the first seven address blocks are allocated for LANs and WANs, as shown in Figure 6-61.

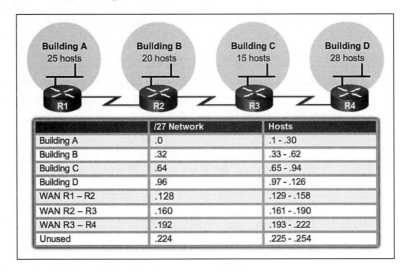

	/27 Network	Hosts
Building A	.0	.1 - .30
Building B	.32	.33 - .62
Building C	.64	.65 - .94
Building D	.96	.97 - .126
WAN R1 – R2	.128	.129 - .158
WAN R2 – R3	.160	.161 - .190
WAN R3 – R4	.192	.193 - .222
Unused	.224	.225 - .254

Figure 6-61 Subnetting 192.168.20.0/24 to 192.168.20.0/27

This scheme results in 8 subnets with 30 usable addresses each (/27). While this scheme works for the LAN segments, there are many wasted addresses in the WAN segments.

If an addressing scheme is designed for a new network, the address blocks can be assigned in a way that minimizes waste and keeps unused blocks of addresses contiguous. It can be more difficult to do this when adding to an existing network.

As shown in Figure 6-62, to use the address space more efficiently, /30 subnets are created for WAN links. To keep the unused blocks of addresses together, the last /27 subnet is further subnetted to create the /30 subnets. The first three subnets were assigned to WAN links creating subnets 192.168.20.224/30, 192.168.20.228/30, and 192.168.20.232/30. Designing the addressing scheme in this way leaves three unused /27 subnets and five unused /30 subnets.

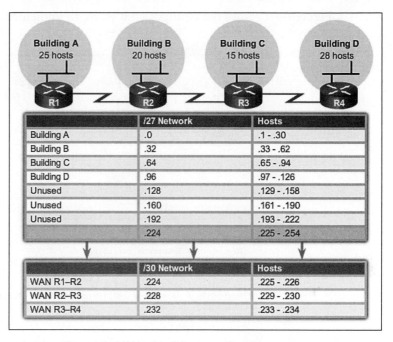

Figure 6-62 Subnetting 192.168.20.224/27 to 192.168.20.224/30

Figure 6-63 shows the configuration on R1 to implement the VLSM addressing scheme.

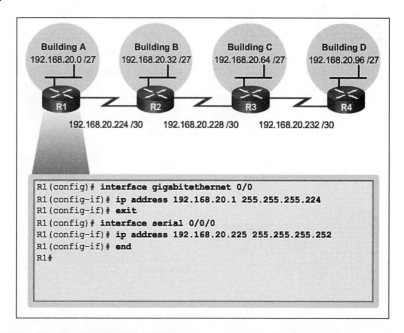

Figure 6-63 Configuring VLSM on R1

Figure 6-64 shows the configuration on R2 to implement the VLSM addressing scheme.

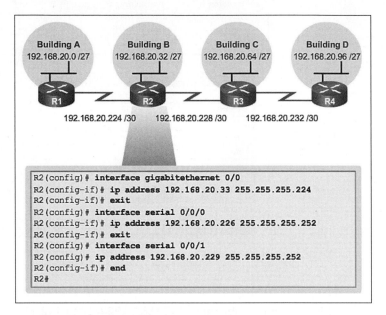

Figure 6-64   Configuring VLSM on R2

Figure 6-65 shows the configuration on R3 to implement the VLSM addressing scheme.

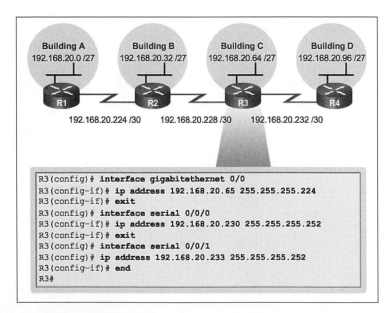

Figure 6-65   Configuring VLSM on R3

Figure 6-66 shows the configuration on R4 to implement the VLSM addressing scheme.

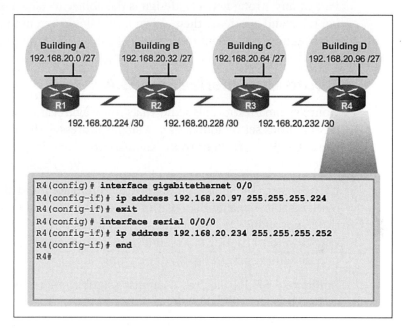

Figure 6-66   Configuring VLSM on R4

Packet Tracer Activity 6.3.3.6: Designing and Implementing a VLSM Addressing Scheme

Background/Scenario

In this activity, you are given a network address to develop a VLSM addressing scheme for the network shown in the included topology.

Go to the course online to complete this Packet Tracer activity.

Lab Activity 6.3.3.7: Designing and Implementing Addressing with VLSM

In this lab, you will complete the following objectives:

- Part 1: Examine the Network Requirements
- Part 2: Design the VLSM Address Scheme
- Part 3: Cable and Configure the IPv4 Network

Configure IPv4 Summary Routes (6.4.1)

Part of any strong network design is the ability to take a number of routes in a routing table and condense them down into a single line in that same routing table. This next section talks about route summarization and how to configure summary routes.

Route Summarization (6.4.1.1)

Route summarization, also known as route aggregation, is the process of advertising a contiguous set of addresses as a single address with a less-specific, shorter subnet mask. CIDR is a form of route summarization and is synonymous with the term supernetting.

CIDR ignores the limitation of classful boundaries, and allows summarization with masks that are smaller than that of the default classful mask. This type of summarization helps reduce the number of entries in routing updates and lowers the number of entries in local routing tables. It also helps reduce bandwidth utilization for routing updates and results in faster routing table lookups.

In Figure 6-67, R1 requires a summary static route to reach networks in the range of 172.20.0.0/16 to 172.23.0.0/16.

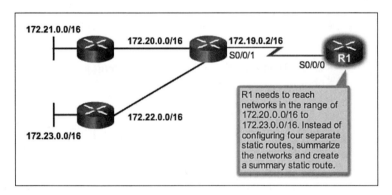

Figure 6-67 Basic Topology for Summary Routes

Calculate a Summary Route (6.4.1.2)

Summarizing networks into a single address and mask can be done in three steps:

Step 1. List the networks in binary format. Figure 6-68 lists networks 172.20.0.0/16 to 172.23.0.0/16 in binary format.

Step 1: List the networks in binary format.

172.20.0.0	10101100 .	00010100 .	00000000 .	00000000
172.21.0.0	10101100 .	00010101 .	00000000 .	00000000
172.22.0.0	10101100 .	00010110 .	00000000 .	00000000
172.23.0.0	10101100 .	00010111 .	00000000 .	00000000

Figure 6-68   Calculating a Route Summary

Step 2.   Count the number of far-left matching bits to determine the mask for the summary route. Figure 6-69 highlights the 14 far-left matching bits. This is the prefix, or subnet mask, for the summarized route: /14 or 255.252.0.0.

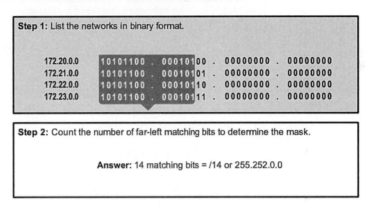

Figure 6-69   Calculating a Route Summary

Step 3.   Copy the matching bits and then add zero bits to determine the summarized network address. Figure 6-70 shows that the matching bits with zeros at the end results in the network address 172.20.0.0. The four networks—172.20.0.0/16, 172.21.0.0/16, 172.22.0.0/16, and 172.23.0.0/16—can be summarized into the single network address and prefix 172.20.0.0/14.

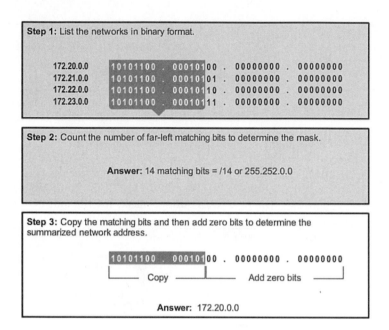

Figure 6-70   Calculating a Route Summary

Figure 6-71 displays R1 configured with a summary static route to reach networks 172.20.0.0/16 to 172.23.0.0/16.

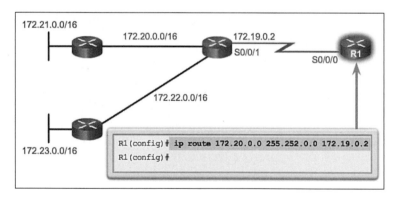

Figure 6-71   One Summary Static Route

Summary Static Route Example (6.4.1.3)

Multiple static routes can be summarized into a single static route if

- The destination networks are contiguous and can be summarized into a single network address.

- The multiple static routes all use the same exit interface or next-hop IP address.

Consider the example in Figure 6-72.

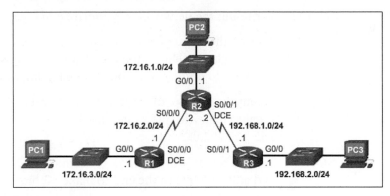

Figure 6-72   Basic Topology

All routers have connectivity using static routes.

Figure 6-73 displays the static routing table entries for R3.

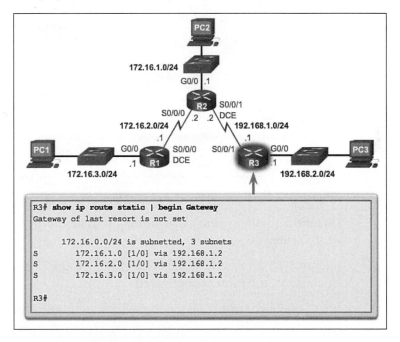

Figure 6-73   Verify the Routing Table

Figure 6-73 has three static routes that can be summarized because they share the same two first octets.

Figure 6-74 displays the steps to summarize those three networks:

How To

Step 1. Write out the networks to summarize in binary.

Step 2. To find the subnet mask for summarization, start with the far-left bit, work to the right, finding all the bits that match consecutively until a column of bits that do not match is found, identifying the summary boundary.

Step 3. Count the number of far-left matching bits; in our example, it is 22. This number identifies the subnet mask for the summarized route as /22 or 255.255.252.0.

Step 4. To find the network address for summarization, copy the matching 22 bits and add all 0 bits to the end to make 32 bits.

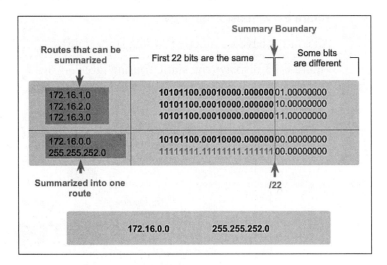

Figure 6-74   Summarize the Networks

After the summary route is identified, replace the existing routes with the one summary route.

Figure 6-75 displays how the three existing routes are removed, and then the new summary static route is configured.

Figure 6-76 confirms that the summary static route is in the routing table of R3.

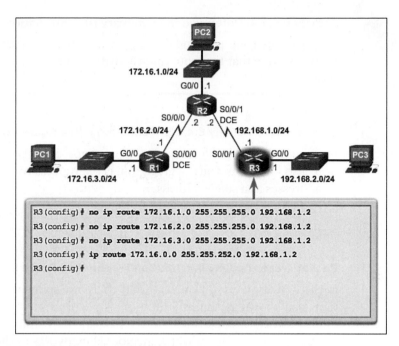

Figure 6-75 Remove Static Routes and Configure Summary Static Routes

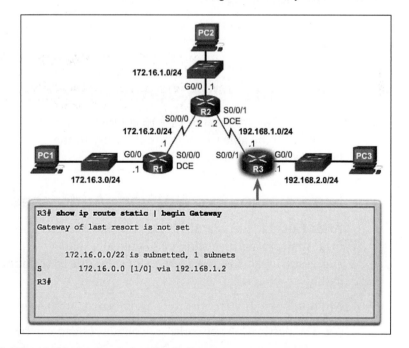

Figure 6-76 Verify the Summary Static Route

Interactive Graphic

Activity 6.4.1.4: Determine the Summary Network Address and Prefix

Go to the course online and complete the activities on summarizing networks and prefixes. Note that there are three activities, one for each of the graphics in this section.

Packet Tracer ☐ Activity

Packet Tracer Activity 6.4.1.5: Configuring IPv4 Route Summarization - Scenario 1

In this activity, you will calculate and configure summary routes. Router summarization, also known as route aggregation, is the process of advertising a contiguous set of addresses as a single address.

Go to the course online to complete this Packet Tracer activity.

Packet Tracer ☐ Activity

Packet Tracer Activity 6.4.1.6: Configuring IPv4 Route Summarization: Scenario 2

In this activity, you will calculate and configure summary routes. Router summarization, also known as route aggregation, is the process of advertising a contiguous set of addresses as a single address. After calculating summary routes for each LAN, you must summarize a route, which includes all networks in the topology in order for the ISP to reach each LAN.

Go to the course online to complete this Packet Tracer activity.

Configure IPv6 Summary Routes (6.4.2)

Just as it is important to be able to configure summary routes in IPv4, it is equally important to be able to configure summary routes in IPv6. This next section shows how to summarize IPv6 network addresses.

Summarize IPv6 Network Addresses (6.4.2.1)

Aside from the fact that IPv6 addresses are 128 bits long and written in hexadecimal, summarizing IPv6 addresses is actually similar to the summarization of IPv4 addresses. It just requires a few extra steps due to the abbreviated IPv6 addresses and hex conversion.

Multiple static IPv6 routes can be summarized into a single static IPv6 route if

- The destination networks are contiguous and can be summarized into a single network address.

- The multiple static routes all use the same exit interface or next-hop IPv6 address.

Refer to the network in the Figure 6-77.

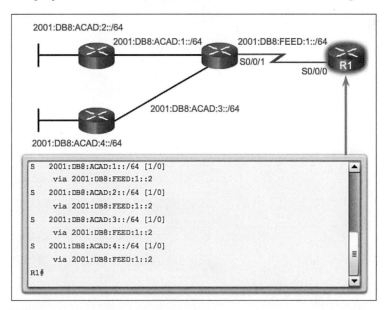

Figure 6-77   Basic Topology

R1 currently has four static IPv6 routes to reach networks 2001:DB8:ACAD:1::/64 to 2001:DB8:ACAD:4::/64.

Figure 6-78 displays the IPv6 static routes installed in the IPv6 routing table.

```
S    2001:DB8:ACAD:1::/64 [1/0]
       via 2001:DB8:FEED:1::2
S    2001:DB8:ACAD:2::/64 [1/0]
       via 2001:DB8:FEED:1::2
S    2001:DB8:ACAD:3::/64 [1/0]
       via 2001:DB8:FEED:1::2
S    2001:DB8:ACAD:4::/64 [1/0]
       via 2001:DB8:FEED:1::2
R1#
```

Figure 6-78   Verify the Routing Table of R1

Interactive Graphic

Activity 6.4.2.1: Configure IPv6 Summary Routes

Go to the course online, and use the slider bar in the second graphic to see the entire output of the **show ipv6 route static** command.

Calculate IPv6 Summary Addresses (6.4.2.2)

Summarizing IPv6 networks into a single IPv6 prefix and prefix-length can be done in seven steps as shown in Figures 6-79 to 6-85:

Step 1.   List the network addresses (prefixes) and identify the part where the addresses differ.

```
2001:0DB8:ACAD:1::/64

2001:0DB8:ACAD:2::/64

2001:0DB8:ACAD:3::/64

2001:0DB8:ACAD:4::/64
```

Figure 6-79   Identify the Part Where the Addresses Differ

Step 2.   Expand the IPv6 if it is abbreviated.

```
2001:0DB8:ACAD:0001::/64

2001:0DB8:ACAD:0002::/64

2001:0DB8:ACAD:0003::/64

2001:0DB8:ACAD:0004::/64
```

Figure 6-80   Expanded Abbreviated Sections of Addresses

Step 3.   Convert the differing section from hex to binary.

```
2001:0DB8:ACAD:0000000000000001::/64

2001:0DB8:ACAD:0000000000000010::/64

2001:0DB8:ACAD:0000000000000011::/64

2001:0DB8:ACAD:0000000000000100::/64
```

Figure 6-81   Convert the Section from Hex to Binary

Step 4. Count the number of far-left matching bits to determine the prefix-length for the summary route.

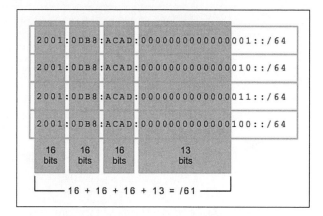

Figure 6-82 Count the Number of Far-Left Matching Bits

Step 5. Copy the matching bits, and then add zero bits to determine the summarized network address (prefix).

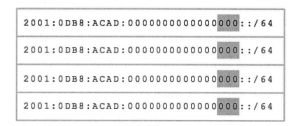

Figure 6-83 Add Zero Bits to Determine the Summarized Network Address

Step 6. Convert the binary section back to hex.

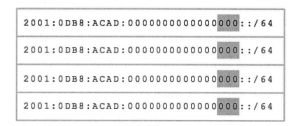

Figure 6-84 Convert the Binary Section Back to Hex

Step 7.   Append the prefix of the summary route (result of Step 4).

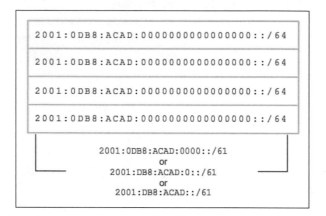

Figure 6-85   Append the Prefix of the Summary Route

Configure an IPv6 Summary Address (6.4.2.3)

After the summary route is identified, replace the existing routes with the single summary route.

Figure 6-86 displays how the four existing routes are removed and then the new summary static IPv6 route is configured.

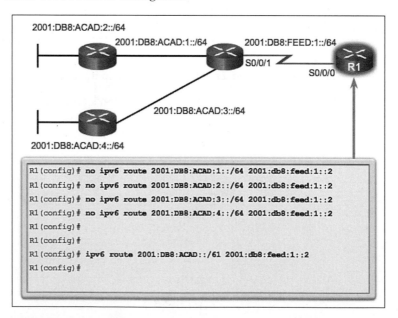

Figure 6-86   Remove Static Routes and Configure Summary IPv6 Route

Figure 6-87 confirms that the summary static route is in the routing table of R1.

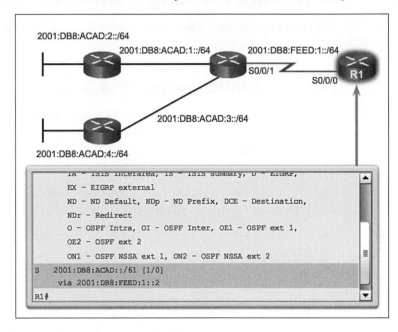

Figure 6-87   Verify the Summary IPv6 Route

Activity 6.4.2.3: Configure an IPv6 Summary Address

Go to the course online, and use the slider bar in the second graphic to see the entire output of the **show ipv6 route static** command.

Packet Tracer Activity 6.4.2.4: Configuring IPv6 Route Summarization

In this activity, you will calculate, configure, and verify a summary route for all the networks R1 can access through R2. R1 is configured with a loopback interface. Instead of adding a LAN or another network to R1, we can use a loopback interface to simplify testing when verifying routing.

Go to the course online to complete this Packet Tracer activity

Lab 6.4.2.5: Calculating Summary Routes with IPv4 and IPv6

In this lab, you will complete the following objectives:

- Part 1: Calculate IPv4 Summary Routes
- Part 2: Calculate IPv6 Summary Routes

Configure Floating Static Routes (6.4.3)

The floating static route is a great way to create a backup route that will not override your dynamic routing protocols.

Floating Static Routes (6.4.3.1)

Floating static routes are static routes that have an administrative distance greater than the administrative distance of another static route or dynamic routes. They are very useful when providing a backup to a primary link, as shown in Figure 6-88.

By default, static routes have an administrative distance of 1, making them preferable to routes learned from dynamic routing protocols. For example, the administrative distances of some common dynamic routing protocols are

- EIGRP = 90
- IGRP = 100
- OSPF = 110
- IS-IS = 115
- RIP = 120

The administrative distance of a static route can be increased to make the route less desirable than that of another static route or a route learned through a dynamic routing protocol. In this way, the static route "floats" and is not used when the route with the better administrative distance is active. However, if the preferred route is lost, the floating static route can take over, and traffic can be sent through this alternate route.

A floating static route can be used to provide a backup route to multiple interfaces or networks on a router. It is also encapsulation independent, meaning it can be used to forward packets out any interface, regardless of encapsulation type.

An important consideration of a floating static route is that it is affected by convergence time. A route that is continuously dropping and re-establishing a connection can cause the backup interface to be activated unnecessarily.

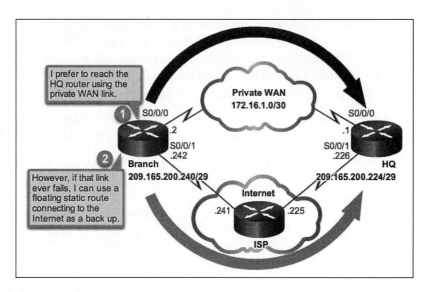

Figure 6-88 Why Configure a Floating Static Route?

Configure a Floating Static Route (6.4.3.2)

IPv4 static routes are configured using the **ip route** global configuration command and specifying an administrative distance. If no administrative distance is configured, the default value (1) is used.

Refer to the topology in Figure 6-89. In this scenario, the preferred route from R1 is to R2. The connection to R3 should be used for backup only.

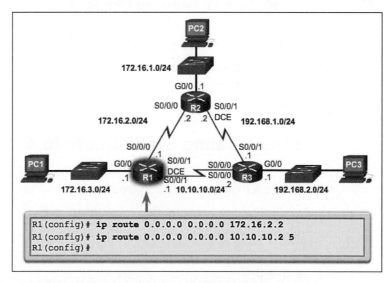

Figure 6-89 Configuring a Floating Static Route to R3

R1 is configured with a default static route pointing to R2. Because no administrative distance is configured, the default value (1) is used for this static route. R1 is also configured with a floating static default pointing to R3 with an administrative distance of 5. This value is greater than the default value of 1 and, therefore, this route floats and is not present in the routing table, unless the preferred route fails.

Figure 6-90 verifies that the default route to R2 is installed in the routing table. Note that the backup route to R3 is not present in the routing table.

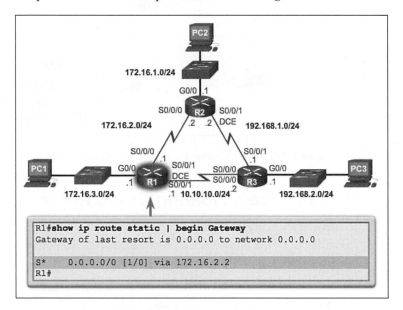

Figure 6-90   Verifying the Routing Table of R1

Interactive Graphic

Activity 6.4.3.2: Configure a Floating Static Route on R3

Go to the course online and use the Syntax Checker in the third graphic to configure a floating static route on router R3.

Test the Floating Static Route (6.4.3.3)

Because the default static route on R1 to R2 has an administrative distance of 1, traffic from R1 to R3 should go through R2.

The output in Figure 6-91 confirms that traffic between R1 and R3 flows through R2.

What would happen if R2 failed? To simulate this failure, both serial interfaces of R2 are shut down, as shown in Figure 6-92.

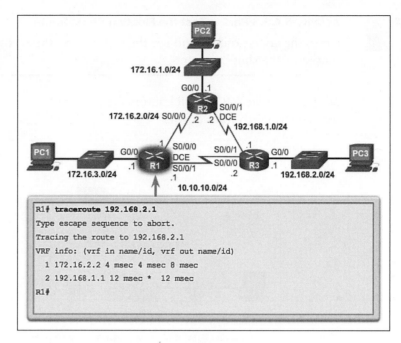

Figure 6-91 Verify the Path to the R3 LAN

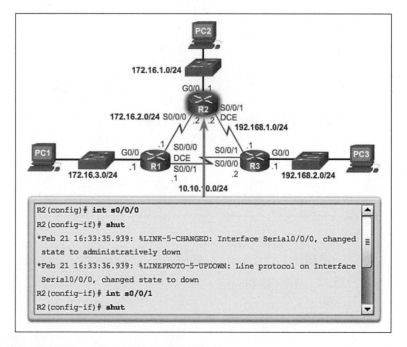

Figure 6-92 Simulate a Router Failure on R2

Activity 6.4.3.3 Part 1: Test the Floating Static Route

Go to the course online, and use the slider bar in the second graphic to see the entire output of the **shut** command.

Notice in Figure 6-93 that R1 automatically generates messages indicating that the serial interface to R2 is down.

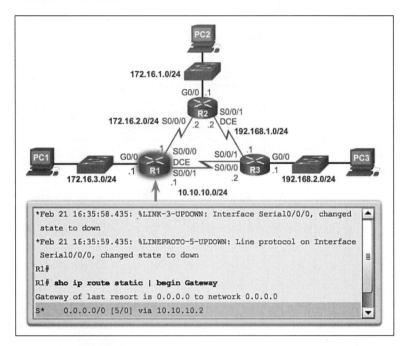

Figure 6-93   Verify the Default Route on R1

Activity 6.4.3.3 Part 2: Verify the Default Route on R1

Go to the course online, and use the slider bar in the third graphic to see the entire output of the **show ip route static** command.

A look at the routing table verifies that the default route is now pointing to R3 using the floating static default route configured for next-hop 10.10.10.2.

The output in Figure 6-94 confirms that traffic now flows directly between R1 and R3.

Note

Configuring IPv6 floating static routes is outside of the scope of this chapter.

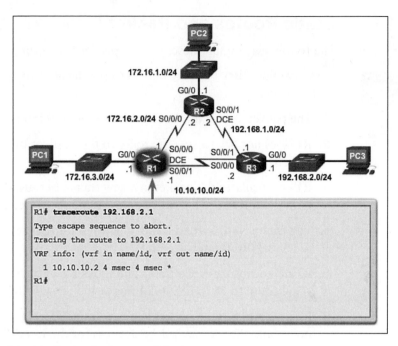

Figure 6-94   Verify the Path to the R3 LAN

Packet Tracer Activity 6.4.3.4: Configuring a Floating Static Route

In this activity, you will configure a floating static route. A floating static route is used as a backup route. It has a manually configured administrative distance greater than that of the primary route and therefore would not be in the routing table until the primary route fails. You will test failover to the backup route, and then restore connectivity to the primary route.

Go to the course online to complete this Packet Tracer activity.

Troubleshoot Static and Default Route Issues (6.5)

Troubleshooting static and default routes are easy, as long as you understand how they work in your network design. The following sections provide some handy steps in the troubleshooting process.

Static Routes and Packet Forwarding (6.5.1.1)

The following example describes the packet-forwarding process with static routes.

In the graphic, click the Play button to see the animation, where PC1 is sending a packet to PC3:

1. The packet arrives on the GigabitEthernet 0/0 interface of R1.

2. R1 does not have a specific route to the destination network, 192.168.2.0/24; therefore, R1 uses the default static route.

3. R1 encapsulates the packet in a new frame. Because the link to R2 is a point-to-point link, R1 adds an "all 1s" address for the Layer 2 destination address.

4. The frame is forwarded out of the Serial 0/0/0 interface. The packet arrives on the Serial 0/0/0 interface on R2.

5. R2 de-encapsulates the frame and looks for a route to the destination. R2 has a static route to 192.168.2.0/24 out of the Serial 0/0/1 interface.

6. R2 encapsulates the packet in a new frame. Because the link to R3 is a point-to-point link, R2 adds an "all 1s" address for the Layer 2 destination address.

7. The frame is forwarded out of the Serial 0/0/1 interface. The packet arrives on the Serial 0/0/1 interface on R3.

8. R3 de-encapsulates the frame and looks for a route to the destination. R3 has a connected route to 192.168.2.0/24 out of the GigabitEthernet 0/0 interface.

9. R3 looks up the ARP table entry for 192.168.2.10 to find the Layer 2 Media Access Control (MAC) address for PC3. If no entry exists, R3 sends an Address Resolution Protocol (ARP) request out of the GigabitEthernet 0/0 interface, and PC3 responds with an ARP reply, which includes the PC3 MAC address.

10. R3 encapsulates the packet in a new frame with the MAC address of the GigabitEthernet 0/0 interface as the source Layer 2 address and the MAC address of PC3 as the destination MAC address.

11. The frame is forwarded out of GigabitEthernet 0/0 interface. The packet arrives on the network interface card (NIC) interface of PC3.

Troubleshoot a Missing Route (6.5.2.1)

Networks are subject to forces that can cause their status to change quite often:

- An interface fails.

- A service provider drops a connection.

- Links become oversaturated.

- An administrator enters a wrong configuration.

When there is a change in the network, connectivity may be lost. Network administrators are responsible for pinpointing and solving the problem. To find and solve these issues, a network administrator must be familiar with tools to help isolate routing problems quickly.

Common IOS troubleshooting commands include

- **ping**

- **traceroute**

- **show ip route**

- **show ip interface brief**

- **show cdp neighbors detail**

Figure 6-95 displays the result of an extended ping from the source interface of R1 to the LAN interface of R3. An extended ping is when the source interface or source IP address is specified.

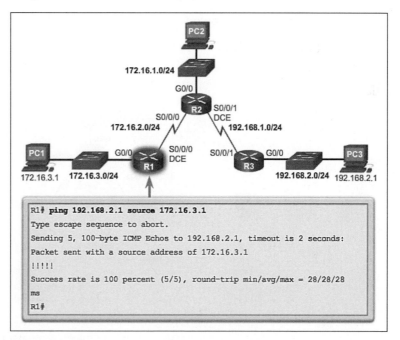

Figure 6-95 Extended Ping

Figure 6-96 displays the result of a traceroute from R1 to the R3 LAN.

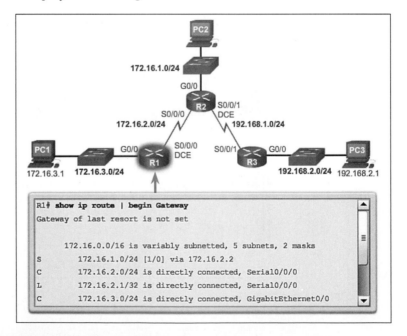

Figure 6-96   Traceroute from R1 to R3

Figure 6-97 displays the routing table of R1.

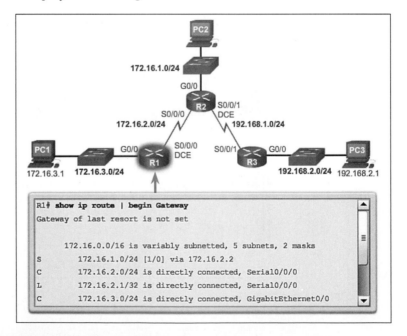

Figure 6-97   Verify the Routing Table

Activity 6.5.2.1 Part 1: Verify the Routing Table

Go to the course online, and use the slider bar in the third graphic to see the entire output of the **show ip route | begin Gateway** command.

Figure 6-98 provides a quick status of all interfaces on the router.

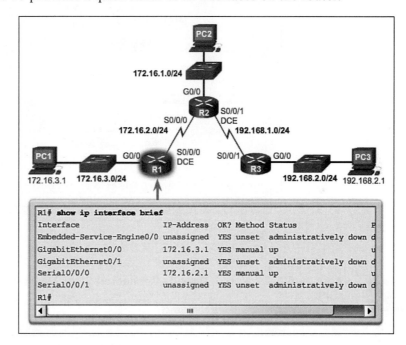

Figure 6-98   Interface Status

Activity 6.5.2.1 Part 2: Interface Status

Go to the course online, and use the slider bar in the fourth graphic to see the entire output of the **show ip interface brief** command.

Figure 6-99 provides a list of directly connected Cisco devices. This command validates Layer 2 (and therefore Layer 1) connectivity. For example, if a neighbor device is listed in the command output, but it cannot be pinged, then Layer 3 addressing should be investigated.

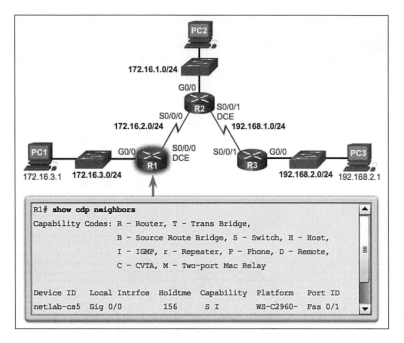

Figure 6-99 Directly Connected Cisco Devices

Activity 6.5.2.1 Part 3: Directly Connected Cisco Devices

Go to the course online, and use the slider bar in the fifth graphic to see the entire output of the **show cdp neighbors** command.

Solve a Connectivity Problem (6.5.2.2)

Finding a missing (or misconfigured) route is a relatively straightforward process if the right tools are used in a methodical manner.

For instance, in Figure 6-100, the user at PC1 reports that he cannot access resources on the R3 LAN. This can be confirmed by pinging the LAN interface of R3 using the LAN interface of R1 as the source. The results show that there is no connectivity between these LANs.

A traceroute in Figure 6-101 reveals that R2 is not responding as expected.

Activity 6.5.2.2 Part 1: Verify Hop-to-Hop Connectivity

Go to the course online, and use the slider bar in the second graphic to see the entire output of the **traceroute** command.

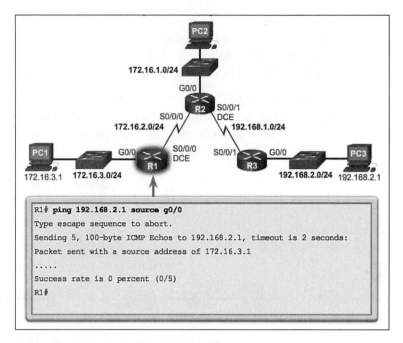

Figure 6-100 Verify Connectivity to the R3 LAN

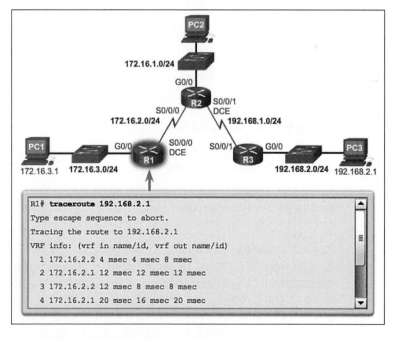

Figure 6-101 Verify Hop-to-Hop Connectivity

For some reason, R2 forwards the traceroute back to R1. R1 returns it to R2. This loop would continue until the time to live (TTL) value decrements to zero, in which case, the router would then send an Internet Control Message Protocol (ICMP) destination unreachable message to R1.

The next step is to investigate the routing table of R2 because it is the router displaying a strange forwarding pattern. The routing table in Figure 6-102 reveals that the 192.168.2.0/24 network is configured incorrectly.

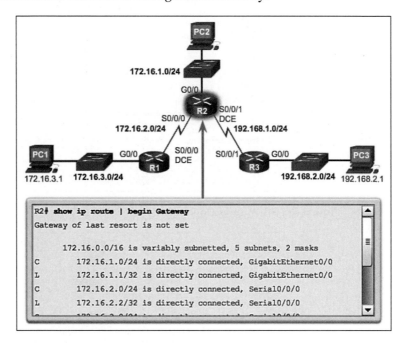

Figure 6-102   Verify the Route Table

Activity 6.5.2.2 Part 2: Verify the Route Table

Go to the course online and use the slider bar in the third graphic to see the entire output of the **show ip route | begin Gateway** command.

A static route to the 192.168.2.0/24 network has been configured using the next-hop address 172.16.2.1. Using the configured next-hop address, packets destined for the 192.168.2.0/24 network are sent back to R1. It is clear from the topology that the 192.168.2.0/24 network is connected to R3, not R1. Therefore, the static route to the 192.168.2.0/24 network on R2 must use next-hop 192.168.1.1, not 172.16.2.1.

Figure 6-103 shows output from the running configuration that reveals the incorrect **ip route** statement. The incorrect route is removed and the correct route is then entered.

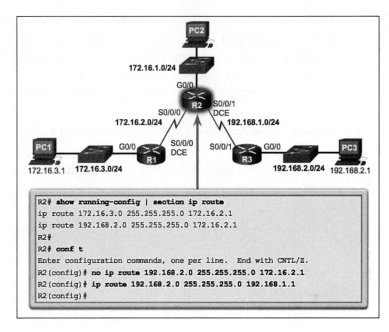

Figure 6-103   Identify and Solve the Problem

Figure 6-104 verifies that R1 can now reach the LAN interface of R3. As a last step in the confirmation, the user on PC1 should also test connectivity to the 192.168.2.0/24 LAN.

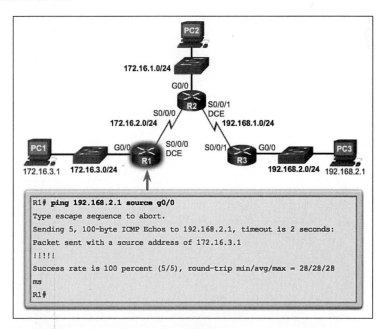

Figure 6-104   Verify Connectivity to the R3 LAN

Packet Tracer Activity 6.5.2.3: Troubleshooting Static Routes

In this activity, PC1 reports that they cannot access resources at Server. Locate the problem, decide on an appropriate solution and resolve the issue. Go to the course online to complete this Packet Tracer activity.

Packet Tracer Activity 6.5.2.4: Troubleshooting VLSM and Route Summarization

In this activity, the network is already addressed using VLSM and configured with static routes. But there is a problem. Locate the issue or issues, determine the best solution, implement the solution, and verify connectivity.

Go to the course online to complete this Packet Tracer activity.

Lab 6.5.2.5: Troubleshooting Static Routes

In this lab, you will complete the following objectives:

- Part 1: Build the Network and Configure Basic Device Settings
- Part 2: Troubleshoot Static Routes in an IPv4 Network
- Part 3: Troubleshoot Static Routes in an IPv6 Network

Summary (6.6)

Class Activity 6.6.1.1: Make It Static

As the use of IPv6 addressing becomes more prevalent, it is important for network administrators to be able to direct network traffic between routers.

To prove that you are able to direct IPv6 traffic correctly and review the IPv6 default static route curriculum concepts, use the topology as shown in the .pdf file provided, specifically for this activity.

Work with a partner to write an IPv6 statement for each of the three scenarios. Try to write the route statements without the assistance of completed labs, Packet Tracer files, etc.

Scenario 1

IPv6 default static route from R2 directing all data through your S0/0/0 interface to the next hop address on R1.

Scenario 2

IPv6 default static route from R3 directing all data through your S0/0/1 interface to the next hop address on R2.

Scenario 3

IPv6 default static route from R2 directing all data through your S0/0/1 interface to the next hop address on R3.

When complete, get together with another group and compare your written answers. Discuss any differences found in your comparisons.

Go to the lab manual to complete this class activity.

Packet Tracer Activity 6.6.1.2: Skills Integration Challenge

The network administrator asked you to implement IPv4 and IPv6 static and default routing in the test environment shown in the topology. Configure each static and default route as directly connected.

Go to the course online to complete this Packet Tracer activity.

In this chapter, you learned how IPv4 and IPv6 static routes can be used to reach remote networks. Remote networks are networks that can be reached only by forwarding the packet to another router. Static routes are easily configured. However, in large networks, this manual operation can become quite cumbersome. Static routes are still used even when a dynamic routing protocol is implemented.

Static routes can be configured with a next-hop IP address, which is commonly the IP address of the next-hop router. When a next-hop IP address is used, the routing table process must resolve this address to an exit interface. On point-to-point serial links, it is usually more efficient to configure the static route with an exit interface. On multi-access networks, such as Ethernet, both a next-hop IP address and an exit interface can be configured on the static route.

Static routes have a default administrative distance of 1. This administrative distance also applies to static routes configured with a next-hop address, as well as an exit interface.

A static route is only entered in the routing table if the next-hop IP address can be resolved through an exit interface. Whether the static route is configured with a next-hop IP address or exit interface, if the exit interface that is used to forward that packet is not in the routing table, the static route is not included in the routing table.

Using CIDR, several static routes can be configured as a single summary route. This means fewer entries in the routing table and results in a faster routing table lookup process. CIDR also manages the IPv4 address space more efficiently.

VLSM subnetting is similar to traditional subnetting in that bits are borrowed to create subnets. With VLSM, the network is first subnetted, and then the subnets are subnetted again. This process can be repeated multiple times to create subnets of various sizes.

The ultimate summary route is a default route configured with a 0.0.0.0 network address and a 0.0.0.0 subnet mask for IPv4 and the prefix/prefix-length ::/0 for IPv6. If there is not a more specific match in the routing table, the routing table uses the default route to forward the packet to another router.

A floating static route can be configured to back up a main link by manipulating its administrative value.

Practice

The following activities provide practice with the topics introduced in this chapter. The Labs and Class Activities are available in the companion *Routing and Switching Essentials Lab Manual* (978-1-58713-320-6). You can find the Packet Tracer Activities PKA files in the online course.

Class Activities

Class Activity 6.0.1.2: Which Way Should We Go?

Class Activity 6.6.1.1: Make It Static!

Labs

Lab 6.2.2.5: Configuring IPv4 Static and Default Routes

Lab 6.2.4.5: Configuring IPv6 Static and Default Routes

Lab 6.3.3.7: Designing and Implementing IPv4 Addressing with VLSM

Lab 6.4.2.5: Calculating Summary Routes with IPv4 and IPv6

Lab 6.5.2.5: Troubleshooting IPv4 and IPv6 Static Routes

Packet Tracer Activities

Packet Tracer Activity 6.2.2.4: Configuring IPv4 Static and Default Routes

Packet Tracer Activity 6.2.4.4: Configuring IPv6 Static and Default Routes

Packet Tracer Activity 6.3.3.6: Designing and Implementing a VLSM Addressing Scheme

Packet Tracer Activity 6.4.1.5: Configuring IPv4 Route Summarization – Part I

Packet Tracer Activity 6.4.1.6: Configuring IPv4 Route Summarization – Part II

Packet Tracer Activity 6.4.2.4: Calculating and Configuring an IP6 Route Summarization

Packet Tracer Activity 6.4.3.4: Configuring a Floating Static Route

Packet Tracer Activity 6.5.2.3: Troubleshooting Static Routes

Packet Tracer Activity 6.5.2.4: Troubleshooting VLSM and Route Summarization

Packet Tracer Activity 6.6.1.2: Skills Integration Challenge

Check Your Understanding Questions

Complete all the review questions listed here to test your understanding of the topics and concepts in this chapter. The appendix, "Answers to the 'Check Your Understanding' Questions," lists the answers.

1. Which statement is true concerning configuring static routes using next-hop addresses?

   A. Routers cannot use more than one static route with a next-hop address.

   B. When the router identifies that a packet is destined for a route associated with a next-hop address in the routing table, the router requires no further information and can immediately forward the packet.

   C. Routers configured with the static route using a next-hop address must either have the exit interface listed in the route or have another route with the network of the next hop and an associated exit interface.

   D. Routes associated with a next-hop address are more efficient than routes going to exit interfaces.

2. Which of the following are three characteristics of a static route? (Choose three.)

   A. Reduces the memory and processing burdens on a router

   B. Ensures that there is always a path available

   C. Used to dynamically find the best path to a destination network

   D. Used for routers that connect to stub networks

   E. Used for networks with a single route to a destination network

   F. Reduces configuration time

3. Which option shows a correctly configured IPv4 default static route?

   A. **ip route 0.0.0.0 0.0.0.0 S0/0/0**

   B. **ip route 0.0.0.0 255.255.255.0 S0/0/0**

   C. **ip route 0.0.0.0 255.255.255.255 S0/0/0**

   D. **ip route 0.0.0.0 255.0.0.0 S0/0/0**

4. A network administrator enters the following command into Router1: **ip route 192.168.0.0 255.255.255.0 S0/1/0**. Router1 then receives a packet that is destined for 192.168.0.22/24. After finding the recently configured static route in the routing table, what does Router1 do next to process the packet?

    A. Drops the packet because the destination host is not listed in the routing table

    B. Looks up the MAC address of the S0/1/0 interface to determine the destination MAC address of the new frame

    C. Performs a recursive lookup for the IP address of the S0/1/0 interface before forwarding the packet

    D. Encapsulates the packet into a frame for the WAN link and forwards the packet out the S0/1/0 interface

5. What type of static route is created when the next-hop IP address and exit interface are specified?

    A. Recursive static route

    B. Directly connected static route

    C. Fully specified static route

    D. Floating static route

6. Why would a summarized static route be configured on a router?

    A. To reduce the number of public IP addresses required by an organization

    B. To provide a better route than a particular routing protocol

    C. To provide a default gateway for a router that connects to an ISP

    D. To reduce the size of the routing table

    E. To reduce the size of the routing protocol update to a neighboring router

7. Which subnet mask would be used for a network that has a maximum of 300 devices?

    A. 255.255.255.0

    B. 255.255.254.0

    C. 255.255.252.0

    D. 255.255.248.0

    E. 255.255.240.0

8. Which two conditions must exist in order to summarize IPv6 routes into a single static IPv6 route? (Choose two.)

   A. The destination networks are contiguous and can be summarized into a single network address.

   B. The multiple static routes all use different exit-interface or next-hop IPv6 address.

   C. The destination networks are not contiguous.

   D. The multiple static routes all use the same exit-interface or next-hop IPv6 address.

   E. The administrative distance is greater than the administrative distance of another static route or dynamic routes.

9. What command, or set of commands, would be used to determine if the following configuration on router HQ works as designed?

   ```
   ip route 0.0.0.0 0.0.0.0 serial 0/0/0 10
   ```

   ```
   ip route 0.0.0.0 0.0.0.0 serial 0/1/0
   ```

   A. `HQ(config)# interface serial 0/1/0`

      `HQ(config-if)# shutdown`

      `HQ(config-if)# end`

      `HQ# show ip route`

   B. `HQ# traceroute 128.107.0.99`

   C. `HQ# show ip interface brief`

   D. `HQ# ping 128.107.0.99`

      `HQ# ping 64.100.0.5`

   E. `HQ# show ip route`

10. Which is a valid summary route for networks 192.168.8.0/22, 192.168.12.0/22, and 192.168.16.0/22?

    A. 192.168.0.0/18

    B. 192.168.0.0/19

    C. 192.168.0.0/20

    D. 192.168.8.0/21

CHAPTER 7

Routing Dynamically

Objectives

Upon completion of this chapter, you will be able to answer the following questions:

- What is the purpose of dynamic routing protocols?

- What is the difference between dynamic routing versus static routing?

- How do dynamic routing protocols share route information and achieve convergence?

- What are the different categories of routing protocols?

- What is the algorithm used by distance vector routing protocols to determine the best path?

- What are the different types of distance vector routing protocols?

- How do you configure the RIP routing protocol?

- How do you configure the RIPng routing protocol?

- What is the algorithm used by link-state routing protocols to determine the best path?

- How does the link-state routing protocol use the information sent in a link-state update?

- What are the advantages and disadvantages of using a link-state routing protocol?

- How do you determine the route source, administrative distance, and metric for any given route?

- Describe the concept of a parent/child relationship in a dynamically built routing table?

- What are the differences between the IPv4 classless route lookup routing process and the IPv6 lookup process?

- How do you determine which route in a route table will be used to forward a packet?

Key Terms

This chapter uses the following key terms. You can find the definitions in the Glossary.

Introduction (7.0.1.1)

The data networks that we use in our everyday lives to learn, play, and work range from small, local networks to large, global internetworks. At home, a user may have a router and two or more computers. At work, an organization may have multiple routers and switches servicing the data communication needs of hundreds or even thousands of PCs.

Routers forward packets by using information in the routing table. Routes to remote networks can be learned by the router in two ways: static routes and dynamic routes.

In a large network with numerous networks and subnets, configuring and maintaining static routes between these networks requires a great deal of administrative and operational overhead. This operational overhead is especially cumbersome when changes to the network occur, such as a down link or implementing a new subnet. Implementing dynamic routing protocols can ease the burden of configuration and maintenance tasks and give the network scalability.

This chapter introduces dynamic routing protocols. It explores the benefits of using dynamic routing protocols, how different routing protocols are classified, and the *metrics* routing protocols use to determine the best path for network traffic. Other topics covered in this chapter include the characteristics of dynamic routing protocols and how the various routing protocols differ. Network professionals must understand the different routing protocols available to make informed decisions about when to use static or dynamic routing. They also need to know which dynamic routing protocol is most appropriate in a particular network environment.

Class Activity 7.0.1.2 How Much Does This Cost

This modeling activity illustrates the network concept of routing cost.

You will be a member of a team of five students who travel routes to complete the activity scenarios. One digital camera or bring your own device (BYOD) with camera, a stopwatch, and the student file for this activity will be required per group. One person will function as the photographer and event recorder, as selected by each group. The remaining four team members will actively participate in the following scenarios.

A school or university classroom, hallway, outdoor track area, school parking lot, or any other location can serve as the venue for these activities.

Activity 1

The tallest person in the group establishes a start and finish line by marking 15 steps from start to finish, indicating the distance of the team route. Each student will take 15 steps from the start line toward the finish line and then stop on the 15th step; no further steps are allowed.

Note

Not all the students may reach the same distance from the start line due to their height and stride differences. The photographer will take a group picture of the entire team's final location after taking the 15 steps required.

Activity 2

A new start and finish line will be established; however, this time, a longer distance for the route will be established than the distance specified in Activity 1. No maximum steps are to be used as a basis for creating this particular route. One at a time, students will "walk the new route from beginning to end twice."

Each team member will count the steps taken to complete the route. The recorder will time each student and at the end of each team member's route, record the time that it took to complete the full route and how many steps were taken, as recounted by each team member and recorded on the team's student file.

After both activities have been completed, teams will use the digital picture taken for Activity 1 and their recorded data from Activity 2 file to answer the reflection questions.

Group answers can be discussed as a class, time permitting.

Dynamic Routing Protocol Operation (7.1.1)

Before you look at the dynamic protocols, you should first look at where they came from, and why they were needed in the first place. This next section looks at the evolution of dynamic routing protocols.

The Evolution of Dynamic Routing Protocols (7.1.1.1)

Dynamic routing protocols have been used in networks since the late 1980s. One of the first routing protocols was Routing Information Protocol (RIP). RIP version 1 (RIPv1) was released in 1988, but some of the basic algorithms within the protocol were used on the Advanced Research Projects Agency Network (ARPANET) as early as 1969.

As networks evolved and became more complex, new routing protocols emerged. The RIP routing protocol was updated to accommodate growth in the network environment, into RIPv2. However, the newer version of RIP still does not scale to the larger network implementations of today. To address the needs of larger networks, two advanced routing protocols were developed: Open Shortest Path First (OSPF) and Intermediate System-to-Intermediate System (IS-IS). Cisco developed the Interior Gateway Routing Protocol (IGRP) and Enhanced IGRP (EIGRP), which also scales well in larger network implementations.

Additionally, there was the need to connect different internetworks and provide routing between them. The Border Gateway Protocol (BGP) is now used between Internet service providers (ISP). BGP is also used between ISPs and their larger private clients to exchange routing information.

Interactive Graphic

Go to the course online and look at the first graphic in section 7.1.1.1. Here you are introduced to a timeline showing when the various protocols were introduced.

Table 7-1 classifies the protocols.

Table 7-1   Routing Protocol Classification

	Interior Gateway Protocols				**Exterior Gateway Protocols**
	Distance Vector		Link-State		Path-Vector
IPv4	RIPv2	EIGRP	OSPFv2	IS-IS	BGP-4
IPv6	RIP ng	EIGRP for IPv6	OSPF v3	IS-IS for IPv6	BGP-MP

With the advent of numerous consumer devices using IP, the IPv4 addressing space is nearly exhausted; thus, IPv6 has emerged. To support the communication based on IPv6, newer versions of the IP routing protocols have been developed; see the IPv6 row in the figure.

RIP is the simplest of dynamic routing protocols and is used in this section to provide a basic level of routing protocol understanding.

Purpose of Dynamic Routing Protocols (7.1.1.2)

Routing protocols are used to facilitate the exchange of routing information between routers. A routing protocol is a set of processes, algorithms, and messages that are used to exchange routing information and populate the routing table with the routing protocol's choice of best paths. The purpose of dynamic routing protocols includes

- Discovery of remote networks

- Maintaining up-to-date routing information

- Choosing the best path to destination networks

- Ability to find a new best path if the current path is no longer available

The main components of dynamic routing protocols include

- *Data structures:* Routing protocols typically use tables or databases for their operations. This information is kept in RAM.

- **Routing protocol messages:** Routing protocols use various types of messages to discover neighboring routers, exchange routing information, and other tasks to learn and maintain accurate information about the network.

- *Algorithm:* An algorithm is a finite list of steps used to accomplish a task. Routing protocols use algorithms for facilitating routing information and for best path determination.

Figure 7-1 highlights the data structures, routing protocol messages, and routing algorithm used by EIGRP.

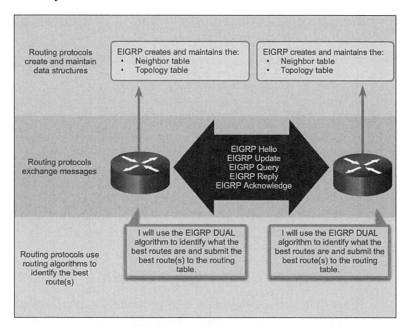

Figure 7-1   Components of Routing Protocols

The Role of Dynamic Routing Protocols (7.1.1.3)

Routing protocols allow routers to dynamically share information about remote networks and automatically add this information to their own routing tables.

Video

Video 7.1.1.3: Routers Dynamically Share Updates

Go to the course and play the video of update packets being exchanged between three routers.

Routing protocols determine the best path, or route, to each network. That route is then added to the routing table. A primary benefit of dynamic routing protocols is that routers exchange routing information when there is a topology change. This exchange allows routers to automatically learn about new networks and also to find alternate paths when there is a link failure to a current network.

Compared to static routing, dynamic routing protocols require less administrative overhead. However, the expense of using dynamic routing protocols is dedicating part of a router's resources for protocol operation, including CPU time and network link bandwidth. Despite the benefits of dynamic routing, static routing still has its place. There are times when static routing is more appropriate and other times when dynamic routing is the better choice. Networks with moderate levels of complexity may have both static and dynamic routing configured.

Interactive Graphic

Activity 7.1.1.4 Part 1: Identify Components of a Routing Protocol - EIGRP

Go to the course online and complete the activity in the first graphic identifying components of EIGRP.

Interactive Graphic

Activity 7.1.1.4 Part 2: Identify Components of a Routing Protocol - EIGRP

Go to the course online and complete the activity in the second graphic identifying components of EIGRP.

Interactive Graphic

Activity 7.1.1.4 Part 3: Identify Components of a Routing Protocol - EIGRP

Go to the course online and complete the activity in the third graphic identifying components of EIGRP.

Dynamic Versus Static Routing (7.1.2)

To understand the power of dynamic routing protocols, review what you know about static routing and compare it to dynamic protocols first.

Using Static Routing (7.1.2.1)

Before identifying the benefits of dynamic routing protocols, consider the reasons why network professionals use static routing. Dynamic routing certainly has several advantages over static routing; however, static routing is still used in networks today. In fact, networks typically use a combination of both static and dynamic routing.

Static routing has several primary uses, including

- Providing ease of routing table maintenance in smaller networks that are not expected to grow significantly

- Routing to and from a stub network, which is a network with only one default route out and no knowledge of any remote networks

- Accessing a single default route (which is used to represent a path to any network that does not have a more specific match with another route in the routing table)

Figure 7-2 provides a sample scenario of static routing.

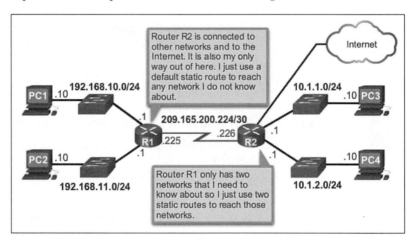

Figure 7-2 Static Routing Scenario

Static Routing Scorecard (7.1.2.2)

Table 7-2 highlights the advantages and disadvantages of static routing. Static routing is easy to implement in a small network. Static routes stay the same, which makes them fairly easy to troubleshoot. Static routes do not send update messages and, therefore, require very little overhead.

The disadvantages of static routing include

- They are not easy to implement in a large network.

- Managing the static configurations can become time-consuming.

- If a link fails, a static route cannot reroute traffic.

Table 7-2   Static Routing Advantages and Disadvantages

Advantage	Disadvantage
Easy to implement in a small network.	Suitable only for simple topologies or for special purposes such as default static route. Configuration complexity increases dramatically as network grows.
Very secure. No advertisements are sent as compared to dynamic routing protocols.	
Route destination is always the same.	Manual intervention required to reroute traffic.
No routing algorithm or update mechanism required; therefore, extra resources (CPU or RAM) are not required.	

Using Dynamic Routing Protocols (7.1.2.3)

Dynamic routing protocols help the network administrator manage the time-consuming and exacting process of configuring and maintaining static routes.

Imagine maintaining the static routing configurations for the seven routers in Figure 7-3.

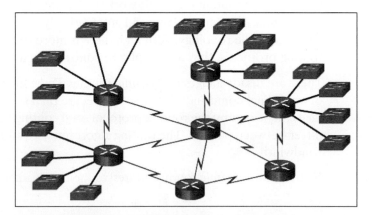

Figure 7-3   Dynamic Routing Scenario

What if the company grew and now had four regions and 28 routers to manage, as shown in Figure 7-4?

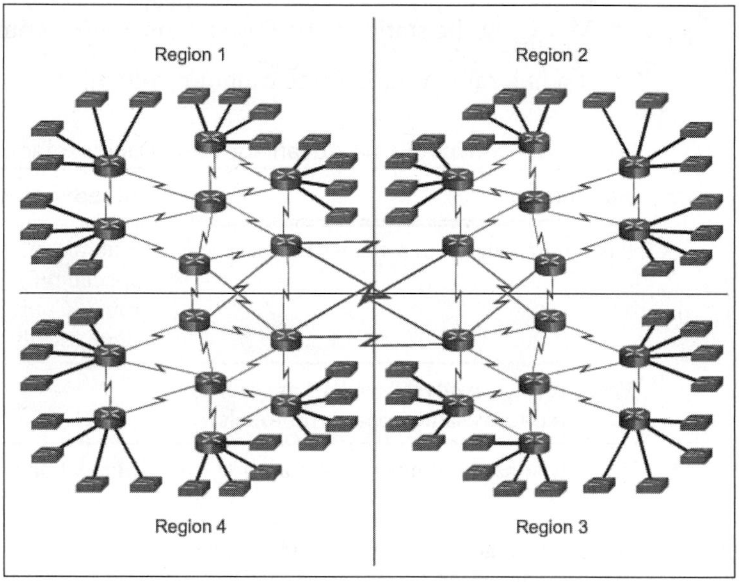

Figure 7-4 Dynamic Routing Scenario

What happens when a link goes down? How do you ensure that redundant paths are available?

Dynamic routing is the best choice for large networks.

Dynamic Routing Scorecard (7.1.2.4)

The table in the figure highlights the advantages and disadvantages of dynamic routing. Dynamic routing protocols work well in any type of network consisting of several routers. They are scalable and automatically determine better routes if there is a change in the topology. Although there is more to the configuration of dynamic routing protocols, they are simpler to configure in a large network.

There are disadvantages to dynamic routing. Dynamic routing requires knowledge of additional commands. It is also less secure than static routing because the interfaces identified by the routing protocol send routing updates out. Routes taken may differ between packets. The routing algorithm uses additional CPU, RAM, and link bandwidth.

Notice how dynamic routing addresses the disadvantages of static routing.

Table 7-3   Dynamic Routing Advantages and Disadvantages

Advantage	Disadvantage
Suitable in all topologies where multiple routers are required	Can be more complex to implement.
Generally independent of the network size	Less secure. Additional configuration settings are required to secure.
Automatically adapts topology to reroute traffic if possible	Route depends on the current topology.
	Requires additional CPU, RAM, and link bandwidth.

Interactive
Graphic

Activity 7.1.2.5: Compare Static and Dynamic Routing

Go to the course online and complete the activity in which you classify each routing type description as either Static or Dynamic Routing.

Routing Protocol Operating Fundamentals (7.1.3)

This next section deals with how dynamic routing protocols operate in a generic fashion. Later you move onto specific dynamic routing protocols to see how they operate.

Dynamic Routing Protocol Operation (7.1.3.1)

All routing protocols are designed to learn about remote networks and to quickly adapt whenever there is a change in the topology. The method that a routing protocol uses to accomplish this depends upon the algorithm it uses and the operational characteristics of that protocol.

In general, the operations of a dynamic routing protocol can be described as follows:

1. The router sends and receives routing messages on its interfaces.

2. The router shares routing messages and routing information with other routers that are using the same routing protocol.

3. Routers exchange routing information to learn about remote networks.

4. When a router detects a topology change, the routing protocol can advertise this change to other routers.

Video 7.1.3.1: Routing Protocol Operation.

Go to the course online and play the video of dynamic routing protocols in operation.

Cold Start (7.1.3.2)

All routing protocols follow the same patterns of operation. To help illustrate this, consider the following scenario in which all three routers are running RIPv2.

When a router powers up, it knows nothing about the network topology. It does not even know that there are devices on the other end of its links. The only information that a router has is from its own saved configuration file stored in NVRAM. After a router boots successfully, it applies the saved configuration. If the IP addressing is configured correctly, then the router initially discovers its own directly connected networks.

Video 7.1.3.2: Initial Discovery of Directly Connected Networks

Go to the course online and play the video of the initial discovery of connected networks for each router.

Notice how the routers proceed through the boot up process and then discovers any directly connected networks and subnet masks. This information is added to their routing tables as follows:

- R1 adds the 10.1.0.0 network available through interface FastEthernet 0/0 and 10.2.0.0 is available through interface Serial 0/0/0.

- R2 adds the 10.2.0.0 network available through interface Serial 0/0/0 and 10.3.0.0 is available through interface Serial 0/0/1.

- R3 adds the 10.3.0.0 network available through interface Serial 0/0/1 and 10.4.0.0 is available through interface FastEthernet 0/0.

With this initial information, the routers then proceed to find additional route sources for their routing tables.

Network Discovery (7.1.3.3)

After initial boot up and discovery, the routing table is updated with all directly connected networks and the interfaces those networks reside on.

If a routing protocol is configured, the next step is for the router to begin exchanging routing updates to learn about any remote routes.

The router sends an update packet out all interfaces that are enabled on the router. The update contains the information in the routing table, which currently are all directly connected networks.

At the same time, the router also receives and processes similar updates from other connected routers. Upon receiving an update, the router checks it for new network information. Any networks that are not currently listed in the routing table are added.

Refer to Figure 7-5 for a topology setup between three routers: R1, R2, and R3.

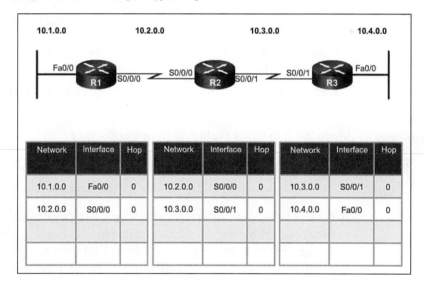

Figure 7-5 Initial Exchange of Information

Based on this topology, following is a listing of the different updates that R1, R2, and R3 send and receive during initial convergence.

R1:

- Sends an update about network 10.1.0.0 out the Serial0/0/0 interface.
- Sends an update about network 10.2.0.0 out the FastEthernet0/0 interface.
- Receives update from R2 about network 10.3.0.0 and increments the hop count by 1.
- Stores network 10.3.0.0 in the routing table with a metric of 1.

R2:

- Sends an update about network 10.3.0.0 out the Serial 0/0/0 interface.

- Sends an update about network 10.2.0.0 out the Serial 0/0/1 interface.

- Receives an update from R1 about network 10.1.0.0 and increments the hop count by 1.

- Stores network 10.1.0.0 in the routing table with a metric of 1.

- Receives an update from R3 about network 10.4.0.0 and increments the hop count by 1.

- Stores network 10.4.0.0 in the routing table with a metric of 1.

R3:

- Sends an update about network 10.4.0.0 out the Serial 0/0/1 interface.

- Sends an update about network 10.3.0.0 out the FastEthernet0/0.

- Receives an update from R2 about network 10.2.0.0 and increments the hop count by 1.

- Stores network 10.2.0.0 in the routing table with a metric of 1.

Video

Video 7.1.3.3: Initial Exchange Between Routers

Go to the course online and play the video of the initial exchange of information between three routers.

After this first round of update exchanges, each router knows about the connected networks of their directly connected neighbors. However, did you notice that R1 does not yet know about 10.4.0.0 and that R3 does not yet know about 10.1.0.0? Full knowledge and a converged network do not take place until there is another exchange of routing information.

Exchanging the Routing Information (7.1.3.4)

At this point the routers have knowledge about their own directly connected networks and about the connected networks of their immediate neighbors. Continuing the journey toward convergence, the routers exchange the next round of *periodic updates*. Each router again checks the updates for new information.

Refer to Figure 7-6 for a topology setup between three routers: R1, R2, and R3. After initial discovery is complete, each router continues the convergence process by sending and receiving the following updates.

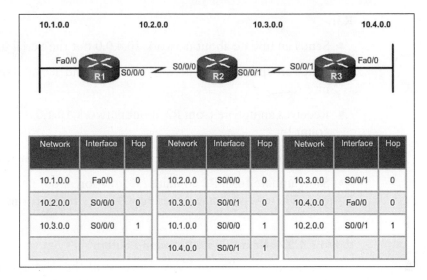

Figure 7-6 Next Update

R1:

- Sends an update about network 10.1.0.0 out the Serial 0/0/0 interface.

- Sends an update about networks 10.2.0.0 and 10.3.0.0 out the FastEthernet0/0 interface.

- Receives an update from R2 about network 10.4.0.0 and increments the hop count by 1.

- Stores network 10.4.0.0 in the routing table with a metric of 2.

- Same update from R2 contains information about network 10.3.0.0 with a metric of 1. There is no change; therefore, the routing information remains the same.

R2:

- Sends an update about networks 10.3.0.0 and 10.4.0.0 out of Serial 0/0/0 interface.

- Sends an update about networks 10.1.0.0 and 10.2.0.0 out of Serial 0/0/1 interface.

- Receives an update from R1 about network 10.1.0.0. There is no change; therefore, the routing information remains the same.

- Receives an update from R3 about network 10.4.0.0. There is no change; therefore, the routing information remains the same.

R3:

- Sends an update about network 10.4.0.0 out the Serial 0/0/1 interface.

- Sends an update about networks 10.2.0.0 and 10.3.0.0 out the FastEthernet0/0 interface.

- Receives an update from R2 about network 10.1.0.0 and increments the hop count by 1.

- Stores network 10.1.0.0 in the routing table with a metric of 2.

- Same update from R2 contains information about network 10.2.0.0 with a metric of 1. There is no change; therefore, the routing information remains the same.

Video 7.1.3.4: Next Update Between Routers

Go to the course online and play the video of the next update of information between three routers.

Distance vector routing protocols typically implement a routing loop prevention technique known as *split horizon*. Split horizon prevents information from being sent out the same interface from which it was received. For example, R2 does not send an update containing the network 10.1.0.0 out of Serial 0/0/0 because R2 learned about network 10.1.0.0 through Serial 0/0/0.

After routers within a network have converged, the router can then use the information within the route table to determine the best path to reach a destination. Different routing protocols have different ways of calculating the best path.

Achieving Convergence (7.1.3.5)

The network has converged when all routers have complete and accurate information about the entire network, as shown in Figure 7-7.

Convergence time is the time it takes routers to share information, calculate best paths, and update their routing tables. A network is not completely operable until the network has converged; therefore, most networks require short convergence times.

Convergence is both collaborative and independent. The routers share information with each other but must independently calculate the impacts of the topology change on their own routes. Because they develop an agreement with the new topology independently, they are said to converge on this consensus.

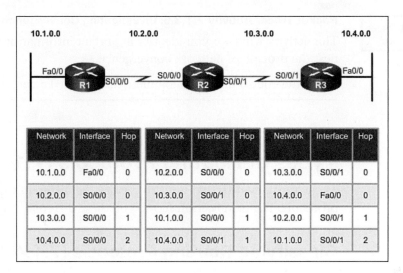

Figure 7-7 Convergence

Convergence properties include the speed of propagation of routing information and the calculation of optimal paths. The speed of propagation refers to the amount of time it takes for routers within the network to forward routing information.

As shown in Figure 7-8, routing protocols can be rated based on the speed to convergence; the faster the convergence, the better the routing protocol. Generally, older protocols, such as RIP, are slow to converge, whereas modern protocols, such as EIGRP and OSPF, converge more quickly.

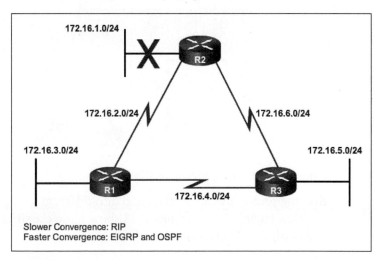

Figure 7-8 Convergence Speeds

Packet Tracer
☐ Activity

Packet Tracer Activity 7.1.3.6: Investigating Convergence

This activity will help you identify important information in routing tables and witness the process of network convergence.

Go to the course online to complete this Packet Tracer activity.

Types of Routing Protocols (7.1.4)

There are many different ways to classify the different types of dynamic routing protocols. The next section shows you these different ways.

Classifying Routing Protocols (7.1.4.1)

Figure 7-9 displays a hierarchical view of dynamic routing protocol classification.

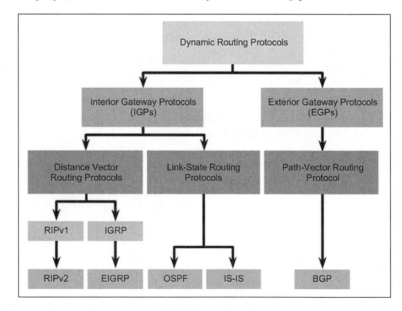

Figure 7-9   Routing Protocols Classification

Routing protocols can be classified into different groups according to their characteristics. Figures 7-10 through 7-13 show these classifications. Specifically, routing protocols can be classified by their

- **Purpose:** *Interior Gateway Protocol (IGP)* or *Exterior Gateway Protocol (EGP)*

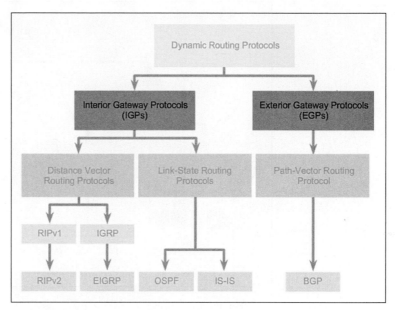

Figure 7-10   Classifying Routing Protocols by Purpose

- **Operation:** Distance vector, link-state protocol, or path-vector protocol

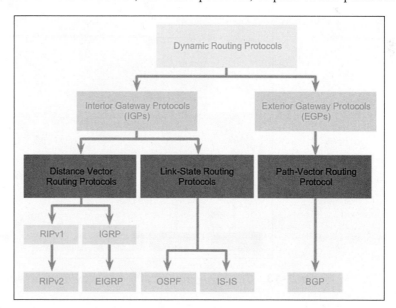

Figure 7-11   Classifying Routing Protocols by Operation

■ **Behavior:** Classful (legacy) or classless protocol

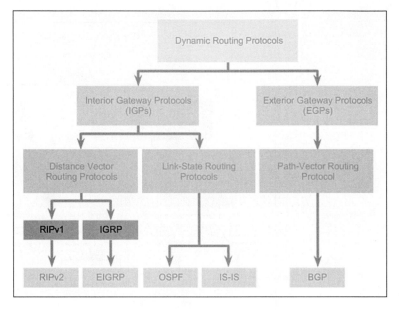

Figure 7-12   Classifying Routing Protocols by Classful Behavior

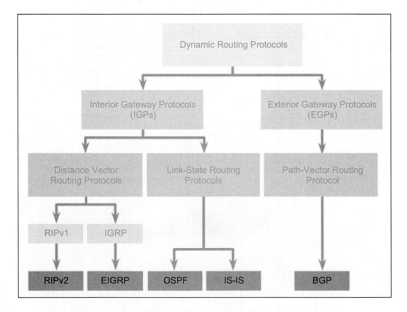

Figure 7-13   Classifying Routing Protocols by Classless Behavior

For example, IPv4 routing protocols are classified as follows:

- **RIPv1 (legacy):** IGP, distance vector, classful protocol
- **IGRP (legacy):** IGP, distance vector, classful protocol developed by Cisco (deprecated from 12.2 IOS and later)
- **RIPv2:** IGP, distance vector, classless protocol
- **EIGRP:** IGP, distance vector, classless protocol developed by Cisco
- **OSPF:** IGP, link-state, classless protocol
- **IS-IS:** IGP, link-state, classless protocol
- **BGP:** EGP, path-vector, classless protocol

The classful routing protocols, RIPv1 and IGRP, are *legacy protocols* and are used only in older networks. These routing protocols have evolved into the classless routing protocols, RIPv2 and EIGRP, respectively. Link-state routing protocols are classless by nature.

IGP and EGP Routing Protocols (7.1.4.2)

An *autonomous system (AS)* is a collection of routers under a common administration such as a company or an organization. An AS is also known as a routing domain. Typical examples of an AS are a company's internal network and an ISP's network.

The Internet is based on the AS concept; therefore, two types of routing protocols are required:

- **Interior Gateway Protocols (IGP):** Used for routing within an AS. It is also referred to as intra-AS routing. Companies, organizations, and even service providers use an IGP on their internal networks. IGPs include RIP, EIGRP, OSPF, and IS-IS.
- **Exterior Gateway Protocols (EGP):** Used for routing between AS. It is also referred to as inter-AS routing. Service providers and large companies may interconnect using an EGP. The Border Gateway Protocol (BGP) is the only currently viable EGP and is the official routing protocol used by the Internet.

Note

Because BGP is the only EGP available, the term EGP is rarely used; instead, most engineers simply refer to BGP.

The example in Figure 7-14 provides simple scenarios highlighting the deployment of IGPs, BGP, and static routing.

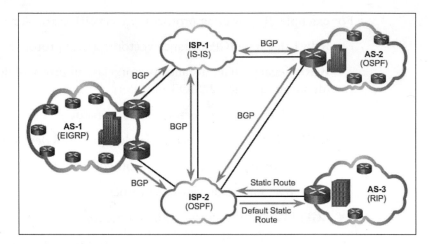

Figure 7-14 IGP Versus EGP Routing Protocols

- **ISP-1:** This is an AS and it uses IS-IS as the IGP. It interconnects with other autonomous systems and service providers using BGP to explicitly control how traffic is routed.

- **ISP-2:** This is an AS and it uses OSPF as the IGP. It interconnects with other autonomous systems and service providers using BGP to explicitly control how traffic is routed.

- **AS-1:** This is a large organization and it uses EIGRP as the IGP. Because it is multihomed (that is, connects to two different service providers), it uses BGP to explicitly control how traffic enters and leaves the AS.

- **AS-2:** This is a medium-sized organization and it uses OSPF as the IGP. It is also multihomed; therefore, it uses BGP to explicitly control how traffic enters and leaves the AS.

- **AS-3:** This is a small organization with older routers within the AS; it uses RIP as the IGP. BGP is not required because it is single-homed (that is, connects to one service provider). Instead, static routing is implemented between the AS and the service provider.

Note

BGP is beyond the scope of this course and is not discussed in detail.

Distance Vector Routing Protocols (7.1.4.3)

Distance vector means that routes are advertised by providing two characteristics:

- *Distance*: Identifies how far it is to the destination network and is based on a metric such as the hop count, cost, bandwidth, delay, and more.

- *Vector*: Specifies the direction of the next-hop router or exit interface to reach the destination.

For example, in Figure 7-15, R1 knows that the distance to reach network 172.16.3.0/24 is one hop and that the direction is out of the interface S0/0/0 toward R2.

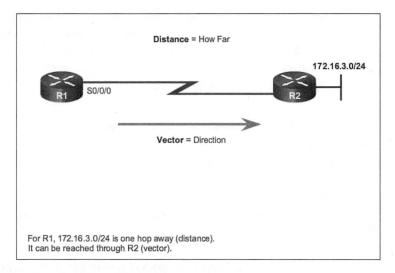

Figure 7-15   The Meaning of Distance Vector

A router using a distance vector routing protocol does not have the knowledge of the entire path to a destination network. Distance vector protocols use routers as sign posts along the path to the final destination. The only information a router knows about a remote network is the distance or metric to reach that network and which path or interface to use to get there. Distance vector routing protocols do not have an actual map of the network topology.

There are four distance vector IPv4 IGPs:

- **RIPv1:** First-generation legacy protocol

- **RIPv2:** Simple distance vector routing protocol

- **IGRP:** First-generation Cisco-proprietary protocol (obsolete and replaced by EIGRP)

- **EIGRP:** Advanced version of distance vector routing

Link-State Routing Protocols (7.1.4.4)

In contrast to distance vector routing protocol operation, a router configured with a link-state routing protocol can create a complete view or topology of the network by gathering information from all of the other routers.

To continue the analogy of sign posts, using a link-state routing protocol is like having a complete map of the network topology. The sign posts along the way from source to destination are not necessary because all link-state routers are using an identical map of the network. A link-state router uses the link-state information to create a topology map and to select the best path to all destination networks in the topology.

RIP-enabled routers send periodic updates of their routing information to their neighbors. Link-state routing protocols do not use periodic updates. After the network has converged, a link-state update is only sent when there is a change in the topology. For example, the link-state update in the animation is not sent until the 172.16.3.0 network goes down.

Video

Video 7.1.4.4: Link-State Protocol Operation

Go to the course and play the video of link-state protocols forwarding updates when the state of a link changes.

Link-state protocols work best in situations where

- The network design is hierarchical, usually occurring in large networks.
- Fast convergence of the network is crucial.
- The administrators have good knowledge of the implemented link-state routing protocol.

There are two link-state IPv4 IGPs:

- **OSPF:** Popular standards-based routing protocol
- **IS-IS:** Popular in provider networks

Classful Routing Protocols (7.1.4.5)

The biggest distinction between classful and classless routing protocols is that classful routing protocols do not send subnet mask information in their routing updates. Classless routing protocols include subnet mask information in the routing updates.

The two original IPv4 routing protocols developed were RIPv1 and IGRP. They were created when network addresses were allocated based on classes (that is, class A, B, or C). At that time, a routing protocol did not need to include the subnet mask in the routing update because the network mask could be determined based on the first octet of the network address.

> **Note**
>
> Only RIPv1 and IGRP are classful. All other IPv4 and IPv6 routing protocols are classless. Classful addressing has never been a part of IPv6.

The fact that RIPv1 and IGRP do not include subnet mask information in their updates means that they cannot provide variable-length subnet masks (VLSMs) and classless interdomain routing (CIDR).

Classful routing protocols also create problems in discontiguous networks. A discontiguous network is when subnets from the same classful major network address are separated by a different classful network address.

To illustrate the shortcoming of classful routing, refer to the topology in Figure 7-16.

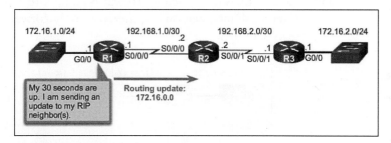

Figure 7-16   R1 Forwards a Classful Update to R2

Notice that the LANs of R1 (172.16.1.0/24) and R3 (172.16.2.0/24) are both subnets of the same class B network (172.16.0.0/16). They are separated by different classful network addresses (192.168.1.0/30 and 192.168.2.0/30).

When R1 forwards an update to R2, RIPv1 does not include the subnet mask information with the update; it only forwards the class B network address 172.16.0.0.

R2 receives and processes the update. It then creates and adds an entry for the class B 172.16.0.0/16 network in the routing table, as shown in Figure 7-17.

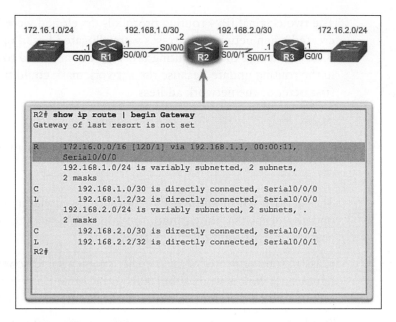

Figure 7-17   R2 Adds the Routing Entry

Figure 7-18 shows that when R3 forwards an update to R2, it also does not include the subnet mask information and therefore only forwards the classful network address 172.16.0.0.

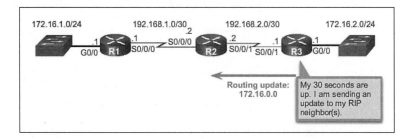

Figure 7-18   R3 Forwards a Classful Update to R2

In Figure 7-19, R2 receives and processes the update and adds another entry for the classful network address 172.16.0.0/16 to its routing table. When there are two entries with identical metrics in the routing table, the router shares the load of the traffic equally among the two links. This is known as load balancing.

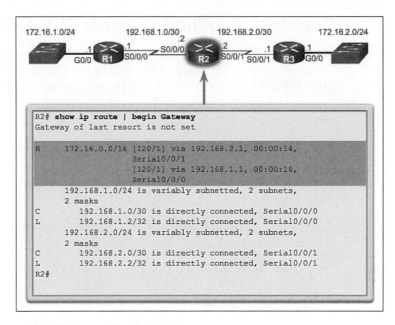

Figure 7-19   R2 Adds the Entry from R3

As shown in Figure 7-20, this has a negative effect on a discontiguous network. Notice the erratic behavior of the **ping** and **traceroute** commands.

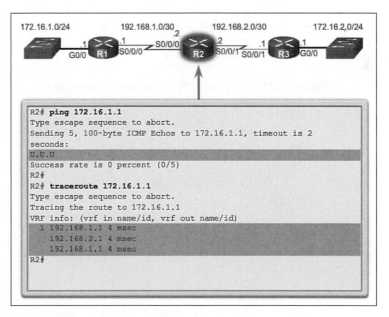

Figure 7-20   Connectivity Failure

Classless Routing Protocols (7.1.4.6)

Modern networks no longer use classful IP addressing, and the subnet mask cannot be determined by the value of the first octet. The classless IPv4 routing protocols (RIPv2, EIGRP, OSPF, and IS-IS) all include the subnet mask information with the network address in routing updates. Classless routing protocols support VLSM and CIDR.

IPv6 routing protocols are classless. The distinction whether a routing protocol is classful or classless typically only applies to IPv4 routing protocols. All IPv6 routing protocols are considered classless because they include the prefix-length with the IPv6 address.

Figures 7-21 through 7-25 illustrate how classless routing solves the issues created with classful routing:

- **Figure 7-21:** In this discontiguous network design, the classless protocol RIPv2 has been implemented on all three routers. When R1 forwards an update to R2, RIPv2 includes the subnet mask information with the update 172.16.1.0/24.

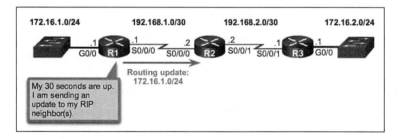

Figure 7-21   R1 Forwards a Classless Update to R2

- **Figure 7-22:** R2 receives, processes, and adds two entries in the routing table. The first line displays the classful network address 172.16.0.0 with the /24 subnet mask of the update. This is known as the *parent route*. The second entry displays the VLSM network address 172.16.1.0 with the exit and next-hop address. This is referred to as the *child route*. Parent routes never include an exit interface or next-hop IP address.

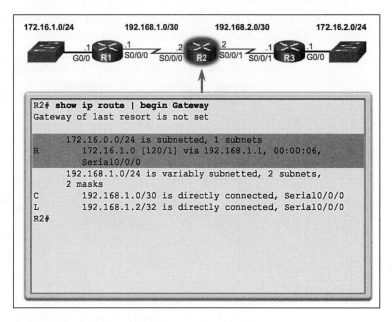

Figure 7-22 R2 Adds Routing Entry Learned from R1

- **Figure 7-23:** When R3 forwards an update to R2, RIPv2 includes the subnet mask information with the update 172.16.2.0/24.

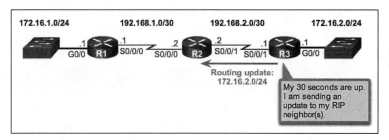

Figure 7-23 R3 Forwards a Classless Update to R2

■ **Figure 7-24:** R2 receives, processes, and adds another child route entry 172.16.2.0/24 under the parent route entry 172.16.0.0.

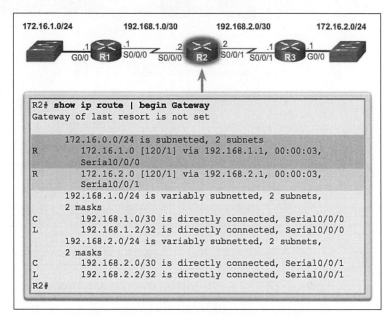

Figure 7-24   R2 Adds Routing Entry Learned from R3

■ **Figure 7-25:** R2 is now aware of the subnetted networks.

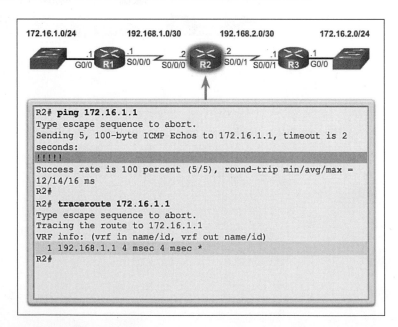

Figure 7-25   Connectivity Success

Routing Protocol Characteristics (7.1.4.7)

Routing protocols can be compared based on the following characteristics:

- **Speed of Convergence:** Speed of convergence defines how quickly the routers in the network topology share routing information and reach a state of consistent knowledge. The faster the convergence, the more preferable the protocol. Routing loops can occur when inconsistent routing tables are not updated due to slow convergence in a changing network.

- **Scalability:** Scalability defines how large a network can become, based on the routing protocol that is deployed. The larger the network is, the more scalable the routing protocol needs to be.

- **Classful or Classless (Use of VLSM):** Classful routing protocols do not include the subnet mask and cannot support VLSM. Classless routing protocols include the subnet mask in the updates. Classless routing protocols support VLSM and better route summarization.

- **Resource Usage:** Resource usage includes the requirements of a routing protocol such as memory space (RAM), CPU utilization, and link bandwidth utilization. Higher resource requirements necessitate more powerful hardware to support the routing protocol operation, in addition to the packet forwarding processes.

- **Implementation and Maintenance:** Implementation and maintenance describes the level of knowledge that is required for a network administrator to implement and maintain the network based on the routing protocol deployed.

Table 7-4 summarizes the characteristics of each routing protocol.

Table 7-4 Comparing Routing Protocols

	Distance Vector			Link State		
	RIPv1	RIPv2	IGRP	EIGRP	OSPF	IS-IS
Speed Convergence	Slow	Slow	Slow	Fast	Fast	Fast
Scalability – Size of Network	Small	Small	Small	Large	Large	Large
Use of VLSM	No	Yes	No	Yes	Yes	Yes
Resource Usage	Low	Low	Low	Medium	High	High
Implementation and Maintenance	Simple	Simple	Simple	Complex	Complex	Complex

Routing Protocol Metrics (7.1.4.8)

There are cases when a routing protocol learns of more than one route to the same destination. To select the best path, the routing protocol must be able to evaluate and differentiate between the available paths. This is accomplished through the use of routing metrics.

A metric is a measurable value that is assigned by the routing protocol to different routes based on the usefulness of that route. In situations where there are multiple paths to the same remote network, the routing metrics are used to determine the overall "cost" of a path from source to destination. Routing protocols determine the best path based on the route with the lowest cost.

Different routing protocols use different metrics. The metric used by one routing protocol is not comparable to the metric used by another routing protocol. Two different routing protocols might choose different paths to the same destination.

Video

Video 7.1.4.8: Routing Protocols and Their Metrics

Go to the course and play the animation of two different protocols demonstrating their metrics.

Interactive Graphic

Activity 7.1.4.9 Part 1: Classify Dynamic Routing Protocols

Go to the course and perform the activity (7.1.4.9 Part 1) where you will drag and drop the appropriate protocols into the distance vector routing protocol fields provided.

Interactive Graphic

Activity 7.1.4.9 Part 2: Classify Dynamic Routing Protocols

Go to the course and perform the activity (7.1.4.9 Part 2) where you will drag and drop the appropriate protocols into the link-state routing protocol fields provided.

Interactive Graphic

Activity 7.1.4.9 Part 3: Classify Dynamic Routing Protocols

Go to the course and perform the activity (7.1.4.9 Part 3) where you will drag and drop the appropriate protocols into the path-vector routing protocol fields provided.

Interactive Graphic

Activity 7.1.4.10 Part 1: Compare Routing Protocols

Go to the course and perform the activity (7.1.4.10 Part 1) where you will drag and drop each item to the appropriate routing protocol that matches the characteristic.

Interactive Graphic

Activity 7.1.4.10 Part 2: Compare Routing Protocols

Go to the course and perform the activity (7.1.4.10 Part 2) where you will drag and drop each item to the appropriate routing protocol that matches the characteristic.

Interactive Graphic

Activity 7.1.4.10 Part 3: Compare Routing Protocols

Go to the course and perform the activity (7.1.4.10 Part 3) where you will drag and drop each item to the appropriate routing protocol that matches the characteristic.

Interactive Graphic

Activity 7.1.4.11: Match the Metric to the Protocol

Go to the course and perform the activity (7.1.4.11) where you will check the protocol which best matches the metric described.

Distance Vector Routing Protocol Operation (7.2.1)

This next section deals with how distance vector routing protocols operate.

Distance Vector Technologies (7.2.1.1)

Distance vector routing protocols share updates between neighbors. *Neighbors* are routers that share a link and are configured to use the same routing protocol. The router is only aware of the network addresses of its own interfaces and the remote network addresses it can reach through its neighbors. Routers using distance vector routing are not aware of the network topology.

Some distance vector routing protocols send periodic updates. For example, RIP sends a periodic update to all of its neighbors every 30 seconds. RIP does this even if the topology has not changed; it continues to send updates. RIPv1 reaches all of its neighbors by sending updates to the all-hosts IPv4 address of 255.255.255.255, a broadcast.

The broadcasting of periodic updates is inefficient because the updates consume bandwidth and consume network device CPU resources. Every network device has to process a broadcast message. RIPv2 and EIGRP, instead, use multicast addresses so that only neighbors that need updates will receive them. EIGRP can also send a unicast message to only the affected neighbor. In addition, EIGRP will only send an update when needed, instead of periodically.

As shown in Figure 7-26, the two modern IPv4 distance vector routing protocols are RIPv2 and EIGRP. RIPv1 and IGRP are listed only for historical accuracy.

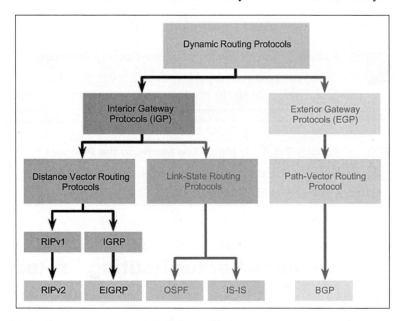

Figure 7-26   Distance Vector Routing Protocols

Distance Vector Algorithm (7.2.1.2)

At the core of the distance vector protocol is the routing algorithm. The algorithm is used to calculate the best paths and then send that information to the neighbors.

The algorithm used for the routing protocols defines the following processes:

- Mechanism for sending and receiving routing information

- Mechanism for calculating the best paths and installing routes in the routing table

- Mechanism for detecting and reacting to topology changes

Video 7.2.1.2: Purpose of Routing Algorithms

Go to the course and play the animation of a packet being sent through two routers from sender to receiver.

In the animation in the online course, R1 and R2 are configured with the RIP routing protocol.

The algorithm sends and receives updates. Both R1 and R2 then glean new information from the update. In this case, each router learns about a new network. The algorithm on each router makes its calculations independently and updates the routing table with the new information. When the LAN on R2 goes down, the algorithm constructs a *triggered update* and sends it to R1. R1 then removes the network from the routing table.

Different routing protocols use different algorithms to install routes in the routing table, send updates to neighbors, and make path determination decisions. For example:

- RIP uses the *Bellman-Ford algorithm* as its routing algorithm. It is based on two algorithms developed in 1958 and 1956 by Richard Bellman and Lester Ford, Jr.

- IGRP and EIGRP use the *Diffusing Update Algorithm (DUAL)* routing algorithm developed by Dr. J.J. Garcia-Luna-Aceves at SRI International.

Activity 7.2.1.3: Identify Distance Vector Terminology

Go to the course and perform the activity where you will drag and drop each item matching it with its corresponding description.

Types of Distance Vector Routing Protocols (7.2.2)

There are many different distance vector protocols that have been used over time. The two most commonly used in today's networks are Routing Information Protocol (RIP) and Enhanced Interior Gateway Protocol (EIGRP).

Routing Information Protocol (7.2.2.1)

The Routing Information Protocol (RIP) was a first-generation routing protocol for IPv4 originally specified in RFC 1058. It is easy to configure, making it a good choice for small networks.

RIPv1 has the following key characteristics:

- Routing updates are broadcasted (255.255.255.255) every 30 seconds.

- The hop count is used as the metric for path selection.

- A hop count greater than 15 hops is deemed infinite (too far). That 15th hop router would not propagate the routing update to the next router.

In 1993, RIPv1 evolved to a classless routing protocol known as RIP version 2 (RIPv2). RIPv2 introduced the following improvements:

- **Classless routing protocol:** It supports VLSM and CIDR because it includes the subnet mask in the routing updates.

- **Increased efficiency:** It forwards updates to multicast address 224.0.0.9, instead of the broadcast address 255.255.255.255.

- **Reduced routing entries:** It supports manual route summarization on any interface.

- **Secure:** It supports an authentication mechanism to secure routing table updates between neighbors. Table 7-5 summarizes the differences between RIPv1 and RIPv2.

Table 7-5 RIPv1 Versus RIPv2

Characteristics and Features	RIPv1	RIPv2
Metric	Both use hop count as a simple metric. The maximum number of hops is 15.	
Updates Forwarded to Addresses	255.255.255.255	224.0.0.9
Supports VLSM	NO	YES
Supports CIDR	NO	YES
Supports Summarization	NO	YES
Supports Authentication	NO	YES

RIP updates are encapsulated into a UDP segment, with both source and destination port numbers set to UDP port 520.

In 1997, the IPv6-enabled version of RIP was released. RIPng is based on RIPv2. It still has a 15-hop limitation and the administrative distance is 120.

Enhanced Interior-Gateway Routing Protocol (7.2.2.2)

The Interior Gateway Routing Protocol (IGRP) was the first proprietary IPv4 routing protocol developed by Cisco in 1984. It used the following design characteristics:

- Bandwidth, delay, load, and reliability are used to create a composite metric.

- Routing updates are broadcast every 90 seconds, by default.

In 1992, IGRP was replaced by Enhanced IGRP (EIGRP). Like RIPv2, EIGRP also introduced support for VLSM and CIDR. EIGRP increases efficiency, reduces routing updates, and supports secure message exchange.

Table 7-6 summarizes the differences between IGRP and EIGRP.

Table 7-6   IGRP Versus EIGRP

Characteristics and Features	IGRP	EIGRP
Metric	Both use a composite metric consisting of Bandwidth and Delay. Reliability and Load can also be used in the metric calculation.	
Updates Forwarded to Addresses	255.255.255.255	224.0.0.10
Supports VLSM	NO	YES
Supports CIDR	NO	YES
Supports Summarization	NO	YES
Supports Authentication	NO	YES

EIGRP also introduced:

- *Bounded triggered updates:* It does not send periodic updates. Only routing table changes are propagated whenever a change occurs. This reduces the amount of load the routing protocol places on the network. Bounded triggered updates mean that EIGRP sends only to the neighbors that need it. It uses less bandwidth, especially in large networks with many routes.

- **Hello keepalive mechanism:** A small Hello message is periodically exchanged to maintain adjacencies with neighboring routers. This means a low usage of network resources during normal operation, instead of the periodic updates.

- **Maintains a topology table:** Maintains all the routes received from neighbors (not only the best paths) in a topology table. DUAL can insert backup routes into the EIGRP topology table.

- **Rapid convergence:** In most cases, it is the fastest IGP to converge because it maintains alternative routes, enabling almost instantaneous convergence. If a primary route fails, the router can use the alternate route identified. The switchover to the alternate route is immediate and does not involve interaction with other routers.

- **Multiple network layer protocol support:** EIGRP uses *Protocol Dependent Modules (PDM)*, which means that it is the only protocol to include support for protocols other than IPv4 and IPv6, such as legacy IPX and AppleTalk.

Interactive Graphic

Activity 7.2.2.3: Compare RIP and EIGRP

Go to the course and perform the activity (7.2.2.3) where you will match the distance vector protocol with each descriptor. Click Button #2 to go to the second screen to continue the activity.

Packet Tracer ☐ Activity

Packet Tracer Activity 7.2.2.4: Comparing RIP and EIGRP Path Selection

PCA and **PCB** need to communicate. The path that the data takes between these end devices can travel through **R1**, **R2**, and **R3**, or it can travel through **R4** and **R5**. The process by which routers select the best path depends on the routing protocol. You examine the behavior of two distance vector routing protocols, Enhanced Interior Gateway Routing Protocol (EIGRP) and Routing Information Protocol version 2 (RIPv2).

Go to the course online to complete this Packet Tracer activity.

RIP and RIPng Routing (7.3)

Although it is now considered a legacy routing protocol, RIP is still available in Cisco IOS and is a great learning routing protocol. These next sections deal with both RIP and the IPv6 version of RIP: RIPng.

Router RIP Configuration Mode (7.3.1.1)

Although RIP is rarely used in modern networks, it is useful as a foundation for understanding basic network routing. For this reason, this section provides a brief overview of how to configure basic RIP settings and to verify RIPv2.

Refer to the reference topology in Figure 7-27 and the addressing table in Table 7-7.

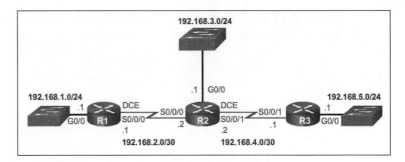

Figure 7-27   Reference Topology

Table 7-7   Addressing Table

Device	Interface	IP Address	Subnet Mask
R1	G0/0	192.168.1.1	255.255.255.0
	S0/0/0	192.168.2.1	255.255.255.0
R2	G0/0	192.168.3.1	255.255.255.0
	S0/0/0	192.168.2.2	255.255.255.0
	S0/0/1	192.168.4.2	255.255.255.0
R3	G0/0	192.168.5.1	255.255.255.0
	S0/01	192.168.4.1	255.255.255.0

In this scenario, all routers have been configured with basic management features and all interfaces identified in the reference topology are configured and enabled. There are no static routes configured and no routing protocols enabled; therefore, remote network access is currently impossible. RIPv2 is used as the dynamic routing protocol. To enable RIP, use the **router rip** command, as shown in the following output.

```
R1# conf t
Enter configuration commands, one per line. End with CNTL/Z.
R1 (config)# router rip
R1 (config-router)#
```

This command does not directly start the RIP process. Instead, it provides access to the router configuration mode where the RIP routing settings are configured.

To disable and eliminate RIP, use the **no router rip** global configuration command. This command stops the RIP process and erases all existing RIP configurations.

Figure 7-28 displays the various RIP commands that can be configured. The high-lighted keywords are covered in this section.

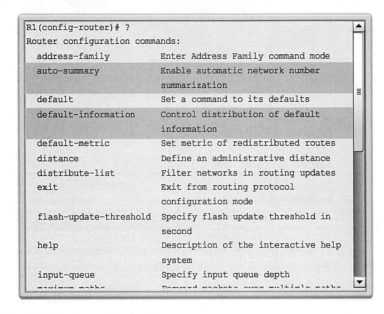

```
R1(config-router)# ?
Router configuration commands:
  address-family          Enter Address Family command mode
  auto-summary            Enable automatic network number
                          summarization
  default                 Set a command to its defaults
  default-information     Control distribution of default
                          information
  default-metric          Set metric of redistributed routes
  distance                Define an administrative distance
  distribute-list         Filter networks in routing updates
  exit                    Exit from routing protocol
                          configuration mode
  flash-update-threshold  Specify flash update threshold in
                          second
  help                    Description of the interactive help
                          system
  input-queue             Specify input queue depth
```

Figure 7-28   RIP Configuration Options

Interactive Graphic

Activity 7.3.1.1: RIP Configuration Options

Go to the course online and use the slider bar in the fourth graphic to see all the RIP Configuration Options.

Advertising Networks (7.3.1.2)

By entering the RIP router configuration mode, the router is instructed to run RIP. But the router still needs to know which local interfaces it should use for communication with other routers, as well as which locally connected networks it should advertise to those routers.

To enable RIP routing for a network, use the **network** *network-address* router configuration mode command. Enter the classful network address for each directly connected network. This command

- Enables RIP on all interfaces that belong to a specific network. Associated interfaces now both send and receive RIP updates.

- Advertises the specified network in RIP routing updates sent to other routers every 30 seconds.

Note

If a subnet address is entered, the IOS automatically converts it to the classful network address. Remember RIPv1 is a classful routing protocol for IPv4. For example, entering the **network 192.168.1.32** command would automatically be converted to **network 192.168.1.0** in the running configuration file. The IOS does not give an error message, but instead corrects the input and enters the classful network address.

In Figure 7-29, the **network** command is used to advertise the R1 directly connected networks.

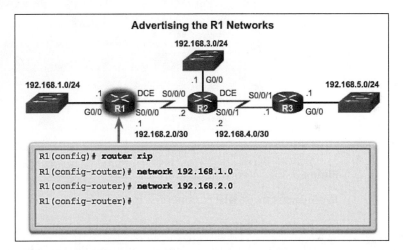

Figure 7-29 Advertising the R1 Networks

Activity 7.3.1.2: Advertising the R2 and R3 Networks

Go to the course online and use the Syntax Checker in the second graphic to configure the RIP routing process on routers R2 and R3.

Examining Default RIP Settings (7.3.1.3)

The **show ip protocols** command displays the IPv4 routing protocol settings currently configured on the router. This output is displayed in Figure 7-30.

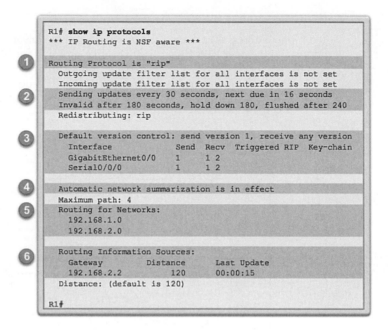

```
R1# show ip protocols
*** IP Routing is NSF aware ***

Routing Protocol is "rip"
  Outgoing update filter list for all interfaces is not set
  Incoming update filter list for all interfaces is not set
  Sending updates every 30 seconds, next due in 16 seconds
  Invalid after 180 seconds, hold down 180, flushed after 240
  Redistributing: rip

  Default version control: send version 1, receive any version
    Interface              Send  Recv  Triggered RIP  Key-chain
    GigabitEthernet0/0     1     1 2
    Serial0/0/0            1     1 2

  Automatic network summarization is in effect
  Maximum path: 4
  Routing for Networks:
    192.168.1.0
    192.168.2.0

  Routing Information Sources:
    Gateway          Distance        Last Update
    192.168.2.2          120         00:00:15
  Distance: (default is 120)

R1#
```

Figure 7-30   Verifying RIP Settings on R1

It confirms most RIP parameters, including

1. RIP routing is configured and running on router R1.

2. The values of various timers; for example, the next routing update, is sent by R1 in 16 seconds.

3. The version of RIP configured is currently RIPv1.

4. R1 is currently summarizing at the classful network boundary.

5. The classful networks are advertised by R1. These are the networks that R1 include in its RIP updates.

6. The RIP neighbors are listed including their next-hop IP address, the associated AD that R2 uses for updates sent by this neighbor, and when the last update was received from this neighbor.

Note

This command is also very useful when verifying the operations of other routing protocols (that is, EIGRP and OSPF).

The **show ip route** command displays the RIP routes installed in the routing table. In the following output, R1 now knows about the highlighted networks.

```
R1# show ip route | begin Gateway
Gateway of last resort is not set

   192.138.1.0/24 is variably subnetted, 2 subnets, 2masks
C     192.168.1.0/24 is directly connected, GigabitEthernet0/0
L     192.168.1.1/32 is directly connected, GigabitEthernet0/0
   192.168.2.0/24 is variably subnetted, 2 subnets, 2 masks
C     192.168.2.0/24 is directly connected, Serial0/0/0
L     192.168.2.1/32 is directly connected Serial0/0/0
R  192.168.3.0/24 [120/1] via 192.168.2.2, 00:00:24, Serial0/0/0
R  192.168.4.0/24 [120/1] via 192.168.2.2, 00:00:24, Serial0/0/0
R  192.168.5.0/24 [120/2] via 192.168.2.2, 00:00:24, Serial0/0/0
R1#
```

Interactive Graphic

Activity 7.3.1.3: Verifying RIP Settings and Routes on the R2 and R3 Routers

Go to the course online and use the Syntax Checker in the second graphic to verify the R2 and R3 RIP settings and routes.

Enabling RIPv2 (7.3.1.4)

By default, when a RIP process is configured on a Cisco router, it is running RIPv1, as shown in Figure 7-31.

```
R1# show ip protocols
*** IP Routing is NSF aware ***

Routing Protocol is "rip"
  Outgoing update filter list for all interfaces is not
set
  Incoming update filter list for all interfaces is not
set
  Sending updates every 30 seconds, next due in 16 seconds
  Invalid after 180 seconds, hold down 180, flushed after
240
  Redistributing: rip
  Default version control: send version 1, receive any
version
    Interface        Send  Recv  Triggered RIP  Key-chain
    GigabitEthernet0/0  1    1 2
    Serial0/0/0          1    1 2
  Automatic network summarization is in effect
  Maximum path: 4
  Routing for Networks:
    192.168.1.0
    192.168.2.0
  Routing Information Sources:
    Gateway        Distance     Last Update
```

Figure 7-31   Verifying RIP Settings on R1

Interactive Graphic

Activity 7.3.1.4: Verifying RIP Settings on R1

Go to the course online and use the slider bar in the first graphic to see the entire output of the **show ip protocols** command.

However, even though the router only sends RIPv1 messages, it can interpret both RIPv1 and RIPv2 messages. A RIPv1 router ignores the RIPv2 fields in the route entry.

Use the **version 2** router configuration mode command to enable RIPv2, as shown in Figure 7-32.

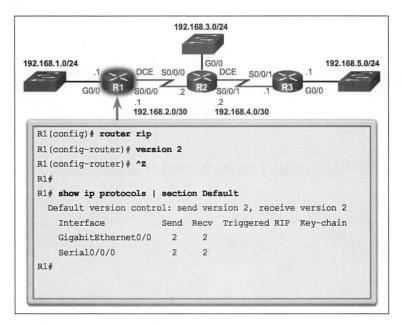

```
R1(config)# router rip
R1(config-router)# version 2
R1(config-router)# ^Z
R1#
R1# show ip protocols | section Default
  Default version control: send version 2, receive version 2
    Interface          Send  Recv  Triggered RIP  Key-chain
    GigabitEthernet0/0   2     2
    Serial0/0/0          2     2
R1#
```

Figure 7-32 Enable and Verify RIPv2 on R1

Notice how the **show ip protocols** command verifies that R2 is now configured to send and receive version 2 messages only. The RIP process now includes the subnet mask in all updates, making RIPv2 a classless routing protocol.

Note

Configuring **version 1** enables RIPv1 only, while configuring **no version** returns the router to the default setting of sending version 1 updates but listening for version 1 or version 2 updates.

Figure 7-33 verifies that there are no RIP routes still in the routing table.

This is because R1 is now only listening for RIPv2 updates. R2 and R3 are still sending RIPv1 updates. Therefore, the **version 2** command must be configured on all routers in the routing domain.

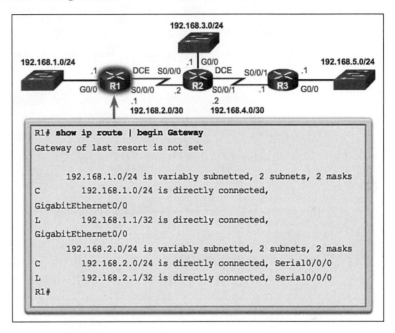

```
R1# show ip route | begin Gateway
Gateway of last resort is not set

        192.168.1.0/24 is variably subnetted, 2 subnets, 2 masks
C          192.168.1.0/24 is directly connected,
GigabitEthernet0/0
L          192.168.1.1/32 is directly connected,
GigabitEthernet0/0
        192.168.2.0/24 is variably subnetted, 2 subnets, 2 masks
C          192.168.2.0/24 is directly connected, Serial0/0/0
L          192.168.2.1/32 is directly connected, Serial0/0/0
R1#
```

Figure 7-33   Verify R1 Routes

Activity 7.3.1.4: Enable and Verify RIPv2 on the R2 and R3 Routers

Go to the course online and use the Syntax Checker in the fourth graphic to enable RIPv2 on R2 and R3.

Disabling Auto Summarization (7.3.1.5)

As shown in Figure 7-34, RIPv2 automatically summarizes networks at major network boundaries by default, just like RIPv1.

```
R1# show ip protocols
*** IP Routing is NSF aware ***

Routing Protocol is "rip"
 Outgoing update filter list for all interfaces is not set
 Incoming update filter list for all interfaces is not set
 Sending updates every 30 seconds, next due in 16 seconds
 Invalid after 180 seconds, hold down 180, flushed after
 240
 Redistributing: rip
 Default version control: send version 2, receive version 2
    Interface          Send  Recv  Triggered RIP  Key-chain
    GigabitEthernet0/0   1    1 2
    Serial0/0/0          1    1 2
 Automatic network summarization is in effect
 Maximum path: 4
 Routing for Networks:
    192.168.1.0
    192.168.2.0
 Routing Information Sources:
    Gateway          Distance      Last Update
    192.168.2.2          120       00:00:15
 Distance: (default is 120)
R1#
```

Figure 7-34 Automatic Summarization with RIPv2

To modify the default RIPv2 behavior of automatic summarization, use the
no auto-summary router configuration mode command, as shown in Figure 7-35.

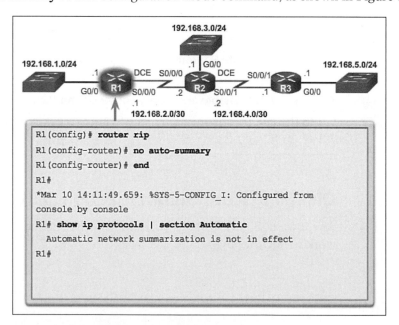

Figure 7-35 Disable Automatic Summarization on R1

This command has no effect when using RIPv1. When automatic summarization has been disabled, RIPv2 no longer summarizes networks to their classful address at boundary routers. RIPv2 now includes all subnets and their appropriate masks in its routing updates. The **show ip protocols** now states that `automatic network summarization is not in effect`.

> **Note**
>
> RIPv2 must be enabled before automatic summarization is disabled.

Activity 7.3.1.5: Disable Automatic Summarization on the R2 and R3 Routers

Go to the course online and use the Syntax Checker in the third graphic to disable automatic summarization on R2 and R3.

Configuring Passive Interfaces (7.3.1.6)

By default, RIP updates are forwarded out all RIP-enabled interfaces. However, RIP updates really only need to be sent out interfaces connecting to other RIP-enabled routers.

For instance, refer to the topology in Figure 7-36.

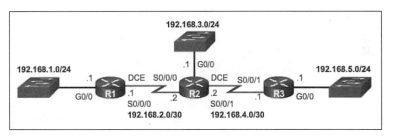

Figure 7-36 Configuring Passive Interfaces on R1

RIP sends updates out of its G0/0 interface even though no RIP device exists on that LAN. R1 has no way of knowing this and, as a result, sends an update every 30 seconds. Sending out unneeded updates on a LAN impacts the network in three ways:

- **Wasted bandwidth:** Bandwidth is used to transport unnecessary updates. Because RIP updates are either broadcasted or multicasted, therefore, switches also forward the updates out all ports.

- **Wasted resources:** All devices on the LAN must process the update up to the transport layers, at which point the devices will discard the update.

■ **Security risk:** Advertising updates on a broadcast network is a security risk. RIP updates can be intercepted with packet sniffing software. Routing updates can be modified and sent back to the router, corrupting the routing table with false metrics that misdirect traffic.

Use the **passive-interface** router configuration command to prevent the transmission of routing updates through a router interface, but still allow that network to be advertised to other routers. The command stops routing updates out the specified interface. However, the network that the specified interface belongs to is still advertised in routing updates that are sent out other interfaces.

There is no need for R1, R2, and R3 to forward RIP updates out of their LAN interfaces. The configuration in the following output identifies the R1 G0/0 interface as passive.

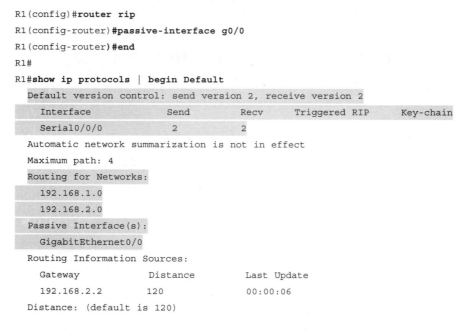

```
R1(config)#router rip
R1(config-router)#passive-interface g0/0
R1(config-router)#end
R1#
R1#show ip protocols | begin Default
  Default version control: send version 2, receive version 2
    Interface           Send         Recv        Triggered RIP      Key-chain
    Serial0/0/0          2            2
  Automatic network summarization is not in effect
  Maximum path: 4
  Routing for Networks:
    192.168.1.0
    192.168.2.0
  Passive Interface(s):
    GigabitEthernet0/0
  Routing Information Sources:
    Gateway            Distance       Last Update
    192.168.2.2        120            00:00:06
  Distance: (default is 120)

R1#
```

The **show ip protocols** command is then used to verify that the Gigabit Ethernet interface was passive. Notice that the G0/0 interface is no longer listed as sending or receiving version 2 updates but instead is now listed under the Passive Interface(s) section. Also notice that the network 192.168.1.0 is still listed under Routing for Networks, which means that this network is still included as a route entry in RIP updates that are sent to R2.

Note

All routing protocols support the **passive-interface** command.

Activity 7.3.1.6: Configuring and Verifying a Passive Interface on the R2 and R3 Routers

Go to the course online and use the Syntax Checker in the third graphic to configure the LAN interface as a passive interface on R2 and R3.

As an alternative, all interfaces can be made passive using the **passive-interface default** command. Interfaces that should not be passive can be re-enabled using the **no passive-interface** command.

Propagating a Default Route (7.3.1.7)

Refer to Figure 7-37.

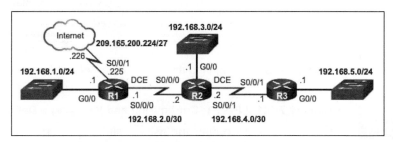

Figure 7-37   Propagating a Default Route on R1

In this scenario, R1 is single-homed to a service provider. Therefore, all that is required for R1 to reach the Internet is a default static route going out of the Serial 0/0/1 interface.

Similar default static routes could be configured on R2 and R3, but it is much more scalable to enter it one time on the edge router R1 and then have R1 propagate it to all other routers using RIP. To provide Internet connectivity to all other networks in the RIP routing domain, the default static route needs to be advertised to all other routers that use the dynamic routing protocol.

To propagate a default route, the edge router must be configured with

- A default static route using the **ip route 0.0.0.0 0.0.0.0** *exit-intf next-hop-ip* command.

- The **default-information originate** router configuration command. This instructs R1 router to originate default information, by propagating the static default route in RIP updates.

The example in Figure 7-38 configures a fully specified default static route to the service provider and then the route is propagated by RIP. Notice that R1 now has a Gateway of Last Resort and default route installed in its routing table.

```
R1(config)# ip route 0.0.0.0 0.0.0.0 S0/0/1 209.165.200.226
R1(config)# router rip
R1(config-router)# default-information originate
R1(config-router)# ^Z
R1#
*Mar 10 23:33:51.801: %SYS-5-CONFIG_I: Configured from console by
console
R1# show ip route | begin Gateway
Gateway of last resort is 209.165.200.226 to network 0.0.0.0

S*    0.0.0.0/0 [1/0] via 209.165.200.226, Serial0/0/1
      192.168.1.0/24 is variably subnetted, 2 subnets, 2 masks
C        192.168.1.0/24 is directly connected, GigabitEthernet0/0
L        192.168.1.1/32 is directly connected, GigabitEthernet0/0
      192.168.2.0/24 is variably subnetted, 2 subnets, 2 masks
C        192.168.2.0/24 is directly connected, Serial0/0/0
L        192.168.2.1/32 is directly connected, Serial0/0/0
R     192.168.3.0/24 [120/1] via 192.168.2.2, 00:00:08,
Serial0/0/0
R     192.168.4.0/24 [120/1] via 192.168.2.2, 00:00:08,
Serial0/0/0
R     192.168.5.0/24 [120/2] via 192.168.2.2, 00:00:08,
Serial0/0/0
      209.165.200.0/24 is variably subnetted, 2 subnets, 2 masks
C        209.165.200.0/24 is directly connected, Serial0/0/1
```

Figure 7-38   Configuring and Verifying a Default Route on R1

Interactive Graphic

Activity 7.3.1.7 Part 1: Configuring and Verifying a Default Route on R1

Go to the course online and use the slider bar in the second graphic to see the entire output of the **show ip route | begin Gateway** command.

Interactive Graphic

Activity 7.3.1.7 Part 2: Verifying the Gateway of Last Resort on the R2 and R3 Routers

Go to the course online and use the Syntax Checker in the third graphic to verify that the default route has been propagated to R2 and R3.

Packet Tracer Activity 7.3.1.8: Configuring RIPv2

Although RIP is rarely used in modern networks, it is useful as a foundation for understanding basic network routing. In this activity, you will configure a default route, RIP version 2 with appropriate network statements and passive interfaces and verify full connectivity.

Go to the course online to complete this Packet Tracer activity.

Configuring the RIPng Protocol (7.3.2)

The RIPng protocol is needed if you want to use RIP with IPv6 networks. Although not used very often in newer networks, it is still a great learning protocol and is presented here as such.

Advertising IPv6 Networks (7.3.2.1)

As with its IPv4 counterpart, RIPng is rarely used in modern networks. It is also useful as a foundation for understanding basic network routing. For this reason, this section provides a brief overview of how to configure basic RIPng.

Refer to the reference topology in Figure 7-39.

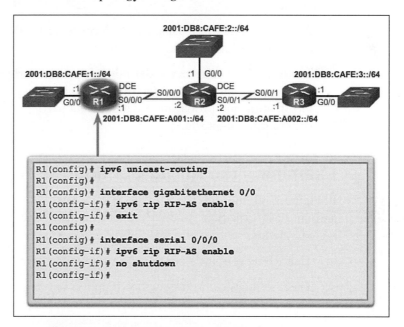

Figure 7-39   Enabling RIPng on IPv6 Interfaces on R1

In this scenario, all routers have been configured with basic management features and all interfaces identified in the reference topology are configured and enabled. There are no static routes configured and no routing protocols enabled; therefore, remote network access is currently impossible.

To enable an IPv6 router to forward IPv6 packets, the **ipv6 unicast-routing** must be configured.

Unlike RIPv2, RIPng is enabled on an interface and not in router configuration mode. In fact, there is no **network** *network-address* command available in RIPng. Instead, use the **ipv6 rip** *domain-name* **enable** interface configuration command.

In Figure 7-39, IPv6 unicast routing is enabled and the Gigabit Ethernet 0/0 and Serial 0/0/0 interfaces are enabled for RIPng using the domain name RIP-AS.

Activity 7.3.2.1: Enabling RIPng on IPv6 Interfaces on R2 and R3

Go to the course online and use the Syntax Checker in the second graphic to enable RIPng on IPv6 interfaces on R2 and R3.

The process to propagate a default route in RIPng is identical to RIPv2 except that an IPv6 default static route must be specified. For example, assume that R1 had an Internet connection from a Serial 0/0/1 interface to IP address 2001:DB8:FEED:1::1/64. To propagate a default route, R3 would have to be configured with

- A default static route using the **ipv6 route 0::/0 2001:DB8:FEED:1::1** global configuration command.

- The **ipv6 rip** *domain-name* **default-information originate** interface configuration mode command. This instructs R3 to be the source of the default route information and propagate the default static route in RIPng updates sent out of the configured interface.

Examining the RIPng Configuration (7.3.2.2)

In Figure 7-40, the **show ipv6 protocols** command does not provide the same amount of information as its IPv4 counterpart. However, it does confirm the following parameters:

1. That RIPng routing is configured and running on router R1.

2. The interfaces configured with RIPng.

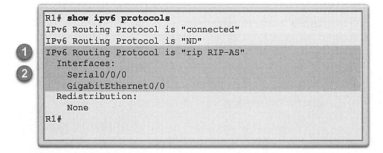

```
R1# show ipv6 protocols
IPv6 Routing Protocol is "connected"
IPv6 Routing Protocol is "ND"
IPv6 Routing Protocol is "rip RIP-AS"
  Interfaces:
    Serial0/0/0
    GigabitEthernet0/0
  Redistribution:
    None
R1#
```

Figure 7-40   Verifying RIPng Settings on R1

The **show ipv6 route** command displays the routes installed in the routing table, as shown in Figure 7-41. The output confirms that R1 now knows about the highlighted RIPng networks.

```
R1# show ipv6 route
IPv6 Routing Table - default - 8 entries
Codes: C - Connected, L - Local, S - Static, U - Per-user
Static route
       B - BGP, R - RIP, I1 - ISIS L1, I2 - ISIS L2
       IA - ISIS interarea, IS - ISIS summary, D - EIGRP,
       EX - EIGRP external, ND - ND Default,
       NDp - ND Prefix, DCE - Destination, NDr - Redirect,
       O - OSPF Intra, OI - OSPF Inter, OE1 - OSPF ext 1,
       OE2 - OSPF ext 2, ON1 - OSPF NSSA ext 1,
       ON2 - OSPF NSSA ext 2
C   2001:DB8:CAFE:1::/64 [0/0]
       via GigabitEthernet0/0, directly connected
L   2001:DB8:CAFE:1::1/128 [0/0]
       via GigabitEthernet0/0, receive
R   2001:DB8:CAFE:2::/64 [120/2]
       via FE80::FE99:47FF:FE71:78A0, Serial0/0/0
R   2001:DB8:CAFE:3::/64 [120/3]
       via FE80::FE99:47FF:FE71:78A0, Serial0/0/0
C   2001:DB8:CAFE:A001::/64 [0/0]
       via Serial0/0/0, directly connected
L   2001:DB8:CAFE:A001::1/128 [0/0]
       via Serial0/0/0, receive
R   2001:DB8:CAFE:A002::/64 [120/2]
```

Figure 7-41   Verifying Routes on R1

Activity 7.3.2.2: Verifying Routes on R1

Go to the course online and use the slider bar in the second graphic to see the entire output of the **show ipv6 route** command.

Notice that the R2 LAN is advertised as two hops away. This is because there is a difference in the way RIPv2 and RIPng calculate the hop counts. With RIPv2 (and RIPv1), the metric to the R2 LAN would be one hop. This is because the metric (hop count) that is displayed in the IPv4 routing table is the number of hops required to reach the remote network (counting the next-hop router as the first hop). In RIPng, the sending router already considers itself to be one hop away; therefore, R2 advertises its LAN with a metric of 1. When R1 receives the update, it adds another hop count of 1 to the metric. Therefore, R1 considers the R2 LAN to be two hops away. Similarly it considers the R3 LAN to be three hops away.

Appending the **rip** keyword to the command as shown in Figure 7-42 only lists RIPng networks.

```
R1# show ipv6 route rip
IPv6 Routing Table - default - 8 entries
Codes: C - Connected, L - Local, S - Static, U - Per-user
Static route
       B - BGP, R - RIP, I1 - ISIS L1, I2 - ISIS L2
       IA - ISIS interarea, IS - ISIS summary, D - EIGRP,
       EX - EIGRP external, ND - ND Default,
       NDp - ND Prefix, DCE - Destination, NDr - Redirect,
       O - OSPF Intra, OI - OSPF Inter, OE1 - OSPF ext 1,
       OE2 - OSPF ext 2, ON1 - OSPF NSSA ext 1,
       ON2 - OSPF NSSA ext 2
R    2001:DB8:CAFE:2::/64 [120/2]
       via FE80::FE99:47FF:FE71:78A0, Serial0/0/0
R    2001:DB8:CAFE:3::/64 [120/3]
       via FE80::FE99:47FF:FE71:78A0, Serial0/0/0
R    2001:DB8:CAFE:A002::/64 [120/2]
       via FE80::FE99:47FF:FE71:78A0, Serial0/0/0
R1#
```

Figure 7-42   Verifying RIPng Routes on R1

Activity 7.3.2.2: Verifying RIPng Settings and Routes on R2 and R3

Go to the course online and use the Syntax Checker in the fourth graphic to verify RIPng settings and routes on R2 and R3.

Packet Tracer Activity 7.3.2.3: Configuring RIPng

RIPng (RIP Next Generation) is a distance vector routing protocol for routing IPv6 addresses. RIPng is based on RIPv2 and has the same administrative distance and 15-hop limitation. This activity will help you become more familiar with RIPng.

Go to the course online to complete this Packet Tracer activity.

Lab 7.3.2.4: Configuring RIPv2

In this lab you will complete the following objectives:

- Part 1: Build the Network and Configure Basic Device Settings
- Part 2: Configure and Verify RIPv2 Routing
- Part 3: Configure IPv6 on Devices
- Part 4: Configure and Verify RIPng Routing

Link-State Dynamic Routing (7.4)

Now that we have looked at distance vector routing protocols, it is time to look at the other type of IGP known as Link-State Routing Protocols.

Shortest Path First Protocols (7.4.1.1)

Link-state routing protocols are also known as shortest path first protocols and are built around Edsger *Dijkstra's shortest path first (SPF) algorithm*. The SPF algorithm is discussed in more detail in a later section.

The IPv4 link-state routing protocols as shown in Figure 7-43 are

- Open Shortest Path First (OSPF)

- Intermediate System-to-Intermediate System (IS-IS)

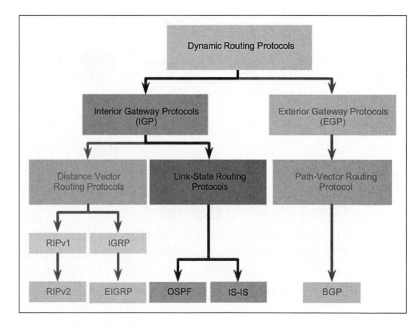

Figure 7-43   Link-State Routing Protocols

Link-state routing protocols have the reputation of being much more complex than their distance vector counterparts. However, the basic functionality and configuration of link-state routing protocols is equally straightforward.

Just like RIP and EIGRP, basic OSPF operations can be configured using the

- **router ospf** *process-id* global configuration command

- **network** command to advertise networks

Dijkstra's Algorithm (7.4.1.2)

All link-state routing protocols apply Dijkstra's algorithm to calculate the best path route. The algorithm is commonly referred to as the shortest path first (SPF) algorithm. This algorithm uses accumulated costs along each path, from source to destination, to determine the total cost of a route.

In Figure 7-44, each path is labeled with an arbitrary value for cost.

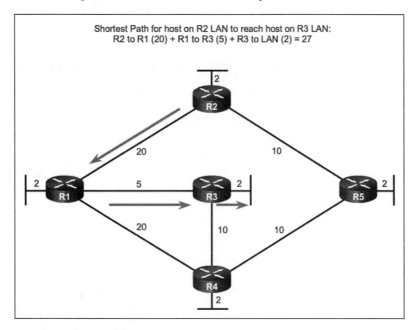

Figure 7-44 Dijkstra's Shortest Path Algorithm

The cost of the shortest path for R2 to send packets to the LAN attached to R3 is 27. Each router determines its own cost to each destination in the topology. In other words, each router calculates the SPF algorithm and determines the cost from its own perspective.

> **Note**
>
> The focus of this section is on cost, which is determined by the SPF tree. For this reason, the graphics throughout this section show the connections of the SPF tree, not the topology. All links are represented with a solid black line.

SPF Example (7.4.1.3)

The table in Figure 7-45 displays the shortest path and the accumulated cost to reach the identified destination networks from the perspective of R1.

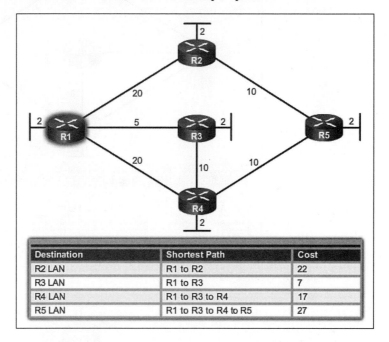

Destination	Shortest Path	Cost
R2 LAN	R1 to R2	22
R3 LAN	R1 to R3	7
R4 LAN	R1 to R3 to R4	17
R5 LAN	R1 to R3 to R4 to R5	27

Figure 7-45   R1 SPF Tree

The shortest path is not necessarily the path with the least number of hops. For example, look at the path to the R5 LAN. It might be assumed that R1 would send directly to R4 instead of to R3. However, the cost to reach R4 directly (22) is higher than the cost to reach R4 through R3 (17).

Observe the shortest path for each router to reach each of the LANs, as shown in Figures 7-46 through 7-49.

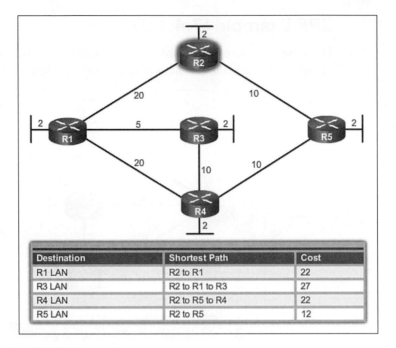

Destination	Shortest Path	Cost
R1 LAN	R2 to R1	22
R3 LAN	R2 to R1 to R3	27
R4 LAN	R2 to R5 to R4	22
R5 LAN	R2 to R5	12

Figure 7-46   R2 SPF Tree

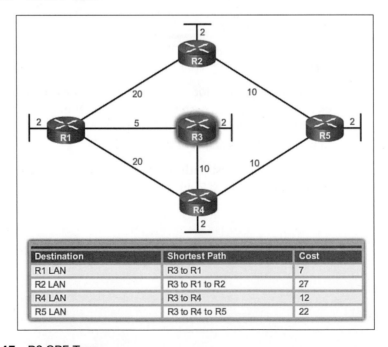

Destination	Shortest Path	Cost
R1 LAN	R3 to R1	7
R2 LAN	R3 to R1 to R2	27
R4 LAN	R3 to R4	12
R5 LAN	R3 to R4 to R5	22

Figure 7-47   R3 SPF Tree

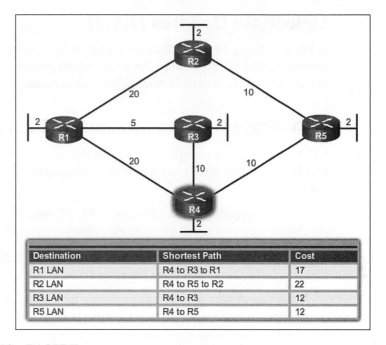

Figure 7-48 R4 SPF Tree

Destination	Shortest Path	Cost
R1 LAN	R4 to R3 to R1	17
R2 LAN	R4 to R5 to R2	22
R3 LAN	R4 to R3	12
R5 LAN	R4 to R5	12

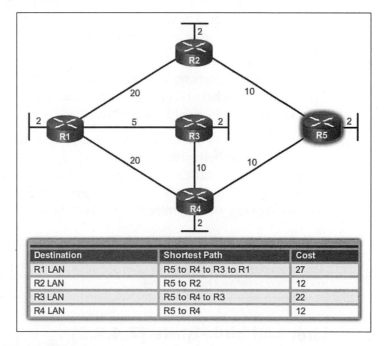

Destination	Shortest Path	Cost
R1 LAN	R5 to R4 to R3 to R1	27
R2 LAN	R5 to R2	12
R3 LAN	R5 to R4 to R3	22
R4 LAN	R5 to R4	12

Figure 7-49 R5 SPF Tree

Link-State Updates (7.4.2)

A big difference between distance vector and link state routing protocols is how changes to the network cause the protocols to update their information. This next section shows the link state routing process in action.

Link-State Routing Process (7.4.2.1)

So exactly how does a link-state routing protocol work? With link-state routing protocols, a link is an interface on a router. Information about the state of those links is known as link-states.

Examine the topology back in Figure 7-44. All routers in the topology will complete the following generic link-state routing process to reach a state of convergence:

1. Each router learns about its own links and its own directly connected networks. This is done by detecting that an interface is in the up state.

2. Each router is responsible for meeting its neighbors on directly connected networks. Link state routers do this by exchanging Hello packets with other link-state routers on directly connected networks.

3. Each router builds a *Link-State Packet (LSP)* containing the state of each directly connected link. This is done by recording all the pertinent information about each neighbor, including neighbor ID, link type, and bandwidth.

4. Each router floods the LSP to all neighbors. Those neighbors store all LSPs received in a database. They then flood the LSPs to their neighbors until all routers in the area have received the LSPs. Each router stores a copy of each LSP received from its neighbors in a local database.

5. Each router uses the database to construct a complete map of the topology and computes the best path to each destination network. Like having a road map, the router now has a complete map of all destinations in the topology and the routes to reach them. The SPF algorithm is used to construct the map of the topology and to determine the best path to each network.

Note

This process is the same for both OSPF for IPv4 and OSPF for IPv6. The examples in this section will refer to OSPF for IPv4.

Link and Link-State (7.4.2.2)

The first step in the link-state routing process is that each router learns about its own links, its own directly connected networks. When a router interface is configured with an IP address and subnet mask, the interface becomes part of that network.

Refer to the topology in Figure 7-50.

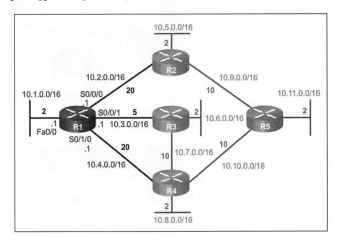

Figure 7-50   R1 Links

For purposes of this discussion, assume that R1 was previously configured and had full connectivity to all neighbors. However, R1 lost power briefly and had to restart.

During boot up R1 loads the saved startup configuration file. As the previously configured interfaces become active, R1 learns about its own directly connected networks. Regardless of the routing protocols used, these directly connected networks are now entries in the routing table.

As with distance vector protocols and static routes, the interface must be properly configured with an IPv4 address and subnet mask, and the link must be in the up state before the link-state routing protocol can learn about a link. Also, like distance vector protocols, the interface must be included in one of the **network** router configuration statements before it can participate in the link-state routing process.

Figure 7-53 shows R1 linked to four directly connected networks:

- FastEthernet 0/0 - 10.1.0.0/16
- Serial 0/0/0 - 10.2.0.0/16
- Serial 0/0/1 - 10.3.0.0/16
- Serial 0/1/0 - 10.4.0.0/16

As shown in Figures 7-51 through 7-54, the link-state information includes

- The interface's IPv4 address and subnet mask
- The type of network, such as Ethernet (broadcast) or Serial point-to-point link
- The cost of that link
- Any neighbor routers on that link

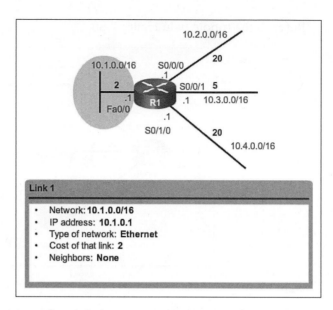

Figure 7-51   Link-State of Interface Fa0/0

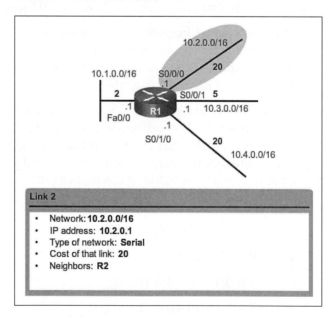

Figure 7-52   Link-State of Interface S0/0/0

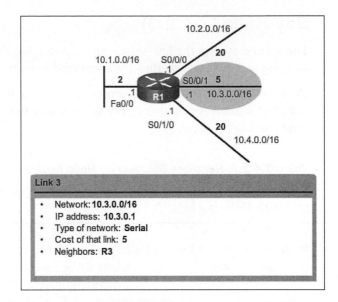

Figure 7-53   Link-State of Interface S0/0/1

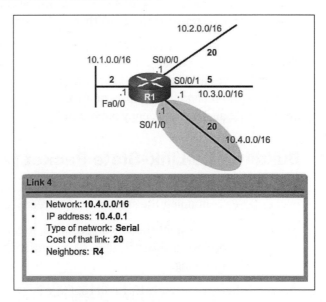

Figure 7-54   Link-State of Interface S0/1/0

Say Hello (7.4.2.3)

The second step in the link-state routing process is that each router is responsible for meeting its neighbors on directly connected networks.

Routers with link-state routing protocols use a Hello protocol to discover any neighbors on its links. A neighbor is any other router that is enabled with the same link-state routing protocol.

Video

Video 7.4.2.3: Neighbor Discovery – Hello Packets.

Go to the course and play the animation on the link-state neighbor discovery process with Hello packets.

In the animation, R1 sends Hello packets out of its links (interfaces) to discover if there are any neighbors. R2, R3, and R4 reply to the Hello packet with their own Hello packets because these routers are configured with the same link-state routing protocol. There are no neighbors out the FastEthernet 0/0 interface. Because R1 does not receive a Hello on this interface, it does not continue with the link-state routing process steps for the FastEthernet 0/0 link.

When two link-state routers learn that they are neighbors, they form an *adjacency*. These small Hello packets continue to be exchanged between two adjacent neighbors and serves as a keepalive function to monitor the state of the neighbor. If a router stops receiving Hello packets from a neighbor, that neighbor is considered unreachable and the adjacency is broken.

Building the Link-State Packet (7.4.2.4)

The third step in the link-state routing process is that each router builds a link-state packet (LSP) containing the state of each directly connected link.

After a router has established its adjacencies, it can build its LSPs that contain the link-state information about its links. A simplified version of the LSP from R1 would contain the following:

1. R1; Ethernet network 10.1.0.0/16; Cost 2

2. R1 -> R2; Serial point-to-point network; 10.2.0.0/16; Cost 20

3. R1 -> R3; Serial point-to-point network; 10.3.0.0/16; Cost 5

4. R1 -> R4; Serial point-to-point network; 10.4.0.0/16; Cost 20

Flooding the LSP (7.4.2.5)

The fourth step in the link-state routing process is that each router floods the LSP to all neighbors, who then store all LSPs received in a database.

Each router floods its link-state information to all other link-state routers in the routing area. Whenever a router receives an LSP from a neighboring router, it immediately sends that LSP out all other interfaces except the interface that received the LSP. This process creates a flooding effect of LSPs from all routers throughout the routing area.

Video

Video 7.4.2.5: Flooding the LSP

Go to the course and play the animation on LSP flooding.

In the animation, notice how the LSPs are flooded almost immediately after being received without any intermediate calculations. Link-state routing protocols calculate the SPF algorithm after the flooding is complete. As a result, link-state routing protocols reach convergence very quickly.

Remember that LSPs do not need to be sent periodically. An LSP only needs to be sent

- During initial startup of the routing protocol process on that router (for example, router restart)

- Whenever there is a change in the topology (for example, a link going down or coming up, a neighbor adjacency being established or broken)

In addition to the link-state information, other information is included in the LSP, such as sequence numbers and aging information, to help manage the flooding process. This information is used by each router to determine if it has already received the LSP from another router or if the LSP has newer information than what is already contained in the link-state database. This process allows a router to keep only the most current information in its link-state database.

Building the Link-State Database (7.4.2.6)

The final step in the link-state routing process is that each router uses the database to construct a complete map of the topology and computes the best path to each destination network.

Eventually, all routers receive an LSP from every other link-state router in the routing area. These LSPs are stored in the link-state database.

Table 7-8 displays the link-state database content of R1.

Table 7-8   Link-State Database Content of R1

R1 Link-State Database

R1 Link-States:
- Connected to network 10.1.0.0/16, cost = 2
- Connected to R2 on network 10.2.0.0/16, cost = 20
- Connected to R3 on network 10.3.0.0/16, cost = 5
- Connected to R4 on network 10.4.0.0/16, cost = 20

R2 Link-States:
- Connected to network 10.5.0.0/16, cost = 2
- Connected to R1 on network 10.2.0.0/16, cost = 20
- Connected to R5 on network 10.9.0.0/16, cost = 10

R3 Link-States:
- Connected to network 10.6.0.0/16, cost = 2
- Connected to R1 on network 10.3.0.0/16, cost = 5
- Connected to R4 on network 10.7.0.0/16, cost = 10

R4 Link-States:
- Connected to network 10.8.0.0/16, cost = 2
- Connected to R1 on network 10.4.0.0/16, cost = 20
- Connected to R3 on network 10.7.0.0/16, cost = 10
- Connected to R5 on network 10.10.0.0/16, cost = 10

R5 Link-States:
- Connected to network 10.11.0.0/16, cost = 2
- Connected to R2 on network 10.9.0.0/16, cost = 10
- Connected to R4 on network 10.10.0.0/16, cost = 10

As a result of the flooding process, R1 has learned the link-state information for each router in its routing area. Notice that R1 also includes its own link-state information in the link-state database.

With a complete link-state database, R1 can now use the database and the shortest path first (SPF) algorithm to calculate the preferred path or shortest path to each network resulting in the SPF tree.

Building the SPF Tree (7.4.2.7)

Each router in the routing area uses the link-state database and SPF algorithm to construct the SPF tree.

For example, using the link-state information from all other routers, R1 can now begin to construct an SPF tree of the network. To begin, the SPF algorithm interprets each router's LSP to identify networks and associated costs. R1 identifies its directly connected networks and costs, and keeps adding any unknown network and associated costs to the SPF tree. R1 ignores any networks it has already identified.

Note

To see the complete progression of the SPF tree of R1, go to the online curriculum and view graphics 1 through 6 of 7.4.2.7.

Interactive Graphic

Activity 7.4.2.7: Identifying Unknown Networks

Go to the course online and use the slider bar in the first through fifth graphics to see the entire link-state database of R1.

The SPF algorithm then calculates the shortest paths to reach each individual network resulting in the SPF tree, as shown in Figure 7-55.

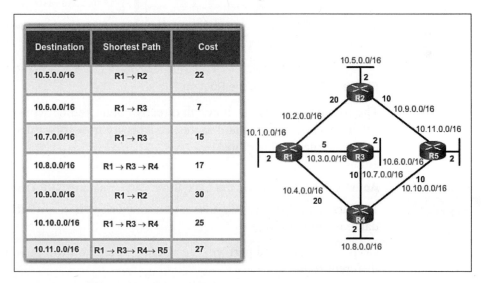

Destination	Shortest Path	Cost
10.5.0.0/16	R1 → R2	22
10.6.0.0/16	R1 → R3	7
10.7.0.0/16	R1 → R3	15
10.8.0.0/16	R1 → R3 → R4	17
10.9.0.0/16	R1 → R2	30
10.10.0.0/16	R1 → R3 → R4	25
10.11.0.0/16	R1 → R3→ R4→ R5	27

Figure 7-55 Resulting SPF Tree of R1

R1 now has a complete topology view of the link-state area.

Each router constructs its own SPF tree independently from all other routers. To ensure proper routing, the link-state databases used to construct those trees must be identical on all routers.

Adding OSPF Routes to the Routing Table (7.4.2.8)

Using the shortest path information determined by the SPF algorithm, these paths can now be added to the routing table. Figure 7-56 shows the routes that have now been added to R1's IPv4 routing table.

Destination	Shortest Path	Cost
10.5.0.0/16	R1 → R2	22
10.6.0.0/16	R1 → R3	7
10.7.0.0/16	R1 → R3	15
10.8.0.0/16	R1 → R3 → R4	17
10.9.0.0/16	R1 → R2	30
10.10.0.0/16	R1 → R3 → R4	25
10.11.0.0/16	R1 → R3→ R4→ R5	27

R1 Routing Table

Directly Connected Networks
- 10.1.0.0/16 Directly Connected Network
- 10.2.0.0/16 Directly Connected Network
- 10.3.0.0/16 Directly Connected Network
- 10.4.0.0/16 Directly Connected Network

Remote Networks
- 10.5.0.0/16 via R2 serial 0/0/0, cost = 22
- 10.6.0.0/16 via R3 serial 0/0/1, cost = 7
- 10.7.0.0/16 via R3 serial 0/0/1, cost = 15
- 10.8.0.0/16 via R3 serial 0/0/1, cost = 17
- 10.9.0.0/16 via R2 serial 0/0/0, cost = 30
- 10.10.0.0/16 via R3 serial 0/0/1, cost = 25
- 10.11.0.0/16 via R3 serial 0/0/1, cost = 27

Figure 7-56 Populate the Routing Table

The routing table also includes all directly connected networks and routes from any other sources, such as static routes. Packets are now forwarded according to these entries in the routing table.

Activity 7.4.2.9: Building the Link-State Database and SPF Tree

This drag and drop activity allows you to check your knowledge of the link-state database and SPF tree.

Go to the course and perform the activity where you will build the SPF tree for two different routers.

Why Use Link-State Routing Protocols (7.4.3)

With all of the added complexity of link-state protocols, a common question asked is, "Why use them if they are so complex?" These next three sections show you the advantages and disadvantages of link-state routing protocols, along with a list of link-state routing protocols from which to choose as your solution.

Why Use Link-State Protocols? (7.4.3.1)

There are several advantages of link-state routing protocols compared to distance vector routing protocols.

- **Builds a Topological Map:** Link-state routing protocols create a topological map, or SPF tree of the network topology. Because link-state routing protocols exchange link-states, the SPF algorithm can build an SPF tree of the network. Using the SPF tree, each router can independently determine the shortest path to every network.

- **Fast Convergence:** When receiving an LSP, link-state routing protocols immediately flood the LSP out all interfaces except for the interface from which the LSP was received. In contrast, RIP needs to process each routing update and update its routing table before flooding them out other interfaces.

- **Event-Driven Updates:** After the initial flooding of LSPs, link-state routing protocols only send out an LSP when there is a change in the topology. The LSP contains only the information regarding the affected link. Unlike some distance vector routing protocols, link-state routing protocols do not send periodic updates.

- **Hierarchical Design:** Link-state routing protocols use the concept of areas. Multiple areas create a hierarchical design to networks, allowing for better route aggregation (summarization) and the isolation of routing issues within an area.

Link-state protocols also have a few disadvantages compared to distance vector routing protocols:

- **Memory Requirements:** Link-state protocols require additional memory to create and maintain the link-state database and SPF tree.

- **Processing Requirements:** Link-state protocols can also require more CPU processing than distance vector routing protocols. The SPF algorithm requires more CPU time than distance vector algorithms such as Bellman-Ford because link-state protocols build a complete map of the topology.

- **Bandwidth Requirements:** The flooding of link-state packets can adversely affect the available bandwidth on a network. This should only occur during initial startup of routers but can also be an issue on unstable networks.

Disadvantages of Link-State Protocols (7.4.3.2)

Modern link-state routing protocols are designed to minimize the effects on memory, CPU, and bandwidth. The use and configuration of multiple areas can reduce the size of the link-state databases. Multiple areas can also limit the amount of link-state information flooding in a routing domain and send LSPs only to those routers that need them. When there is a change in the topology, only those routers in the affected area receive the LSP and run the SPF algorithm. This can help isolate an unstable link to a specific area in the routing domain.

For example, in Figure 7-57, there are three separate routing domains: area 1, area 0, and area 51.

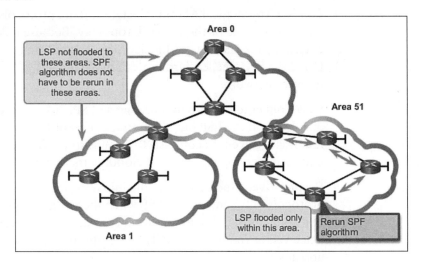

Figure 7-57   Create Areas to Minimize Router Resource Usage

If a network in area 51 goes down (shown by an X in Figure 7-57), the LSP with the information about this downed link is only flooded to other routers in that area. Only those routers in area 51 need to update their link-state databases, rerun the SPF algorithm, create a new SPF tree, and update their routing tables. Routers in other areas learn that this route is down, but this is done with a type of LSP that does not cause them to rerun their SPF algorithm. Routers in other areas can update their routing tables directly.

Protocols That Use Link-State (7.4.3.3)

There are only two link-state routing protocols, OSPF and IS-IS.

Open Shortest Path First (OSPF) is the most popular implementation. It was designed by the Internet Engineering Task Force (IETF) OSPF Working Group. The development of OSPF began in 1987 and there are two current versions in use:

- **OSPFv2:** OSPF for IPv4 networks (RFC 1247 and RFC 2328)

- **OSPFv3:** OSPF for IPv6 networks (RFC 2740)

Note

With the OSPFv3 Address Families feature, OSPFv3 includes support for both IPv4 and IPv6.

IS-IS was designed by the International Organization for Standardization (ISO) and is described in ISO 10589. The first incarnation of this routing protocol was developed at Digital Equipment Corporation (DEC) and is known as DECnet Phase V. Radia Perlman was the chief designer of the IS-IS routing protocol.

IS-IS was originally designed for the OSI protocol suite and not the TCP/IP protocol suite. Later, Integrated IS-IS, or Dual IS-IS, included support for IP networks. Although IS-IS has been known as the routing protocol used mainly by ISPs and carriers, more enterprise networks are beginning to use IS-IS.

OSPF and IS-IS share many similarities and also have many differences. There are many pro-OSPF and pro-IS-IS factions who discuss and debate the advantages of one routing protocol over the other. Both routing protocols provide the necessary routing functionality.

Parts of an IPv4 Route Entry (7.5.1)

To understand how a router can determine where to send a packet, you must look closely at the routing table. This section breaks down a routing table entry into smaller pieces for ease of understanding.

Routing Table Entries (7.5.1.1)

The topology displayed in Figure 7-58 is used as the reference topology for this section.

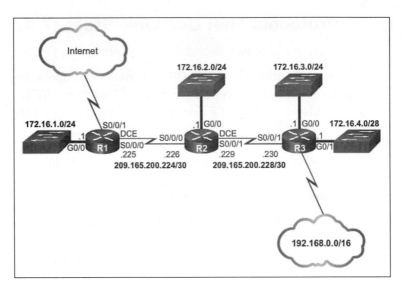

Figure 7-58 Reference Topology

Notice that in the topology

- R1 is the edge router that connects to the Internet. Therefore, it is propagating a default static route to R2 and R3.

- R1, R2, and R3 contain discontiguous networks separated by another classful network.

- R3 is also introducing a 192.168.0.0/16 supernet route.

Figure 7-59 displays the IPv4 routing table of R1 with directly connected, static, and dynamic routes.

```
R1# show ip route | begin Gateway
Gateway of last resort is 209.165.200.234 to network 0.0.0.0

S*  0.0.0.0/0 [1/0] via 209.165.200.234, Serial0/0/1
                  is directly connected, Serial0/0/1
    172.16.0.0/16 is variably subnetted, 5 subnets, 3 masks
C     172.16.1.0/24 is directly connected, GigabitEthernet0/0
L     172.16.1.1/32 is directly connected, GigabitEthernet0/0
R     172.16.2.0/24 [120/1] via 209.165.200.226, 00:00:12, Serial0/0/0
R     172.16.3.0/24 [120/2] via 209.165.200.226, 00:00:12, Serial0/0/0
R     172.16.4.0/28 [120/2] via 209.165.200.226, 00:00:12, Serial0/0/0
R   192.168.0.0/16 [120/2] via 209.165.200.226, 00:00:03, Serial0/0/0
    209.165.200.0/24 is variably subnetted, 5 subnets, 2 masks
C     209.165.200.224/30 is directly connected, Serial0/0/0
L     209.165.200.225/32 is directly connected, Serial0/0/0
R     209.165.200.228/30 [120/1] via 209.165.200.226, 00:00:12,
                  Serial0/0/0
C     209.165.200.232/30 is directly connected, Serial0/0/1
L     209.165.200.233/30 is directly connected, Serial0/0/1
R1#
```

Figure 7-59 Routing Table of R1

> **Note**
>
> The routing table hierarchy in Cisco IOS was originally implemented with the classful routing scheme. Although the routing table incorporates both classful and classless addressing, the overall structure is still built around this classful scheme.

Directly Connected Entries (7.5.1.2)

As highlighted in Figure 7-60, the routing table of R1 contains three directly connected networks.

```
R1# show ip route | begin Gateway
Gateway of last resort is 209.165.200.234 to network 0.0.0.0

S*   0.0.0.0/0 [1/0] via 209.165.200.234, Serial0/0/1
              is directly connected, Serial0/0/1
     172.16.0.0/16 is variably subnetted, 5 subnets, 3 masks
C       172.16.1.0/24 is directly connected, GigabitEthernet0/0
L       172.16.1.1/32 is directly connected, GigabitEthernet0/0
R       172.16.2.0/24 [120/1] via 209.165.200.226, 00:00:12, Serial0/0/0
R       172.16.3.0/24 [120/2] via 209.165.200.226, 00:00:12, Serial0/0/0
R       172.16.4.0/28 [120/2] via 209.165.200.226, 00:00:12, Serial0/0/0
R       192.168.0.0/16 [120/2] via 209.165.200.226, 00:00:03, Serial0/0/0
     209.165.200.0/24 is variably subnetted, 5 subnets, 2 masks
C       209.165.200.224/30 is directly connected, Serial0/0/0
L       209.165.200.225/32 is directly connected, Serial0/0/0
R       209.165.200.228/30 [120/1] via 209.165.200.226, 00:00:12, Serial0/0/0
C       209.165.200.232/30 is directly connected, Serial0/0/1
L       209.165.200.233/32 is directly connected, Serial0/0/1
R1#
```

Figure 7-60   Directly Connected Interfaces of R1

Notice that two routing table entries are automatically created when an active router interface is configured with an IP address and subnet mask.

Figure 7-61 displays one of the routing table entries on R1 for the directly connected network 172.16.1.0.

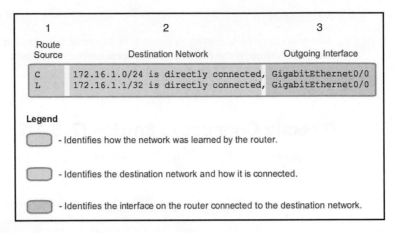

Figure 7-61   Directly Connected Routes of R1

These entries were automatically added to the routing table when the Gigabit-Ethernet 0/0 interface was configured and activated. The entries contain the following information:

- **Route source:** Identifies how the route was learned. Directly connected interfaces have two route source codes. C identifies a directly connected network. Directly connected networks are automatically created whenever an interface is configured with an IP address and activated. L identifies that this is a local route. Local routes are automatically created whenever an interface is configured with an IP address and activated.

- **Destination network:** The address of the remote network and how that network is connected.

- **Outgoing interface:** Identifies the exit interface to use when forwarding packets to the destination network.

Note

Local routing table entries did not appear in routing tables prior to IOS release 15.

A router typically has multiple interfaces configured. The routing table stores information about both directly connected and remote routes. As with directly connected networks, the route source identifies how the route was learned. For instance, common codes for remote networks include

- **S:** Identifies that the route was manually created by an administrator to reach a specific network. This is known as a static route.

- **D:** Identifies that the route was learned dynamically from another router using the EIGRP routing protocol.

- **O:** Identifies that the route was learned dynamically from another router using the OSPF routing protocol.

- **R:** Identifies that the route was learned dynamically from another router using the RIP routing protocol.

Remote Network Entries (7.5.1.3)

Figure 7-62 displays an IPv4 routing table entry on R1 for the route to remote network 172.16.4.0 on R3.

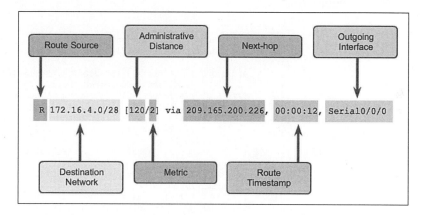

Figure 7-62   Remote Network Route Entry on R1

The entry identifies the following information:

- **Route source:** Identifies how the route was learned.

- **Destination network:** Identifies the address of the remote network.

- **Administrative distance:** Identifies the trustworthiness of the route source.

- **Metric:** Identifies the value assigned to reach the remote network. Lower values indicate preferred routes.

- **Next hop:** Identifies the IPv4 address of the next router to forward the packet to.

- **Route timestamp:** Identifies from when the route was last heard.

- **Outgoing interface:** Identifies the exit interface to use to forward a packet toward the final destination.

Interactive Graphic

Activity 7.5.1.4: Identify Parts of an IPv4 Routing Table Entry

Go to the course online and analyze the routes in the routing table. Then drag each value to its corresponding field in the table

Dynamically Learned IPv4 Routes (7.5.2)

When a routing table is being built, a lot of information is presented to you. These next sections go over some of the terms presented along with the information needed to understand how routing is being used in your network.

Routing Table Terms (7.5.2.1)

A dynamically built routing table provides a great deal of information, as shown in Figure 7-63.

```
R1#show ip route | begin Gateway
Gateway of last resort is 209.165.200.234 to network 0.0.0.0

S*    0.0.0.0/0 [1/0] via 209.165.200.234, Serial0/0/1
               is directly connected, Serial0/0/1
      172.16.0.0/16 is variably subnetted, 5 subnets, 3 masks
C        172.16.1.0/24 is directly connected, GigabitEthernet0/0
L        172.16.1.1/32 is directly connected, GigabitEthernet0/0
R        172.16.2.0/24 [120/1] via 209.165.200.226, 00:00:12,
         Serial0/0/0
R        172.16.3.0/24 [120/2] via 209.165.200.226, 00:00:12,
         Serial0/0/0
R        172.16.4.0/28 [120/2] via 209.165.200.226, 00:00:12,
         Serial0/0/0
R     192.168.0.0/16 [120/2] via 209.165.200.226, 00:00:03,
      Serial0/0/0
      209.165.200.0/24 is variably subnetted, 5 subnets, 2 masks
C        209.165.200.224/30 is directly connected, Serial0/0/0
L        209.165.200.225/32 is directly connected, Serial0/0/0
R        209.165.200.228/30 [120/1] via 209.165.200.226, 00:00:12,
         Serial0/0/0
C        209.165.200.232/30 is directly connected, Serial0/0/1
L        209.165.200.233/32 is directly connected, Serial0/0/1
R1#
```

Figure 7-63   Routing Table of R1

Therefore, it is crucial to understand the output generated by the routing table. Special terms are applied when discussing the contents of a routing table.

The Cisco IP routing table is not a flat database. The routing table is actually a hierarchical structure that is used to speed up the lookup process when locating routes and forwarding packets. Within this structure, the hierarchy includes several levels.

Routes are discussed in terms of

- Ultimate route
- Level 1 route
- Level 1 parent route
- Level 2 child routes

Ultimate Route (7.5.2.2)

An *ultimate route* is a routing table entry that contains either a next-hop IPv4 address or an exit interface. Directly connected, dynamically learned, and local routes are ultimate routes.

In Figure 7-64, the highlighted areas are examples of ultimate routes.

```
R1# show ip route | begin Gateway
Gateway of last resort is 209.165.200.234 to network 0.0.0.0

S*    0.0.0.0/0 [1/0] via 209.165.200.234, Serial0/0/1
              is directly connected, Serial0/0/1
      172.16.0.0/16 is variably subnetted, 5 subnets, 3 masks
C         172.16.1.0/24 is directly connected, GigabitEthernet0/0
L         172.16.1.1/32 is directly connected, GigabitEthernet0/0
R         172.16.2.0/24 [120/1] via 209.165.200.226, 00:00:12,
          Serial0/0/0
R         172.16.3.0/24 [120/2] via 209.165.200.226, 00:00:12,
           Serial0/0/0
R         172.16.4.0/28 [120/2] via 209.165.200.226, 00:00:12,
          Serial0/0/0
R     192.168.0.0/16 [120/2] via 209.165.200.226, 00:00:03,
      Serial0/0/0
      209.165.200.0/24 is variably subnetted, 5 subnets, 2 masks
C         209.165.200.224/30 is directly connected, Serial0/0/0
L         209.165.200.225/32 is directly connected, Serial0/0/0
R         209.165.200.228/30 [120/1] via 209.165.200.226, 00:00:12,
          Serial0/0/0
C         209.165.200.232/30 is directly connected, Serial0/0/1
L         209.165.200.233/32 is directly connected, Serial0/0/1
R1#
```

Figure 7-64   Ultimate Routes of R1

Notice that all these routes specify either a next-hop IPv4 address or an exit interface.

Level 1 Route (7.5.2.3)

A *level 1 route* is a route with a subnet mask equal to or less than the classful mask of the network address. Therefore, a level 1 route can be a

- *Network route:* A network route that has a subnet mask equal to that of the classful mask.

- *Supernet route:* A supernet route is a network address with a mask less than the classful mask, for example, a summary address.

- **Default route:** A default route is a static route with the address 0.0.0.0/0.

The source of the level 1 route can be a directly connected network, static route, or a dynamic routing protocol.

Figure 7-65 highlights how level 1 routes are also ultimate routes.

Figure 7-65   Sources of Level 1 Routes

Figure 7-66 highlights level 1 routes.

```
R1# show ip route | begin Gateway
Gateway of last resort is 209.165.200.234 to network
0.0.0.0

S*      0.0.0.0/0 [1/0] via 209.165.200.234, Serial0/0/1
                  is directly connected, Serial0/0/1
        172.16.0.0/16 is variably subnetted, 5 subnets, 3
masks
C         172.16.1.0/24 is directly connected,
GigabitEthernet0/0
L         172.16.1.1/32 is directly connected,
GigabitEthernet0/0
R         172.16.2.0/24 [120/1] via 209.165.200.226,
00:00:12, Serial0/0/0
R         172.16.3.0/24 [120/2] via 209.165.200.226,
00:00:12, Serial0/0/0
R         172.16.4.0/28 [120/2] via 209.165.200.226,
00:00:12, Serial0/0/0
R      192.168.0.0/16 [120/2] via 209.165.200.226, 00:00:03,
Serial0/0/0
        209.165.200.0/24 is variably subnetted, 5 subnets, 2
masks
C         209.165.200.224/30 is directly connected,
Serial0/0/0
```

Figure 7-66   Examples of Level 1 Routes

Interactive Graphic

Activity 7.5.2.3: Example of Level 1 Routes

Go to the course online and use the slider bar in the second graphic to see the entire output of the **show ip route | begin Gateway** command.

Level 1 Parent Route (7.5.2.4)

As illustrated in Figure 7-67, a level 1 parent route is a level 1 network route that is subnetted. A parent route can never be an ultimate route.

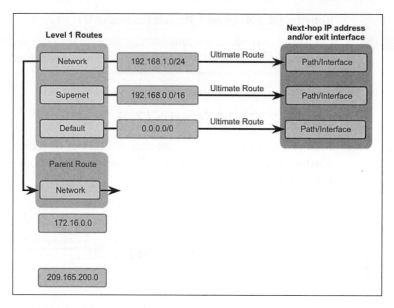

Figure 7-67 Level 1 Parent Route

Figure 7-68 highlights the level 1 parent routes in the routing table of R1.

```
R1# show ip route | begin Gateway
Gateway of last resort is 209.165.200.234 to network
0.0.0.0

S*    0.0.0.0/0 [1/0] via 209.165.200.234, Serial0/0/1
                is directly connected, Serial0/0/1
      172.16.0.0/16 is variably subnetted, 5 subnets, 3
masks
C        172.16.1.0/24 is directly connected,
GigabitEthernet0/0
L        172.16.1.1/32 is directly connected,
GigabitEthernet0/0
R        172.16.2.0/24 [120/1] via 209.165.200.226,
00:00:12, Serial0/0/0
R        172.16.3.0/24 [120/2] via 209.165.200.226,
00:00:12, Serial0/0/0
R        172.16.4.0/28 [120/2] via 209.165.200.226,
00:00:12, Serial0/0/0
R     192.168.0.0/16 [120/2] via 209.165.200.226, 00:00:03,
Serial0/0/0
      209.165.200.0/24 is variably subnetted, 5 subnets, 2
masks
C        209.165.200.224/30 is directly connected,
Serial0/0/0
```

Figure 7-68 Level 1 Parent Routes of R1

In the routing table, it basically provides a heading for the specific subnets it contains. Each entry displays the classful network address, the number of subnets, and the number of different subnet masks that the classful address has been subdivided into.

Activity 7.5.2.4: Level 1 Parent Routes of R1

Go to the course online and use the slider bar in the second graphic to see the entire output of the **show ip route | begin Gateway** command.

Level 2 Child Route (7.5.2.5)

A level 2 child route is a route that is a subnet of a classful network address. As illustrated in Figure 7-69, a level 1 parent route is a level 1 network route that is subnetted.

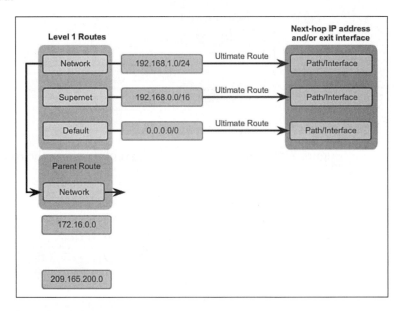

Figure 7-69   Level 2 Child Route

A level 1 parent routes contain level 2 child routes, as shown in Figure 7-70.

Like a level 1 route, the source of a *level 2 route* can be a directly connected network, a static route, or a dynamically learned route. Level 2 child routes are also ultimate routes.

Note

The routing table hierarchy in Cisco IOS has a classful routing scheme. A level 1 parent route is the classful network address of the subnet route. This is the case even if a classless routing protocol is the source of the subnet route.

Figure 7-71 highlights the child routes in the routing table of R1.

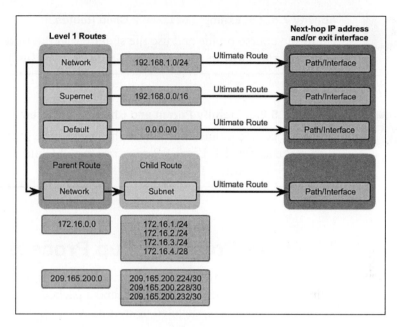

Figure 7-70   Child Routes Are Ultimate Routes

```
R1#show ip route | begin Gateway
Gateway of last resort is 209.165.200.234 to network
0.0.0.0

S*   0.0.0.0/0 [1/0] via 209.165.200.234, Serial0/0/1
             is directly connected, Serial0/0/1
     172.16.0.0/16 is variably subnetted, 5 subnets, 3
masks
C       172.16.1.0/24 is directly connected,
GigabitEthernet0/0
L       172.16.1.1/32 is directly connected,
GigabitEthernet0/0
R       172.16.2.0/24 [120/1] via 209.165.200.226,
00:00:12, Serial0/0/0
R       172.16.3.0/24 [120/2] via 209.165.200.226,
00:00:12, Serial0/0/0
R       172.16.4.0/28 [120/2] via 209.165.200.226,
00:00:12, Serial0/0/0
R    192.168.0.0/16 [120/2] via 209.165.200.226, 00:00:03,
Serial0/0/0
     209.165.200.0/24 is variably subnetted, 5 subnets, 2
masks
C       209.165.200.224/30 is directly connected,
Serial0/0/0
```

Figure 7-71   Example of Level 2 Child Routes

Activity 7.5.2.5: Example of Level 2 Child Routes

Go to the course online and use the slider bar in the third graphic to see the entire output of the **show ip route | begin Gateway** command.

Activity 7.5.2.6: Identify Parent and Child IPv4 Routes

Go to the course online and analyze the routes in the routing table. Then classify each route as Level 1, Level 1 Parent, or Level 2 Child routes and drag the appropriate term to the Route Type file provided.

The IPv4 Route Lookup Process (7.5.3)

One of the most important skills that a network administrator needs to understand is how a router determines where to send a packet that has entered the router. The router lookup process, detailed next, is something that all administrators need to understand.

Route Lookup Process (7.5.3.1)

When a packet arrives on a router interface, the router examines the IPv4 header, identifies the destination IPv4 address, and proceeds through the router lookup process.

In Figure 7-72, the router examines level 1 network routes for the best match with the destination address of the IPv4 packet.

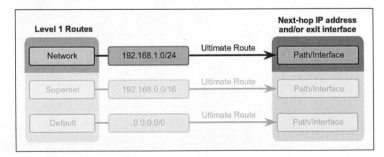

Figure 7-72   Match Level 1 Routes

1. If the best match is a level 1 ultimate route, then this route is used to forward the packet.

2. If the best match is a level 1 parent route, proceed to the next step.

In Figure 7-73, the router examines child routes (the subnet routes) of the parent route for a best match.

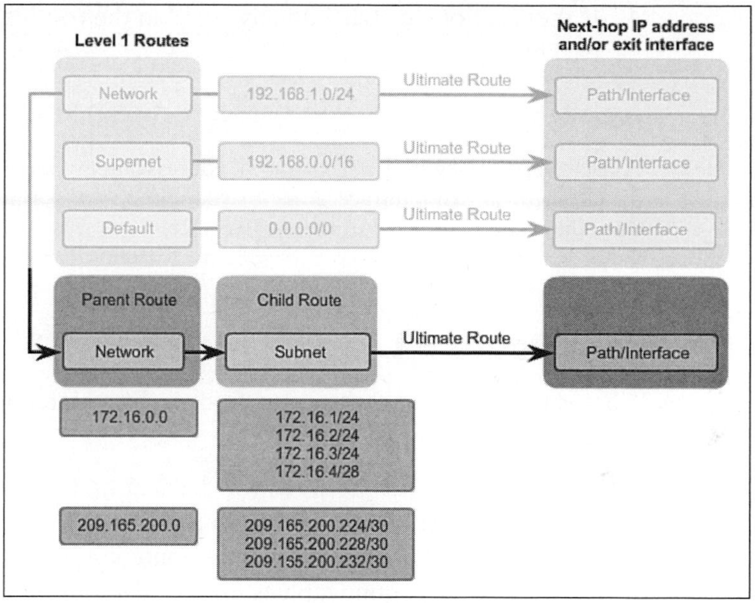

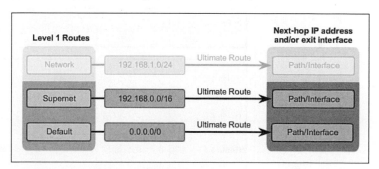

Figure 7-73   Match Level 2 Child Routes

1. If there is a match with a level 2 child route, that subnet is used to forward the packet.

2. If there is not a match with any of the level 2 child routes, proceed to the next step.

   In Figure 7-74, the router continues searching level 1 supernet routes in the routing table for a match, including the default route, if there is one.

Figure 7-74   Match Supernet and the Default Route

3. If there is now a lesser match with a level 1 supernet or default routes, the router uses that route to forward the packet.

4. If there is not a match with any route in the routing table, the router drops the packet.

Note

A route referencing only a next-hop IP address and not an exit interface must be resolved to a route with an exit interface. A recursive lookup is performed on the next-hop IP address until the route is resolved to an exit interface.

Best Route = Longest Match (7.5.3.2)

What is meant by the router must find the best match in the routing table? Best match is equal to the longest match.

For there to be a match between the destination IPv4 address of a packet and a route in the routing table, a minimum number of far-left bits must match between the IPv4 address of the packet and the route in the routing table. The subnet mask of the route in the routing table is used to determine the minimum number of far-left bits that must match. Remember that an IPv4 packet only contains the IPv4 address and not the subnet mask.

The best match is the route in the routing table that has the most number of far-left matching bits with the destination IPv4 address of the packet. The route with the greatest number of equivalent far-left bits, or the longest match, is always the preferred route.

In Figure 7-75, a packet is destined for 172.16.0.10.

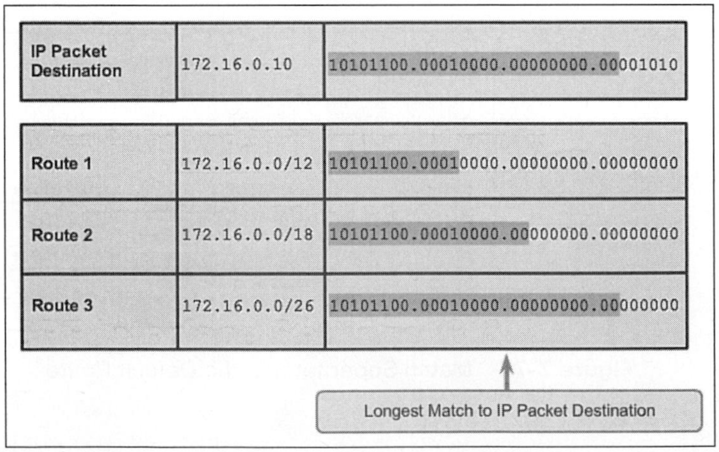

IP Packet Destination	172.16.0.10	10101100.00010000.00000000.00001010
Route 1	172.16.0.0/12	10101100.00010000.00000000.00000000
Route 2	172.16.0.0/18	10101100.00010000.00000000.00000000
Route 3	172.16.0.0/26	10101100.00010000.00000000.00000000

Longest Match to IP Packet Destination

Figure 7-75   Matches for Packet Destined to 172.16.0.10

The router has three possible routes that match this packet: 172.16.0.0/12, 172.16.0.0/18, and 172.16.0.0/26. Of the three routes, 172.16.0.0/26 has the longest match and is therefore chosen to forward the packet. Remember, for any of these routes to be considered a match, there must be at least the number of matching bits indicated by the subnet mask of the route.

Activity 7.5.3.3: Determine the Longest Match Route

Go to the course online and drag each destination IPv4 address to its best route choice.

Analyze an IPv6 Routing Table (7.5.4)

The other routing table that IT Professionals need to understand and use is the routing table for IPv6.

IPv6 Routing Table Entries (7.5.4.1)

Components of the IPv6 routing table are very similar to the IPv4 routing table. For instance, it is populated using directly connected interfaces, static routes, and dynamically learned routes.

Because IPv6 is classless by design, all routes are effectively level 1 ultimate routes. There is no level 1 parent of level 2 child routes.

The topology displayed in Figure 7-76 is used as the reference topology for this section.

Notice that in the topology

- R1, R2, and R3 are configured in a full mesh topology. All routers have redundant paths to various networks.

- R2 is the edge router and connects to the ISP; however, a default static route is not being advertised.

- EIGRP for IPv6 has been configured on all three routers.

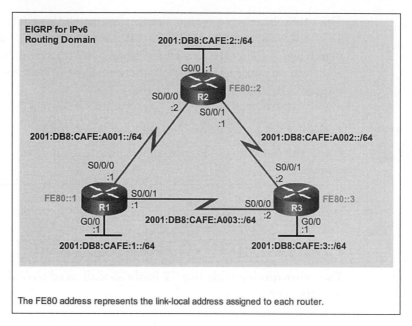

Figure 7-76   Reference IPv6 Topology

Directly Connected Entries (7.5.4.2)

The routing table of R1 is displayed in Figure 7-77 using the **show ipv6 route** command.

```
R1# show ipv6 route
<output omitted>

C   2001:DB8:CAFE:1::/64 [0/0]
      via GigabitEthernet0/0, directly connected
L   2001:DB8:CAFE:1::1/128 [0/0]
      via GigabitEthernet0/0, receive
D   2001:DB8:CAFE:2::/64 [90/3524096]
      via FE80::3, Serial0/0/1
D   2001:DB8:CAFE:3::/64 [90/2170112]
      via FE80::3, Serial0/0/1
C   2001:DB8:CAFE:A001::/64 [0/0]
      via Serial0/0/0, directly connected
L   2001:DB8:CAFE:A001::1/128 [0/0]
      via Serial0/0/0, receive
D   2001:DB8:CAFE:A002::/64 [90/3523840]
      via FE80::3, Serial0/0/1
C   2001:DB8:CAFE:A003::/64 [0/0]
      via Serial0/0/1, directly connected
L   2001:DB8:CAFE:A003::1/128 [0/0]
      via Serial0/0/1, receive
L   FF00::/8 [0/0]
      via Null0, receive
R1#
```

Figure 7-77   IPv6 Routing Table of R1

Although the command output is displayed slightly differently than in the IPv4 version, it still contains the relevant route information.

Figure 7-78 highlights the connected network and local routing table entries of the directly connected interfaces.

```
R1# show ipv6 route
<output omitted>

C    2001:DB8:CAFE:1::/64 [0/0]
       via GigabitEthernet0/0, directly connected
L    2001:DB8:CAFE:1::1/128 [0/0]
       via GigabitEthernet0/0, receive
D    2001:DB8:CAFE:2::/64 [90/3524096]
       via FE80::3, Serial0/0/1
D    2001:DB8:CAFE:3::/64 [90/2170112]
       via FE80::3, Serial0/0/1
C    2001:DB8:CAFE:A001::/64 [0/0]
       via Serial0/0/0, directly connected
L    2001:DB8:CAFE:A001::1/128 [0/0]
       via Serial0/0/0, receive
D    2001:DB8:CAFE:A002::/64 [90/3523840]
       via FE80::3, Serial0/0/1
C    2001:DB8:CAFE:A003::/64 [0/0]
       via Serial0/0/1, directly connected
L    2001:DB8:CAFE:A003::1/128 [0/0]
       via Serial0/0/1, receive
L    FF00::/8 [0/0]
       via Null0, receive
R1#
```

Figure 7-78   Directly Connected Routes on R1

The three entries were added when the interfaces were configured and activated.

As shown in Figure 7-79, directly connected route entries display the following information:

- **Route source:** Identifies how the route was learned. Directly connected interfaces have two route source codes. (C identifies a directly connected network while L identifies that this is a local route.)

- **Directly connected network:** The IPv6 address of the directly connected network.

- **Administrative distance:** Identifies the trustworthiness of the route source. IPv6 uses the same distances as IPv4. A value of 0 indicates the best, most trustworthy source.

- **Metric:** Identifies the value assigned to reach the remote network. Lower values indicate preferred routes.

- **Outgoing interface:** Identifies the exit interface to use when forwarding packets to the destination network.

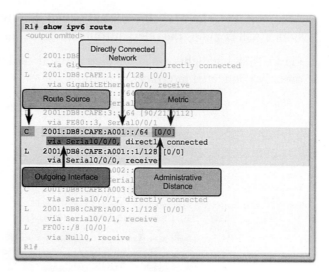

Figure 7-79   Directly Connected Routes on R1

Note

The serial links have reference bandwidths configured to observe how EIGRP metrics select the best route. The reference bandwidth is not a realistic representation of modern networks. It is used only to provide a visual sense of link speed.

Remote IPv6 Network Entries (7.5.4.3)

Figure 7-80 highlights the routing table entries for the three remote networks (that is, R2 LAN, R3 LAN, and the link between R2 and R3). The three entries were added by the EIGRP.

```
R1# show ipv6 route
<output omitted>

C    2001:DB8:CAFE:1::/64 [0/0]
     via GigabitEthernet0/0, directly connected
L    2001:DB8:CAFE:1::1/128 [0/0]
     via GigabitEthernet0/0, receive
D    2001:DB8:CAFE:2::/64 [90/3524096]
     via FE80::3, Serial0/0/1
D    2001:DB8:CAFE:3::/64 [90/2170112]
     via FE80::3, Serial0/0/1
C    2001:DB8:CAFE:A001::/64 [0/0]
     via Serial0/0/0, directly connected
L    2001:DB8:CAFE:A001::1/128 [0/0]
     via Serial0/0/0, receive
D    2001:DB8:CAFE:A002::/64 [90/3523840]
     via FE80::3, Serial0/0/1
C    2001:DB8:CAFE:A003::/64 [0/0]
     via Serial0/0/1, directly connected
L    2001:DB8:CAFE:A003::1/128 [0/0]
     via Serial0/0/1, receive
L    FF00::/8 [0/0]
     via Null0, receive
R1#
```

Figure 7-80   Remote Network Entries on R1

Figure 7-81 displays a routing table entry on R1 for the route to remote network 2001:DB8:CAFE:3::/64 on R3. The entry identifies the following information:

- **Route source:** Identifies how the route was learned. Common codes include O (OSPF), D (EIGRP), R (RIP), and S (Static route).

- **Destination network:** Identifies the address of the remote IPv6 network.

- **Administrative distance:** Identifies the trustworthiness of the route source. IPv6 uses the same distances as IPv4.

- **Metric:** Identifies the value assigned to reach the remote network. Lower values indicate preferred routes.

- **Next hop:** Identifies the IPv6 address of the next router to forward the packet to.

- **Outgoing interface:** Identifies the exit interface to use to forward a packet toward the final destination.

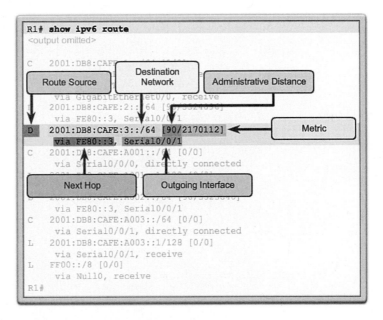

Figure 7-81   Remote Network Entries on R1

When an IPv6 packet arrives on a router interface, the router examines the IPv6 header and identifies the destination IPv6 address. The router then proceeds through the following router lookup process.

The router examines level 1 network routes for the best match with the destination address of the IPv6 packet. Just like IPv4, the longest match is the best match. For example, if there are multiple matches in the routing table, the router chooses the route with the longest match. A match is made by matching the far-left bits of the packet's destination IPv6 address with the IPv6 prefix and prefix-length in the IPv6 routing table.

Interactive Graphic

Activity 7.5.4.4: Identify Parts of an IPv6 Routing Table Entry

Go to the course online and analyze the IPv6 routing table to determine the different parts of a routing entry. Then drag each value to its corresponding field in the table. Do this for all three graphics in this section.

Summary (7.6)

Class Activity 7.6.1.1: IPv6 - Details, Details...

After studying the concepts presented in this chapter concerning IPv6, you should be able to read a routing table easily and interpret the IPv6 routing information listed within it.

With a partner, use the IPv6 routing table diagram and the .pdf provided with this activity.

Record your answers to the Reflection questions.

Then compare your answers with, at least, one other group from the class.

Dynamic routing protocols are used by routers to facilitate the exchange of routing information between routers. The purpose of dynamic routing protocols includes discovery of remote networks, maintaining up-to-date routing information, choosing the best path to destination networks, and ability to find a new best path if the current path is no longer available. Although dynamic routing protocols require less administrative overhead than static routing, they do require dedicating part of a router's resources for protocol operation, including CPU time and network link bandwidth.

Networks typically use a combination of both static and dynamic routing. Dynamic routing is the best choice for large networks and static routing is better for stub networks.

Routing protocols are responsible for discovering remote networks, as well as maintaining accurate network information. When there is a change in the topology, routing protocols propagate that information throughout the routing domain. The process of bringing all routing tables to a state of consistency, where all of the routers in the same routing domain or area have complete and accurate information about the network, is called convergence. Some routing protocols converge faster than others.

Routing protocols can be classified as either classful or classless, distance-vector or link-state, and an interior gateway protocol or an exterior gateway protocol.

Distance vector protocols use routers as "sign posts" along the path to the final destination. The only information a router knows about a remote network is the distance or metric to reach that network and which path or interface to use to get there. Distance vector routing protocols do not have an actual map of the network topology.

A router configured with a link-state routing protocol can create a complete view or topology of the network by gathering information from all of the other routers.

Metrics are used by routing protocols to determine the best path or shortest path to reach a destination network. Different routing protocols may use different metrics. Typically, a lower metric means a better path. Metrics can be determined by hops, bandwidth, delay, reliability, and load.

Routers sometimes learn about multiple routes to the same network from both static routes and dynamic routing protocols. When a router learns about a destination network from more than one routing source, Cisco routers use the administrative distance value to determine which source to use. Each dynamic routing protocol has a unique administrative value, along with static routes and directly connected networks. The lower the administrative value, the more preferred the route source. A directly connected network is always the preferred source, followed by static routes and then various dynamic routing protocols.

The **show ip protocols** command displays the IPv4 routing protocol settings currently configured on the router. For IPv6, use **show ipv6 protocols**.

With link-state routing protocols such as OSPF, a link is an interface on a router. Information about the state of those links is known as link-states. All link-state routing protocols apply Dijkstra's algorithm to calculate the best path route. The algorithm is commonly referred to as the shortest path first (SPF) algorithm. This algorithm uses accumulated costs along each path, from source to destination, to determine the total cost of a route.

Practice

The following activities provide practice with the topics introduced in this chapter. The Labs and Class Activities are available in the companion *Routing and Switching Essentials Lab Manual* (978-1-58713-320-6). The Packet Tracer Activities PKA files are found in the online course.

Class Activities

Class Activity 7.0.1.2: How Much Does This Cost?

Class Activity 7.6.1.1: IPv6 – Details, Details

Labs

Lab 7.3.2.4: Configuring RIPv2

Packet Tracer Activities

Packet Tracer 7.1.3.6: Investigating Convergence

Packet Tracer 7.2.2.4: Comparing RIP and EIGRP Path Selection

Packet Tracer 7.3.1.8: Configuring RIPv2

Packet Tracer 7.3.2.3: Configuring RIPng

Check Your Understanding Questions

Complete all the review questions listed here to test your understanding of the topics and concepts in this chapter. The appendix, "Answers to the 'Check Your Understanding' Questions," lists the answers.

1. What is the difference between interior and exterior routing protocols?

   A. Exterior routing protocols are used only by large ISPs. Interior routing protocols are used by small ISPs.

   B. Interior routing protocols are used to route on the Internet. Exterior routing protocols are used inside organizations.

   C. Exterior routing protocols are used to administer a single autonomous system. Interior routing protocols are used to administer several domains.

   D. Interior routing protocols are used to communicate within a single autonomous system. Exterior routing protocols are used to communicate between multiple autonomous systems.

2. Which factor directly affects the time to convergence?

   A. Data link layer protocol used

   B. Number of hosts

   C. Size of the network

   D. Type of applications used

3. Which classless routing protocol supports VLSM and CIDR, supports manual route summarization, and uses the multicast address 224.0.0.9?

   A. RIPv1

   B. RIPv2

   C. OSPF

   D. EIGRP

4. What are two characteristics of link-state protocols compared to distance vector protocols? (Choose two.)

   A. They require a lot of hardware resources.

   B. They know of the network topology from the perspective of their neighbors.

   C. They compute their own knowledge of the network topology.

   D. They use hop counts to compute the network topology.

   E. They flood the routing table periodically.

5. Which classless routing protocol supports VLSM and CIDR, bounded and triggered updates, and uses the multicast address of 224.0.0.10?

   A. RIPv1

   B. RIPv2

   C. OSPF

   D. EIGRP

6. Which algorithm is used by the OSPF routing process to construct the SPF tree on a router?

   A. DUAL algorithm

   B. Bellman-Ford algorithm

   C. Dijkstra's algorithm

   D. Path vector protocol

7. What is an advantage of OSPF compared to RIP?

   A. Fast convergence

   B. Less complexity

   C. Less CPU processing

   D. Low memory requirements

8. A network administrator has examined the routing table of a router and noted that the entry for the destination network 172.16.4.0/24 begins with the letter **D**. What does this letter signify?

   A. The route to network 172.16.4.0/24 is directly connected.

   B. The route source was learned dynamically.

   C. That is the direct route for packets to that network.

   D. The route to this network is configured statically on the router.

9. What is the purpose of classifying Cisco IP routing table entries as ultimate route, level 1 route, level 1 parent route, and level 2 child routes?

   A. To enable the implementation of dynamic routing protocols

   B. To explain the operation of the routing table as a flat database

   C. To enable Cisco routers to implement both IPv4 and IPv6 routing

   D. To explain the operation of the hierarchical structure of the routing table

10. What are two functions of dynamic routing protocols? (Choose two.)

    A. To maintain routing tables

    B. To assure low router overhead

    C. To avoid exposing network information

    D. To discover the network

    E. To choose the path that is specified by the administrator

CHAPTER 8

Single-Area OSPF

Objectives

Upon completion of this chapter, you will be able to answer the following questions:

- What is the process by which link-state routers learn about other networks?

- What are the types of packets used by Cisco IOS routers to establish and maintain an OSPF network?

- How do Cisco IOS routers achieve convergence in an OSPF network?

- How do you configure an OSPF router ID?

- How do you configure single-area OSPFv2 in a small, routed IPv4 network?

- How does OSPF use cost to determine best path?

- How do you verify the operation of OSPFv2 in a small routed network?

- What are the main similarities and differences between OSPFv2 and OSPFv3?

- How do you configure OSPFv3 in a small routed IPv6 network?

- How do you verify OSPFv3 in a small routed IPv6 network?

Key Terms

This chapter uses the following key terms. You can find the definitions in the Glossary.

Introduction (8.0.1.1)

Open Shortest Path First (OSPF) is a *link-state routing protocol* that was developed as a replacement for the distance vector routing protocol, RIP. RIP was an acceptable routing protocol in the early days of networking and the Internet. However, RIP's reliance on hop count as the only metric for determining best route quickly became problematic. Using hop count does not scale well in larger networks with multiple paths of varying speeds. OSPF has significant advantages over RIP in that it offers faster convergence and scales to much larger network implementations.

OSPF is a classless routing protocol that uses the concept of areas for scalability. This chapter covers basic, *single-area OSPF* implementations and configurations.

Class Activity 8.0.1.2: Can Submarines Swim?

Scenario

Edsger Wybe Dijkstra was a famous computer programmer and theoretical physicist. One of his most famous quotes was, "The question of whether computers can think is like the question of whether submarines can swim." Dijkstra's work has been applied, among other things, to routing protocols. He created the *Shortest Path First (SPF) algorithm* for network routing.

Now, open the PDF provided with this activity and answer the reflection questions. Save your work.

Get together with two of your classmates to compare your answers.

After completing this activity, do you have an idea as to how the OSPF protocol may work?

Characteristics of OSPF (8.1)

OPSF was one of the first link-state routing protocols to be created. This next section deals with the evolution of OSPF.

Evolution of OSPF (8.1.1.1)

As shown in Table 8-1, OSPF version 2 (*OSPFv2*) is available for IPv4, whereas OSPF version 3 (*OSPFv3*) is available for IPv6.

Table 8-1   Routing Protocol Classification

	Interior Gateway Protocols				Exterior Gateway Protocols
	Distance Vector		Link-State		Path Vector
IPv4	RIPv2	EIGRP	OSPFv2	IS-IS	BGP-4
IPv6	RIP ng	EIGRP for IPv6	OSPF v3	IS-IS for IPv6	BGP-MP

Interactive Graphic

Go to the course online and look at the second graphic in section 8.1.1.1.

Here you are introduced to a timeline showing historical events related to OSPF.

The initial development of OSPF began in 1987 by the Internet Engineering Task Force (IETF) OSPF Working Group. At that time, the Internet was largely an academic and research network funded by the U.S. government.

In 1989, the specification for OSPFv1 was published in RFC 1131. Two implementations were written. One implementation was developed to run on routers and the other to run on UNIX workstations. The latter implementation became a widespread UNIX process known as GATED. OSPFv1 was an experimental routing protocol and was never deployed.

In 1991, OSPFv2 was introduced in RFC 1247 by John Moy. OSPFv2 offered significant technical improvements over OSPFv1. It is classless by design; therefore, it supports VLSM and CIDR.

At the same time the OSPF was introduced, ISO was working on a link-state routing protocol of its own, Intermediate System-to-Intermediate System (IS-IS). IETF chose OSPF as its recommended Interior Gateway Protocol (IGP).

In 1998, the OSPFv2 specification was updated in RFC 2328, which remains the current RFC for OSPF.

In 1999, OSPFv3 for IPv6 was published in RFC 2740. OSPF for IPv6, created by John Moy, Rob Coltun, and Dennis Ferguson, is not only a new protocol implementation for IPv6, but also a major rewrite of the operation of the protocol.

In 2008, OSPFv3 was updated in RFC 5340 as OSPF for IPv6.

Note

In this chapter, unless explicitly identified as OSPFv2 or OSPFv3, the term OSPF is used to indicate concepts that are shared by both.

Features of OSPF (8.1.1.2)

OSPF features include

- **Classless:** It is classless by design; therefore, it supports VLSM and CIDR.

- **Efficient:** Routing changes trigger routing updates (no periodic updates). It uses the SPF algorithm to choose the best path.

- **Fast convergence:** It quickly propagates network changes.

- **Scalable:** It works well in small and large network sizes. Routers can be grouped into areas to support a hierarchical system.

- **Secure:** It supports Message Digest 5 (MD5) authentication. When enabled, OSPF routers accept only encrypted routing updates from peers with the same preshared password.

Administrative distance (AD) is the trustworthiness (or preference) of the route source. OSPF has a default administrative distance of 110. Because of this, OSPF is preferred over IS-IS (AD 115) and RIP (AD 120).

Components of OSPF (8.1.1.3)

All routing protocols share similar components. They all use routing protocol messages to exchange route information. The messages help build *data structures*, which are then processed using a routing algorithm.

The three main components of the OSPF routing protocol follow.

Data Structures

OSPF creates and maintains three databases:

- **Adjacency database:** Creates the neighbor table.

- *Link-state database (LSDB):* Creates the topology table.

- **Forwarding database:** Creates the routing table.

Table 8-2 summarizes these three OSPF databases.

Table 8-2 OSPF Data Structures

Database	Table	Description
Adjacency Database	Neighbor Table	■ List of all neighbor routers to which a router has established bidirectional communication. ■ This table is unique for each router. ■ Can be viewed with the **show ip ospf neighbor** command.
Link-State Database (LSDB)	Topology Table	■ Lists information about all other routers in the network. ■ This database represents the network topology. ■ All routers within an area have the same LSDB. ■ Can be viewed with the **show ip ospf database** command.
Forwarding Database	Routing Table	■ List of routes generated when an algorithm is run on the link-state database. ■ Each router's routing table is unique and contains information on how and where to send packets to other routers. ■ Can be viewed with the **show ip route** command.

These tables contain a list of neighboring routers to exchange routing information with and are kept and maintained in RAM.

Routing Protocol Messages

OSPF exchanges messages to convey routing information using five types of packets. These packets, as shown in Figure 8-1, follow:

- *Hello packet*
- *Database description* packet
- *Link-state request* packet
- *Link-state update* packet
- *Link-state acknowledgment* packet

These packets are used to discover neighboring routers and also to exchange routing information to maintain accurate information about the network.

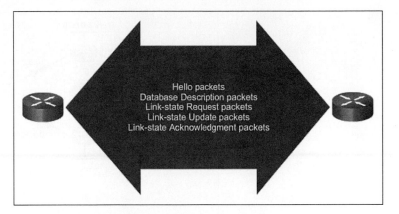

Figure 8-1   OSPF Routers Exchange Packets

Algorithm

The CPU processes the neighbor and topology tables using Dijkstra's SPF algorithm. The SPF algorithm is based on the cumulative *cost* to reach a destination.

The SPF algorithm creates an SPF tree by placing each router at the root of the tree and calculating the shortest path to each node. The SPF tree is then used to calculate the best routes. OSPF places the best routes into the forwarding database, which is used to make the routing table.

Link-State Operation (8.1.1.4)

To maintain routing information, OSPF routers complete the following generic link-state routing process to reach a state of convergence:

1. Establish Neighbor Adjacencies (see Figure 8-2). OSPF-enabled routers must recognize each other on the network before they can share information. An OSPF-enabled router sends Hello packets out all OSPF-enabled interfaces to determine if neighbors are present on those links. If a neighbor is present, the OSPF-enabled router attempts to establish a neighbor adjacency with that neighbor.

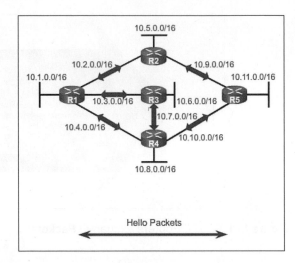

Figure 8-2   Routers Exchange Hello Packets

2. Exchange Link-State Advertisements (Figure 8-3). After adjacencies are established, routers then exchange *link-state advertisements (LSA)*. LSAs contain the state and cost of each directly connected link. Routers flood their LSAs to adjacent neighbors. Adjacent neighbors receiving the LSA immediately flood the LSA to other directly connected neighbors, until all routers in the area have all LSAs.

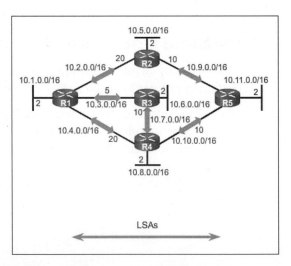

Figure 8-3   Routers Exchange LSAs

3. Build the Topology Table (Figure 8-4). After LSAs are received, OSPF-enabled routers build the topology table (LSDB) based on the received LSAs. This database eventually holds all the information about the topology of the network.

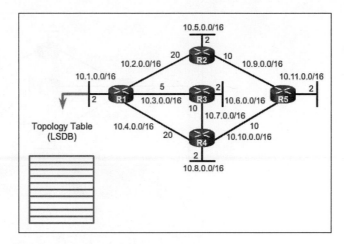

Figure 8-4   R1 Creates Its Topological Database

4. Execute the SPF Algorithm (Figure 8-5). Routers then execute the SPF algorithm. The gears in the figure are used to indicate the execution of the SPF algorithm. The SPF algorithm creates the SPF tree.

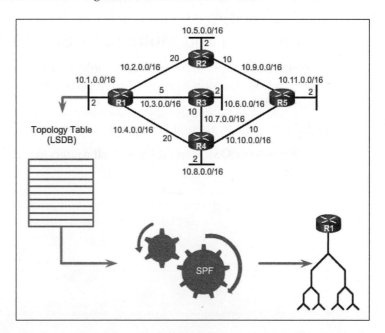

Figure 8-5   R1 Executes the SPF Algorithm and Creates the SPF Tree

The content of the R1 SPF tree is displayed in Figure 8-6.

From the SPF tree, the best paths are inserted into the routing table. Routing decisions are made based on the entries in the routing table.

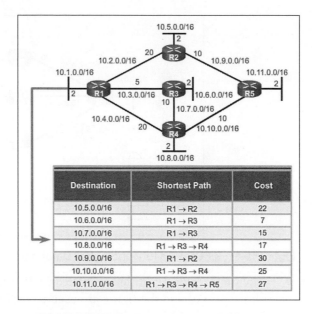

Destination	Shortest Path	Cost
10.5.0.0/16	R1 → R2	22
10.6.0.0/16	R1 → R3	7
10.7.0.0/16	R1 → R3	15
10.8.0.0/16	R1 → R3 → R4	17
10.9.0.0/16	R1 → R2	30
10.10.0.0/16	R1 → R3 → R4	25
10.11.0.0/16	R1 → R3 → R4 → R5	27

Figure 8-6   Content of the R1 SPF Tree

Single-Area and Multiarea OSPF (8.1.1.5)

To make OSPF more efficient and scalable, OSPF supports hierarchical routing using areas. An *OSPF area* is a group of routers that share the same link-state information in their LSDBs.

OSPF can be implemented in one of two ways:

- **Single-Area OSPF:** In Figure 8-7, all routers are in one area called the backbone area (area 0).

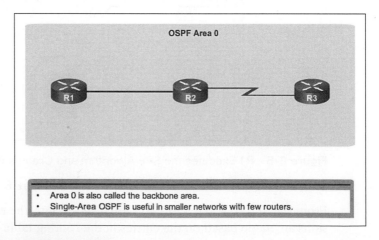

Figure 8-7   Single-Area OSPF

- *Multiarea OSPF*: In Figure 8-8, OSPF is implemented using multiple areas, in a hierarchal fashion. All areas must connect to the backbone area (area 0). Routers interconnecting the areas are referred to as *Area Border Routers (ABR)*.

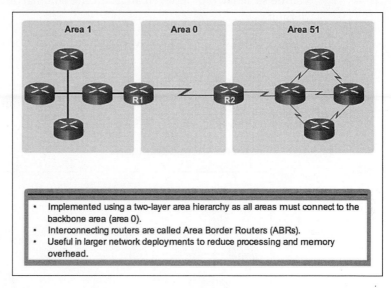

Figure 8-8   Multiarea OSPF

With multiarea OSPF, OSPF can divide one large autonomous system (AS) into smaller areas to support hierarchical routing. With hierarchical routing, routing still occurs between the areas (interarea routing), while many of the processor-intensive routing operations, such as recalculating the database, are kept within an area.

For instance, any time a router receives new information about a topology change within the area (including the addition, deletion, or modification of a link), the router must rerun the SPF algorithm, create a new SPF tree, and update the routing table. The SPF algorithm is CPU-intensive, and the time it takes for calculation depends on the size of the area.

Note

Topology changes are distributed to routers in other areas in a distance vector format. In other words, these routers update only their routing tables and do not need to rerun the SPF algorithm.

Too many routers in one area would make the LSDBs large and increase the load on the CPU. Therefore, arranging routers into areas effectively partitions a potentially large database into smaller and more manageable databases.

The hierarchical-topology possibilities of multiarea OSPF have these advantages:

- **Smaller routing tables:** Fewer routing table entries because network addresses can be summarized between areas. Route summarization is not enabled by default.

- **Reduced link-state update overhead:** Minimizes processing and memory requirements.

- **Reduced frequency of SPF calculations:** Localizes the impact of a topology change within an area. For instance, it minimizes routing update impact because LSA flooding stops at the area boundary.

Figure 8-9 illustrates these advantages.

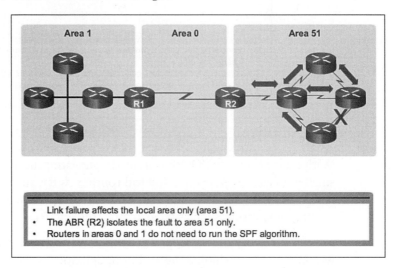

Figure 8-9   Link Changes Impacts Local Area Only

In Figure 8-9, R2 is an ABR for area 51. As an ABR, it would summarize the area 51 routes into area 0. When one of the summarized links fails, LSAs are exchanged within area 51 only. Routers in area 51 must rerun the SPF algorithm to identify the best routes. However, the routers in area 0 and area 1 do not receive any updates; therefore, they do not execute the SPF algorithm.

The focus of this chapter is on single-area OSPF.

Activity 8.1.1.6 Part 1: Identify OSPF Features

Go to the course online and complete the activity in the first graphic identifying features of OSPF.

Activity 8.1.1.6 Part 2: Identify OSPF Terminology

Go to the course online and complete the activity in the second graphic identifying terminology related to OSPF.

OSPF Messages (8.1.2)

There are many different types of OSPF messages. After looking at the encapsulation of OSPF in a frame, the next sections describe and define the different type of OSPF packets.

Encapsulating OSPF Messages (8.1.2.1)

OSPF messages transmitted over an Ethernet link contain the following information:

- **Data Link Ethernet Frame Header:** Identifies the destination multicast MAC addresses 01-00-5E-00-00-05 or 01-00-5E-00-00-06, as shown in Figure 8-10.

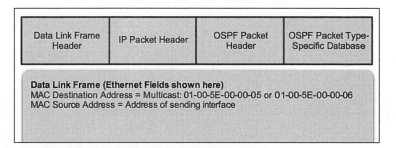

Figure 8-10   Data Link Ethernet Frame Header

- **IP Packet Header:** Identifies the IPv4 protocol field 89, which indicates that this is an OSPF packet. It also identifies one of two OSPF multicast addresses, 224.0.0.5 or 224.0.0.6, as shown in Figure 8-11.

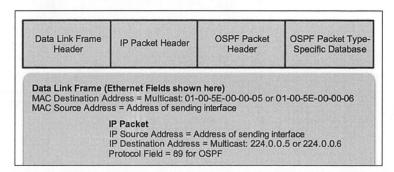

Figure 8-11   IP Packet Header

■ **OSPF Packet Header:** Identifies the OSPF packet type, the router ID and the area ID, as shown in Figure 8-12.

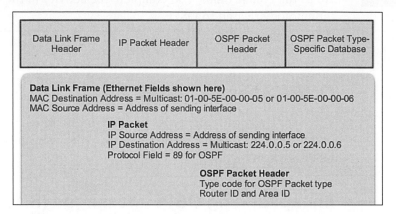

Figure 8-12   OSPF Packet Header

■ **OSPF Packet Type Specific Data:** Contains the OSPF packet type information. The content differs depending on the packet type. In this case, it is an IPv4 Header, as shown in Figure 8-13.

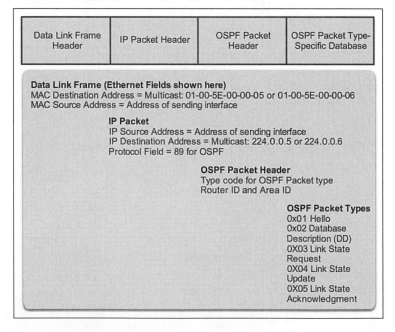

Figure 8-13   OSPF IPv4 Header Fields

Types of OSPF Packets (8.1.2.2)

OSPF uses *link-state packets (LSP)* to establish and maintain neighbor adjacencies and exchange routing updates.

There are five different types of LSPs used by OSPF. Each packet serves a specific purpose in the OSPF routing process:

- **Type 1: Hello packet:** Used to establish and maintain adjacency with other OSPF routers.

- **Type 2: Database Description (DBD) packet:** Contains an abbreviated list of the sending router's LSDB and is used by receiving routers to check against the local LSDB. The LSDB must be identical on all link-state routers within an area to construct an accurate SPF tree.

- **Type 3: Link-State Request (LSR) packet:** Receiving routers can then request more information about any entry in the DBD by sending an LSR.

- **Type 4: Link-State Update (LSU) packet:** Used to reply to LSRs and to announce new information. LSUs contain seven different types of LSAs.

- **Type 5: Link-State Acknowledgment (LSAck) packet:** When an LSU is received, the router sends an LSAck to confirm receipt of the LSU. The LSAck data field is empty.

Hello Packet (8.1.2.3)

The OSPF Type 1 packet is the Hello packet. Hello packets are used to

- Discover OSPF neighbors and establish neighbor adjacencies.

- Advertise parameters on which two routers must agree to become neighbors.

- Elect the *Designated Router (DR)* and *Backup Designated Router (BDR)* on multiaccess networks like Ethernet and Frame Relay. Point-to-point links do not require DR or BDR.

Figure 8-14 displays the fields contained in the Type 1 Hello packet.

Interactive Graphic

Activity 8.1.2.3: OSPF Hello Packet Content

Go to the course online and click any of the Blue packet fields to see a description of the field. Those descriptions are listed here.

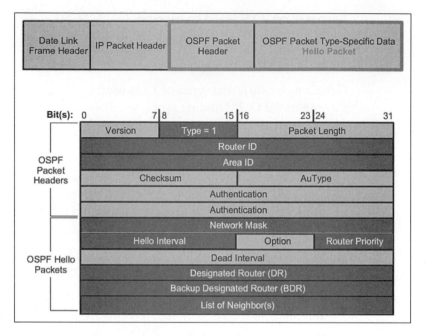

Figure 8-14 OSPF Hello Packet Content

Important fields shown in the figure include

- **Type:** Identifies the type of packet. A one (1) indicates a Hello packet. A value 2 identifies a DBD packet, 3 an LSR packet, 4 an LSU packet, and 5 an LSAck packet.

- *Router ID*: A 32-bit value expressed in dotted decimal notation (an IPv4 address) used to uniquely identifying the originating router.

- **Area ID:** Area from which the packet originated.

- **Network Mask:** Subnet mask associated with the sending interface.

- *Hello Interval*: Specifies the frequency, in seconds, at which a router sends Hello packets. The default Hello interval on multiaccess networks is 10 seconds. This timer must be the same on neighboring routers; otherwise, an adjacency is not established.

- *Router Priority*: Used in a DR/BDR election. The default priority for all OSPF routers is 1 but can be manually altered from 0 to 255. The higher the value, the more likely the router becomes the DR on the link.

- *Dead Interval*: The time in seconds that a router waits to hear from a neighbor before declaring the neighboring router out of service. By default, the router Dead Interval is four times the Hello interval. This timer must be the same on neighboring routers; otherwise, an adjacency is not established.

- **Designated Router (DR):** Router ID of the DR.

- **Backup Designated Router (BDR):** Router ID of the BDR.

- **List of Neighbors:** List that identifies the router IDs of all adjacent routers.

Hello Packet Intervals (8.1.2.4)

As shown in Figure 8-15, OSPF Hello packets are transmitted to multicast address 224.0.0.5 in IPv4 and FF02::5 in IPv6 (all OSPF routers) every

- 10 seconds (default on multiaccess and point-to-point networks)

- 30 seconds (default on nonbroadcast multiaccess [NBMA] networks; for example, Frame Relay)

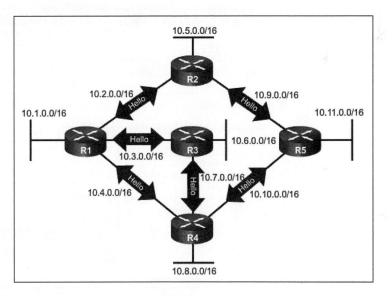

Figure 8-15   Hello Packets Sent Periodically

The Dead interval is the period that the router waits to receive a Hello packet before declaring the neighbor down. If the Dead interval expires before the routers receive a Hello packet, OSPF removes that neighbor from its LSDB. The router floods the LSDB with information about the down neighbor out all OSPF-enabled interfaces.

Cisco uses a default of 4 times the Hello interval:

- 40 seconds (default on multiaccess and point-to-point networks)

- 120 seconds (default on NBMA networks; for example, Frame Relay)

Link-State Updates (8.1.2.5)

Routers initially exchange Type 2 DBD packets, which is an abbreviated list of the sending router's LSDB and is used by receiving routers to check against the local LSDB.

A Type 3 LSR packet is used by the receiving routers to request more information about an entry in the DBD.

The Type 4 LSU packet is used to reply to an LSR packet.

LSUs are also used to forward OSPF routing updates, such as link changes. Specifically, an LSU packet can contain 11 different types of OSPFv2 LSAs, as shown in Figure 8-16.

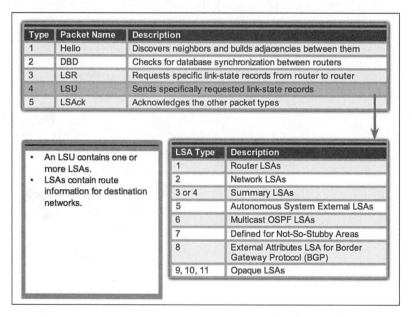

Figure 8-16   LSUs Contain LSAs

OSPFv3 renamed several of these LSAs and also contains two additional LSAs.

Note

The difference between the LSU and LSA terms can sometimes be confusing because these terms are often used interchangeably. However, an LSU contains one or more LSAs.

Activity 8.1.2.6 Part 1: Identify OSPF Packet Types

Go to the course online and complete the activity in the first graphic dragging the OSPF packet types to their corresponding fields.

Activity 8.1.2.6 Part 2: Identify OSPF Packet Types

Go to the course online and complete the activity in the second graphic dragging the OSPF packet types to their corresponding fields.

OSPF Operation (8.1.3)

OSPF has a reputation of being difficult to understand because it is more complex than other routing protocols that are available. But it is no more complex than other routing protocols. It is definitely more powerful and has more features than other protocols, which is why we use it. These next sections deal with how OSPF works as a dynamic routing protocol.

OSPF Operational States (8.1.3.1)

When an OSPF router is initially connected to a network, it attempts to

- Create adjacencies with neighbors.
- Exchange routing information.
- Calculate the best routes.
- Reach convergence.

OSPF progresses through several states while attempting to reach convergence:

- *Down state*
- *Init state*
- *Two-Way state*
- *ExStart state*
- *Exchange state*
- *Loading state*
- *Full state*

Activity 8.1.3.1: Transitioning Through the OSPF States

Go to the course online and click any of the Blue OSPF States to see a description of the State.

Establish Neighbor Adjacencies (8.1.3.2)

When OSPF is enabled on an interface, the router must determine if there is another OSPF neighbor on the link. To accomplish this, the router forwards a Hello packet that contains its router ID out all OSPF-enabled interfaces. The OSPF router ID is used by the OSPF process to uniquely identify each router in the OSPF area. A router ID is an IP address assigned to identify a specific router among OSPF peers.

When a neighboring OSPF-enabled router receives a Hello packet with a router ID that is not within its neighbor list, the receiving router attempts to establish an adjacency with the initiating router.

Refer to R1 in Figure 8-17.

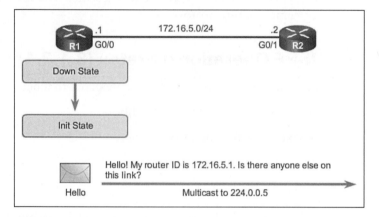

Figure 8-17   Down State to Init State

When OSPF is enabled, the enabled Gigabit Ethernet 0/0 interface transitions from the Down state to the Init state. R1 starts sending Hello packets out all OSPF-enabled interfaces to discover OSPF neighbors to develop adjacencies with.

In Figure 8-18, R2 receives the Hello packet from R1 and adds the R1 router ID to its neighbor list.

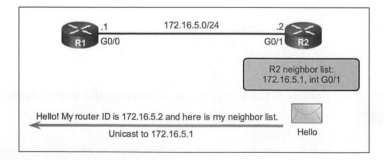

Figure 8-18   The Init State

R2 then sends a Hello packet to R1. The packet contains the R2 Router ID and the R1 Router ID in its list of neighbors on the same interface.

In Figure 8-19, R1 receives the Hello and adds the R2 Router ID in its list of OSPF neighbors.

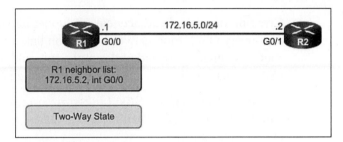

Figure 8-19   Two-Way State

It also notices its own Router ID in the Hello packet's list of neighbors. When a router receives a Hello packet with its Router ID listed in the list of neighbors, the router transitions from the Init state to the Two-Way state.

The action performed in Two-Way state depends on the type of interconnection between the adjacent routers:

- If the two adjacent neighbors are interconnected over a point-to-point link, then they immediately transition from the Two-Way state to the database synchronization phase.

- If the routers are interconnected over a common Ethernet network, then a designated router DR and a BDR must be elected.

Because R1 and R2 are interconnected over an Ethernet network, a DR and BDR election takes place. As shown in Figure 8-20, R2 becomes the DR and R1 is the BDR. This process occurs only on multiaccess networks such as Ethernet LANs.

Hello packets are continually exchanged to maintain router information.

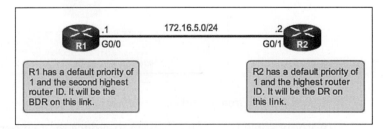

Figure 8-20   Elect the DR and BDR

OSPF DR and BDR (8.1.3.3)

Why is a DR and BDR election necessary?

Multiaccess networks can create two challenges for OSPF regarding the flooding of LSAs:

- **Creation of multiple adjacencies:** Ethernet networks could potentially interconnect many OSPF routers over a common link. Creating adjacencies with every router is unnecessary and undesirable. It would lead to an excessive number of LSAs exchanged between routers on the same network.

- **Extensive flooding of LSAs:** *Link-state routers* flood their LSAs any time OSPF is initialized, or when there is a change in the topology. This flooding can become excessive.

To understand the problem with multiple adjacencies, you must study a formula:

For any number of routers (designated as *n*) on a multiaccess network, there are *n* (*n* − 1) / 2 adjacencies.

Figure 8-21 shows a simple topology of five routers, all of which are attached to the same multiaccess Ethernet network.

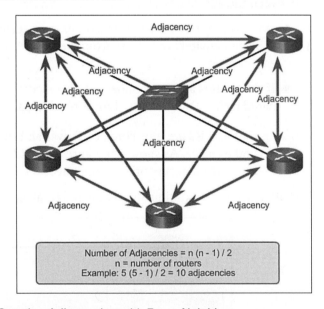

Figure 8-21   Creating Adjacencies with Every Neighbor

Without some type of mechanism to reduce the number of adjacencies, collectively these routers would form 10 adjacencies:

5 (5 − 1) / 2 = 10

This may not seem like much, but as routers are added to the network, the number of adjacencies increases dramatically, as shown in Table 8-3.

Table 8-3   More Routers = More Adjacencies

Routers	Adjacencies
n	n(n−1)/2
5	10
10	45
20	190
100	4950

Video 8.1.3.3: Flooding LSAs

Go to the course and play the animation in the third graphic of LSAs being flooded throughout a network.

In the animation, R2 sends out an LSA. This event triggers every other router to also send out an LSA. Not shown in the animation are the required acknowledgments sent for every LSA received. If every router in a multiaccess network had to flood and acknowledge all received LSAs to all other routers on that same multiaccess network, the network traffic would become quite chaotic.

The solution to managing the number of adjacencies and the flooding of LSAs on a multiaccess network is the DR. On multiaccess networks, OSPF elects a DR to be the collection and distribution point for LSAs sent and received. A BDR is also elected in case the DR fails. All other routers become *DROTHERs*. A DROTHER is a router that is neither the DR nor the BDR.

Video 8.1.3.3: LSAs and DR

Go to the course and play the animation in the fourth graphic of LSAs being flooded throughout a network using a DR to manage the number of adjacencies.

Synchronizing OSPF Databases (8.1.3.4)

After the Two-Way state, routers transition to database synchronization states. Although the Hello packet was used to establish neighbor adjacencies, the other four types of OSPF packets are used during the process of exchanging and synchronizing LSDBs.

In the ExStart state, a master and slave relationship is created between each router and its adjacent DR and BDR. The router with the higher router ID acts as the master for the Exchange state. In Figure 8-22, R2 becomes the master.

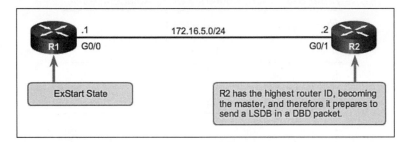

Figure 8-22   Decide Which Router Sends the First DBD

In the Exchange state, the master and slave routers exchange one or more DBD packets. A DBD packet includes information about the LSA entry header that appears in the router's LSDB. The entries can be about a link or about a network. Each LSA entry header includes information about the link-state type, the address of the advertising router, the link's cost, and the sequence number. The router uses the sequence number to determine the newness of the received link-state information.

In Figure 8-23, R2 sends a DBD packet to R1.

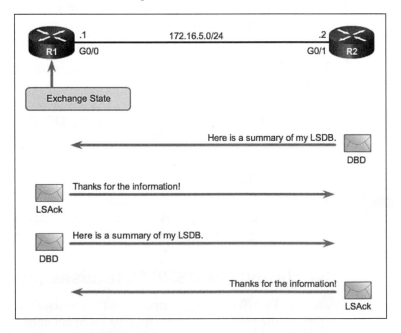

Figure 8-23   Exchange DBD Packets

When R1 receives the DBD, it performs the following actions:

1. It acknowledges the receipt of the DBD using the LSAck packet.

2. R1 then sends DBD packets to R2.

3. R2 acknowledges R1.

R1 compares the information received with the information it has in its own LSDB. If the DBD packet has a more current link-state entry, the router transitions to the Loading state.

For example, in Figure 8-24, R1 sends an LSR regarding network 172.16.6.0 to R2. R2 responds with the complete information about 172.16.6.0 in an LSU packet. Again, when R1 receives an LSU, it sends an LSAck. R1 then adds the new link-state entries into its LSDB.

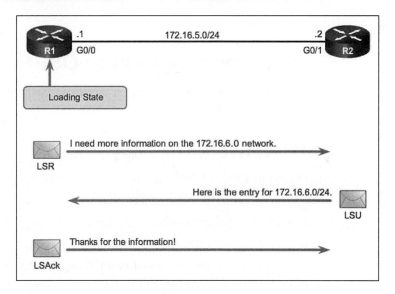

Figure 8-24   Getting Additional Routing Information

After all LSRs have been satisfied for a given router, the adjacent routers are considered synchronized and in a full state.

As long as the neighboring routers continue receiving Hello packets, the network in the transmitted LSAs remain in the topology database. After the topological databases are synchronized, updates (LSU) are sent only to neighbors when

- A change is perceived (incremental updates)

- Every 30 minutes

Interactive Graphic

Activity 8.1.3.5 Part 1: Identify OSPF States for Establishing Adjacency

Go to the course online and complete the activity in the first graphic dragging the OSPF states to their corresponding fields.

Interactive Graphic

Activity 8.1.3.5 Part 2: Identify OSPF States for Establishing Adjacency

Go to the course online and complete the activity in the second graphic dragging the OSPF states to their corresponding fields.

Video

Video 8.1.3.6: Observing OSPF Protocol Communications

Go to the course and play the video "Observing OSPF Protocol Communications."

Configuring Single-Area OSPFv2 (8.2.1)

The following sections go through the steps necessary to configure single-area OSPFv2 in an IPv4 network.

OSPF Network Topology (8.2.1.1)

Introduced in 1991, OSPFv2 is a link-state routing protocol for IPv4. OSPF was designed as an alternative to another IPv4 routing protocol, RIP.

Figure 8-25 shows the topology used for configuring OSPFv2 in this section.

The types of serial interfaces and their associated bandwidths may not necessarily reflect the more common types of connections found in networks today. The bandwidths of the serial links used in this topology were chosen to help explain the calculation of the routing protocol metrics and the process of best path selection.

The routers in the topology have a starting configuration, including interface addresses. There is currently no static routing or dynamic routing configured on any of the routers. All interfaces on routers R1, R2, and R3 (except the loopback on R2) are within the OSPF backbone area. The ISP router is used as the routing domain's gateway to the Internet.

Note

In this topology, the loopback interface is used to simulate the WAN link to the Internet.

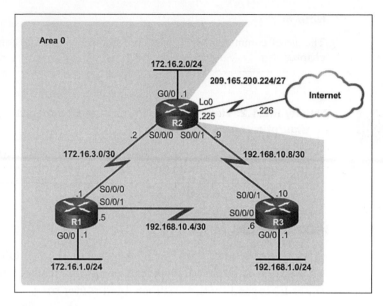

Figure 8-25 OSPF Reference Topology

Router OSPF Configuration Mode (8.2.1.2)

OSPFv2 is enabled using the **router ospf** *process-id* global configuration mode command. The *process-id* value represents a number between 1 and 65,535 and is selected by the network administrator. The *process-id* value is locally significant, which means that it does not have to be the same value on the other OSPF routers to establish adjacencies with those neighbors.

Figure 8-26 provides an example of entering router OSPF configuration mode on R1.

```
R1(config)# router ospf 10
R1(config-router)# ?
Router configuration commands:
  auto-cost               Calculate OSPF interface cost
                          according to bandwidth
  network                 Enable routing on an IP network
  no                      Negate a command or set its defaults
  passive-interface       Suppress routing updates on an
                          interface
  priority                OSPF topology priority
  router-id               router-id for this OSPF process
```

Note: Output has been altered to display only the commands that will be used in this chapter.

Figure 8-26 Entering Router OSPF Configuration Mode on R1

> **Note**
>
> The list of commands has been altered to display only the commands that are used in this chapter.

Interactive Graphic

Activity 8.2.1.2: View the Complete List of Commands Available in Router Configuration Mode

Go to the course online and use the Syntax Checker in the third graphic to enter router configuration mode on R2 and list the commands available at the prompt.

Router IDs (8.2.1.3)

Every router requires a router ID to participate in an OSPF domain. The router ID can be defined by an administrator or automatically assigned by the router. The router ID is used by the OSPF-enabled router to

- **Uniquely identify the router:** The router ID is used by other routers to uniquely identify each router within the OSPF domain and all packets that originate from them.

- **Participate in the election of the DR:** In a multiaccess LAN environment, the election of the DR occurs during initial establishment of the OSPF network. When OSPF links become active, the routing device configured with the highest priority is elected the DR. Assuming there is no priority configured, or there is a tie, then the router with the highest router ID is elected the DR. The routing device with the second highest router ID is elected the BDR.

But how does the router determine the router ID? As illustrated in Figure 8-27, Cisco routers derive the router ID based on one of three criteria, in the following preferential order:

- The router ID is explicitly configured using the OSPF **router-id** *rid* router configuration mode command. The *rid* value is any 32-bit value expressed as an IPv4 address. This is the recommended method to assign a router ID.

- If the router ID is not explicitly configured, the router chooses the highest IPv4 address of any of the configured loopback interfaces. This is the next best alternative to assigning a router ID.

- If no loopback interfaces are configured, then the router chooses the highest active IPv4 address of any of its physical interfaces. This is the least recommended method because it makes it more difficult for administrators to distinguish between specific routers.

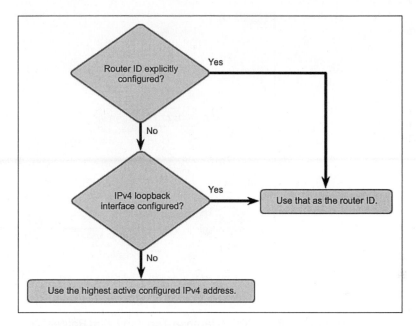

Figure 8-27   Router ID Order of Precedence

If the router uses the highest IPv4 address for the router ID, the interface does not need to be OSPF-enabled. This means that the interface address does not need to be included in one of the OSPF **network** commands for the router to use that IP address as the router ID. The only requirement is that the interface is active and in the up state.

Note

The router ID looks like an IP address, but it is not routable and, therefore, is not included in the routing table, unless the OSPF routing process chooses an interface (physical or loopback) that is appropriately defined by a **network** command.

Configuring an OSPF Router ID (8.2.1.4)

Use the **router-id** *rid* router configuration mode command to manually assign a 32-bit value expressed as an IPv4 address to a router. An OSPF router identifies itself to other routers using this router ID.

As shown in Figure 8-28, R1 is configured with a router ID of 1.1.1.1, R2 with 2.2.2.2, and R3 with 3.3.3.3.

In Figure 8-29, the router ID 1.1.1.1 is assigned to R1. Use the **show ip protocols** command to verify the router ID.

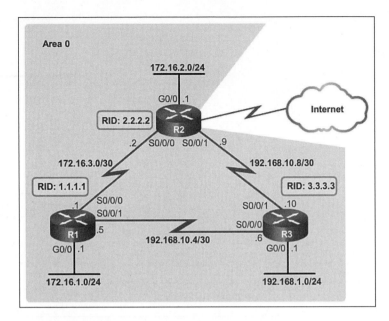

Figure 8-28   OSPF Reference Topology with Router IDs

```
R1(config)# router ospf 10
R1(config-router)# router-id 1.1.1.1
R1(config-router)# end
R1#
*Mar 25 19:50:36.595: %SYS-5-CONFIG_I: Configured from
console by console
R1#
R1# show ip protocols
*** IP Routing is NSF aware ***

Routing Protocol is "ospf 10"
  Outgoing update filter list for all interfaces is not set
  Incoming update filter list for all interfaces is not set
  Router ID 1.1.1.1
  Number of areas in this router is 0. 0 normal 0 stub 0
nssa
  Maximum path: 4
  Routing for Networks:
  Routing Information Sources:
    Gateway         Distance      Last Update
  Distance: (default is 110)

R1#
```

Figure 8-29   Assigning a Router ID to R1

Note

R1 had never been configured with an OSPF router ID. If it had, then the router ID would have to be modified.

If the router ID is the same on two neighboring routers, the router displays an error message similar to the one here:

```
%OSPF-4-DUP_RTRID1: Detected router with duplicate router ID.
```

To correct this problem, configure all routers so that they have unique OSPF router IDs.

Activity 8.2.1.4: Assigning a Router ID on R2 and R3

Go to the course online and use the Syntax Checker in the third graphic to enter router configuration mode first on R2 and then on R3 to assign a Router ID to both routers.

Modifying a Router ID (8.2.1.5)

Sometimes a router ID needs to be changed, for example, when a network administrator establishes a new router ID scheme for the network. However, after a router selects a router ID, an active OSPF router does not allow the router ID to be changed until the router is reloaded or the OSPF process cleared.

In Figure 8-30, notice that the current router ID is 192.168.10.5. The router ID should be 1.1.1.1.

```
R1# show ip protocols
*** IP Routing is NSF aware ***

Routing Protocol is "ospf 10"
  Outgoing update filter list for all interfaces is not set
  Incoming update filter list for all interfaces is not set
  Router ID 192.168.10.5
  Number of areas in this router is 1. 1 normal 0 stub 0
nssa
  Maximum path: 4
  Routing for Networks:
    172.16.1.0 0.0.0.255 area 0
    172.16.3.0 0.0.0.3 area 0
    192.168.10.4 0.0.0.3 area 0
  Routing Information Sources:
    Gateway          Distance      Last Update
    209.165.200.225      110       00:07:02
    192.168.10.10        110       00:07:02
  Distance: (default is 110)

R1#
```

Figure 8-30   Verifying the Router ID

In the following output, the router ID 1.1.1.1 is being assigned to R1.

```
R1(config)#router ospf 10
R1(config-router)#router-id 1.1.1.1
%OSPF: Reload or use "clear ip ospf process" command, for
this to take effect.
R1(config-router)#end
R1#
*Mar 25 19:46:09.711: %SYS-5-CONFIG_I: Configured from
Console by console
```

Notice how an informational message appears stating that the OSPF process must be cleared or that the router must be reloaded. The reason is because R1 already has adjacencies with other neighbors using the router ID 192.168.10.5. Those adjacencies must be renegotiated using the new router IP 1.1.1.1.

Clearing the OSPF process is the preferred method to reset the router ID.

In Figure 8-31, the OSPF routing process is cleared using the **clear ip ospf process** privileged EXEC mode command.

```
R1# clear ip ospf process
Reset ALL OSPF processes? [no]: y
R1#
*Mar 25 19:46:22.423: %OSPF-5-ADJCHG: Process 10, Nbr
3.3.3.3 on Serial0/0/1 from FULL to DOWN, Neighbor Down:
Interface down or detached
*Mar 25 19:46:22.423: %OSPF-5-ADJCHG: Process 10, Nbr
2.2.2.2 on Serial0/0/0 from FULL to DOWN, Neighbor Down:
Interface down or detached
*Mar 25 19:46:22.475: %OSPF-5-ADJCHG: Process 10, Nbr
3.3.3.3 on Serial0/0/1 from LOADING to FULL, Loading Done
*Mar 25 19:46:22.475: %OSPF-5-ADJCHG: Process 10, Nbr
2.2.2.2 on Serial0/0/0 from LOADING to FULL, Loading Done
R1#
R1# show ip protocols | section Router ID
  Router ID 1.1.1.1
R1#
```

Figure 8-31   Clearing the OSPF Process

This forces OSPF on R1 to transition to the Down and Init states. Notice the adjacency changes messages from full to down and then from loading to full. The **show ip protocols** command verifies that the router ID has changed.

Activity 8.2.1.5: Modifying the Router ID

Go to the course online and use the Syntax Checker in the fourth graphic to modify the router ID for R1.

Using a Loopback Interface as the Router ID (8.2.1.6)

A router ID can also be assigned using a loopback interface.

The IPv4 address of the loopback interface should be configured using a 32-bit subnet mask (255.255.255.255). This effectively creates a host route. A 32-bit host route does not get advertised as a route to other OSPF routers.

The following output displays how to configure a loopback interface with a host route on R1.

```
R1(config)# interface loopback 0
R1(config-if)# ip address 1.1.1.1 255.255.255.255
R1(config-if)# end
R1#
```

R1 uses the host route as its router ID, assuming there is no router ID explicitly configured or previously learned.

> **Note**
>
> Some older versions of the IOS do not recognize the **router-id** command; therefore, the best way to set the router ID on those routers is by using a loopback interface.

Configure Single-Area OSPFv2 (8.2.2)

For this course, we are concerned only with single-area OSPF. Multiarea OSPF is out of scope for this course.

Enabling OSPF on Interfaces (8.2.2.1)

The **network** command determines which interfaces participate in the routing process for an OSPF area. Any interfaces on a router that match the network address in the **network** command are enabled to send and receive OSPF packets. As a result, the network (or subnet) address for the interface is included in OSPF routing updates.

The basic command syntax is **network** *network-address wildcard-mask* **area** *area-id*.

The **area** *area-id* syntax refers to the OSPF area. When configuring single-area OSPF, the **network** command must be configured with the same *area-id* value on all routers. Although any area ID can be used, it is good practice to use an area ID of 0 with single-area OSPF. This convention makes it easier if the network is later altered to support multiarea OSPF.

Wildcard Mask (8.2.2.2)

OSPFv2 uses the argument combination of `network-address wildcard-mask` to enable OSPF on interfaces. OSPF is classless by design; therefore, the *wildcard mask* is always required. When identifying interfaces that are participating in a routing process, the wildcard mask is typically the inverse of the subnet mask configured on that interface.

A wildcard mask is a string of 32 binary digits used by the router to determine which bits of the address to examine for a match. In a subnet mask, binary 1 is equal to a match and binary 0 is not a match. In a wildcard mask, the reverse is true:

- **Wildcard mask bit 0:** Matches the corresponding bit value in the address.

- **Wildcard mask bit 1:** Ignores the corresponding bit value in the address.

The easiest method for calculating a wildcard mask is to subtract the network subnet mask from 255.255.255.255.

The example in Figure 8-32 calculates the wildcard mask from the network address of 192.168.10.0/24.

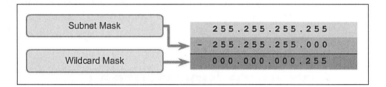

Figure 8-32   Calculating a Wildcard Mask for /24

To do so, the subnet mask 255.255.255.0 is subtracted from 255.255.255.255, providing a result of 0.0.0.255. Therefore, 192.168.10.0/24 is 192.168.10.0 with a wildcard mask of 0.0.0.255.

The example in Figure 8-33 calculates the wildcard mask from the network address of 192.168.10.64/26.

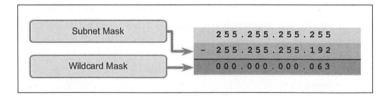

Figure 8-33   Calculating a Wildcard Mask for /26

Again, the subnet mask 255.255.255.192 is subtracted from 255.255.255.255 providing a result of 0.0.0.63. Therefore, 192.168.10.0/26 is 192.168.10.0 with a wildcard mask of 0.0.0.63.

The network Command (8.2.2.3)

There are several ways to identify the interfaces that will participate in the OSPFv2 routing process.

The following output displays the required commands to determine which interfaces on R1 participate in the OSPFv2 routing process for an area. Notice the use of wildcard masks to identify the respective interfaces based on their network addresses. Because this is a single-area OSPF network, all area IDs are set to 0.

Assigning Interfaces to an OSPF Area:

```
R1(config)# router ospf 10
R1(config-router)# network 172.16.1.0 0.0.0.255 area 0
R1(config-router)# network 172.16.3.0 0.0.0.3 area 0
R1(config-router)# network 192.168.10.4 0.0.0.3 area 0
R1(config-router)#
R1#
```

As an alternative, OSPFv2 can be enabled using the **network** *intf-ip-address* **0.0.0.0** *area area-id* router configuration mode command.

The following output provides an example of specifying the interface IPv4 address with a quad 0 wildcard mask. Entering **network 172.16.3.1 0.0.0.0 area 0** on R1 tells the router to enable interface Serial0/0/0 for the routing process. As a result, the OSPFv2 process will advertise the network that is on this interface (172.16.3.0/30).

Assigning Interfaces to an OSPF Area with a Quad Zero:

```
R1(config)# router ospf 10
R1(config-router)# network 172.16.1.1 0.0.0.0 area 0
R1(config-router)# network 172.16.3.1 0.0.0.0 area 0
R1(config-router)# network 192.168.10.5 0.0.0.0 area 0
R1(config-router)#
R1#
```

The advantage of specifying the interface is that the wildcard mask calculation is not necessary. OSPFv2 uses the interface address and subnet mask to determine the network to advertise.

Some IOS versions allow the subnet mask to be entered instead of the wildcard mask. The IOS then converts the subnet mask to the wildcard mask format.

Interactive Graphic

Activity 8.2.2.3: Assigning Networks in OSPF

Go to the course online and use the Syntax Checker in the fourth graphic to advertise the networks connected to R2.

Note

While completing the syntax checker, observe the informational messages describing the adjacency between R1 (1.1.1.1) and R2 (2.2.2.2). The IPv4 addressing scheme used for the router ID makes it easy to identify the neighbor.

Passive Interface (8.2.2.4)

By default, OSPF messages are forwarded out all OSPF-enabled interfaces. However, these messages need to be sent out only interfaces connecting to other OSPF-enabled routers.

Refer to the topology in Figure 8-34.

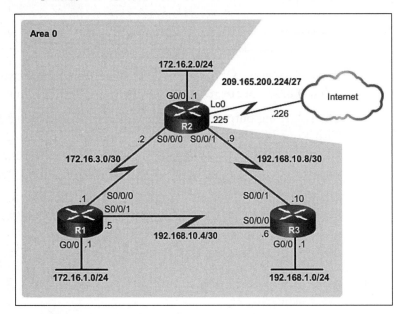

Figure 8-34   OSPF Topology

OSPF messages are forwarded out of all three routers G0/0 interface even though no OSPF neighbor exists on that LAN. Sending out unneeded messages on a LAN affects the network in three ways:

- **Inefficient use of bandwidth:** Available bandwidth is consumed transporting unnecessary messages. Messages are multicasted; therefore, switches are also forwarding the messages out all ports.

- **Inefficient use of resources:** All devices on the LAN must process the message and eventually discard the message.

- **Increased security risk:** Advertising updates on a broadcast network is a security risk. OSPF messages can be intercepted with packet sniffing software. Routing updates can be modified and sent back to the router, corrupting the routing table with false metrics that misdirect traffic.

Configuring Passive Interfaces (8.2.2.5)

Use the **passive-interface** router configuration mode command to prevent the transmission of routing messages through a router interface, but still allow that network to be advertised to other routers, as shown in the following output.

Configuring a *Passive Interface* on R1:

```
R1(config)# router ospf 10
R1(config-router)# passive-interface GigabitEthernet0/0
R1(config-router)# end
R1#
```

Specifically, the command stops routing messages from being sent out the specified interface. However, the network that the specified interface belongs to is still advertised in routing messages that are sent out other interfaces.

For instance, there is no need for R1, R2, and R3 to forward OSPF messages out of their LAN interfaces. The configuration identifies the R1 G0/0 interface as passive.

It is important to know that a neighbor adjacency cannot be formed over a passive interface. This is because link-state packets cannot be sent or acknowledged.

The **show ip protocols** command is then used to verify that the Gigabit Ethernet interface was passive, as shown in Figure 8-35.

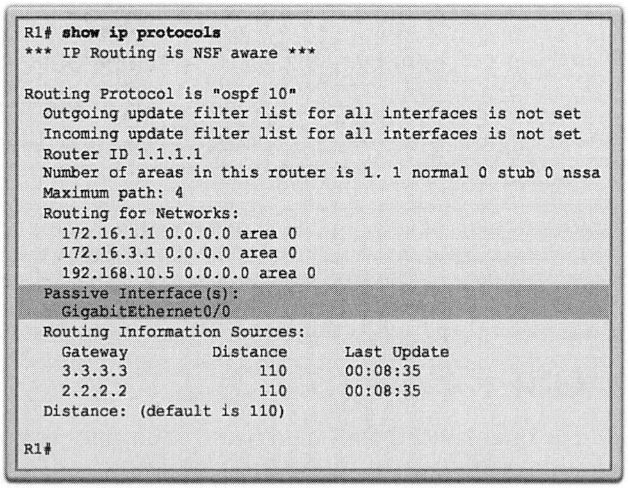

```
R1# show ip protocols
*** IP Routing is NSF aware ***

Routing Protocol is "ospf 10"
  Outgoing update filter list for all interfaces is not set
  Incoming update filter list for all interfaces is not set
  Router ID 1.1.1.1
  Number of areas in this router is 1. 1 normal 0 stub 0 nssa
  Maximum path: 4
  Routing for Networks:
    172.16.1.1 0.0.0.0 area 0
    172.16.3.1 0.0.0.0 area 0
    192.168.10.5 0.0.0.0 area 0
  Passive Interface(s):
    GigabitEthernet0/0
  Routing Information Sources:
    Gateway         Distance      Last Update
    3.3.3.3              110      00:08:35
    2.2.2.2              110      00:08:35
  Distance: (default is 110)

R1#
```

Figure 8-35   Verifying a Default Route on R1

Notice that the G0/0 interface is now listed under the Passive Interface(s) section. The network 172.16.1.0 is still listed under Routing for Networks, which means that this network is still included as a route entry in OSPF updates that are sent to R2 and R3.

> **Note**
>
> OSPFv2 and OSPFv3 both support the **passive-interface** command.

Interactive Graphic

Activity 8.2.2.5: Configuring Passive Interfaces in OSPF

Go to the course online and use the Syntax Checker in the third graphic to configure passive interfaces on R2 and R3.

> **Note**
>
> While completing the syntax checker, notice the OSPF informational state messages as the interfaces are all rendered passive and then the two serial interfaces are made nonpassive.

As an alternative, all interfaces can be made passive using the **passive-interface default** command. Interfaces that should not be passive can be re-enabled using the **no passive-interface** command.

Interactive Graphic

Activity 8.2.2.6: Calculating Subnet and Wildcard Masks

Go to the course online and complete the activity calculating the subnet and wildcard masks. Click New Problem to continue the activity.

Packet Tracer
☐ Activity

Packet Tracer Activity 8.2.2.7: Configuring OSPFv2 in a Single-Area

In this activity, the IP addressing is already configured. You are responsible for configuring the three router topologies with basic single-area OSPFv2 and then verifying connectivity between end devices.

Go to the course online to complete this Packet Tracer activity.

OSPF Cost (8.2.3)

The original RFC for OSPF had cost an amount that was to be manually set by every individual network administrator. To help out, some companies made the default cost of every interface a value of 1. That made OSPF an expensive way to implement

RIPs as essentially they turned routers into counting hop count only. Cisco decided to change this to a more reasonable measurement by using the Bandwidth of each interface. These next sections deal with understanding the Cisco implementation of the OSPF Metric.

OSPF Metric = Cost (8.2.3.1)

Recall that a routing protocol uses a metric to determine the best path of a packet across a network. A metric gives indication of the overhead that is required to send packets across a certain interface. OSPF uses cost as a metric. A lower cost indicates a better path than a higher cost.

The cost of an interface is inversely proportional to the bandwidth of the interface. Therefore, a higher bandwidth indicates a lower cost. More overhead and time delays equal a higher cost. Therefore, a 10-Mb/s Ethernet line has a higher cost than a 100-Mb/s Ethernet line.

The formula used to calculate the OSPF cost is

- **Cost** = *reference bandwidth/interface bandwidth*

The default *reference bandwidth* is 10^8 (100,000,000); therefore, the formula is

- **Cost** = *100,000,000 bps/interface bandwidth in bps*

Refer to Figure 8-36 for a breakdown of the cost calculation.

Interface Type	Reference Bandwidth in bps		Default Bandwidth in bps	Cost	
10 Gigabit Ethernet 10 Gbps	100,000,000	÷	10,000,000,000	1	Same Cost due to reference bandwidth
Gigabit Ethernet 1 Gbps	100,000,000	÷	1,000,000,000	1	
Fast Ethernet 100 Mbps	100,000,000	÷	100,000,000	1	
Ethernet 10 Mbps	100,000,000	÷	10,000,000	10	
Serial 1.544 Mbps	100,000,000	÷	1,544,000	64	
Serial 128 kbps	100,000,000	÷	128,000	781	
Serial 64 kbps	100,000,000	÷	64,000	1562	

Figure 8-36   Default Cisco OSPF Cost Values

Notice that FastEthernet, Gigabit Ethernet, and 10 GigE interfaces share the same cost because the OSPF cost value must be an integer. Consequently, because the default reference bandwidth is set to 100 Mb/s, all links that are faster than Fast Ethernet also have a cost of 1.

OSPF Accumulates Costs (8.2.3.2)

The cost of an OSPF route is the accumulated value from one router to the destination network.

For example, in Figure 8-37, the cost to reach the R2 LAN 172.16.2.0/24 from R1 should be as follows:

- Serial link from R1 to R2 cost = 64

- Gigabit Ethernet link on R2 cost = 1

- Total cost to reach 172.16.2.0/24 = 65

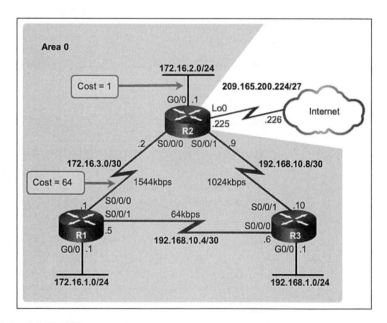

Figure 8-37   OSPF Reference Topology

The routing table of R1 in the following output confirms that the metric to reach the R2 LAN is a cost of 65.

Verifying the Cost to the R2 LAN:

```
R1# show ip route | include 172.16.2.0
O    172.16.2.0/24 [110/65] via 172.16.3.2, 03:39:07,
     Serial0/0/0
```

```
R1#
R1# show ip route 172.16.2.0
Routing entry for 172.16.2.0/24
  Known via "ospf 10", distance 110, metric 65, type intraarea
  Last update from 172.16.3.2 on Serial0/0/0, 03:39:15 ago
  Routing Descriptor Blocks:
  * 172.16.3.2, from 2.2.2.2, 03:39:15 ago, via Serial0/0/0
    Route Metric is 65, traffic share is 1
R1#
```

Adjusting the Reference Bandwidth (8.2.3.3)

OSPF uses a reference bandwidth of 100 Mb/s for any links that are equal to or faster than a fast Ethernet connection. Therefore, the cost assigned to a fast Ethernet interface with an interface bandwidth of 100 Mb/s would equal 1.

```
Cost = 100,000,000 bps / 100,000,000 = 1
```

Although this calculation works for fast Ethernet interfaces, it is problematic for links that are faster than 100 Mb/s because the OSPF metric uses only integers as its final cost of a link. If something less than an integer is calculated, OSPF rounds up to the nearest integer. For this reason, from the OSPF perspective, an interface with an interface bandwidth of 100 Mb/s (a cost of 1) has the same cost as an interface with a bandwidth of 100 Gb/s (a cost of 1).

To assist OSPF in making the correct path determination, the reference bandwidth must be changed to a higher value to accommodate networks with links faster than 100 Mb/s.

Adjusting the Reference Bandwidth

Changing the reference bandwidth does not actually affect the bandwidth capacity on the link; rather, it simply affects the calculation used to determine the metric. To adjust the reference bandwidth, use the **auto-cost reference-bandwidth** *Mb/s* router configuration command. This command must be configured on every router in the OSPF domain. Notice that the value is expressed in Mb/s; therefore, to adjust the costs for

- Gigabit Ethernet—auto-cost reference-bandwidth 1000

- 10 Gigabit Ethernet—auto-cost reference-bandwidth 10000

To return to the default reference bandwidth, use the **auto-cost reference-bandwidth 100** command.

Table 8-4 displays the OSPF cost if the reference bandwidth is set to Gigabit Ethernet.

Table 8-4   auto-cost reference bandwidth 1000

Interface Type	Reference Bandwidth in bps		Default Bandwidth in bps	Cost
10 Gigabit Ethernet 10 Gbps	1,000,000,000	÷	10,000,000,000	1
Gigabit Ethernet 1 Gbps	1,000,000,000	÷	1,000,000,000	1
Fast Ethernet 100Mbps	1,000,000,000	÷	100,000,000	10
Ethernet 10 Mbps	1,000,000,000	÷	10,000,000	100
Serial 1.544 Mbps	1,000,000,000	÷	1,544,000	647
Serial 128 kbps	1,000,000,000	÷	128,000	7812
Serial 64 kbps	1,000,000,000	÷	64,000	15625

Although the metric values increase, OSPF makes better choices because it can now distinguish between FastEthernet and Gigabit Ethernet links.

Table 8-5 displays the OSPF cost if the reference bandwidth is adjusted to accommodate 10 Gigabit Ethernet links.

Table 8-5   auto-cost reference-bandwidth 10 000

Interface Type	Reference Bandwidth in bps		Default Bandwidth in bps	Cost
10 Gigabit Ethernet 10 Gbps	10,000,000,000	÷	10,000,000,000	1
Gigabit Ethernet 1 Gbps	10,000,000,000	÷	1,000,000,000	10
Fast Ethernet 100Mbps	10,000,000,000	÷	100,000,000	100

Interface Type	Reference Bandwidth in bps		Default Bandwidth in bps	Cost
Ethernet 10 Mbps	10,000,000,000	÷	10,000,000	1000
Serial 1.544 Mbps	10,000,000,000	÷	1,544,000	6477
Serial 128 kbps	10,000,000,000	÷	128,000	78125
Serial 64 kbps	10,000,000,000	÷	64,000	156250

The reference bandwidth should be adjusted anytime there are links faster than FastEthernet (100 Mb/s).

Note

The costs represent whole numbers that have been rounded down.

In Figure 8-38, all routers have been configured to accommodate the Gigabit Ethernet link with the **auto-cost reference-bandwidth 1000 router** configuration command.

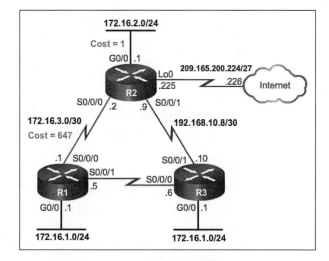

Figure 8-38 OSPF Reference Topology with Modified Auto-Cost

The new accumulated cost to reach the R2 LAN 172.16.2.0/24 from R1:

- Serial link from R1 to R2 cost = 647

- Gigabit Ethernet link on R2 cost = 1

- Total cost to reach 172.16.2.0/24 = **648**

Use the **show ip ospf interface s0/0/0** command to verify the current OSPF cost assigned to the R1 serial 0/0/0 interface, as shown in Figure 8-39. Notice how it displays a cost of 647.

```
R1# show ip ospf interface serial 0/0/0
Serial0/0/0 is up, line protocol is up
 Internet Address 172.16.3.1/30,Area 0,Attached via Network Statement
 Process ID 10,Router ID 1.1.1.1,Network Type POINT_TO_POINT,Cost:647
 Topology-MTID    Cost    Disabled    Shutdown      Topology Name
         0         647       no          no             Base
 Transmit Delay is 1 sec, State POINT_TO_POINT
 Timer intervals configured, Hello 10, Dead 40, Wait 40, Retransmit 5
   oob-resync timeout 40
   Hello due in 00:00:01
 Supports Link-local Signaling (LLS)
 Cisco NSF helper support enabled
 IETF NSF helper support enabled
 Index 3/3, flood queue length 0
 Next 0x0(0)/0x0(0)
 Last flood scan length is 1, maximum is 1
 Last flood scan time is 0 msec, maximum is 0 msec
 Neighbor Count is 1, Adjacent neighbor count is 1
   Adjacent with neighbor 2.2.2.2
 Suppress hello for 0 neighbor(s)
R1#
```

Figure 8-39 Verifying the S0/0/0 Link Cost

The routing table of R1 in the following output confirms that the metric to reach the R2 LAN is a cost of 648.

```
R1# show ip route | include 172.16.2.0
O        172.16.2.0/24 [110/648] via 172.16.3.2, 03:39:07, Serial0/0/0
R1#
R1# show ip route 172.16.2.0
Routing entry for 172.16.2.0/24
  Known via "ospf 10", distance 110, metric 648, type intra area
  Last update from 172.16.3.2 on Serial0/0/0, 00:06:17 ago
  Routing Descriptor Blocks:
  * 172.16.3.2, from 2.2.2.2, 03:39:15 ago, via Serial0/0/0
      Route Metric is 648, traffic share is 1
R1#
```

Default Interface Bandwidths (8.2.3.4)

All interfaces have default bandwidth values assigned to them. As with reference bandwidth, interface bandwidth values do not actually affect the speed or capacity of the link. Instead, they are used by OSPF to compute the routing metric. Therefore, it is important that the bandwidth value reflect the actual speed of the link so that the routing table has accurate best path information.

Although the bandwidth values of Ethernet interfaces usually match the link speed, some other interfaces may not. For instance, the actual speed of serial interfaces is often different than the default bandwidth. On Cisco routers, the default bandwidth on most serial interfaces is set to 1.544 Mb/s.

Note

Older serial interfaces may default to 128 kb/s.

Refer to the example in Figure 8-40. Notice that the link between

- R1 and R2 should be set to 1,544 kb/s (default value)

- R2 and R3 should be set to 1,024 kb/s

- R1 and R3 should be set to 64 kb/s

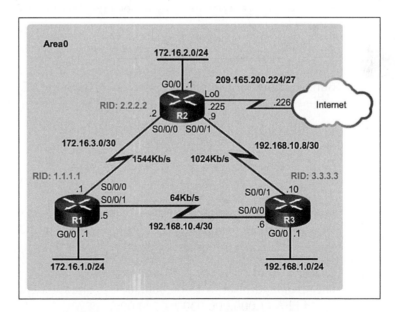

Figure 8-40   OSPF Reference Topology

Use the **show interfaces** command to view the interface bandwidth setting. Figure 8-41 displays the serial interface 0/0/0 settings for R1. The bandwidth setting is accurate and therefore the serial interface does not have to be adjusted.

```
R1# show interfaces serial 0/0/0
Serial0/0/0 is up, line protocol is up
  Hardware is WIC MBRD Serial
  Description: Link to R2
  Internet address is 172.16.3.1/30
  MTU 1500 bytes, BW 1544 Kbit/sec, DLY 20000 usec,
     reliability 255/255, txload 1/255, rxload 1/255
  Encapsulation HDLC, loopback not set
  Keepalive set (10 sec)
  Last input 00:00:05, output 00:00:03, output hang never
  Last clearing of "show interface" counters never
  Input queue: 0/75/0/0 (size/max/drops/flushes); Total
output drops: 0
  Queueing strategy: fifo
  Output queue: 0/40 (size/max)
  5 minute input rate 0 bits/sec, 0 packets/sec
  5 minute output rate 0 bits/sec, 0 packets/sec
     215 packets input, 17786 bytes, 0 no buffer
     Received 109 broadcasts (0 IP multicasts)
     0 runts, 0 giants, 0 throttles
     0 input errors, 0 CRC, 0 frame, 0 overrun, 0 ignored,
0 abort
     216 packets output, 17712 bytes, 0 underruns
     0 output errors, 0 collisions, 5 interface resets
```

Figure 8-41 Verifying the Default Settings of R1 Serial 0/0/0

Activity 8.2.3.4: Verifying the Default Settings of R1 Serial 0/0/0

Go to the course online and use the slider bar in the second graphic to see the entire output of the **show interfaces serial 0/0/0** command.

The following output displays the serial interface 0/0/1 settings for R1.

```
R1# show interfaces serial 0/0/1 | include BW
  MTU 1500 bytes, Bw 1544 Kbit/sec, DLY 20000 usec,
R1#
```

It also confirms that the interface is using the default interface bandwidth 1,544 kb/s. According to the reference topology, this should be set to 64 kb/s. Therefore, the R1 serial 0/0/1 interface must be adjusted.

Figure 8-42 displays the resulting cost metric of 647, which is based on the reference bandwidth set to 1,000,000,000 bps and the default interface bandwidth of 1,544 kb/s (1,000,000,000 / 1,544,000).

```
R1# show ip ospf interface serial 0/0/1
Serial0/0/1 is up, line protocol is up
  Internet Address 192.168.10.5/30, Area 0, Attached via
  Network Statement
  Process ID 10, Router ID 1.1.1.1, Network Type
  POINT_TO_POINT, Cost: 647
  Topology-MTID    Cost  Disabled  Shutdown    Topology Name
        0           647     no        no            Base
  Transmit Delay is 1 sec, State POINT_TO_POINT
  Timer intervals configured, Hello 10, Dead 40, Wait 40,
  Retransmit 5
     oob-resync timeout 40
     Hello due in 00:00:04
  Supports Link-local Signaling (LLS)
  Cisco NSF helper support enabled
  IETF NSF helper support enabled
  Index 3/3, flood queue length 0
  Next 0x0(0)/0x0(0)
  Last flood scan length is 1, maximum is 1
  Last flood scan time is 0 msec, maximum is 0 msec
  Neighbor Count is 1, Adjacent neighbor count is 1
     Adjacent with neighbor 3.3.3.3
  Suppress hello for 0 neighbor(s)
R1#
```

Figure 8-42   R1 Serial 0/0/1 Settings

Activity 8.2.3.4: R1 Serial 0/0/1 Settings

Go to the course online and use the slider bar in the fourth graphic to see the entire output of the **show ip ospf interface serial 0/0/1** command.

Adjusting the Interface Bandwidths (8.2.3.5)

To adjust the interface bandwidth use the **bandwidth** *kilobits* interface configuration command. Use the **no bandwidth** command to restore the default value.

The following example adjusts the R1 Serial 0/0/1 interface bandwidth to 64 kb/s. A quick verification confirms that the interface bandwidth setting is now 64 kb/s.

```
R1(config)# int s0/0/1
R1(config-if)# bandwidth 64
R1(config-if)# end
R1#
*Mar 27 10:10:07.735: %Sys-5-Config_I: Configured from console by console
R1#
R1# show interfaces serial 0/0/1 | include BW
  MTU 1550 bytes, BW 64 Kbit/sec, DLY 20000
R1#
R1# show ip ospf interface serial 0/0/1 | include Costs
```

```
Process ID 10, Router ID 1.1.1.1, Network Type
POINT_TO_POINT, Cost: 15625
R1#
```

The bandwidth must be adjusted at each end of the serial links, therefore

- R2 requires its S0/0/1 interface to be adjusted to 1024 kb/s.

- R3 requires its serial 0/0/0 to be adjusted to 64 kb/s and its serial 0/0/1 to be adjusted to 1024 kb/s.

Activity 8.2.3.5: Adjusting Interface Bandwidths

Go to the course online and use the Syntax Checker in the second graphic to adjust the bandwidth settings in both R2 and R3.

Note

A common misconception for students who are new to networking and the Cisco IOS is to assume that the **bandwidth** command changes the physical bandwidth of the link. The command modifies only the bandwidth metric used by EIGRP and OSPF. The command does not modify the actual bandwidth on the link.

Manually Setting the OSPF Cost (8.2.3.6)

As an alternative to setting the default interface bandwidth, the cost can be manually configured on an interface using the **ip ospf cost** *value* interface configuration command.

An advantage of configuring a cost over setting the interface bandwidth is that the router does not have to calculate the metric when the cost is manually configured. In contrast, when the interface bandwidth is configured, the router must calculate the OSPF cost based on the bandwidth. The **ip ospf cost** command is useful in multivendor environments where non-Cisco routers may use a metric other than bandwidth to calculate the OSPF costs.

Both the **bandwidth** interface command and the **ip ospf cost** interface command achieve the same result, which is to provide an accurate value for use by OSPF in determining the best route.

For instance, in the example in the following output, the interface bandwidth of serial 0/0/1 is reset to the default value and the OSPF cost is manually set to 15,625. Although the interface bandwidth is reset to the default value, the OSPF cost is set as if the bandwidth was still calculated.

```
R1(config)# int s0/0/1
R1(config-if)# no bandwidth 64
R1(config-if)# ip ospf cost 15625
R1(config-if)# end
R1#
R1# show interface serial 0/0/1 | include BW
    MTU 1500 bytes, BW 1544 Kbit/sec, DLY 20000 usec,
R1#
R1# show ip ospf interface serial 0/0/1 | include Cost:
    Process ID 0, Router ID 1.1.1.1, Network Type POINT-TO-POINT,
    Cost: 15625
R1#
```

Table 8-6 shows the two alternatives that can be used in modifying the costs of the serial links in the topology. The right side of the figure shows the **ip ospf cost** command equivalents of the **bandwidth** commands on the left.

Table 8-6 Bandwidth and **ip ospf cost**

Adjusting the Interface Bandwidth	=	Manually Setting the OSPF Cost
R1(config)# interface s0/0/1	=	R1(config)# interface s0/0/1
R1(config-if)# bandwidth 64		R1(config)# ip ospf cost 15625
R2(config)# interface s0/0/1	=	R2(config)# interface s0/0/1
R2(config-if)# bandwidth 1024		R2(config-if)# ip ospf cost 976
R3(config)# interface s0/0/0	=	R3(config)# interface s0/0/0
R3(config-if)# bandwidth 64		R3(config-if)#ip ospf cost 15625
R3(config)# interface s0/0/1	=	R3(config)# interface s0/0/1
R3(config-if)# bandwidth 1024		R3(config-if)# ip ospf cost 976

Verify OSPF (8.2.4)

To verify the operation of OSPF, first look at verifying your OSPF neighbors, which is described in the next section.

Verify OSPF Neighbors (8.2.4.1)

Continue to refer to Figure 8-28 for this section.

Use the **show ip ospf neighbor** command to verify that the router has formed an adjacency with its neighboring routers. If the router ID of the neighboring router is not displayed, or if it does not show as being in a state of FULL, the two routers have not formed an OSPF adjacency.

If two routers do not establish adjacency, link-state information is not exchanged. Incomplete LSDBs can cause inaccurate SPF trees and routing tables. Routes to destination networks may not exist or may not be the most optimum path.

Figure 8-43 displays the neighbor adjacency of R1.

```
R1# show ip ospf neighbor

Neighbor ID  Pri  State   Dead Time  Address       Interface
3.3.3.3       0   FULL/-  00:00:37   192.168.10.6  Serial0/0/1
2.2.2.2       0   FULL/-  00:00:30   172.16.3.2    Serial0/0/0
R1#
```

Figure 8-43 Verify R1's OSPF Neighbors

For each neighbor, this command displays the following output:

- **Neighbor ID:** The router ID of the neighboring router.

- **Pri:** The OSPF priority of the interface. This value is used in the DR and BDR election.

- **State:** The OSPF state of the interface. FULL state means that the router and its neighbor have identical OSPF LSDBs. On multiaccess networks, such as Ethernet, two routers that are adjacent may have their states displayed as 2WAY. The dash indicates that no DR or BDR is required because of the network type.

- **Dead Time:** The amount of time remaining that the router waits to receive an OSPF Hello packet from the neighbor before declaring the neighbor down. This value is reset when the interface receives a Hello packet.

- **Address:** The IPv4 address of the neighbor's interface to which this router is directly connected.

- **Interface:** The interface on which this router has formed adjacency with the neighbor.

Interactive Graphic

Activity 8.2.4.1: Verifying OSPF Neighbors

Go to the course online and use the Syntax Checker in the third graphic to verify the neighbors in both R2 and R3.

Two routers may not form an OSPF adjacency if

- The subnet masks do not match, causing the routers to be on separate networks.

- OSPF Hello or Dead Timers do not match.

- OSPF Network Types do not match.

- There is a missing or incorrect OSPF **network** command.

Verify OSPF Protocol Settings (8.2.4.2)

As shown in Figure 8-44, the **show ip protocols** command is a quick way to verify vital OSPF configuration information.

```
R1# show ip protocols
*** IP Routing is NSF aware ***

Routing Protocol is "ospf 10"
  Outgoing update filter list for all interfaces is not
  set
  Incoming update filter list for all interfaces is not
  set
  Router ID 1.1.1.1
  Number of areas in this router is 1. 1 normal 0 stub 0
  nssa
  Maximum path: 4
  Routing for Networks:
    172.16.1.0 0.0.0.255 area 0
    172.16.3.0 0.0.0.3 area 0
    192.168.10.4 0.0.0.3 area 0
  Routing Information Sources:
    Gateway         Distance      Last Update
    2.2.2.2              110      00:17:18
    3.3.3.3              110      00:14:49
  Distance: (default is 110)

R1#
```

Figure 8-44   Verify R1's OSPF Neighbors

This includes the OSPF process ID, router ID, networks the router is advertising, neighbors the router is receiving updates from, and default administrative distance, which is 110 for OSPF.

Activity 8.2.4.2: Verifying OSPF Protocol Settings

Go to the course online and use the Syntax Checker in the second graphic to verify the OSPF protocol settings in both R2 and R3.

Verify OSPF Process Information (8.2.4.3)

The **show ip ospf** command can also be used to examine the OSPF process ID and router ID, as shown in Figure 8-45.

```
R1# show ip ospf
Routing Process "ospf 10" with ID 1.1.1.1
Start time: 01:37:15.156, Time elapsed: 01:32:57.776
Supports only single TOS(TOS0) routes
Supports opaque LSA
Supports Link-local Signaling (LLS)
Supports area transit capability
Supports NSSA (compatible with RFC 3101)
Event-log enabled, Maximum number of events: 1000, Mode:
cyclic
Router is not originating router-LSAs with maximum metric
Initial SPF schedule delay 5000 msecs
Minimum hold time between two consecutive SPFs 10000 msecs
Maximum wait time between two consecutive SPFs 10000 msecs
Incremental-SPF disabled
Minimum LSA interval 5 secs
Minimum LSA arrival 1000 msecs
LSA group pacing timer 240 secs
Interface flood pacing timer 33 msecs
Retransmission pacing timer 66 msecs
Number of external LSA 0. Checksum Sum 0x000000
Number of opaque AS LSA 0. Checksum Sum 0x000000
Number of DCbitless external and opaque AS LSA 0
Number of DoNotAge external and opaque AS LSA 0
```

Figure 8-45 Verifying R1's OSPF Process

Activity 8.2.4.3 Part 1: Verifying R1's OSPF Process

Go to the course online and use the slider bar in the first graphic to see the entire output of the **show ip ospf** command.

This command displays the OSPF area information and the last time the SPF algorithm was calculated.

Activity 8.2.4.3 Part 2: Verifying OSPF Process Information

Go to the course online and use the Syntax Checker in the second graphic to verify OSPF process information in both R2 and R3.

Verify OSPF Interface Settings (8.2.4.4)

The quickest way to verify OSPF interface settings is to use the **show ip ospf interface** command. This command provides a detailed list for every OSPF-enabled interface. The command is useful to determine whether the **network** statements were correctly composed.

To get a summary of OSPF-enabled interfaces, use the **show ip ospf interface brief** command, as shown in Figure 8-46.

```
R1# show ip ospf interface brief
Interface   PID   Area   IP Address/Mask   Cost    State   Nbrs F/C
Se0/0/1     10    0      192.168.10.5/30   15625   P2P     1/1
Se0/0/0     10    0      172.16.3.1/30     647     P2P     1/1
Gi0/0       10    0      172.16.1.1/24     1       DR      0/0
R1#
```

Figure 8-46   Verifying R1's OSPF Interfaces

Activity 8.2.4.4: Verifying OSPF Interface Settings

Use the Syntax Checker in the second graphic to retrieve and view a summary of OSPF-enabled interfaces on R2 using the **show ip ospf interface brief** command. Notice that specifying the interface name as done in the **show ip ospf interface serial 0/0/1** command provides detailed OSPF information.

Continue using the Syntax Checker in the second graphic to get a summary of OSPF-enabled interfaces on R3 using the **show ip ospf interface brief** command. Retrieve and view additional information for the Serial 0/0/0 interface using the **show ip ospf interface serial 0/0/0** command.

Lab 8.2.4.5: Configuring Basic Single-Area OSPFv2

In this lab, you will complete the following objectives:

- Part 1: Build the Network and Configure Basic Device Settings
- Part 2: Configure and Verify OSPF Routing
- Part 3: Change Router ID Assignments
- Part 4: Configure OSPF Passive Interfaces
- Part 5: Change OSPF Metrics

OSPFv2 vs. OSPFv3 (8.3.1)

If you want to use OSPF in an IPv6 network, you need to use OSPFv3. This next section covers the basics of OSPFv3.

OSPFv3 (8.3.1.1)

OSPFv3 is the OSPFv2 equivalent for exchanging IPv6 prefixes. Recall that in IPv6, the network address is referred to as the prefix and the subnet mask is called the prefix-length.

Similar to its IPv4 counterpart, OSPFv3 exchanges routing information to populate the IPv6 routing table with remote prefixes, as shown in Figure 8-47.

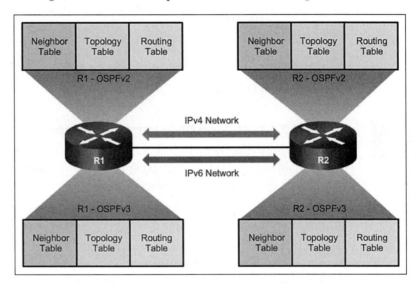

Figure 8-47   OSPFv2 and OSPFv3 Data Structures

Note

With the OSPFv3 Address Families feature, OSPFv3 includes support for both IPv4 and IPv6.

OSPFv2 runs over the IPv4 network layer, communicating with other OSPF IPv4 peers, and advertising only IPv4 routes.

OSPFv3 has the same functionality as OSPFv2 but uses IPv6 as the network layer transport, communicating with OSPFv3 peers and advertising IPv6 routes. OSPFv3 also uses the SPF algorithm as the computation engine to determine the best paths throughout the routing domain.

As with all IPv6 routing protocols, OSPFv3 has separate processes from its IPv4 counterpart. The processes and operations are basically the same as in the IPv4 routing protocol, but run independently. OSPFv2 and OSPFv3 each have separate adjacency tables, OSPF topology tables, and IP routing tables, as shown in the figure.

The OSPFv3 configuration and verification commands are similar to those used in OSPFv2.

Similarities Between OSPFv2 to OSPFv3 (8.3.1.2)

The following are similarities between OSPFv2 and OSPFv3:

- **Link-state:** OSPFv2 and OSPFv3 are both classless link-state routing protocols.

- **Routing algorithm:** OSPFv2 and OSPFv3 use the SPF algorithm to make routing decisions.

- **Metric:** The RFCs for both OSPFv2 and OSPFv3 define the metric as the cost of sending packets out the interface. OSPFv2 and OSPFv3 can be modified using the **auto-cost reference-bandwidth** `ref-bw` router configuration mode command. The command influences only the OSPF metric where it was configured. For example, if this command were entered for OSPFv3, it does not affect the OSPFv2 routing metrics.

- **Areas:** The concept of multiple areas in OSPFv3 is the same as in OSPFv2.

- **OSPF packet types:** OSPFv3 uses the same five basic packet types as OSPFv2 (Hello, DBD, LSR, LSU, and LSAck).

- **Neighbor discovery mechanism:** The neighbor state machine, including the list of OSPF neighbor states and events, remains unchanged. OSPFv2 and OSPFv3 use the Hello mechanism to learn about neighboring routers and form adjacencies. However, in OSPFv3, there is no requirement for matching subnets to form neighbor adjacencies. This is because neighbor adjacencies are formed using link-local addresses, not global unicast addresses.

- **DR/BDR election process:** The DR/BDR election process remains unchanged in OSPFv3.

- **Router:** Both OSPFv2 and OSPFv3 use a 32-bit number for the router ID represented in dotted-decimal notation. Typically, this is an IPv4 address. The OSPF **router-id** command must be used to configure the router ID. The process in determining the 32-bit Router ID is the same in both protocols. Use an explicitly configured router ID; otherwise, the highest loopback IPv4 address becomes the router ID.

Differences Between OSPFv2 and OSPFv3 (8.3.1.3)

The following are differences between OSPFv2 and OSPFv3:

- **Advertises:** OSPFv2 advertises IPv4 routes, whereas OSPFv3 advertises routes for IPv6.

- **Source address:** OSPFv2 messages are sourced from the IPv4 address of the exit interface. In OSPFv3, OSPF messages are sourced using the link-local address of the exit interface.

- **All OSPF router multicast addresses:** OSPFv2 uses 224.0.0.5; whereas, OSPFv3 uses FF02::5.

- **DR/BDR multicast address:** OSPFv2 uses 224.0.0.6; whereas, OSPFv3 uses FF02::6.

- **Advertise networks:** OSPFv2 advertises networks using the **network** router configuration command; whereas, OSPFv3 uses the **ipv6 ospf** *process-id* **area** *area-id* interface configuration command.

- **IP unicast routing:** Enabled, by default, in IPv4; whereas, the **ipv6 unicast-routing** global configuration command must be configured.

- **Authentication:** OSPFv2 uses either plaintext authentication or MD5 authentication. OSPFv3 uses IPv6 authentication.

Link-Local Addresses (8.3.1.4)

Routers running a dynamic routing protocol, such as OSPF, exchange messages between neighbors on the same subnet or link. Routers need to send and receive routing protocol messages only with their directly connected neighbors. These messages are always sent from the source IPv4 address of the router doing the forwarding.

IPv6 link-local addresses are ideal for this purpose. An IPv6 link-local address enables a device to communicate with other IPv6-enabled devices on the same link and only on that link (subnet). Packets with a source or destination link-local address cannot be routed beyond the link from where the packet originated.

As shown in Figure 8-48, OSPFv3 messages are sent using

- **Source IPv6 address:** This is the IPv6 link-local address of the exit interface.

- **Destination IPv6 address:** OSPFv3 packets can be sent to a unicast address using the neighbor IPv6 link-local address. They can also be sent using a multicast address. The FF02::5 address is the all OSPF router address, whereas the FF02::6 is the DR/BDR multicast address.

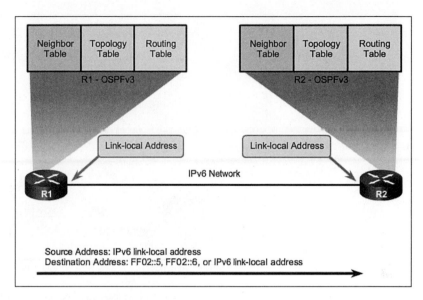

Figure 8-48   OSPFv3 Packet Destination

Activity 8.3.1.5: Compare and Contrast OSPFv2 and OSPFv3

This drag-and-drop activity allows you to check your knowledge of the similarities and differences between OSPFv2 and OSPFv3.

Go to the course and perform the activity (8.3.1.5) where you will compare and contrast OSPFv2 and OSPFv3. You will click the second graphic in order to continue the activity.

Configuring OSPFv3 (8.3.2)

Configuring OSPFv3 is quite easy; most of the commands are the same except for the addition of the keyword of v6, as shown in the next sections.

OSPFv3 Network Topology (8.3.2.1)

Figure 8-49 displays the network topology that is used to configure OSPFv3.

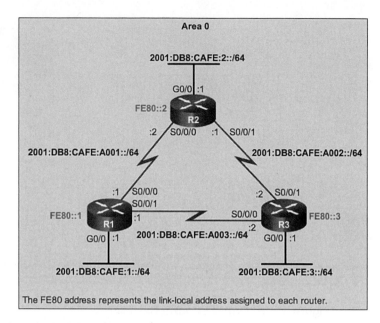

Figure 8-49   OSPFv3 Topology

The following output shows IPv6 unicast routing and the configuration of the global unicast addresses of R1, as identified in the reference topology:

```
R1(config)# ipv6 unicast-routing
R1(config)#
R1(config)# interface GigabitEthernet 0/0
R1(config-if)# description R1 LAN
R1(config-if)# ipv6 address 2001:DB8:CAFÉ:1::1/64
R1(config-if)# no shut
R1(config-if)#
R1(config-if)# interface Serial0/0/0
R1(config-if)# description Link to R2
R1(config-if)# ipv6 address 2001:CAFE:A001::1/64
R1(config-if)# clock rate 128000
R1(config-if)# no shut
R1(config-if)#
R1(config-if)# interface Serial 0/0/1
R1(config-if)# description Link to R3
R1(config-if)# ip av6 address 2001:DB8:CAFE:A003::1/64R1(config-if)# no shut
R1(config-if)# exit
R1#
```

Assume that the interfaces of R2 and R3 have also been configured with their global unicast addresses, as identified in the referenced topology.

In this topology, none of the routers have IPv4 addresses configured. A network with router interfaces configured with IPv4 and IPv6 addresses is referred to as dual-stacked. A dual-stacked network can have OSPFv2 and OSPFv3 simultaneously enabled.

Table 8-7 displays the steps to configure basic OSPFv3 in a single area.

Table 8-7   Steps to Configure OSPFv3

Step #	Description
1	Enable IPv6 unicast routing: **ipv6 unicast-routing**
2 (Optional)	Configure Link-Local Addresses.
3	Configure a 32-bit router ID in OSPFv3 router configuration mode using the **router-id** *rid* command.
4	Configure optional routing specifics such as adjusting the reference bandwidth.
5 (optional)	Configure OSPFv3 interface-specific settings. For example, adjust the interface bandwidth.
6	Enable IPv6 routing by using the **ipv6 ospf area**.

Link-Local Addresses (8.3.2.2)

In the following output, the output of the **show ipv6 interface brief** command confirms that the correct global IPv6 addresses have been successfully configured and that the interfaces are enabled. Also, notice that each interface automatically generated a link-local address, as highlighted.

```
R1# show ipv6 interface brief
Em0/0                            [administratively down/down]
    unassigned
GigabitEthernet0/0               [up/up]
    FE80::32F7:DFF:FEA3:DA0
    2001:DB8:CAFE:1::1
GigabitEthernet0/1               [administratively down/down]
    unassigned
Serial0/0/0                      [up/up]
    FE80::32F7:DFF:FEA3:DA0
    2001:DB8:CAFE:A001::1
Serial0/0/1                      [up/up]
    FE80::32F7:DFF:FEA3:DA0
    2001:DB8:CAFE:A003::1
R1#
```

Link-local addresses are automatically created when an IPv6 global unicast address is assigned to the interface. Global unicast addresses are not required on an interface; however, IPv6 link-local addresses are.

Unless configured manually, Cisco routers create the link-local address using FE80::/10 prefix and the EUI-64 process. EUI-64 involves using the 48-bit Ethernet MAC address, inserting FFFE in the middle and flipping the seventh bit. For serial interfaces, Cisco uses the MAC address of an Ethernet interface. Notice in the figure that all three interfaces use the same link-local address.

Assigning Link-Local Addresses (8.3.2.3)

Link-local addresses created using the EUI-64 format or in some cases, random interface IDs, make it difficult to recognize and remember those addresses. Because IPv6 routing protocols use IPv6 link-local addresses for unicast addressing and next-hop address information in the routing table, it is common practice to make it an easily recognizable address.

Configuring the link-local address manually provides the ability to create an address that is recognizable and easier to remember. As well, a router with several interfaces can assign the same link-local address to each IPv6 interface. This is because the link-local address is required only for local communications.

Link-local addresses can be configured manually using the same interface command used to create IPv6 global unicast addresses, but appending the **link-local** keyword to the **ipv6 address** command.

A link-local address has a prefix within the range FE80 to FEBF. When an address begins with this hextet (16-bit segment), the **link-local** keyword must follow the address.

The example configures the same link-local address FE80::1 on the three R1 interfaces. FE80::1 was chosen to make it easy to remember the link-local addresses of R1.

```
R1(config)# interface GigabitEthernet 0/0
R1(config-if)# ipv6 address fe80::1 link-local
R1(config-if)# exit
R1(config)# interface Serial0/0/0
R1(config-if)# ipv6 address fe80::1 link-local
R1(config-if)# exit
R1(config)# interface Serial0/0/1
R1(config-if)# ipv6 address fe80::1 link-local
R1(config-if)#
```

A quick look at the interfaces as shown in the following output confirms that the R1 interface link-local addresses have been changed to FE80::1.

```
R1# show ipv6 interface brief
Em0/0                    [administratively down/down]
    unassigned
GigabitEthernet0/0       [up/up]
    FE80::1
    2001:DB8:CAFE:1::1
GigabitEthernet0/1       [administratively down/down]
    unassigned
Serial0/0/0              [up/up]
    FE80::1
    2001:DB8:CAFE:A001::1
Serial0/0/1              [up/up]
    FE80::1
    2001:DB8:CAFE:A003::1
R1#
```

Interactive Graphic

Activity 8.3.2.3: Configuring Link-Local Addresses

Go to the course online and use the Syntax Checker in the third graphic to configure and verify link-local address FE80::2 on R2, and the link-local address FE80::3 on R3.

Configuring the OSPFv3 Router ID (8.3.2.4)

Use the **ipv6 router ospf** *process-id* global configuration mode command to enter router configuration mode. The IPv6 router configuration mode prompt is different than the IPv4 router configuration mode prompt. Use the IPv6 router configuration mode to configure global OSPFv3 parameters, such as assigning a 32-bit OSPF router ID and reference bandwidth.

IPv6 routing protocols are enabled on an interface, and not from router configuration mode, like their IPv4 counterparts. The **network** IPv4 router configuration mode command does not exist in IPv6.

Like OSPFv2, the *process-id* value is a number between 1 and 65,535 and is chosen by the network administrator. The *process-id* value is locally significant, which means that it does not have to match other OSPF routers to establish adjacencies with those neighbors.

OSPFv3 requires a 32-bit router ID to be assigned before OSPF can be enabled on an interface. The logic diagram in Figure 8-50 displays how a router ID is chosen.

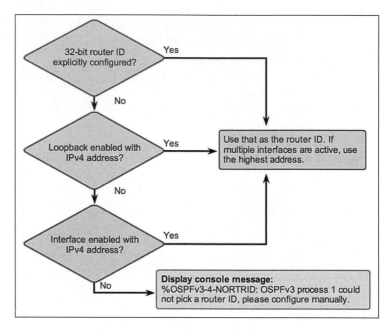

Figure 8-50   Router ID Order of Precedence

Like OSPFv2, OSPFv3 uses

- An explicitly configured router ID first.

- If none are configured, then the router uses the highest configured IPv4 address of a loopback interface.

- If none are configured, then the router uses the highest configured IPv4 address of an active interface.

- If there are no sources of IPv4 addresses on a router, then the router displays a console message to configure the router ID manually.

Note

For consistency, all three routers use the process ID of 10.

As shown in the topology in Figure 8-51, routers R1, R2, and R3 are to be assigned the router IDs indicated.

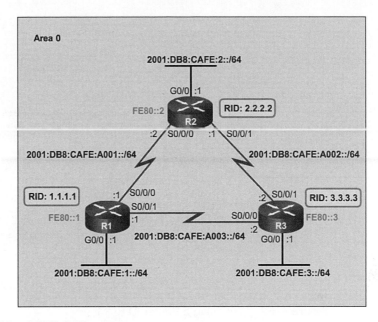

Figure 8-51   OSPFv3 Topology

The **router-id** *rid* command used to assign a router ID in OSPFv2 is the same command used in OSPFv3.

The example in Figure 8-52 shows the following:

- Enters the router OSPFv3 configuration mode. Notice how the router prompt is different than the default IPv4 routing protocol mode router prompt. Also notice how an informational console message appeared when the OSPFv3 router configuration mode was accessed.

- Assigns the router ID 1.1.1.1.

- Adjusts the reference bandwidth to 1,000,000,000 bps (1 Gb/s), because there are Gigabit Ethernet links in the network. Notice the information console message that this command must be configured on all routers in the routing domain.

- The **show ipv6 protocols** command is used to verify that the OSPFv3 process ID 10 is using the router ID 1.1.1.1.

Activity 8.3.2.4: Assigning a Router ID

Interactive Graphic

Go to the course online and use the Syntax Checker in the fourth graphic to configure global OSPFv3 settings on R2 and R3.

```
R1(config)# ipv6 router ospf 10
R1(config-rtr)#
*Mar 29 11:21:53.739: %OSPFv3-4-NORTRID: Process OSPFv3-1-
IPv6 could not pick a router-id, please configure manually
R1(config-rtr)#
R1(config-rtr)# router-id 1.1.1.1
R1(config-rtr)#
R1(config-rtr)# auto-cost reference-bandwidth 1000
% OSPFv3-1-IPv6: Reference bandwidth is changed. Please
ensure reference bandwidth is consistent across all routers.
R1(config-rtr)#
R1(config-rtr)# end
R1#
R1# show ipv6 protocols
IPv6 Routing Protocol is "connected"
IPv6 Routing Protocol is "ND"
IPv6 Routing Protocol is "ospf 10"
  Router ID 1.1.1.1
  Number of areas: 0 normal, 0 stub, 0 nssa
  Redistribution:
    None
R1#
```

Figure 8-52   Assigning a Router ID to R1

Modifying an OSPFv3 Router ID (8.3.2.5)

Router IDs sometimes must be changed, for example, if the network administrator has established a new router ID identification scheme. However, after an OSPFv3 router establishes a router ID, that router ID cannot be changed until the router is reloaded or the OSPF process is cleared.

In the following output, notice that the current router ID is 10.1.1.1. The OSPFv3 router ID should be 1.1.1.1.

```
R1# show ipv6 protocols
IPv6 Routing Protocol is "connected"
IPv6 Routing Protocol is "ND"
IPv6 Routing Protocol is "ospf 10"
  Router ID 10.1.1.1
  Number of areas: 0 normal, 0 stub, 0 nssa
Redistribution:
    None
R1#
```

In the following output, the router ID 1.1.1.1 is being assigned to R1:

```
R1(config)# ipv6 router ospf 10
R1(config-rtr)# router-id 1.1.1.1
R1(config-rtr)#   end
R1#
```

Note

Clearing the OSPF process is the preferred method to reset the router ID.

In the following output, the OSPF routing process is cleared using the **clear ipv6 ospf process** privileged EXEC mode command.

```
R1# clear ipv6 ospf processes
Reset selected OSPFv3 processes? [no]: y
R1#
R1# show ipv6 protocols
IPv6 Routing Protocol is "connected"
IPv6 Routing Protocol is "ND"
IPv6 Routing Protocol is "ospf 10"
  Router ID 1.1.1.1
  Number of areas: 0 normal, 0 stub, 0 nssa
Redistribution:
     None
R1#
```

Doing this forces OSPF on R1 to renegotiate neighbor adjacencies using the new router ID.

The **show ipv6 protocols** command verifies that the router ID has changed.

Interactive Graphic

Activity 8.3.2.5: Modifying a Router ID

Go to the course online and use the Syntax Checker in the fourth graphic to modify the router ID for R1.

Enabling OSPFv3 on Interfaces (8.3.2.6)

OSPFv3 uses a different method to enable an interface for OSPF. Instead of using the **network** router configuration mode command to specify matching interface addresses, OSPFv3 is configured directly on the interface.

To enable OSPFv3 on an interface, use the **ipv6 ospf** *process-id* **area** *area-id* interface configuration mode command.

The *process-id* value identifies the specific routing process and must be the same as the process ID used to create the routing process in the **ipv6 router ospf** *process-id* command.

The *area-id* value is the area to be associated with the OSPFv3 interface. Although any value could have been configured for the area, 0 was selected because area 0 is the backbone area to which all other areas must attach. This helps in the migration to multiarea OSPF, if the need arises.

In Figure 8-53, OSPFv3 is enabled on the R1 interfaces using the **ipv6 ospf 10 area 0** command. The **show ipv6 ospf interface brief** command displays the active OSPFv3 interfaces.

```
R1(config)# interface GigabitEthernet 0/0
R1(config-if)# ipv6 ospf 10 area 0
R1(config-if)#
R1(config-if)# interface Serial0/0/0
R1(config-if)# ipv6 ospf 10 area 0
R1(config-if)#
R1(config-if)# interface Serial0/0/1
R1(config-if)# ipv6 ospf 10 area 0
R1(config-if)#
R1(config-if)# end
R1#
R1# show ipv6 ospf interfaces brief
Interface   PID   Area        Intf ID  Cost    State   Nbrs F/C
Se0/0/1     10    0           7        15625   P2P     0/0
Se0/0/0     10    0           6        647     P2P     0/0
Gi0/0       10    0           3        1       WAIT    0/0
R1#
```

Figure 8-53   Enable OSPFv3 on the R1 Interfaces

Activity 8.3.2.6: Enabling OSPFv3 on Interfaces

Go to the course online and use the Syntax Checker in the third graphic to enable OSPFv3 on the R2 and R3 interfaces.

Verify OSPFv3 (8.3.3)

Just like in OSPFv2, to verify the operation of OSPF, you must first look at verifying your OSPF neighbors, which is described in the next section.

Verify OSPFv3 Neighbors (8.3.3.1)

Use the **show ipv6 ospf neighbor** command to verify that the router has formed an adjacency with its neighboring routers. If the router ID of the neighboring router is not displayed, or if it does not show as being in a state of FULL, the two routers have not formed an OSPF adjacency.

If two routers do not establish a neighbor adjacency, link-state information is not exchanged. Incomplete LSDBs can cause inaccurate SPF trees and routing tables. Routes to destination networks may not exist or may not be the most optimum path.

Figure 8-54 displays the neighbor adjacency of R1.

```
R1# show ipv6 ospf neighbor

OSPFv3 Router with ID (1.1.1.1) (Process ID 10)

Neighbor ID  Pri  State     Dead Time  Interface ID  Interface
3.3.3.3        0  FULL/  -  00:00:39   6             Serial0/0/1
2.2.2.2        0  FULL/  -  00:00:36   6             Serial0/0/0
R1#
```

Figure 8-54   Verifying OSPFv3 Neighbors for R1

For each neighbor, this command displays the following output:

- **Neighbor ID:** The router ID of the neighboring router.

- **Pri:** The OSPF priority of the interface. Value is used in the DR and BDR election.

- **State:** The OSPF state of the interface. FULL state means that the router and its neighbor have identical OSPF LSDBs. On multiaccess networks such as Ethernet, two routers that are adjacent may have their states displayed as 2WAY. The dash indicates that no DR or BDR is required because of the network type.

- **Dead Time:** The amount of time remaining that the router waits to receive an OSPF Hello packet from the neighbor before declaring the neighbor down. This value is reset when the interface receives a Hello packet.

- **Interface ID:** The interface ID or link ID.

- **Interface:** The interface on which this router has formed adjacency with the neighbor.

Activity 8.3.3.1: Verifying OSPFv3 Neighbors

Go to the course online and use the Syntax Checker in the second graphic to verify OSPFv3 neighbors for R2 and R3.

Verify OSPFv3 Protocol Settings (8.3.3.2)

As shown in the following output, the **show ipv6 protocols** command is a quick way to verify vital OSPFv3 configuration information, including the OSPF process ID, the router ID, and the interfaces enabled for OSPFv3.

```
R1# show ipv6 protocols
IPv6 Routing Protocol is "connected"
IPv6 Routing Protocol is "ND"
```

```
IPv6 Routing Protocol is "ospf 10"
  Router ID 1.1.1.1
  Number of areas: 1 normal, 0 stub, 0 nssa
  Interfaces (Area 0):
    Serial0/0/1
    Serial0/0/0
    GigabitEthernet0/0
  Redistribution:
    None
R1#
```

Activity 8.3.3.2: Verifying OSPFv3 Protocol Settings

Go to the course online and use the Syntax Checker in the second graphic to verify OSPFv3 protocol settings for R2 and R3.

Use the **show ipv6 ospf** command to also examine the OSPFv3 process ID and router ID. This command displays the OSPF area information and the last time the SPF algorithm was calculated.

Verify OSPFv3 Interfaces (8.3.3.3)

The quickest way to verify OSPF interface settings is to use the **show ipv6 ospf interface** command. This command provides a detailed list for every OSPF-enabled interface.

To retrieve and view a summary of OSPFv3-enabled interfaces on R1, use the **show ipv6 ospf interface brief** command, as shown in the following output.

```
R1# show ipv6 ospf interface brief
Interface    PID    Area    Intf ID    Cost    State    Nbrs F/C
SE0/0/1      10     0          7        15625   P2P      1/1
SE0/0/0      10     0          6        647     P2P      1/1
Gi0/0        10     0          3        1       DR       0/0
R1#
```

Activity 8.3.3.3: Verifying OSPFv3 Interfaces on R2 and R3

Go to the course online and use the Syntax Checker in the second graphic to verify OSPFv3 interfaces for R2 and R3.

Verify the IPv6 Routing Table (8.3.3.4)

In Figure 8-55, the **show ipv6 route ospf** command provides specifics about OSPF routes in the routing table.

```
R1# show ipv6 route ospf
IPv6 Routing Table - default - 10 entries
Codes: C - Connected, L - Local, S - Static, U - Per-user
Static route
       B - BGP, R - RIP, H - NHRP, I1 - ISIS L1
       I2 - ISIS L2, IA - ISIS interarea, IS - ISIS
summary, D - EIGRP
       EX - EIGRP external, ND - ND Default, NDp - ND
Prefix, DCE - Destination
       NDr - Redirect, O - OSPF Intra, OI - OSPF Inter,
OE1 - OSPF ext 1
       OE2 - OSPF ext 2, ON1 - OSPF NSSA ext 1, ON2 - OSPF
NSSA ext 2
O   2001:DB8:CAFE:2::/64 [110/657]
     via FE80::2, Serial0/0/0
O   2001:DB8:CAFE:3::/64 [110/1304]
     via FE80::2, Serial0/0/0
O   2001:DB8:CAFE:A002::/64 [110/1294]
     via FE80::2, Serial0/0/0
R1#
```

Figure 8-55   Verifying the IPv6 Routing Table of R1

Activity 8.3.3.4: Verifying the IPv6 Routing Table

Go to the course online and use the Syntax Checker in the second graphic to verify the IPv6 Routing Table of R2 and R3.

Packet Tracer Activity 8.3.3.5: Configuring Basic OSPFv3

In this activity, the IPv6 addressing is already configured. You are responsible for configuring the three router topology with a basic single-area OSPFv3, and then verifying connectivity between end devices.

Go to the course online to complete this Packet Tracer activity.

Lab 8.3.3.6: Configuring Basic Single-Area OSPFv3

In this lab, you will complete the following objectives:

- Part 1: Build the Network and Configure Basic Device Settings
- Part 2: Configure OSPFv3 Routing
- Part 3: Configure OSPFv3 Passive Interfaces

Summary (8.4)

Class Activity 8.4.1.1: Stepping Through OSPFv3

Scenario

This class activity is designed for groups of three students. The objective is to review the Shortest Path First (SPF) routing process.

You will design and address a network, communicate the network address scheme and operation of network links to your group members, and compute the SPF.

Complete the steps as shown on the PDF for this class activity.

If you have time, share your network design and Open Shortest Path First (OSPF) process with another group.

Packet Tracer Activity 8.4.1.2: Skills Integration Challenge

In this Skills Integration Challenge, your focus is OSPFv2 and OSPFv3 configurations. You configure IP addressing for all devices. Then you configure OSPFv2 routing for the IPv4 portion of the network and OSPFv3 routing for the IPv6 portion of the network. One router will be configured with both IPv4 and IPv6 configurations. Finally, you verify your configurations and test connectivity between end devices.

Go to the course online to complete this Packet Tracer activity.

The current version of OSPF for IPv4 is OSPFv2 introduced in RFC 1247 and updated in RFC 2328 by John Moy. In 1999, OSPFv3 for IPv6 was published in RFC 2740.

OSPF is a classless, link-state routing protocol with a default administrative distance of 110 and is denoted in the routing table with a route source code of **o**.

OSPF is enabled with the **router ospf** *process-id* global configuration mode command. The *process-id* value is locally significant, which means that it does not need to match other OSPF routers to establish adjacencies with those neighbors.

The **network** command used with OSPF has the same function as when used with other IGP routing protocols, but with slightly different syntax. The *wildcard-mask* value is the inverse of the subnet mask, and the *area-id* value should be set to **0**.

By default, OSPF Hello packets are sent every 10 seconds on multiaccess and point-to-point segments and every 30 seconds on NBMA segments (Frame Relay, X.25, and ATM) and are used by OSPF to establish neighbor adjacencies. The Dead interval is four times the Hello interval, by default.

For routers to become adjacent, their Hello interval, Dead interval, network types, and subnet masks must match. Use the **show ip ospf neighbors** command to verify OSPF adjacencies.

OSPF elects a DR to act as collection and distribution point for LSAs sent and received in the multiaccess network. A BDR is elected to assume the role of the DR should the DR fail. All other routers are known as DROTHERs. All routers send their LSAs to the DR, which then floods the LSA to all other routers in the multi-access network.

The **show ip protocols** command is used to verify important OSPF configuration information, including the OSPF process ID, the router ID, and the networks the router is advertising.

OSPFv3 is enabled on an interface and not under router configuration mode. OSPFv3 needs link-local addresses to be configured. IPv6 Unicast routing must be enabled for OSPFv3. A 32-bit router-ID is required before an interface can be enabled for OSPFv3.

Practice

The following activities provide practice with the topics introduced in this chapter. The Labs and Class Activities are available in the companion *Routing and Switching Essentials Lab Manual* (978-1-58713-320-6). The Packet Tracer Activities PKA files are found in the online course.

Class Activities

Class Activity 8.0.1.2: Can Submarines Swim?

Class Activity 8.4.1.1: Stepping Through OSPFv3

Labs

Lab 8.2.4.5: Configuring Basic Single-Area OSPFv2

Lab 8.3.3.6: Configuring Basic Single-Area OSPFv3

Packet Tracer
☐ Activity

Packet Tracer Activities

Packet Tracer 8.2.2.7: Configuring OSPFv2 in a Single Area

Packet Tracer 8.3.3.5: Configuring Basic OSPFv3

Packet Tracer 8.4.1.2: Skills Integration Challenge

Check Your Understanding Questions

Complete all the review questions listed here to test your understanding of the topics and concepts in this chapter. The appendix, "Answers to the 'Check Your Understanding' Questions," lists the answers.

1. What will an OSPF router prefer to use first as a router ID?

   A. Any IP address that is configured using the **router-id** command

   B. A loopback interface that is configured with the highest IP address on the router

   C. The highest active interface IP that is configured on the router

   D. The highest active interface that participates in the routing process because of a specifically configured **network** statement

2. At which OSPF state are neighbor routers converged and can exchange routing updates?

   A. Two-Way

   B. ExStart

   C. Exchange

   D. Full

3. Which OSPF wildcard mask would be appropriate to use for the given network prefix?

   A. /30 and 0.0.0.2

   B. /13 and 0.7.255.255

   C. /23 and 0.0.2.255

   D. /18 and 0.0.64.255

4. Which statement is correct about multiarea OSPF?

    A. OSPF can consolidate a fragmented OSPF area into one large area.

    B. All routers are in one area called the backbone area (area 0).

    C. Arranging routers into areas partitions a large autonomous system to lighten the load on routers.

    D. OSPF multiarea increases the frequency of SPF calculation.

5. A network technician issues the following commands when configuring a router:

    ```
    R1(config)# router ospf 11
    R1(config-router)# network 10.10.10.0 0.0.0.255 area 0
    ```

    What does the number 11 represent?

    A. The autonomous system number to which R1 belongs

    B. The area number where R1 is located

    C. The cost of the link to R1

    D. The OSPF process ID on R1

    E. The administrative distance that is manually assigned to R1

6. The OSPF Hello timer has been set to 15 seconds on a router in a point-to-point network. By default, what is the dead interval on this router?

    A. 15 seconds

    B. 30 seconds

    C. 45 seconds

    D. 60 seconds

7. A network administrator configures a loopback interface as the OSPF router ID with the IP address of 192.168.1.1/30. What could be the consequence of using this 30-bit mask for the loopback interface?

    A. Older routers do not recognize the **router-id** command.

    B. The interface is not enabled for OSPF.

    C. OSPF routers must also be configured with a router priority value.

    D. This loopback interface may be advertised as a reachable network.

8. What are three entries that are displayed by the **show ip ospf neighbor** command? (Choose three.)

   A. The route metric and neighbor next-hop address

   B. The router ID of the neighboring routers

   C. The OSPF state of each interface

   D. The OSPF process ID used to establish the adjacency

   E. The OSPF area number shared by the neighbor routers

   F. The IP address of the neighbor router interface to which this router is directly connected

9. Which statement describes a difference or similarity between OSPFv2 and OSPFv3?

   A. OSPFv2 requires the DR/BDR election to occur on multiaccess networks only, whereas OSPv3 requires DR/BDR elections for all network types.

   B. Both OSPFv2 and OSPFv3 use the router configuration **network** command to advertise networks.

   C. Both OSPFv2 and OSPFv3 use multicast destination addresses for link-state packets.

   D. OSPFv2 uses a 32-bit router ID and OSPFv3 uses a 128 bit router ID.

10. Refer to the exhibit. With the default metric settings, the OSPF cost for R1 to reach the network 172.16.1.0 is

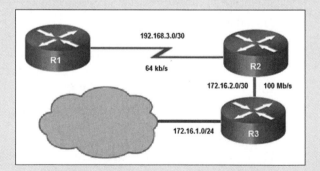

   A. 64

   B. 1563

   C. 65

   D. 1564

   E. 10

   F. 1

CHAPTER 9

Access Control Lists

Objectives

Upon completion of this chapter, you will be able to answer the following questions:

- How do ACLs filter traffic?

- What are the differences between standard and extended IPv4 ACLs?

- How do ACLs use wildcard masks?

- What are the guidelines for placing ACLs?

- How do you configure a standard IPv4 ACL to filter traffic?

- How do you use sequence numbers to modify a standard IPv4 ACL?

- How do you use standard ACLs to secure vty access?

- What is the structure of an extended access control entry (ACE)?

- How do you configure an extended IPv4 ACL to filter traffic?

- How do you use ACLs to limit debug output?

- How does a router process packets when an ACL is applied?

- How do you troubleshoot an ACL?

- What are the main differences between UPv4 and IPV6 ACLs?

- How do you configure IPv6 ACLs to filter traffic?

Key Terms

This chapter uses the following key terms. You can find the definitions in the Glossary.

Introduction (9.0.1.1)

Network security is a huge subject, and much of it is far beyond the scope of this course. However, one of the most important skills a network administrator needs is mastery of *access control lists (ACL)*.

Network designers use firewalls to protect networks from unauthorized use. Firewalls are hardware or software solutions that enforce network security policies. Consider a lock on a door to a room inside a building. The lock allows only authorized users with a key or access card to pass through the door. Similarly, a firewall filters unauthorized or potentially dangerous packets from entering the network. On a Cisco router, you can configure a simple firewall that provides basic traffic filtering capabilities using ACLs. Administrators use ACLs to stop traffic or permit only specified traffic on their networks.

An ACL is a sequential list of permit or deny statements that apply to addresses or upper-layer protocols. ACLs provide a powerful way to control traffic into and out of a network. ACLs can be configured for all routed network protocols.

The most important reason to configure ACLs is to provide security for a network. This chapter explains how to use standard and *extended ACLs* on a Cisco router as part of a security solution. Included are tips, considerations, recommendations, and general guidelines on how to use ACLs.

This chapter includes an opportunity to develop your mastery of ACLs with a series of lessons, activities, and lab exercises.

Class Activity 9.0.1.2: Permit Me to Assist You

Permit Me to Assist You

Scenario

Each individual in the class will record five questions they would ask a candidate who is applying for a security clearance for a network assistant position within a small- to medium-sized business. The list of questions should be listed in order of importance to selecting a good candidate for the job. The preferred answers will also be recorded.

Two interviewers from the class will be selected. The interview process will begin. Candidates will be allowed or denied the opportunity to move to the next level of questions based upon their answers to the interviewer's questions.

Refer to the accompanying PDF for further instructions for this activity.

The entire class will then get together and discuss their observations regarding the process to permit or deny them the opportunity to continue to the next level of interviews.

IP ACL Operation (9.1)

ACLs are only part of a larger solution to the question of network security. These next sections define what is an ACL and how *packet filtering* is used as a means of securing your network.

What Is an ACL? (9.1.1.1)

An ACL is a series of IOS commands that control whether a router forwards or drops packets based on information found in the packet header. ACLs are among the most commonly used features of Cisco IOS software.

When configured, ACLs perform the following tasks:

- Limit network traffic to increase network performance. For example, if corporate policy does not allow video traffic on the network, ACLs that block video traffic could be configured and applied. This would greatly reduce the network load and increase network performance.

- Provide traffic flow control. ACLs can restrict the delivery of routing updates. If updates are not required because of network conditions, bandwidth is preserved.

- Provide a basic level of security for network access. ACLs can allow one host to access a part of the network and prevent another host from accessing the same area. For example, access to the Human Resources network can be restricted to authorized users.

- Filter traffic based on traffic type. For example, an ACL can permit email traffic but block all Telnet traffic.

- Screen hosts to permit or deny access to network services. ACLs can permit or deny a user to access file types, such as FTP or HTTP.

By default, a router does not have ACLs configured; therefore, by default a router does not filter traffic. Traffic that enters the router is routed solely based on information within the routing table. However, when an ACL is applied to an interface, the router performs the additional task of evaluating all network packets as they pass through the interface to determine if the packet can be forwarded.

In addition to either permitting or denying traffic, ACLs can be used for selecting types of traffic to be analyzed, forwarded, or processed in other ways. For example, ACLs can be used to classify traffic to enable priority processing. This capability is similar to having a VIP pass at a concert or sporting event. The VIP pass gives selected guests privileges not offered to general admission ticket holders, such as priority entry or being able to enter a restricted area.

Figure 9-1 shows a sample topology with ACLs applied.

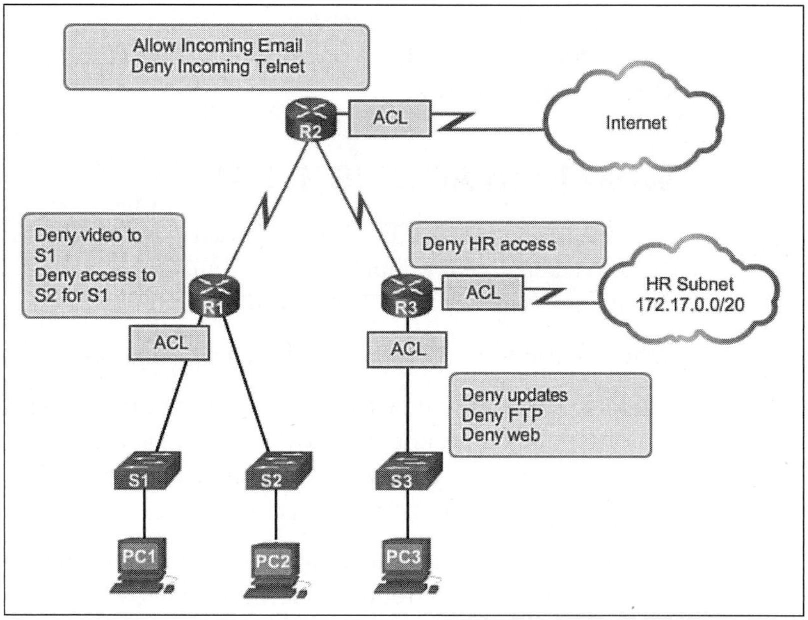

Figure 9-1   What Is an ACL?

A TCP Conversation (9.1.1.2)

ACLs enable administrators to control traffic into and out of a network. This control can be as simple as permitting or denying traffic based on network addresses or as complex as controlling network traffic based on the TCP port being requested. It is easier to understand how an ACL filters traffic by examining the dialogue that occurs during a TCP conversation, such as when requesting a web page.

TCP Communication

When a client requests data from a web server, IP manages the communication between the PC (source) and the server (destination). TCP manages the communication between the web browser (application) and the network server software.

When you send an email, look at a web page, or download a file, TCP is responsible for breaking data down into segments for IP before they are sent. TCP also manages assembling the data from the segments when they arrive. The TCP process is very much like a conversation in which two nodes on a network agree to pass data between one another.

TCP provides a connection-oriented, reliable, byte stream service. Connection-oriented means that the two applications must establish a TCP connection prior to exchanging data. TCP is a full-duplex protocol, meaning that each TCP connection supports a pair of byte streams, each stream flowing in one direction. TCP includes a flow-control mechanism for each byte stream that allows the receiver to limit how much data the sender can transmit. TCP also implements a congestion-control mechanism.

Video 9.1.1.2: "A TCP Conversation."

Go to the course and play the animation of a TCP conversation.

TCP segments are marked with flags that denote their purpose: a SYN starts (synchronizes) the session; an ACK is an acknowledgment that an expected segment was received, and a FIN finishes the session. A SYN/ACK acknowledges that the transfer is synchronized. TCP data segments include the higher level protocol needed to direct the application data to the correct application.

The TCP data segment also identifies the port that matches the requested service. For example, HTTP is port 80, SMTP is port 25, and FTP is port 20 and port 21. Table 9-1 shows ranges of UDP and TCP ports.

Table 9-1   Port Numbers

Port Number Range	Port Group
0 to 1023	Well-Known Ports
1024 to 49151	Registered Ports
49152 to 65535	Private and/or Dynamic Ports

Figure 9-2 explores TCP ports.

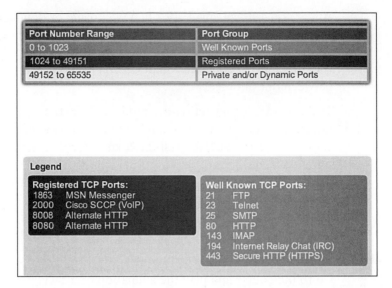

Figure 9-2 TCP Ports

Figure 9-3 explores UDP ports.

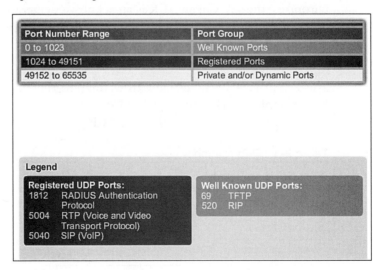

Figure 9-3 UDP Ports

Figure 9-4 explores TCP/UDP common ports.

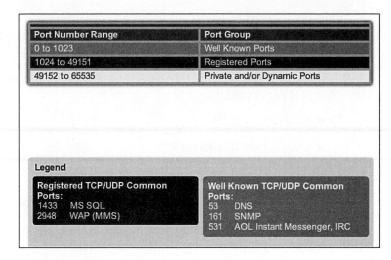

Port Number Range	Port Group
0 to 1023	Well Known Ports
1024 to 49151	Registered Ports
49152 to 65535	Private and/or Dynamic Ports

Legend

Registered TCP/UDP Common Ports:	Well Known TCP/UDP Common Ports:
1433 MS SQL	53 DNS
2948 WAP (MMS)	161 SNMP
	531 AOL Instant Messenger, IRC

Figure 9-4   UDP Ports

Packet Filtering (9.1.1.3, 9.1.1.4)

So how does an ACL use the information passed during a TCP/IP conversation to filter traffic?

Packet filtering, sometimes called static packet filtering, controls access to a network by analyzing the incoming and outgoing packets and passing or dropping them based on given criteria, such as the source IP address, destination IP addresses, and the protocol carried within the packet.

A router acts as a packet filter when it forwards or denies packets according to filtering rules. When a packet arrives at the packet-filtering router, the router extracts certain information from the packet header. Using this information, the router makes decisions, based on configured filter rules, as to whether the packet can pass through or be discarded. Packet filtering can work at different layers of the OSI model or at the Internet layer of TCP/IP.

A packet-filtering router uses rules to determine whether to permit or deny traffic. A router can also perform packet filtering at Layer 4, the transport layer. The router can filter packets based on the source port and destination port of the TCP or UDP segment. These rules are defined using ACLs.

An ACL is a sequential list of permit or deny statements, known as *access control entries (ACE)*. ACEs are also commonly called ACL statements. ACEs can be created to filter traffic based on certain criteria such as the source address, destination address, protocol, and port numbers. When network traffic passes through an interface configured with an ACL, the router compares the information within the packet against each ACE, in sequential order, to determine if the packet matches one of the statements. If a match is found, the packet is processed accordingly. In this way, ACLs can be configured to control access to a network or subnet.

To evaluate network traffic, the ACL extracts the following information from the Layer 3 packet header:

- Source IP address
- Destination IP address
- ICMP message type

The ACL can also extract upper layer information from the Layer 4 header, including

- TCP/UDP source port
- TCP/UDP destination port

To understand the concept of how a router uses packet filtering, imagine that a guard has been posted at a locked door. The guard's instructions are to allow only people whose names appear on a list to pass through the door. The guard is filtering people based on the criterion of having their names on the authorized list. An ACL works in a similar manner, making decisions based on set criteria.

For example, an ACL could be configured to logically, "Permit web access to users from network A but deny all other services to network A users. Deny HTTP access to users from network B, but permit network B users to have all other access."

Refer to Figure 9-5 to examine the decision path the packet filter uses to accomplish this task.

For this scenario, the packet filter looks at each packet as follows:

- If the packet is a TCP SYN from Network A using Port 80, it is allowed to pass. All other access is denied to those users.
- If the packet is a TCP SYN from Network B using Port 80, it is blocked. However, all other access is permitted.

This is just a simple example. Multiple rules can be configured to further permit or deny services to specific users.

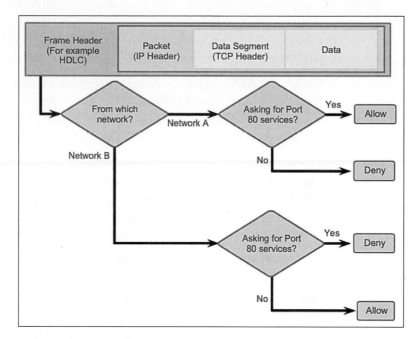

Figure 9-5   Packet Filtering Example

ACL Operation (9.1.1.5)

ACLs define the set of rules that give added control for packets that enter inbound interfaces, packets that relay through the router, and packets that exit outbound interfaces of the router. ACLs do not act on packets that originate from the router itself.

ACLs are configured to apply to *inbound traffic* or to apply to *outbound traffic*, as shown in Figure 9-6.

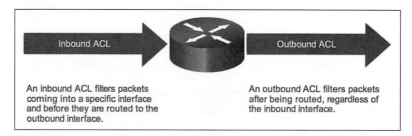

Figure 9-6   Inbound and Outbound ACLs

- **Inbound ACLs:** Incoming packets are processed before they are routed to the outbound interface. An inbound ACL is efficient because it saves the overhead of routing lookups if the packet is discarded. If the packet is permitted by the tests, it is then processed for routing. Inbound ACLs are best used to filter packets when the network attached to an inbound interface is the only source of the packets needed to be examined.

- **Outbound ACLs:** Incoming packets are routed to the outbound interface, and then they are processed through the outbound ACL. Outbound ACLs are best used when the same filter will be applied to packets coming from multiple inbound interfaces before exiting the same outbound interface.

The last statement of an ACL is always an *implicit deny*. This statement is automatically inserted at the end of each ACL even though it is not physically present. The implicit deny blocks all traffic. Because of this implicit deny, an ACL that does not have at least one permit statement will block all traffic.

Packet Tracer Activity 9.1.1.6: ACL Demonstration

In this activity, you will observe how an access control list (ACL) can be used to prevent a ping from reaching hosts on remote networks. After removing the ACL from the configuration, the pings will be successful.

Go to the course online to complete this Packet Tracer activity.

Standard Versus Extended IPv4 ACLS (9.1.2)

The following section deals with the differences between Standard and Extended ACLs for IPv4.

Types of Cisco IPv4 ACLs (9.1.2.1)

The two types of Cisco IPv4 ACLs are standard and extended.

> **Note**
>
> Cisco IPv6 ACLs are similar to IPv4 extended ACLs and are discussed in section 9.5 – IPv6 ACLs.

Standard ACLs

Standard ACLs can be used to permit or deny traffic only from source IPv4 addresses. The destination of the packet and the ports involved are not evaluated. The following example allows all traffic from the 192.168.30.0/24 network. Because of the implied deny any at the end, all other traffic is blocked with this ACL.

Standard ACLs are created in global configuration mode.

```
access-list 10 permit 192.168.30.0.0.0.0.255
```

Standard ACLs filter IP packets based on the source address only.

Extended ACLs

Extended ACLs filter IPv4 packets based on several attributes:

- Protocol type

- Source IPv4 address

- Destination IPv4 address

- Source TCP or UDP ports

- Destination TCP or UDP ports

- Optional protocol type information for finer control

In the following output, ACL 103 permits traffic originating from any address on the 192.168.30.0/24 network to any IPv4 network if the destination host port is 80 (HTTP). Extended ACLs are created in global configuration mode.

```
access-list 103 permit tcp 192.168.30.0.0.0.0.255 any eq 80
```

Extended ACLs filter IP packets based on several attributes, including the following:

- Source and destination IP addresses

- Source and destination TCP and UDP ports

- Protocol type/Protocol number (example: IP, ICMP, UDP, TCP, and so on)

The commands for ACLs are explained in the next few topics.

Note

Standard and extended ACLs are discussed in more detail later in this chapter in sections 9.2 and 9.3.

Numbering and Naming ACLs (9.1.2.2)

Standard and extended ACLs can be created using either a number or a name to identify the ACL and its list of statements.

Using numbered ACLs is an effective method for determining the ACL type on smaller networks with more homogeneously defined traffic. However, a number does not provide information about the purpose of the ACL. For this reason, starting with Cisco IOS Release 11.2, a name can be used to identify a Cisco ACL.

The following lists summarize the rules to follow to designate numbered ACLs and *named ACLs*.

Numbered ACL: Assign a number based on protocol to be filtered.

- (1 to 99) and (1300 to1999): Standard IP ACL
- (100 to 199) and (2000 to 2699): Extended IP ACL

Named ACL: Assign a name to identify the ACL.

- Names can contain alphanumeric characters.
- It is suggested that the name be written in CAPITAL LETTERS.
- Names cannot contain spaces or punctuation.
- Entries can be added or deleted within the ACL.

Regarding numbered ACLs, numbers 200 to 1299 are skipped because those numbers are used by other protocols, many of which are legacy or obsolete. This course focuses only on IP ACLs. Examples of legacy ACL protocol numbers are 600 to 699 used by AppleTalk, and numbers 800 to 899 used by IPX.

Wildcard Masks in ACLs (9.1.3)

This section shows how wildcard masks can be used with ACLs to make them more effective.

Introducing ACL Wildcard Masking (9.1.3.1)

In OSPF, *wildcard masks* are used to make network statements either extremely general or extremely specific. The same principle applies here: Wildcard masks can make ACL statements either extremely general or extremely specific when filtering packets.

Wildcard Masking

IPv4 ACEs include the use of wildcard masks. A wildcard mask is a string of 32 binary digits used by the router to determine which bits of the address to examine for a match.

Note

Unlike IPv4 ACLs, IPv6 ACLs do not use wildcard masks. Instead, the prefix-length is used to indicate how much of an IPv6 source or destination address should be matched. IPv6 ACLs are discussed in section 9.5.

As with subnet masks, the numbers 1 and 0 in the wildcard mask identify how to treat the corresponding IP address bits. However, in a wildcard mask, these bits are used for different purposes and follow different rules.

Subnet masks use binary 1s and 0s to identify the network, subnet, and host portion of an IP address. Wildcard masks use binary 1s and 0s to filter individual IP addresses or groups of IP addresses to permit or deny access to resources.

Wildcard masks and subnet masks differ in the way they match binary 1s and 0s. Wildcard masks use the following rules to match binary 1s and 0s:

- **Wildcard mask bit 0:** Match the corresponding bit value in the address.

- **Wildcard mask bit 1:** Ignore the corresponding bit value in the address.

Figure 9-7 shows how different wildcard masks filter IP addresses. In the example, remember that binary 0 signifies a bit that must match, and binary 1 signifies a bit that can be ignored.

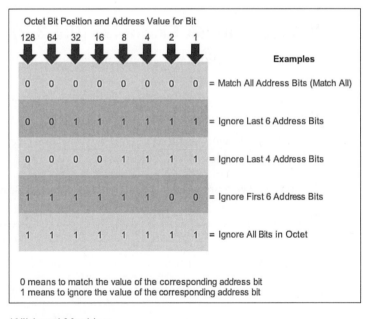

Figure 9-7   Wildcard Masking

Note

A wildcard mask is often referred to as an *inverse mask*. The reason is that, unlike a subnet mask in which binary 1 is equal to a match and binary 0 is not a match, in a wildcard mask the reverse is true.

Using a Wildcard Mask

Table 9-2 shows the results of applying a 0.0.255.255 wildcard mask to a 32-bit IPv4 address. Remember that a binary 0 indicates a value that is matched.

Table 9-2 Wildcard Mask Example

	Decimal Address	Binary Address
IP Address to Be Processed	192.168.10.0	11000000.10101000.00001010.00000000
Wildcard Mask	0.0.255.255	00000000.00000000.11111111.11111111
Resulting IP Address	192.168.0.0	11000000.10101000.00000000.00000000

Wildcard masks are also used when configuring some IPv4 routing protocols, such as OSPF, to enable the protocol on specific interfaces.

Wildcard Mask Examples (9.1.3.2)

The following sections show some of the more commonly used wildcard masks in ACL statements.

Wildcard Masks to Match IPv4 Subnets

Calculating the wildcard mask can take some practice. Tables 9-3 through 9-5 provide three examples of wildcard masks.

Table 9-3 Wildcard Masks to Match IPv4 Hosts and Subnets: Example 1

	Decimal	Binary
IP Address	192.168.1.1	11000000.10101000.00000001.00000001
Wildcard Mask	0.0.0.0	00000000.00000000.00000000.00000000
Result	192.168.1.1	11000000.10101000.00000001.00000001

Table 9-4 Wildcard Masks to Match IPv4 Hosts and Subnets: Example 2

	Decimal	Binary
IP Address	192.168.1.1	11000000.10101000.00000001.00000001
Wildcard Mask	255.255.255.255	11111111.11111111.11111111.11111111
Result	0.0.0.0	00000000.00000000.00000000.00000000

Table 9-5 Wildcard Masks to Match IPv4 Hosts and Subnets: Example 3

	Decimal	Binary
IP Address	192.168.1.1	11000000.10101000.00000001.00000001
Wildcard Mask	0.0.0.255	00000000.00000000.00000000.11111111
Result	192.168.1.0	11000000.10101000.00000001.00000000

In Table 9-3, the wildcard mask stipulates that every bit in the IPv4 192.168.1.1 must match exactly.

In Table 9-4, the wildcard mask stipulates that anything will match.

In Table 9-5, the wildcard mask stipulates that any host within the 192.168.1.0/24 network will match.

These examples were fairly simple and straightforward. However, the calculation of wildcard masks can be more complex.

Wildcard Masks to Match Ranges

Tables 9-6 and 9-7 are more complex.

Table 9-6 Wildcard Masks to Match Ranges: Example 1

	Decimal	Binary
IP Address	192.168.16.0	11000000.10101000.00010000.00000001
Wildcard Mask	0.0.15.255	00000000.00000000.00001111.11111111
Result Range	192.168.16.0 to 192.168.31.255	11000000.10101000.00010000.00000000 to 11000000.10101000.00011111.11111111

Table 9-7 Wildcard Masks to Match Ranges: Example 2

	Decimal	Binary
IP Address	192.168.1.0	11000000.10101000.00000001.00000000
Wildcard Mask	0.0.254.255	00000000.00000000.11111110.11111111
Result	192.168.1.0	11000000.10101000.00000001.00000000
	All odd numbered subnets in the 192.168.0.0 major network	

In Table 9-6, the first 2 octets and first 4 bits of the third octet must match exactly. The last 4 bits in the third octet and the last octet can be any valid number. This results in a mask that checks for the range of networks 192.168.16.0 to 192.168.31.0.

Table 9-7 shows a wildcard mask that matches the first 2 octets, and the least significant bit in the third octet. The last octet and the first 7 bits in the third octet can be any valid number. The result is a mask that would permit or deny all hosts from odd subnets from the 192.168.0.0 major network.

Calculating the Wildcard Mask (9.1.3.3)

Calculating wildcard masks can be challenging. One shortcut method is to subtract the subnet mask from 255.255.255.255. Figure 9-8 shows three examples of this shortcut method.

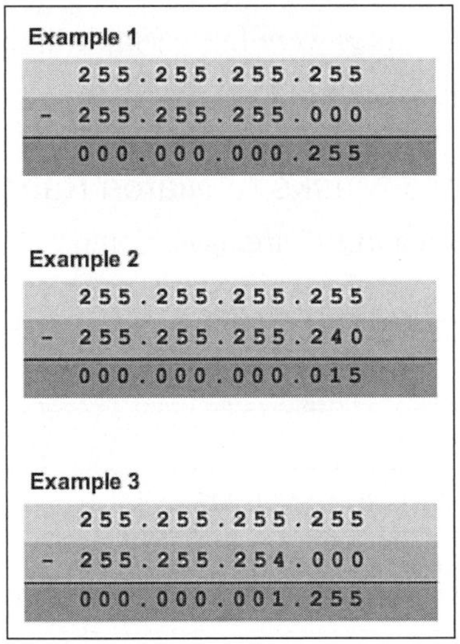

Example 1

```
    255 . 255 . 255 . 255
-   255 . 255 . 255 . 000
    000 . 000 . 000 . 255
```

Example 2

```
    255 . 255 . 255 . 255
-   255 . 255 . 255 . 240
    000 . 000 . 000 . 015
```

Example 3

```
    255 . 255 . 255 . 255
-   255 . 255 . 254 . 000
    000 . 000 . 001 . 255
```

Figure 9-8   Wildcard Mask Calculation

Wildcard Mask Calculation: Example 1

In the first example in Figure 9-8, assume you wanted to permit access to all users in the 192.168.3.0 network. Because the subnet mask is 255.255.255.0, you could take the 255.255.255.255 and subtract the subnet mask 255.255.255.0 as is indicated in the figure. The solution produces the wildcard mask 0.0.0.255.

Wildcard Mask Calculation: Example 2

In the second example in Figure 9-8, assume you wanted to permit network access for the 14 users in the subnet 192.168.3.32/28. The subnet mask for the IP subnet is 255.255.255.240; therefore, take 255.255.255.255 and subtract the subnet mask 255.255.255.240. The solution this time produces the wildcard mask 0.0.0.15.

Wildcard Mask Calculation: Example 3

In the third example in Figure 9-8, assume you wanted to match only networks 192.168.10.0 and 192.168.11.0. Again, you take the 255.255.255.255 and subtract the regular subnet mask, which in this case would be 255.255.252.0. The result is 0.0.3.255.

You could accomplish the same result with statements like the two shown here:

```
R1(config)# access-list 10 permit 192.168.10.0
R1(config)# access-list 10 permit 192.168.11.0
```

It is far more efficient to configure the wildcard mask in the following way:

```
R1(config)# access-list 10 permit 192.168.10.0 0.0.3.255
```

Consider the next configuration to match networks in the range between 192.168.16.0 to 192.168.31.0:

```
R1(config)# access-list 10 permit 192.168.16.0
R1(config)# access-list 10 permit 192.168.17.0
R1(config)# access-list 10 permit 192.168.18.0
R1(config)# access-list 10 permit 192.168.19.0
R1(config)# access-list 10 permit 192.168.20.0
R1(config)# access-list 10 permit 192.168.21.0
R1(config)# access-list 10 permit 192.168.22.0
R1(config)# access-list 10 permit 192.168.23.0
R1(config)# access-list 10 permit 192.168.24.0
R1(config)# access-list 10 permit 192.168.25.0
R1(config)# access-list 10 permit 192.168.26.0
R1(config)# access-list 10 permit 192.168.27.0
R1(config)# access-list 10 permit 192.168.28.0
R1(config)# access-list 10 permit 192.168.29.0
R1(config)# access-list 10 permit 192.168.30.0
R1(config)# access-list 10 permit 192.168.31.0
```

The previous 16 configuration statements can be reduced to a single statement using the correct wildcard mask as shown here:

```
R1(config)# access-list 10 permit 192.168.16.0 0.0.15.255
```

Wildcard Mask Keywords (9.1.3.4)

For some more commonly used wildcard masks, certain keywords can replace strings of 1s and 0s, which are described in the next section.

Wildcard Bit Mask Keywords

Working with decimal representations of binary wildcard mask bits can be tedious. To simplify this task, the keywords **host** and **any** help identify the most common uses of wildcard masking. These keywords eliminate entering wildcard masks when identifying a specific host or an entire network. These keywords also make it easier to read an ACL by providing visual clues as to the source or destination of the criteria.

The **host** keyword substitutes for the 0.0.0.0 mask. This mask states that all IPv4 address bits must match or only one host is matched.

The **any** option substitutes for the IP address and 255.255.255.255 mask. This mask says to ignore the entire IPv4 address or to accept any addresses.

Figure 9-9 shows an example of using the **host** keyword and an example of using the **any** keyword.

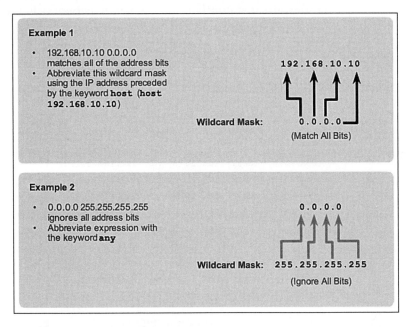

Figure 9-9   Wildcard Bit Mask Abbreviations

Example 1: Wildcard Masking Process with a Single IP Address

In Example 1, instead of entering **192.168.10.10 0.0.0.0**, you can use **host 192.168.10.10**.

Example 2: Wildcard Masking Process with a Match Any IP Address

In Example 2, instead of entering **0.0.0.0 255.255.255.255**, you can use the keyword **any** by itself.

Note

The keywords **host** and **any** can also be used when configuring an IPv6 ACL.

Examples Wildcard Mask Keywords (9.1.3.5)

This next section provides examples of using the **any** and **host** keywords.

The **any** and **host** Keywords

Example 9-1 shows how to use the **any** keyword to substitute for the IPv4 address 0.0.0.0 with a wildcard mask of 255.255.255.255.

Example 9-1   The **any** Keyword

```
R1 (config) #access-list 1 permit 0.0.0.0 255.255.255.255
R1 (config) #access-list 1 permit any
```

Example 9-2 shows how to use the **host** keyword to substitute for the wildcard mask when identifying a single host.

Example 9-2   The **host** Keyword

```
R1 (config) #access-list 1 permit 192.168.10.10 0.0.0.0
R1 (config) #access-list 1 permit host 192.168.10.10
```

Interactive Graphic

Activity 9.1.3.6: Determine the Correct Wildcard Mask

Go to the course online and drag the wildcard mask to the appropriate ACL statement.

Interactive Graphic

Activity 9.1.3.7: Determine the Permit or Deny

Go to the course online and drag the **permit** or **deny** result from comparing each ACL statement as it applies to the comparison address provided. Click the second graphic to continue the scenario.

Guidelines for ACL Creation (9.1.4)

These next sections will help in the creation of ACLs by providing guidelines and best practices.

General Guidelines for Creating ACLs (9.1.4.1)

Writing ACLs can be a complex task. For every interface, there may be multiple policies needed to manage the type of traffic allowed to enter or exit that interface. The router in Figure 9-10 has two interfaces configured for IPv4 and IPv6.

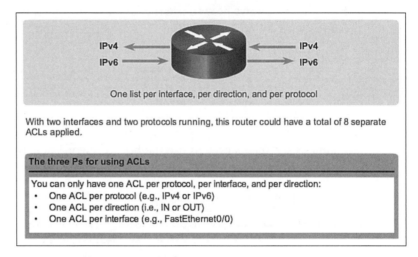

One list per interface, per direction, and per protocol

With two interfaces and two protocols running, this router could have a total of 8 separate ACLs applied.

The three Ps for using ACLs

You can only have one ACL per protocol, per interface, and per direction:
- One ACL per protocol (e.g., IPv4 or IPv6)
- One ACL per direction (i.e., IN or OUT)
- One ACL per interface (e.g., FastEthernet0/0)

Figure 9-10   ACL Traffic Filtering on a Router

If you needed ACLs for both protocols, on both interfaces and in both directions, this would require eight separate ACLs. Each interface would have four ACLs: two ACLs for IPv4 and two ACLs for IPv6. For each protocol, one ACL is for inbound traffic and one for outbound traffic.

Note

ACLs do not have to be configured in both directions. The number of ACLs and their direction applied to the interface will depend on the requirements being implemented.

Here are some guidelines for using ACLs:

- Use ACLs in firewall routers positioned between your internal network and an external network such as the Internet.

- Use ACLs on a router positioned between two parts of your network to control traffic entering or exiting a specific part of your internal network.

- Configure ACLs on border routers, that is, routers situated at the edges of your networks. This provides a basic buffer from the outside network, or between a less controlled area of your own network and a more sensitive area of your network.

- Configure ACLs for each network protocol configured on the border router interfaces.

The Three Ps

A general rule for applying ACLs on a router can be recalled by remembering the three Ps. You can configure one ACL per protocol, per direction, per interface:

- **One ACL per protocol:** To control traffic flow on an interface, an ACL must be defined for each protocol enabled on the interface.

- **One ACL per direction:** ACLs control traffic in one direction at a time on an interface. Two separate ACLs must be created to control inbound and outbound traffic.

- **One ACL per interface:** ACLs control traffic for an interface, for example, GigabitEthernet 0/0.

ACL Best Practices (9.1.4.2)

Using ACLs requires attention to detail and great care. Mistakes can be costly in terms of downtime, troubleshooting efforts, and poor network service. Before configuring an ACL, basic planning is required. Table 9-8 presents guidelines that form the basis of an ACL best practices list.

Table 9-8   ACL Best Practices

Guideline	Benefit
Base your ACLs on the security policy of the organization.	This will ensure you implement organizational security guidelines.
Prepare a description of what you want your ACLs to do.	This will help you avoid inadvertently creating potential access problems.
Use a text editor to create, edit, and save ACLs.	This will help you create a library of reusable ACLs.
Test your ACLs on a development network before implementing them on a production network.	This will help you avoid costly errors.

Activity 9.1.4.3: ACL Operation

Go to the course online and drag the appropriate word or phrase to complete the ACL operation statements.

Guidelines for ACL Placement (9.1.5)

After you have created your ACL, you must be aware of where to place it in the network to achieve maximum efficiency. These next sections deal with the concept of where to place ACLs.

Where to Place ACLs (9.1.5.1)

The proper placement of an ACL can make the network operate more efficiently. An ACL can be placed to reduce unnecessary traffic. For example, traffic that will be denied at a remote destination should not be forwarded using network resources along the route to that destination.

Every ACL should be placed where they have the greatest impact on efficiency. Figure 9-11 shows the basic rules for ACL placement.

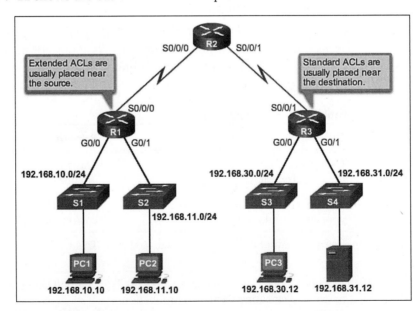

Figure 9-11 ACL Placement

- **Extended ACLs:** Locate extended ACLs as close as possible to the source of the traffic to be filtered. This way, undesirable traffic is denied close to the source network without crossing the network infrastructure.

- **Standard ACLs:** Because standard ACLs do not specify destination addresses, place them as close to the destination as possible. Placing a standard ACL at the source of the traffic will effectively prevent that traffic from reaching any other networks through the interface where the ACL is applied.

Placement of the ACL and therefore the type of ACL used may also depend on

- **The extent of the network administrator's control:** Placement of the ACL can depend on whether the network administrator has control of both the source and destination networks.

- **Bandwidth of the networks involved:** Filtering unwanted traffic at the source prevents transmission of the traffic before it consumes bandwidth on the path to a destination. This is especially important in low bandwidth networks.

- **Ease of configuration:** If a network administrator wants to deny traffic coming from several networks, one option is to use a single standard ACL on the router closest to the destination. The disadvantage is that traffic from these networks will use bandwidth unnecessarily. An extended ACL could be used on each router where the traffic originated. This will save bandwidth by filtering the traffic at the source but requires creating extended ACLs on multiple routers.

Note

For CCNA certification, the general rule is that extended ACLs are placed as close as possible to the source, and standard ACLs are placed as close as possible to the destination.

Standard ACL Placement (9.1.5.2)

A standard ACL can filter traffic only based on a source address. The basic rule for placement of a standard ACL is to place the ACL as close as possible to the destination network. This allows the traffic to reach all other networks except the network where the packets will be filtered.

In Figure 9-12, the administrator wants to prevent traffic originating in the 192.168.10.0/24 network from reaching the 192.168.30.0/24 network.

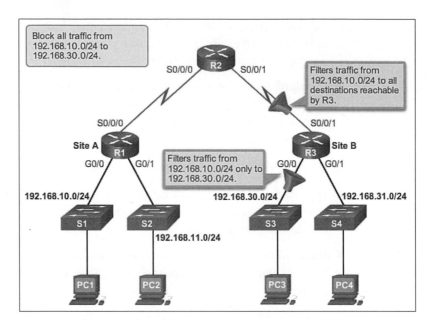

Figure 9-12   Standard ACL Placement

If the standard ACL is placed on the outbound interface of R1, this would prevent traffic on the 192.168.10.0/24 network from reaching any networks reachable through the Serial 0/0/0 interface of R1.

Following the basic placement guidelines of placing the standard ACL close to the destination, the figure shows two possible interfaces on R3 to apply the standard ACL:

- **R3 S0/0/1 interface:** Applying a standard ACL to prevent traffic from 192.168.10.0/24 from entering the S0/0/1 interface will prevent this traffic from reaching 192.168.30.0/24 and all other networks reachable by R3. This includes the 192.168.31.0/24 network. Because the intent of the ACL is to filter traffic destined only for 192.168.30.0/24, a standard ACL should not be applied to this interface.

- **R3 G0/0 interface:** Applying the standard ACL to traffic exiting the G0/0 interface will filter packets from 192.168.10.0/24 to 192.168.30.0/24. This will not affect other networks reachable by R3. Packets from 192.16810.0/24 can still reach 192.168.31.0/24.

Extended ACL Placement (9.1.5.3)

Like a standard ACL, an extended ACL can filter traffic based on the source address. However, an extended ACL can also filter traffic based on the destination address, protocol, and port number. This allows network administrators more flexibility in the type of traffic that can be filtered and where to place the ACL. The basic rule for placing an extended ACL is to place it as close to the source as possible. This prevents unwanted traffic from being sent across multiple networks only to be denied when it reaches its destination.

Network administrators can place ACLs only on devices that they control. Therefore, placement must be determined in the context of where the control of the network administrator extends. In Figure 9-13, the administrator of Company A, which includes the 192.168.10.0/24 and 192.168.11.0/24 networks (referred to as .10 and .11 in this example) wants to control traffic to Company B. Specifically, the administrator wants to deny Telnet and FTP traffic from the .11 network to Company B's 192.168.30.0/24 (.30, in this example) network. At the same time, all other traffic from the .11 network must be permitted to leave Company A without restriction.

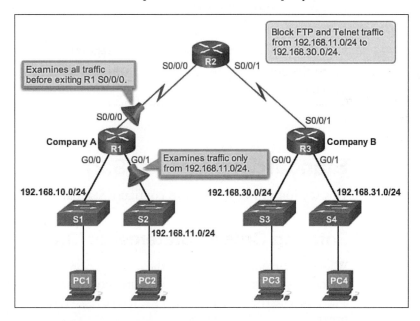

Figure 9-13   Extended ACL Placement

There are several ways to accomplish these goals. An extended ACL on R3 that blocks Telnet and FTP from the .11 network would accomplish the task, but the administrator does not control R3. In addition, this solution also allows unwanted traffic to cross the entire network, only to be blocked at the destination. This affects overall network efficiency.

A better solution is to place an extended ACL on R1 that specifies both source and destination addresses (.11 network and .30 network, respectively), and enforces the rule, "Telnet and FTP traffic from the .11 network is not allowed to go to the .30 network." Figure 9-13 shows two possible interfaces on R1 to apply the extended ACL:

- **R1 S0/0/0 interface (outbound):** One possibility is to apply an extended ACL outbound on the S0/0/0 interface. Because the extended ACL can examine both source and destination addresses, only FTP and Telnet packets from 192.168.11.0/24 will be denied. Other traffic from 192.168.11.0/24 and other networks will be forwarded by R1. The disadvantage of placing the extended ACL on this interface is that all traffic exiting S0/0/0 must be processed by the ACL including packets from 192.168.10.0/24.

- **R1 G0/1 interface (inbound):** Applying an extended ACL to traffic entering the G0/1 interface means that only packets from the 192.168.11.0/24 network are subject to ACL processing on R1. Because the filter is to be limited to only those packets leaving the 192.168.11.0/24 network, applying the extended ACL to G0/1 is the best solution.

Activity 9.1.5.4: Placing Standard and Extended ACLs

Go to the course online and drag and drop the ACL label to the appropriate place in the graphic.

Standard IPv4 ACLs (9.2)

This section shows you how to configure Standard ACLs.

Entering Criteria Statements (9.2.1.1)

When traffic enters the router, the traffic is compared to all ACEs in the order that the entries occur in the ACL. The router continues to process the ACEs until it finds a match. The router will process the packet based on the first match found, and no other ACEs will be examined.

If no matches are found when the router reaches the end of the list, the traffic is denied. This is because, by default, there is an implied deny at the end of all ACLs for traffic that was not matched to a configured entry. A single-entry ACL with only one deny entry has the effect of denying all traffic. At least one permit ACE must be configured in an ACL or all traffic is blocked.

For the network in Figure 9-14, applying either ACL 1 or ACL 2 to the S0/0/0 interface of R1 in the outbound direction will have the same effect. Network 192.168.10.0 will be permitted to access the networks reachable through S0/0/0 while 192.168.11.0 will not be allowed to access those networks.

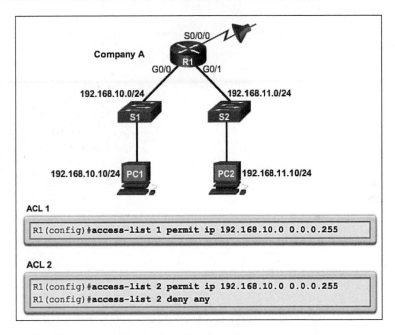

Figure 9-14   R1 Creates Its Topological Database

Configuring a Standard ACL – Standard ACL Logic (9.2.1.2)

In Figure 9-15, packets that enter the router through interface G0/0 are checked for their source addresses based on the following entries:

```
access-list 2 deny 192.168.10.10
access-list 2 permit 192.168.10.0 0.0.0.255
access-list 2 deny 192.168.0.0 0.0.255.255
access-list 2 permit 192.0.0.0 0.255.255.255
```

If packets are permitted, they are routed through the router to an output interface. If packets are denied, they are dropped at the incoming interface.

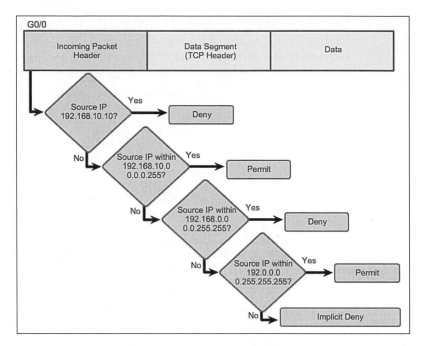

Figure 9-15 R1 Creates Its Topological Database

Configuring a Standard ACL – Configuring Standard ACLs (9.2.1.3)

To use numbered standard ACLs on a Cisco router, you must first create the standard ACL and then activate the ACL on an interface.

The **access-list** global configuration command defines a standard ACL with a number in the range of 1 through 99. Cisco IOS Software Release 12.0.1 extended these numbers by allowing 1300 to 1999 to be used for standard ACLs. This allows for a maximum of 798 possible standard ACLs. These additional numbers are referred to as expanded IP ACLs.

The full syntax of the standard ACL command is as follows:

```
Router(config)# access-list access-list-number {deny | permit | remark} source
    [source-wildcard] [log]
```

Table 9-9 provides a detailed explanation of the syntax for a standard ACL.

Table 9-9   Standard ACL **access-list** Command Syntax

Parameter	Description
access-list-number	Number of an ACL. This is a decimal number from 1–99 or 1300–1999 (for standard ACL).
deny	Denies access if the conditions are met.
permit	Permits access if the conditions are met.
remark	Add a remark about entries in an IP access list to make the list easier to understand and scan.
source	Number of the network or host from which the packet is being sent. There are two ways to specify the *source*: Use a 32-bit quantity in four-part, dotted-decimal format. Use the keyword **any** as an abbreviation for a *source* and *source-wildcard* of 0.0.0.0 255.255.255.255.
source-wildcard	(Optional) 32-bit wildcard mask to be applied to the source. Places ones in the bit positions you want to ignore.
Log	(Optional) Causes an informational logging message about the packet that matches the entry to be sent to the console. (The level of messages logged to the console is controlled by the **logging console** command.) The message includes the ACL number, whether the packet was permitted or denied, the source address, and the number of packets. The message is generated for the first packet that matches and then at 5-minute intervals, including the number of packets permitted or denied in the prior 5-minute interval.

ACEs can deny or permit an individual host or a range of host addresses. To create a host statement in numbered ACL 10 that permits a specific host with the IP address 192.168.10.0, you would enter

```
R1(config)#access-list 10 permit host 192.168.10.10
```

As shown in the following output, to create a statement that will permit a range of IPv4 addresses in a numbered ACL 10 that permits all IPv4 addresses in the network 192.168.10.0/24, you would enter

```
R1(config)# access-list 10 permit 192.168.10.0 0.0.0.255
R1(config)# exit
R1# show access-lists
Standard IP access list 10
    10 permit 192.168.10.0, wildcard bits 0.0.0.255
```

```
R1# conf t
Enter configuration commands, one per line.  End with CNTL/Z.
R1(config)# no access-list 10
R1(config)# exit
R1# show access-lists
R1#
```

To remove the ACL, the global configuration **no access-list** command is used. Issuing the **show access-list** command confirms that access list 10 has been removed. The output also shows this command.

Typically, when an administrator creates an ACL, the purpose of each statement is known and understood. However, to ensure that the administrator and others recall the purpose of a statement, remarks should be included. The **remark** keyword is used for documentation and makes access lists easier to understand. Each remark is limited to 100 characters. The ACL in the following output, although fairly simple, is used to provide an example. When reviewing the ACL in the configuration using the **show running-config** command, the remark is also displayed.

```
R1(config)# access-list 10 remark Permit hosts from the 192.168.10.0 LAN
R1(config)# access-list 10 permit 192.168.10.0 0.0.0.255
R1(config)# exit
R1# show running-config | include access-list 10
access-list 10 remark Permit hosts from the 192.168.10.0 LAN
access-list 10 permit 192.168.10.0 0.0.0.255
R1#
```

Internal Logic (9.2.1.4)

Cisco IOS applies an internal logic when accepting and processing standard ACEs. As discussed previously, ACEs are processed sequentially. Therefore, the order in which ACEs are entered is important.

For example, ACL 3 contains two ACEs:

```
R1(config)# access-list 3 deny 192.168.10.0 0.0.0.255
R1(config)# access-list 3 permit host 192.168.10.10
% Access rule can't be configured at higher sequence num as it is part of the
    existing rule at sequence num 10
R1(config)#
```

ACL 3: Host statement conflicts with previous range statement.

The first ACE uses a wildcard mask to deny a range of addresses, which includes all hosts in the 192.168.10.0/24 network. The second ACE is a host statement that examines a specific host: 192.168.10.10. This is a host within the range of hosts that was configured in the previous statement. In other words, 192.168.10.10 is a host in the 192.168.10.0/24 network. The IOS internal logic for standard access lists rejects the second statement and returns an error message because it is a subset of the previous statement. Notice in the figure that the router automatically assigns sequence num 10 as the sequence number assigned to the first statement entered in this example. The router output includes the message that the rule is "part of the existing rule at sequence num 10" and does not accept the statement.

Note

Currently, extended ACLs do not produce a similar error.

The configuration in the following output of ACL 4 has the same two statements but in reverse order.

```
R1(config)# access-list 4 permit host 192.168.10.10
R1(config)# access-list 4 deny 192.168.10.0 0.0.0.255
R1(config)#
```

ACL 4: Host statements can always be configured before range statements.

This is a valid sequence of statements because the first statement refers a specific host, not a range of hosts.

In the following output, ACL 5 shows that a host statement can be configured after a statement that denotes a range of hosts. The host must not be within the range covered by a previous statement. The 192.168.11.10 host address is not a member of the 192.168.10.0/24 network, so this is a valid statement.

```
R1(config)# access-list 5 deny 192.168.10.0 0.0.0.255
R1(config)# access-list 5 permit host 192.168.11.10
R1(config)#
```

ACL 5: Host statement can be configured after a range statement if there is no conflict.

Note

The order in which standard ACEs are entered may not be the order that they are stored, displayed, or processed by the router. This will be discussed in section 9.2.2.

Applying Standard ACLs to Interfaces – Standard ACL Configuration Procedures (9.2.1.5, 9.2.1.6)

After a standard ACL is configured, it is linked to an interface using the **ip access-group** command in interface configuration mode:

```
Router(config-if)#ip access-group{access-list-number| access-list-name} {in| out}
```

To remove an ACL from an interface, first enter the **no ip access-group** command on the interface, and then enter the global **no access-list** command to remove the entire ACL.

The steps and syntax to configure and apply a numbered standard ACL on a router are shown here:

Step 1: Use the **access-list** global configuration command to create an entry in a standard IPv4 ACL.

```
R1(config) #access-list 1 permit 192.168.10.0 0.0.0.255
```

The example statement matches any address that starts with 192.168.10.x. Use the **remark** option to add a description to your ACL.

Step 2: Use the **interface** configuration command to select an interface to which to apply the ACL.

```
R1(config) #interface serial 0/0/0
```

Step 3: Use the ip access-group interface configuration command to activate the existing ACL on an interface.

```
R1(config-if)#ip access-group 1 out
```

This example activates the standard IPv4 ACL 1 on the interface as an outbound filter.

Figure 9-16 shows an example of an ACL to permit a single network.

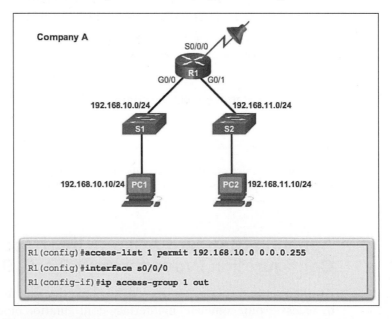

Figure 9-16 Permit a Specific Subnet

This ACL allows only traffic from source network 192.168.10.0 to be forwarded out of interface S0/0/0. Traffic from networks other than 192.168.10.0 is blocked.

The first line identifies the ACL as access list 1. It permits traffic that matches the selected parameters. In this case, the IPv4 address and wildcard mask identifying the source network is 192.168.10.0 0.0.0.255. Recall that there is an implicit 'deny all' statement that is equivalent to adding the line **access-list 1 deny 0.0.0.0 255.255.255.255**.

The **ip access-group 1 out** interface configuration command links and ties ACL 1 to the Serial 0/0/0 interface as an outbound filter.

Therefore, ACL 1 permits only hosts from the 192.168.10.0/24 network to exit router R1. It denies any other network including the 192.168.11.0 network.

Figure 9-17 shows an example of an ACL that permits a specific subnet except for a specific host on that subnet.

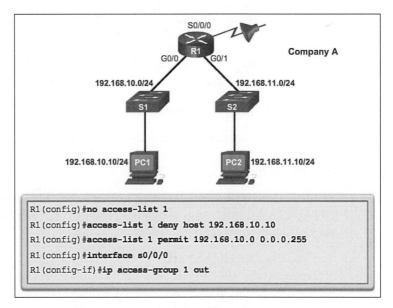

Figure 9-17   Deny a Specific Host and Permit a Specific Subnet

This ACL replaces the previous example but also blocks traffic from a specific address. The first command deletes the previous version of ACL 1. The next ACL statement denies the PC1 host located at 192.168.10.10. Every other host on the 192.168.10.0/24 network is permitted. Again the implicit deny statement matches every other network.

The ACL is reapplied to interface S0/0/0 in an outbound direction.

Figure 9-18 is an example of an ACL that denies a specific host. This ACL replaces the previous example. This example still blocks traffic from host PC1 but permits all other traffic.

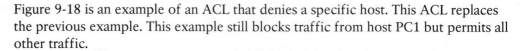

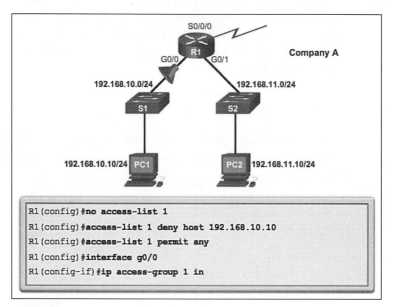

```
R1(config)#no access-list 1
R1(config)#access-list 1 deny host 192.168.10.10
R1(config)#access-list 1 permit any
R1(config)#interface g0/0
R1(config-if)#ip access-group 1 in
```

Figure 9-18 Deny a Specific Host

The first two commands are the same as the previous example. The first command deletes the previous version of ACL 1 and the next ACL statement denies the PC1 host that is located at 192.168.10.10.

The third line is new and permits all other hosts. This means that all hosts from the 192.168.10.0/24 network will be permitted except for PC1, which was denied in the previous statement.

This ACL is applied to interface G0/0 in the inbound direction. Because the filter affects only the 192.168.10.0/24 LAN on G0/0, it is more efficient to apply the ACL to the inbound interface. The ACL could be applied to s0/0/0 in the outbound direction, but then R1 would have to examine packets from all networks including 192.168.11.0/24.

Creating Named Standard ACLs (9.2.1.7)

Naming an ACL makes it easier to understand its function. For example, an ACL configured to deny FTP could be called NO_FTP. When you identify your ACL with a name instead of with a number, the configuration mode and command syntax are slightly different.

The following outputs and steps show what is required to create a standard named ACL.

Step 1. Starting from the global configuration mode, use the **ip access-list** command to create a named ACL. ACL names are alphanumeric, case-sensitive, and must be unique. The **ip access-list standard** *name* is used to create a standard named ACL, whereas the command **ip access-list extended** *name* is for an extended access list. After entering the command, the router is in named standard ACL configuration mode as indicated by the prompt.

```
Router(config)# ip access-list [standard | extended] name
```

Note

Alphanumeric name string must be unique and cannot begin with a number.

Note

Numbered ACLs use the global configuration command access-list, whereas named IPv4 ACLs use the ip access-list command.

Step 2. From the named ACL configuration mode, use **permit** or **deny** statements to specify one or more conditions for determining whether a packet is forwarded or dropped.

```
Router(config-std-nacl)# [permit | deny | remark] {source [source-
wildcard]} [log]
```

Step 3. Apply the ACL to an interface using the **ip access-group** command. Specify if the ACL should be applied to packets as they enter into the interface (**in**) or applied to packets as they exit the interface (**out**).

```
Router(config-if)# ip access-group name [in | out]
```

Figure 9-19 shows the commands used to configure a standard named ACL on router R1, interface G0/0 that denies host 192.168.11.10 access to the 192.168.10.0 network. The ACL is named NO_ACCESS.

Capitalizing ACL names is not required but makes them stand out when viewing the running-config output. It also makes it less likely that you will accidentally create two different ACLs with the same name but with different uses of capitalization.

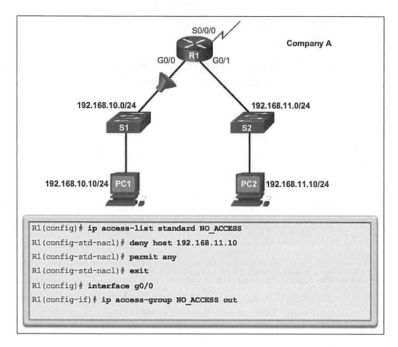

```
R1(config)# ip access-list standard NO_ACCESS
R1(config-std-nacl)# deny host 192.168.11.10
R1(config-std-nacl)# permit any
R1(config-std-nacl)# exit
R1(config)# interface g0/0
R1(config-if)# ip access-group NO_ACCESS out
```

Figure 9-19   Named ACL Example

Commenting ACLs (9.2.1.8)

You can use the **remark** keyword to include comments (remarks) about entries in any IP standard or extended ACL. The remarks make the ACL easier for you to understand and scan. Each remark line is limited to 100 characters.

The remark can go before or after a **permit** or **deny** statement. You should be consistent about where you put the remark so that it is clear which remark describes which **permit** or **deny** statement. For example, it would be confusing to have some remarks before the associated **permit** or **deny** statements and some remarks after the statements.

To include a comment for IPv4 numbered standard or extended ACLs, use the **access-list** *access-list_number* **remark** *remark* global configuration command. To remove the remark, use the **no** form of this command.

In Example 9-3, in the first example, the numbered ACL denies the 192.168.10.10 guest workstation from exiting S0/0/0 but permits all other devices from 192.168.0.0/16.

Example 9-3   Commenting a Numbered ACL

```
R1(config)# access-list 1 remark Do not allow Guest workstation through
R1(config)# access-list 1 deny host 192.168.10.10
R1(config)# access-list 1 remark Allow devices from all other 192.168.x.x subnets
R1(config)# access-list 1 permit 192.168.0.0 0.0.255.255
R1(config)# interface s0/0/0
R1(config-if)# ip access-group 1 out
R1(config-if)#
```

For an entry in a named standard or extended ACL, use the **remark** access-list configuration command. To remove the remark, use the **no** form of this command. Example 9-4 shows a standard named ACL. In this example, the remark statements indicate that the lab workstation with the host address 192.168.11.10 is denied but devices from all other networks are permitted.

Example 9-4   Commenting a Named ACL

```
R1(config)# ip access-list standard NO_ACCESS
R1(config-std-nacl)# remark Do not allow from Lab workstation
R1(config-std-nacl)# deny host 192.168.11.10
R1(config-std-nacl)# remark Allow access from all other networks
R1(config-std-nacl)# permit any
R1(config-std-nacl)# exit
R1(config)# interface G0/0
R1(config-if)# ip access-group NO_ACCESS out
R1(config-if)#
```

Interactive Graphic

Activity 9.2.1.9: Configuring Standard ACLs

Go to the course online and using the first graphic as a reference, answer the questions shown in graphics 2 through 4.

Packet Tracer ☐ Activity

Packet Tracer Activity 9.2.1.10: Configuring Standard ACLs

Standard access control lists (ACL) are router configuration scripts that control whether a router permits or denies packets based on the source address. This activity focuses on defining filtering criteria, configuring standard ACLs, applying ACLs to router interfaces, and verifying and testing the ACL implementation. The routers are already configured, including IP addresses and EIGRP routing.

Go to the course online to complete this Packet Tracer activity.

Packet Tracer Activity 9.2.1.11: Configuring Named Standard ACLs

The senior network administrator has tasked you to create a standard named ACL to prevent access to a file server. All clients from one network and one specific work-station from a different network should be denied access.

Go to the course online to complete this Packet Tracer activity.

Modify IPv4 ACLs (9.2.2)

When ACLs were first introduced into the Cisco IOS, there were no editing features built into the Cisco IOS that allowed you to make changes. You had to retype the entire ACL. However, with more recent versions of Cisco IOS, editing features have been introduced. The next sections go through these editing features.

Editing Standard Numbered ACLs (9.2.2.1, 9.2.2.2)

When configuring a standard ACL, the statements are added to the running-config. However, there is no built-in editing feature that allows you to edit a change in an ACL.

There are two ways that a standard numbered ACL can be edited.

Method 1: Using a Text Editor

After someone is familiar with creating and editing ACLs, it may be easier to con-struct the ACL using a text editor such as Microsoft Notepad. This allows you to create or edit the ACL and then paste it into the router. For an existing ACL, you can use the **show running-config** command to display the ACL, copy and paste it into the text editor, make the necessary changes, and paste it back in.

Configuration: For example, assume that the following host IPv4 address was incor-rectly entered:

```
R1 (config)# access-list 1 deny host 192.168.10.99
R1 (config)# access-list 1 permit 192.168.0.0 0.0.255.255
```

Instead of the 192.168.10.99 host, it should have been the 192.168.10.10 host.

Here are the steps to edit and correct ACL 1:

Step 1.   Display the ACL using the **show running-config** command. The following output uses the **include** keyword to display only the ACEs.

```
R1# show running-config | include access-list 1
access-list 1 deny host 192.168.10.99
access-list 1 permit 192.168.0.0 0.0.255.255
```

Step 2. Highlight the ACL, copy it, and then paste it into Microsoft Notepad. Edit the list as required. After the ACL is correctly displayed in Microsoft Notepad, highlight it and copy it.

```
<Text editor>
access-list 1 deny host 192.168.10.10
access-list permit 192.168.0.0 0.0.255.255
```

Step 3. In global configuration mode, remove the access list using the **no access-list 1** command. Otherwise, the new statements would be appended to the existing ACL. Then paste the new ACL into the configuration of the router.

```
R1# config t
Enter configuration commands, one per line. End with CNTL/Z.
R1(config#) no access-list 1
R1(config#) access-list 1 deny host 192.168.10.10
R1(config#) access-list 1 permit 192.168.0.0 0.0.255.255
```

Step 4. Using the **show running-config** command, verify the changes.

```
R1# show running-config | include access-list 1
access-list 1 deny host 192.168.10.10
access-list 1 permit 192.168.0.0 0.0.255.255
```

It should be mentioned that when using the **no access-list** command, different Cisco IOS Software releases act differently. If the ACL that has been deleted is still applied to an interface, some IOS versions act as if no ACL is protecting your network, whereas others deny all traffic. For this reason, it is good practice to remove the reference to the access list from the interface before modifying the access list. Also, be aware that if there is an error in the new list, disable it and troubleshoot the problem. In that instance, again, the network has no ACL during the correction process.

Method 2: Using the Sequence Number

As shown in the following output, the initial configuration of ACL 1 included a host statement for host 192.168.10.99. This was in error. The host should have been configured as 192.168.10.10.

Original Configuration:

```
R1(config)# access-list 1 deny host 192.168.10.99
R1(config)# access-list 1 permit 192.168.0.0 0.0.255.255
```

To edit the ACL using sequence numbers, follow these steps:

Step 1.   Display the current ACL using the **show access-lists 1** command. The output from this command will be discussed in more detail later in this section. The sequence number is displayed at the beginning of each statement. The sequence number was automatically assigned when the access list statement was entered. Notice that the misconfigured statement has the sequence number 10.

```
R1# show access-lists 1
Standard IP access list 1
    10 deny          192.168.10.99
    20 permit        192.168.0.0, wildcard bits 0.0.255.255
R1#
```

Step 2.   Enter the **ip access-lists standard** command that is used to configure named ACLs. The ACL number, 1, is used as the name. The misconfigured statement needs to be deleted using the **no 10** command with 10 referring to the sequence number. Then, a new sequence number 10 statement is added using the command, **10 deny host 192.168.10.10**.

```
R1# config t
R1(config)# ip access-list standard 1
R1(config-std-nacl)# no 10
R1(config-std-nacl)# 10 deny host 192.168.10.10
R1(config-std-nacl)# end
R1#
```

Note

Statements cannot be overwritten using the same sequence number as an existing statement. The current statement must be deleted first, and then the new one can be added.

Step 3.   Verify the changes using the **show access-lists** command.

```
R1# show access-lists
Standard IP access list 1
    10 deny          192.168.10.10
    20 permit        192.168.0.0, wildcard bits 0.0.255.255
R1#
```

As discussed previously, Cisco IOS implements an internal logic to standard access lists. The order in which standard ACEs are entered may not be the order in which they are stored, displayed, or processed by the router. The **show access-lists** command displays the ACEs with their sequence numbers.

Editing Standard Named ACLs (9.2.2.3)

In a previous example, sequence numbers were used to edit a standard numbered ACL. By referring to the statement sequence numbers, individual statements can easily be inserted or deleted. This method can also be used to edit standard named ACLs.

The following shows an example of inserting a line to a named ACL.

- In the first **show** command output, you can see that the ACL named NO_ACCESS has two numbered lines indicating access rules for a workstation with the IPv4 address 192.168.11.10.

```
R1# show access-lists
Standard IP access list NO_ACCESS
    10 deny    192.168.11.10
    20 permit 192.168.11.0, wildcard bits 0.0.0.255
R1#
```

- The **ip access-list standard** command is used to configure named ACLs. From named access list configuration mode, statements can be inserted or removed. The **no** *sequence-number* command is used to delete individual statements.

- To add a statement to deny another workstation requires inserting a numbered line. In the example, the workstation with the IPv4 address 192.168.11.11 is being added using a new sequence number of 15.

```
R1# config t
Enter configuration commands, one per line. End with
CNTL/Z.
R1(config)# ip access-list standard NO_ACCESS
R1(config-std-nacl)# 15 deny host 192.168.11.11
R1(config-std-nacl)# end
```

- The final **show** command output verifies that the new workstation is now denied access.

```
R1# show access-lists
Standard IP access list NO_ACCESS
    10 deny       192.168.11.10
    15 deny       192.168.11.11
    20 permit     192.168.11.0, wildcard bits 0.0.0.255
R1#
```

Verifying ACLs (9.2.2.4)

As shown in the following output, the **show ip interface** command is used to verify the ACL on the interface.

```
R1# show ip interface s0/0/0
Serial0/0/0 is up, line protocol is up
  Internet address is 10.1.1.1/30
<output omitted>
  Outgoing access list is 1
  Inbound  access list is not set
<output omitted>

R1# show ip interface g0/0
GigabitEthernet0/0 is up, line protocol is up
  Internet address is 192.168.10.1/24
<output omitted>
  Outgoing access list is NO_ACCESS
  Inbound  access list is not set
<output omitted>
R1#
```

The output from this command includes the number or name of the access list and the direction in which the ACL was applied. The output shows router R1 has the access list 1 applied to its S0/0/0 outbound interface and the access list NO_ACCESS applied to its g0/0 interface also in the outbound direction.

The following output shows the result of issuing the **show access-lists** command on router R1.

```
R1# show access-lists
Standard IP access list 1
    10 deny         192.168.10.10
    20 permit       192.168.0.0, wildcard bits 0.0.255.255
Standard IP access list NO_ACCESS
    15 deny         192.168.11.11
    10 deny         192.168.11.10
    20 permit       192.168.11.0, wildcard bits 0.0.0.255
R1#
```

To view an individual access list, use the **show access-lists** command followed by the access list number or name. The NO_ACCESS statements may look strange. Notice that sequence number 15 is displayed prior to sequence number 10. This is a result of the router internal process and will be discussed later in this section.

ACL Statistics (9.2.2.5)

After the ACL has been applied to an interface and some testing has occurred, the **show access-lists** command shows statistics for each statement that has been matched. In the output in Figure 9-20, note that some of the statements have been matched.

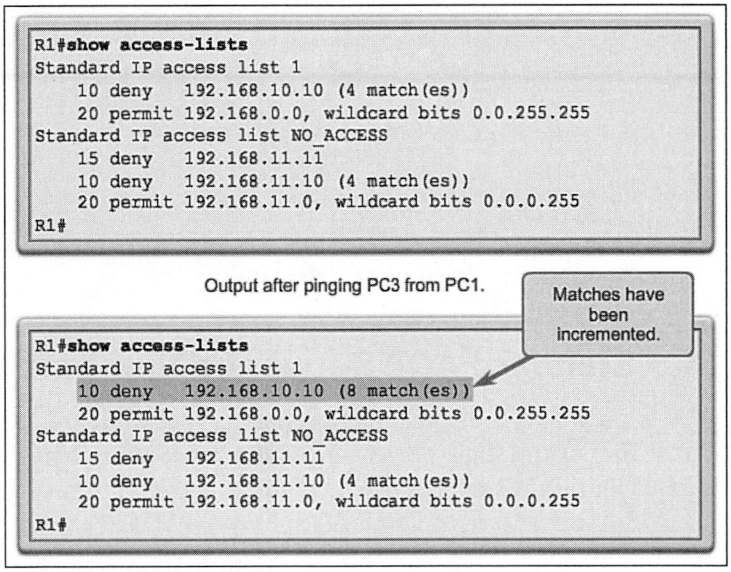

```
R1#show access-lists
Standard IP access list 1
    10 deny   192.168.10.10 (4 match(es))
    20 permit 192.168.0.0, wildcard bits 0.0.255.255
Standard IP access list NO_ACCESS
    15 deny   192.168.11.11
    10 deny   192.168.11.10 (4 match(es))
    20 permit 192.168.11.0, wildcard bits 0.0.0.255
R1#
```

Output after pinging PC3 from PC1.

Matches have been incremented.

```
R1#show access-lists
Standard IP access list 1
    10 deny   192.168.10.10 (8 match(es))
    20 permit 192.168.0.0, wildcard bits 0.0.255.255
Standard IP access list NO_ACCESS
    15 deny   192.168.11.11
    10 deny   192.168.11.10 (4 match(es))
    20 permit 192.168.11.0, wildcard bits 0.0.0.255
R1#
```

Figure 9-20   Viewing ACL Statistics

When traffic is generated that should match an ACL statement, the matches shown in the **show access-lists** command output should increase. For instance in this example, if a ping is issued from PC1 to PC3 or PC4, the output shows an increase in the matches for the deny statement of ACL 1.

Both permit and statements track statistics for matches; however, recall that every ACL has an implied deny any as the last statement. This statement does not appear in the **show access-lists** command; therefore, statistics for that statement do not appear. To view statistics for the implied deny any statement, the statement can be configured manually and appear in the output. Extreme caution should be taken when manually configuring the deny any statement because it will match all traffic. If this statement is not configured as the last statement in the ACL, it could cause unexpected results.

During testing of an ACL, the counters can be cleared using the **clear access-list counters** command. This command can be used alone or with the number or name of a specific ACL. As shown in Figure 9-21, this command clears the statistic counters for an ACL.

```
R1#show access-lists
Standard IP access list 1
    10 deny   192.168.10.10 (8 match(es))
    20 permit 192.168.0.0, wildcard bits 0.0.255.255
Standard IP access list NO_ACCESS
    15 deny   192.168.11.11
    10 deny   192.168.11.10 (4 match(es))
    20 permit 192.168.11.0, wildcard bits 0.0.0.255
R1#clear access-list counters 1
R1#
R1#show access-lists                    ┌─────────────────────────────┐
Standard IP access list 1               │ Matches have been cleared.  │
    10 deny   192.168.10.10  ◄───────────┘                             │
    20 permit 192.168.0.0, wildcard bits 0.0.255.255
Standard IP access list NO_ACCESS
    15 deny   192.168.11.11
    10 deny   192.168.11.10 (4 match(es))
    20 permit 192.168.11.0, wildcard bits 0.0.0.255
```

Figure 9-21   Clearing ACL Statistics

Standard ACL Sequence Numbers (9.2.2.6)

Cisco IOS implements an internal logic to standard ACLs. As discussed previously, part of this logic prevents host statements from being configured after a range statement if the host is a member of that range, as shown in the following output.

```
R1(config)# access-list 3 deny 192.168.10.0 0.0.0.255
R1(config)# access-list 3 permit host 192.168.10.10
% Access rule can't be configured at higher sequence num as
it is part of the existing rule at sequence  num 10
R1(config)#
```

Another part of the IOS internal logic involves the internal sequencing of standard ACEs. Figure 9-22 shows the configuration of a standard access list.

Range statements that deny three networks are configured first followed by five host statements. The host statements are all valid statements because their host IP addresses are not part of the previously entered range statements.

The **show running-config** command is used to verify the ACL configuration. Notice that the statements are listed in a different order than they were entered. You can use the **show access-lists** command to understand the logic behind this.

As shown in Figure 9-23, the **show access-lists** command displays ACEs along with their sequence numbers.

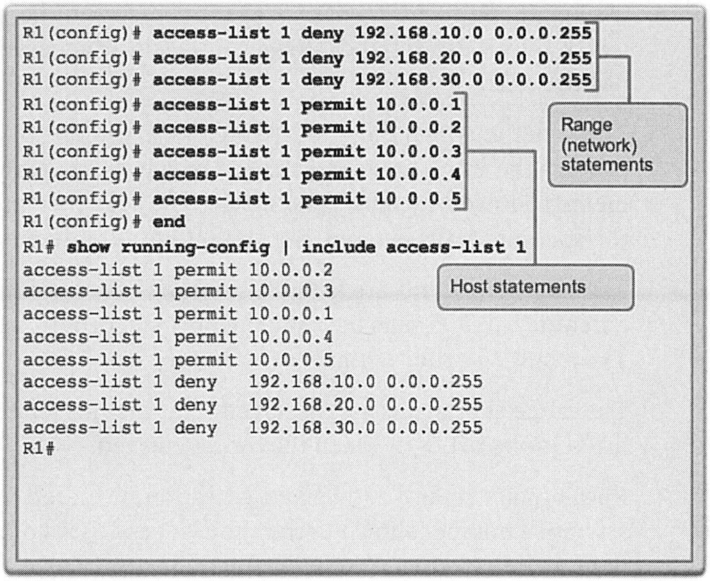

```
R1(config)# access-list 1 deny 192.168.10.0 0.0.0.255
R1(config)# access-list 1 deny 192.168.20.0 0.0.0.255
R1(config)# access-list 1 deny 192.168.30.0 0.0.0.255
R1(config)# access-list 1 permit 10.0.0.1
R1(config)# access-list 1 permit 10.0.0.2
R1(config)# access-list 1 permit 10.0.0.3
R1(config)# access-list 1 permit 10.0.0.4
R1(config)# access-list 1 permit 10.0.0.5
R1(config)# end
R1# show running-config | include access-list 1
access-list 1 permit 10.0.0.2
access-list 1 permit 10.0.0.3
access-list 1 permit 10.0.0.1
access-list 1 permit 10.0.0.4
access-list 1 permit 10.0.0.5
access-list 1 deny   192.168.10.0 0.0.0.255
access-list 1 deny   192.168.20.0 0.0.0.255
access-list 1 deny   192.168.30.0 0.0.0.255
R1#
```

Range (network) statements

Host statements

Figure 9-22   Sequencing Considerations During Configuration

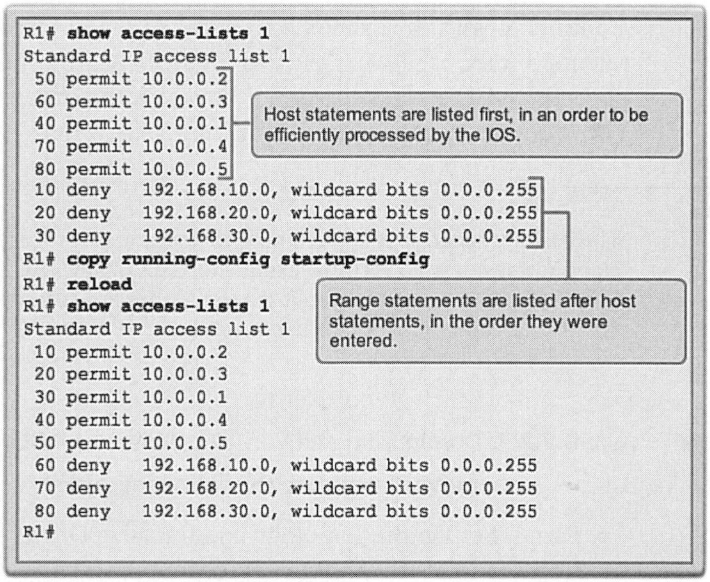

```
R1# show access-lists 1
Standard IP access list 1
  50 permit 10.0.0.2
  60 permit 10.0.0.3
  40 permit 10.0.0.1
  70 permit 10.0.0.4
  80 permit 10.0.0.5
  10 deny   192.168.10.0, wildcard bits 0.0.0.255
  20 deny   192.168.20.0, wildcard bits 0.0.0.255
  30 deny   192.168.30.0, wildcard bits 0.0.0.255
R1# copy running-config startup-config
R1# reload
R1# show access-lists 1
Standard IP access list 1
  10 permit 10.0.0.2
  20 permit 10.0.0.3
  30 permit 10.0.0.1
  40 permit 10.0.0.4
  50 permit 10.0.0.5
  60 deny   192.168.10.0, wildcard bits 0.0.0.255
  70 deny   192.168.20.0, wildcard bits 0.0.0.255
  80 deny   192.168.30.0, wildcard bits 0.0.0.255
R1#
```

Host statements are listed first, in an order to be efficiently processed by the IOS.

Range statements are listed after host statements, in the order they were entered.

Figure 9-23   Sequence Numbers After Reload

You might expect the order of the statements in the output to reflect the order in which they were entered. However, the **show access-lists** output shows that this is not the case.

The order in which the standard ACEs are listed is the sequence used by the IOS to process the list. Notice that the statements are grouped into two sections: host statements followed by range statements. The sequence number indicates the order that the statement was entered, not the order the statement will be processed.

The host statements are listed first but not necessarily in the order that they were entered. The IOS puts host statements in an order using a special hashing function. The resulting order optimizes the search for a host ACL entry.

The range statements are displayed after the host statements. These statements are listed in the order in which they were entered.

Recall that standard and named ACLs can be edited using sequence numbers. The sequence number shown in the **show access-lists** command output is the number used when deleting an individual statement from the list. When inserting a new ACL statement, the sequence number will affect only the location of a range statement in the list. Host statements will always be put in order using the hashing function.

Continuing with the example, after saving the running-configuration the router is reloaded (rebooted). As shown in Figure 9-23, the **show access-lists** command displays the ACL in the same order; however, the statements have been renumbered. The sequence numbers are now in numerical order.

Note

The hashing function is applied only to host statements in an IPv4 standard access list. The algorithm is not used for IPv4 extended ACLs or IPv6 ACLs. This is because extended and IPv6 ACLs filter on more than just a single source address. The details of the hashing function are beyond the scope of this course.

Lab 9.2.2.7: Configuring and Verifying Standard ACLs

In this lab, you will complete the following objectives:

- Part 1: Set Up the Topology and Initialize Devices
- Part 2: Configure Devices and Verify Connectivity
- Part 3: Configure and Verify Standard Numbered and Named ACLs
- Part 4: Modify a Standard ACL

Securing VTY Ports with a Standard IPv4 ACL (9.2.3)

The most commonly used Standard ACL is the one used to secure your VTY ports on the router. This next section shows how to configure a Standard ACL to secure VTY ports.

Configuring a Standard ACL to Secure a VTY Port (9.2.3.1)

Cisco recommends using SSH for administrative connections to routers and switches. If the Cisco IOS software image on your router does not support SSH, you can improve the security of administrative lines by restricting VTY access. Restricting VTY access is a technique that allows you to define which IP addresses are allowed Telnet access to the router EXEC process. You can control which administrative workstation or network manages your router with an ACL and an **access-class** statement configured on your VTY lines. You can also use this technique with SSH to further improve administrative access security.

The **access-class** command configured in line configuration mode restricts incoming and outgoing connections between a particular VTY (into a Cisco device) and the addresses in an access list.

Standard and extended access lists apply to packets that travel through a router. They are not designed to block packets that originate within the router. An outbound Telnet extended ACL does not prevent router-initiated Telnet sessions, by default.

Filtering Telnet or SSH traffic is typically considered an extended IP ACL function because it filters a higher level protocol. However, because the **access-class** command is used to filter incoming or outgoing Telnet/SSH sessions by source address, a standard ACL can be used.

The command syntax of the **access-class** command is

```
Router(config-line)# access-class access-list-number
  {in [vrf-also] | out}
```

The parameter **in** restricts incoming connections between the addresses in the access list and the Cisco device, whereas the parameter **out** restricts outgoing connections between a particular Cisco device and the addresses in the access list.

An example allowing a range of addresses to access VTY lines 0 through 4 is shown in Figure 9-24.

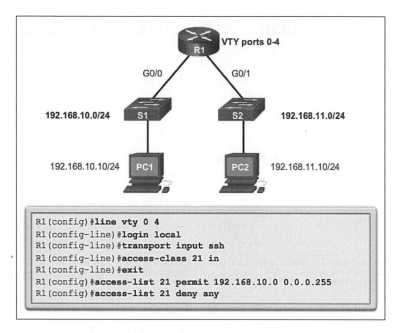

```
R1(config)#line vty 0 4
R1(config-line)#login local
R1(config-line)#transport input ssh
R1(config-line)#access-class 21 in
R1(config-line)#exit
R1(config)#access-list 21 permit 192.168.10.0 0.0.0.255
R1(config)#access-list 21 deny any
```

Figure 9-24   Securing VTY Ports with a Standard IPv4 ACL

The ACL in the figure is configured to permit network 192.168.10.0 to access VTY lines 0 through 4 but deny all other networks.

The following should be considered when configuring access lists on VTYs:

- Only numbered access lists can be applied to VTYs.

- Identical restrictions should be set on all the VTYs because a user can attempt to connect to any of them.

Activity 9.2.3.1: Securing VTY Ports with a Standard IPv4 ACL

Go to the course online and use the Syntax Checker in the second graphic to configure a Standard IPv4 ACL to secure VTY access.

Verifying a Standard ACL Used to Secure a VTY Port (9.2.3.2)

After the ACL to restrict access to the VTY lines is configured, it is important to verify that it is working as expected. Figure 9-25 shows two devices attempting to connect to R1 using SSH.

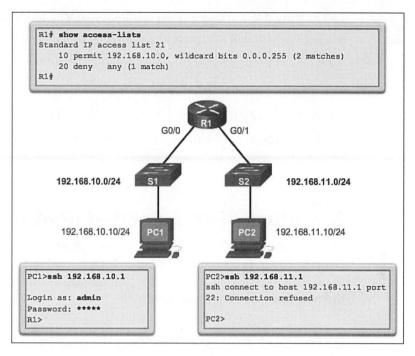

```
R1# show access-lists
Standard IP access list 21
    10 permit 192.168.10.0, wildcard bits 0.0.0.255 (2 matches)
    20 deny   any (1 match)
R1#
```

```
PC1>ssh 192.168.10.1

Login as: admin
Password: *****
R1>
```

```
PC2>ssh 192.168.11.1
ssh connect to host 192.168.11.1 port
22: Connection refused

PC2>
```

Figure 9-25   Verifying a Standard ACL to Secure a VTY Port

PC2 fails to establish an SSH connection. This is the expected behavior because the configured access list permits VTY access from the 192.168.10.0/24 network while denying all other devices.

The output for R1 shows the result of issuing the **show access-lists** command after the SSH attempts by PC1 and PC2. The match in the permit line of the output is a result of a successful SSH connection by PC1. The match in the deny statement is due to the failed attempt to create an SSH connection by PC2, a device on the 192.168.11.0/24 network.

Packet Tracer Activity 9.2.3.3: Configuring an ACL on VTY Lines

As administrator of a network, you need to have remote access to your router. This access should not be available to other users of the network. Therefore, you will configure and apply an ACL that allows PC access to the Telnet lines, but denies all other source IP addresses.

Go to the course online to complete this Packet Tracer activity.

Lab Activity 9.2.3.4: Configuring and Verifying VTY Restrictions

In this lab, you will complete the following objectives:

- Part 1: Configure Basic Device Settings

- Part 2: Configure and Apply the Access Control List on R1

- Part 3: Verify the Access Control List Using Telnet

- Part 4: Challenge - Configure and Apply the Access Control List on S1

Structure of an Extended IPv4 ACL (9.3.1)

The Extended ACL looks similar to a Standard ACL. However, because the Extended ACL has more conditions to look at, and more granularity in its searching, the syntax of an Extended ACL is a bit more complex. These next sections deal with the structure of an Extended IPv4 ACL.

Extended ACLs – Testing Packets with Extended ACLs (9.3.1.1)

For more precise traffic-filtering control, extended IPv4 ACLs can be created. Extended ACLs are numbered 100 to 199 and 2000 to 2699, providing a total of 799 possible extended numbered ACLs. Extended ACLs can also be named.

Extended ACLs are used more often than standard ACLs because they provide a greater degree of control. As shown in Figure 9-26, like standard ACLs, extended ACLs check source addresses of packets, but they also check the destination address, protocols, and port numbers (or services). This provides a greater range of criteria on which to base the ACL. For example, an extended ACL can simultaneously allow email traffic from a network to a specific destination while denying file transfers and web browsing.

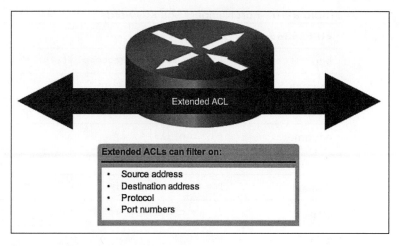

Figure 9-26   Extended ACLs

Extended ACLs – Testing for Ports and Services (9.3.1.2)

The ability to filter on protocol and port number allows network administrators to build specific extended ACLs. An application can be specified by configuring either the port number or the name of a well-known port.

The following outputs show examples of how an administrator specifies a TCP or UDP port number by placing it at the end of the extended ACL statement. Logical operations can be used, such as equal (eq), not equal (neq), greater than (gt), and less than (lt).

Using Port Numbers:

```
access-list 114 permit tcp 192.168.20.0 0.0.0.255 any eq 23
access-list 114 permit tcp 192.168.20.0 0.0.0.255 any eq 21
access-list 114 permit tcp 192.168.20.0 0.0.0.255 any eq 20
```

Using Keywords:

```
access-list 114 permit tcp 192.168.20.0 0.0.0.255 any eq telnet
access-list 114 permit tcp 192.168.20.0 0.0.0.255 any eq ftp
access-list 114 permit tcp 192.168.20.0 0.0.0.255 any eq ftp-data
```

Table 9-10 shows how to display a list of port numbers and keywords that can be used when building an ACL using the command:

```
R1(config)# access-list 101 permit tcp any any eq ?
```

Table 9-10 Port Numbers and Keywords

<0-65535>	Port Number
bgp	Border Gateway Protocol (179)
chargen	Character generator (19)
cmd	Remote commands (rcmd, 514)
daytime	Daytime (13)
discard	Discard (9)
domain	Domain Name Service (53)
drip	Dynamic Routing Information Protocol (3949)
echo	Echo (7)
exec	Exec (rsh, 512)
finger	Finger (79)
ftp	File Transfer Protocol (21)
ftp-data	FTP data connections (20)
gopher	Gopher (70)
hostname	NIC hostname server (101)
ident	Ident Protocol (113)
irc	Internet Relay Chat (194)
klogin	Kerberos login (543)
kshell	Kerberos shell (544)
login	Login (rlogin, 513)
lpd	Printer service (515)
nntp	Network News Transport Protocol (119)
pim-auto-rp	PIM Auto-RP (496)
pop2	Post Office Protocol v2 (109)
pop3	Post Office Protocol v3 (110)
smtp	Simple Mail Transport Protocol (25)
sunrpc	Sun Remote Procedure Call (111)
tacacs	TAC Access Control System (49)
talk	Talk (517)

telnet	(Telnet (23)
time	Time (37)
uucp	Unix-to-Unix Copy Program (540)
whois	Nicname (43)
www	World Wide Web (HTTP, 80)

Interactive Graphic

Activity 9.3.1.2: Extended IPv4 ACLs – Testing for Ports and Services

Go to the course online and use the slider bar in the second graphic to see the entire output of the **access-list 101 permit tcp any any eq ?** command.

Configure Extended IPv4 ACLs (9.3.2)

Configuring an Extended ACL follows the same steps as configuring a Standard ACL. They are shown in the next section.

Configuring Extended ACLs (9.3.2.1)

The procedural steps for configuring extended ACLs are the same as for standard ACLs. The extended ACL is first configured, and then it is activated on an interface. However, the command syntax and parameters are more complex to support the additional features provided by extended ACLs.

Note

The internal logic applied to the ordering of standard ACL statements does not apply to extended ACLs. The order in which the statements are entered during configuration is the order they are displayed and processed.

The following output and Table 9-11 shows the common command syntax for extended IPv4 ACLs. Note that there are many keywords and parameters for extended ACLs. It is not necessary to use all the keywords and parameters when configuring an extended ACL. Recall that the **?** can be used to get help when entering complex commands.

Configuring Extended ACLs:

```
access-list access-list-number {deny | permit | remark} protocol source
    [source-wildcard] [operator operand] [port port-number or name] destination
    [destination-wildcard] [operator operand] [port port-number or name] established
```

Table 9-11   Common Command Syntax Extended IPv4 ACLs

Parameter	Description
`access-list-number`	Identifies the access list using a number in the range 100 to 199 (for an extended IP ACL) and 2000 to 2699 (expanded IP ACLs).
deny	Denies access if the conditions are matched.
permit	Permits access if the conditions are matched.
remark	Used to enter a remark or comment.
`protocol`	Name or number of an Internet Protocol. Common keywords include **icmp**, **ip**, **tcp**, or **udp**. To match any Internet Protocol (including ICMP, TCP, and UDP), use the **ip** keyword.
`source`	Number of the network or host from which the packet is being sent.
`source-wildcard`	Wildcard bits to be applied to the source.
`destination`	Number of the network or host to which the packet is being sent.
`destination-wildcard`	Wildcard bits to be applied to the destination.
`operator`	(Optional) Compares source or destination ports. Possible commands include ■ **lt** (less than) ■ **gt** (greater than) ■ **eq** (equal) ■ **neq** (not equal) ■ **range** (inclusive range)
`port`	(Optional) The decimal number or name of a TCP or UDP port.
established	(Optional) For the TCP protocol only; indicates an established connection.

Activity 9.3.2.1: Configuring Extended ACLs

Go to the course online and use the slider bar in the first graphic to see all the parameters and their descriptions for configuring extended ACLs.

Figure 9-27 shows an example of an extended ACL. In this example, the network administrator has configured ACLs to restrict network access to allow website browsing only from the LAN attached to interface G0/0 to any external network.

ACL 103 allows traffic coming from any address on the 192.168.10.0 network to go to any destination, subject to the limitation that the traffic is using ports 80 (HTTP) and 443 (HTTPS) only.

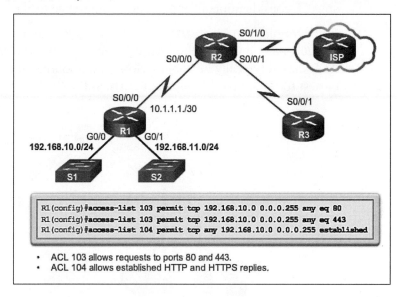

R1(config)#access-list 103 permit tcp 192.168.10.0 0.0.0.255 any eq 80
R1(config)#access-list 103 permit tcp 192.168.10.0 0.0.0.255 any eq 443
R1(config)#access-list 104 permit tcp any 192.168.10.0 0.0.0.255 established

- ACL 103 allows requests to ports 80 and 443.
- ACL 104 allows established HTTP and HTTPS replies.

Figure 9-27 Configuring Extended ACLs

The nature of HTTP requires that traffic flow back into the network from websites accessed from internal clients. The network administrator wants to restrict that return traffic to HTTP exchanges from requested websites, while denying all other traffic. ACL 104 does that by blocking all incoming traffic, except for previously established connections. The permit statement in ACL 104 allows inbound traffic using the **established** parameter.

The **established** parameter allows only responses to traffic that originate from the 192.168.10.0/24 network to return to that network. A match occurs if the returning TCP segment has the ACK or reset (RST) bits set, which indicates that the packet belongs to an existing connection. Without the **established** parameter in the ACL statement, clients could send traffic to a web server, but not receive traffic returning from the web server.

Applying Extended ACLs to Interfaces (9.3.2.2)

In the previous example, the network administrator configured an ACL to allow users from the 192.168.10.0/24 network to browse both insecure and secure websites. Even though it has been configured, the ACL will not filter traffic until it is applied to an interface. To apply an ACL to an interface, first consider whether the traffic to be filtered is going in or out. When a user on the internal LAN accesses a website on the Internet, traffic is going out to the Internet. When an internal user receives an email from the Internet, traffic is coming into the local router. However, when applying an ACL to an interface, in and out take on different meanings. From an ACL consideration, in and out are in reference to the router interface.

In the topology in Figure 9-28, R1 has three interfaces. It has a serial interface, S0/0/0, and two Gigabit Ethernet interfaces, G0/0 and G0/1. Recall that an extended ACL should typically be applied close to the source. In this topology, the interface closest to the source of the target traffic is the G0/0 interface.

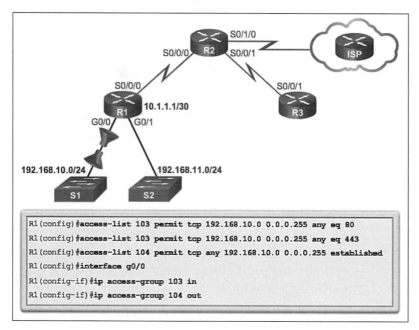

Figure 9-28   Applying an ACL to an Interface

Web request traffic from users on the 192.168.10.0/24 LAN is inbound to the G0/0 interface. Return traffic from established connections to users on the LAN is outbound from the G0/0 interface. The example applies the ACL to the G0/0 interface in both directions. The inbound ACL, 103, checks for the type of traffic leaving the network. The outbound ACL, 104, checks for return traffic from established connections. This will restrict 192.168.10.0 Internet access to allow only website browsing.

Note

The access lists could have been applied to the S0/0/0 interface, but in that case, the router's ACL process would have to examine all packets entering the router, not only traffic to and from 192.168.11.0. This would cause unnecessary processing by the router.

Filtering Traffic with Extended ACLs (9.3.2.3)

The example shown in Figure 9-29 denies FTP traffic from subnet 192.168.11.0 that is going to subnet 192.168.10.0, but permits all other traffic. Note the use of wildcard masks and the explicit deny any statement. Remember that FTP uses TCP ports 20 and 21; therefore, the ACL requires both port name keywords **ftp** and **ftp-data** or **eq 20** and **eq 21** to deny FTP.

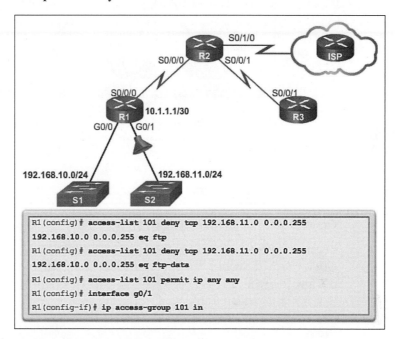

```
R1(config)# access-list 101 deny tcp 192.168.11.0 0.0.0.255
192.168.10.0 0.0.0.255 eq ftp
R1(config)# access-list 101 deny tcp 192.168.11.0 0.0.0.255
192.168.10.0 0.0.0.255 eq ftp-data
R1(config)# access-list 101 permit ip any any
R1(config)# interface g0/1
R1(config-if)# ip access-group 101 in
```

Figure 9-29   Extended ACL to Deny FTP

If using port numbers instead of port names, the commands would be written as

```
access-list 101 permit tcp 192.168.11.0 0.0.0.255 192.168.10.0 0.0.0.255 eq 20
access-list 101 permit tcp 192.168.11.0 0.0.0.255 192.168.10.0 0.0.0.255 eq 21
```

To prevent the implicit deny any statement at the end of the ACL from blocking all traffic, the **permit ip any any** statement is added. Without at least one **permit** statement in an ACL, all traffic on the interface where that ACL was applied would be dropped. The ACL should be applied inbound on the G0/1 interface so that traffic from the 192.168.11.0/24 LAN is filtered as it enters the router interface.

The example shown in Figure 9-30 denies Telnet traffic from any source to the 192.168.11.0/24 LAN but allows all other IP traffic.

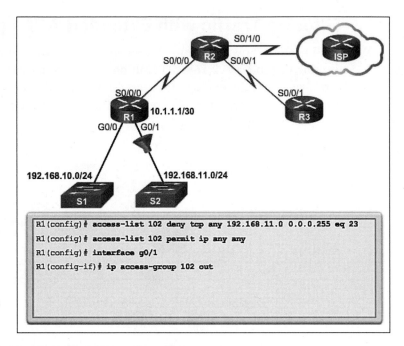

Figure 9-30   Extended ACL to Deny Telnet

Because traffic destined for the 192.168.11.0/24 LAN is outbound on interface G0/1, the ACL would be applied to G0/1 using the **out** keyword. Note the use of the **any** keywords in the permit statement. This permit statement is added to ensure that no other traffic is blocked.

Note

The examples in Figures 9-29 and 9-30 both use the `permit ip any any` statement at the end of the ACL. For greater security, the `permit 192.168.11.0 0.0.0.255 any` command may be used.

Creating Named Extended ACLs (9.3.2.4)

Named extended ACLs are created in essentially the same way that named standard ACLs are created. Follow these steps to create an extended ACL, using names:

Step 1.   From global configuration mode, use the **ip access-list extended** *name* command to define a name for the extended ACL.

Step 2.   In named ACL configuration mode, specify the conditions to **permit** or **deny**.

Step 3. Return to privileged EXEC mode and verify the ACL with the
show access-lists *name* command.

Step 4. Save the entries in the configuration file with the **copy running-config
startup-config** command.

To remove a named extended ACL, use the **no ip access-list extended** *name* global
configuration command.

Figure 9-31 shows the named versions of the ACLs created in the previous examples.
The named ACL, SURFING, permits the users on the 192.168.10.0/24 LAN to
access websites. The named ACL, BROWSING, allows the return traffic from established connections. Using the ACL names, the rules are applied inbound and outbound on the G0/0 interface.

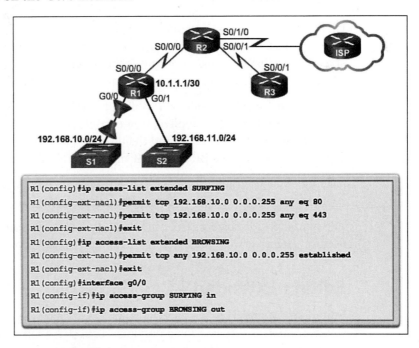

Figure 9-31   Creating Named Extended ACLs

Verifying Extended ACLs (9.3.2.5)

After an ACL has been configured and applied to an interface, use Cisco IOS **show**
commands to verify the configuration. In the following output, the top example
shows the Cisco IOS command used to display the contents of all ACLs. The bottom example shows the result of issuing the **show ip interface g0/0** command on
router R1.

```
R1#show access-lists
Extended IP access list BROWSING
10 permit tcp any 192.168.10.0 0.0.0.255 established
Extended IP access list SURFING
        10 permit tcp 192.168.10.0 0.0.0.255 any eq www
        20 permit tcp 192.168.10.0 0.0.0.255 any eq 443
R1#
R1#show ip interface g0/0
GigabitEthernet0/0 is up, line protocol is up
  Internet address is 192.168.10.1/24
<output omitted for brevity>
  Outgoing access list is BROWSING
  Inbound access list is SURFING
<output omitted for brevity>
```

Unlike standard ACLs, extended ACLs do not implement the same internal logic and hashing function. The output and sequence numbers displayed in the **show access-lists** command output is the order in which the statements were entered. Host entries are not automatically listed prior to range entries.

The **show ip interface** command is used to verify the ACL on the interface and the direction in which it was applied. The output from this command includes the number or name of the access list and the direction in which the ACL was applied. The capitalized ACL names BROWSING and SURFING stand out in the screen output.

After an ACL configuration has been verified, the next step is to confirm that the ACLs work as planned; blocking and permitting traffic as expected.

The guidelines discussed earlier in this section suggest that ACLs should be configured on a test network and then implemented on the production network.

Editing Extended ACLs (9.3.2.6)

Editing an extended ACL can be accomplished using the same process as editing a standard ACL as discussed in a previous section. An extended ACL can be modified using

- **Method 1 Text editor:** Using this method, the ACL is copied and pasted into the text editor where the changes are made. The current access list is removed using the **no access-list** command. The modified ACL is then pasted back into the configuration.

- **Method 2 Sequence numbers:** Sequence numbers can be used to delete or insert an ACL statement. The **ip access-list extended** *name* command is used to enter named-ACL configuration mode. If the ACL is numbered instead of named, the ACL number is used in the *name* parameter. ACEs can be inserted or removed.

In Figure 9-32, the administrator needs to edit the ACL named SURFING to correct a typo in the source network statement. To view the current sequence numbers, the **show access-lists** command is used. The statement to be edited is identified as statement 10. The original statement is removed with the **no** *sequence_#* command. The corrected statement is added replacing the original statement.

```
R1# show access-lists
Extended IP access list BROWSING
    10 permit tcp any 192.168.10.0 0.0.0.255 established
Extended IP access list SURFING
    10 permit tcp 192.168.11.0 0.0.0.255 any eq www
    20 permit tcp 192.168.10.0 0.0.0.255 any eq 443
R1#
R1# configure terminal
R1(config)# ip access-list extended SURFING
R1(config-ext-nacl)# no 10
R1(config-ext-nacl)# 10 permit tcp 192.168.10.0 0.0.0.255 any eq
www
R1(config-ext-nacl)# end
R1#
R1# show access-lists
Extended IP access list BROWSING
    10 permit tcp any 192.168.10.0 0.0.0.255 established
Extended IP access list SURFING
    10 permit tcp 192.168.10.0 0.0.0.255 any eq www
    20 permit tcp 192.168.10.0 0.0.0.255 any eq 443
```

Should be 192.168.10.0

Figure 9-32 Editing Extended ACLs

Interactive Graphic

Activity 9.3.2.7: Creating an Extended ACL Statement

Go to the course online and create an extended ACL based on the topology and requirements shown. Click the second graphic for scenario 2 and the third graphic for scenario 3.

Interactive Graphic

Activity 9.3.2.8: Evaluating Extended ACEs

Go to the course online and using the first graphic as a reference, answer the questions shown in graphics 2 through 4.

Activity 9.3.2.9: ACL Testlet

Go to the course online and using the first graphic as a reference, answer the five questions shown in graphics 2 through 6.

Packet Tracer Activity 9.3.2.10: Configuring Extended ACLs - Scenario 1

Scenario

Two employees need access to services provided by the server. PC1 needs only FTP access while PC2 needs only web access. Both computers can ping the server, but not each other.

Go to the course online to complete this Packet Tracer activity.

Packet Tracer Activity 9.3.2.11: Configuring Extended ACLs - Scenario 2

Scenario

In this scenario, devices on one LAN are allowed to remotely access devices in another LAN using the Telnet protocol. Besides ICMP, all traffic from other networks is denied.

Go to the course online to complete this Packet Tracer activity.

Packet Tracer Activity 9.3.2.12: Configuring Extended ACLs - Scenario 3

Background / Scenario

In this scenario, specific devices on the LAN are allowed to various services on servers located on the Internet.

Go to the course online to complete this Packet Tracer activity.

Lab 9.3.2.13: Configuring and Verifying Extended ACLs

In this lab, you will complete the following objectives:

- Part 1: Set Up the Topology and Initialize Devices
- Part 2: Configure Devices and Verify Connectivity
- Part 3: Configure and Verify Extended Numbered and Named ACLs
- Part 4: Modify and Verify Extended ACLs

Troubleshoot ACLs (9.4)

Part of every network administrator's job is to troubleshoot ACLs. This next section looks at the logic between inbound and outbound ACLs.

Inbound and Outbound ACL Logic (9.4.1.1)

Inbound ACL Logic

Figure 9-33 shows the logic for an inbound ACL.

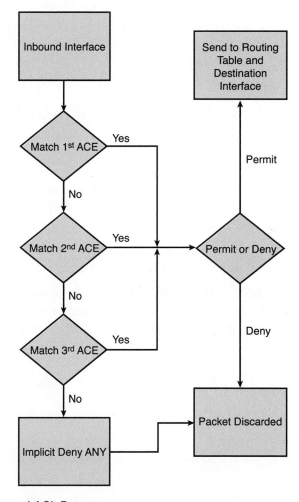

Figure 9-33   Inbound ACL Process

If the information in a packet header and an ACL statement match, the rest of the statements in the list are skipped, and the packet is permitted or denied as specified by the matched statement. If a packet header does not match an ACL statement, the packet is tested against the next statement in the list. This matching process continues until the end of the list is reached.

At the end of every ACL is an implicit deny any statement. This statement is not shown in output. This final implied statement applied to all packets for which conditions did not test true. This final test condition matches all other packets and results in a `deny` action. Instead of proceeding into or out of an interface, the router drops all these remaining packets. This final statement is often referred to as the `implicit deny any statement` or the `deny all traffic` statement. Because of this statement, an ACL should have at least one permit statement in it; otherwise, the ACL blocks all traffic.

Outbound ACL Logic

Figure 9-34 shows the logic for an outbound ACL.

Before a packet is forwarded to an outbound interface, the router checks the routing table to see if the packet is routable. If the packet is not routable, it is dropped and is not tested against the ACEs. Next, the router checks to see whether the outbound interface is grouped to an ACL. If the outbound interface is not grouped to an ACL, the packet can be sent to the output buffer. Examples of outbound ACL operation are as follows:

- **No ACL applied to the interface:** If the outbound interface is not grouped to an outbound ACL, the packet is sent directly to the outbound interface.

- **ACL applied to the interface:** If the outbound interface is grouped to an outbound ACL, the packet is not sent out on the outbound interface until it is tested by the combination of ACEs that are associated with that interface. Based on the ACL tests, the packet is permitted or denied.

For outbound lists, `permit` means to send the packet to the output buffer, and `deny` means to discard the packet.

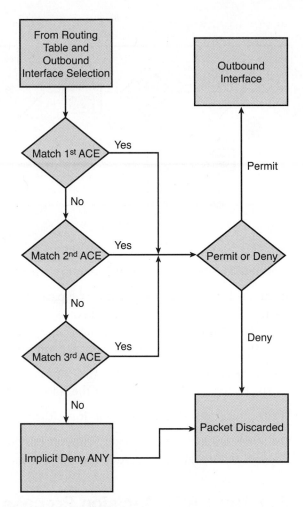

Figure 9-34   Outbound ACL Process

ACL Logic Operations (9.4.1.2)

Figure 9-35 shows the logic of routing and ACL processes.

When a packet arrives at a router interface, the router process is the same, regardless of whether ACLs are used. As a frame enters an interface, the router checks to see whether the destination Layer 2 address matches its interface Layer 2 address, or whether the frame is a broadcast frame.

If the frame address is accepted, the frame information is stripped off and the router checks for an ACL on the inbound interface. If an ACL exists, the packet is tested against the statements in the list.

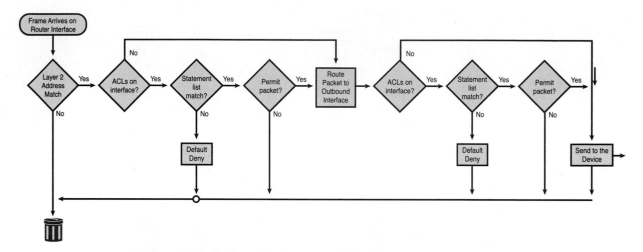

Figure 9-35 ACL and Routing Processes in a Router

If the packet matches a statement, the packet is either permitted or denied. If the packet is accepted, it is then checked against routing table entries to determine the destination interface. If a routing table entry exists for the destination, the packet is then switched to the outgoing interface; otherwise, the packet is dropped.

Next, the router checks whether the outgoing interface has an ACL. If an ACL exists, the packet is tested against the statements in the list.

If the packet matches a statement, it is either permitted or denied.

If there is no ACL or the packet is permitted, the packet is encapsulated in the new Layer 2 protocol and forwarded out the interface to the next device.

Standard ACL Decision Process (9.4.1.3)

Standard ACLs examine only the source IPv4 address. The destination of the packet and the ports involved are not considered.

The decision process for a standard ACL is mapped in Figure 9-36.

Cisco IOS Software tests addresses against the conditions in the ACL one by one. The first match determines whether the software accepts or rejects the address. Because the software stops testing conditions after the first match, the order of the conditions is critical. If no conditions match, the address is rejected.

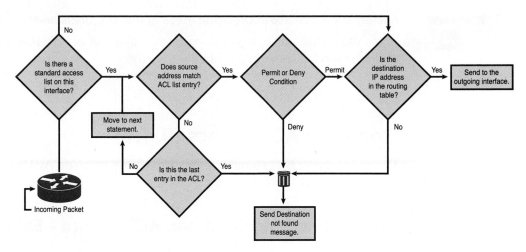

Figure 9-36   How a Standard ACL Works

Extended ACL Decision Process (9.4.1.4)

Figure 9-37 shows the logical decision path used by an extended ACL built to filter on source and destination addresses, and protocol and port numbers.

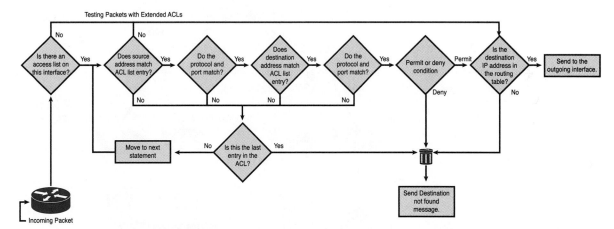

Figure 9-37   Testing Packets with Extended ACLs

In this example, the ACL first filters on the source address and then on the port and protocol of the source. It then filters on the destination address and then on the port and protocol of the destination, and makes a final permit or deny decision.

Recall that entries in ACLs are processed one after the other, so a No decision does not necessarily equal a Deny. As you go through the logical decision path, note that a No means go to the next entry until a condition is matched.

Interactive Graphic

Activity 9.4.1.5: Place in Order the Steps of the ACL Decision-Making Process

Go to the course online to check your understanding of how routers process ACLs. Click the second graphic to continue the activity.

Common ACL Errors (9.4.2)

This next section goes through some of the more common ACL errors and how they can be corrected.

Troubleshooting Common ACL Errors - Example 1 (9.4.2.1)

Using the **show** commands described earlier reveals most of the more common ACL errors. The most common errors are entering ACEs in the wrong order and not applying adequate criteria to the ACL rules.

In Figure 9-38, host 192.168.10.10 has no connectivity with 192.168.30.12.

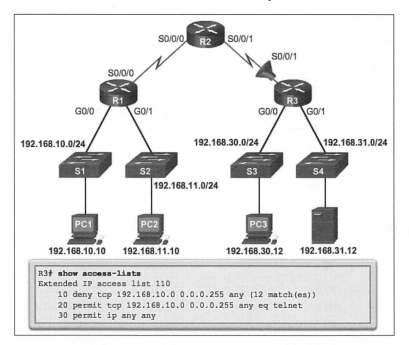

Figure 9-38 ACL Network Topology

When viewing the output of the **show access-lists** command, matches are shown for the first `deny` statement. This is an indicator that this statement has been matched by traffic.

Solution: Look at the order of the ACEs. Host 192.168.10.10 has no connectivity with 192.168.30.12 because of the order of rule 10 in the access list. Because the router processes ACLs from the top down, statement 10 denies host 192.168.10.10, so statement 20 can never be matched. Statements 10 and 20 should be reversed. The last line allows all other non-TCP traffic that falls under IP (ICMP, UDP, and so on).

Troubleshooting Common ACL Errors - Example 2 (9.4.2.2)

In Figure 9-39, the 192.168.10.0/24 network cannot use TFTP to connect to the 192.168.30.0/24 network.

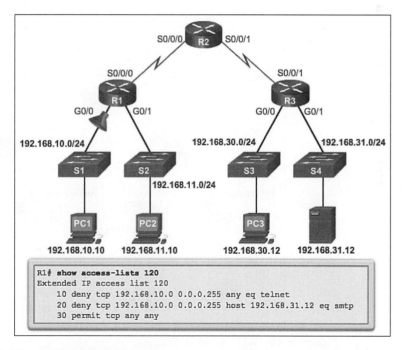

Figure 9-39   ACL Network Topology

Solution: The 192.168.10.0/24 network cannot use TFTP to connect to the 192.168.30.0/24 network because TFTP uses the transport protocol UDP. Statement 30 in access list 120 allows all other TCP traffic. However, because TFTP uses UDP instead of TCP, it is implicitly denied. Recall that the implied `deny any` statement does not appear in **show access-lists** output and therefore matches are not shown.

Statement 30 should be **ip any any**.

This ACL works whether it is applied to G0/0 of R1, S0/0/1 of R3, or S0/0/0 of R2 in the incoming direction. However, based on the rule about placing extended ACLs closest to the source, the best option is to place it inbound on G0/0 of R1 because it allows undesirable traffic to be filtered without crossing the network infrastructure.

Troubleshooting Common ACL Errors - Example 3 (9.4.2.3)

In Figure 9-40, the 192.168.11.0/24 network can use Telnet to connect to 192.168.30.0/24, but according to company policy, this connection should not be allowed. The results of the **show access-lists 130** command indicate that the permit statement has been matched.

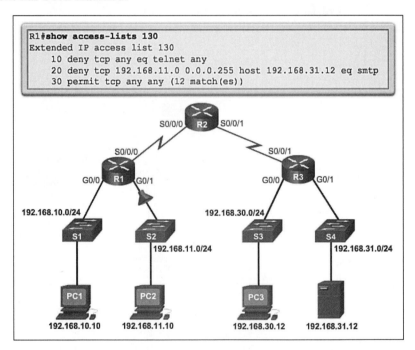

Figure 9-40 ACL Network Topology

Solution: The 192.168.11.0/24 network can use Telnet to connect to the 192.168.30.0/24 network because the Telnet port number in statement 10 of access list 130 is listed in the wrong position in the ACL statement. Statement 10 currently denies any source packet with a port number that is equal to Telnet. To deny Telnet traffic inbound on G0/1, deny the destination port number that is equal to Telnet; for example, **deny tcp any any eq telnet**.

Troubleshooting Common ACL Errors - Example 4 (9.4.2.4)

In Figure 9-41, host 192.168.30.12 can Telnet to connect to 192.168.31.12, but company policy states that this connection should not be allowed. Output from the **show access-lists 140** command indicates that the `permit` statement has been matched.

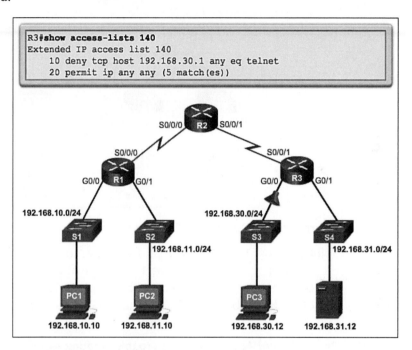

```
R3#show access-lists 140
Extended IP access list 140
    10 deny tcp host 192.168.30.1 any eq telnet
    20 permit ip any any (5 match(es))
```

Figure 9-41   ACL Network Topology

Solution: Host 192.168.30.12 can use Telnet to connect to 192.168.31.12 because there are no rules that deny host 192.168.30.12 or its network as the source. Statement 10 of access list 140 denies the router interface on which traffic enters the router. The host IPv4 address in statement 10 should be 192.168.30.12.

Troubleshooting Common ACL Errors - Example 5 (9.4.2.5)

In Figure 9-42, host 192.168.30.12 can use Telnet to connect to 192.168.31.12, but according to the security policy, this connection should not be allowed. Output from the **show access-lists 150** command indicate that no matches have occurred for the `deny` statement as expected.

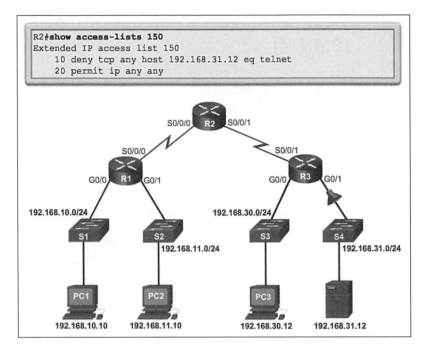

```
R2#show access-lists 150
Extended IP access list 150
    10 deny tcp any host 192.168.31.12 eq telnet
    20 permit ip any any
```

Figure 9-42 ACL Network Topology

Solution: Host 192.168.30.12 can use Telnet to connect to 192.168.31.12 because of the direction in which access list 150 is applied to the G0/1 interface. Statement 10 denies any source address to connect to host 192.168.31.12 using Telnet. However, this filter should be applied outbound on G0/1 to filter correctly.

Packet Tracer Activity 9.4.2.6: Troubleshooting ACLs

Scenario

Create a network that has the following three policies implemented:

- Hosts from the 192.168.0.0/24 network are unable to access any TCP service of Server3.

- Hosts from the 10.0.0.0/8 network are unable to access the HTTP service of Server1.

- Hosts from the 172.16.0.0/16 network are unable to access the FTP service of Server2.

Go to the course online to complete this Packet Tracer activity.

Lab 9.4.2.7: Troubleshooting ACL Configuration and Placement

In this lab, you will complete the following objectives:

- Part 1: Build the Network and Configure Basic Device Settings
- Part 2: Troubleshoot Internal Access
- Part 3: Troubleshoot Remote Access

Packet Tracer Activity 9.4.2.8: Skills Integration Challenge

In this challenge activity, you will finish the addressing scheme, configure routing, and implement named access control lists.

Go to the course online to complete this Packet Tracer activity.

IPv6 ACLs (9.5)

When working with IPv6 ACLs, the logic behind creating them is similar to the logic found in IPv4 logic. These next sections deal with IPv6 ACLs.

Type of IPv6 ACLs (9.5.1.1)

IPv6 ACLs are similar to IPv4 ACLs in both operation and configuration. Being familiar with IPv4 access lists makes IPv6 ACLs easy to understand and configure.

In IPv4, there are two types of ACLs, standard and extended. Both types of ACLs can be either numbered or named ACLs.

With IPv6, there is only one type of ACL, which is equivalent to an IPv4 extended named ACL. There are no numbered ACLs in IPv6.

To summarize, IPv6 ACLs are

- Named ACLs only
- Equivalent to the functionality of an IPv4 Extended ACL

An IPv4 ACL and an IPv6 ACL cannot share the same name.

Comparing IPv4 and IPv6 ACLs (9.5.1.2)

Although IPv4 and IPv6 ACLs are similar, there are three significant differences between them.

- **Applying an IPv6 ACL**

  The first difference is the command used to apply an IPv6 ACL to an interface. IPv4 uses the command **ip access-group** to apply an IPv4 ACL to an IPv4 interface. IPv6 uses the **ipv6 traffic-filter** command to perform the same function for IPv6 interfaces.

- **No Wildcard Masks**

  Unlike IPv4 ACLs, IPv6 ACLs do not use wildcard masks. Instead, the prefix-length is used to indicate how much of an IPv6 source or destination address should be matched.

- **Additional Default Statements**

  The last major difference has to do with the addition of two implicit `permit` statements at the end of each IPv6 access list. At the end of every IPv4 standard or extended ACL is an implicit **deny any** or **deny any any**. IPv6 includes a similar **deny ipv6 any any** statement at the end of each IPv6 ACL. The difference is IPv6 also includes two other implicit statements by default:

  - **permit icmp any any nd-na**
  - **permit icmp any any nd-ns**

These two statements allow the router to participate in the IPv6 equivalent of ARP for IPv4. Recall that ARP is used in IPv4 to resolve Layer 3 addresses to Layer 2 MAC addresses. As shown in Figure 9-43, IPv6 uses ICMP Neighbor Discovery (ND) messages to accomplish the same thing. ND uses Neighbor Solicitation (NS) and Neighbor Advertisement (NA) messages.

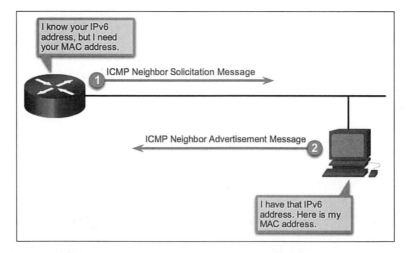

Figure 9-43   IPv6 Neighbor Discovery

ND messages are encapsulated in IPv6 packets and require the services of the IPv6 network layer, whereas ARP for IPv4 does not use Layer 3. Because IPv6 uses the Layer 3 service for neighbor discovery, IPv6 ACLs need to implicitly permit ND packets to be sent and received on an interface. Specifically, both Neighbor Discovery - Neighbor Advertisement (nd-na) and Neighbor Discovery - Neighbor Solicitation (nd-ns) messages are permitted.

Configuring IPv6 Topology (9.5.2.1)

Figure 9-44 shows the topology that will be used for configuring IPv6 ACLs.

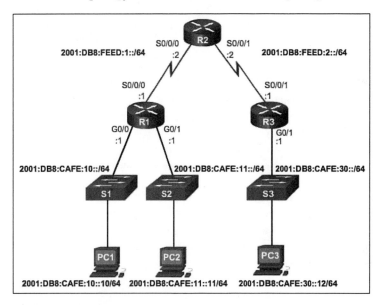

Figure 9-44   IPv6 Topology

The topology is similar to the previous IPv4 topology except for the IPv6 addressing scheme. There are three 2001:DB8:CAFE::/64 subnets: 2001:DB8:CAFE:10::/64, 2001:DB8:CAFE:11::/64, and 2001:DB8:CAFE:30::/64. Two serial networks connect the three routers: 2001:DB8:FEED:1::/64 and 2001:DB8:FEED:2::/64.

The following output shows the IPv6 address configuration for R1.

```
R1(config)# interface g0/0
R1(config-if)# ipv6 address 2001:db8:cafe:10::1/64
R1(config-if)# exit
R1(config)# interface s0/0/0
R1(config-if)# ipv6 address 2001:db8:feed:1::1/64
R1(config)# interface g0/1
R1(config-if)# ipv6 address 2001:db8:cafe:11::1/64
R1(config-if)# end
```

```
R1# show ipv6 interface brief
GigabitEthernet0/0        [up/up]
        FE80::FE99:47FF:FE75:C3E0
        2001:DB8:CAFE:10::1
GigabitEthernet0/1        [up/up]
        FE80::FE99:47FF:FE75:C3E1
        2001:DB8:CAFE:11::1
Serial0/0/0               [up/up]
        FE80::FE99:47FF:FE75:C3E0
        2001:DB8:FEED:1::1
<output omitted>
R1#
```

The **show ipv6 interface brief** command is used to verify the address and the state of the interface.

The following output shows the IPv6 address configuration for R2.

```
R2(config)# interface s0/0/0
R2(config-if)# ipv6 address 2001:db8:feed:1::2/64
R2(config-if)# exit
R2(config)# interface s0/0/1
R2(config-if)# ipv6 address 2001:db8:feed:2::2/64
R2(config-if)# end
R2# show ipv6 interface brief
Serial0/0/0        [up/up]
        FE80::FE99:47FF:FE75:78A0
        2001:DB8:FEED:1::2
Serial0/0/1        [up/up]
        FE80::FE99:47FF:FE75:C3E0
        2001:DB8:FEED:2::2
<output omitted>
R2#
```

The **show ipv6 interface brief** command is used to verify the address and the state of the interface.

The following output shows the IPv6 address configuration for R3.

```
R3(config)# interface s0/0/1
R3(config-if)# ipv6 address 2001:db8:feed:2::1/64
R3(config-if)# exit
R3(config)# interface g0/0
R3(config-if)# ipv6 address 2001:db8:cafe:30::1/64
R3(config-if)# end
R3# show ipv6 interface brief
GigabitEthernet0/0/0    [up/up]
        FE80::FE99:47FF:FE71:7A20
```

```
        2001:DB8:CAFE:30::1
Serial0/0/1              [up/up]
        FE80::FE99:47FF:FE71:7A20
        2001:DB8:FEED:2::1
<output omitted>
R3#
```

The **show ipv6 interface brief** command is used to verify the address and the state of the interface.

Note

The **no shutdown** command and the **clock rate** command are not shown.

Configuring IPv6 ACLs (9.5.2.2)

In IPv6, there are only named ACLs. The configuration is similar to that of an IPv4 extended named ACL.

The following output along with Table 9-12 show the command syntax for IPv6 ACLs. The syntax is similar to the syntax used for an IPv4 extended ACL. One significant difference is the use of the IPv6 prefix-length instead of an IPv4 wildcard mask.

```
R1(config)# ipv6 access-list access-list-name
R1(config-ipv6-acl)# deny | permit protocol {source-ipv6-prefix/prefix-length | any
    | host source-ipv6-address} [operator [port-number]] {destination-ipv6-prefix/
    prefix-length | any | host destination-ipv6-address} [operator [port-number]]
```

Table 9-12 ipv6 access-list access-list-name Command

Parameter	Description
**deny	permit**	Specifies whether to deny or permit the packet.
protocol	Enter the name or number of an Internet protocol or an integer representing an IPv6 protocol number.
source-ipv6-prefix/ prefix-length	The source or destination IPv6 network or class of networks for which to set deny or permit conditions.
destination-ipv6- address	
any	Enter **any** as an abbreviation for the IPv6 prefix ::/0. This matches all addresses.

continues

Parameter	Description
host	For **host** *source-ipv6-address* or *destination-ipv6-address*, enter the source or destination IPv6 host address for which to set deny or permit conditions.
operator	(Optional) An operand that compares the source or destination ports of the specified protocols. Operands are lt (less than) gt (greater than) eq (equal) neq (not equal) range
port-number	(Optional) A decimal number or the name of a TCP or UDP port for filtering TCP or UDP, respectively.

There are three basic steps to configure an IPv6 ACL:

Step 1.   From global configuration mode, use the **ipv6 access-list** *name* command to create an IPv6 ACL. Like IPv4 named ACLs, IPv6 names are alphanumeric, case-sensitive, and must be unique. Unlike IPv4, there is no need for a standard or extended option.

Step 2.   From the named ACL configuration mode, use the **permit** or **deny** statements to specify one or more conditions to determine if a packet is forwarded or dropped.

Step 3   Return to privileged EXEC mode with the **end** command.

The following output demonstrates the steps to create an IPv6 ACL with a simple example based on the previous topology.

```
R1(config)# ipv6 access-list NO-R3-LAN-ACCESS
R1(config-ipv6-acl)# deny ipv6 2001:db8:cafe:30::/64 any
R1(config-ipv6-acl)# permit ipv6 any any
R1(config-ipv6-acl)# end
R1#
```

The first statement names the IPv6 access list NO-R3-LAN-ACCESS. Similar to IPv4 named ACLs, capitalizing IPv6 ACL names is not required, but makes them stand out when viewing the running-config output.

The second statement denies all IPv6 packets from the 2001:DB8:CAFE:30::/64 destined for any IPv6 network. The third statement allows all other IPv6 packets.

Figure 9-45 shows the ACL in context with the topology.

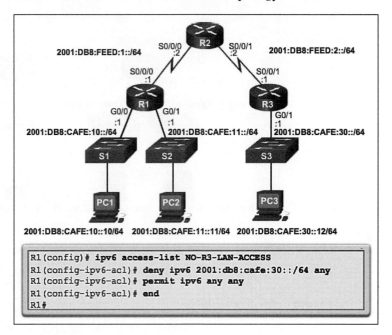

Figure 9-45   R3 IPv6 Configuration and Topology

Applying an IPv6 ACL to an Interface (9.5.2.3)

After an IPv6 ACL is configured, it is linked to an interface using the **ipv6 traffic-filter** command:

```
Router(config-if)# ipv6 traffic-filter access-list-name {in | out}
```

Figure 9-46 shows the NO-R3-LAN-ACCESS ACL configured previously and the commands used to apply the IPv6 ACL inbound to the S0/0/0 interface. Applying the ACL to the inbound S0/0/0 interface will deny packets from 2001:DB8:CAFE:30::/64 to both of the LANs on R1.

To remove an ACL from an interface, first enter the **no ipv6 traffic-filter** command on the interface, and then enter the global **no ipv6 access-list** command to remove the access list.

Note

IPv4 and IPv6 both use the **ip access-class** command to apply an access list to VTY ports.

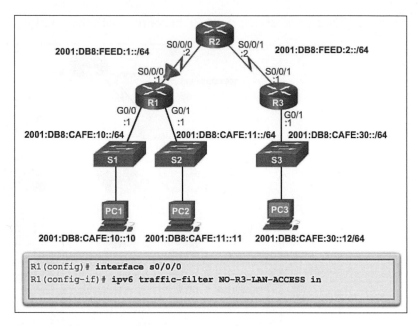

Figure 9-46   IPv6 Topology

IPv6 ACL Examples (9.5.2.4)

Here are two examples of IPv6 ACLs: **Deny FTP** and **Restricted Access**.

The topology for the examples is shown in Figure 9-47.

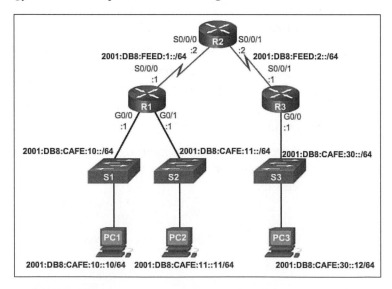

Figure 9-47   IPv6 Topology

Deny FTP

In the following output, router R1 is configured with an IPv6 access list to deny FTP traffic to 2001:DB8:CAFE:11::/64. Ports for both FTP data (port 20) and FTP control (port 21) need to be blocked. Because the filter is applied inbound on the G0/0 interface on R1, only traffic from the 2001:DB8:CAFE:10::/64 network will be denied.

```
R1(config)# ipv6 access-list NO-FTP-TO-11
R1(config-ipv6-acl)# deny tcp any 2001:db8:cafe:11::/64 eq ftp
R1(config-ipv6-acl)# deny tcp any 2001:db8:cafe:11::/64 eq ftp-data
R1(config-ipv6-acl)# permit ipv6 any any
R1(config-ipv6-acl)# exit
R1(config)# interface g0/0
R1(config-if)# ipv6 traffic-filter NO-FTP-TO-11 in
R1(config-if)#
```

Restricted Access

In the second example shown in Figure 9-48, an IPv6 ACL is configured to give the LAN on R3 limited access to the LANs on R1. Comments are added in the configuration to document the ACL.

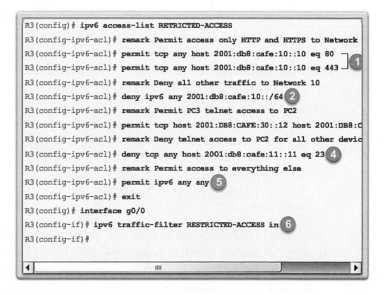

Figure 9-48 Restricted Access

Activity 9.5.2.4: IPv6 ACL Examples – Restricted Access

Go to the course online and use the slider bar in the third graphic to see the entire output of the **ipv6 access-list RESTRICTED-ACCESS** ACL.

The following features have been labeled in the ACL:

1. The first two permit statements allow access from any device to the web server at 2001:DB8:CAFE:10::10.

2. All other devices are denied access to the 2001:DB8:CAFE:10::/64 network.

3. PC3 at 2001:DB8:CAFE:30::12 is permitted Telnet access to PC2, which has the IPv6 address 2001:DB8:CAFE:11::11.

4. All other devices are denied Telnet access to PC2.

5. All other IPv6 traffic is permitted to all other destinations.

6. The IPv6 access list is applied to interface G0/0 in the inbound direction, so only the 2001:DB8:CAFE:30::/64 network is affected.

Verifying IPv6 ACLs (9.5.2.5)

The commands used to verify an IPv6 access list are similar to those used for IPv4 ACLs. Using these commands, the IPv6 access list RESTRICTED-ACCESS that was configured previously can be verified. The following output shows the output of the **show ipv6 interface** command. The output confirms that RESTRICTED-ACCESS ACL is configured inbound on the G0/0 interface.

```
R3# show ipv6 interface g0/0
GigabitEthernet0/0 is up, line protocol is up
   Global unicast address(es):
      2001:DB8:CAFE:30::1, subnet is 2001:DB8:CAFE:30::/64
   Input features: Access List
   Inbound access list RESTRICTED-ACCESS
<output omitted>
```

As shown in the following output, the **show access-lists** command displays all access lists on the router including both IPv4 and IPv6 ACLs.

```
R3#  show access-lists
IPv6 access list RESTRICTED-ACCESS
     permit tcp any host 2001:DB8:CAFE:10::10 eq www sequence 20
     permit tcp any host 2001:DB8:CAFE:10::10 eq 443 sequence 30
     deny ipv6 any 2001:DB8:CAFE:10::/64 SEQUENCE 50
     permit tcp host 2001:DB8:CAFE:30::12 host 2001:DB8:CAFE:11::11
```

```
            eq telnet sequence 70
            deny tcp any host 2001:DB8:CAFE:11::11 eq telnet sequence 90
            permit ipv6 any any sequence 110
      R3#
```

Notice that with IPv6 ACLs the sequence numbers occur at the end of the statement and not the beginning as with IPv4 access lists. Although the statements appear in the order they were entered, they are not always incremented by 10. This is because the remark statements that were entered use a sequence number but are not displayed in the output of the **show access-lists** command.

Similar to extended ACLs for IPv4, IPv6 access lists are displayed and processed in the order the statements are entered. Remember, IPv4 standard ACLs use an internal logic, which changes their order and processing sequence.

As shown in the following output, the output from the **show running-config** command includes all the ACEs and remark statements. Remark statements can come before or after **permit** or **deny** statements but should be consistent in their placement.

```
R3# show running-config
<output omitted>
ipv6 access-list RESTRICTED-ACCESS
 remark Permit access only HTTP and HTTPS to Network 10
 permit tcp any host 2001:DB8:CAFE:10::10 eq www
 permit tcp any host 2001:DB8:CAFE:10::10 eq 443
 remark Deny all other traffic to Network 10
 deny ipv6 any 2001:DB8:CAFE:10::/64
 remark Permit PC3 telnet access to PC2
 permit tcp host 2001:DB8:CAFE:30::12 host 2001:DB8:CAFE:11::11
 eq telnet
 remark Deny telnet access to PC2 for all other devices
 deny tcp any host 2001:DB8:CAFE:11::11 eq telnet
 remark Permit access to everything else
 permit ipv6 any any
```

Packet Tracer Activity 9.5.2.6: Configuring IPv6 ACLs

Objectives

- Part 1: Configure, Apply, and Verify an IPv6 ACL

- Part 2: Configure, Apply, and Verify a Second IPv6 ACL

Go to the course online to complete this Packet Tracer activity.

Lab 9.5.2.7: Configuring and Verifying IPv6 ACLs

In this lab, you will complete the following objectives:

- Part 1: Set Up the Topology and Initialize Devices
- Part 2: Configure Devices and Verify Connectivity
- Part 3: Configure and Verify IPv6 ACLs
- Part 4: Edit IPv6 ACLs

Summary (9.6)

Class Activity 9.6.1.1: FTP Denied

Scenario

It was recently reported that viruses are on the rise within your small- to medium-sized business network. Your network administrator has been tracking network performance and has determined that one particular host is constantly downloading files from a remote FTP server. This host just may be the virus source perpetuating throughout the network!

Use Packet Tracer to complete this activity. Write a named ACL to deny the host access to the FTP server. Apply the ACL to the most effective interface on the router.

To complete the physical topology, you must use

- One PC host station

- Two switches

- One Cisco 1941 series Integrated Services Router

- One server

Using the Packet Tracer text tool, record the ACL you prepared. Validate that the ACL works to deny access to the FTP server by trying to access the FTP server's address. Observe what happens while in simulation mode.

Save your file and be prepared to share it with another student, or with the entire class.

Go to the lab manual to complete this class activity.

By default, a router does not filter traffic. Traffic that enters the router is routed solely based on information within the routing table.

Packet filtering controls access to a network by analyzing the incoming and outgoing packets and passing or dropping them based on criteria such as the source IP address, destination IP addresses, and the protocol carried within the packet. A packet-filtering router uses rules to determine whether to permit or deny traffic. A router can also perform packet filtering at Layer 4, the transport layer.

An ACL is a sequential list of permit or deny statements. The last statement of an ACL is always an implicit **deny**, which blocks all traffic. To prevent the implied **deny any** statement at the end of the ACL from blocking all traffic, the **permit ip any any** statement can be added.

When network traffic passes through an interface configured with an ACL, the router compares the information within the packet against each entry, in sequential order, to determine if the packet matches one of the statements. If a match is found, the packet is processed accordingly.

ACLs are configured to apply to inbound traffic or to apply to outbound traffic.

Standard ACLs can be used to permit or deny traffic only from a source IPv4 address. The destination of the packet and the ports involved are not evaluated. The basic rule for placing a standard ACL is to place it close to the destination.

Extended ACLs filter packets based on several attributes: protocol type, source or destination IPv4 address, and source or destination ports. The basic rule for placing an extended ACL is to place it as close to the source as possible.

The **access-list** global configuration command defines a standard ACL with a number in the range of 1 through 99 and 1300 through 1999 or an extended ACL with numbers in the range of 100 through 199 and 2000 through 2699. Both standard and extended ACLs can also be named. The **ip access-list standard** *name* is used to create a standard named ACL, whereas the command **ip access-list extended** *name* is for an extended access list. IPv4 ACEs include the use of wildcard masks.

After an ACL is configured, it is linked to an interface using the **ip access-group** command in interface configuration mode. Remember the three Ps: one ACL per protocol, per direction, per interface.

To remove an ACL from an interface, first enter the **no ip access-group** command on the interface, and then enter the global **no access-list** command to remove the entire ACL.

The **show running-config** and **show access-lists** commands are used to verify ACL configuration. The **show ip interface** command is used to verify the ACL on the interface and the direction in which it was applied.

The **access-class** command configured in line configuration mode restricts incoming and outgoing connections between a particular VTY and the addresses in an access list.

Like IPv4 named ACLs, IPv6 names are alphanumeric, case-sensitive, and must be unique. Unlike IPv4, there is no need for a standard or extended option.

From global configuration mode, use the **ipv6 access-list** *name* command to create an IPv6 ACL. Unlike IPv4 ACLs, IPv6 ACLs do not use wildcard masks. Instead, the prefix-length is used to indicate how much of an IPv6 source or destination address should be matched.

After an IPv6 ACL is configured, it is linked to an interface using the **ipv6 traffic-filter** command.

Practice

The following activities provide practice with the topics introduced in this chapter. The Labs and Class Activities are available in the companion *Routing and Switching Essentials Lab Manual* (978-1-58713-320-6). The Packet Tracer Activities PKA files are found in the online course.

Class Activities

Class Activity 9.0.1.2: Permit Me to Assist You

Class Activity 9.6.1.1: FTP Denied

Labs

Lab 9.2.2.7: Configuring and Verifying Standard ACLs

Lab 9.2.3.4: Configuring and Verifying VTY Restrictions

Lab 9.3.2.13: Configuring and Verifying Extended ACLs

Lab 9.4.2.7: Troubleshooting ACL Configuration and Placement

Lab 9.5.2.7: Configuring and Verifying IPv6 ACLs

Packet Tracer Activities

Packet Tracer Activity 9.1.1.6: ACL Demonstration

Packet Tracer Activity 9.2.1.10: Configuring Standard ACLs

Packet Tracer Activity 9.2.1.11: Configuring Named Standard ACLs

Packet Tracer Activity 9.2.3.3: Configuring an ACL on VTY Lines

Packet Tracer Activity 9.3.2.10: Configuring Extended ACLs – Scenario 1

Packet Tracer Activity 9.3.2.11: Configuring Extended ACLs – Scenario 2

Packet Tracer Activity 9.3.2.12: Configuring Extended ACLs – Scenario 3

Packet Tracer Activity 9.4.2.6: Troubleshooting ACLs

Packet Tracer Activity 9.4.2.8: Skills Integration Challenge

Packet Tracer Activity 9.5.2.6: Configuring IPv6 ACL

Check Your Understanding Questions

Complete all the review questions listed here to test your understanding of the topics and concepts in this chapter. The appendix, "Answers to the 'Check Your Understanding' Questions," lists the answers.

1. What range of IP addresses is represented by the network and wildcard mask 192.168.70.0 0.0.0.127?

   A. 192.168.70.0 to 192.168.70.127

   B. 192.168.70.0 to 192.168.70.255

   C. 192.168.70.0 to 192.168.70.63

   D. 192.168.70.0 to 192.168.71.255

2. What range of IP addresses is represented by the network and wildcard mask 192.168.70.0 0.0.1.255?

   A. 192.168.70.0 to 192.168.71.255

   B. 192.168.70.0 to 192.168.70.255

   C. 192.168.70.0 to 192.168.73.255

   D. 192.168.70.0 to 192.168.76.255

3. What range of IP addresses is represented by the network and wildcard mask 172.16.32.0 0.0.15.255?

   A. 172.16.32.0 to 172.16.47.255

   B. 172.16.32.0 to 172.16.34.255

   C. 172.16.32.0 to 172.16.63.255

   D. 172.16.32.0 to 172.16.240.255

4. Which set of access control entries would allow all users on the 192.168.10.0/24 network to access a web server that is located at 172.17.80.1, but would not allow them to use Telnet?

   A. access-list 103 deny tcp host 192.168.10.0 any eq 23
      access-list 103 permit tcp host 192.168.10.1 eq 80

   B. access-list 103 permit 192.168.10.0 0.0.0.255 host 172.17.80.1
      access-list 103 deny tcp 192.168.10.0 0.0.0.255 any eq telnet

   C. access-list 103 permit tcp 192.168.10.0 0.0.0.255 host 172.17.80.1 eq 80
      access-list 103 deny tcp 192.168.10.0 0.0.0.255 any eq 23

   D. access-list 103 permit tcp 192.168.10.0 0.0.0.255 any eq 80
      access-list 103 deny tcp 192.168.10.0 0.0.0.255 any eq 23

5. In applying an ACL to a router interface, which traffic is designated as outbound?

   A. Traffic that is coming from the source IP address into the router

   B. Traffic that is leaving the router and going toward the destination host

   C. Traffic that is going from the destination IP address into the router

   D. Traffic for which the router can find no routing table entry

6. In the creation of an IPv6 ACL, what is the purpose of the implicit final command entries **permit icmp any any nd-na** and **permit icmp any any nd-ns**?

   A. To allow IPv6 to MAC address resolution

   B. To allow forwarding of IPv6 multicast packets

   C. To allow automatic address configuration

   D. To allow forwarding of ICMPv6 packets

7. What is the effect of the **established** parameter in an extended ACL?

   A. Blocks all incoming traffic from reaching a network

   B. Allows external traffic into a network only if it is part of an existing connection with an internal host

   C. Allows external sources to send unsolicited requests for information to source IP addresses in the network

   D. Allows traffic from a permitted source address to go to any destination outside the network

8. ACLs are used primarily to filter traffic. What are two additional uses of ACLs? (Choose two.)

   A. Specifying source addresses for authentication

   B. Specifying internal hosts for NAT

   C. Identifying traffic for QoS

   D. Reorganizing traffic into VLANs

   E. Filtering VTP packets

9. Which two statements are correct about extended ACLs? (Choose two.)

   A. Extended ACLs use a number range from 1 through 99.

   B. Extended ACLs end with an implicit permit statement.

   C. Extended ACLs evaluate the source and destination addresses.

   D. Port numbers can be used to add greater definition to an ACL.

   E. Multiple ACLs can be placed on the same interface as long as they are in the same direction.

10. Which command is used to activate an IPv6 ACL named ENG_ACL on an interface so that the router filters traffic prior to accessing the routing table?

    A. **access-group ipv6_ENG_ACL in**

    B. **access-group ipv6_ENG_ACL out**

    C. **ipv6 access-class ENG_ACL in**

    D. **ipv6 access-class ENG_ACL out**

    E. **ipv6 traffic-filter ENG_ACL in**

    F. **ipv6 traffic-filter ENG_ACL out**

CHAPTER 10

DHCP

Objectives

Upon completion of this chapter, you will be able to answer the following questions:

- What is the purpose of DHCP?

- How is DHCPv4 different from DHCPv6?

- How do you configure a router for DHCPv4 or DHCPv6?

- What do you do if a DHCP server is on a different network than the network device needing IP addressing configuration?

- What are the three methods used by a client to obtain an IPv6 address?

- What is SLAAC?

- What are the most important **show** commands used when troubleshooting DHCP?

- What are the most common problems found when implementing DHCP?

Key Terms

This chapter uses the following key terms. You can find the definitions in the Glossary.

Dynamic Host Configuration Protocol (DHCP)   page 640

DHCPv4   page 640

DHCPv6   page 640

DHCPDISCOVER   page 643

DHCPOFFER   page 643

DHCPREQUEST   page 643

DHCPACK   page 644

DHCPv4 relay agent   page 657

Stateless Address Autoconfiguration (SLAAC)   page 666

Router Solicitation (RS) message   page 666

Router Advertisement (RA) message   page 666

Duplicate Address Detection (DAD)   page 668

stateless DHCPv6   page 670

stateful DHCPv6   page 671

DHCPv6 relay agent   page 682

Introduction (10.0.1.1)

Every device that connects to a network needs a unique IP address. Network administrators assign static IP addresses to routers, servers, printers, and other network devices whose locations (physical and logical) are not likely to change. These are usually devices that provide services to users and devices on the network; therefore, the addresses assigned to them should remain constant. Additionally, static addresses enable administrators to manage these devices remotely. It is easier for network administrators to access a device when they can easily determine its IP address.

However, computers and users in an organization often change locations, physically and logically. It can be difficult and time consuming for administrators to assign new IP addresses every time an employee moves. Additionally, for mobile employees working from remote locations, manually setting the correct network parameters can be challenging. Even for desktop clients, the manual assignment of IP addresses and other addressing information presents an administrative burden, especially as the network grows.

Dynamic Host Configuration Protocol (DHCP) is a protocol used for deploying IP address-related configuration information to network devices. Introducing a DHCP server to the local network simplifies IP address assignment to both desktop and mobile devices. Using a centralized DHCP server enables organizations to administer all dynamic IP address assignments from a single server. This practice makes IP address management more effective and ensures consistency across the organization, including branch offices.

DHCP is available for both IPv4 (*DHCPv4*) and for IPv6 (*DHCPv6*). This chapter explores the functionality, configuration, and troubleshooting of both DHCPv4 and DHCPv6.

Class Activity 10.0.1.2: Own or Lease?

This chapter presents the concept of using the DHCP process in a small- to medium-sized business network. This modeling activity describes how very basic wireless ISR devices work using the DHCP process.

Visit `http://ui.linksys.com/WRT54GL/4.30.0/Setup.htm`, which is a web-based simulator that helps you learn to configure DHCP using a Linksys wireless 54GL router. To the right of the simulator (in the blue description column), you can click `More` to read information about configuring DHCP settings on this particular integrated services router (ISR) simulator.

Practice configuring the ISRs:

- Hostname
- Local IP address with subnet mask

- DHCP (enable and disable)

- Starting IP address

- Maximum number of users to receive an IP DHCP address

- Lease time

- Time zone (use yours or a favorite as an alternative)

When you have completed configuring the settings as listed for this assignment, take a screen shot of your settings by using the **PrtScrn** key command. Copy and place your screen shot into a word processing document. Save it and be prepared to discuss your configuration choices with the class.

Dynamic Host Configuration Protocol v4 (10.1)

DHCPv4 is the most widely used protocol for IP addressing in the world. You might be familiar with this protocol due to your home network. A wireless router commonly provides IP addresses to mobile devices using DHCPv4. Let's take a deeper look into how DHCP works.

Introducing DHCPv4 (10.1.1.1)

DHCPv4 assigns IPv4 addresses and other network configuration information dynamically. Because desktop clients typically make up the bulk of network nodes, DHCPv4 is an extremely useful and timesaving tool for network administrators.

A dedicated DHCPv4 server is scalable and relatively easy to manage. However, in a small branch or SOHO location, a Cisco router can be configured to provide DHCPv4 services without the need for a dedicated server. A Cisco IOS feature set (called "Easy IP") offers an optional, full-featured DHCPv4 server.

DHCPv4 includes three different address allocation mechanisms to provide flexibility when assigning IP addresses:

- **Manual Allocation:** The administrator assigns a pre-allocated IPv4 address to the client, and DHCPv4 communicates only the IPv4 address to the device.

- **Automatic Allocation:** DHCPv4 automatically assigns a static IPv4 address permanently to a device, selecting it from a pool of available addresses. There is no lease, and the address is permanently assigned to the device.

- **Dynamic Allocation:** DHCPv4 dynamically assigns, or leases, an IPv4 address from a pool of addresses for a limited period of time chosen by the server, or until the client no longer needs the address.

Dynamic allocation is the most commonly used DHCPv4 mechanism and is the focus of this section. When using dynamic allocation, clients lease the information from the server for an administratively defined period, as shown in Figure 10-1. Administrators configure DHCPv4 servers to set the leases to time out at different intervals. The lease is typically anywhere from 24 hours to a week or more. When the lease expires, the client must ask for another address, although, the client is typically reassigned the same address.

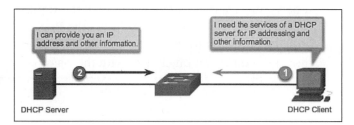

Figure 10-1   What is Dynamic Host Configuration Protocol (DHCP)?

DHCPv4 Operation (10.1.1.2)

As shown in Figure 10-2, DHCPv4 works in a client/server mode. When a client communicates with a DHCPv4 server, the server assigns or leases an IPv4 address to that client. The client connects to the network with that leased IP address until the lease expires. The client must contact the DHCP server periodically to extend the lease. This lease mechanism ensures that clients that move or power off do not keep addresses that they no longer need. When a lease expires, the DHCP server returns the address to the pool where it can be reallocated as necessary.

Figure 10-2   DHCPv4 Operation Overview

Lease Origination

When the client boots (or otherwise wants to join a network), it begins a four-step process to obtain a lease. As shown in Figure 10-3, a client starts the process with a broadcast DHCPDISCOVER message with its own MAC address to discover available DHCPv4 servers.

DHCP Discover (DHCPDISCOVER)

The *DHCPDISCOVER* message finds DHCPv4 servers on the network. Because the client has no valid IPv4 information at bootup, it uses Layer 2 and Layer 3 broadcast addresses to communicate with the server.

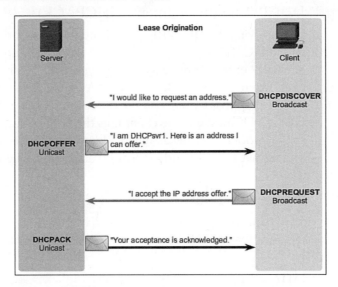

Figure 10-3   DHCPv4 Operation - Lease Origination

DHCP Offer (DHCPOFFER)

When the DHCPv4 server receives a DHCPDISCOVER message, it reserves an available IPv4 address to lease to the client. The server also creates an ARP entry consisting of the MAC address of the requesting client and the leased IPv4 address of the client. As shown in Figure 10-3, the DHCPv4 server sends the binding *DHCPOFFER* message to the requesting client. The DHCPOFFER message is sent as a unicast, using the Layer 2 MAC address of the server as the source address and the Layer 2 MAC address of the client as the destination.

DHCP Request (DHCPREQUEST)

When the client receives the DHCPOFFER from the server, the client sends back a *DHCPREQUEST* message, as shown in Figure 10-3. This message is used for both lease origination and lease renewal. When used for lease origination, the DHCPREQUEST serves as a binding acceptance notice to the selected server for the parameters it has offered and an implicit decline to any other servers that may have provided the client a binding offer.

Many enterprise networks use multiple DHCPv4 servers. The DHCPREQUEST message is sent in the form of a broadcast to inform this DHCPv4 server and any other DHCPv4 servers about the accepted offer.

DHCP Acknowledgment (DHCPACK)

On receiving the DHCPREQUEST message, the server verifies the lease information with an ICMP ping to that address to ensure it is not being used already, creates a new ARP entry for the client lease, and replies with a unicast *DHCPACK* message, as shown in Figure 10-3. The DHCPACK message is a duplicate of the DHCPOFFER, except for a change in the message type field. When the client receives the DHCPACK message, the client logs the configuration information and performs an ARP lookup for the assigned address. If there is no reply to the ARP, the client knows that the IPv4 address is valid and starts using it as its own.

Lease Renewal

DHCP information provided by a DHCP server commonly has a specific lease time. Let's explore what happens when that lease time expires.

DHCP Request (DHCPREQUEST)

As shown in Figure 10-4, when the lease has expired, the client sends a DHCPREQUEST message directly to the DHCPv4 server that originally offered the IPv4 address. If a DHCPACK is not received within a specified amount of time, the client broadcasts another DHCPREQUEST so that one of the other DHCPv4 servers can extend the lease.

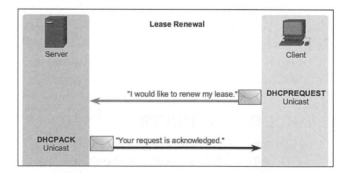

Figure 10-4 DHCPv4 Operation - Lease Renewal

DHCP Acknowledgment (DHCPACK)

On receiving the DHCPREQUEST message, the server verifies the lease information by returning a DHCPACK, as shown in Figure 10-4.

DHCPv4 Message Format (10.1.1.3)

The DHCPv4 message format is used for all DHCPv4 transactions. DHCPv4 messages are encapsulated within the UDP transport protocol. DHCPv4 messages sent from the client use UDP source port 68 and destination port 67. DHCPv4 messages sent from the server to the client use UDP source port 67 and destination port 68.

Table 10-1 shows the format of a DHCPv4 message.

Table 10-1   DHCPv4 Message Format

8	16	24	32
OP Code (1)	Hardware Type (1)	Hardware Address Length (1)	Hops (1)
Transaction Identifier			
Seconds - 2 bytes		Flags - 2 bytes	
Client IP Address (CIADDR) - 4 bytes			
Your IP Address (YIADDR) - 4 bytes			
Server IP Address (SIADDR) - 4 bytes			
Gateway IP Address (GIADDR) - 4 bytes			
Client Hardware Address (CHADDR) - 16 bytes			
Server Name (SNAME) - 64 bytes			
Boot Filename - 128 bytes			
DHCP Options - variable			

The DHCPv4 fields are as follows:

- **Operation (OP) Code:** Specifies the general type of message. A value of 1 indicates a request message; a value of 2 is a reply message.

- **Hardware Type:** Identifies the type of hardware used in the network. For example, 1 is Ethernet, 15 is Frame Relay, and 20 is a serial line. These are the same codes used in ARP messages.

- **Hardware Address Length:** Specifies the length of the address.

- **Hops:** Controls the forwarding of messages. Set to 0 by a client before transmitting a request.

- **Transaction Identifier:** Used by the client to match the request with replies received from DHCPv4 servers.

- **Seconds:** Identifies the number of seconds elapsed since a client began attempting to acquire or renew a lease. Used by DHCPv4 servers to prioritize replies when multiple client requests are outstanding.

- **Flags:** Used by a client that does not know its IPv4 address when it sends a request. Only one of the 16 bits is used, which is the broadcast flag. A value of 1 in this field tells the DHCPv4 server or relay agent receiving the request that the reply should be sent as a broadcast.

- **Client IP Address:** Used by a client during lease renewal when the address of the client is valid and usable, not during the process of acquiring an address. The client puts its own IPv4 address in this field if and only if it has a valid IPv4 address while in the bound state; otherwise, the client sets the field to 0.

- **Your IP Address:** Used by the server to assign an IPv4 address to the client.

- **Server IP Address:** Used by the server to identify the address of the server that the client should use for the next step in the bootstrap process, which may or may not be the server sending this reply. The sending server always includes its own IPv4 address in a special field called the Server Identifier DHCPv4 option.

- **Gateway IP Address:** Routes DHCPv4 messages when DHCPv4 relay agents are involved. The gateway address facilitates communications of DHCPv4 requests and replies between the client and a server that are on different subnets or networks.

- **Client Hardware Address:** Specifies the physical layer of the client.

- **Server Name:** Used by the server sending a DHCPOFFER or DHCPACK message. The server may optionally put its name in this field. This can be a simple text nickname or a DNS domain name, such as dhcpserver.netacad.net.

- **Boot Filename:** Optionally used by a client to request a particular type of boot file in a DHCPDISCOVER message. Used by a server in a DHCPOFFER to fully specify a boot file directory and filename.

- **DHCP Options:** Holds DHCP options, including several parameters required for basic DHCP operation. This field is variable in length. Both client and server may use this field.

DHCPv4 Discover and Offer Messages (10.1.1.4)

If a client is configured to receive its IPv4 settings dynamically and wants to join the network, the client requests addressing values from the DHCPv4 server. The client transmits a DHCPDISCOVER message on its local network when it boots or senses an active network connection. Because the client has no way of knowing the subnet to which it belongs, the DHCPDISCOVER message is an IPv4 broadcast (destination IPv4 address of 255.255.255.255). The client does not have a configured IPv4 address yet, so the source IPv4 address of 0.0.0.0 is used.

As shown in Figure 10-5, the client IPv4 address (CIADDR), default gateway address (GIADDR), and subnet mask are all marked to indicate that the address 0.0.0.0 is used.

Note

Unknown information is sent as 0.0.0.0.

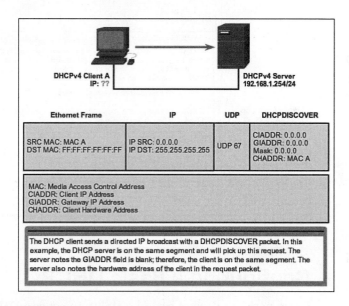

Figure 10-5 DHCPv4 Discover Message

When the DHCPv4 server receives the DHCPDISCOVER message, the server responds with a DHCPOFFER message. This message contains initial configuration information for the client, including the IPv4 address that the server offers, the subnet mask, the lease duration, and the IPv4 address of the DHCPv4 server making the offer.

The DHCPOFFER message can be configured to include other information, such as the lease renewal time and DNS address.

As shown in Figure 10-6, the DHCP server responds to the DHCPDISCOVER by assigning values to the CIADDR and subnet mask. The frame is constructed using the client hardware address (CHADDR) and sent to the requesting client.

The client and server send acknowledgment messages, and the process is complete.

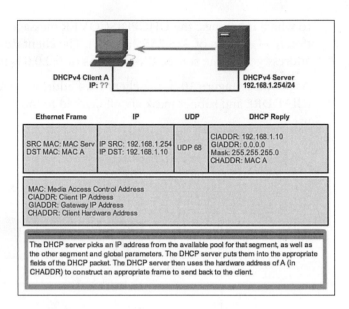

Figure 10-6   DHCPv4 Offer Message

Activity 10.1.1.5: Identify the Steps in the DHCPv4 Operation

Go to the online curriculum to practice placing the four steps of the DHCPv4 process in the correct order.

Configuring a Basic DHCPv4 Server (10.1.2)

Many network devices have the ability to act as a DHCP server; for example, a server, router, Layer 3 switch, and wireless router. In this course, we will examine how to configure DHCPv4 on a router.

Configuring a Basic DHCPv4 Server (10.1.2.1)

A Cisco router running Cisco IOS software can be configured to act as a DHCPv4 server. The Cisco IOS DHCPv4 server assigns and manages IPv4 addresses from specified address pools within the router to DHCPv4 clients. The topology shown in Figure 10-7 is used to illustrate this functionality.

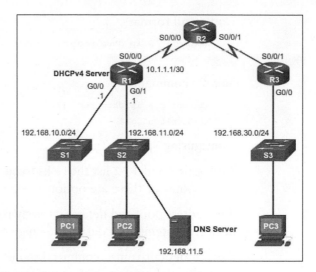

Figure 10-7   Router R1 as a DHCPv4 Server

Step 1.   **Excluding IPv4 Addresses**

The router functioning as the DHCPv4 server assigns all IPv4 addresses in a DHCPv4 address pool unless configured to exclude specific addresses. Typically, some IPv4 addresses in a pool are assigned to network devices that require static address assignments. Therefore, these IPv4 addresses should not be assigned to other devices. To exclude specific addresses, use the **ip dhcp excluded-address** command, as shown in the following output.

A single address or a range of addresses can be excluded by specifying the low-address and high-address of the range. Excluded addresses should include the addresses assigned to routers, servers, printers, and other devices that have been manually configured.

Command format:

```
R1(config)# ip dhcp excluded-address low-address [high-address]
```

Sample commands:

```
R1(config)# ip dhcp excluded-address 192.168.10.1 192.168.10.9
R1(config)# ip dhcp excluded-address 192.168.10.254
```

Step 2.   **Configuring a DHCPv4 Pool**

Configuring a DHCPv4 server involves defining a pool of addresses to assign. As shown in the following output, the **ip dhcp pool** *pool-name* command creates a pool with the specified name and puts the router in DHCPv4 configuration mode, which is identified by this prompt `Router(dhcp-config)#`.

Command format:

```
R1(config)# ip dhcp pool pool-name
R1(dhcp-config)#
```

Sample commands:

```
R1(config)# ip dhcp pool LAN-POOL-1
R1(dhcp-config)#
```

Step 3.   **Configuring Specific Tasks**

Tables 10-2 and 10-3 list the tasks to complete the DHCPv4 pool configuration. Some of these are optional, whereas others must be configured.

The address pool and default gateway router must be configured. Use the **network** statement to define the range of available addresses.

Use the **default-router** command to define the default gateway router. Typically, the gateway is the LAN interface of the router closest to the client devices. One gateway is required, but you can list up to eight addresses if there are multiple gateways.

Table 10-2   Configuring DHCPv4 Step 3: Configuring Specific Required Tasks

Required Task	Command
Define the address pool.	**network** *network-number* [*mask* | */prefix-length*]
Define the default router or gateway.	**default-router** *address* [*address2...address8*]

Table 10-3   Configuring DHCPv4 Step 3: Configuring Optional Tasks

Optional Task	Command
Define a DNS server.	**dns-server** *address* [*address2...address8*]
Define the domain name.	**domain-name** *domain*
Define the duration of the DHCP lease.	**lease** {*days* [*hours*] [*minutes*] | **infinite**}
Define the NetBIOS WINS server.	**netbios-name-server** *address* [*address2...address8*]

Other DHCPv4 pool commands are optional. For example, the IPv4 address of the DNS server that is available to a DHCPv4 client is configured using the **dns-server** command. The **domain-name** *domain* command is used to define the domain name. The duration of the DHCPv4 lease can be changed using the **lease** command. The default lease value is one day. The **netbios-name-server** command is used to define the NetBIOS WINS server.

DHCPv4 Example

A sample configuration with basic DHCPv4 parameters configured on router R1, a DHCPv4 server for the 192.168.10.0/24 LAN is shown in the following output using the example topology from Figure 10-7:

```
R1(config)# ip dhcp excluded-address 192.168.10.1 192.168.10.9
R1(config)# ip dhcp excluded-address 192.168.10.254
R1(config)# ip dhcp pool LAN-POOL-1
R1(dhcp-config)# network 192.168.10.0 255.255.255.0
R1(dhcp-config)# default-router 192.168.10.1
R1(dhcp-config)# dns-server 192.168.11.5
R1(dhcp-config)# domain-name example.com
```

Disabling DHCPv4

The DHCPv4 service is enabled, by default, on versions of Cisco IOS software that support it. To disable the service, use the **no service dhcp** global configuration mode command. Use the **service dhcp** global configuration mode command to re-enable the DHCPv4 server process. Enabling the service has no effect if the parameters are not configured.

Activity 10.1.2.1: Configure DHCPv4

Go to the online course and select the sixth graphic to configure similar DHCPv4 parameters on R1 for the 192.168.11.0/24 LAN.

Verifying DHCPv4 (10.1.2.2)

The topology shown in Figure 10-8 is used in the example output. In this example, R1 has been configured to provide DHCPv4 services. PC1 has not been powered up and, therefore, does not have an IP address.

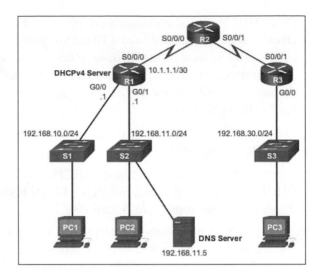

Figure 10-8   Examining R1 as a DHCPv4 Server

As shown in the output that follows, the **show running-config | section dhcp** command output displays the DHCPv4 commands configured on R1. The **| section** parameter displays only the commands associated with DHCPv4 configuration.

```
R1# show running-config | section dhcp
ip dhcp excluded-address 192.168.10.1 192.168.10.9
ip dhcp excluded-address 192.168.10.254
ip dhcp excluded-address 192.168.11.1 192.168.11.9
ip dhcp excluded-address 192.168.11.254
ip dhcp pool LAN-POOL-1
 network 192.168.10.0 255.255.255.0
 default-router 192.168.10.1
 dns-server 192.168.11.5
 domain-name example.com
ip dhcp pool LAN-POOL-2
 network 192.168.11.0 255.255.255.0
 default-router 192.168.11.1
 dns-server 192.168.11.5
 domain-name example.com
R1#
```

As shown in the output that follows, the operation of DHCPv4 can be verified using the **show ip dhcp binding** command. This command displays a list of all IPv4 addresses to MAC address bindings that have been provided by the DHCPv4 service. The second command in the output that follows, **show ip dhcp server statistics**, is used to verify that messages are being received or sent by the router.

This command displays count information regarding the number of DHCPv4 messages that have been sent and received.

As seen in the output for these commands, currently there are no bindings, and the statistics indicate no messages sent or received. At this point, no devices have requested DHCPv4 services from router R1.

```
R1# show ip dhcp binding
Bindings from all pools not associated with VRF:
IP address         Client-ID/               Lease expiration      Type
                   Hardware address/
                   User name

R1# show ip dhcp server statistics
Memory usage           23543
Address pools          2
Database agents        0
Automatic bindings     0
Manual bindings        0
Expired bindings       0
Malformed messages     0
Secure arp entries     0
Renew messages         0

Message                Received
BOOTREQUEST            0
DHCPDISCOVER           0
DHCPREQUEST            0
DHCPDECLINE            0
DHCPRELEASE            0
DHCPINFORM             0

Message                Sent
BOOTREPLY              0
DHCPOFFER              0
DHCPACK                0
DHCPNAK                0
```

In the output that follows, the commands are issued after PC1 and PC2 have been powered on and have completed the boot process.

Notice that the binding information now displays that the IPv4 addresses of 192.168.10.10 and 192.168.11.10 have been bound to MAC addresses. The statistics are also displaying DHCPDISCOVER, DHCPREQUEST, DHCPOFFER, and DHCPACK activity.

```
R1# show ip dhcp binding
Bindings from all pools not associated with VRF:
IP address         Client-ID/                      Lease expiration        Type
                   Hardware address/
                   User name
192.168.10.10      0100.e018.5bdd.35       May 28 2013 01:06 PM     Automatic
192.168.11.10      0100.b0d0.d817.e6       May 28 2013 01:06 PM     Automatic

R1# show ip dhcp server statistics
Memory usage           25307
Address pools          2
Database agents        0
Automatic bindings     2
Manual bindings        0
Expired bindings       0
Malformed messages     0
Secure arp entries     0

Message                    Received
BOOTREQUEST                0
DHCPDISCOVER               8
DHCPREQUEST                3
DHCPDECLINE                0
DHCPRELEASE                0
DHCPINFORM                 0

Message                    Sent
BOOTREPLY                  0
DHCPOFFER                  3
DHCPACK                    3
DHCPNAK                    0
R1#
```

As shown in the output that follows, the **ipconfig /all** command, when issued on PC1, displays the TCP/IP parameters. Because PC1 was connected to the network segment 192.168.10.0/24, it automatically received a DNS suffix, IPv4 address, subnet mask, default gateway, and DNS server address from that pool. No router interface configuration is required. If a PC is connected to a network segment that has a DHCPv4 pool available, the PC can obtain an IPv4 address from the appropriate pool automatically.

```
C:\Documents and Settings\SpanPC> ipconfig /all

Windows IP Configuration
```

```
   Host Name             : ciscolab
   Primary Dns Suffix   :
   Node Type             : Unknown
   IP Routing Enabled    : No
   WINS Proxy Enabled    : No

Ethernet Adapter Local Area Connection

   Connection-specific DNS Suffix   : example.com          ←————————
   Description                      : SiS 900 PCI Fast Ethernet Adapter
   Physical Address                 : 00-E0-18-5B-DD-35
   Dhcp Enabled                     : Yes
   Autoconfiguration Enabled        : Yes
   IP Address                       : 192.168.10.10        ←————————
   Subnet Mask                      : 255.255.255.0        ←————————
   Default Gateway                  : 192.168.10.1         ←————————
   DHCP Server                      : 192.168.10.1
   Lease Obtained                   : Monday, May 27, 2013 1:06:22PM


   Lease Expires                    : Tuesday, May 28, 2013 1:06:22PM


   DNS Servers                      : 192.168.11.5         ←————————

C:\Documents and Settings\SpanPC>
```

DHCPv4 Relay (10.1.2.3)

Companies do not normally place a DCHP server on every LAN. So what do they do? DHCP servers are normally centrally located, but something special has to be done to handle the DHCPv4 broadcasts. That is where DHCP Relay comes into play.

What Is DHCP Relay?

In a complex hierarchical network, enterprise servers are usually located in a server farm. These servers may provide DHCP, DNS, TFTP, and FTP services for the network. Network clients are not typically on the same subnet as those servers. In order to locate the servers and receive services, clients often use broadcast messages.

In Figure 10-9, PC1 is attempting to acquire an IPv4 address from a DHCP server using a broadcast message. In this scenario, router R1 is not configured as a DHCPv4 server and does not forward the broadcast. Because the DHCPv4 server is located on a different network, PC1 cannot receive an IP address using DHCP.

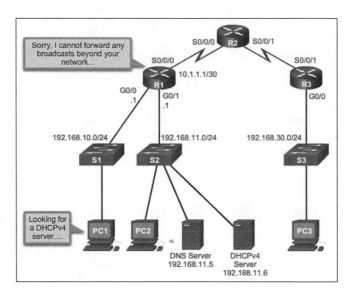

Figure 10-9   DHCPv4 Problems

In the output that follows, PC1 is attempting to renew its IPv4 address. To do so, the **ipconfig /release** command is issued. Notice that the IPv4 address is released and the address is shown to be 0.0.0.0.

```
C:\Documents and Settings\Administrator> ipconfig /release


Windows IP Configuration


Ethernet adapter Local Area Connection:


        Connection-specific DNS Suffix.:
        IP Address......................: 0.0.0.0
        Subnet Mask.....................: 0.0.0.0
        Default Gateway.................:
```

Next, the **ipconfig /renew** command is issued. This command causes PC1 to broadcast a DHCPDISCOVER message. The output shows that PC1 is unable to locate the DHCPv4 server. Because routers do not forward broadcasts, the request is not successful.

```
C:\Documents and Settings\Administrator> ipconfig /renew


Windows IP Configuration


An error occurred while renewing interface Local Area Connection:
unable to contact your DHCP server. Request has timed out.
```

As a solution to this problem, an administrator can add DHCPv4 servers on all the subnets. However, running these services on several computers creates additional cost and administrative overhead.

A better solution is to configure a DHCPv4 relay agent using a Cisco IOS helper address. A *DHCPv4 relay agent* enables a network device such as a router to forward DHCPv4 broadcasts to the DHCPv4 server. When a router forwards address assignment/parameter requests, it is acting as a DHCPv4 relay agent. In the example topology, PC1 would broadcast a request to locate a DHCPv4 server. If R1 was configured as a DHCPv4 relay agent, it would forward the request to the DHCPv4 server located on subnet 192.168.11.0.

As shown in the following commands, the interface on R1 receiving the broadcast is configured with the **ip helper-address** interface configuration mode command. The address of the DHCPv4 server is configured as the only parameter. When R1 has been configured as a DHCPv4 relay agent, it accepts broadcast requests for the DHCPv4 service and then forwards those requests as a unicast to the IPv4 address 192.168.11.6. The **show ip interface** command is used to verify the configuration.

```
R1(config)# interface g0/0
R1(config-if)# ip helper-address 192.168.11.6
R1(config-if)# end
R1# show ip interface g0/0
GigabitEthernet0/0 is up, line protocol is up
  Internet address is 192.168.10.1/24
  Broadcast address is 255.255.255.255
  Address determined by setup command
  MTU is 1500 bytes
  Helper address is 192.168.11.6
<output omitted>
```

As shown in the following output, PC1 is now able to acquire an IPv4 address from the DHCPv4 server.

```
C:\Documents and Settings\Administrator> ipconfig /release

Windows IP Configuration

Ethernet adapter Local Area Connection:

        Connection-specific DNS Suffix.:
        IP Address.....................: 0.0.0.0
        Subnet Mask....................: 0.0.0.0
        Default Gateway................:
C:\Documents and Settings\Administrator> ipconfig /renew
```

```
Windows IP Configuration

Ethernet adapter Local Area Connection:

        Connection-specific DNS Suffix.:
        IP Address......................: 192.168.10.11
        Subnet Mask.....................: 255.255.255.0
        Default Gateway.................: 192.168.10.1
C:\Documents and Settings\Administrator>
```

DHCPv4 is not the only service that the router can be configured to relay. By default, the **ip helper-address** command forwards the following eight UDP services:

- Port 37: Time
- Port 49: TACACS
- Port 53: DNS
- Port 67: DHCP/BOOTP client
- Port 68: DHCP/BOOTP server
- Port 69: TFTP
- Port 137: NetBIOS name service
- Port 138: NetBIOS datagram service

Activity 10.1.2.3: Configure DHCPv4 Relay

Go to the online course and select the fifth graphic to use the Syntax Checker to configure the DHCPv4 relay commands on the correct router so that PC3 can receive IPv4 addressing information from the DHCPv4 server. Refer to Figure 10-9 to view the network topology.

Lab 10.1.2.4: Configuring Basic DHCPv4 on a Router (10.1.2.4)

In this lab, you will complete the following objectives:

- Part 1: Build the Network and Configure Basic Device Settings
- Part 2: Configure a DHCPv4 Server and a DHCP Relay Agent

Lab 10.1.2.5: Configuring Basic DHCPv4 on a Switch (10.1.2.5)

In this lab, you will complete the following objectives:

■ Part 1: Build the Network and Configure Basic Device Settings

■ Part 2: Change the SDM Preference

■ Part 3: Configure DHCPv4

■ Part 4: Configure DHCP for Multiple VLANs

■ Part 5: Enable IP Routing

Configure DHCPv4 Client (10.1.3)

This section shows how you might configure DHCPv4 clients in a similar manner to client computers with a Cisco router or a Linksys router.

Configuring a Router as DHCPv4 Client (10.1.3.1)

Sometimes, Cisco routers in small office/home office (SOHO) and branch sites have to be configured as DHCPv4 clients in a similar manner to client computers. The method used depends on the ISP. However, in its simplest configuration, the Ethernet interface is used to connect to a cable or DSL modem. To configure an Ethernet interface as a DHCP client, use the **ip address dhcp** interface configuration mode command.

In the topology shown in Figure 10-10, assume that an ISP has been configured to provide select customers with IP addresses from the 209.165.201.0/27 network range.

Figure 10-10   Configuring a Router as a DHCP Client

After the G0/1 interface is configured with the **ip address dhcp** command, the **show ip interface g0/1** command confirms that the interface is up and that the address was allocated by a DHCPv4 server, as shown in the output that follows.

```
SOHO(config)# interface g0/1
SOHO(config-if)# ip address dhcp
SOHO(config-if)# no shutdown
SOHO(config-if)#
```

```
*Jan 31 17:31:11.507: %DHCP-6-ADDRESS_ASSIGN: Interface GigabitEthernet0/1 assigned
   DHCP address 209.165.201.12, mask 255.255.255.224, hostname SOHO
SOHO(config-if)# end
SOHO# show ip interface g0/1
GigabitEthernet0/1 is up, line protocol is up
   Internet address is 209.165.201.12/27
   Broadcast address is 255.255.255.255
   Address determined by DHCP
<output omitted>
```

Activity 10.1.3.1: Configure a Router as a DHCP Client

Go to the online course and select the second graphic to use the Syntax Checker to configure the interface that is connected to the ISP to acquire an address from the DHCP server.

Configuring a SOHO Router as a DHCPv4 Client (10.1.3.2)

Typically, small broadband routers for home use, such as Linksys routers, can be configured to connect to an ISP using a DSL or cable modem. In most cases, SOHO routers are set to acquire an IPv4 address automatically from the ISP.

For example, Figure 10-11 shows the default WAN setup page for a Linksys EA6500 router. The Internet connection type is set to Automatic Configuration - DHCP. This means that when the router is connected to a cable modem, for example, it is a DHCPv4 client and requests an IPv4 address from the ISP.

Figure 10-11 Linksys Router as a DHCP Client

> **Note**
>
> The MAC Address Clone feature uses a specified address as the source MAC address on the ISP facing interface of the router. Many ISPs assign IPv4 addresses based on the MAC address of the device during the initial installation. When a different device, such as a SOHO router, is connected to the ISP, the ISP may require that the MAC address of the original device be configured on the WAN interface.

Packet Tracer Activity 10.1.3.3: Configuring DHCPv4 Using Cisco IOS

A dedicated DHCP server is scalable and relatively easy to manage but can be costly to have one at every location in a network. However, a Cisco router can be configured to provide DHCP services without the need for a dedicated server. Cisco routers use the Cisco IOS feature set, Easy IP, as an optional, full-featured DHCP server. Easy IP leases configurations for 24 hours by default. As the network technician for your company, you are tasked with configuring a Cisco router as a DHCP server to provide dynamic allocation of addresses to clients on the network. You are also required to configure the edge router as a DHCP client so that it receives an IP address from the ISP network.

Troubleshoot DHCPv4 (10.1.4)

The most common problems with DHCPv4 are misconfiguration. Remember to always remove any DHCP pools that you start with the wrong name, for example. Having a DHCP pool with no configured parameters causes IP addresses to not be assigned from other correctly configured DHCP pools. Some of the issues commonly seen are described in the next two sections.

Troubleshooting Tasks (10.1.4.1)

DHCPv4 problems can arise for a multitude of reasons, such as software defects in operating systems, NIC drivers, or DHCP relay agents, but the most common are configuration issues. Because of the number of potentially problematic areas, a systematic approach to troubleshooting is required, as shown in Table 10-4.

Table 10-4   Troubleshooting DHCPv4

Task 1	Resolve address conflicts.
Task 2	Verify physical connectivity.
Task 3	Test with a static IPv4 address.
Task 4	Verify switch port configuration.
Task 5	Test from the same subnet or VLAN.

Troubleshooting Task 1: Resolve IPv4 Address Conflicts

An IPv4 address lease can expire on a client still connected to a network. If the client does not renew the lease, the DHCPv4 server can reassign that IPv4 address to another client. When the client reboots, it requests an IPv4 address. If the DHCPv4 server does not respond quickly, the client uses the last IPv4 address. The situation then arises where two clients are using the same IPv4 address, creating a conflict.

The **show ip dhcp conflict** command displays all address conflicts recorded by the DHCPv4 server, as shown in the output:

```
R1# show ip dhcp conflict
IP address Detection Method Detection time
192.168.10.32 Ping Feb 16 2013 12:28 PM
192.168.10.64 Gratuitous ARP Feb 23 2013 08:12 AM
```

The server uses the **ping** command to detect clients. The client uses Address Resolution Protocol (ARP) to detect conflicts. If an address conflict is detected, the address is removed from the pool and not assigned until an administrator resolves the conflict.

This output displays IP addresses that have conflicts with the DHCP server. It shows the detection method and detection time for conflicting IP addresses that the DHCP server has offered.

Troubleshooting Task 2: Verify Physical Connectivity

First, use the **show interfaces** *interface* command to confirm that the router interface acting as the default gateway for the client is operational. If the state of the interface is anything other than up, the port does not pass traffic, including DHCP client requests.

Troubleshooting Task 3: Test Connectivity Using a Static IP Address

When troubleshooting any DHCPv4 issue, verify network connectivity by configuring static IPv4 address information on a client workstation. If the workstation is unable to reach network resources with a statically configured IPv4 address, the root cause of the problem is not DHCPv4. At this point, network connectivity troubleshooting is required.

Troubleshooting Task 4: Verify Switch Port Configuration

If the DHCPv4 client is unable to obtain an IPv4 address from the DHCPv4 server on startup, attempt to obtain an IPv4 address from the DHCPv4 server by manually forcing the client to send a DHCPv4 request.

Note

If there is a switch between the client and the DHCPv4 server, and the client is unable to obtain the DHCP configuration, switch port configuration issues may be the cause. These causes may include issues from trunking and channeling, STP, and RSTP. PortFast configuration and edge port configurations resolve the most common DHCPv4 client issues that occur with an initial installation of a Cisco switch.

Troubleshooting Task 5: Test DHCPv4 Operation on the Same Subnet or VLAN

It is important to distinguish whether DHCPv4 is functioning correctly when the client is on the same subnet or VLAN as the DHCPv4 server. If DHCPv4 is working correctly when the client is on the same subnet or VLAN, the problem may be the DHCP relay agent. If the problem persists even with testing DHCPv4 on the same subnet or VLAN as the DHCPv4 server, the problem may actually be with the DHCPv4 server.

Verify Router DHCPv4 Configuration (10.1.4.2)

When the DHCPv4 server is located on a separate LAN from the client, the router interface facing the client must be configured to relay DHCPv4 requests by configuring the IPv4 helper address. If the IPv4 helper address is not configured properly, client DHCPv4 requests are not forwarded to the DHCPv4 server.

Follow these steps to verify the router configuration:

How To

Step 1.   Verify that the **ip helper-address** command is configured on the correct interface. It must be present on the inbound interface of the LAN containing the DHCPv4 client workstations and must be directed to the correct DHCPv4 server. The output of the **show running-config** command verifies that the DHCPv4 relay IPv4 address is referencing the DHCPv4 server address at 192.168.11.6.

```
R1# show running-config | section interface GigabitEthernet0/0
interface GigabitEthernet0/0
 ip address 192.168.10.1 255.255.255.0
 ip helper-address 192.168.11.6
 duplex auto
 speed auto
R1#
```

The **show ip interface** command can also be used to verify the DHCPv4 relay on an interface.

Step 2.   Verify that the global configuration command **no service dhcp** has not been configured. This command disables all DHCP server and relay functionality on the router. The command **service dhcp** does not appear in the **running-config** because it is the default configuration. In the output, the **show running-config | include no service dhcp** command verifies that the DHCPv4 service is enabled because there is no match for the **show running-config | include no service dhcp** command.

```
R1# show running-config | include no service dhcp
```

If the service had been disabled, the **no service dhcp** command would be displayed in the output.

Debugging DHCPv4 (10.1.4.3)

On routers configured as DHCPv4 servers, the DHCPv4 process fails if the router is not receiving requests from the client. As a troubleshooting task, verify that the router is receiving the DHCPv4 request from the client. This troubleshooting step involves configuring an ACL for debugging output.

The output that follows shows an extended ACL permitting only packets with UDP destination ports of 67 or 68. These are the typical ports used by DHCPv4 clients and servers when sending DHCPv4 messages. The extended ACL is used with the **debug ip packet** command to display only DHCPv4 messages:

```
R1(config)# access-list 100 permit udp any any eq 67
R1(config)# access-list 100 permit udp any any eq 68
R1(config)# end
R1# debug ip packet 100
IP packet debugging is on for access list 100
*IP: s=0.0.0.0 (GigabitEthernet0/1), d=255.255.255.255, len 333,
rcvd 2
*IP: s=0.0.0.0 (GigabitEthernet0/1), d=255.255.255.255, len 333,
stop process pak for forus packet
*IP: s=192.168.11.1 (local), d=255.255.255.255
(GigabitEthernet0/1), len 328, sending broad/multicast
<output omitted>

R1# debug ip dhcp server events
DHCPD: returned 192.168.10.11 to address pool LAN-POOL-1
DHCPD: assigned IP address 192.168.10.12 to client
0100.0103.85e9.87.
DHCPD: checking for expired leases.
DHCPD: the lease for address 192.168.10.10 has expired.
DHCPD: returned 192.168.10.10 to address pool LAN-POOL-1
```

The preceding output shows that the router is receiving DHCP requests from the client. The source IP address is 0.0.0.0 because the client does not yet have an IP address. The destination is 255.255.255.255 because the DHCP discovery message from the client is sent as a broadcast. This output shows only a summary of the packet and not the DHCPv4 message itself. Nevertheless, the router did receive a broadcast packet with the source and destination IP and UDP ports that are correct for DHCPv4. The complete debug output shows all the packets in the DHCPv4 communications between the DHCPv4 server and client.

Another useful command for troubleshooting DHCPv4 operation is the **debug ip dhcp server events** command. This command reports server events, like address assignments and database updates. It is also used for decoding DHCPv4 receptions and transmissions.

Lab 10.1.4.4: Troubleshooting DHCPv4

In this lab, you will complete the following objectives:

- Part 1: Build the Network and Configure Basic Device Settings
- Part 2: Troubleshoot DHCPv4 Issues

Dynamic Host Configuration Protocol v6 (10.2)

DHCPv6 has more options than DHCPv4. A DHCPv4 client either uses a DHCPv4 server or information is statically assigned. This section explores what options are available for IPv6 addressing-related information to be assigned and how to configure and enable these options.

Stateless Address Autoconfiguration (SLAAC) (10.2.1.1)

Similar to IPv4, IPv6 global unicast addresses can be configured manually or dynamically. However, there are two methods in which IPv6 global unicast addresses can be assigned dynamically:

- Stateless Address Autoconfiguration (SLAAC), as shown in Figure 10-12
- Dynamic Host Configuration Protocol for IPv6 (Stateful DHCPv6)

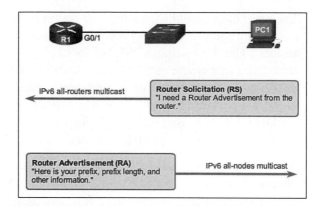

Figure 10-12 ICMPv6 Stateless Address Autoconfiguration

Introducing SLAAC

Stateless Address Autoconfiguration (SLAAC) is a method in which a device can obtain an IPv6 global unicast address without the services of a DHCPv6 server. At the core of SLAAC is ICMPv6. ICMPv6 is similar to ICMPv4 but includes additional functionality and is a much more robust protocol. SLAAC uses ICMPv6 Router Solicitation and Router Advertisement messages to provide addressing and other configuration information that would normally be provided by a DHCP server:

- *Router Solicitation (RS) message:* When a client is configured to obtain its addressing information automatically using SLAAC, the client sends an RS message to the router. The RS message is sent to the IPv6 all-routers multicast address FF02::2.

- *Router Advertisement (RA) message:* RA messages are sent by routers to provide addressing information to clients configured to obtain their IPv6 addresses automatically. The RA message includes the prefix and prefix length of the local segment. A client uses this information to create its own IPv6 global unicast address. A router sends an RA message periodically or in response to an RS message. By default, Cisco routers send RA messages every 200 seconds. RA messages are always sent to the IPv6 all-nodes multicast address FF02::1.

As the name indicates, SLAAC is stateless. A stateless service means there is no server that maintains network address information. Unlike DHCP, there is no SLAAC server that knows which IPv6 addresses are being used and which ones are available.

SLAAC Operation (10.2.1.2)

A router must be enabled as an IPv6 router before it can send RA messages. To enable IPv6 routing, a router is configured with the following command:

```
Router(config)# ipv6 unicast-routing
```

Figure 10-13 shows how SLAAC works.

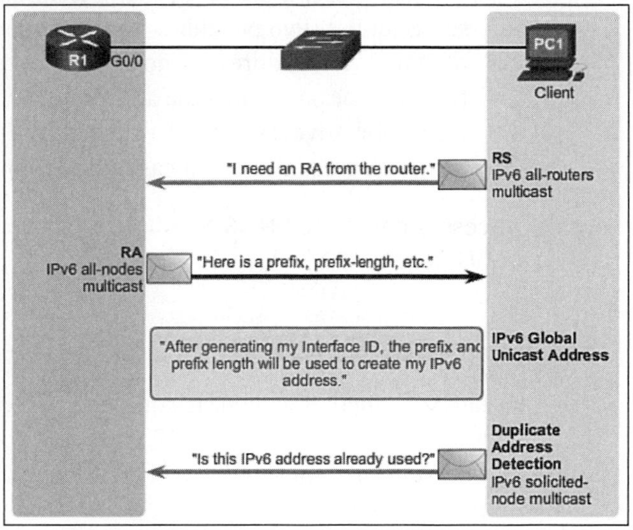

Figure 10-13   SLAAC Operation

Step 1.   In the example topology shown in Figure 10-13, PC1 is configured to obtain IPv6 addressing automatically. Since booting, PC1 has not received an RA message, so it sends an RS message to the all-routers multicast address to inform the local IPv6 router that it needs an RA.

Step 2.   As shown in Figure 10-13, R1 receives the RS message and responds with an RA message. Included in the RA message are the prefix and prefix length of the network. The RA message is sent to the IPv6 all-nodes multicast address FF02::1 with the link-local address of the router as the IPv6 source address.

Step 3.   PC1 receives the RA message containing the prefix and prefix length for the local network. PC1 will use this information to create its own IPv6 global unicast address. PC1 now has a 64-bit network prefix, but needs a 64-bit Interface ID (IID) to create a global unicast address.

There are two ways PC1 can create its own unique IID:

- **EUI-64:** Using the EUI-64 process, PC1 will create an IID using its 48-bit MAC address.

- **Randomly generated:** The 64-bit IID can be a random number generated by the client operating system.

As shown in Figure 10-13, PC1 can create a 128-bit IPv6 global unicast address by combining the 64-bit prefix with the 64-bit IID. PC1 will use the link-local address of the router as its IPv6 default gateway address.

Step 4.   Because SLAAC is a stateless process, before PC1 can use this newly created IPv6 address it must verify that it is unique. As shown in Figure 10-13, PC1 sends an ICMPv6 Neighbor Solicitation message with its own address as the target IPv6 address. If no other devices respond with a Neighbor Advertisement message, then the address is unique and can be used by PC1. If a Neighbor Advertisement is received by PC1, then the address is not unique and the operating system has to determine a new Interface ID to use.

This process is part of ICMPv6 Neighbor Discovery and is known as *Duplicate Address Detection (DAD)*.

SLAAC and DHCPv6 (10.2.1.3)

The decision of whether a client is configured to obtain its IPv6 addressing information automatically using SLAAC, DHCPv6, or a combination of both depends on the settings within the RA message. ICMPv6 RA messages contain two flags to indicate which option the client should use.

The two flags are the Managed Address Configuration flag (M flag) and the Other Configuration flag (O flag).

Using different combinations of the M and O flags, RA messages have one of three addressing options for the IPv6 device, as shown in Figure 10-14:

- SLAAC (Router Advertisement only)

- Stateless DHCPv6 (Router Advertisement and DHCPv6)

- Stateful DHCPv6 (DHCPv6 only)

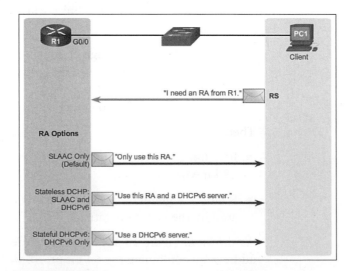

Figure 10-14   SLAAC Options

Regardless of the option used, it is recommended by RFC 4861 that all IPv6 devices perform Duplicate Address Detection (DAD) on any unicast address, including addresses configured using SLAAC or DHCPv6.

> **Note**
>
> Although the RA message specifies the process the client should use in obtaining an IPv6 address dynamically, the client operating system may choose to ignore the RA message and use the services of a DHCPv6 server exclusively.

SLAAC Option (10.2.1.4)

One of the simplest ways to obtain an IPv6 address is through SLAAC. Let us examine this option first.

SLAAC Option (Router Advertisement Only)

SLAAC is the default option on Cisco routers. Both the M flag and the O flag are set to 0 in the RA, as shown in Figure 10-15.

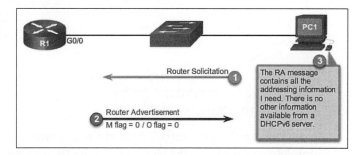

Figure 10-15   SLAAC Option

This option instructs the client to use the information in the RA message exclusively. This includes prefix, prefix-length, DNS server, MTU, and default gateway information. There is no further information available from a DHCPv6 server. The IPv6 global unicast address is created by combining the prefix from RA and an Interface ID using either EUI-64 or a randomly generated value.

RA messages are configured on an individual interface of a router. To re-enable an interface for SLAAC that might have been set to another option, the M and O flags need to be reset to their initial values of 0. This is done using the following interface configuration mode commands:

```
Router(config-if)# no ipv6 nd managed-config-flag
Router(config-if)# no ipv6 nd other-config-flag
```

Stateless DHCPv6 Option (10.2.1.5)

Although DHCPv6 is similar to DHCPv4 in what it provides, the two protocols are independent of each other. DHCPv6 is defined in RFC 3315. There has been a lot of work done on this specification over the years as indicated by the fact that DHCPv6 RFC has the highest revision number of any Internet draft.

Stateless DHCPv6 Option (Router Advertisement and DHCPv6)

As shown in Figure 10-16, the *stateless DHCPv6* option informs the client to use the information in the RA message for addressing, but additional configuration parameters are available from a DHCPv6 server.

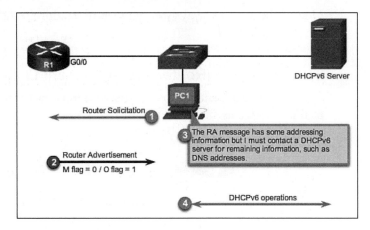

Figure 10-16   Stateless DHCPv6 Option

Using the prefix and prefix length in the RA message, along with EUI-64 or a randomly generated IID, the client creates its IPv6 global unicast address.

The client will then communicate with a stateless DHCPv6 server to obtain additional information not provided in the RA message. This may be a list of DNS server IPv6 addresses, for example. This process is known as stateless DHCPv6 because the server is not maintaining any client state information (i.e., a list of available and allocated IPv6 addresses). The stateless DHCPv6 server is only providing configuration parameters for clients, not IPv6 addresses.

For stateless DHCPv6, the O flag is set to 1 and the M flag is left at the default setting of 0. The O flag value of 1 is used to inform the client that additional configuration information is available from a stateless DHCPv6 server.

To modify the RA message sent on the interface of a router to indicate stateless DHCPv6, use the following command:

```
Router(config-if)#ipv6 nd other-config-flag
```

Stateful DHCPv6 Option (10.2.1.6)

This option is the most similar to DHCPv4. *Stateful DHCPv6* requires the client to obtain all addressing and configuration information from a stateful DHCPv6 server.

Stateful DHCPv6 (DHCPv6 Only)

As shown in Figure 10-17, the RA message informs the client not to use the information in the RA message.

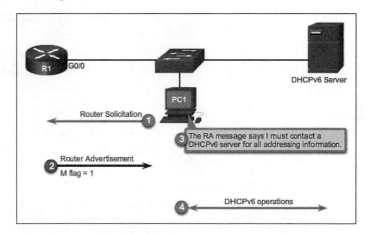

Figure 10-17   Stateful DHCPv6 Option

This is known as stateful DHCPv6 because the DHCPv6 server maintains IPv6 state information. This is similar to a DHCPv4 server allocating addresses for IPv4.

The M flag indicates whether to use stateful DHCPv6. The O flag is not involved. The following command is used to change the M flag from 0 to 1 to signify stateful DHCPv6:

```
Router(config-if)#ipv6 nd managed-config-flag
```

DHCPv6 Operations (10.2.1.7)

As shown in Figure 10-18, stateless or stateful DHCPv6, or both, begin with an ICMPv6 RA message from the router. The RA message might have been a periodic message or solicited by the device using an RS message.

If stateless or stateful DHCPv6 is indicated in the RA message, then the device begins DHCPv6 client/server communications.

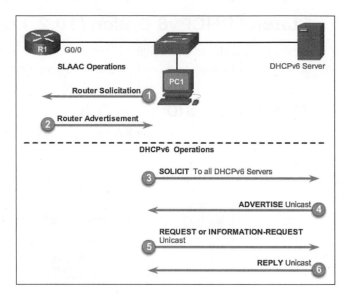

Figure 10-18   DHCPv6 Operations

DHCPv6 Communications

When stateless DHCPv6 or stateful DHCPv6 is indicated by the RA, DHCPv6 operation is invoked. DHCPv6 messages are sent over UDP. DHCPv6 messages from the server to the client use UDP destination port 546. The client sends DHCPv6 messages to the server using UDP destination port 547.

The client, now a DHCPv6 client, needs to locate a DHCPv6 server. In Figure 10-18, the client sends a DHCPv6 SOLICIT message to the reserved IPv6 multicast all-DHCPv6-servers address FF02::1:2. This multicast address has link-local scope, which means routers do not forward the messages to other networks.

One or more DHCPv6 servers respond with a DHCPv6 ADVERTISE message as shown in Figure 10-18. The ADVERTISE message informs the DHCPv6 client that the server is available for DHCPv6 service.

In Figure 10-18, the client responds with a DHCPv6 REQUEST or INFORMATION-REQUEST message to the server, depending on whether it is using stateful or stateless DHCPv6.

- **Stateless DHCPv6 client:** The client sends a DHCPv6 INFORMATION-REQUEST message to the DHCPv6 server requesting only configuration parameters, such as the DNS server address. The client generated its own IPv6 address using the prefix from the RA message and a self-generated Interface ID.

- **Stateful DHCPv6 client:** The client sends a DHCPv6 REQUEST message to the server to obtain an IPv6 address and all other configuration parameters from the server.

The server sends a DHCPv6 REPLY to the client containing the information requested in the REQUEST or INFORMATION-REQUEST message, as shown in Figure 10-18.

Interactive Graphic

Activity 10.2.1.8: Identify the Steps in DHCPv6 Operation

Go to the online course to practice putting the DHCPv6 steps into the correct order.

Stateless DHCPv6 (10.2.2)

A router can be configured as a stateless DHCPv6 server. This is a little different than a DHCPv4 server. This section details how to configure and verify this service on a Cisco router.

Configuring a Router as a Stateless DHCPv6 Server (10.2.2.1)

There are four steps to configure a router as a DHCPv6 server:

Step 1.   Enable IPv6 Routing

The **ipv6 unicast-routing** command is required to enable IPv6 routing. This command is not necessary for the router to be a stateless DHCPv6 server but is required for sending ICMPv6 RA messages.

```
Router (config)# ipv6 unicast-routing
```

Step 2.   Configure a DHCPv6 Pool

The **ipv6 dhcp pool** *pool-name* command creates a pool and enters the router in DHCPv6 configuration mode, which is identified by the Router(config-dhcpv6)# prompt:

```
Router(config)# ipv6 dhcp pool pool-name
Router(config-dhcpv6)#
```

Step 3.   Configure Pool Parameters

During the SLAAC process, the client received the information it needed to create an IPv6 global unicast address. The client also received the default gateway information using the source IPv6 address from the RA message, which is the link-local address of the router. However, the stateless DHCPv6 server can be configured to provide other information that might not have been included in the RA message such as DNS server address and the domain name:

```
Router(config-dhcpv6)# dns-server dns-server-address
Router(config-dhcpv6)# domain-name domain-name
```

Step 4.   Configure the DHCPv6 Interface

The **ipv6 dhcp server** *pool-name* interface configuration mode command binds the DHCPv6 pool to the interface. The router responds to stateless DHCPv6 requests on this interface with the information contained in the pool. The O flag needs to be changed from 0 to 1 using the interface command **ipv6 nd other-config-flag**. RA messages sent on this interface indicate that additional information is available from a stateless DHCPv6 server:

```
Router(config)# interface type number
Router(config-if)# ipv6 dhcp server pool-name
Router(config-if)# ipv6 nd other-config-flag
```

DHCPv6 Stateless Server Example

Figure 10-19 shows a topology where a router might need to be made a DHCPv6 stateless server.

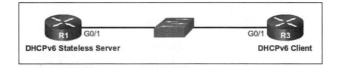

Figure 10-19   Router R1 as a Stateless DHCPv6 Server

What follows is a sample configuration for a router to be configured as a stateless DHCPv6 server. Notice that router R3 is shown as a DHCPv6 client. R3 is configured as a client to help verify the stateless DHCPv6 operations:

```
R1(config)# ipv6 unicast-routing
R1(config)# ipv6 dhcp pool IPV6-STATELESS
R1(config-dhcpv6)# dns-server 2001:db8:cafe:aaaa::5
R1(config-dhcpv6)# domain-name example.com
R1(config-dhcpv6)# exit
R1(config)# interface g0/1
R1(config-if)# ipv6 address 2001:db8:cafe:1::1/64
R1(config-if)# ipv6 dhcp server IPV6-STATELESS
R1(config-if)# ipv6 nd other-config-flag
```

Configuring a Router as a Stateless DHCPv6 Client (10.2.2.2)

In the topology shown in Figure 10-20, a Cisco router is used as the stateless DHCPv6 client. This is not a typical scenario and is used for demonstration purposes only. Typically, a stateless DHCPv6 client is a device, such as a computer, tablet, mobile device, or webcam.

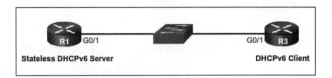

Figure 10-20   Router R1 as a Stateless DHCPv6 Client

The client router needs an IPv6 link-local address on the interface to send and receive IPv6 messages, such as RS messages and DHCPv6 messages. The link-local address of a router is created automatically when IPv6 is enabled on the interface. This can happen when a global unicast address is configured on the interface or by using the **ipv6 enable** command. After the router receives a link-local address, it can send RS messages and participate in DHCPv6. Here is how the configuration would look:

```
R3(config)# interface g0/1
R3(config-if)# ipv6 enable
R3(config-if)# ipv6 address autoconfig
```

In this example, the **ipv6 enable** command is used because the router does not yet have a global unicast address.

The **ipv6 address autoconfig** command enables automatic configuration of IPv6 addressing using SLAAC. An RA message is then used to inform the client router to use stateless DHCPv6.

Verifying Stateless DHCPv6 (10.2.2.3)

As with all configurations, you should verify the Stateless DHCPv6 configuration on both the server and on the clients.

Verifying the Stateless DHCPv6 Server

The **show ipv6 dhcp pool** command verifies the name of the DHCPv6 pool and its parameters. The number of active clients is 0 because there is no state being maintained by the server:

```
R1# show ipv6 dhcp pool
DHCPv6 pool: IPV6-STATELESS
   DNS server: 2001:DB8:CAFE:AAAA::5
   Domain name: example.com
   Active clients: 0
R1#
```

The **show running-config** command can also be used to verify all the commands that were previously configured.

Verifying the Stateless DHCPv6 Client

In this example, a router is used as a stateless DHCPv6 client. The **show ipv6 interface** command can be used to verify the configuration.

```
R3# show ipv6 interface g0/1
GigabitEthernet0/1 is up, line protocol is up
   IPv6 is enabled, link-local address is
FE80::32F7:DFF:FE25:2DE1
   No Virtual link-local address(es):
   Stateless address autoconfig enabled
   Global unicast address(es):
     2001:DB8:CAFE:1:32F7:DFF:FE25:2DE1, subnet is
2001:DB8:CAFE:1::/64 [EUI/CAL/PRE]
     valid lifetime 291935 preferred lifetime 604735
   Joined group address(es):
     FF02::1
     FF02::1:FF25:2DE1
   MTU is 1500 bytes
   ICMP error messages limited to one every 100 milliseconds
   ICMP redirects are enabled
   ICMP unreachables are sent
   ND DAD is enabled, number of DAD attempts: 1
   ND reachable time is 30000 milliseconds (using 30000)
   ND NS retransmit interval is 1000 milliseconds
   Default router is FE80::D68C:B5FF:FECE:A0C1 on
   GigabitEthernet0/1
R3#
```

The output from the **show ipv6 interface** command shows that the router has "Stateless address autoconfig enabled" and has an IPv6 global unicast address. The IPv6 global unicast address was created using SLAAC, which includes the prefix contained in the RA message. The IID was generated using EUI-64. DHCPv6 was not used to assign the IPv6 address.

The default router information is also from the RA message. This was the source IPv6 address of the packet that contained the RA message and the link-local address of the router.

The output from the **debug ipv6 dhcp detail** command shows the DHCPv6 messages exchanged between the client and the server:

```
R3# debug ipv6 dhcp detail
    IPv6 DHCP debugging is on (detailed)
R3#
*Feb  3 02:39:10.454: IPv6 DHCP: Sending INFORMATION-REQUEST
to FF02::1:2 on GigabitEthernet0/1
*Feb  3 02:39:10.454: IPv6 DHCP: detailed packet contents
*Feb  3 02:39:10.454:     src FE80::32F7:DFF:FE25:2DE1
*Feb  3 02:39:10.454:     dst FF02::1:2 (GigabitEthernet0/1)
*Feb  3 02:39:10.454:     type INFORMATION-REQUEST(11),xid 12541745
<output omitted>
*Feb  3 02:39:10.424: IPv6 DHCP: Adding server
                       FE80::D68C:B5FF:FECE:A0C1
*Feb  3 02:39:10.454: IPv6 DHCP: Processing options
*Feb  3 02:39:10.454: IPv6 DHCP: Configuring DNS server
                       2001:DB8:CAFE:AAAA::5
*Feb  3 02:39:10.454: IPv6 DHCP: Configuring domain name
                       example.com
*Feb  3 02:39:10.454: IPv6 DHCP: DHCPv6 changes state from
INFORMATION-REQUEST to IDLE (REPLY_RECEIVED) on GigabitEthernet0/1
```

In this example, the command has been entered on the client. The INFORMATION-REQUEST message is shown because it is sent from a stateless DHCPv6 client. Notice that the client, router R3, is sending the DHCPv6 messages from its link-local address to the All_DHCPv6_Relay_Agents_and_Servers address FF02::1:2.

The debug output displays all the DHCPv6 messages sent between the client and the server including the DNS server and domain name options that were configured on the server.

Interactive Graphic

Activity 10.2.2.3: Configuring and Verifying Stateless DHCPv6

Go to the online course and select the fourth graphic. Use the Syntax Checker to configure and verify stateless DHCPv6 on the router.

Stateful DHCPv6 Server (10.2.3)

A Cisco router can also be configured as a stateful DHCPv6 server. This is what technicians normally have in mind when they think of DHCP because this method is similar to DHCPv4 operations. Let's examine how the stateful DHCPv6 server is different.

Configuring a Router as a Stateful DHCPv6 Server (10.2.3.1)

Configuring a stateful DHCPv6 server is similar to configuring a stateless server. The most significant difference is that a stateful server also includes IPv6 addressing information similar to a DHCPv4 server.

Step 1.   Enable IPv6 Routing

Use of the **ipv6 unicast-routing** command is required to enable IPv6 routing. This command is not necessary for the router to be a stateful DHCPv6 server, but is required for sending ICMPv6 RA messages.

```
Router(config)# ipv6 unicast-routing
```

Step 2.   Configure a DHCPv6 Pool

The **ipv6 dhcp pool** *pool-name* command creates a pool and enters the router in DHCPv6 configuration mode, which is identified by the Router(config-dhcpv6)# prompt:

```
Router(config)# ipv6 dhcp pool pool-name
Router(config-dhcpv6)#
```

Step 3.   Configure Pool Parameters

With stateful DHCPv6, all addressing and other configuration parameters must be assigned by the DHCPv6 server. The **address** *prefix/length* command is used to indicate the pool of addresses to be allocated by the server. The **lifetime** option indicates the valid and preferred lease times in seconds. As with stateless DHCPv6, the client uses the source IPv6 address from the packet that contained the RA message.

Other information provided by the stateful DHCPv6 server typically includes the DNS server address and the domain name:

```
Router(config-dhcpv6)# address prefix/length [lifetime
valid-lifetime preferred-lifetime | infinite]
Router(config-dhcpv6)# dns-server dns-server-address
Router(config-dhcpv6)# domain-name domain-name
```

Step 4.   Interface Commands

The **ipv6 dhcp server** *pool-name* interface command binds the DHCPv6 pool to the interface. The router responds to stateless DHCPv6 requests on this interface with the information contained in the pool. The M flag needs to be changed from 0 to 1 using the interface command **ipv6 nd managed-config-flag**. This informs the device not to use SLAAC but to obtain IPv6 addressing and all configuration parameters from a stateful DHCPv6 server:

```
Router(config)# interface type number
Router(config-if)# ipv6 dhcp server pool-name
Router(config-if)# ipv6 nd managed-config-flag
```

DHCPv6 Stateful Server Example

Figure 10-21 shows the topology where R1 is acting as a stateful DHCPv6 server.

Figure 10-21   Router R1 as a Stateful DHCPv6 Server

The commands that follow are an example of stateful DHCPv6 server commands for a router configured on R1. Notice that a default gateway is not specified because the router will automatically send its own link-local address as the default gateway.

```
R1(config)# ipv6 unicast-routing
R1(config)# ipv6 dhcp pool IPV6-STATEFUL
R1(config-dhcpv6)# address prefix 2001:DB8:CAFE:1::/64 lifetime infinite
R1(config-dhcpv6)# dns-server 2001:db8:cafe:aaaa::5
R1(config-dhcpv6)# domain-name example.com
R1(config-dhcpv6)# exit
R1(config)# interface g0/1
R1(config-if)# ipv6 address 2001:db8:cafe:1::1/64
R1(config-if)# ipv6 dhcp server IPV6-STATEFUL
R1(config-if)# ipv6 nd managed-config-flag
```

Router R3 will be configured next as an IPv6 client to help verify the stateful DHCPv6 operations.

Configuring a Router as a Stateful DHCPv6 Client (10.2.3.2)

The topology in Figure 10-22 shows how a router might be connected as a DHCPv6 client in order to verify DHCPv6 operations.

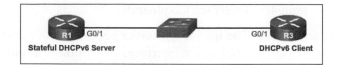

Figure 10-22   Router R1 as a Stateful DHCPv6 Client

The commands needed to configure R3 as a DHCPv6 client are entered as follows:

```
R3(config)# interface g0/1
R3(config-if)# ipv6 enable
R3(config-if)# ipv6 address dhcp
```

Use the **ipv6 enable** interface configuration mode command to allow the router to receive a link-local address to send RS messages and participate in DHCPv6. The **ipv6 address dhcp** interface configuration mode command enables the router to behave as a DHCPv6 client on this interface.

Verifying Stateful DHCPv6 (10.2.3.3)

Use the **show ipv6 dhcp pool** command to verify the name of the DHCPv6 pool and its parameters. The number of active clients is 1, which reflects client R3 receiving its IPv6 global unicast address from this server:

```
R1# show ipv6 dhcp pool
DHCPv6 pool: IPV6-STATEFUL
  Address allocation prefix: 2001:DB8:CAFE:1::/64 valid 4294967295 preferred
  429467295 (1 in use, 0 conflicts)
  DNS server: 2001:DB8:CAFE:AAAA::5
  Domain name: example.com
  Active clients: 1
R1#
```

Use the **show ipv6 dhcp binding** command to display the automatic binding between the link-local address of the client and the address assigned by the server:

```
R1# show ipv6 dhcp binding
Client: FE80::32F7:DFF:FE25:2DE1
  DUID: 003000130F70D252DE0
  Username : unassigned
  IA NA: IA ID 0x00040001, T1 43200, T2 69120
    Address: 2001:DB8:CAFE:1:5844:47B2:2603:C171
        preferred lifetime INFINITY, , valid lifetime INFINITY,
```

FE80::32F7:DFF:FE25:2DE1 is the link-local address of the client. In this example, this is the G0/1 interface of R3. This address is bound to the IPv6 global unicast address, 2001:DB8:CAFE:1:5844:47B2:2603:C171, which was assigned by R1, the DHCPv6 server. This information is maintained by a stateful DHCPv6 server and not by a stateless DHCPv6 server.

Verifying the Stateful DHCPv6 Client

Use the output from the **show ipv6 interface** command to verify the IPv6 global unicast address on DHCPv6 client R3 that was assigned by the DHCPv6 server. The default router information is not from the DHCPv6 server, but was determined by using the source IPv6 address from the RA message. Although the client does not use the information contained in the RA message, it is able to use the source IPv6 address for its default gateway information.

```
R3# show ipv6 interface g0/1
GigabitEthernet0/1 is up, line protocol is up
  IPv6 is enabled, link-local address is
FE80::32F7:DFF:FE25:2DE1
  No Virtual link-local address(es):
  Global unicast address(es):
    2001:DB8:CAFE:1:5844:47B2:2603:C171, subnet is
2001:DB8:CAFE:1:5844:47B2:2603:C171/128
  Joined group address(es):
    FF02::1
    FF02::1:FF03:C171
    FF02::1:FF25:2DE1
  MTU is 1500 bytes
  ICMP error messages limited to one every 100 milliseconds
  ICMP redirects are enabled
  ICMP unreachables are sent
  ND DAD is enabled, number of DAD attempts: 1
  ND reachable time is 30000 milliseconds (using 30000)
  ND NS retransmit interval is 1000 milliseconds
  Default router is FE80::D68C:B5FF:FECE:A0C1 on
  GigabitEthernet0/1
R3#
```

Interactive Graphic

Activity 10.2.3.3: Configuring and Verifying Stateful DHCPv6

Go to the online course and select the fourth graphic. Use the Syntax Checker to configure and verify stateful DHCPv6 on the router.

Configuring a Router as a DHCPv6 Relay Agent (10.2.3.4)

If the DHCPv6 server is located on a different network than the client, then the IPv6 router can be configured as a *DHCPv6 relay agent*, which is used to relay messages between a DHCPv6 server and a client that are not on the same link. The configuration of a DHCPv6 relay agent is similar to the configuration of an IPv4 router as a DHCPv4 relay.

Note

Although the configuration of a DHCPv6 relay agent is similar to DHCPv4, IPv6 router or relay agents forward DHCPv6 messages slightly differently than DHCPv4 relays. The messages and the process are beyond the scope of this curriculum.

Figure 10-23 shows an example topology where a DHCPv6 server is located on the 2001:DB8:CAFE:1::/64 network. The network administrator wants to use this DHCPv6 server as a central, stateful DHCPv6 server to allocate IPv6 addresses to all clients. Therefore, clients on other networks, such as PC1 on the 2001:DB8:CAFE:A::/64 network, must communicate with the DHCPv6 server.

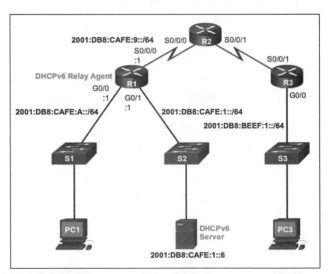

Figure 10-23 DHCPv6 Relay Agent

DHCPv6 messages from clients are sent to the IPv6 multicast address FF02::1:2. All_DHCPv6_Relay_Agents_and_Servers address. This address has link-local scope, which means routers do not forward these messages. The router must be configured as a DHCPv6 relay agent to enable the DHCPv6 client and server to communicate.

Configuring the DHCPv6 Relay Agent

A DHCPv6 relay agent is configured using the **ipv6 dhcp relay destination** command. This command is configured on the interface facing the DHCPv6 client using the address of the DHCPv6 server as the destination:

```
R1(config)# interface g0/0
R1(config-if)# ipv6 dhcp relay destination 2001:db8:cafe:1::6
R1(config-if)# end
```

The **show ipv6 dhcp interface** command verifies the G0/0 interface is in relay mode with 2001:DB8:CAFE:1::6 configured as the DHCPv6 server:

```
R1# show ipv6 dhcp interface g0/0
GigabitEthernet0/0 is in relay mode
  Relay destinations:
    2001:DB8:CAFE:1::6
```

Interactive Graphic

Activity 10.2.3.4: Configuring and Verifying DHCPv6 Relay

Go to the online course and select the third graphic. Use the Syntax Checker to configure the DHCPv6 relay commands on the correct router so that PC3 can receive IPv6 addressing information from the DHCPv6 server. Refer to Figure 10-23 to view the network topology.

Lab 10.2.3.5: Configuring Stateless and Stateful DHCPv6 (10.2.3.5)

In this lab, you will complete the following objectives:

- Part 1: Build the Network and Configure Basic Device Settings
- Part 2: Configure the Network for SLAAC
- Part 3: Configure the Network for Stateless DHCPv6
- Part 4: Configure the Network for Stateful DHCPv6

Troubleshoot DHCPv6 (10.2.4)

Troubleshooting DHCPv6 is similar to troubleshooting DHCPv4.

Troubleshooting Tasks (10.2.4.1)

The same four tasks used to troubleshoot DHCPv4 are used to troubleshoot DHCPv6. The commands are a little different.

Troubleshooting Task 1. Resolve Conflicts

Similar to IPv4 addresses, an IPv6 address lease can expire on a client that still needs to connect to the network. The **show ipv6 dhcp conflict** command displays any address conflicts logged by the stateful DHCPv6 server. If an IPv6 address conflict is detected, the client typically removes the address and generates a new address using either SLAAC or stateful DHCPv6.

Troubleshooting Task 2. Verify Allocation Method

The **show ipv6 interface** *interface* command can be used to verify the method of address allocation indicated in the RA message as indicated by the settings of the M and O flags. This information is displayed in the last lines of the output. If a client is not receiving its IPv6 address information from a stateful DHCPv6 server, it could be due to incorrect M and O flags in the RA message.

Troubleshooting Task 3. Test with a Static IPv6 Address

When troubleshooting any DHCP issue, whether it is DHCPv4 or DHCPv6, network connectivity can be verified by configuring a static IP address on a client workstation. In the case of IPv6, if the workstation is unable to reach network resources with a statically configured IPv6 address, the root cause of the problem is not SLAAC or DHCPv6. At this point, network connectivity troubleshooting is required.

Troubleshooting Task 4. Verify Switch Port Configuration

If the DHCPv6 client is unable to obtain information from a DHCPv6 server, verify that the switch port is enabled and is operating correctly.

Note

If there is a switch between the client and the DHCPv6 server, and the client is unable to obtain the DHCP configuration, switch port configuration issues may be the cause. These causes may include issues from trunking and channeling, STP, and RSTP. PortFast and edge port configurations resolve the most common DHCPv6 client issues that occur with an initial installation of a Cisco switch.

Troubleshooting Task 5. Test DHCPv6 Operation on the Same Subnet or VLAN

If the stateless or stateful DHCPv6 server is functioning correctly, but is on a different IPv6 network or VLAN than the client, the problem may be with the DHCPv6 relay agent. The client facing interface on the router must be configured with the **ipv6 dhcp relay destination** command.

Verify Router DHCPv6 Configuration (10.2.4.2)

The router configurations for stateless and stateful DHCPv6 services have many similarities but also include significant differences.

Stateful DHCPv6

As shown in the output that follows, a router configured for stateful DHCPv6 services has the **address prefix** command to provide addressing information. For stateful DHCPv6 services the **ipv6 nd managed-config-flag** interface configuration mode command is used. In this instance, the client ignores the addressing information in the RA message and communicates with a DHCPv6 server for both addressing and other information:

```
R1(config)# ipv6 unicast-routing
R1(config)# ipv6 dhcp pool IPV6-STATEFUL
R1(config-dhcpv6)# address prefix 2001:DB8:CAFE:1::/64 lifetime infinite
R1(config-dhcpv6)# dns-server 2001:db8:cafe:aaaa::5
R1(config-dhcpv6)# domain-name example.com
R1(config-dhcpv6)# exit
R1(config)# interface g0/1
R1(config-if)# ipv6 address 2001:db8:cafe:1::1/64
R1(config-if)# ipv6 dhcp server IPV6-STATEFUL
R1(config-if)# ipv6 nd managed-config-flag
```

Stateless DHCPv6

For stateless DHCPv6 services, the **ipv6 nd other-config-flag** interface configuration mode command is used as shown in the output that follows. This informs the device to use SLAAC for addressing information and a stateless DHCPv6 server for other configuration parameters.

```
R1(config)# ipv6 unicast-routing
R1(config)# ipv6 dhcp pool IPV6-STATELESS
R1(config-dhcpv6)# dns-server 2001:db8:cafe:aaaa::5
R1(config-dhcpv6)# domain-name example.com
R1(config-dhcpv6)# exit
R1(config)# interface g0/1
R1(config-if)# ipv6 address 2001:db8:cafe:1::1/64
R1(config-if)# ipv6 dhcp server IPV6-STATELESS
R1(config-if)# ipv6 nd other-config-flag
```

The **show ipv6 interface** command can be used to view the current configuration for allocation method. No matter which method is used for DHCPv6, the last line of the output indicates how clients obtain addresses and other parameters, as shown in the output that follows:

SLAAC

```
R3# show ipv6 interface g0/1
GigabitEthernet0/1 is up, line protocol is up
  IPv6 is enabled, link-local address is
FE80::D68C:B5FF:FECE:A0C1
<output omitted>
Hosts use stateless autoconfig for addresses.
```

Stateless DHCPv6

```
R3# show ipv6 interface g0/1
GigabitEthernet0/1 is up, line protocol is up
  IPv6 is enabled, link-local address is
FE80::D68C:B5FF:FECE:A0C1
<output omitted>
Hosts uses DHCP to obtain other configuration.
```

Stateful DHCPv6

```
R3# show ipv6 interface g0/1
GigabitEthernet0/1 is up, line protocol is up
  IPv6 is enabled, link-local address is
FE80::D68C:B5FF:FECE:A0C1
<output omitted>
Hosts uses DHCP to obtain routable addresses.
```

Debugging DHCPv6 (10.2.4.3)

When the router is configured as a stateless or stateful DHCPv6 server, the **debug ipv6 dhcp detail** command is useful to verify the receipt and transmission of DHCPv6 messages. As shown in the output that follows, a stateful DHCPv6 router has received a SOLICIT message from a client. The router is using the addressing information in its IPV6-STATEFUL pool for binding information.

```
R1# debug ipv6 dhcp detail
    IPv6 DHCP debugging is on (detailed)
R1#
*Feb  3 21:27:41.123: IPv6 DHCP: Received SOLICIT from
FE80::32F7:DFF:FE25:2DE1 on GigabitEthernet0/1
*Feb  3 21:27:41.123: IPv6 DHCP: detailed packet contents
*Feb  3 21:27:41.123:   src FE80::32F7:DFF:FE25:2DE1
(GigabitEthernet0/1)
*Feb  3 21:27:41.123:   dst FF02::1:2
*Feb  3 21:27:41.123:   type SOLICIT(1),xid 13190645
*Feb  3 21:27:41.123:   option ELAPSED-TIME(8), len 2
*Feb  3 21:27:41.123:     elapsed-time 0
```

```
*Feb  3 21:27:41.123:   option CLIENTID(1), len 10
*Feb  3 21:27:41.123:      000
*Feb  3 21:27:41.123: IPv6 DHCP: Using interface pool IPV6-STATEFUL
*Feb  3 21:27:41.123: IPv6 DHCP: Creating binding for
FE80::32F7:DFF:FE25:2DE1 in pool IPV6-STATEFUL
<output omitted>
```

Lab 10.2.4.4: Troubleshooting DHCPv6

In this lab, you will complete the following objectives:

- Part 1: Build the Network and Configure Basic Device Settings

- Part 2: Troubleshoot IPv6 Connectivity

- Part 3: Troubleshoot Stateless DHCPv6

Summary (10.3)

Now, do you think you know all there is to know about DHCPv4 and DHCPv6? Take a moment to review and challenge yourself with an activity, the skills integration challenge, and some review questions.

Class Activity 10.3.1.1: IoE and DHCP

This chapter presents the concept of using the DHCP process in a small- to medium-sized business network; however, DHCP also has other uses!

With the advent of the Internet of Everything (IoE), any device in your home capable of wired or wireless connectivity to a network will be able to be accessed from just about anywhere.

Using Packet Tracer for this modeling activity, perform the following tasks:

- Configure a Cisco 1941 router (or DHCP-server-capable ISR device) for IPv4 or IPv6 DHCP addressing.

- Think of five devices in your home you would like to receive IP addresses from the router's DHCP service. Set the end devices to claim DHCP addresses from the DHCP server.

- Show output validating that each end device secures an IP address from the server. Save your output information via a screen capture program or use the **PrtScrn** key command.

- Present your findings to a fellow classmate or to the class.

Packet Tracer Activity 10.3.1.2: Skills Integration Challenge

In this culminating activity, you will configure VLANs, trunks, DHCP Easy IP, DHCP relay agents, and configure a router as a DHCP client.

All nodes on a network require a unique IP address to communicate with other devices. The static assignment of IP addressing information on a large network results in an administrative burden that can be eliminated by using DHCPv4 or DHCPv6 to dynamically assign IPv4 and IPv6 addressing information, respectively.

DHCPv4 includes three different address allocation mechanisms to provide flexibility when assigning IP addresses:

- **Manual Allocation:** The administrator assigns a pre-allocated IPv4 address to the client, and DHCPv4 communicates only the IPv4 address to the device.

- **Automatic Allocation:** DHCPv4 automatically assigns a static IPv4 address permanently to a device, selecting it from a pool of available addresses. There is no lease and the address is permanently assigned to the device.

- **Dynamic Allocation:** DHCPv4 dynamically assigns, or leases, an IPv4 address from a pool of addresses for a limited period of time as configured on the server, or until the client no longer needs the address.

Dynamic allocation is the most commonly used DHCPv4 mechanism and involves the exchange of several different packets between the DHCPv4 server and the DHCPv4 client resulting in the lease of valid addressing information for a predefined period of time.

Messages originating from the client (DHCPDISCOVER, DHCPREQUEST) are broadcast to allow all DHCPv4 servers on the network to hear the client request for, and receipt of, addressing information. Messages originating from the DHCPv4 server (DHCPOFFER, DHCPACK) are sent as unicasts directly to the client requesting the information.

There are two methods available for the dynamic configuration of IPv6 global unicast addresses:

- Stateless Address Autoconfiguration (SLAAC)

- Dynamic Host Configuration Protocol for IPv6 (Stateful DHCPv6)

With stateless autoconfiguration, the client uses information provided by the IPv6 RA message to automatically select and configure a unique IPv6 address. The stateless DHCPv6 option informs the client to use the information in the RA message for addressing, but additional configuration parameters are available from a DHCPv6 server.

Stateful DHCPv6 is similar to DHCPv4. In this case, the RA message informs the client not to use the information in the RA message. All addressing information and configuration information is obtained from a stateful DHCPv6 server. The DHCPv6 server maintains IPv6 state information similar to a DHCPv4 server allocating addresses for IPv4.

If the DHCP server is located on a different network segment than the DHCP client, then it is necessary to configure a relay agent. The relay agent forwards specific broadcast messages originating from a LAN segment to a specified server located on a different LAN segment. (In this case, a DHCP broadcast message would be forwarded to a DHCP server.)

Troubleshooting issues with DHCPv4 and DHCPv6, involves the same tasks:

- Resolve Address Conflicts

- Verify Physical Connectivity

- Test Connectivity Using a Static IP Address
- Verify Switch Port Configuration
- Test Operation on the Same Subnet or VLAN

Practice

The following activities provide practice with the topics introduced in this chapter. The Labs and Class Activities are available in the companion *Introduction to Routing and Switching Essentials Lab Manual* (978-1-58713-320-6). You can find the Packet Tracer Activities PKA files in the online course.

Class Activities

Class Activity 10.0.1.2: Own or Lease

Class Activity 10.3.1.1: IoE and DHCP

Packet Tracer
☐ **Activity**

Packet Tracer Activities

Packet Tracer Activity 10.1.3.3: Configuring DHCPv4 Using Cisco IOS

Packet Tracer Activity 10.3.1.2: Skills Integration Challenge

Check Your Understanding Questions

Complete all the review questions listed here to test your understanding of the topics and concepts in this chapter. The appendix, "Answers to the 'Check Your Understanding' Questions," lists the answers.

1. Which statements are true about the DHCP server functions? (Choose two.)

   A. When a client requests an IP address, the DHCP server searches the binding table for an entry that matches the client's MAC address. If an entry exists, the corresponding IP address for the entry is returned to the client.

   B. Clients can be assigned an IP address from a predefined DHCP pool for a finite lease period.

   C. DHCP services must be installed on a dedicated network server to define the pool of IP addresses available to the client.

   D. The DHCP server can answer requests and assign IP addresses for a particular subnet only.

   E. Each subnet in the network requires a dedicated DHCP server to assign IP addresses to the host on the subnet.

   F. DHCP provides clients with an IP address, a subnet mask, a default gateway, and optionally, a domain name.

2. Consider the following configuration:

   ```
   R1(config)# ip dhcp pool 192.168.10.0
   ```

   What is the function of the **192.168.10.0** argument?

   A. Name of the DCHP pool

   B. Pool of IP addresses available for lease

   C. Range of excluded IP addresses

   D. Subnet where the DHCP server resides

3. Which three statements about DHCPv4 are true? (Choose three.)

   A. DHCP messages use UDP as a transport protocol.

   B. The DHCPOFFER message is sent by a DHCP server after receiving a DHCPDISCOVER message from a client.

   C. DHCP uses ports 67 and 68.

   D. The DHCPREQUEST message is sent by a DHCP client to locate a DHCP server.

   E. The DHCPACK message is sent by the DHCP server to provide the DHCP client with the DHCP server MAC address for further communications.

   F. All DHCP communications are broadcast.

4. Refer to Figure 10-7. If PC3 used R1 as a DHCPv4 server, on what interface would the **ip helper-address** be configured?

   A. R3 S0/0/0

   B. Any interface on R3

   C. R3 S0/0/1

   D. R3 G0/0

5. If a DHCPv6 client resides on subnet 192.168.30.0/24 and the DHCPv6 server resides on subnet 192.168.10.0/24, why is it necessary for a DHCPv6 Relay Agent?

   A. Because DHCPv6 does not use broadcasts

   B. Because a DHCPv6 client cannot use a DHCP server on a remote network

   C. Because DHCPv6 messages still need to be relayed if the DHCPv6 server resides on a different network

   D. Because DHCP v6 messages must be converted to a broadcast to be heard across multiple networks

6. Which two methods of assigning an IPv6 address to a router interface are automatic and can be used in conjunction with one another? (Choose two.)

   A. EUI-64

   B. Static assignment

   C. DNS

   D. DHCPv6

   E. Stateless autoconfiguration

7. Place the four DHCPv4 steps in the order they occur. Note that not all options will be used.

   DHCPREQUEST

   DHCPLEASE

   DHCPACK

   DHCPDISCOVER

   DHCPREPLY

   DHCPOFFER

   First: _____

   Second: _____

   Third: _____

   Fourth: _____

8. Which DHCP message types are originated by a DHCPv4 server? (Select all that apply.)

   [DHCPREQUEST | DHCPLEASE | DHCPACK | DHCPDISCOVER | DHCPREPLY | DHCPOFFER]

9. What type of IPv6 message is used by an IPv6 host to automatically obtain an IPv6 address from a router?

   A. broadcast

   B. DNS

   C. RS

   D. ARP

10. Which DHCPv6 option is most like DHCPv4?

   A. SLAAC

   B. Stateful DHCPv6

   C. Stateless DHCPv6

   D. EUI-64

11. Match the DHCPv6 command with the purpose. Note that not all options are used.

   _____ Enables IPv6 routing.

   _____ RA messages sent to an interface with this command indicates that additional information is available from a stateless DHCPv6 server.

   _____ Used on a router interface connected to a DHCPv6 client, and the DHCPv6 server is on a different link.

   _____ Causes a router interface to request a DHCPv6 address.

   _____ RA messages sent to an interface with this command indicates that the client is to obtain IP addressing information from a stateful DHCPv6 server.

   A. ipv6 nd other-config-flag

   B. ipv6 dhcp relay destination

   C. ipv6 dhcp

   D. ipv6 unicast-routing

   E. ipv6 nd managed-config-flag

   F. ipv6 routing

   G. ipv6 address dhcp

12. What are the two port numbers used by DHCPv6? (Choose two.)

[67 | 68 | 546 | 547 | 1025 | 1026 | 34768 | 34769]

Network Address Translation for IPv4

Objectives

Upon completion of this chapter, you will be able to answer the following questions:

- What is NAT for IPv4 and IPv6?

- What IPv4 private IP addresses are used with NAT?

- When is NAT used?

- What are the three types of NAT and where would each one be used?

- What are the disadvantages and advantages of NAT?

- How do you configure the three types of NAT for IPv4?

- What are the most common commands used when troubleshooting NAT for IPv4?

- What type of addresses are translated when NAT for IPv6 is used?

- When would NAT for IPv6 be used?

Key Terms

This chapter uses the following key terms. You can find the definitions in the Glossary.

Network Address Translation (NAT)
  page 696

NAT for IPv4   page 697

*RFC 1918 Address Allocation for Private
  Internets   page 697*

inside local address   page 700

inside global address   page 701

outside global address   page 701

static NAT   page 703

dynamic NAT   page 703

Port Address Translation (PAT)   page 703

dual-stack   page 739

tunneling for IPv6   page 739

*Network Address Translation-Protocol
  Translation (NAT-PT)   page 739*

NAT64   page 739

Introduction (11.0.1.1)

All public IPv4 addresses that transverse the Internet must be registered with a Regional Internet Registry (RIR). Organizations can lease public addresses from an SP, but only the registered holder of a public Internet address can assign that address to a network device. However, with a theoretical maximum of 4.3 billion addresses, IPv4 address space is severely limited. When Bob Kahn and Vint Cerf first developed the suite of TCP/IP protocols including IPv4 in 1981, they never envisioned what the Internet would become. At the time, the personal computer was mostly a curiosity for hobbyists, and the World Wide Web was still more than a decade away.

With the proliferation of personal computing and the advent of the World Wide Web, it soon became obvious that 4.3 billion IPv4 addresses would not be enough. The long-term solution was IPv6, but more immediate solutions to address exhaustion were required. For the short term, several solutions were implemented by the IETF including *Network Address Translation (NAT)* and RFC 1918 private IPv4 addresses. This chapter discusses how NAT, combined with the use of private address space, is used to both conserve and more efficiently use IPv4 addresses to provide networks of all sizes access to the Internet.

Class Activity 11.0.1.2: Conceptual NAT

You work for a large university or school system.

Because you are the network administrator, many professors, administrative workers, and other network administrators need your assistance with their networks on a daily basis. They call you at all working hours of the day, and because of the number of telephone calls, you cannot complete your regular network administration tasks.

You need to find a way to limit when you take calls and from whom. You also need to mask your telephone number so that when you call someone, another number displays to the recipient.

This scenario describes a very common problem for most small- to medium-sized businesses. Visit, "How Network Address Translation Works" located at `http://computer.howstuffworks.com/nat.htm/printable` to view more information about how the digital world handles these types of workday interruptions.

Use the PDF provided accompanying this activity to reflect further on how a process, known as NAT, could be the answer to this scenario's challenge.

NAT Operation (11.1)

When someone says the term "NAT," the concept the person is describing is most likely NAT for IPV4. *NAT for IPv4* is a term used to describe when a company uses private IP addresses inside a company, but these addresses get translated to public IP addresses so the data can be transmitted across the Internet. As you will find out, NAT can be used with IPv6 addresses but operates differently than NAT for IPv4.

IPv4 Private Address Space (11.1.1.1)

There are not enough public IPv4 addresses to assign a unique address to each device connected to the Internet. Networks are commonly implemented using private IPv4 addresses, as defined in *RFC 1918 Address Allocation for Private Internets.* Table 11-1 shows the range of addresses included in RFC 1918. It is very likely that the computer that you use to view this course is assigned a private address.

Table 11-1   Private Internet Addresses as Defined in RFC 1918

Class	RFC 1918 Internal Address Range	CIDR Prefix
A	10.0.0.0–10.255.255.255	10.0.0.0/8
B	172.16.0.0–172.31.255.255	172.16.0.0/12
C	192.168.0.0–192.168.255.255	192.168.0.0/16

These private addresses are used within an organization or site to allow devices to communicate locally. However, because these addresses do not identify any single company or organization, private IPv4 addresses cannot be routed over the Internet. To allow a device with a private IPv4 address to access devices and resources outside of the local network, the private address must first be translated to a public address.

As shown in Figure 11-1, NAT provides the translation of private addresses to public addresses.

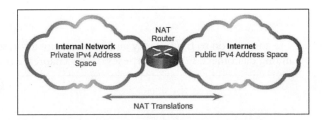

Figure 11-1   Translating Between Private and Public IP Addresses

This allows a device with a private IPv4 address to access resources outside of their private network, such as those found on the Internet. NAT combined with private IPv4 addresses has proven to be a useful method of preserving public IPv4 addresses. A single, public IPv4 address can be shared by hundreds, even thousands of devices, each configured with a unique private IPv4 address.

Without NAT, the exhaustion of the IPv4 address space would have occurred well before the year 2000. However, NAT has certain limitations, which are explored later in this chapter. The solution to the exhaustion of IPv4 address space and the limitations of NAT is the eventual transition to IPv6.

What Is NAT? (11.1.1.2)

NAT has many uses, but its primary use is to conserve public IPv4 addresses. It does this by allowing networks to use private IPv4 addresses internally and providing translation to a public address only when needed. NAT has an added benefit of adding a degree of privacy and security to a network because it hides internal IPv4 addresses from outside networks.

NAT-enabled routers can be configured with one or more valid public IPv4 addresses. These public addresses are known as the NAT pool. When an internal device sends traffic out of the network, the NAT-enabled router translates the internal IPv4 address of the device to a public address from the NAT pool. To outside devices, all traffic entering and exiting the network appears to have a public IPv4 address from the provided pool of addresses.

A NAT router typically operates at the border of a stub network. A stub network is a network that has a single connection to its neighboring network, one way in and one way out of the network. In the example in Figure 11-2, R2 is a border router. As seen from the ISP, R2 forms a stub network.

When a device inside the stub network wants to communicate with a device outside of its network, the packet is forwarded to the border router. The border router performs the NAT process, translating the internal private address of the device to a public, outside, routable address.

Note

The connection to the ISP may also use a private address or a public address that is shared among customers. For the purposes of this chapter, a public address is shown.

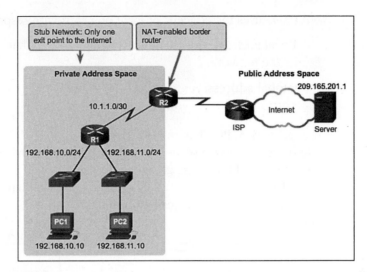

Figure 11-2 NAT Border

NAT Terminology (11.1.1.3, 11.1.1.4)

In NAT terminology, the inside network is the set of networks that is subject to translation. The outside network refers to all other networks.

When using NAT, IPv4 addresses have different designations based on whether they are on the private network, or on the public network (Internet), and whether the traffic is incoming or outgoing.

NAT includes four types of addresses:

- Inside local address
- Inside global address
- Outside local address
- Outside global address

When determining which type of address is used, it is important to remember that NAT terminology is always applied from the perspective of the device with the translated address:

- **Inside address:** The address of the device which is being translated by NAT.
- **Outside address:** The address of the destination device.

NAT also uses the concept of local or global with respect to addresses:

- **Local address:** A local address is any address that appears on the inside portion of the network.

- **Global address:** A global address is any address that appears on the outside portion of the network.

In Figure 11-3, PC1 has an inside local address of 192.168.10.10. From the perspective of PC1, the web server has an outside address of 209.165.201.1. When packets are sent from PC1 to the global address of the web server, the inside local address of PC1 is translated to 209.165.200.226 (inside global address). The address of the outside device is not typically translated because that address is usually a public IPv4 address.

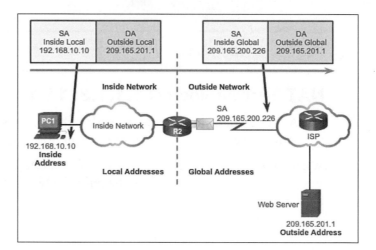

Figure 11-3   Types of NAT Addresses

Notice that PC1 has different local and global addresses, whereas the web server has the same public IPv4 address for both. From the perspective of the web server, traffic originating from PC1 appears to have come from 209.165.200.226, the inside global address.

The NAT router, R2 in Figure 11-3, is the demarcation point between the inside and outside networks and also between local and global addresses.

The terms inside and outside are combined with the terms local and global to refer to specific addresses. In Figure 11-4, router R2 has been configured to provide NAT. It has a pool of public addresses to assign to inside hosts.

- *Inside local address:* The address of the source as seen from inside the network. In Figure 11-4, the IPv4 address 192.168.10.10 is assigned to PC1. This is the inside local address of PC1.

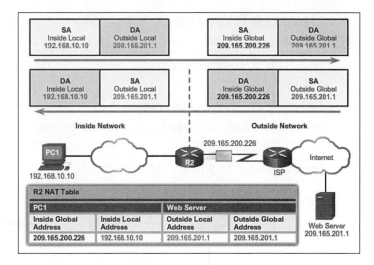

Figure 11-4   NAT Addresses Examples

- *Inside global address:* The address of source as seen from the outside network. In Figure 11-4, when traffic from PC1 is sent to the web server at 209.165.201.1, R2 translates the inside local address to an inside global address. In this case, R2 changes the IPv4 source address from 192.168.10.10 to 209.165.200.226. In NAT terminology, the inside local address of 192.168.10.10 is translated to the inside global address of 209.165.200.226.

- *Outside global address:* The address of the destination as seen from the outside network. It is a globally routable IPv4 address assigned to a host on the Internet. For example, the web server is reachable at IPv4 address 209.165.201.1. Most often the outside local and outside global addresses are the same.

- **Outside local address:** The address of the destination as seen from inside the network. In this example, PC1 sends traffic to the web server at the IPv4 address 209.165.201.1. While uncommon, this address could be different than the globally routable address of the destination.

Figure 11-4 shows how traffic is addressed that is sent from an internal PC to an external web server, across the NAT-enabled router. It also shows how return traffic is initially addressed and translated.

Note

The use of the outside local address is outside the scope of this course.

How NAT Works (11.1.1.5)

In this example, PC1 with private address 192.168.10.10 wants to communicate with an outside web server with public address 209.165.201.1.

Activity 11.1.1.5: NAT in Action

Go to the online course and click the Play button in the figure to start the animation.

Look at Figure 11-5 to see the NAT topology.

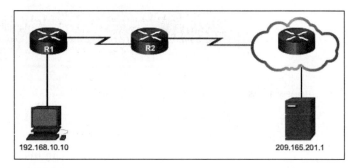

Figure 11-5   NAT topology

PC1 sends a packet addressed to the web server. The packet is forwarded by R1 to R2.

When the packet arrives at R2, the NAT-enabled router for the network, R2 reads the source IPv4 address of the packet to determine if the packet matches the criteria specified for translation.

In this case, the source IPv4 address does match the criteria and is translated from 192.168.10.10 (inside local address) to 209.165.200.226 (inside global address). R2 adds this mapping of the local to global address to the NAT table.

R2 sends the packet with the translated source address toward the destination.

The web server responds with a packet addressed to the inside global address of PC1 (209.165.200.226).

R2 receives the packet with destination address 209.165.200.226. R2 checks the NAT table and finds an entry for this mapping. R2 uses this information and translates the inside global address (209.165.200.226) to the inside local address (192.168.10.10), and the packet is forwarded toward PC1.

Interactive Graphic

Activity 11.1.1.6: Identify the NAT Terminology

Go to the online course. Use this activity to drag the NAT term to the appropriate place in the topology where the term would be applied.

Types of NAT (11.1.2)

The three types of NAT translation can be confusing, but take each type one at a time and understand it. Keep in mind that a company may implement more than one type of NAT.

Static NAT (11.1.2.1)

There are three types of NAT translation:

- **Static address translation (*static NAT*)**: One-to-one address mapping between local and global addresses.

- **Dynamic address translation (*dynamic NAT*)**: Many-to-many address mapping between local and global addresses.

- *Port Address Translation (PAT):* Many-to-one address mapping between local and global addresses. This method is also known as overloading (NAT overloading).

Static NAT uses a one-to-one mapping of local and global addresses. These mappings are configured by the network administrator and remain constant.

Look at the static NAT table shown in Table 11-2 and the topology shown in Figure 11-6.

Table 11-2   Static NAT Table

Inside Local Address	Inside Global Address (Reachable via R2)
192.168.10.10	209.165.200.226
192.168.10.11	209.165.200.227
192.168.10.12	209.165.200.228

In Figure 11-6, R2 is configured with static mappings for the inside local addresses of Svr1, PC2, and PC3. When these devices send traffic to the Internet, their inside local addresses are translated to the configured inside global addresses. To outside networks, these devices have public IPv4 addresses.

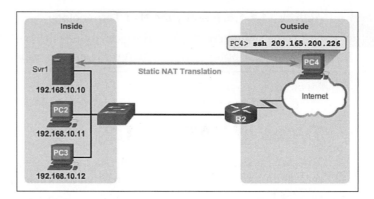

Figure 11-6   Static NAT Topology

Static NAT is particularly useful for web servers or devices that must have a consistent address that is accessible from the Internet, such as a company web server. It is also useful for devices that must be accessible by authorized personnel when offsite, but not by the general public on the Internet. For example, a network administrator from PC4 can SSH to Svr1's inside global address (209.165.200.226). R2 translates this inside global address to the inside local address and connects the administrator's session to Svr1.

Static NAT requires that enough public addresses are available to satisfy the total number of simultaneous user sessions.

Dynamic NAT (11.1.2.2)

Dynamic NAT uses a pool of public addresses and assigns them on a first-come, first-served basis. When an inside device requests access to an outside network, dynamic NAT assigns an available public IPv4 address from the pool.

Look at Figure 11-7. PC3 needs to send data to the Internet.

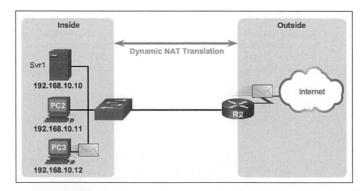

Figure 11-7   Dynamic NAT Topology

Refer to Table 11-3; PC3 has accessed the Internet using the first available address in the dynamic NAT pool. The other addresses are still available for use.

Table 11-3   Dynamic NAT: IPv4 NAT Pool

Inside Local Address	Inside Global Address (Reachable via R2)
192.168.10.12	209.165.200.226
Available	209.165.200.227
Available	209.165.200.228
Available	209.165.200.229
Available	209.165.200.230

Similar to static NAT, dynamic NAT requires that enough public addresses are available to satisfy the total number of simultaneous user sessions.

Port Address Translation (PAT) (11.1.2.3)

Port Address Translation (PAT), also known as NAT overloading, maps multiple private IPv4 addresses to a single public IPv4 address or a few addresses, as shown in Figure 11-8. This is what most home routers do. The ISP assigns one address to the router, yet several members of the household can simultaneously access the Internet. This is the most common form of NAT.

With PAT, multiple addresses can be mapped to one or to a few addresses because each private address is also tracked by a port number. When a device initiates a TCP/IP session, it generates a TCP or UDP source port value to uniquely identify the session. When the NAT router receives a packet from the client, it uses its source port number to uniquely identify the specific NAT translation.

PAT ensures that devices use a different TCP port number for each session with a server on the Internet. When a response comes back from the server, the source port number, which becomes the destination port number on the return trip, determines to which device the router forwards the packets. The PAT process also validates that the incoming packets were requested, thus adding a degree of security to the session.

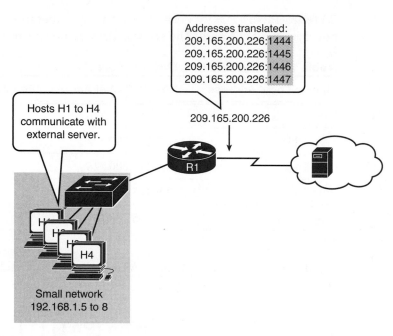

Figure 11-8   PAT Topology

Activity 11.1.2.3: The PAT Process

Go to the online course. Use the Play and Pause buttons to see the address translations in action. The animation illustrates the PAT process. PAT adds unique source port numbers to the inside global address to distinguish between translations.

In the animation, as R2 processes each packet, it uses a port number (1331 and 1555, in this example) to identify the device from which the packet originated. The source address (SA) is the inside local address with the TCP/IP assigned port number added. The destination address (DA) is the outside local address with the service port number added. In this example, the service port is 80: HTTP.

For the source address, R2 translates the inside local address to an inside global address with the port number added. The destination address is not changed but is now referred to as the outside global IP address. When the web server replies, the path is reversed.

Next Available Port (11.1.2.4)

In the previous example, the client port numbers, 1331 and 1555, did not change at the NAT-enabled router. This is not a likely scenario because there is a good chance that these port numbers may have already been attached to other active sessions.

PAT attempts to preserve the original source port. However, if the original source port is already used, PAT assigns the first available port number starting from the beginning of the appropriate port group 0–511, 512–1,023, or 1,024–65,535. When there are no more ports available and there is more than one external address in the address pool, PAT moves to the next address to try to allocate the original source port. This process continues until there are no more available ports or external IP addresses.

Activity 11.1.2.4: Next Available Port

Go to the online course and click the Play button in the graphic to view PAT operation. In the animation, the hosts have chosen the same port number 1444. This is acceptable for the inside address because the hosts have unique private IP addresses. However, at the NAT router, the port numbers must be changed; otherwise, packets from two different hosts would exit R2 with the same source address. In this example, PAT has assigned the next available port (1445) to the second host address, as shown in Figure 11-9.

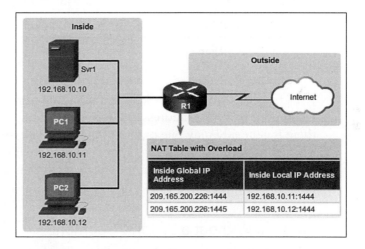

Figure 11-9   PAT Using Varying Port Numbers

Comparing NAT and PAT (11.1.2.5)

Summarizing the differences between NAT and PAT helps your understanding of each.

As Table 11-4 shows, NAT translates IPv4 addresses on a 1:1 basis between private IPv4 addresses and public IPv4 addresses.

Table 11-4   NAT Example

Inside Global Address Pool	Inside Local Address
209.165.200.226	192.168.10.10
209.165.200.227	192.168.10.11
209.165.200.228	192.168.10.12
209.165.200.229	192.168.10.13

PAT, on the other hand, modifies both the address and the port number, as shown in Table 11-5.

Table 11-5   PAT Example

Inside Global Address	Inside Local Address
209.165.200.226:1444	192.168.10.10:1444
209.165.200.226:1445	192.168.10.11:1444
209.165.200.226:1555	192.168.10.12:1555
209.165.200.226:1556	192.168.10.13:1555

NAT forwards incoming packets to their inside destination by referring to the incoming source IPv4 address given by the host on the public network. With PAT, there is generally only one or a very few publicly exposed IPv4 addresses. Incoming packets from the public network are routed to their destinations on the private network by referring to a table in the NAT router. This table tracks public and private port pairs. This is called connection tracking.

Packets Without a Layer 4 Segment

What about IPv4 packets carrying data other than a TCP or UDP segment? These packets do not contain a Layer 4 port number. PAT translates most common protocols carried by IPv4 that do not use TCP or UDP as a transport layer protocol. The most common of these is ICMPv4. Each of these types of protocols is handled differently by PAT. For example, ICMPv4 query messages, echo requests, and echo replies include a Query ID. ICMPv4 uses the Query ID to identify an echo request with its corresponding echo reply. The Query ID is incremented with each echo request sent. PAT uses the Query ID instead of a Layer 4 port number.

> **Note**
>
> Other ICMPv4 messages do not use the Query ID. These messages and other protocols that do not use TCP or UDP port numbers vary and are beyond the scope of this curriculum.

Packet Tracer Activity 11.1.2.6: Investigating NAT Operation

You know that as a frame travels across a network, the MAC addresses change. But IP addresses can also change when a packet is forwarded by a device configured with NAT. In this activity, you see what happens to IP addresses during the NAT process.

Benefits of NAT (11.1.3)

NAT is common in home networks, small business, and multisite corporations. Understanding the benefits and the disadvantages associated with NAT helps to have a deeper understanding of the NAT concepts.

Benefits of NAT (11.1.3.1)

NAT provides many benefits, including

- NAT conserves the legally registered addressing scheme by allowing the privatization of intranets. NAT conserves addresses through application port-level multiplexing. With NAT overload, internal hosts can share a single public IPv4 address for all external communications. In this type of configuration, very few external addresses are required to support many internal hosts.

- NAT increases the flexibility of connections to the public network. Multiple pools, backup pools, and load-balancing pools can be implemented to ensure reliable public network connections.

- NAT provides consistency for internal network addressing schemes. On a network not using private IPv4 addresses and NAT, changing the public IPv4 address scheme requires the readdressing of all hosts on the existing network. The costs of readdressing hosts can be significant. NAT allows the existing private IPv4 address scheme to remain while allowing for easy change to a new public addressing scheme. This means an organization could change ISPs and not need to change any of its inside clients.

- NAT provides network security. Because private networks do not advertise their addresses or internal topology, they remain reasonably secure when used with NAT to gain controlled external access. However, NAT does not replace firewalls.

Disadvantages of NAT (11.1.3.2)

NAT does have some drawbacks. The fact that hosts on the Internet appear to communicate directly with the NAT-enabled device, rather than with the actual host inside the private network, creates a number of issues.

One disadvantage of using NAT is related to network performance, particularly for real-time protocols such as VoIP. NAT increases switching delays because the translation of each IPv4 address within the packet headers takes time. The first packet is process-switched; it always goes through the slower path. The router must look at every packet to decide whether it needs translation. The router must alter the IPv4 header and possibly alter the TCP or UDP header. The IPv4 header checksum, along with the TCP or UDP checksum, must be recalculated each time a translation is made. Remaining packets go through the fast-switched path if a cache entry exists; otherwise, they, too, are delayed.

Another disadvantage of using NAT is that end-to-end addressing is lost. Many Internet protocols and applications depend on end-to-end addressing from the source to the destination. Some applications do not work with NAT. For example, some security applications, such as digital signatures, fail because the source IPv4 address changes before reaching the destination. Applications that use physical addresses, instead of a qualified domain name, do not reach destinations that are translated across the NAT router. Sometimes, this problem can be avoided by implementing static NAT mappings.

End-to-end IPv4 traceability is also lost. It becomes much more difficult to trace packets that undergo numerous packet address changes over multiple NAT hops, making troubleshooting challenging.

Using NAT also complicates tunneling protocols, such as IPsec, because NAT modifies values in the headers that interfere with the integrity checks done by IPsec and other tunneling protocols.

Services that require the initiation of TCP connections from the outside network, or stateless protocols, such as those using UDP, can be disrupted. Unless the NAT router has been configured to support such protocols, incoming packets cannot reach their destination. Some protocols can accommodate one instance of NAT between participating hosts (passive mode FTP, for example), but fail when both systems are separated from the Internet by NAT.

Configuring NAT (11.2)

Now that you know some information about NAT, you should learn how to configure this technology. In this section, you learn how to configure static NAT, dynamic NAT, and PAT. Keep in mind that you can do more than one NAT type on a single border device such as a router.

Configuring Static NAT (11.2.1.1)

Static NAT is a one-to-one mapping between an inside address and an outside address. Static NAT allows external devices to initiate connections to internal devices using the statically assigned public address. For instance, an internal web server may be mapped to a specific inside global address so that it is accessible from outside networks.

Figure 11-10 and Table 11-6 show an inside network containing a web server with a private IPv4 address.

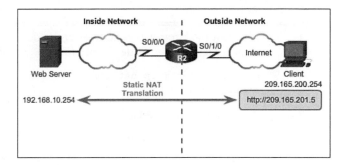

Figure 11-10   Static NAT Topology

Table 11-6   Static NAT Table

Inside Global Address	Inside Local Address
209.165.201.5	192.168.10.254

Router R2 is configured with static NAT to allow devices on the outside network (Internet) to access the web server. The client on the outside network accesses the web server using a public IPv4 address. Static NAT translates the public IPv4 address to the private IPv4 address.

There are two basic tasks when configuring static NAT translations.

Step 1.   The first task is to create a mapping between the inside local address and the inside global addresses. For example, the 192.168.10.254 inside local address and the 209.165.201.5 inside global address shown in both Figure 11-10 and Table 11-6 are configured as a static NAT translation.

Step 2.   After the mapping is configured, the interfaces participating in the translation are configured as inside or outside relative to NAT. In the example, the Serial 0/0/0 interface of R2 is an inside interface and Serial 0/1/0 is an outside interface.

Packets arriving on the inside interface of R2 (Serial 0/0/0) from the configured inside local IPv4 address (192.168.10.254) are translated and then forwarded toward the outside network. Packets arriving on the outside interface of R2 (Serial 0/1/0), which are addressed to the configured inside global IPv4 address (209.165.201.5), are translated to the inside local address (192.168.10.254) and then forwarded to the inside network.

Table 11-7 outlines the commands needed to configure static NAT.

Table 11-7 Static NAT Commands

Step	Action	Notes
1	Establish static translation between an inside local address and an inside global address. `Router(config)# ip nat inside source static local-ip global-ip`	Enter the **no ip nat inside source static** global configuration mode command to remove the static source translation.
2	Access the inside interface. `Router(config)# interface type number`	Enter the **interface** command. The CLI prompt changes from `Router(config)#` to `Router(config-if)#`.
3	Designate the interface as connected to the inside network. `Router(config-if)# ip nat inside`	
4	Exit interface configuration mode. `Router(config-if)# exit`	
5	Access the outside interface. `Router(config)# interface type number`	
6	Designate the interface as connected to the outside network. `Router(config-if)# ip nat outside`	

The commands that follow are used to configure the static NAT topology shown in Figure 11-10.

```
!Establishes static translation between an inside local address and an inside global
   address.
R2(config)# ip nat inside source static 192.168.10.254 209.165.201.5


!Identifies interface serial 0/0/0 as an inside NAT interface.
R2(config)# interface serial0/0/0
R2(config-if)# ip address 10.1.1.2 255.255.255.252
```

```
R2(config-if)# ip nat inside
R2(config-if)# exit

!Identifies interface serial 0/1/0 as the outside NAT interface.
R2(config)# interface serial0/1/0
R2(config-if)# ip address 209.165.200.225 255.255.255.224
R2(config-if)# ip nat outside
R2(config-if)# exit
```

With the configuration shown, R2 translates packets from the web server with address 192.168.10.254 to public IPv4 address 209.165.201.5. The Internet client directs web requests to the public IPv4 address 209.165.201.5. R2 forwards that traffic to the web server at 192.168.10.254.

Interactive Graphic

Activity 11.2.1.1: Configure Static NAT

Go to the online course and select the fourth graphic. Use the Syntax Checker to configure an additional static NAT entry on R2.

Analyzing Static NAT (11.2.1.2)

Using the previous configuration, Figure 11-11 illustrates the static NAT translation process between the client and the web server. Usually static translations are used when clients on the outside network (Internet) need to reach servers on the inside (internal) network.

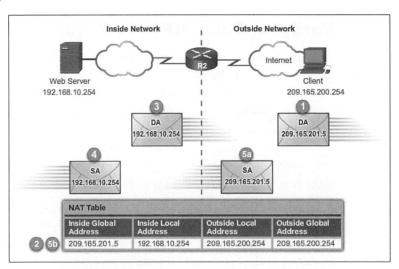

Figure 11-11   Static NAT Process

How To ⌕

Step 1.   The client wants to open a connection to the web server. The client sends a packet to the web server using the public IPv4 destination address of 209.165.201.5. This is the inside global address of the web server.

Step 2.   The first packet that R2 receives from the client on its NAT outside interface causes R2 to check its NAT table. The destination IPv4 address is located in the NAT table and is translated.

Step 3.   R2 replaces the inside global address of 209.165.201.5 with the inside local address of 192.168.10.254. R2 then forwards the packet toward the web server.

Step 4.   The web server receives the packet and responds to the client using the inside local address, 192.168.10.254.

Step 5.   R2 receives the packet from the web server on its NAT inside interface with source address of the inside local address of the web server, 192.168.10.254.

   R2 checks the NAT table for a translation for the inside local address. The address is found in the NAT table. R2 translates the source address to the inside global address of 209.165.201.5 and forwards the packet out of its serial 0/1/0 interface toward the client.

Step 6.   The client receives the packet and continues the conversation. The NAT router performs Steps 2 to 5b for each packet. (Step 6 is not shown in Figure 11-11.)

Verifying Static NAT (11.2.1.3)

A useful command to verify NAT operation is the **show ip nat translations** command. This command shows active NAT translations. Static translations, unlike dynamic translations, are always in the NAT table. The following shows the output from this command using the previous configuration example.

```
R2# show ip nat translations
Pro   Inside global   Inside local     Outside local  Outside global
---   209.165.201.5   192.168.10.254   ---            ---
```

Note how the static translation is always present in the NAT table.

Because the example is a static NAT configuration, the translation is always present in the NAT table regardless of any active communications. If the command is issued during an active session, the output also indicates the address of the outside device, as shown in the following output.

```
R2# show ip nat translations
Pro   Inside global   Inside local     Outside local     Outside global
---   209.165.201.5   192.168.10.254   209.165.200.254   209.165.200.254
```

Another useful command is the **show ip nat statistics** command, but to verify that the NAT translation is working, it is best to clear statistics from any past translations using the **clear ip nat statistics** command before testing, as shown in the following output.

```
R2# clear ip nat statistics

R2# show ip nat statistics
Total translations: 1 (1 static, 0 dynamic, 0 extended)
Peak translations: 0
Outside interfaces:
  Serial0/1/0
Inside interfaces:
  Serial0/0/0
Hits: 0  Misses: 0
<output omitted>
```

The output of the **show ip nat statistics** command displays information about the total number of active translations, NAT configuration parameters, the number of addresses in the pool, and the number of addresses that have been allocated.

Prior to any communications with the web server, the **show ip nat statistics** command shows no current hits. After the client establishes a session with the web server, the **show ip nat statistics** command has been incremented to five hits, as shown in the following output. This verifies that the static NAT translation is taking place on R2.

```
R2# show ip nat statistics
Total translations: 1 (1 static, 0 dynamic, 0 extended)
Peak translations: 2, occurred 00:00:14 ago
Outside interfaces:
    Serial0/1/0
Inside interfaces:
    Serial0/0/0
Hits: 5  Misses: 0
<output omitted>
```

Packet Tracer Activity 11.2.1.4: Configuring Static NAT

In IPv4-configured networks, clients and servers use private addressing. Before packets with private addressing can cross the Internet, they need to be translated to public addressing. Servers that are accessed from outside the organization are usually assigned both a public and a private static IP address. In this activity, you configure static NAT so that outside devices can access an inside server at its public address.

Configuring Dynamic NAT (11.2.2)

Dynamic NAT is used for the bulk of internal corporate devices. It is important that you know how to configure this type of NAT. Dynamic NAT has a little more complexity to the configuration, so go slowly through this section to ensure you get the purpose of each command.

Dynamic NAT Operation (11.2.2.1)

While static NAT provides a permanent mapping between an inside local address and an inside global address, dynamic NAT allows the automatic mapping of inside local addresses to inside global addresses. These inside global addresses are typically public IPv4 addresses. Dynamic NAT uses a group or pool of public IPv4 addresses for translation.

Dynamic NAT, like static NAT, requires the configuration of the inside and outside interfaces participating in NAT. However, where static NAT creates a permanent mapping to a single address, dynamic NAT uses a pool of addresses.

Note

Translating between public and private IPv4 addresses is by far the most common use of NAT. However, NAT translations can occur between any pair of addresses.

The example topology shown in Figure 11-12 has an inside network using addresses from the RFC 1918 private address space. Attached to router R1 are two LANs, 192.168.10.0/24 and 192.168.11.0/24. Router R2, the border router, is configured for dynamic NAT using a pool of public IPv4 addresses 209.165.200.226 through 209.165.200.240, as shown in Table 11-8.

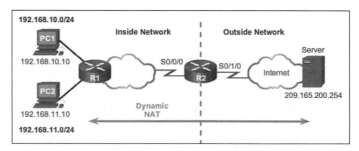

Figure 11-12   Dynamic NAT Topology

Table 11-8   IPv4 Dynamic NAT Pool

Inside Global Address	Inside Local Address
209.165.200.226	192.168.10.10
209.165.200.227	192.168.11.10
209.165.200.228	Available
…	…
209.165.200.240	Available

The pool of public IPv4 addresses (inside global address pool) is available to any device on the inside network on a first-come first-served basis. With dynamic NAT, a single inside address is translated to a single outside address. With this type of translation, there must be enough addresses in the pool to accommodate all the inside devices needing access to the outside network at the same time. If all the addresses in the pool have been used, a device must wait for an available address before it can access the outside network.

Configuring Dynamic NAT (11.2.2.2)

Table 11-9 shows the steps and the commands used to configure dynamic NAT.

Table 11-9   Dynamic NAT Configuration Steps

Step 1	Define a pool of global addresses to be used for translation.
	ip nat pool *name start-ip end-ip* {**netmask** *netmask* | **prefix-length** *prefix-length*}
Step 2	Configure a standard access list permitting the addresses that should be translated.
	access-list *access-list-number* **permit** *source* [*source-wildcard*]
Step 3	Establish dynamic source translation by specifying the access list and pool that was defined in prior steps.
	ip nat inside source list *access-list-number* **pool** *name*
Step 4	Identify the inside interface.
	interface *type number*
	ip nat inside
Step 5	Identify the outside interface.
	interface *type number*
	ip nat outside

How To

Step 1. Define the pool of addresses that will be used for translation using the **ip nat pool** command. This pool of addresses is typically a group of public addresses. The addresses are defined by indicating the starting IP address and the ending IP address of the pool. The **netmask** or **prefix-length** keyword indicates which address bits belong to the network and which bits belong to the host for the range of addresses.

Step 2. Configure a standard ACL to identify (permit) only those addresses that are to be translated. An ACL that is too permissive can lead to unpredictable results. Remember there is an implicit **deny all** statement at the end of each ACL.

Step 3. Bind the ACL to the pool. The **ip nat inside source list** *access-list-number* **pool** *name* command is used to bind the ACL to the pool. This configuration is used by the router to identify which devices (**list**) receive which addresses (**pool**).

Step 4. Identify which interfaces are inside, in relation to NAT; that is, any interface that connects to the inside network.

Step 5. Identify which interfaces are outside, in relation to NAT; that is, any interface that connects to the outside network.

Figure 11-13 shows an example topology, and the configuration follows.

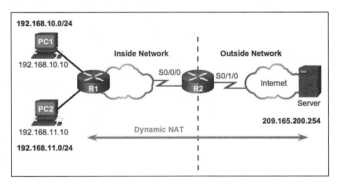

Figure 11-13 Example Dynamic NAT Topology

```
!Define a pool of public IPv4 addresses under the pool name NAT-POOL1.
R2(config)# ip nat pool NAT-POOL1 209.165.200.226 209.165.200.240 netmask
   255.255.255.224
!Define which addresses are eligible to be translated.
R2(config)# access-list 1 permit 192.168.0.0 0.0.255.255

!Bind NAT-POOL1 with access list 1.
R2(config)# ip nat inside source list 1 pool NAT-POOL1
```

```
!Identify interface serial 0/0/0 as an inside NAT interface.
R2(config)# interface serial0/0/0
  R2(config-if)# ip nat inside


!Identify interface serial 0/1/0 as an outside NAT interface.
R2(config)# interface serial0/1/0
  R2(config-if)# ip nat outside
```

This configuration allows translation for all hosts on the 192.168.0.0/16 network, which includes the 192.168.10.0 and 192.168.11.0 LANs, when they generate traffic that enters S0/0/0 and exits S0/1/0. These hosts are translated to an available address in the pool in the range 209.165.200.226-209.165.200.240.

Interactive Graphic

Activity 11.2.2.2: Configure Static NAT

Go to the online course and select the third graphic to see the topology used for the Syntax Checker. Then use the fourth graphic to access the Syntax Checker you can use to practice configuring dynamic NAT on R2.

Analyzing Dynamic NAT (11.2.2.3)

Using the previous configuration, Figures 11-14 and 11-15 illustrate the dynamic NAT translation process between two clients and the web server.

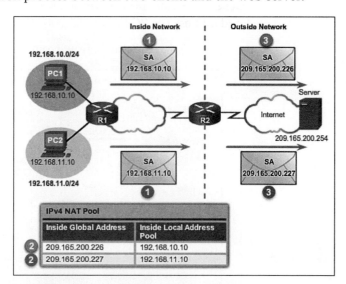

Figure 11-14   Dynamic NAT Process-Inside to Outside

In Figure 11-14, the traffic flow from inside to outside is shown.

Step 1.   The hosts with the source IPv4 addresses (192.168.10.10 [PC1] and 192.168.11.10 [PC2]) send packets requesting a connection to the server at the public IPv4 address (209.165.200.254).

Step 2.   R2 receives the first packet from host 192.168.10.10. Because this packet was received on an interface configured as an inside NAT interface, R2 checks the NAT configuration to determine if this packet should be translated. The ACL permits this packet, so R2 will translate the packet. R2 checks its NAT table. Because there is no translation entry for this IP address, R2 determines that the source address 192.168.10.10 must be translated dynamically. R2 selects an available global address from the dynamic address pool and creates a translation entry, 209.165.200.226. The original source IPv4 address (192.168.10.10) is the inside local address, and the translated address is the inside global address (209.165.200.226) in the NAT table.

For the second host, 192.168.11.10, R2 repeats the procedure, selects the next available global address from the dynamic address pool and creates a second translation entry, 209.165.200.227.

Step 3.   R2 replaces the inside local source address of PC1, 192.168.10.10, with the translated inside global address of 209.165.200.226, and forwards the packet. The same process occurs for the packet from PC2 using the translated address for PC2 (209.165.200.227).

In Figure 11-15, the traffic flow from outside to inside is shown.

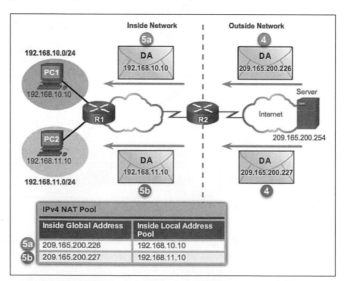

Figure 11-15   Dynamic NAT Process-Outside to Inside

Step 4. The server receives the packet from PC1 and responds using the IPv4 destination address of 209.165.200.226. When the server receives the second packet, it responds to PC2 using the IPv4 destination address of 209.165.200.227.

Step 5. When R2 receives the packet with the destination IPv4 address of 209.165.200.226, it performs a NAT table lookup. Using the mapping from the table, R2 translates the address back to the inside local address (192.168.10.10) and forwards the packet toward PC1.

When R2 receives the packet with the destination IPv4 address of 209.165.200.227, it performs a NAT table lookup. Using the mapping from the table, R2 translates the address back to the inside local address (192.168.11.10) and forwards the packet toward PC2.

Step 6. PC1 at 192.168.10.10 and PC2 at 192.168.11.10 receive the packets and continue the conversation. The router performs Steps 2 through 5 for each packet. (Step 6 is not shown in the figures.)

Verifying Dynamic NAT (11.2.2.4)

The output of the **show ip nat translations** command shown in the following output displays the details of the two previous NAT assignments. The command output shows that all static translations that have been configured and any dynamic translations that have been created by traffic.

```
R2# show ip nat translations
Pro  Inside global     Inside local     Outside local     Outside global
---  209.165.200.226   192.168.10.10    ---               ---
---  209.165.200.227   192.168.11.10    ---               ---
```

Adding the **verbose** keyword displays additional information about each translation, including how long ago the entry was created and used.

```
R2# show ip nat translations verbose
Pro Inside global     Inside local     Outside local Outside global
--- 209.165.200.226   192.168.10.10    ---             ---
    create 00:17:25, use 00:01:54, timeout: 86400000,left
23:58:05,Map-Id(In):1,
    flags:
none, use count: 0, entry-id: 32, lc_entries: 0
--- 209.165.200.227   192.168.11.10    ---             ---
    create 00:17:25, use 00:01:51, timeout: 86400000,left
23:58:08,Map-Id(In):1,
    flags:
none, use count: 0, entry-id: 34, lc_entries: 0
```

By default, translation entries time out after 24 hours, unless the timers have been reconfigured with the **ip nat translation timeout** *timeout-seconds* command in global configuration mode. To clear dynamic entries before the timeout has expired, use the **clear ip nat translation** global configuration mode command as shown.

```
R2# clear ip nat translation *
R2# show ip nat translations
```

It is useful to clear the dynamic entries when testing the NAT configuration. As shown in Table 11-10, this command can be used with keywords and variables to control which entries are cleared. Specific entries can be cleared to avoid disrupting active sessions. Use the **clear ip nat translation** * global configuration command to clear all translations from the table.

Note

Only the dynamic translations are cleared from the table. Static translations cannot be cleared from the translation table.

Table 11-10   Clearing NAT Translations

`clear ip nat translation *`	Clears all dynamic address translation entries from the NAT translation table
`clear ip nat translation inside` *global-ip local-ip* [**outside** *local-ip global-ip*]	Clears a single dynamic translation entry containing an inside translation or both inside and outside translation
`clear ip nat translation` *protocol* **inside** *global-ip global-port local-ip local-port* [**outside** *local-ip local-port global-ip global-port*]	Clears an extended dynamic translation entry

In the following output, the **show ip nat statistics** command displays information about the total number of active translations, NAT configuration parameters, the number of addresses in the pool, and how many of the addresses have been allocated.

```
R2# clear ip nat statistics
<PC1 and PC2 establish sessions with the external server.>

R2# show ip nat statistics
Total active translations: 0 (0 static, 2 dynamic, 0 extended)
Peak translations: 6, occurred 00:27:07 ago
```

```
Outside interfaces:
  Serial0/1/0
Inside interfaces:
  Serial0/0/0
Hits: 24  Misses: 0
CEF Translated packets: 24, CEF Punted packets: 0
Expired translations: 4
Dynamic mappings:
-- Inside Source
[ID: 1] access-list 1 pool NAT-POOL1 refCount 2
 pool NAT-POOL1: netmask 255.255.255.224
 start 209.165.200.226 end 209.165.200.240
 type generic, total addresses 15 , allocated 2 (13%), misses 0

Total doors: 0
Appl doors: 0
Normal doors: 0
Queued Packets: 0
R2#
```

Alternatively, use the **show running-config** command and look for NAT, ACL, interface, or pool commands with the required values. Examine these carefully and correct any errors discovered.

Packet Tracer Activity 11.2.2.5: Configuring Dynamic NAT

In this Packet Tracer, you complete the following objectives:

- Part 1: Configure Dynamic NAT

- Part 2: Verify NAT Implementation

Lab 11:2.2.6: Configuring Dynamic and Static NAT

In this lab, you complete the following objectives:

- Part 1: Build the Network and Verify Connectivity

- Part 2: Configure and Verify Static NAT

- Part 3: Configure and Verify Dynamic NAT

Configuring Port Address Translation (PAT) (11.2.3)

PAT is commonly used in small companies and large companies. PAT can be implemented using one of two methods. One method uses a pool of addresses. The second method uses the IP address of the router interface that connects to the Internet. First, learn how to configure the address pool method.

Configuring PAT: Address Pool (11.2.3.1)

PAT (also called NAT overload) conserves addresses in the inside global address pool by allowing the router to use one inside global address for many inside local addresses. In other words, a single public IPv4 address can be used for hundreds, even thousands of internal private IPv4 addresses. When this type of translation is configured, the router maintains enough information from higher-level protocols (TCP or UDP port numbers, for example) to translate the inside global address back into the correct inside local address. When multiple inside local addresses map to one inside global address, the TCP or UDP port numbers of each inside host distinguish between the local addresses.

> **Note**
>
> The total number of internal addresses that can be translated to one external address could theoretically be as high as 65,536 per IP address. However, the number of internal addresses that are assigned a single IP address does not normally exceed 4000.

There are two ways to configure PAT, depending on how the ISP allocates public IPv4 addresses. In the first instance, the ISP allocates more than one public IPv4 address to the organization, and in the other, it allocates a single public IPv4 address that is required for the organization to connect to the ISP.

Configuring PAT for a Pool of Public IP Addresses

If a site has been issued more than one public IPv4 address, these addresses can be part of a pool that is used by PAT. This is similar to dynamic NAT, except that there are not enough public addresses for a one-to-one mapping of inside to outside addresses. The small pool of addresses is shared among a larger number of devices.

Table 11-11 shows the steps to configure PAT to use a pool of addresses. The primary difference between this configuration and the configuration for dynamic, one-to-one NAT is that the **overload** keyword is used. The **overload** keyword enables PAT.

Table 11-11   PAT Configuration Steps

Step 1	Define a pool of global addresses to be used for translation.
	`ip nat pool` *name start-ip end-ip* {`netmask` *netmask* | `prefix-length` *prefix-length*}
Step 2	Configure a standard access list permitting the addresses that should be translated.
	`access-list` *access-list-number* `permit` *source* [*source-wildcard*]
Step 3	Establish overload translation by specifying the access list and pool that was defined in prior steps.
	`ip nat inside source list` *access-list-number* `pool` *name* `overload`
Step 4	Identify the inside interface.
	`interface` *type number*
	`ip nat inside`
Step 5	Identify the outside interface.
	`interface` *type number*
	`ip nat outside`

An example topology is shown in Figure 11-16.

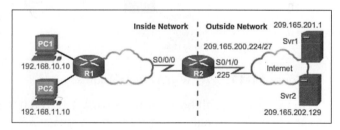

Figure 11-16   Example PAT Topology

```
!Define a pool of public IPv4 addresses under the pool name NAT-POOL2.
R2(config)# ip nat pool NAT-POOL2 209.165.200.226 209.165.200.240 netmask
   255.255.255.224
!Define which addresses are eligible to be translated.
R2(config)# access-list 1 permit 192.168.0.0 0.0.255.255

!Bind NAT-POOL2 with access list 1.
R2(config)# ip nat inside source list 1 pool NAT-POOL2 overload

!Identify interface serial 0/0/0 as an inside NAT interface.
R2(config)# interface serial0/0/0
R2(config-if)# ip nat inside
```

```
!Identify interface serial 0/1/0 as an outside NAT interface.
R2(config)# interface serial0/1/0
R2(config-if)# ip nat outside
```

The previous configuration establishes overload translation for the NAT pool named NAT-POOL2. NAT-POOL2 contains addresses 209.165.200.226 to 209.165.200.240. Hosts in the 192.168.0.0/16 network are subject to translation. The S0/0/0 interface is identified as an inside interface, and the S0/1/0 interface is identified as an outside interface.

Activity 11.2.3.1: Configure PAT: Address Pool

Go to the online course and select the third graphic. Use the Syntax Checker to configure PAT using an address pool on R2.

Configuring PAT: Single Address (11.2.3.2)

Figure 11-17 shows the topology of a PAT implementation for a single public IPv4 address translation.

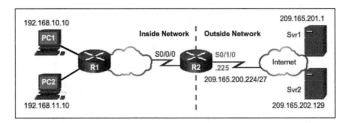

Figure 11-17   PAT with a Single Address

In the example, all hosts from network 192.168.0.0/16 (matching ACL 1) that send traffic through router R2 to the Internet will be translated to IPv4 address 209.165.200.225 (IPv4 address of interface S0/1/0) as shown in the NAT table (Table 11-12). The traffic flows will be identified by port numbers in the NAT table because the **overload** keyword was used.

Table 11-12   NAT Table with PAT Implemented

Inside Global Address	Inside Local Address	Outside Local Address	Outside Global Address
209.165.200.225:1444	192.168.10.10:1444	209.165.201.1:80	209.165.201.1:80
209.165.200.225:1445	192.168.10.11:1444	209.165.202.129:80	209.165.202.129:80

The following steps are used to configure PAT with a single IPv4 address. If only a single public IPv4 address is available, the overload configuration typically assigns the public address to the outside interface that connects to the ISP. All inside addresses are translated to the single IPv4 address when leaving the outside interface.

Step 1. Define a standard access list to permit the traffic to be translated.

```
access-list access-list-number permit source [source-wildcard]
```

Step 2. Configure source translation using the access list number, **interface**, and **overload** keywords. The **interface** keyword identifies which interface IP address to use when translating inside addresses. The **overload** keyword directs the router to track port numbers with each NAT entry.

```
ip nat inside source list access-list-number interface type number
overload
```

Step 3. Identify which interfaces are inside in relation to NAT; that is, any interface that connects to the inside network.

```
interface type number
ip nat inside
```

Step 4. Identify which interface is outside in relation to NAT. This should be the same interface identified in the source translation statement from Step 2.

```
interface type number
ip nat  outside
```

The configuration is similar to dynamic NAT, except that instead of a pool of addresses, the **interface** keyword is used to identify the outside IPv4 address, and the **overload** keyword is used. Therefore, no NAT pool is defined.

Interactive Graphic

Activity 11.2.3.2: Configure PAT: Single Address

Go to the online course and select the third graphic in order to use the Syntax Checker to configure PAT using a single address on R2.

Analyzing PAT (11.2.3.3)

The process of NAT overload is the same whether a pool of addresses is used or a single address is used. Continuing with the previous PAT example, using a single public IPv4 address, PC1 wants to communicate with the web server, Svr1. At the same time, another client, PC2, wants to establish a similar session with the web server Svr2. Both PC1 and PC2 are configured with private IPv4 addresses, with R2 enabled for PAT.

PC to Server Process

1. Figure 11-18 shows both PC1 and PC2 sending packets to Svr1 and Svr2, respectively. PC1 has the source IPv4 address 192.168.10.10 and is using TCP source port 1444. PC2 has the source IPv4 address 192.168.10.11 and is coincidentally assigned the same source port of 1444.

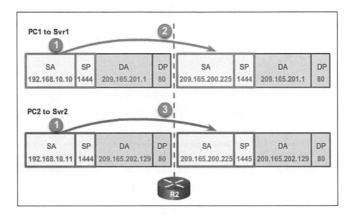

Figure 11-18   PAT Analysis from PCs to Servers

2. The packet from PC1 reaches R2 first. Using PAT, R2 modifies the source IPv4 address to 209.165.200.225 (inside global address) as shown in Table 11-13. There are no other devices in the NAT table using port 1444, so PAT maintains the same port number. The packet is then forwarded toward Svr1 at 209.165.201.1.

Table 11-13   NAT Table to Show PAT Analysis from PCs

Inside Local Address	Inside Global Address	Outside Global Address	Outside Local Address
192.168.10.10:1444	209.165.200.225:1444	209.165.201.1:80	209.165.201.1:80
192.168.11.10:1444	209.165.200.225:1445	209.165.202.129:80	209.165.202.129:80

3. Next, the packet from PC2 arrives at R2. PAT is configured to use a single inside global IPv4 address for all translations, 209.165.200.225. Similar to the translation process for PC1, PAT changes PC2's source IPv4 address to the inside global address 209.165.200.225. However, PC2 has the same source port number as a current PAT entry, the translation for PC1. PAT increments the source port number until it is a unique value in its table. In this instance, the source port entry in the NAT table and the packet for PC2 receives 1445.

Although PC1 and PC2 are using the same translated address, the inside global address of 209.165.200.225, and the same source port number of 1444, the modified port number for PC2 (1445) makes each entry in the NAT table unique. This will become evident with the packets sent from the servers back to the clients.

Server to PC Process

4. As shown in Figure 11-19, in a typical client-server exchange, Svr1 and Svr2 respond to the requests received from PC1 and PC2, respectively. The servers use the source port from the received packet as the destination port and the source address as the destination address for the return traffic. The servers seem as if they are communicating with the same host at 209.165.200.225; however, this is not the case.

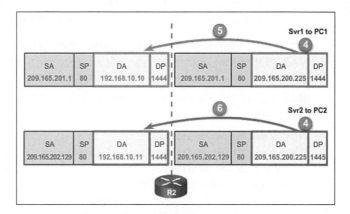

Figure 11-19   PAT Analysis from Servers to PCs

5. As the packets arrive, R2 locates the unique entry in its NAT table (see Table 11-13) using the destination address and the destination port of each packet. In the case of the packet from Svr1, the destination IPv4 address of 209.165.200.225 has multiple entries but only one with the destination port 1444. Using the entry in its table, R2 changes the destination IPv4 address of the packet to 192.168.10.10, with no change required for the destination port. The packet is then forwarded toward PC1.

6. When the packet from Svr2 arrives, R2 performs a similar translation. The destination IPv4 address of 209.165.200.225 is located, again with multiple entries. However, using the destination port of 1445, R2 is able to uniquely identify the translation entry. The destination IPv4 address is changed to 192.168.11.10. In this case, the destination port must also be modified back to its original value of 1444, which is stored in the NAT table. The packet is then forwarded toward PC2.

Verifying PAT (11.2.3.4)

Router R2 has been configured to provide PAT to the 192.168.0.0/16 clients. When the internal hosts exit router R2 to the Internet, they are translated to an IPv4 address from the PAT pool with a unique source port number.

The same commands used to verify static and dynamic NAT are used to verify PAT, as shown in the following output. The **show ip nat translations** command displays the translations from two different hosts to different web servers. Notice that two different inside hosts are allocated the same IPv4 address of 209.165.200.226 (inside global address). The source port numbers in the NAT table differentiate the two transactions.

```
R2# show ip nat translations
Pro  Inside global       Inside local       Outside local      Outside global
tcp  209.165.200.226:51839 192.168.10.10:51839 209.165.201.1:80 209.165.201.1:80
tcp  209.165.200.226:42558 192.168.11.10:42558 209.165.202.129:80 209.165.202.129:80
```

As shown in the following output, the **show ip nat statistics** command verifies that NAT-POOL2 has allocated a single address for both translations. Included in the output is information about the number and type of active translations, NAT configuration parameters, the number of addresses in the pool, and how many have been allocated.

```
R2# clear ip nat statistics
<PC1 and PC2 establish sessions with the external server.>
R2# show ip nat statistics
Total active translations: 0 (0 static, 2 dynamic, 2 extended)
Peak translations: 6, occurred 00:00:05 ago
Outside interfaces:
  Serial0/1/0
Inside interfaces:
  Serial0/0/0
Hits: 4  Misses: 0
CEF Translated packets: 4, CEF Punted packets: 0
Expired translations: 4
Dynamic mappings:
-- Inside Source
[ID: 3] access-list 1 pool NAT-POOL2 refCount 2
 pool NAT-POOL2: netmask 255.255.255.224
 start 209.165.200.226 end 209.165.200.240
 type generic, total addresses 15 , allocated 1 (6%), misses 0

Total doors: 0
Appl doors: 0
```

```
Normal doors: 0
Queued Packets: 0
R2#
```

Activity 11.2.3.5: Identify the Address Information at Each Hop

Go to the online course and select the first graphic to see the topology. Click the second through fifth graphics to drag the appropriate source address, source port number, destination address, and destination port numbers to the appropriate location.

Packet Tracer Activity 11.2.3.6: Implementing Static and Dynamic NAT

In this Packet Tracer, you complete the following objectives:

- Part 1: Configure Dynamic NAT with PAT
- Part 2: Configure Static NAT
- Part 3: Verify NAT Implementation

Lab 11.2.3.7: Configuring NAT Pool Overload and PAT

In this lab, you complete the following objectives:

- Part 1: Build the Network and Verify Connectivity
- Part 2: Configure and Verify NAT Pool Overload
- Part 3: Configure and Verify PAT

Port Forwarding (11.2.4)

Port forwarding (sometimes referred to as tunneling) is the act of forwarding a network port from one network node to another. This technique allows an external user to reach a port on a private IPv4 address (inside a LAN) from an outside network through a NAT-enabled router.

Typically, peer-to-peer file-sharing programs and operations, such as web serving and outgoing FTP, require that router ports be forwarded or opened to allow these applications to work, as shown in Figure 11-20. Because NAT hides internal addresses, peer-to-peer works only from the inside out where NAT can map outgoing requests against incoming replies.

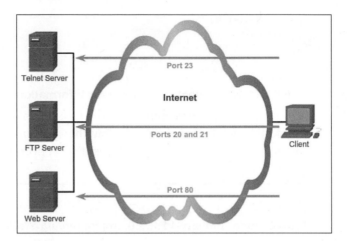

Figure 11-20   TCP and UDP Destination Ports

The problem is that NAT does not allow requests to be initiated from the outside. This situation can be resolved with manual intervention. Port forwarding can be configured to identify specific ports that can be forwarded to inside hosts.

Recall that Internet software applications interact with user ports that need to be open or available to those applications. Different applications use different port numbers. This makes it predictable for applications and routers to identify network services. For example, HTTP operates through the well-known port 80. When someone enters the `http://cisco.com` address, the browser displays the Cisco Systems, Inc. website. Notice that they do not have to specify the HTTP port number for the page request because the application assumes port 80.

If a different port number is required, it can be appended to the URL separated by a colon (:). For example, if the web server is listening on port 8080, the user would type `http://www.example.com:8080`.

Port forwarding allows users on the Internet to access internal servers by using the WAN port address of the router and the matched external port number. The internal servers are typically configured with RFC 1918 private IPv4 addresses. When a request is sent to the IPv4 address of the WAN port via the Internet, the router forwards the request to the appropriate server on the LAN. For security reasons, broadband routers do not, by default, permit any external network request to be forwarded to an inside host.

Figure 11-21 shows a small business owner using a point of sale (PoS) server to track sales and inventories at the store.

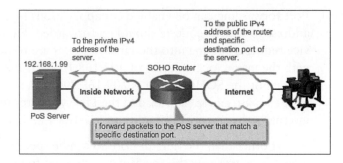

Figure 11-21   PoS Server Port Forwarding Example

The server can be accessed within the store, but because it has a private IPv4 address, it is not publically accessible from the Internet. Enabling the local router for port forwarding allows the owner to access the point of sale server from anywhere on the Internet. Port forwarding on the router is configured using the destination port number and the private IPv4 address of the point of sale server. To access the server, the client software would use the public IPv4 address of the router and the destination port of the server.

SOHO Example (11.2.4.2)

Figure 11-22 shows the Single Port Forwarding configuration window of a Linksys EA6500 SOHO router. By default, port forwarding is not enabled on the router.

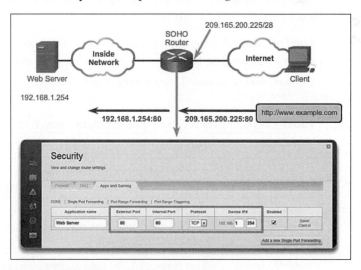

Figure 11-22   SOHO Router Port Forwarding Example

Port forwarding can be enabled for applications by specifying the inside local address to which requests should be forwarded. Figure 11-22 shows HTTP service requests coming into the Linksys router are forwarded to the web server with the inside local address of 192.168.1.254. If the external WAN IPv4 address of the SOHO router is 209.165.200.225, the external user can enter `http://www.example.com`, and the Linksys router redirects the HTTP request to the internal web server at IPv4 address 192.168.1.254, using the default port number 80.

A port other than the default port 80 can be specified. However, the external user would have to know the specific port number to use. To specify a different port, the value of the External Port in the Single Port Forwarding window would be modified.

The approach taken to configure port forwarding depends on the brand and model of the broadband router in the network. However, there are some generic steps to follow. If the instructions supplied by the ISP, or those that came with the router, do not provide adequate guidance, the website `http://www.portforward.com` provides guides for several broadband routers. You can follow the instructions to add or delete ports as required to meet the needs of any applications you want to allow or deny.

Configuring Port Forwarding with IOS (11.2.4.3)

Implementing port forwarding with IOS commands is similar to the commands used to configure static NAT. Port forwarding is essentially a static NAT translation with a specified TCP or UDP port number.

The following configuration and Table 11-14 shows the static NAT command and parameters needed to configure port forwarding using IOS.

```
ip nat inside source {static {tcp | udp local-ip local-port global-ip global-port}
   [extendable]
```

Table 11-14 Port Forwarding Parameters Using IOS

tcp or **udp**	Indicates if the source is a TCP or UDP port number.
local-ip	An IPv4 address assigned to the host on the inside network, typically from the RFC 1918 private address space.
local-port	Sets the TCP/UDP port number chosen from a range of numbers from 1 to 65,535. This is the port number through which the server listens for network traffic.
global-ip	This is the globally unique IPv4 address of the inside host. This is the IP address the outside client(s) will use to reach the internal server.

global-port	Sets the TCP/UDP port number chosen from a range of numbers from 1 to 65,535. This is the port number the outside client will use to reach the internal server.
extendable	The **extendable** option is applied automatically. The **extendable** keyword allows the user to configure several ambiguous static translations, where ambiguous translations are translations with the same local or global address. It allows the router to extend the translation to more than one port if necessary.

Figure 11-23 shows an example of configuring port forwarding using IOS commands on router R2.

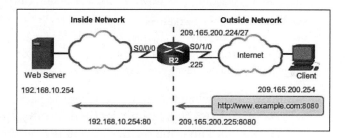

Figure 11-23   Port Forwarding Example Using IOS

192.168.10.254 is the inside local IPv4 address of the web server listening on port 80. Users will access this internal web server using the global IP address 209.165.200.225, a globally unique public IPv4 address. In this case, it is the address of the Serial 0/1/0 interface of R2. The global port is configured as 8080. This will be the destination port used, along with the global IPv4 address of 209.165.200.225 to access the internal web server. Notice within the NAT configuration, the following command parameters:

- *local-ip* = 192.168.10.254
- *local-port* = 80
- *global-ip* = 209.165.200.225
- *global-port* = 8080

When a well-known port number is not being used, the client must specify the port number in the application.

Like other types of NAT, port forwarding requires the configuration of both the inside and outside NAT interfaces. The following configuration shows how all of this would be configured.

```
!Establishes static translation between an inside local address and local port and
  an inside global address and global port.
R2(config)# ip nat inside source static tcp 192.168.10.254 80 209.165.200.225 8080

!Identifies interface serial 0/0/0 as an inside NAT interface.
R2(config)# interface serial0/0/0
R2(config-if)# ip nat inside

!Identifies interface serial 0/1/0 as an outside NAT interface.
R2(config)# interface serial0/1/0
R2(config-if)# ip nat outside
```

Similar to static NAT, the **show ip nat translations** command can be used to verify the port forwarding, as shown in the following output.

```
R2# show ip nat translations
Pro Inside global       Inside local     Outside local          Outside global
tcp 209.165.200.225:8080 192.168.10.254:80 209.165.200.254:46088 209.165.200.254:46088
tcp 209.165.200.225:8080 192.168.10.254:80 ---                    ---
```

In the example, when the router receives the packet with the inside global IPv4 address of 209.165.200.225 and a TCP destination port 8080, the router performs a NAT table lookup using the destination IPv4 address and destination port as the key. The router then translates the address to the inside local address of host 192.168.10.254 and destination port 80. R2 then forwards the packet to the web server. For return packets from the web server back to the client, this process is reversed.

Packet Tracer
☐ Activity

Packet Tracer Activity 11.2.4.4: Configuring Port Forwarding on a Linksys Router

Scenario

Your friend wants to play a game with you on your server. Both of you are at your respective homes, connected to the Internet. You need to configure your SOHO (Small Office, Home Office) router to port forward HTTP requests to your server so that your friend can access the game lobby web page.

Configuring NAT and IPv6 (11.2.5)

IPv6 is different from IPv4. With so many bits and with IPv6 having private addressing integral to the protocol, NAT for IPv6 is implemented differently. This section explores how NAT might be implemented in an IPv6 environment.

NAT for IPv6? (11.2.5.1)

Since the early 1990s, the concern about the depletion of IPv4 address space has been a priority of the IETF. The combination of RFC 1918 private IPv4 addresses and NAT has been instrumental in slowing this depletion. NAT has significant disadvantages, and in January of 2011, IANA allocated the last of its IPv4 addresses to RIRs.

One of the unintentional benefits of NAT for IPv4 is that it hides the private network from the public Internet. NAT has the advantage of providing a perceived level of security by denying computers in the public Internet from accessing internal hosts. However, it should not be considered a substitute for proper network security, such as that provided by a firewall. Figure 11-24 shows where NAT can be used with varying private IPv4 addressing schemes.

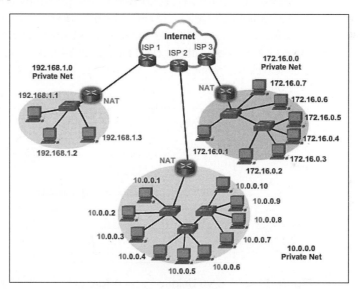

Figure 11-24   IPv4 Private Addresses and NAT

In RFC 5902, the Internet Architecture Board (IAB) included the following quote concerning IPv6 network address translation:

"It is commonly perceived that a NAT box provides one level of protection because external hosts cannot directly initiate communication with hosts behind a NAT. However, one should not confuse NAT boxes with firewalls. As discussed in [RFC4864], Section 2.2, the act of translation does not provide security in itself. The stateful filtering function can provide the same level of protection without requiring a translation function."

IPv6 with a 128-bit address provides 340 undecillion addresses. Therefore, address space is not an issue. IPv6 was developed with the intention of making NAT for IPv4 with its translation between public and private IPv4 addresses unnecessary. However, IPv6 does implement a form of NAT. IPv6 includes both its own IPv6 private address space and NAT, which are implemented differently than they are for IPv4.

IPv6 Unique Local Addresses (11.2.5.2)

IPv6 unique local addresses (ULA) are similar to RFC 1918 private addresses in IPv4, but there are significant differences as well. The intent of ULA is to provide IPv6 address space for communications within a local site; it is not meant to provide additional IPv6 address space, nor is it meant to provide a level of security.

As shown in Figure 11-25, ULA have the prefix FC00::/7, which results in a first hextet range of FC00 to FDFF. The next 1 bit is set to 1 if the prefix is locally assigned. Set to 0 may be defined in the future. The next 40 bits is a global ID followed by a 16-bit Subnet ID. These first 64 bits combine to make the ULA prefix. This leaves the remaining 64 bits for the interface ID, or in IPv4 terms, the host portion of the address.

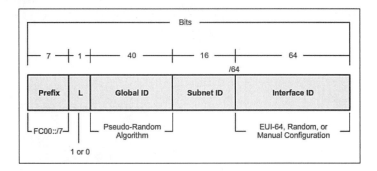

Figure 11-25 IPv6 Unique Local Address

Unique local addresses are defined in RFC 4193. ULAs are also known as local IPv6 addresses (not to be confused with IPv6 link-local addresses) and have several characteristics including

- Allows sites to be combined or privately interconnected, without creating any address conflicts or requiring renumbering of interfaces that use these prefixes.

- Independent of any ISP and can be used for communications within a site without having any Internet connectivity.

- Not routable across the Internet, however, if accidentally leaked by routing or DNS, there is not conflict with other addresses.

ULA is not quite as straightforward as RFC 1918 addresses. Unlike private IPv4 addresses, it has not been the intention of the IETF to use a form of NAT to translate between unique local addresses and IPv6 global unicast addresses.

The implementation and potential uses for IPv6 unique local addresses are still being examined by the Internet community. For example, the IETF is considering allowing the option to have the ULA prefix created locally using FC00::/8, or to have it assigned automatically by a third-party beginning with FD00::/8.

Note

The original IPv6 specification allocated address space for site-local addresses, defined in RFC 3513. Site-local addresses have since been deprecated by the IETF in RFC 3879 because the term "site" was somewhat ambiguous. Site-local addresses had the prefix range of FEC0::/10 and may still be found in some older IPv6 documentation.

NAT for IPv6 (11.2.5.3)

NAT for IPv6 is used in a much different context than NAT for IPv4. The varieties of NAT for IPv6 are used to transparently provide access between IPv6-only and IPv4-only networks. It is not used as a form of private IPv6 to global IPv6 translation.

Ideally, IPv6 should be run natively wherever possible. This means IPv6 devices communicating with each other over IPv6 networks. However, to aid in the move from IPv4 to IPv6, the IETF has developed several transition techniques to accommodate a variety of IPv4-to-IPv6 scenarios, including dual-stack, tunneling, and translation.

Dual-stack is when the devices are running protocols associated with both the IPv4 and IPv6. *Tunneling for IPv6* is the process of encapsulating an IPv6 packet inside an IPv4 packet. This allows the IPv6 packet to be transmitted over an IPv4-only network.

NAT for IPv6 should not be used as a long term strategy but as a temporary mechanism to assist in the migration from IPv4 to IPv6. Over the years, there have been several types of NAT for IPv6 including *Network Address Translation-Protocol Translation (NAT-PT)*. NAT-PT has been deprecated by IETF in favor of its replacement, *NAT64*. See Figure 11-26 for a basic NAT64 scenario. NAT64 is beyond the scope of this curriculum.

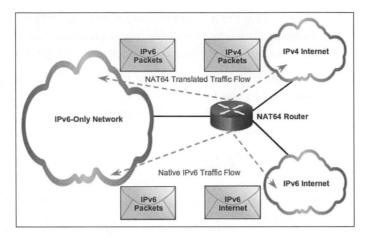

Figure 11-26 NAT64

Troubleshooting NAT (11.3)

As with all technical things, troubleshooting common problems is expected of technicians (even new technicians). NAT issues are sometimes difficult to detect because technicians suspect other issues. Because of the complexity and inter-dependence among the commands, NAT troubleshooting continues to challenge Cisco students.

Troubleshooting NAT: show Commands (11.3.1.1)

Figure 11-27 shows R2 enabled for PAT, using the range of addresses 209.165.200.226 to 209.165.200.240.

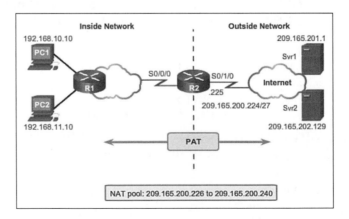

Figure 11-27 Troubleshooting NAT

When there are IPv4 connectivity problems in a NAT environment, it is often difficult to determine the cause of the problem. The first step in solving the problem is to rule out NAT as the cause. Follow these steps to verify that NAT is operating as expected:

Step 1. Based on the configuration, clearly define what NAT is supposed to achieve. This may reveal a problem with the configuration.

Step 2. Verify that correct translations exist in the translation table using the **show ip nat translations** command.

Step 3. Use the **clear** and **debug** commands to verify that NAT is operating as expected. Check to see if dynamic entries are recreated after they are cleared.

Step 4. Review in detail what is happening to the packet, and verify that routers have the correct routing information to move the packet.

Later output shows the output of the **show ip nat statistics** and **show ip nat translations** commands. Prior to using the **show** commands, the NAT statistics and entries in the NAT table are cleared with the **clear ip nat statistics** and **clear ip nat translation** * commands.

```
R2# clear ip nat statistics
R2# clear ip nat translation *
```

After the host at 192.168.10.10 telnets to the server at 209.165.201.1, the NAT statistics and NAT table are displayed to verify NAT is working as expected.

In a simple network environment, it is useful to monitor NAT statistics with the **show ip nat statistics** command. The **show ip nat statistics** command displays information about the total number of active translations, NAT configuration parameters, the number of addresses in the pool, and the number that have been allocated. However, in a more complex NAT environment, with several translations taking place, this command may not clearly identify the issue. It may be necessary to run **debug** commands on the router. The following output shows a sample output when NAT is working.

```
R2# show ip nat statistics
Total active translations: 0 (0 static, 1 dynamic, 1 extended)
Peak translations: 1, occurred 00:00:09 ago
Outside interfaces:
  Serial0/1/0
Inside interfaces:
  Serial0/0/0
Hits: 31  Misses: 0
CEF Translated packets: 31, CEF Punted packets: 0
Expired translations: 0
```

```
Dynamic mappings:
-- Inside Source
[ID: 5] access-list 1 pool NAT-POOL2 refCount 1
 pool NAT-POOL2: netmask 255.255.255.224
 start 209.165.200.226 end 209.165.200.240
 type generic, total addresses 15 , allocated 1 (6%), misses 0
<output omitted>


R2# show ip nat translations
Pro  Inside global         Inside local        Outside local       Outside global
tcp  209.165.200.226:19005  192.168.10.10:19005  209.165.201.1:23   209.165.201.1:23
```

Troubleshooting NAT: debug Command (11.3.1.2)

Use the **debug ip nat** command to verify the operation of the NAT feature by displaying information about every packet that is translated by the router. The **debug ip nat detailed** command generates a description of each packet considered for translation. This command also provides information about certain errors or exception conditions, such as the failure to allocate a global address. The **debug ip nat detailed** command generates more overhead than the **debug ip nat** command, but it can provide the detail that may be needed to troubleshoot the NAT problem. Always turn off debugging when finished.

The following shows a sample **debug ip nat** output. The output shows that the inside host (192.168.10.10) initiated traffic to the outside host (209.165.201.1) and the source address was translated to address 209.165.200.226.

```
R2# debug ip nat
IP NAT debugging is on
R2#
*Feb 15 20:01:311.670: NAT*: s=192.168.10.10->209.165.200.226, d=209.165.201.1 [2817]
*Feb 15 20:01:311.682: NAT*: s=209.165.201.1, d=209.165.200.226->192.168.10.10 [4180]
*Feb 15 20:01:311.698: NAT*: s=192.168.10.10->209.165.200.226, d=209.165.201.1 [2818]
*Feb 15 20:01:311.702: NAT*: s=192.168.10.10->209.165.200.226, d=209.165.201.1 [2819]
*Feb 15 20:01:311.710: NAT*: s=192.168.10.10->209.165.200.226, d=209.165.201.1 [2820]
*Feb 15 20:01:311.682: NAT*: s=209.165.201.1, d=209.165.200.226->192.168.10.10 [4181]
*Feb 15 20:01:311.682: NAT*: s=209.165.201.1, d=209.165.200.226->192.168.10.10 [4182]
*Feb 15 20:01:311.710: NAT*: s=192.168.10.10->209.165.200.226, d=209.165.201.1 [2821]
*Feb 15 20:01:311.682: NAT*: s=209.165.201.1, d=209.165.200.226->192.168.10.10 [4183]
*Feb 15 20:01:311.710: NAT*: s=192.168.10.10->209.165.200.226, d=209.165.201.1 [2822]
*Feb 15 20:01:311.682: NAT*: s=209.165.201.1, d=209.165.200.226->192.168.10.10 [4184]
<output omitted>
```

When decoding the debug output, note what the following symbols and values indicate:

- *** (asterisk):** The asterisk next to NAT indicates that the translation is occurring in the fast-switched path. The first packet in a conversation is always process-switched, which is slower. The remaining packets go through the fast-switched path if a cache entry exists.

- **s=:** This symbol refers to the source IP address.

- **a.b.c.d--->w.x.y.z:** This value indicates that source address a.b.c.d is translated to w.x.y.z.

- **d=:** This symbol refers to the destination IP address.

- **[xxxx]:** The value in brackets is the IP identification number. This information may be useful for debugging in that it enables correlation with other packet traces from protocol analyzers.

Note

Verify that the ACL referenced in the NAT command reference is permitting all the necessary networks. In Figure 11-28, only 192.168.0.0/16 addresses are eligible to be translated. Packets from the inside network destined for the Internet with source addresses that are not explicitly permitted by ACL 1 are not translated by R2.

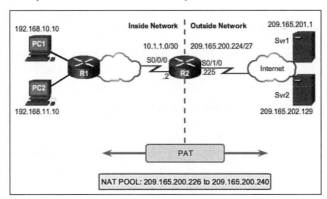

Figure 11-28   Troubleshooting PAT

Use the **show access-lists** command to verify what internal addresses are to be translated as shown. Note that when there are matches, the access list is working for NAT.

```
R2# show access-lists
Standard IP access list 1
    10 permit 192.168.0.0, wildcard bits 0.0.255.255 (29 matches)
R2#
```

Case Study (11.3.1.3)

The following case demonstrates a situation where NAT is not working. The given commands are essential to troubleshooting NAT or PAT.

Case Study 1

Figure 11-29 shows that hosts from the 192.168.0.0/16 LANs, PC1, and PC2 cannot ping servers on the outside network Svr1 and Svr2.

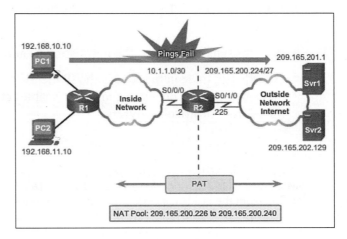

Figure 11-29   Troubleshooting PAT Case Study

To begin troubleshooting the problem, use the **show ip nat translations** command to see if any translations are currently in the NAT table. The output that follows shows that no translations are in the table.

```
R2# show ip nat translations
R2#
```

The **show ip nat statistics** command is used to determine whether any translations have taken place. It also identifies the interfaces that translation should be occurring between. As shown in the output that follows, the NAT counters are at 0, verifying that no translation has occurred. By comparing the output with the topology shown in Figure 11-29, notice that the router interfaces are incorrectly defined as NAT inside or NAT outside. The incorrect configuration can also be verified using the **show running-config** command.

The current NAT interface configuration must be deleted from the interfaces before applying the correct configuration.

```
R2# show ip nat statistics
Total active translations: 0 (0 static, 1 dynamic, 1 extended)
Peak translations: 1, occurred 00:00:09 ago
```

```
Outside interfaces:
  Serial0/0/0
Inside interfaces:
  Serial0/1/0
Hits: 0  Misses: 0
CEF Translated packets: 20, CEF Punted packets: 0
Expired translations: 1
Dynamic mappings:
-- Inside Source
[ID: 5] access-list 1 pool NAT-POOL2 refCount 1
 pool NAT-POOL2: netmask 255.255.255.224
 start 209.165.200.226 end 209.165.200.240
 type generic, total addresses 15 , allocated 1 (6%), misses 0
<output omitted>


R2(config)# interface serial0/0/0
R2(config-if)# no ip nat outside
R2(config-if)# ip nat inside
R2(config-if)# exit
R2(config)# interface serial0/1/0
R2(config-if)# no ip nat inside
R2(config-if)# ip nat outside
```

After correctly defining the NAT inside and outside interfaces, another ping from PC1 to Svr1 fails. Using the **show ip nat translations** and **show ip nat statistics** commands again verifies that translations are still not occurring.

As shown in the output that follows, the **show access-lists** command is used to determine whether the ACL that the NAT command references is permitting all the necessary networks. Examining the output indicates that an incorrect wildcard bit mask has been used in the ACL that defines the addresses that need to be translated. The wildcard mask is permitting only the 192.168.0.0/24 subnet.

```
R2# show access-lists
Standard IP access list 1
   10 permit 192.168.0.0, wildcard bits 0.0.0.255
R2#
```

The access list is first removed and then reconfigured using the correct wildcard mask, as shown in the configuration.

```
R2(config)# no access-list 1
R2(config)# access-list 1 permit 192.168.0.0 0.0.255.255
```

After configurations are corrected, another ping is generated from PC1 to Svr1, and this time the ping succeeds. As shown, the **show ip nat translations** and **show ip nat statistics** commands are used to verify that the NAT translation is occurring.

```
R2# show ip nat statistics
Total active translations: 0 (0 static, 1 dynamic, 1 extended)
Peak translations: 1, occurred 00:00:09 ago
Outside interfaces:
  Serial0/1/0
Inside interfaces:
  Serial0/0/0
Hits: 20  Misses: 0
<output omitted>
```

```
R2# show ip nat translations
Pro  Inside global      Inside local      Outside local     Outside global
tcp  209.165.200.226:38  192.168.10.10:38  209.165.201.1:38  209.165.201.1:38
```

Packet Tracer Activity 11.3.1.4: Verifying and Troubleshooting NAT Configurations

A contractor restored an old configuration to a new router running NAT. But the network has changed and a new subnet was added after the old configuration was backed up. It is your job to get the network working again.

Lab 11.3.1.5: Troubleshooting NAT Configurations

In this lab, you complete the following objectives:

- Part 1: Build the Network and Configure Basic Device Settings
- Part 2: Troubleshoot Static NAT
- Part 3: Troubleshoot Dynamic NAT

Summary (11.4)

This chapter has probably been quite challenging. Take a few moments and read through the summary. Try the Skills Integration Challenge to see if your skills are up to par. Then, try the review questions to see what you retained.

Class Activity 11.4.1.1: NAT Check

NAT Check

Scenario

Network address translation is not currently included in your company's network design. It has been decided to configure some devices to use NAT services for connecting to the mail server.

Before deploying NAT live on the network, you prototype it using a network simulation program.

For further instructions, refer to the PDF which accompanies this activity.

Packet Tracer Activity 11.4.1.2: Skills Integration Challenge

Scenario

This culminating activity includes many of the skills that you have acquired during this course. First, you complete the documentation for the network. So make sure you have a printed version of the instructions. During implementation, you configure VLANs, trunking, port security, and SSH remote access on a switch. Then, you implement inter-VLAN routing and NAT on a router. Finally, you use your documentation to verify your implementation by testing end-to-end connectivity.

This chapter has outlined how NAT is used to help alleviate the depletion of IPv4 address space. NAT for IPv4 allows network administrators to use RFC 1918 private address space while providing connectivity to the Internet, using a single or limited number of public addresses.

NAT conserves public address space and saves considerable administrative overhead in managing adds, moves, and changes. NAT and PAT can be implemented to conserve public address space and build private secure intranets without affecting the ISP connection. However, NAT has drawbacks in terms of its negative effects on device performance, security, mobility, and end-to-end connectivity and should be considered a short-term implementation for address exhaustion with the long-term solution being IPv6.

This chapter discussed NAT for IPv4, including

- NAT characteristics, terminology, and general operations

- The different types of NAT including static NAT, dynamic NAT, and PAT

- The benefits and disadvantages of NAT

- The configuration, verification, and analysis of static NAT, dynamic NAT, and PAT

- How port forwarding can be used to access internal devices from the Internet

- Troubleshooting NAT using **show** and **debug** commands

Practice

The following activities provide practice with the topics introduced in this chapter. The Labs and Class Activities are available in the companion *Introduction to Routing and Switching Essentials Lab Manual* (978-1-58713-320-6). The Packet Tracer Activities PKA files are found in the online course.

Class Activities

Class Activity 11.0.1.2: Conceptual NAT

Class Activity 11.4.1.1: NAT Check

Labs

Lab 11:2.2.6: Configuring Dynamic and Static NAT

Lab 11.2.3.7: Configuring NAT Pool Overload and PAT

Lab 11.3.1.5: Troubleshooting NAT Configurations

Packet Tracer Activities

Packet Tracer Activity 11.1.2.6: Investigating NAT Operation

Packet Tracer Activity 11.2.1.4: Configuring Static NAT

Packet Tracer Activity 11.2.2.5: Configuring Dynamic NAT

Packet Tracer Activity 11.2.3.6: Implementing Static and Dynamic NAT

Packet Tracer Activity 11.3.1.4: Verifying and Troubleshooting NAT Configurations

Packet Tracer Activity 11.4.1.2: Skills Integration Challenge

Check Your Understanding Questions

Complete all the review questions listed here to test your understanding of the topics and concepts in this chapter. The appendix, "Answers to the 'Check Your Understanding' Questions," lists the answers.

1. Refer to the following output:

```
NAT1# show ip nat translations
Pro   Inside global        Inside local       Outside local      Outside global
udp   198.133.24.211:123   192.168.254.7:123   192.31.7.4:123     192.31.7.4:123
tcp   198.133.24.211:4509 192.168.254.66:4509 192.135.250.184:
80   192.135.250.184:80
tcp   198.133.24.211:4643 192.168.254.66:4643 192.135.250.71:
5190   192.135.250.71:5190
```

Based on the output, which statement is true about the NAT configuration?

A. Static NAT is configured.

B. Dynamic NAT is configured.

C. NAT Overload (PAT) is configured.

D. NAT is configured incorrectly.

2. What is the default timeout value for NAT translations?

A. One hour

B. One day

C. One week

D. Indefinite

3. Match the characteristic to the NAT technique. Note that a technique can have more than one characteristic.

   A. Provides one-to-one fixed mappings of local and global addresses

   B. Assigns the translated address of IP hosts from a pool of public addresses

   C. Can map multiple addresses to a single address of an external interface

   D. Assigns unique source port numbers of an inside global address on a session-by-session basis

   E. Allows an external host to establish sessions with an internal host

   _____   Dynamic NAT

   _____   PAT

   _____   Static NAT

4. Consider the following configuration:

   ```
   R2(config)# ip nat inside source static 192.168.0.100 209.165.200.2
   R2(config)# interface serial0/0/0
   R2(config-if)# ip address 10.1.1.2 255.255.255.252
   R2(config-if)# ip nat inside
   R2(config-if)# exit
   R2(config)# interface serial0/1/0
   R2(config-if)# ip address 209.165.200.225 255.255.255.224
   R2(config-if)# ip nat outside
   R2(config-if)# exit
   ```

   Which host(s) will be translated by NAT?

   A. 10.1.1.2

   B. 192.168.0.100

   C. 209.165.200.2

   D. All hosts on the 10.1.1.0 network

   E. All hosts on the 192.168.0.0 network

5. Consider the following configuration:

```
R2(config)# ip nat pool nat-pool1 209.165.200.225 209.165.200.240 netmask
255.255.255.0
R2(config)# ip nat inside source list 1 pool nat-pool1
R2(config)# interface serial0/0/0
R2(config-if)# ip address 10.1.1.2 255.255.255.252
R2(config-if)# ip nat inside
R2(config-if)# exit
R2(config)# interface serial0/1/0
R2(config-if)# ip address 209.165.200.1 255.255.255.224
R2(config-if)# ip nat outside
R2(config-if)# exit
R2(config)# access-list 1 permit 192.168.0.0 0.0.0.31
```

Which addresses will be translated by NAT?

A. 10.1.1.2 to 10.1.1.255

B. 192.168.0.0 to 192.168.0.255

C. 192.168.0.0 to 192.168.0.31

D. 209.165.200.240 to 209.165.200.255

E. Only host 10.1.1.2

F. Only host 209.165.200.255

6. Consider the following topology.

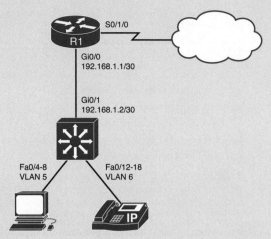

On which interface(s) would NAT be applied?

A. Only S0/1/0

B. Only Gi0/0

C. Only on S0/1/0 and Gi0/0

D. Only on Gi0/0 and Gi0/1

E. Only on S0/1/0, Gi0/0, and Gi0/1

F. On all interfaces

7. Which NAT solution allows external users to access an internal SFTP server on a network that uses private IP addresses?

A. Dynamic NAT

B. PAT

C. Static NAT

D. NAT overload

8. What are two disadvantages of NAT? (Choose two.)

A. Uses too many legally registered addresses.

B. Decreases the number of connections that can be used to the public network.

C. Network device performance.

D. End-to-end traceability is lost.

E. Increased network costs.

F. Increased provider costs.

9. What is the last step in configuring PAT with an address pool?

   A. Creating the access list

   B. Defining the address pool

   C. Binding the access list to the address pool

   D. Applying NAT to at least two interfaces

10. What parameter defines what internal addresses are translated by NAT?

    A. The access list

    B. The address pool

    C. The interface(s) that have the command **ip nat inside** applied

    D. The interface(s) that have the command **ip nat outside** applied

11. What is the effect of adding the keyword **overload** to a NAT configuration?

    A. More interfaces can participate in NAT.

    B. More internal address can be translated into one or more public addresses.

    C. The router is placed into stealth mode verifying that the address translation is not overtaxing the router hardware.

    D. Public IP addresses can be added to the NAT pool dynamically.

12. What is the most commonly deployed IPv6 NAT method recommended for all IPv6-based companies?

    A. NAT for IPv6

    B. IPv6 tunneling

    C. PAT for IPv6

    D. None of these

Answers to the "Check Your Understanding" Questions

Chapter 1

1. **B, C, and F. Explanation:** The access layer is concerned with end device connectivity. Switches and access points provide connectivity for wired and wireless devices. Distribution layer aggregates connections from access layer switches. This layer can also define Layer 3 routing boundaries and policy-based network connectivity. The core layer is known as the high speed backbone.

2. **C. Explanation:** The hierarchical goal specifies a specific role for each device in the network design. Modularity allows the network to expand in a planned fashion. Flexibility ensures that network resources are available to provide traffic load sharing.

3. **D and F. Explanation:** The three layers of the hierarchical design model are access, distribution, and core. The two design models are three layer and two layer. The two layer design is also known as a collapsed-core design because the distribution layer and core layer are combined.

4. **C. Explanation:** Convergence of network services that involve voice, video, and data requires a structured network design so that traffic flow reaches the destination network.

5. **A, D, and F. Explanation:** A converged network requires more complex configuration, maintenance, and hierarchical design than a traditional data network.

6. **A and D. Explanation:** Port density is the number of ports available on a single switch. Rack unit is used to describe the switch height and is used in network rack space planning. A modular configuration switch allows great flexibility in configuration through the use of line cards in the various available chassis sizes.

7. **B. Explanation:** MAC addresses are associated with Ethernet frames and are also known as a Layer 2 address.

8. **B. Explanation:** When a switch is first powered on, it has no entries in the MAC address table. A switch adds to the MAC address table by examining the Layer 2 header source MAC address. If the MAC address is not already in the switch MAC address table, the switch adds it. The switch forwards the frame based on the destination MAC address found in the Layer 2 header. If the destination MAC address is not in the MAC address table, the switch forwards the data to all ports that have devices attached except for the ingress port through which the switch received the frame.

9. A. Explanation: Access layer switches commonly provide Power over Ethernet (PoE) to end devices such as access points and IP phones.

10. B. Explanation: Because the source MAC address is already known, the switch then turns to the destination MAC address to determine how to forward the frame. Because the destination MAC address for port 5 is not in the switch MAC address table, the switch sends the frame out all ports except the ingress port (the port through which the frame was received).

11. A. Explanation: Because the source MAC address is not known, the switch adds the source MAC address to the MAC address. Remember, the switch "learns" from the source MAC address. The switch "forwards" based on the destination MAC address.

Chapter 2

1. C, D, and E. Explanation: Know the switch port security types and violation modes is important *before* configuring port security. Port security can be configured using (1) static secure MAC addresses, (2) dynamic secure MAC addresses, and (3) sticky secure MAC addresses. The three violation modes are protect, restrict, and shutdown. Shutdown is the default violation mode.

2. C. Explanation: The switch will connect with full duplex when autonegotiating with a peer device. The default configuration for a switch port is auto negotiating.

3. A and C. Explanation: Autonegotiation sets duplex and speed. Autonegotiation is the default mode for a Cisco switch port.

4. D. Explanation: The default gateway provides a means for the administrator of the switch (from the switch command prompt) to access networks not directly connected to the switch. It also allows for remote connectivity from a different network because when connected, the return packets from the switch can be sent to the remote network device. Answer A would be possible from devices on the same network.

5. C. Explanation: A Layer 2 switch is allotted a single Layer 3 logical address in the form of a switch virtual interface (SVI) used for managing the switch.

6. D. Explanation: The description in A goes with DHCP starvation, in B goes with CDP attack, in C goes with MAC address flooding.

7. A. Explanation: SSH is a more secure method of accessing a device from a remote network.

8. C and E. Explanation: SSH version 2 is the default version. The **transport input ssh** command would not be entered in interface configuration mode, but in line configuration mode (Switch(config-line)#).

9. A. Explanation: By using NTP or manually configuring the date and time on a network device, log messages are time stamped accurately. This is especially important when troubleshooting problems.

10. B. Explanation: When DHCP snooping is configured, switch ports are configured as either a trusted port or an untrusted port. A device connected to a trusted port can send any type of DHCP message into the switch. An untrusted port only allows incoming DHCP requests.

11. A. Explanation: Gigabit Ethernet and 10Gb Ethernet NICs can only run in full duplex. Speed should be manually configured on a port that has an important device such as a server. A network engineer would not want to chance the auto-negotiation configuring a slower speed. No normal word (whether compound or not) should be used as a password. Passwords should include uppercase and lowercase letters as well as special symbols. SSH is the preferred method of remote connectivity for a switch.

12. D. Explanation: Auto-MDIX is not supported on every Cisco device, but if supported, this feature will allow the interface to automatically detect the required connection type (straight-through or crossover) and configure the port appropriately.

Chapter 3

1. D. Explanation: The whole purpose of a trunk port is to "carry" multiple VLANs across a single link. Ports placed in access mode can only belong to one VLAN. Two devices can attach to an access port such as an IP phone that connects to a PC and a switch. Trunk ports have a native (untagged) VLAN.

2. D. Explanation: Each VLAN needs its own network number. A VLAN is simply a virtual network. Each VLAN ID is a separate virtual network.

3. A. Explanation: 802.1p is used for prioritization, multiplexing is a telecommunications term, and the native VLAN is not used to differentiate between VLANs on a trunk. (It is associated with untagged traffic on a trunk link.)

4. B and C. Explanation: Port security is used only on access ports. The native VLAN must be the same on both ends of an 802.1Q trunk.

5. A and D. Explanation: Ports are administratively disabled only with the **no shutdown** command. Access ports never default to trunk ports. Ports do not automatically get reassigned to another VLAN upon deletion of their respective VLAN.

6. A, C, and E. Explanation: A router is needed for inter-VLAN communication. Each port on a switch is associated with a separate collision domain. Hosts on the same VLAN can all be on distinct physical segments.

7. B. Explanation: PC3 is on VLAN 3. Other hosts on VLAN 3 will hear the broadcast which is only PC4.

8. N

   E

   N

   1

   1

   1

   E

9. B, C, and F. Explanation: Hosts within the same VLAN that have the proper IP addressing (they are on the same network) can ping each other. A Layer 3 device such as a router is needed for inter-VLAN communication.

10. A, B, and D.

11. C

    A

    B

    D

12. D

    A

    B

    C

13. IEEE 802.1Q

14. A. Explanation: An attacker using a double-tagging attack attaches two VLAN IDs to the header. The second VLAN ID is examined by a second switch that forwards frames to a destination VLAN that has a host controlled by the attacker.

15. B, C, F, and G. Explanation: DTP autonegotiates a trunk and could be a security risk. DTP should be disabled. Unused switch ports should be placed in an unused VLAN known as a black hole VLAN.

Chapter 4

1. B and D. Explanation: **Read-Only Memory (ROM):** Provides permanent storage for bootup instructions, basic diagnostic software, and a limited IOS in case the router cannot load the full featured IOS. **Flash:** Provides permanent storage for the IOS and other system-related files. The IOS is copied from flash into RAM during the bootup process. Flash is nonvolatile and does not lose its contents when power is turned off.

2. A, C, and D. Explanation: A routing table entry for a directly connected IPv4 or IPv6 network is automatically added to the routing table when the corresponding interface is up. The **interface vlan** and **ip address** commands are used on a switch to assign an IP address to the device. As seen in the chapter content and lab activities, addressing and activating LAN and WAN interfaces automatically trigger the building of a routing table in a Layer 3 device.

3. A. Explanation: The IPv6 address and prefix for a default static route is ::/0. This represents all zeros in the address and a prefix length of zero.

4. D.

5. C and D. Explanation: The command history feature is useful because it temporarily stores the list of executed commands to be recalled. By default, command history is enabled and the system captures the last 10 command lines in its history buffer.

6. D. Explanation: When a PC needs to encapsulate a frame to send a data packet, it first performs an AND operation with its own IP and subnet mask, which yields the network address. Then it performs another AND operation using the destination IP and the same subnet mask. By comparing the two AND operations results, the PC knows if the destination is on the local LAN or on a remote network.

7. A. Explanation: When a router learns that multiple paths are available to a destination network from the same routing protocol, the route with the lowest metric is put into the routing table to forward packets toward that network.

8. C and D. Explanation: When a router has two or more paths to a destination with equal cost metrics, then the router forwards the packets using both paths equally. Only EIGRP supports unequal cost load balancing.

9. A. Explanation: Even though a gateway of last resort could be an IP address of an ISP router, this does not have to be the case. A gateway of last resort, as seen in a Cisco routing table, is simply the IP address that is used to route packets addressed to networks not explicitly listed in the routing table. A Windows-based computer uses the term default gateway, not gateway of last resort.

10. B. Explanation: The exhibited port is a USB port that is found on some Cisco router models. This USB port provides console access to the router, which allows access to the CLI for configuration purposes. The pale blue background behind the icon is also the standard color that is used on Cisco devices to indicate a console connection.

11. B. Explanation: Each route in a routing table has a code that identifies how the route was learned by the router. The code letter D is used to identify routes learned through EIGRP.

12. B and D. Explanation: Static routes are manually configured. They define an explicit path between two networking devices. Unlike a dynamic routing protocol, static routes are not automatically updated and must be manually reconfigured if the network topology changes. A static route is identified in the routing table with the code s.

13. C. Explanation: In the routing table entry, S 10.2.0.0 [1/0] via 172.16.2.2, the numbers inside the bracket indicate the administrative distance and metric, respectively.

Chapter 5

1. subinterface

   subinterface

   physical interface

   physical interface

   subinterface

   physical interface

   Explanation: Physical interface solutions involve more complex cabling, access port switch configurations, and one physical router interface per VLAN.

2. router-on-a-stick

router-on-a-stick

Layer 3 switch routing

Layer 3 switch routing

router-on-a-stick

both

Layer 3 switch routing

Explanation: A Layer 3 switch routed port is commonly used when Layer 3 switching is used to route between VLANs. The router-on-a-stick model involves setting up a trunk port on the switch and using subinterfaces on the router.

3. A, B, and E. Explanation: Keep in mind that the solution decreases available bandwidth and increases troubleshooting and configuration complexity.

4. A. Explanation: Some Layer 3 switches do not have an image loaded that supports Layer 3 switching; if it does, IP routing needs to be enabled by typing **ip routing** from global configuration mode. Layer 3 switches preclude the need for router-on-a-stick.

5. D. Explanation: Router-on-a-stick only requires a single trunk port with a native VLAN assigned to one subinterface.

6. C. Explanation: Router-on-a-stick uses subinterfaces on the participating router.

7. B. Explanation: **ping** tests the connectivity between the source and destination devices.

8. A, C, and E. Explanation: Traditional or legacy routing means one physical router interface per VLAN. There is no such thing as spanning-tree routing or 802.1Q routing.

9. D. Explanation: G0/0 is a physical interface, and the command given is configured only on subinterfaces.

10. one physical port per VLAN

one physical interface (but multiple subinterfaces)

Explanation: A company could implement routing between VLANs on just a multilayer switch. The switch would have devices connected to a physical interface, but these interfaces do not require any configuration to support inter-VLAN routing.

11. B. Explanation: The **show ip interface brief** command is used on either a Layer 2 switch, multilayer switch, or a router to see if an interface (virtual or physical) is "up and up."

12. A and E. Explanation: Common problems in a router on-a-stick configuration include the physical port on the router being shut down, native VLAN mismatch between the router and the switch, and improper IP addressing to match the VLAN. Remember that each VLAN must have a different network number. On the switch side, ensure VLANs 10 and 11 are in the VLAN database, ensure the port connecting to the router is a trunk, and ensure the native VLAN matches the configured native VLAN on the router (or is the default of 1).

Chapter 6

1. C. Explanation: All routes in the routing table must be resolved to an exit interface in the routing table. If a route has only a next-hop IP address, that next-hop address must eventually be resolved to another route in the routing table that does include an exit interface, such as a directly connected network. Some static routes, such as those with Ethernet exit interfaces, can include both an exit interface and a next-hop IP address.

2. D and E. Explanation: Configuring a static route does not ensure that the path is always available. If the exit interface or next-hop IP address is in the up state, the static route will be included in the routing table, regardless of whether the destination network is available. Dynamic routing protocols are typically a better option when there are multiple routes to the same destination network. The routing protocol will be able to automatically determine the best path.

3. A. Explanation: The static route **ip route 0.0.0.0 0.0.0.0 S0/0/0** is considered a default static route and will match all destination networks.

4. D. Explanation: The router will encapsulate the packet for the WAN link and then forward the packet out the S0/1/0 interface. The packet will not be dropped because the destination is in the routing table. The MAC address lookup will not be the next item to do to process the packet. A recursive lookup will not be required as the exit interface is identified in the route statement.

5. C. Explanation: A fully specified static route has the next-hop IP address and exit interface specified. A recursive static route has only the next-hop IP address specified. A directly attached static route has only the router exit interface specified. A floating static route has a higher metric than the dynamic routes and serves as a backup route.

6. D. Explanation: A summary route represents multiple networks. A summarized static route does not necessarily provide a better route than a routing protocol does. A default static route would provide a default gateway for a router that is connected to an ISP. Routing protocol updates may not necessarily be reduced in if static route routes are also used.

7. B. Explanation: A subnet mask of 255.255.255.0 accommodates 254 devices ($2^8 = 256 - 2$ for the network number and broadcast). A subnet mask of 255.255.254.0 accommodates 510 devices. A subnet mask of 255.255.252.0 handles up to 1022 devices. A subnet mask of 255.255.248.0 supports up to 2046 devices. Finally, a mask of 255.255.240.0 is used for a network that needs up to 4094 addresses.

8. A and D. Explanation: Static IPv6 routes can be summarized into a single static IPv6 route if the destination networks are contiguous and can be summarized into a single network address. Moreover, all static routes have to use the same exit-interface or next-hop IPv6 address. Floating static routes are static routes that have an administrative distance greater than the administrative distance of another static or dynamic route.

9. A. Explanation: To test a floating static route, take down the main route/link in order to see whether the backup link appears in the routing table. The **show ip route** command simply shows the routing table. Only one of the static routes would be shown at any one time.

10. B. Explanation: The third octet of the network addresses represented in binary are

    8 = 00001000

    12 = 00001100

    16 = 00010000

    The common leftmost bits are 000 in all three octets. Thus, the summary route will be 192.168.0.0/19.

Chapter 7

1. D

2. C. The factors that directly affect the time to convergence are the speed of the links, the type of protocol used, and the size of the network. The number of hosts, the applications, and the Layer 2 protocol that is used have no direct impact on the time to reach convergence.

3. B

4. A and C

5. D. RIPv1 uses broadcast, not multicast. RIPv2 uses the multicast address 224.0.0.9.

6. C. OSPF routing process uses Dijkstra's algorithm to construct the SPF tree. DUAL algorithm is used by the EIGRP routing protocol. Bellman-Ford algorithm is used by RIP routing protocol. Path vector protocol is the protocol used by BGP.

7. A. Link-state routing protocols require more CPU processing and memory to compute the routes using the Dijkstra algorithm. They are more complex but converge much faster than distance vector protocols like RIP.

8. B. Routing table entries that begin with the letter **D** are learned dynamically using the EIGRP routing protocol. Static route entries on the routing table are identified with **S**. Directly connected route entries are denoted by the letter **C**.

9. D. The Cisco IP routing table is not a flat database. It has a hierarchical structure that is used to expedite the lookup process when locating routes and forwarding packets. The terms ultimate route, level 1 route, level 1 parent route, and level 2 child routes describe the operation and the hierarchical nature of the routing table contents.

10. A and D. Dynamic routing protocols exist to discover the network, maintain routing tables, and calculate the best path. Having low levels of routing overhead, using the path specified by the administrator, and avoiding the exposure of network information are functions of static routing.

Chapter 8

1. A. Explanation: The first preference for an OSPF router ID is an explicitly configured 32-bit address. This address is not included in the routing table and is not defined by the **network** command. If a router ID that is configured through the **router-id** command is not available, OSPF routers next use the highest IP address available on a loopback interface because loopbacks used as router IDs are also not routable addresses. Lacking either of these alternatives, an OSPF router will use the highest IP address from its active physical interfaces.

2. D. Explanation: OSPF neighbors that reach the Full state are converged and can exchange routing information.

3. B. Explanation: To calculate wildcard masks, follow these steps:

    1. Change the subnet mask into dotted-decimal format.

    2 Subtract the resulting mask from 255.255.255.255.

    3. The result is the wildcard mask.

    Example: A mask of /18 equals 255.255.192.0. A mask of 255.255.192.0 subtracted from 255.255.255.255 yields a wildcard mask of 0.0.63.255.

4. C. Explanation: A company with one large autonomous system (AS) can be divided into smaller areas. When this occurs and the OSPF routing protocol is implemented, the design is called multi-area OSPF. Multi-area OSPF decreases the frequency of the SPF calculation, thus lightening the load on the router. In a single area OSPF design, all the routers are located in area 0 or the backbone area.

5. D. Explanation: There is no autonomous system number to configure on OSPF. The area number is located at the end of the network statement. The cost of a link can be modified in the interface configuration mode. The process ID is local to the router.

6. D. Explanation: By default, the dead interval is calculated as 4 times the Hello interval.

7. D. Explanation: A loopback interface used as an OSPF router ID normally uses a 32-bit mask that creates a host route. This route is not advertised as a route to other routers unless a network statement including this interface is added.

8. B, C, and F. Explanation: The route metric and neighbor next-hop address are routing table entries that are displayed by the **show ip route** command. The **show ip ospf neighbor** command does not display the OSPF process ID or the OSPF area number.

9. C. Explanation: OSPFv2 uses the router configuration **network** command to advertise networks. OSPFv3 uses the **ipv6 ospf** *process-id* **area** *area-id* interface configuration command. Both OSPFv2 and OSPFv3 use a 32 bit router ID. Both OSPFv2 and OSPFv3 require the DR/BDR election to occur on multiaccess networks. Neither protocol requires a DR/BDR election for point-to-point networks.

10. B. Explanation: The OSPF cost metric is the accumulated value from R1 to network 172.16.1.0. The cost for the first link is 100,000,000/64,000 (1562). The cost for the second link is 100,000,000/100,000,000 (1). The OSPF cost metric from R1 to 172.16.1.0 is therefore 1563.

Chapter 9

1. A
2. A
3. A
4. C
5. B
6. A
7. B
8. B and C
9. C and D
10. E

Chapter 10

1. B and F. Explanation: DHCP can provide the IP address, subnet mask, default gateway, domain name, DNS server, NetBIOS, and WINS server. The duration of the DHCP lease is by default 1 day, but you can change it by using the **lease** command.

2. A. Explanation: The argument that follows the command **ip dhcp pool** is the *pool-name* argument.

3. A, B, and C. Explanation: DHCP uses User Datagram Protocol (UDP) as its transport protocol. The client sends messages to the server on port 67. The server sends messages to the client on port 68. When the DHCP server receives a DHCPDISCOVER message, it finds an available IP address to lease, creates an ARP entry consisting of the MAC address of the requesting host and the leased IP address, and transmits a binding offer with a DHCPOFFER message. The DHCPOFFER message is sent as a unicast, using the server's Layer 2 MAC address as the source address and the client's Layer 2 address as the destination.

4. D. Explanation: The helper address (DHCPv4 relay) should be configured on the interface that hears the DHCP broadcast. Otherwise, the DHCP broadcast will be dropped by the router.

5. C. Explanation: DHCPv6 relay is still used when the DHCPv6 server is on a different link than the client.

6. D and E. Explanation: Stateless autoconfiguration automatically configures the IPv6 address for the host, and DHCPv6 enables the automatic allocation of reusable network addresses. DHCPv6 is a stateful counterpart to IPv6 stateless autoconfiguration. It can be used separately or concurrently with IPv6 stateless autoconfiguration to obtain configuration parameters.

7. DHCPDISCOVER

   DHCPOFFER

   DHCPREQUEST

   DHCPACK

   Explanation: The four message types in order are as follows: DHCP Discover, DHCP Offer, DHCP Request, and DHCP Acknowledgment.

8. DHCPACK

   DHCPOFFER

   Explanation: The DHCPv4 process starts with a client sending a DHCPDISCOVER to probe for a DHCPv4 server using a broadcast message. When a DHCPv4 server hears the discover message, the server reserves an available IPv4 address for the client and creates an ARP entry containing the client MAC address. The server responds with a DHCPOFFER message. The client responds to the server with a DHCP request. The server responds with a DHCPACK (acknowledgment) message.

9. C. Explanation: The Router Solicitation (RS) message is sent by a client when it obtains addressing information automatically using stateless address autoconfiguration (SLAAC).

10. B. Explanation: SLAAC is used when the client automatically receives basic IP addressing configuration from the router. Stateless DHCPv6 is when the client automatically gets IP addressing information but uses the DHCPv6 server for additional configuration information.

11. D

A

B

G

E

Explanation: The ICMPv6 RA message contains two flags that indicate which IPv6 addressing option the client should use: the Managed Address Configuration (M) flag and the Other Configuration (O) flag. When stateful DHCPv6 is to be used, the M flag is set and the O flag is not used. When stateless DHCPv6 is used, the O flag is enabled (set) and the M flag is left at the default setting of disabled or 0.

12. 546

547

Explanation: DHCPv4 uses UDP ports 67 and 68. DHCPv6 uses UDP ports 546 and 547.

Chapter 11

1. C. Explanation: Because port numbers are shown beside the IP addresses in the NAT translations, PAT is being used.

2. B. Explanation: NAT translations time out after 24 hours. This value can be modified. NAT timeout values are configured in seconds. 86,400 seconds equals 24 hours.

3.   B   Dynamic NAT

  C, D   PAT

  A, E   Static NAT

4. B. Explanation: The host with the address 192.168.0.100 will be translated into 209.165.200.2.

5. C. Explanation: The access-list determines what IP addresses can be translated. With a wildcard of 0.0.0.31, the first 27 bits have to match. Write 192.168.0.0 in binary and draw a line after the first 27 bits. If you place all 0s after the line, you get the first number translated (192.168.0.0). Then place all 1s to the right of the line and determine that IP address to determine the last number translated (192.168.0.31).

6. C. Explanation: R1 is the connection to the Internet, so R1 should have NAT configured. The external interface is S0/1/0. The internal interface is Gi0/0.

7. C. Explanation: Servers need addresses that do not change; therefore, a static NAT is needed.

8. C and D. Explanation: The device doing the NAT must track network conversations. If there are quite a few network conversations occurring, the device doing the translations might have performance issues. Disadvantages of NAT include the following.

   - Hosts on the Internet appear to communicate directly with the NAT-enabled device instead of the actual host.

   - NAT affects time-sensitive packets such as VoIP.

   - End-to-end addressing is lost.

   - End-to-end traceability is lost.

   - Tunneling protocols such as IPsec are negatively affected.

9. D. Explanation: Applying NAT to an interface before the other configuration parameters have been created will cause a loss of connectivity.

10. A. Explanation: The access list determines that addresses must be "matched" in order to be translated using NAT.

11. B. Explanation: The **overload** keyword is used in PAT configurations. PAT can use the IP address of the external interface for all translations or can use an address pool of addresses that is fewer in number than the actual number of private, internal addresses that need translation.

12. D. Explanation: IPv6 should be run natively whenever possible. At times during IPv4 to IPv6 conversion, a company must either run both protocols, use tunneling for IPv6, or use NAT64.

2-way state   This state designates that bidirectional communication has been established between two routers. Bidirectional means that each router has seen the other's hello packet.

Access Control Entry (ACE)   A single line in an ACL. Also known as ACL Statement.

access control list (ACL)   A series of IOS commands that controls whether a router forwards or drops packets based on information found in the packet header.

access layer   A tier in the two- and three-layer hierarchical network design model where devices connect to the network and includes services such as power to network end points.

addressing table   A table that captures device names, interfaces, IPv4 addresses, subnet masks, and default gateway addresses.

adjacency   A relationship formed between selected neighboring routers and end nodes for the purpose of exchanging routing information. Adjacency is based on the use of a common media segment.

Administrative Distance (AD)   The feature that routers use to select the best path when there are two or more different routes to the same destination from two different routing protocols. The AD represents the "trustworthiness" or reliability of the route.

algorithm   Well-defined rule or process for arriving at a solution to a problem. In networking, algorithms are commonly used to determine the best route for traffic from a particular source to a particular destination.

ALLSPFRouters   A multicast group used in the OSPF routing protocol. The ALLSPFRouters address is 224.0.0.5.

application-specific integrated circuit (ASIC)   Electronics added to a switch that allowed it to have more ports without degrading performance.

Area Border Router (ABR)   Routers interconnecting the areas in a multi-area OSPF network.

automatic medium-dependent interface crossover (auto-MDIX)   A feature that allows a port to automatically sense what type of cable (crossover or straight-through) is attached and configure the port so it will function properly.

autonomous system   A collection of routers under a common administration such as a company or an organization.

Autonomous System Boundary Router (ASBR)   The OSPF router located between an OSPF autonomous system network and a non-OSPF network. ASBRs run both OSPF and another routing protocol, such as RIP. ASBRs must reside in a nonstub OSPF area.

availability   A measure of the probability that the network is available for use when it is required.

backbone area   Also known as Area 0. In any OSPF network design, there must be at least one area. Traditionally, this area is numbered 0 and is known as the backbone area. In single-area OSPF, the lone area is area 0. In Multi-Area OSPF, Area 0 forms the core of the network as all other areas attach to the backbone area to facilitate interarea communication.

backup designated router (BDR)   A router that becomes the designated router if the current designated router fails. The BDR is the OSPF router with the second-highest priority at the time of the last DR election.

Bellman-Ford Algorithm   The routing algorithm of the RIP routing protocol.

best path   The path with the lowest metric to a destination network.

black hole VLAN   A VLAN assigned to unused switch ports.

boot loader   A small program stored in ROM that runs immediately after POST successfully completes. It is used to initialize a network device like a router or a switch. The boot loader locates and launches the operating system.

boundary router   A router that sits on the edge of two discontiguous classful networks. A boundary router can also be known as a router that sits on the edge of two different networks that have different routing protocols. Sometimes, the term boundary router is loosely used when discussing OSPF and Autonomous System Boundary Routers.

Branch Router   A router used in a remote or branch office to connect to the main network.

broadcast domain   All nodes that are part of a network segment, vlan, or subnet, and all devices on the LAN receive broadcast frames from a host within the LAN. A broadcast domain is bounded by a Layer 3 device. A Layer 3 device such as a router sets the boundary of the broadcast domain.

broadcast interfaces   An interface on a router in which there may be multiple possible destinations. An example is an Ethernet interface on a router that is connected to a switch. Multiple other routers may also be connected into the same switch, leaving multiple possible destinations.

brute force password attack   Uses a trial-and-error approach to password cracking using software programs that run combinations of characters and common dictionary words to decipher passwords.

child route   A route that is a subnet of a classful network address. Also known as a level 2 route.

Cisco Discovery Protocol (CDP)   A media- and protocol-independent device-discovery protocol that runs on Cisco equipment such as routers, access servers, bridges, and switches. With CDP enabled, a device can advertise its existence to other directly connected devices and receive information about other devices on the same LAN or on the remote side of a WAN.

Cisco Express Forwarding (CEF)   CEF is an advanced, Layer 3 switching technology inside a router. It defines the fastest method by which a Cisco router forwards packets from ingress to egress interfaces.

Class A address   Network address class that contains all addresses in which the most significant bit is zero. The network number for this class is given by the next 7 bits, therefore accommodating 128 networks in total, including the zero network, and including the existing IP networks already allocated.

Class B address   Network address class in which all addresses have the two most-significant bits set to 1 and 0. For these networks, the network address is given by the next 14 bits of the address, thus leaving 16 bits for numbering host on the network for a total of 65536 addresses per network.

Class C address   Network address class which is defined with the 3 high-order bits set to 1, 1, and 0, and designating the next 21 bits to number the networks, leaving each network with 256 local addresses.

Class D address   Network address class in which all addresses have the four most-significant bits set to 1, 1, 1, and 0. These networks have been reserved for multicast traffic.

Class E address   Network address class in which all addresses have the four most-significant bits set to 1, 1, 1, and 1. These networks have been reserved and are not assignable to devices.

classful routing protocol   A routing protocol that does not carry subnet mask information in its routing updates.

Classless Inter-Domain Routing (CIDR)   IP addressing technique based on route aggregation. CIDR allows for routers to group routes together to minimize the quantity of routing information carried by routers.

classless routing protocol   A routing protocol that carries subnet mask information in its routing updates. Classless routing protocols can take advantage of VLSM and supernet routes.

collapsed core network design   See two-tier campus network design.

collision domain   A network segment that shares the same bandwidth between the devices such as between a switch and a PC. Each port on a switch is its own collision domain. Every device connected to a hub is within a single collision domain meaning that when two devices attempt communication simultaneously, collisions occur.

console cable   A cable connected between the serial port of the host and the console port on the device.

converge   Speed and ability of a group of internetworking devices running a specific routing protocol to agree on the topology of an internetwork after a change in that topology.

converged   See *converged network.*

converged network   Convergence means several things in networking: (1) combining voice and video with the traditional data network, (2) providing a loop-free Layer 2 topology for a switched LAN through the use of spanning tree, and (3) providing a stable Layer 3 network where the routers have completed providing each other updates and the routing tables are complete.

core layer   A tier in the three-layer hierarchical network design model that creates the network backbone. All traffic to and from peripheral networks must pass through the core layer. It includes high-speed switching devices that can handle relatively large amounts of traffic. In a two-layer hierarchical design model, the core layer is combined with the distribution layer for small-to-medium-sized business networks.

cost   An arbitrary value, typically based on hop count, media bandwidth, or other measures, that is assigned by a network administrator and used to compare various paths through an internetwork environment. Routing protocols use cost values to calculate the most favorable path to a particular destination: the lower the cost, the better the path.

CRC error   The cyclic redundancy check (CRC) is a process to check for errors within the Layer 2 frame. The sending device generates a CRC and includes this value in the frame check sequence (FCS) field. The receiving device generates a CRC and compares it to the received CRC to look for errors. If the calculations match, no error has occurred. If the calculations do not match, the frame is dropped. CRC errors on Ethernet and serial interfaces usually mean a media or cable problem.

cut-through switching   A method used inside a switch where, after the destination MAC address has been received, the frame is sent to the appropriate port if the destination MAC address was found in the MAC address table or the frame is broadcasted to all ports except the ingress port.

data structures   A group of data elements that are stored together under one name. The adjacency database, link-state database, and forwarding database are all examples of data structures.

data VLAN   A VLAN that is configured to carry only user-generated traffic. In particular, a data VLAN does not carry voice-based traffic or traffic used to manage a switch.

database description (DBD)   A packet used in OSPF that contains link-state advertisement (LSA) headers only and describes the contents of the entire link-state database. Routers exchange DBDs during the exchange phase of adjacency creation. A DBD is an OSPF Type 2 packet.

dead interval   The time in seconds that a router waits to hear from a neighbor before declaring the neighboring router out of service.

default gateway   Identifies the router to send a packet to when the destination is not on the same local network subnet.

default static route   A route that matches all packets and identifies the gateway IP address to which the router sends all packets that it does not have a learned or static route.

default VLAN   The VLAN that all the ports on a switch are members of when a switch is reset to factory defaults or new. All switch ports are members of the default VLAN after the initial boot of the switch. On a Cisco switch, VLAN 1 is the default VLAN.

denial-of-service (DoS) attack   Any attack that prevents legitimate network devices from sending data on or participating in the network.

designated router (DR)   OSPF router that generates LSAs for a multiaccess network and has other special responsibilities in running OSPF. Each multiaccess OSPF network that has at least two attached routers has a designated router that is elected by the OSPF Hello protocol. The designated router enables a reduction in the number of adjacencies required on a multiaccess network, which in turn reduces the amount of routing protocol traffic and the size of the topological database.

DHCP snooping   An optional switch security feature that acts as a firewall between untrusted network devices and trusted DHCP servers.

DHCP spoofing attack   A server is inserted into the network after launching a DHCP starvation attack. The illegitimate DHCP server issues inappropriate IP address-associated information so that clients send network traffic to a machine controlled by the attacker.

DHCP starvation attack   This type of attack overloads a DHCP server with illegitimate requests. When the DHCP pool of IP addresses is empty, DHCP requests from legitimate network clients cannot be fulfilled, and as a result the devices cannot participate in the network. This attack is commonly used before a DHCP spoofing attack.

DHCPACK   A unicast message sent by a DHCP server in response to a device that sends a DHCPREQUEST. The DHCPACK message is used by the DHCP server to complete the DHCP process.

DHCPDISCOVER   A broadcast message sent by a network device to discover an IPv4 DHCP server.

DHCPOFFER   A unicast message returned by a DHCP server in response to a client device sending a DHCPDISCOVER broadcast message. The DHCPOFFER message typically contains an IP address, subnet mask, default gateway address, and other information.

DHCPREQUEST   A broadcast message sent by a network device in response to a DHCPOFFER made by a DHCP server that sent a DHCPOFFER message. The DHCPREQUEST message is used by the device to accept the IP addressing offer made by the DHCP server.

DHCPv4 relay agent   Allows relaying DHCP messages between a DHCP client and a DHCP server located on a different network.

DHCPv4   A method of deploying IP address-related information to IPv4 devices. DHCPv4 uses four types of messages: DHCP discover, DHCP offer, DHCP request, and DHCP acknowledgment.

DHCPv6 relay agent   Allows relaying DHCP messages between an IPv6 DHCP server and a DHCP client when they are not on the same link.

DHCPv6   IPv6 network devices can obtain IPv6 addressing information using one of three options: SLAAC, stateless DHCPv6, and stateful DHCPv6.

Diffusing Update Algorithm   The routing algorithm of both IGRP and EIGRP.

Dijkstra Algorithm   The routing algorithm of the OSPF routing protocol.

directly connected network   Networks that can be reached by the local router.

directly connected static route   A static route in which only the router exit interface is specified.

distance   Identifies how far it is to a destination network. Based on a metric such as hop count, cost, bandwidth, delay, or others.

distribution layer   A tier in the three-layer hierarchical network design model that connects the access layer to the core layer. The distribution layer aggregates connectivity from multiple access layer devices, Layer 2 broadcast domains, and Layer 3 routing boundaries. In a two-layer hierarchical design model, the distribution layer is combined with the core layer for small-to-medium-sized business networks.

double tagging   This type of VLAN hopping attack requires that the attacker be connected to a port that is in the same VLAN as the native VLAN of a trunk port. The attacker sends an 802.1Q frame that has two VLAN tags; the second tag is that fake one that is read by a second switch and sent to an unattended VLAN that has a target host controlled by the attacker.

Down State   This is the first OSPF neighbor state. It means that no information (hellos) has been received from this neighbor, but hello packets can still be sent to the neighbor in this state.

DROthers   Routers that are not a DR or BDR. They are the other routers in the OSPF network.

dual stack   A transition mechanism used when converting from IPv4 to IPv6. Basically when using a dual stack, a router runs both IPv4 and IPv6.

Duplicate Address Detection (DAD)   A process used by IPv6 devices using an ICMPv6 Neighbor Solicitation message to verify whether any other device has the same IPv6 address.

Dynamic Host Configuration Protocol (DHCP)   A protocol used to deploy IP addressing-related configuration to network devices such as PCs, IP phones, and mobile devices.

dynamic NAT   A type of network address translation (NAT) where many local addresses (normally private IP addresses) are mapped to many global IP addresses (which are normally public IP addresses).

dynamic routes   A remote network in a routing table that has been automatically learned using a dynamic routing protocol such as EIGRP or OSPF.

dynamic secure MAC address   A port security method used when MAC addresses are dynamically learned from frames entering a switch port. The address is added to the MAC address table but is removed when the switch restarts.

Dynamic Trunking Protocol (DTP)   A Cisco-proprietary protocol that negotiates both the status and encapsulation of trunk ports.

dynamically assigned IP address   IP address information is provided by a server using the Dynamic Host Configuration Protocol (DHCP).

egress   The port through which a frame exits a switch.

exchange state   In the exchange state, OSPF routers exchange database descriptor (DBD) packets. Database descriptors contain link-state advertisement (LSA) headers only and describe the contents of the entire link-state database.

exit interface   The interface through which frames leave a device.

Exstart State   In this state, the routers and their DR and BDR establish a master-slave relationship and choose the initial sequence number for adjacency formation. The router with the higher router ID becomes the master and starts the exchange.

extended ACL   Filters traffic based upon multiple attributes including protocol type, Source IPv4 addresses, destination IPv4 addresses, source ports, and destination ports.

Exterior Gateway Protocol   A routing protocol used for routing between autonomous systems (AS).

fast switching   In fast switching, the first packet is copied to packet memory, and the destination network or host is found in the fast-switching cache. The frame is rewritten and sent to the outgoing interface that services the destination. Subsequent packets for the same destination use the same switching path.

fixed configuration switch   A type of switch commonly used in the access layer of the hierarchical network design model that supports only the features and options shipped with the switch. This type of switch is not upgradable. Contrast with a modular configuration switch.

Fixed Length Subnet Mask (FLSM)   Divides a large network into smaller subnetworks of equal hosts per subnet. Also known as traditional subnetting.

Flash memory   Provides permanent storage for the IOS and other system-related files. The IOS is copied from flash into RAM during the bootup process. Flash is nonvolatile and does not lose its contents when power is turned off.

flexibility   A network design model goal that allows intelligent and efficient traffic load sharing by network devices and resources.

floating static route   Static routes used to provide a backup path to a primary static or dynamic route, in the event of a link failure. Used only when the primary route is not available.

Forwarding Information Base (FIB)   Used with CEF to provide optimized lookups for more efficient packet forwarding.

frame check sequence (FCS)   A checksum value found in the last field of a datagram that is used by the switch to validate that the frame is free of errors.

Full State   In this state, routers are fully adjacent with each other. All the router and network LSAs are exchanged and the routers' databases are fully synchronized.

fully specified static route   A static route in which both the output interface and next-hop address are identified.

gateway of last resort   Used to direct packets addressed to networks not explicitly listed in the routing table. Also known as a default route.

giant   A problematic Ethernet frame of excess size caused by a malfunctioning NIC or an improperly terminated or unterminated cable.

Hello interval   Specifies the frequency, in seconds, at which a router sends Hello packets.

Hello packet   Hello packets are Type 1 OSPF packets. They are used to establish and maintain adjacency with other OSPF routers.

hierarchical   A design model goal that simplifies deployments because each device at every tier is understood and identified.

high order bits   The far left bits in a 32-bit address.

High-Speed WAN Interface Card (HWIC) Single-wide interface cards that provide Cisco modular and integrated services routers with additional line-rate Layer 3 routed ports.

HQ router   A router at the main network site used to connect to remote or branch offices.

implicit deny   A hard-coded ACL statement in all ACLs that denies all traffic from passing through the interface. This statement is called implicit because it is not shown in output when you list ACL statements using show commands. It is always the last line of any ACL.

inbound traffic   Direction of packet flow. Incoming packets are processed before they are routed to the outbound interface.

ingress   The port through which a frame enters a switch.

Init State   This state specifies that the router has received a hello packet from its neighbor, but the receiving router's ID was not included in the hello packet.

inside global address   Used with NAT for IPv4, a valid public IPv4 address that is given to the packet sourced from an inside host. Normally, the IPv4 public address is assigned as the packet exits the NAT router.

inside local address   Used with NAT for IPv4, this address is usually an RFC 1918 private address, which is a type of address that is not usually assigned by a Regional Internet Registry (RIR) or a service provider. The private IP address is assigned to a device inside a home or corporate environment.

Interior Gateway Protocol   A routing protocol used for routing within an autonomous system (AS).

inter-VLAN routing   The process of routing data between VLANs so that communication can occur between the different networks.

inverse mask   Sometimes used as another name for a wildcard mask.

IP address   The unique number ID assigned to one host or interface in a network.

late collision   A collision that occurs after 512 bytes of an Ethernet frame (the preamble) have been transmitted.

Layer 3 (routed) port   Sometimes called simply a routed port, this type of port is found on a multilayer switch. Any of the Layer 2 ports can be converted into a port that can have an IP address and mask assigned. Layer 3 (routed) ports are commonly implemented between the distribution layer switches and core layer switches in the hierarchical switch design model.

Layer 3 switching   A switch that can have routing enabled to route between VLANs and on some models exchange routing updates with other Layer 3 devices such as routers or multilayer switches.

legacy protocol   Routing protocols that are no longer used due to changed technologies. Examples are RIPv1 and IGRP.

Level 1 route   A route with a subnet mask equal to or less than the classful mask of the network address.

Level 2 route   A route that is a subnet of a classful network address. Also known as a child route.

link state   Refers to the status of a link, including the interface IP address/subnet mask, type of network, cost of the link, and any neighbor routers on that link.

link-state acknowledgment (LSAck)   Acknowledges receipt of link-state advertisement (LSA) packets. Link-state acknowledgment packets are Type 5 OSPF packets.

link-state advertisement (LSA)   Broadcast packet used by link-state protocols that contains information about neighbors and path costs. LSAs are used by the receiving routers to maintain their routing tables.

link-state database   A table used in OSPF that is a representation of the topology of the autonomous system. It is the method by which routers "see" the state of the links in the autonomous system.

link-state packet (LSP)   *See link-state advertisement.*

link-state request (LSR)   Link-state request packets are Type 3 OSPF packets. The link-state request packet is used to request the pieces of the neighbor's database that are more up to date.

link-state router   A router that uses a link-state routing protocol.

link-state routing protocol   A routing protocol in which routers exchange information with one another about the reachability of other networks and the cost or metric to reach the other networks. Link-state routers use Dijkstra's algorithm to calculate shortest paths to a destination, and normally update other routers with whom they are connected only when their own routing tables change.

link-state update (LSU)   Link-state update packets are Type 4 OSPF packets. A link-state update packet carries a collection of link-state advertisements one hop farther from its origin.

load balancing   The capability of a router to distribute traffic over all the router network ports that are the same distance from the destination address.

Loading State   In this state, the actual exchange of link state information occurs. Based on the information provided by the DBDs, routers send link-state request packets. The neighbor then provides the requested link-state information in link-state update packets. During the adjacency, if a router receives an outdated or missing LSA, it requests that LSA by sending a link-state request packet. All link-state update packets are acknowledged.

logical topology   The path over which the data is transferred in a network.

loopback interface   A software-only interface that emulates a physical interface. A loopback interface is always up and never goes down.

MAC address table overflow attack   A security issue when an attacker sends multiple frames that contain fake source MAC addresses that are entered into and fill the MAC address table of a switch. The switch is forced to broadcast all frames out all ports allowing an attacker to capture and view addresses. Configuring port security can be used to prevent this type of attack.

MAC address table   Also known as a CAM or SAT table, which stores source MAC addresses and port numbers learned from frames entering the switch.

MAC flooding attack   *See MAC address table overflow attack.*

management VLAN   A VLAN defined by the network administrator as a means of accessing the management capabilities of a switch. The management VLAN SVI is assigned an IP address and subnet mask. It is a security best practice to define the management VLAN to be a VLAN distinct from all other VLANs defined in the switched LAN.

metric   The quantitative value used to measure the distance to a given network.

microsegmentaton   Dividing a network into smaller segments. Switches use microsegmentation to prevent collisions.

modular configuration switch   A type of switch commonly used in the distribution and core layers of the hierarchical network design model that allows flexibility and customization by adding various line cards. Contrast with a fixed configuration switch.

modularity   A network design model goal that allows the network to expand in a planned fashion.

Multiarea OSPF   In an OSPF Network Design, one large autonomous system (AS) is divided into smaller areas, to support hierarchical routing. All areas must connect to the backbone area (area 0).

multicast addresses   Addresses that are used to identify a group of hosts that are part of a multicast group. Sending traffic to a multicast address is more efficient than broadcasting traffic to all devices on a segment.

multipoint interfaces   Single interfaces on a router that may be partitioned into multiple virtual interfaces. Used in Frame Relay network topologies.

named ACL   An ACL that uses a text string to describe the ACL, rather than a number.

NAT for IPv4   When private IP addresses are translated into public IPv4 addresses so that data may be transmitted across the Internet.

NAT64   A method of using both IPv4 and IPv6 addresses.

native VLAN   A native VLAN is assigned to an IEEE 802.1Q trunk port. An IEEE 802.1Q trunk port supports tagged and untagged traffic coming from VLANs. The 802.1Q trunk port places untagged traffic on the native VLAN. It is a security best practice to define a native VLAN to be a dummy VLAN distinct from all other VLANs defined in the switched LAN. The native VLAN is not used for any traffic in the switched network.

neighbor   In OSPF, two routers that have interfaces to a common network. On multiaccess networks, neighbors are discovered dynamically by the OSPF Hello protocol.

network address translation (NAT)   A mechanism used to translate one IP address into another IP address. *See NAT for IPv4 and NAT for IPv6.*

network address translation-protocol translation (NAT-PT)   A mechanism used when using both IPv4 and IPv6 addresses. This method has been deprecated by IETF in favor of NAT64.

network prefix   In CIDR, the network portion of an IP address is defined by the subnet mask, now known as the network prefix or prefix length. A network prefix of /18 means that the first 18 bits of the address are network bits, and therefore the last 14 bits define the host portion of the address.

network route   A route that has a subnet mask equal to that of the classful mask.

Network Time Protocol (NTP)   A protocol used to synchronize the date and time for networked devices.

next hop address   The address of the next closest router a packet can go through on its way to a destination network.

next-hop route   A static route in which only the next-hop IP address is specified.

Non-Volatile Random Access Memory (NVRAM)   Provides permanent storage for the startup configuration file (startup-config). NVRAM is nonvolatile and does not lose its contents when power is turned off.

OSPF   Open Shortest Path First. Link-state, hierarchical IGP routing algorithm proposed as a successor to RIP in the Internet community. OSPF features include least-cost routing, multipath routing, and load balancing. OSPF was derived from an early version of the IS-IS Protocol.

OSPF area   A logical set of network segments (CLNS-, DECnet-, or OSPF-based) and their attached devices. Areas are usually connected to other areas through routers, making up a single autonomous system.

OSPFv2   Version 2 of the OSPF routing protocol. It is used to support IPv4 unicast address families.

OSPFv3   Version 3 of the OSPF routing protocol. It is used to support both IPv4 and IPv6 unicast address families.

outbound traffic   Direction of packet flow. Outbound packets are processed before they are passed through the outbound interface.

outside global address   A reachable IP address used in NAT for IPv4 and assigned to hosts located out in the Internet.

packet filtering   Controls access to a network by analyzing the incoming and outgoing packets and passing or dropping them based on given criteria, such as the source IP address, destination IP addresses, and the protocol carried within the packet.

parent route   A level 1 route that has been subnetted. A parent route can never be an ultimate route.

passive interface   An interface that does not take part in the advertisement of routing information. The **passive interface** command enables the suppression of routing updates over some interfaces while it allows updates to be exchanged normally over other interfaces. A neighbor adjacency cannot be formed over a passive interface. This is because link-state packets cannot be sent or acknowledged.

penetration testing   An intentional attack by authorized personnel against a network to determine network vulnerabilities.

periodic update   At the end of a certain time period, updates will be transmitted between routers. The periodic update for RIP is 30 seconds.

physical topology   The arrangement of the cables, network devices, and end systems. It describes how the network devices are actually interconnected with wires and cables.

point-to-point interfaces   An interface on a router in which there is only one possible destination. An example is a serial interface on one router connected directly to a serial interface on another Cisco router.

Port Address Translation (PAT)   Many internal local IP addresses are mapped to one global IP address.

port security   A generic term meaning procedures and configurations performed on a switch interface to protect the network from attacks and unauthorized wired devices.

prefix aggregation   Another name for Route Summarization.

prefix length   Another name for a network prefix.

Private VLAN (PVLAN) edge   A locally significant switch feature that provides protection for a particular port. Some applications require that no Layer 2 traffic be forwarded between ports on the same switch. The PVLAN edge feature ensures that no unicast, broadcast, or multicast traffic is exchanged between protected ports.

process switching   In process switching the first packet is copied to the system buffer. The router looks up the Layer 3 network address in the routing table and initializes the fast-switch cache. The frame is rewritten with the destination address and sent to the outgoing interface that services that destination. Subsequent packets for that destination are sent by the same switching path.

Protocol Dependent Modules (PDM)
A feature of EIGRP. Individual modules are responsible for the tasks related to a specific routing protocol. EIGRP has PDMs for IP, IPX, AppleTalk, and IPv6.

quad-zero route   An IPv4 default static route. Referred to as quad-zero route because of its syntax of 0.0.0.0 for the network address and 0.0.0.0 for the subnet mask.

random-access memory (RAM)   Provides temporary storage for various applications and processes including the running IOS, the running configuration file, various tables (that is, IP routing table and Ethernet ARP table) and buffers for packet processing. RAM is referred to as volatile because it loses its contents when power is turned off.

read-only memory (ROM)   Provides permanent storage for bootup instructions, basic diagnostic software, and a limited IOS in case the router cannot load the full featured IOS. ROM is firmware and referred to as nonvolatile because it does not lose its contents when power is turned off.

recursive lookup   Occurs when a router has to perform multiple lookups in a routing table before forwarding a packet.

reference bandwidth   The number, measured in Mb/s, which is used by OSPF routers to calculate cost. The default reference bandwidth is 100 Mb/s. Changing the reference bandwidth does not actually affect the bandwidth capacity on the link; rather, it simply affects the calculation used to determine the metric.

reliability   Indicates the dependability of the components that make up the network, such as the routers, switches, PCs, and servers.

remote network   Networks that can be reached only by forwarding packets to another router.

resiliency   A network design model goal that satisfies user expectations that the network is always up and operational.

reverse route   A route pointing back to the router from which packets were received.

RFC 1918 Address Allocation for Private Internets   Private IP addresses that are reserved blocks of numbers that can be used by anyone; however, ISPs configure border routers to prevent such IP addresses from being forwarded over the Internet.

route summarization   The process of taking multiple contiguous routes and representing them with a single route statement.

routed port   Sometimes called a Layer 3 (routed) port, this type of port is found on a multilayer switch. Any of the Layer 2 ports can be converted into a port that can have an IP address and mask assigned. Layer 3 (routed) ports are commonly implemented between the distribution layer switches and core layer switches in the hierarchical switch design model.

router   A network device, typically connected to a range of LAN and WAN interfaces that forwards packets based on their destination IP addresses.

Router Advertisement (RA) message   A message type used by an IPv6 router to provide IPv6 addressing information to clients. The router sends the message using the IPv6 all-nodes multicast address of FF02::1.

Router ID   A field in an OSPF Hello packet that is a 32-bit value expressed in dotted decimal notation (an IPv4 address) used to uniquely identify the originating router.

Router Priority   Used in a DR/BDR election. The default priority for all OSPF routers is 1 but can be manually altered from 0 to 255. The higher the value, the more likely the router becomes the DR on the link.

Router Solicitation (RS) message   A message type used by an IPv6 client that sends a multicast to address FF02::2 (all-routers) to obtain an IPv6 address using SLAAC, which does not require the services of a DHCPv6 router.

routing table   A data file in RAM that is used to store route information about directly connected and remote networks.

runt   A problematic Ethernet frame of a size less than 64 bytes, the minimum frame size. Runts are caused by malfunctioning NICs and improperly terminated Ethernet cables.

scalability   Indicates how easily the network can accommodate more users and data transmission requirements.

Secure Shell (SSH)   A protocol that supports secure communication with a remote device that has been configured to accept an SSH connection.

security audit   A gathering of information to determine the type of information an attacker could obtain by capturing and analyzing network traffic.

shortest path first (SPF) algorithm   This algorithm uses accumulated costs along each path, from source to destination, to determine the total cost of a route. Routing algorithm that iterates on the length of path to determine a shortest-path spanning tree. Commonly used in link-state routing algorithms. Sometimes called Dijkstra's algorithm.

Single-Area OSPF   In an OSPF Network design, all routers are in one area called the backbone area (area 0).

Split Horizon   a technique for preventing reverse routes between two routers.

stackable configuration switch   Switches cabled together through a special port and managed as a single switch to provide fault tolerance and bandwidth in an area where a modular switch is not financially feasible.

standard ACL   Used to filter traffic only from source IPv4 addresses.

stateful DHCPv6   An IPv6 client using this option obtains all addressing and configuration information from a stateful DHCPv6 server.

Stateless Address Autoconfiguration (SLAAC)   An IPv6 addressing option that allows a device to obtain an IPv6 global unicast address without communicating with a DHCPv6 server. The address is obtained using ICMPv6 RS and RA messages.

stateless DHCPv6   An IPv6 client using this option automatically obtains some addressing information but contacts a DHCPv6 server for an additional addressing configuration to use, such as DNS addresses.

static NAT   A type of network address translation (NAT) where there is a one-to-one address mapping between a local address (normally a private IP address) and a global address (normally a public IP address).

static routes   A remote network in a routing table that has been manually entered into the table by a Network administrator.

static secure MAC address   A port security method used when MAC addresses are manually configured on a switch port.

statically assigned IP address   The host is manually assigned the correct IP address, subnet mask, and default gateway.

sticky secure MAC address   A port security method used where MAC addresses are either manually configured or dynamically learned from frames entering a switch port. The addresses are stored in the MAC address table and automatically added to the switch running configuration.

store-and-forward switching   A method used inside a switch where the entire frame is received, and the cyclic redundancy check (CRC) is calculated. If valid, the frame is sent to the appropriate port if the destination MAC address was found in the MAC address table or the frame is broadcasted to all ports except the ingress port.

stub network   A network with only one exit point. A hub-and-spoke network would be an example of a stub network.

stub router   A router that has only one exit interface from the routing domain and forwards all traffic to a central or distribution router.

subnet mask   A dotted decimal number that helps identify the structure of IP addresses. The mask represents the network and subnet parts of related IP addresses with binary 1s and the host part of related IP addresses with binary 0s.

summary static route   A single static route that can represent multiple contiguous networks to reduce the number of entries in a routing table.

supernet route   A route that has a subnet mask less than the classful mask. A summary address is an example of a supernet route.

supernetting   Occurs when the route summarization mask is a smaller value than the default traditional classful mask.

switch spoofing   A type of VLAN hopping attack that works by taking advantage of an incorrectly configured trunk port. The attacker configures a system to form a trunk with an incorrectly configured switch. The attacker then gains access to all VLANs allowed on the trunk.

Switched Virtual Interface (SVI)   Provides basic Layer 3 functions for a switch, which does not have a dedicated physical interface for IP addressing.

tagging   The process of adding a 4 byte IEEE 802.1Q header to a standard Ethernet frame to identify the VLAN the frame belongs to so that it can be sent across a trunk link with the identifying information.

Telnet DoS attack   An attack that locks a legitimate network administrator from remotely accessing a network device using Telnet.

Terminal Emulation software   A software program that transmits keystrokes to a remote device, receives output from the remote device, and displays it in a window, which simulates the screen that was used historically as a dumb terminal.

three-tier campus network design   A hierarchical network design model that consists of the following layers from bottom to top: access, distribution, and core.

topology diagram   Provides a visual reference that indicates the physical connectivity and logical Layer 3 addressing.

triggered update   Also known as *flash updates.* Updates are sent immediately upon being discovered without waiting for a timer to expire.

trunk   A switch port mode configured so that the switch can transmit traffic from multiple VLANs over a single link.

trusted port   A switch port that has been identified as one that can source any type of DHCP message. Trusted ports have a DHCP server attached or can be a port that is a link that connects toward the DHCP server.

tunneling for IPv6   A method used when a company has both IPv4 and IPv6 addresses in use. Tunneling encapsulates an IPv6 packet inside an IPv4 packet for transmission over an IPv4 network.

two-tier campus network design   A hierarchical network design model that collapses the core and distribution layers into a single layer that connects to the access layer where wired and wireless end devices attach.

ultimate route   A routing table entry that contains either a next-hop IPv4 address or an exit interface. Directly connected, dynamically learned, and local routes are all considered to be ultimate routes.

unequal cost load balancing   The capability of a router to distribute traffic over all the router network ports even those that are different distances from the destination address. EIGRP supports unequal cost load balancing by using the variance command.

untrusted port   A switch port that has been identified as one that is allowed to accept (source) only DHCP request messages. All other types of DHCP message types are denied. Untrusted ports are used with enabling DHCP snooping to prevent an unauthorized device from providing IP address-related information to legitimate network devices.

Variable Length Subnet Mask (VLSM)   Allows for the use of different subnet masks for individual subnets. It allows a network space to be divided into unequal parts. With VLSM, the network is first subnetted, and then the subnets are subnetted again. This process can be repeated multiple times to create subnets of various sizes. Creates a more efficient use of address space.

vector   Identifies the direction of the next-hop router or exit interface needed to reach a destination network.

virtual local area network (VLAN)   A group of hosts with a common set of requirements that communicate as if they were attached to the same wire, regardless of their physical location. A VLAN has the same attributes as a physical LAN, but it allows for end stations to be grouped together even if they are not located on the same LAN segment.

VLAN hopping   Frames from one VLAN can be seen by another VLAN.

VLAN leaking   Frames are accepted from a VLAN that is different from the one assigned to a particular switch port.

VLAN Trunking Protocol (VTP)   A Cisco-proprietary Layer 2 protocol that enables a network manager to configure one or more switches so that they propagate VLAN configuration information to other switches in the network, as well as synchronizes the VLAN information with the other switches in the VTP domain.

vlan.dat   Cisco switch VLAN configuration information is stored within a VLAN database file called vlan.dat. The vlan.dat file is located in Flash memory of the switch.

voice VLAN   Voice VLANs are designed for and dedicated to the transmission of voice traffic involving IP phones or softphones (voice software used instead of a physical phone). QoS configurations are applied to voice VLANs to prioritize voice traffic.

wildcard mask   A string of 32 binary digits used by the router to determine which bits of the address to examine for a match.

Numbers

A

M

P-Q

R